D1596770

MEIROKU ZASSHI

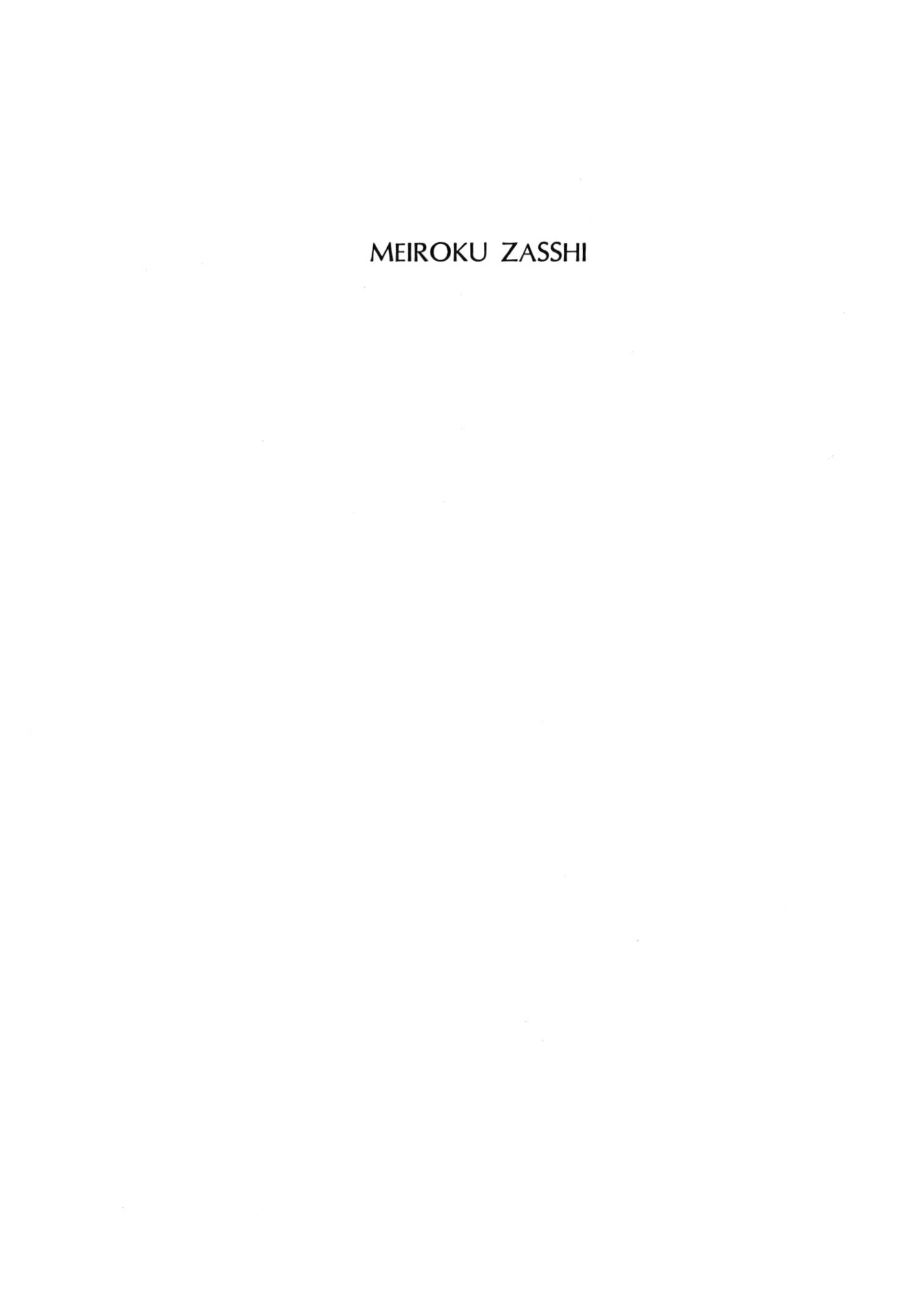

MEIROKU ZASSHI

Journal of the Japanese Enlightenment

Translated and with an introduction by
William Reynolds Braisted

Assisted by
Adachi Yasushi and Kikuchi Yūji

Harvard University Press
Cambridge, Massachusetts
1976

Printed in the United States of America
Library of Congress Catalog Card Number 76-27134
ISBN 0-674-56467-7

In Memory of
Suehiro Fuyuko
A True Daughter of Enlightened Japan

故末弘冬子に捧ぐ

CONTENTS

ACKNOWLEDGMENTS

My involvement with the Meirokusha began nearly two decades ago when I started to collect materials for a monograph on this remarkable group of Japanese enlighteners during a fifteen-month stay in Japan as a Fulbright scholar. My work on the Meirokusha, however, was delayed by an earlier commitment to naval history. Yet, once I was free to devote full attention to the group, I found that others were already well advanced on studies of the society and of its individual members. It seemed, therefore, that I could contribute most to an understanding of the Japanese enlightenment by translating the journal of the Meirokusha, the *Meiroku Zasshi,* which is surely the richest single source on thought in Japan during the initial years after the Meiji Restoration. I could not have completed such a task, however, without the assistance of many persons and important institutional support. Two people who were really essential to the project's success were Mr. Adachi Yasushi and Mr. Kikuchi Yūji. Both read the manuscript carefully and contributed suggestions and corrections throughout. Mr. Adachi also spent countless hours in laborious dictionary work, checking the meanings of doubtful words and phrases. While I myself must accept full responsibility for mistakes or errors in judgment in the translation, Mr. Adachi and Mr. Kikuchi deserve full share of the credit for its merits. Mrs. Suehiro Izutarō, to whom the volume is dedicated, contributed the full run of the original *Meiroku Zasshi* that had belonged to her grandfather, Mitsukuri Shūhei, the second president of the Meirokusha. Of the numerous others to whom I am indebted, Professors Oka Yoshitake and Ōkubo Toshiaki have generously answered questions through the years, as did Professor Yanagida Izumi, Professor Matsumoto Sannosuke, and Mr. Kanai Madoka during the final phase. Mr. Satake Daisetsu, the deputy director of the Tokyo University Library, opened the resources of that library, and Mr. Nishida Taketoshi made available the rich materials of the Meiji Shimbun Zasshi Bunko. Of the many helpful staff members at the International House of Japan, I would especially mention Miss Fukuda Naomi, formerly the house librarian, and Mr. Katō Mikio, both of whom moved to save the project on several occasions. Mr. Sakiyama Teruji contributed numerous suggestions regarding the journal before the translation was really started. Miss Tsuchiyama Tamie, librarian of the Asian Collection at the University of Texas, helped to secure materials from Japan. Miss Elizabeth Powers prepared the manuscript for the press. Sophia University was my host institution when I was a Fulbright research scholar in 1955–1956. Generous monetary support was provided by the Conference Board of the Associated Research Councils, the American Council of Learned Societies, and the University Research Institute at the University of Texas at Austin.

The University of Texas at Austin William R. Braisted

INTRODUCTION

> We companions have recently gathered together, sometimes to discuss reason and sometimes to discourse on foreign news. On the one hand, we have polished our scholarly faculties while, on the other, we have refreshed our minds. The transcriptions of these discussions have mounted to become a volume that we are printing and distributing to gentlemen of like mind. We shall be happy if, its small size notwithstanding, the volume promotes enlightenment among our countrymen.

With these sentiments, the Meirokusha (明六社), or the Meiji Six Society, announced in February 1874 its purpose in publishing the *Meiroku Zasshi* (明六雜誌), the magazine that has been generally regarded as the most luminous of several early journals of opinion that spread knowledge of the West during the first years of the Meiji Period. The Meirokusha was a select group of pioneer Japanese scholars in Western studies (*Yōgakusha,* 洋學者) who joined the society to discuss the issues of the day and to disseminate their views among their less well informed countrymen. A full appreciation of the Meirokusha and its significance would require volumes.[1] This introduction is an attempt to review in only the most general terms the origin and purposes of the society and its journal, the major interests of the journal's most significant contributors, their views on the great public issue of a popularly elected assembly, and the termination of the society's enlightenment activities hardly two years after its inception.

The Meirokusha was established on the prompting of Mori Arinori, the young, education-minded official of samurai extraction from the former domain (*han,* 藩) of Satsuma (薩摩). In the summer of 1873, the sixth year of Meiji, Mori returned to Tokyo after serving as Japan's first diplomatic representative in

Washington, D.C., with the intention of establishing a society of scholars modeled after the literary and scientific societies of the West. Through the introduction of one Yokoyama Magoichirō (横山孫一郎), Mori won the assistance of Nishimura Shigeki, a prestigious scholar soon to join the Education Ministry, in persuading eight other leading authorities on the West to join with himself and Nishimura as the ten charter members of the Meirokusha: Nishi Amane, Tsuda Mamichi, Katō Hiroyuki, Nakamura Masanao, Fukuzawa Yukichi, Sugi Kōji, Mitsukuri Shūhei, and Mitsukuri Rinshō.[2]

Preliminary discussions were protracted until the members finally agreed in February 1874 on the society's regulations and on the previously quoted statement of purpose that appeared on the reverse of the title page in each issue of their journal. While the regulations gave promotion of education as the society's objective, the Meirokusha clearly intended to use the word education in the broadest sense. The regulations also provided for meetings on the 1st and 16th days of each month, for four types of membership, for the election of officers, and for keeping records and accounts.[3] After the great enlightener Fukuzawa Yukichi refused the society's presidency, Mori Arinori himself assumed the chair. The secretary and the treasurer were, respectively, Sera Taiichi and Shimizu Usaburō.

The Meirokusha was formed in one of the most stimulating and optimistic eras of modern Japanese history. Japan had passed through a decade of strife and uncertainty since concluding the first unequal treaties with the West, and the anachronistic Tokugawa bakufu (徳川幕府) had been replaced during the Meiji Restoration of 1868 by the new imperial government dedicated to progressive reform aimed at strengthening the nation so that it might stand on the same level as the nations of the West. The spirit of the new day was epitomized by the popular slogans "civilization and enlightenment" (*bummei kaika,* 文明開化) and "a prosperous country and a strong army" (*fukoku kyōhei,* 富國強兵). Accepting the Western concept of progress as expounded by Buckle and Guizot, the more Western-oriented among Japan's leaders assumed that their people had reached a level of semi-civilization in their advance from savagery to civilization. Moreover, if Japan were to achieve the prosperity and strength necessary for the nation to compete on equal terms with the West, they believed it essential to raise the Japanese people to the level of civilization and enlightenment achieved by the West. To this end, between 1868 and the founding of the Meirokusha, the last institutional vestiges of feudalism were destroyed to make way for the emergence of a modern state as the proud domains returned their powers to the new central government, the legal props of the old class structure were destroyed, and a host of outmoded customs were swept away. In place of the old, the government moved to establish the structure of a national state supported by a new national land tax and a new conscript army. It also proclaimed a program to provide education for every Japanese and reforms to encourage a strong, stable economy.

The names of the ten charter members of the Meirokusha are practically synonymous with the term *keimō gakusha* (啓蒙學者), scholars who illuminate the darkness. Nishi Amane undoubtedly spoke for the group when he wrote in the first article of the *Meiroku Zasshi* that the enlightened few in Japan should "guide the people tenderly by the hand from ignorance to the level of enlightenment, just as one gently removes all the weeds without pulling up the seedlings."[4] The men of the Meirokusha were also practical scholars who combined in their thought the spirit of their country's practical studies (*jitsugaku,* 實學) with the utilitarianism and positivism of the nineteenth-century West. Tsuda Mamichi stressed that the Japanese could not call theirs a civilized society until the minds of their countrymen had been illumined by practical, scientific studies."[5] Although individual Meirokusha members identified with particular areas of interest, they are also called the Japanese encyclopedists because they were often as interested in determining the broad limits of knowledge as in acquiring deep understanding within a specific sphere. Being publicists for civilization and enlightenment, their writings and lectures dealt with such diverse themes as the separation of church and state, the position of women, economic policy, chemistry, and language reform. As converts to science and its methods, they crusaded against everything that smacked of bigotry and superstition in Old Japan.

Averaging thirty-nine years of age and ranging in 1873 from Mitsukuri Rinshō at twenty-seven to Mitsukuri Shūhei at forty-eight, the original ten were from the generation of Japanese who, as young men, were startled into an appreciation of Japan's utter weakness when the American Commodore Matthew Calbraith Perry suddenly appeared with his black ships in Edo (江戸) Bay to request the reopening of Japan. They were also from the first generation of Japanese scholars who were able to direct their attention to the whole of Western civilization, as distinguished from those in Dutch studies (*Rangaku,* 蘭學) whose Western knowledge before the reopening of Japan had been largely limited to the Dutch language and to such information on Western medicine, astronomy, and gunnery as they could acquire through the Dutch trading post at Nagasaki (長崎). All save Mori Arinori had gained experience in Western studies while serving the Tokugawa bakufu directly or indirectly, seven as members of the Institute of Barbarian Letters (Bansho Shirabesho, 蕃書調所), the school for Western studies that the bakufu established in 1856. Most were born into samurai families of fairly modest rank. Mori alone was from one of the great exterior domains (*tozama han,* 外様藩) that engineered the Meiji Restoration, and only Nishimura Shigeki held positions of administrative importance during the old regime. Even as they were valuable to the bakufu because of their knowledge of the West, the Meiji government sought their expertise after 1868, notwithstanding their previous association with its former enemy. It is commonly stated that only two of the original ten, Fukuzawa Yukichi and Nakamura Masanao, resisted government service. The nature and degree of attachment of the remaining eight to government varied greatly, however.

The most important contribution of the Meirokusha as a group to enlightenment was undoubtedly its journal, the *Meiroku Zasshi.* While the average circulation of 3000 for each issue during the journal's first year seems small in a nation of thirty million, Japanese historians point out that the circulation of such a leading Tokyo newspaper as the *Nichi Nichi Shimbun* (日日新聞) was then only 8000. Presumably, the *Meiroku Zasshi* reached the intellectual elite of the capital. It was also sold in Ōsaka (大阪) after the sixteenth issue. Printed by the Hōchisha (報知社), the publisher of the *Yūbin Hōchi Shimbun* (郵便報知新聞), the journal was first advertised in March 1874 to appear twice monthly, perhaps because the members expected that materials prepared for their thrice monthly meetings would suffice for two issues.[6] While Mori stated in his first anniversary address that the number had been increased to thrice monthly in November 1874, the frequency of the issues obviously varied with the productiveness of the members. Six issues appeared before the journal was first dated in May 1874, leading to the conjecture that it was probably inaugurated in March when it was first advertised. Production reached a peak of five issues in June 1874, but it slackened during the summer and New Year seasons. Measuring 4 1/2 by 6 3/4 inches, the issues averaged twenty pages each and were printed with wood blocks on double sheets bound butterfly fashion in traditional (*wahon,* 和本) manner.

Except for Sakatani Shiroshi, whose writing was heavily loaded with Chinese phrases, the contributors to the *Meiroku Zasshi* strove for a prose style that would be more widely understood than the highly artificial traditional literary styles, yet sufficiently dignified to retain the respect of scholars. Their articles, therefore, are usually written in terse, dignified prose transcribed in a mixture of Chinese ideographs and the *katakana* syllabary that fell far short of anything so radical as writing Japanese as it is spoken (*gembun itchi,* 言文一致). Nevertheless, Nishi Amane and Shimizu Usaburō clearly anticipated that the Japanese spoken and written forms would eventually become one.[7]

The members of the Meirokusha were as much transmitters as they were original thinkers. Too definite a distinction, therefore, should not be drawn between their articles in the *Meiroku Zasshi* in which they are given as authors or as translators. The translations convey ideas that the translators themselves held valid for their day while the other articles and speeches commonly transmit themes that the authors would never have claimed as uniquely their own. Thus, Katō Hiroyuki and Nishi Amane both promoted separation of church and state, the former as a translator and the latter as an author. Where translations in the journal can be compared with the originals, they prove to be very faithful. The translations of Nakamura Masanao, however, carry the imprint of Nakamura the Confucian scholar, and there were occasions when translators introduced new material, as when Katō Hiroyuki inserted in his translation of Joseph Parrish Thompson that the superiority of Western civilization could be ascribed to the deeply rooted Western tradition of monogamy or when Mitsukuri Rinshō put in his rendering of Montesquieu that, whereas Western peoples had achieved full liberty, the Asians had not gained any liberty since antiquity.[8] While the sources of Nakamura's outline of Western history and Sugi Kōji's essays on social intercourse are not given, both were probably paraphrasing from one or a few Western sources, although Nakamura is given as translator while to Sugi is attributed full authorship.

Nishimura Shigeki was guilty of exaggeration when he claimed in his memoirs that the Meirokusha was the first to publish a journal and to inagurate public lectures. Fukuzawa Yukichi probably first introduced public lecturing at his private school, Keiō Gijuku (慶應義塾), in the summer of 1874, several months before the Meirokusha adopted the lecture technique as a vehicle for spreading enlightenment. According to Fukuzawa, when he proposed that the Meirokusha also undertake public lectures, there was doubt in the society, especially on the part of Mori Arinori, that Japanese was appropriate for oration. At the succeeding meeting, Fukuzawa asked the others to gather around a table and launched into a discourse on the settlement of the Formosan crisis between Japan and China that was published in the second November issue of the journal. When he had concluded, none denied that he had spoken successfully, and the Meirokusha was committed to public lectures.[9]

Mori had previously startled his countrymen by suggesting that they shift from Japanese to English as the more appropriate language for modern usage.[10] Although he chided others in the society for their failure to modify their language to meet the requirements of speech-making, his misgivings regarding the appropriateness of Japanese for oral communication apparently disappeared as the Meirokusha meetings became crowded with guests who came to hear. Indeed, so popular were the Meirokusha lectures that Mori suggested in his first-anniversary address that the society issue tickets to its lecture sessions and employ the proceeds from the sale of the *Meiroku Zasshi* to support construction of a hall, which could be rented to others for a variety of purposes when not needed by the society. The Meirokusha never pushed ahead with the lecture hall, and it experimented only briefly in February and March 1875 with offering tickets. Thereafter, non-members were allowed to attend the lecture meetings by introduction of members. Judging from the fact that the Meirokusha membership probably never greatly exceeded thirty and that Mori proposed to build a hall of only 70 *tsubo,* about 840 square feet, it would appear that the society's meetings were never large by Western standards. Members would commonly meet in a Western-style restaurant, the Seiyōken (精養軒), in the foreign settlement of Tsukiji (築地), deal with the society's business in the forenoon, eat between 12:00 and 1:00, and then turn to speeches and discussion.[11]

It was also at the first anniversary meeting of the society that Mori Arinori resigned its presidency in favor of Mitsukuri Shūhei. Three months later, in accordance with its revised regulations, the Meirokusha replaced its president with six directors: Mitsukuri Shūhei, Nishi Amane, Nishimura Shigeki, Tsuda Mamichi, Fukuzawa Yukichi, and Mori Arinori.[12]

The *Meiroku Zasshi* Contributors

Fukuzawa Yukichi was clearly the most celebrated of the dozen contributors to the *Meiroku Zasshi.* Fukuzawa's refusal of the society's presidency, however, was an indication of the rather prickly relations that existed between him and others in the society. About fifteen years earlier, when he was still but a lowly samurai from Nakatsu (中津) *han,* Fukuzawa had registered as a day student at the Bansho Shirabesho so that he might use the institute's fine collection of Western books, but he never returned to the school when he was not allowed to borrow a valuable dictionary.[13] Thereafter, he acquired knowledge of the West, founded his famous school, Keiō Gijuku, and became the most famous publicist of Western studies independently of the Bansho group. Whereas the Bansho scholars tended to join the new government after the Meiji Restortaion, Fukuzawa opted to remain in private life surrounded by his group at the new Keiō campus in the Mita (三田) district of Tokyo. Contemporaneous with the *Meiroku Zasshi,* he and his Keio followers published their own journal, the *Minkan Zasshi* (民間雜誌), or the *People's Journal,* in which they repeatedly took issue with the more government-oriented members of the Meirokusha. Rather than contribute to the *Meiroku Zasshi,* Fukuzawa usually wrote for the *Minkan Zasshi*[14] and other publications that would bring fame to himself and Keiō rather than to the Meirokusha.

While the Meirokusha was still organizing in January 1874, Fukuzawa published his famous essay on the role of scholars in which he called on scholars in Western studies to follow his example by resigning from government and undertaking to guide the people in private life. Fukuzawa held that Japan could not achieve equality with the West unless her traditionally subservient people were instilled with a spirit of independence sufficient to challenge and stimulate the government and that only scholars in Western studies acting in private life could sweep away servility in the people and despotism in government. Although Fukuzawa prepared the essay for discussion in the Meirokusha, he characteristically published it as the fourth essay in his series on the *Encouragement of Learning* (*Gakumon no Susume,* 學問のすゝめ) rather than in the *Meiroku Zasshi.*[15] Obviously disgruntled by Fukuzawa's disdainful, even insulting, tone, the Meirokusha devoted the entire second issue of its journal to answering that scholars might properly serve either outside or inside the government. The four responses were by Mori Arinori and three former Bansho scholars who had joined the government: Nishi Amane, Tsuda Mamichi, and Katō Hiroyuki.

Irritating though Fukuzawa may have been to other Meirokusha members, they could hardly aspire to represent enlightened Japanese thought without him. In addition to *Gakumon no Susume,* his writings, such as *Conditions in the West* (*Seiyō Jijō,* 西洋事情) and *An Outline of a Theory of Civilization* (*Bummeiron no Gairyaku,* 文明論之概略), were best sellers that won him first place among the enlighteners. No other Japanese of the day spoke out more eloquently on behalf of achievement-oriented individualism as the source of true civilization and national strength. While he boasted his independence from government and his commitment to the practical, empirical ways of the West, he was neither so independent of his government nor so free of his East Asian heritage as he supposed.[16]

The youthful Mori Arinori was surely one of the most enthusiastic and impetuous of the Meirokusha enlighteners. Like Fukuzawa, Mori achieved his position in Western studies outside the Bansho route, but he fully qualified as a scholar in government. Through most of his official career, Mori's government employed his services more in diplomacy than in education, and it was only in 1885 that his aspirations in education were officially rewarded by his appointment as education minister. Born into a samurai family of comfortable circumstance, Mori briefly attended Satsuma *han*'s Western studies institute (Kaiseijo, 開成所) before his domain in 1865 despatched him with a group to study in England. His letters and a diary of a trip to Russia indicate that he was then deeply impressed by British justice, the rising power of the United States, and Russia's failures. After funds from Japan were cut off by disturbances of the approaching Restoration, Mori spent almost a year in the United States in a religious community in Brocton, New York, headed by Thomas Lake Harris, a follower of Emanuel Swedenborg. Harris' moral teachings apparently had a lasting impact on the young Mori.

Returning to Japan in 1868 to share in the excitement of the new day, Mori served only briefly as president of the Kōgisho (公議所), an early deliberative assembly, before he earned the wrath of his fellow samurai by moving that samurai be ordered to lay aside the cherished swords that were their class symbols. After a brief enforced retirement to Satsuma, he was despatched to Washington as chargé d'affaires, where his energies were largely devoted to supervising the education of Japanese students in the United States, exchanging with American scholars and educators, and writing. His publications while in Washington, all of them in English, included an appeal for religious toleration entitled *Religious Freedom in Japan* (1872) and tracts on *Life and Resources in America* (1871) and *Education in Japan* (1872). While there remains doubt as to whether Mori intended them more for Western than Japanese consumption, these writings are proof positive of his earnestness on behalf of education and uplift. Again, however, Mori caused public shock when he proposed replacing Japanese with English, and he was recalled to Tokyo after he obstructed his government's effort to float a loan in the United States for the commutation of samurai stipends.

Returning to Tokyo somewhat under a cloud, Mori threw himself into enlightenment activities as evidenced by the organization of the Meirokusha, his founding of the commercial school, the Shōhō Kōshūjo (商法講習所), that later became Hitotsubashi (一橋) University, and his efforts to enhance the position of women. While his political attitudes were somewhat ambivalent, his fervor for social betterment and his patriotism ring clear and true in his Meirokusha articles. His most important contributions to the *Meiroku Zasshi* are undoubtedly his essays on "Wives and Concubines" ("Saishōron," 妻妾論) in which he advocated radical changes in the traditional Japanese family to elevate the status of women. Although Mori insisted that he did not favor anything so radical as complete equality between the sexes, he again made headlines when he exchanged marriage vows on an equal contractual basis with Hirose Otsune (廣瀬阿常) before the governor of Tokyo, Fukuzawa Yukichi serving as witness.[17]

The lives of Nishi Amane and Tsuda Mamichi were so closely linked that it is impossible to discuss one without referring to the other. Born, respectively, in the Tsuwano (津和野) and Tsuyama (津山) domains of modest samurai families in 1829, Nishi and Tsuda were both admitted to the Bansho Shirabesho in 1857, after they had broken with their domains to enter Western studies. Chosen by the Tokugawa bakufu to study abroad, the two received tutelage in law and economics in Leiden from Professor Simon Vissering from 1863 to 1865. In addition, they became deeply interested in European philosophy. Although Tsuda reminisced that he favored Comte while Nishi inclined toward Kant in their philosophical disputations, their later writings suggest that they were both influenced more by British and French than by German thought. Upon their return to Japan, they were restored to the bakufu's institute of Western studies, now known as the Institute for Development (Kaiseijo, 開成所), where they translated Vissering's lectures on law and statistics and advised on parliamentary government. After retiring briefly with the Tokugawa family to Shizuoka (靜岡) in 1868, both were attracted into government service, Nishi into the War Ministry and Tsuda initially into the Justice Ministry. It appears, however, that Nishi was perhaps temperamentally better suited to work in government than Tsuda. Whereas Nishi assisted Yamagata Aritomo (山縣有朋) in drafting the conscription law of 1872 and other important military policies, Tsuda served in a number of posts after he resigned from the Justice Ministry when he was unable to agree with the impetuous minister, Etō Shimpei (江藤新平).

Nishi is especially remembered for introducing the Japanese to Western philosophy. Perhaps more than any other of the Meirokusha members, Nishi was a genuine intellectual whose sophisticated mind was fascinated by ideas and systems of thought. He was early influenced by the writings of the practical, utility-oriented Confucian scholar Ogyū Sorai (荻生徂徠), and his thought moved by the Meirokusha period to a position close to the utilitarianism of John Stuart Mill, as expressed in his major philosophical statement in the *Meiroku Zasshi* articles on "The Three Human Treasures" ("Jinsei Sambōsetsu," 人世三寶說). Indeed, "The Three Human Treasures" along with Nishi's articles on "Religion" ("Kyōmonron," 教門論) and "Knowledge" ("Chisetsu," 知說) epitomize his thought after the Meiji Restoration as found in his lectures at his school, the Ikueisha (育英舍), on the *Relation of the Hundred Studies* (*Hyakugaku Renkan,* 百學連環) and his *New Theory of One Hundred and One* (*Hyakuichi Shinron,* 百一新論). While Nishi was obviously influenced by Comte insofar as he sought a systematic organization of the various studies, his scheme in *Hyakugaku Renkan* and his "Chisetsu" articles is characteristically his own. His *Hyakuichi Shinron* is noteworthy for its attack on traditional Confucian thought and its assertion that government and ethics should be separated. It anticipated his insistence on the separation of government and religion in the "Kyōmonron" articles. His break with the orthodox Confucian tradition is also succinctly stated in his fifth "Chisetsu" article in which he divided knowledge into disciplines devoted to studying physical principles (*butsuri,* 物理) and mental principles (*shinri,* 心理), a denial of the all-embracing Principle or Reason (*Ri,* 理) that the followers of Chu Hsi (朱熹) sought in all things physical and metaphysical. Nishi was from the last generation of Japanese who tried to express Western concepts in Chinese ideographs, and several of his inventions survive in common usage to the present day, among them *tetsugaku* (哲學) for philosophy. Although he looked to the state as an instrument for promoting progress, his American biographer was surely correct in asserting that Nishi never conceived of his scholarship as support for the state.[18]

Tsuda Mamichi has received less attention than several other Meirokusha members, although he contributed more than any other to the *Meiroku Zasshi,* some twenty-nine articles on a wide variety of topics. Using modern terminology, Professor Ōkubo Toshiaki has described Tsuda as farthest to the left in the Meirokusha.[19] Tsuda's most important published work before the Meirokusha period was a fine translation from Vissering's lectures on law entitled *Taisei Kokuhōron* (泰西國法論), which is a source for Tsuda's own views as well as those of his teacher. His articles in the *Meiroku Zasshi* are clear evidence of his continued attachment to ninteenth-century European liberalism and humanitarianism. Apart from government and politics, Tsuda was much concerned for the dignity of man and man's treatment of man. He went as far as any other Meirokusha member to accept a popularly elected assembly, perhaps as far as the contemporary advocates of people's rights themselves. His philosophical orientation, already evident in the *Meiroku Zasshi,* was toward materialism, on which he later wrote for the Tokyo Academy (Tōkyō Gakushi Kaiin, 東京學士會院). Like most others in the Meirokusha, he probably admired Christianity more for its enlightenment than out of faith. It was perhaps in recognition of his genuine independence and humanity that Tsuda was elected to the first Diet in 1890 and thereafter served as vice speaker of the House of Representatives.[20]

Fukuzawa Yukichi surely had Katō Hiroyuki in mind when he disparaged scholars in government in *Gakumon no Susume.* A pioneer in German studies and law who later served for many years as president of Tokyo Imperial University, Katō is well known for his opposition to the advocates of an early popularly elected assembly and his denunciation of his previous writings on natural rights after he had been converted to Social Darwinism. Katō was first attracted to Germany in 1860 when, as a recent appointee to the Bansho Shirabesho, he was ordered to prepare for the reception of an emissary from the king of Prussia. Two years later, according to his own recollection, he completed a manuscript entitled *Neighboring Grass* (*Tonari-gusa,* 隣草) that was possibly the first exposition by a Japanese on parliamentary government. Katō quickly joined the Meiji government after the Restoration and achieved fame by publishing a trilogy on natural rights and other Western legal concepts.[21] For the first, he drew heavily from the work of Tsuda Mamichi and thence indirectly from the liberal views of Simon Vissering, but the third shows signs of Katō's increasing conservatism. It was probably influenced by his translations from Johann Kaspar Bluntschli and Friederich Karl Biedermann that he undertook while preparing to lecture before the Meiji Emperor on Western institutions. Katō's American biographer holds that, through all his writings, Katō was concerned to serve the state he believed in, to guarantee that its sovereignty would never be threatened, and to prevent the horrors of revolution.[22] It would be mistaken, however, to judge the Meirokusha only by Katō since his contributions were small as compared with such stellar performers as Tsuda Mamichi, Nishi Amane, and Sakatani Shiroshi. All but one of his six articles in the *Meiroku Zasshi* came out early in the journal's history, and his name does not appear among the society's directors in 1875.[23]

Very similar in background to the above three Bansho scholar officials was Kanda Kōhei who joined the Meirokusha as a corresponding member since he was then governor of Hyōgo (兵庫) Prefecture, the present Kōbe (神戸). Born into an impoverished samurai family in Mino (美濃), Kanda was attracted to economics after joining the Bansho Shirabesho. Six years before the Meiji Restoration, he wrote the short *Tract on Agriculture and Commerce* (*Nōshōben,* 農商辨) in which he ascribed the wealth of Western nations to commerce:

> Countries established by commerce are always rich; and countries based on agriculture are always poor. Eastern countries are based on agriculture, while those of the West are founded on commerce. Therefore, Eastern countries are always poor; Western countries essentially wealthy.[24]

Kanda's principal contributions to Western studies included translations of William Ellis' *Outlines of Social Economy* (*Keizai Shōgaku,* 經濟小學) and Simon Vissering's lectures on natural law (*Seihōryaku,* 性法略) that Nishi Amane and Tsuda Mamichi had brought back from Holland. While serving in the Kōgisho, the early deliberative assembly, Kanda submitted recommendations for a national land tax based on private ownership of property and a civil service examination system that clearly anticipated policies later adopted by the government, as did his articles on a convertible currency in the *Meiroku Zasshi*.[25] Kanda was also interested in parliaments and introduced assemblies at the village and town levels while serving as governor of Hyōgo. He was, in short, the very model of an enlightened scholar-bureaucrat as well as Japan's leading expert on economics.[26]

Distinct from Fukuzawa Yukichi, Mori Arinori, and those from the Bansho Shirabesho were three members who remained attached to East Asian traditions even as they sought knowledge of the West: Nakamura Masanao, Nishimura Shigeki, and Sakatani Shiroshi. Nakamura is reputed to have been one of the most brilliant students at the Shōheikō (昌平黌), the Confucian college in the orthodox Chu Hsi tradition that was supported by the Tokugawa bakufu. There were other elements in his background, however, that may have contributed to the breadth of his vision. His father was born into an affluent farm family and only acquired samurai status by adoption; there was a strong Buddhist influence in the Nakamura family; and the younger Nakamura's Confucian studies were apparently tinged with a strong practical flavor. Moreover, Nakamura began secretly to study Dutch after he learned of China's defeat by England in the first Opium War, 1839–1842. Entering English studies in the 1860s, Nakamura like Nishi Amane and Tsuda Mamichi was one of the first Japanese to recognize that Western studies included metaphysical as well as physical disciplines, and he secured an appointment from the Tokugawa bakufu to chaperone a group of teen-age students to England because he felt that a Confucian scholar like himself should become familiar with English thought.[27] So impressed was he with the moral rectitude of the British nation that he returned to Japan after the Meiji Restoration to translate two best sellers: Samuel Smiles' *Self Help* (*Saigoku Risshihen,* 西國立志編) and John Stuart Mill's *On Liberty* (*Jiyū no Ri,* 自由之理). Although translations, they leave no doubt as to Nakamura's commitment to Western ideals of liberty and independence. For Nakamura the God of the Christians was fully compatible with the Confucian Heaven (*Ten,* 天). When the religion was still officially proscribed in 1872, Nakamura published a memorial in which, masking as a foreigner, he urged the emperor to open Japan to Christianity, the root of Western civilization.[28] Two years later, he was himself baptized a Christian. He also founded a school, Dōninsha (同人社), that ranked with Fukuzawa Yukichi's Keiō in prestige. Whereas Fukuzawa stressed utilitarian, scientific education and heaped scorn on traditional Chinese studies, Nakamura emphasized moral training and included Chinese in his curriculum. While not an active politician, Nakamura was elected to the Tokyo city council and to his ward council shortly before his death. His articles in the *Meiroku Zasshi* are a true reflection of his continued commitment to China, to moral philosophy, and to elevating womanhood.[29]

Nishimura Shigeki's activities as an enlightener have been obscured by his later leadership of a movement aimed at reviving ethics that was strongly tinged with Chinese morality and directed toward loyalty to Japan's imperial system. Nishimura differed from others in the Meirokusha in that he had a long record of honorable and significant public service in the administrations of the Sakura (佐倉) and Sano (佐野) domains of the Hotta (堀田) family. When Commodore Perry appeared in Japan, Nishimura unsuccessfully sought permission to study military science in the West, and he advised Hotta Masayoshi (堀田正睦) on opening the country and domestic problems when Hotta served the Tokugawa bakufu as an elder (*rōjū,* 老中) in the 1850s. With the abolition of the domains, Nishimura accepted appointment from the Meiji government as chief of the Education Ministry's Compilation Bureau (Hensho Kachō, 編書課長), which was charged with the preparation of school texts as well as several magnificent research tools.

Nishimura's reputation in Western studies rested largely on translation and general informational works: two histories of the West, chapters on geography, a chronology, and a translation of Laurens Hickok's *Moral Science.* During the Meirokusha period, he was deeply troubled by the fate of the samurai class and by the absence of ethics from the Japanese government's new educational program. The moralist in him led him to deny the assertion by men like Nishi Amane that government and ethics are separate and to interpret Western history in terms of moral decay and regeneration. Finding advantages as well as disadvantages in both the old and the new, he was a conservative who wanted his countrymen to understand the Western concepts of liberty, freedom, human rights, and civilization.[30]

Perhaps because they have been put off by the difficult prose style of Sakatani Shiroshi [Rōro 朗廬], students of the Meirokusha have generally ignored this scholar in Chinese studies of the Chu Hsi tradition. Yet Sakatani's contributions to the *Meiroku Zasshi* were exceeded in number only by those of Nishi Amane and Tsuda Mamichi. Once the reader penetrates Sakatani's Chinese phrases and obscure references, he finds a vigorous conservative who favored moving ahead judiciously in order to avoid the chaos and even revolution likely to follow any effort to halt orderly and guided progress. The oldest of the Meirokusha authors, having reached fifty in 1874, Sakatani reputedly abandoned an early ambition to enter Western studies so that he might remain in his native Bitchū (備中) to care for his ailing mother. Nevertheless, he established a school in Chinese studies, the Kōjōkan (興讓館), that attracted national attention in the last years of Tokugawa rule. After the Restoration, Sakatani induced his mother to move with the family to Tokyo only to find that his character and traditional training were more prized by scholars than by the Western-oriented government that he wanted to serve. After the Meirokusha ceased its enlightening activities, Sakatani worked with Nishimura and other conservatives in the movement to promote a revival of ethics. It was perhaps characteristics of his open mind and independence, however, that he also associated amiably with the more liberal Fukuzawa Yukichi and his friends in their society, the Kōjunsha (交詢社).[31]

Of the remaining *Meiroku Zasshi* contributors, Sugi Kōji, Mitsukuri Shūhei, and Mitsukuri Rinshō were all former Bansho Shirabesho scholars. The Nagasaki-born Sugi focused his interests primarily on statistics.[32] Mitsukuri Rinshō and Mitsukuri Shūhei were members of a family celebrated in Dutch studies. The brilliant young Rinshō trained in France and worked for the Justice Ministry as a specialist in and translator of French law.[33] The more mature Shūhei, a Mitsukuri by adoption, founded a well-known private school, Sansha Gakusha (三叉學舍), and helped lay the foundations for normal school education. Kashiwabara Takaaki, formerly physician to the main Tokugawa house, joined the Meirokusha as a corresponding member so that he might keep his area of Shizuoka informed on intellectual trends in the capital. The Christian convert Tsuda Sen founded an agricultural school, Nōgakkō (農學校), and published the agricultural journal *Nōgyō Zasshi* (農業雜誌) for more than thirty years. Two years before the founding of the Meirokusha, he had sent his seven-year-old daughter, Tsuda Umeko (津田梅子), to the United States for the education that would prepare her to found Tsuda College for Women.[34]

Shimizu Usaburō, the treasurer of the Meirokusha, was probably its only commoner. The son of a prosperous producer of saké, Shimizu was attracted to Dutch studies and Western chemistry after reading a book on chemistry in translation. After the British bombardment of Kagoshima (鹿兒島) in 1863, he provided valuable service as an intermediary between the British and Satsuma, partly because of his fluency in English but also because he was free as a commoner to negotiate with the British as could no Satsuma samurai. In 1867 he accompanied the mission led by Tokugawa Akitake (德川昭武) to the Paris Expedition where he experimented with the French ethnographer Leon Rosny with printing a paper in the *hiragana* syllabary and collected printing and lithograph machinery and minerals. After the Restoration, Shimizu opened a bookstore and printing establishment, *Mizuhoya,* where he printed educational materials as well as the works of Meirokusha members Nishi Amane and Tsuda Mamichi. Shimizu's two articles in the *Meiroku Zasshi* represent his two major interests: chemistry and the promotion of the *hiragana* syllabary. His *Seimi no Kai* (舎密ノ階) of the Meirokusha period is a three-volume outline of Western chemistry written entirely in *hiragana.* In 1880 he joined with the great dictionary compiler Ōtsuki Fumihiko (大槻文彥) to found the *Kana no Kai,* the *Kana* Society, to push writing with *hiragana.*[35]

A Popularly Elected Assembly

Although Mori Arinori held that the Meirokusha was formed to discuss cultural matters rather than politics, its members inevitably responded to the movement for a popularly elected assembly (*minsen giin undō*, 民選議院運動) that erupted while they were still debating the society's purposes. Since the degree of their enlightenment has often been judged in terms of their supposed attitudes toward this movement, their comments on the proposed popularly elected assembly (*minsen giin*) deserve careful attention.

The movement for an elective assembly was sparked in January 1874 when Itagaki Taisuke (板垣退助) of Tosa (土佐) and several other former ministers and associates submitted to the government their famous memorial in which they called for the assembly's convening. Having resigned from government only three months earlier over the Korean question, the former ministers charged that those still in office were separating the throne from the people by arbitrarily grasping and misusing power. The memorialists claimed that, aside from curbing bureaucratic despotism, the assembly would propel the people toward enlightenment by broadening their wisdom and by instilling in them a spirit of independence. Their proposal, they claimed, conformed to the principle that taxpayers had the right to participate in government. Why, they asked, should the Japanese delay introduction of a Western-style popularly elected assembly when they were adopting steam engines without waiting to invent these machines themselves? Denying that their plan was premature, they later stated that they would limit suffrage to those who had provided the push behind the Meiji Restoration: samurai, rich peasants, and merchants.[36]

On no other issue did the Meirokusha members write more fully than on the question of a popularly elected assembly. Indeed, the Meirokusha could ill afford to ignore the memorial by Itagaki and his associates both because the proposal, like the society, was directed at least ostensibly toward promoting civilization and enlightenment and because it charged with usurping power the government with which the scholar-bureaucrats in the society were identified. On the whole, the Meirokusha members responded with gradualist arguments that Japan was not yet ready for a genuine popularly elected assembly. A review of their attitudes, however, reveals that they were far from united on the question, still less spokesmen for an emerging despotism. Of the ten charter members, four and possibly five (Nishimura Shigeki,

Fukuzawa Yukichi, Nakamura Masanao, Tsuda Mamichi, and possibly Mitsukuri Rinshō)[37] leaned toward some sort of an assembly chosen by restricted franchise; one (Nishi Amane) favored a largely appointive assembly that he claimed would be all inclusive; one (Mori Arinori) verbally evaded the issue; and one (Katō Hiroyuki) held that the Japanese people were not yet ready for the assembly. Two members not of the original ten, Kanda Kōhei and Sakatani Shiroshi, also held the proposed assembly to be premature. All accepted the assembly as an ultimate objective to be achieved as Japan moved toward civilization and enlightenment.

The most celebrated public rebuttal against the memorialists came from the eminent authority on statecraft and German thought, Katō Hiroyuki. Indeed, Katō's response in the *Nichi Nichi Shimbun* (日日新聞) presented the gradualist position so effectively that it has overshadowed the differing views of other Meirokusha members. Whereas the memorialists saw in the assembly a means for leading the people to enlightenment, the Japanese farmers and townsmen were to Katō so stupid, ignorant, and without spirit that they could only elect an assembly of fools capable of causing mischief, if not worse.[38] In the same vein was Katō's translation from Bluntschli for the *Meiroku Zasshi* in which the German-Swiss theoretician stressed how important it was for statesmen to govern resolutely without heeding ignorant parliamentary majorities, as had the younger Pitt and Bismarck.[39]

Also ranged with the gradualists was the philosopher-bureaucrat of the War Ministry, Nishi Amane. Seven years before, Nishi had drawn up a plan for the last Tokugawa shogun that provided for a two-house legislative body without seriously reducing the shogun's authority. Holding in 1874 that human laws, unlike scientific principles, vary from country to country, Nishi denied the contention by the memorialists that parliaments could be introduced as easily as steam engines. Nor did he admit a link between the payment of taxes and the right to participate in government or the theory that government arises from a contract between governed and governing. He looked to the impartial administration of justice, rather than to a popularly elected assembly, for protection of the people's rights. Nishi would establish what he called "an all inclusive assembly" (*mōra giin,* 網羅議院) composed of prefectural governors, eminent subjects, ministerial officials appointed by the government, and representatives elevated from prefectural legislatures. Indeed, Nishi had in mind a hierarchy of similar assemblies at the national, prefectural, and district levels. Although he would reserve to the government absolute veto powers over the assemblies, he argued that his system would provide the government with valuable council as well as enable the people to gain the understanding of parliamentary methods essential for successful operation of a popularly elected assembly.[40]

The entire *minsen giin* controversy undoubtedly was wholly unwelcome to Mori Arinori, the chief promoter of the Meirokusha. His earlier reputation for being somewhat of an iconoclast notwithstanding, Mori responded to the memorialists like a government official on the defensive. He denied that the memorialists were justified in attacking the government for its repressive measures since they had accepted these policies while in office. He also claimed that the people, rather than the government, should establish the elective assembly without, however, suggesting how they could do so.[41]

Kanda Kōhei fully accepted the introduction of a popularly elected assembly in due course. In his article on public finance, Kanda assumed the existence of a national parliament endowed with responsibility for approving the budget, reviewing the accounts of expenditures made, and authorizing any bond issues necessary to meet emergencies. Yet he held that the season had not yet come for a popularly elected assembly if only because the people were too meek to force the assembly on their rulers. Still more, he dreaded the season's coming as he expected it to be attended by conflict between rulers and ruled during a national crisis.[42]

Predictably, Tsuda Mamichi was the most friendly among the scholars in government to the early convening of an elected assembly. Thus, Tsuda declared that there was nothing comparable to a popularly elected assembly to stimulate a spirit of independence among the people and thence to enhance Japan's national prestige, and he heaped scorn on those who would establish a chamber of former great lords or an assembly of regional governors, who were themselves government appointees. Nevertheless, he favored an assembly of sixty to one hundred members chosen by electors who had themselves been elected by an elite constituency drawn from the former samurai and the highest taxpayers, and he would reserve to the throne a complete veto power over the assembly's legislation. He also warned that Japan might confront horrors exceeding those of the French Revolution should the government fail to educate the people so that they could successfully conduct representative government.[43]

Perhaps one of the more remarkable converts to an elected assembly was the Confucian scholar Sakatani Shiroshi. Although Sakatani was a gradualist, he emphatically warned of troubles ahead, perhaps danger to Japan's unique unbroken imperial line, should measures not be undertaken promptly to establish the political structure (*seitai,* 政體) and to demonstrate that the country was moving toward a parliamentary system. Sakatani would forthwith create an officially appointed assembly that he hoped to transform into a genuine popularly elected body over a period of a dozen years by gradually replacing appointed legislators with elected representatives. Sakatani asserted that Japan might already have established the most enlightened government in the world had the Emperor Go-Daigo (後醍醐) introduced a parliament at the time of the Kemmu Restoration (Kemmu no Chūkō, 建武中興) in the fourteenth century![44]

Two others in the Meirokusha sympathetic to the proposed assembly were the two who, like Sakatani, preserved strong attachment for Confucian traditions: Nishimura Shigeki and Nakamura Masanao. Even before the former ministers presented their memorial, Nishimura had lobbied for a consultative assembly of ex-great lords and former samurai, hoping thereby to provide a constructive role for those who had been shorn of their privileges by the new government.[45] To *Meiroku Zasshi* readers, Nishimura also affirmed his faith in constitutional government by equating autocracy with traditional government, limited monarchy with government modified by reason, and democratic republics with government by pure reason.[46] Given such views, it is not surprising that Nishimura submitted a memorial to the left chamber (*sain,* 左院) of the government in support of the popularly elected assembly proposed by Itagaki and the other ex-ministers. To the gradualists who argued that the Japanese were not yet ready, Nishimura countered that the Japanese were not inferior to the English at the inception of their parliament six centuries earlier. For Nishimura, the political system (*seitai*, 政體) was the root of enlightenment, and nothing should take precedence over establishing a popularly elected assembly when determining the political system. Nishimura recommended, therefore, that the authors of the January 1874 memorial be asked how they proposed to establish an assembly. If their plan proved feasible, he would adopt it forthwith.[47]

While Nakamura Masanao was primarily interested in changing the character of the Japanese people through education, he declared in the *Meiroku Zasshi* that a popularly elected assembly would undoubtedly invigorate the public mind since it would develop among the people the will to hold and defend their country and reduce their traditional spirit of subservience.[48] It was partly because he regarded the assembly as a means for guiding the people toward enlightenment that he affirmed its establishment to be the most urgent business of the day in his introduction to a volume on popularly elected assemblies (*Minsen Giin Ronkō*, 民選議院論綱) by Yamada Shunzō (山田俊蔵). Nakamura observed that, when we cannot perceive things in this world, we do what seems right. He favored a popularly elected assembly, therefore, because it seemed right. Since nothing is all profit without loss, he would establish the assembly in the expectation that its injurious features could be eliminated as they arose.[49]

Fukuzawa Yukichi preserved a low profile during the early debates over a popularly elected assembly. He may well have doubted whether Itagaki Taisuke and his fellow memorialists, being themselves former government officials, were really more committed to genuine parliamentary government than those still in office. There survives, however, a report in the Tokyo newspaper, *Chōya Shimbun* (朝野新聞), of an exchange at the meeting of the Meirokusha on 1 May 1874 in which Fukuzawa challenged Katō Hiroyuki's view that the Japanese people were too ignorant and subservient to make good use of a popularly elected assembly. Whereas Katō claimed that to be appreciated liberty must be gained through struggle even as the barons of England had won the Magna Charta from King John, Fukuzawa retorted that creation of a popularly elected assembly should be no more deplored than the recent abolition of the domains (*han*) since both were gates through which the Japanese would necessarily pass on their progress to the great hall of liberty.[50]

That Fukuzawa wanted to avoid a split in Japan's leadership over the *minsen giin* controversy is evident from his article on "The Divisibility of National Power" ("Kokken Kabun," 國權可分) that he published a month later in the *Minkan Zasshi*. To gradualists like Katō, Fukuzawa affirmed that the lower classes of England were fully as ignorant as the rickshaw men and tenant farmers of Japan while Japan possessed scholars, doctors, and ex-government officials in the middle classes and above who were quite as able to participate in parliaments as was the enlightened British upper class that ran the House of Commons. If scholars in government doubted this, then he proposed that they strengthen the ranks of the people by resigning their offices. To those who saw the Meiji government as no more than a perpetuation of traditional Japanese despotism, Fukuzawa countered that the people had set the nation's course toward liberty when they destroyed the despotism of the Tokugawa bakufu during the Meiji Restoration. Only if the new government set up by the people altered this liberal course did Fukuzawa anticipate serious popular outbursts. To Fukuzawa, the urgent business of the moment was to establish some sort of discussion chamber in accordance with an agreement between government and people. He was not too concerned as to the exact nature of the assembly if it provided an opportunity for debate between opposing factions. As for Katō's prediction that the body would be an assembly of fools, Fukuzawa chided: "Those who imagine fools they do not see are as foolish as the fools they imagine." One may well wonder if Fukuzawa's professed faith in Japan's liberal course was wishful thinking since it appeared in the final (June) issue of the *Minkan Zasshi*, even as the government promulgated the strict press and libel law that would provide at least the pretext for halting publication of the *Meiroku Zasshi* later in the year.[51]

When dealing with the popularly elected assembly, the members of the Meirokusha thus wrote as individuals from a small self-conscious elite whose outlook was shaped by their common background and shared experiences. Like other elites elsewhere, they took positions natural to persons convinced of their own enlightenment and reluctant to share responsibility with countrymen just emerging from darkness. For all in the society who wrote on the subject, a popularly elected assembly was an institution especially suited to the most advanced societies. None denied that Japan would ultimately progress to such a point, but they differed considerably on how and when the assembly should be established. Three who leaned toward the assembly idea (Nishimura, Nakamura, and Sakatani) were also the three who remained most attached to their East Asian heritage, while the assembly's most bitter critic, Katō Hiroyuki, had gone perhaps as far as any in breaking with non-Western traditions. Even those most friendly to the assembly, such as Tsuda Mamichi and Fukuzawa Yukichi, contemplated a body representative of a carefully restricted constituency, as did Itagaki Taisuke and his fellow memorialists.

The Meirokusha members were nationalists whose first loyalty was to Japan, and they undoubtedly judged the popularly elected assembly, as they did other gifts from the West, in terms of whether it would help Japan to win equality with the various countries of Europe and America. This was a basic consideration implicit in all their discussions on such varied topics as the position of women, mixed residence, separation of church and state, and foreign trade. They were also loyal to the samurai class from which they sprang and to their government. Their writings, however, were directed far beyond the confines of their class, and their loyalty to as well as participation in the government surely derived in large part from their faith in the government as an agent of progress. Indeed, the Meiji government was far more effective in promoting the enlightenment desired by the Meirokusha than had been the Tokugawa bakufu, whose support had enabled many in the society to acquire their knowledge of the West. As demonstrated by their articles in the *Meiroku Zasshi,* their government employment did not prevent the Meirokusha members from severely criticizing government leadership and explaining at length the meaning of liberty, freedom, civilization, and the rights of man.

The End of the Meiroku Zasshi

After an initial period of repression while it was suppressing the partisans of the Tokugawa, the Meiji government adopted a liberal attitude toward development of a public press, presumably on the assumption that newspapers and journals were attributes of enlightenment. With the split in the government over Korea and the rising criticism from the people's rights advocates and others, however, the government turned to restrictions, such as the press regulations of October 1873 that forbad attacks on the government's actions, moral teachings injurious to government, and works likely to disturb the people. Among the few who stood up for freedom of the press were Tsuda Mamichi and Obata Tokujirō (小幡篤次郎), one of Fukuzawa Yukichi's collaborators on the *Minkan Zasshi*. Obata drew from Alexis de Tocqueville's *De la Démocratie en Amérique* to prepare the first treatise in Japanese on freedom of the press (*Jōboku Jiyūron,* 上木自由論).[52] Tsuda urged the government in the sixth issue of the *Meiroku Zasshi* that the fastest way to advance civilization and enlightenment was to provide for freedom of the press with regulations "whose truth, justice, and clarity are like the sun and the moon hanging from Heaven." In his second appeal six months later, however, Tsuda indicated that the press was exceeding its rightful role when it published stories that were lewd and personally injurious.[53]

More specifically directed to the Meirokusha was the admonition by Mori Arinori in his address at the society's first anniversary meeting that members should refrain from unproductive political discussions likely to bring injury to the society. Mori clearly hoped that the Meirokusha might survive the government's restrictions unscathed if it confined its discussions to literary, scientific, and philosophical matters conducive to education but unrelated to contemporary politics.[54] The blow feared by Obata, Tsuda, and Mori fell on 28 June 1875 when the government promulgated strict new press and libel ordinances that held editors accountable for the material they published.[55] In accordance with the new regulations, Mori's name as responsible editor appeared thereafter on each issue of the *Meiroku Zasshi.*

The Meirokusha members debated the effect of the government's new regulations when they met on 1 September after a summer recess. Presumably because he believed that the Meirokusha could still escape the government's censors if it avoided politics, Mori opposed a move by Mitsukuri Shūhei to suspend publication of the journal. Fukuzawa argued at length, however, that the Meirokusha had no alternative but to halt publication. Insisting that freedom of discussion could not survive under the government's regulations, Fukuzawa held that the members could either lay down their brushes or revise their thought to conform to the government's dictates. Fukuzawa also claimed that the scholar-bureaucrats among the members were prevented by a further government order of the previous July from publishing articles comparable to those by Nishi Amane on travel by foreigners within the country or by Kanda Kōhei on currency reform. Nor did he think the Meirokusha sufficiently united as a group to respond effectively against the government's repression.

To those who believed that the *Meiroku Zasshi* could continue publication since the government's regulations were really directed elsewhere, Fukuzawa insisted that the members should judge the laws by what they said without relying on presumed leniency of officials. Since all areas of human activity in Japan were invariably related to government, Fukuzawa denied that the society could steer clear of trouble by confining its publication to non-political matters. "[I] must say that Japan of today is the government's Japan, not the people's Japan," Fukuzawa lamented. When Fukuzawa advised the members thereafter to publish on their own responsibility without relying on the name of the *Meiroku Zasshi,* he was calling on the Meirokusha to follow the example of his group at Mita, which had ceased printing the *Minkan Zasshi* the previous June.[56]

Members attending the meeting voted nine to four in favor of Fukuzawa's move to suspend publication. Those in favor included Fukuzawa and two of his followers (Furukawa Masao and Akiyama Kōtarō), two Education Ministry officials (Tanaka Fujimaro and Tsuji Shinji), the agricultural expert Tsuda Sen, the senior educator Mitsukuri Shūhei, the statistician Sugi Kōji, and the bookseller Shimizu Usaburō. Those opposed were the society's principal sponsor, Mori, and the journal's three most prolific contributors: Tsuda Mamichi, Nishi Amane, and Sakatani Shiroshi. The society's attending directors split on the issue:

two for (Fukuzawa and Mitsukuri) and three against (Mori, Tsuda, and Nishi). After the meeting, affirmative votes were obtained from three other leading members at their homes: Nakamura Masanao, Nishimura Shigeki, and Katō Hiroyuki. These last three affirmative votes, however, may well have signified unwillingness to reopen the issue as much as approval.[57]

The vote to halt publication of the *Meiroku Zasshi* proved to be the death knell of the Meirokusha as an agent of enlightenment. Three issues of the *Zasshi* appeared thereafter containing articles, all but one by those who had opposed suspension. The lecture sessions ended in February 1876, according to the diary of the youthful Ueki Emori (植木枝盛). Members continued to meet for lunch and talk as the more intimate Meirokukai (明六會), their numbers diminishing through the years until only four were left in 1910.[58]

While hard evidence is difficult to find on this point, one gains the impression that the Meirokusha halted its journal and its other group enlightenment activities as much because the energies of the members were attracted elsewhere by their individual callings as because of the government's restrictive measures. The contents of the *Meiroku Zasshi* during its final months suggest the declining interest of the members as compared with their enthusiastic participation during the journal's first year. Moreover, Japan was moving quickly, and Japanese intellectual currents were proliferating. Under such conditions, the Meirokusha members may well have sensed that it was no longer practical or even desirable for them to pose as the vanguard of progress toward an agreed goal of enlightenment. Its brief public life notwithstanding, the Meirokusha produced in the *Meiroku Zasshi* a journal that epitomized the spirit of the period of the Japanese enlightenment more truthfully than any other single source. Indeed, few journals of any age anywhere outshine the *Meiroku Zasshi* as a journal that included representative contributions from distinguished intellectuals on a variety of problems important in their day.

Individual Meirokusha members remained active and productive intellectual leaders for many years. When the Education Ministry in 1879 sought to establish the Tokyo Academy (Tōkyō Gakushi-in, 東京學士院), in emulation of the national academies of the West, it turned first for assistance to seven former members of the Meirokusha: Nishi Amane, Katō Hiroyuki, Kanda Kōhei, Tsuda Mamichi, Nakamura Masanao, Mitsukuri Shūhei, and Fukuzawa Yukichi. Moreover, Fukuzawa Yukichi, who had declined the Meirokusha presidency, accepted that of the Tokyo Academy, its government sponsorship notwithstanding.[59] Professor Honjō Eijirō was doubtless correct when he denied that the Tokyo Academy was only a revival of the Meirokusha under official auspices. The academy eventually included scholars in Chinese and Japanese as well as in Western studies, and the seven Meirokusha members were clearly selected first because they were still leading intellectuals in 1879 as well as because they were friends of Tanaka Fujimaro, the Western-oriented vice minister of education who promoted the project and who had himself been a member of the Meirokusha.[60]

Notes for Introduction

[1]Undoubtedly the distinguished elder in Meirokusha studies is Professor Ōkubo Toshiaki 大久保利謙. Among Ōkubo's many books and articles, especially useful is his volume on enlightened thought during the Meiji era, *Meiji Keimō Shisō Shū* (明治啓蒙思想集), the third volume in *Meiji Bungaku Zenshū* (明治文學全集) published by Chikuma Shobō (筑摩書房), (Tokyo, 1967). In addition to representative selections from the writings of Meirokusha members other than Fukuzawa Yukichi, the volume includes extensive biographical and bibliographical material on the members as well as appraisals of the group by Ōkubo, Miyagawa Tōru (宮川透), and Hattori Shisō (服部之總). Still very helpful for the Meirokusha and other Japanese pioneers in Western studies is Asō Yoshiteru (麻生義輝), *Kinsei Nihon Tetsugaku Shi* (近世日本哲學史), (Tokyo, 1942). Valuable for his sketches of individual Meirokusha members is Motoyama Yukihiko (本山幸彦), *Meiji Shisō no Keisei* (明治思想の形成), (Tokyo, 1969). Tōyama Shigeki (遠山茂樹) presents a classic leftist view of the Meirokusha members as defenders of despotism in his *Meiji Ishin* (明治維新), (Tokyo, 1953), a theme that is largely absent from his more recent article "Meiroku Zasshi—Nihon Shisō Zasshi" (明六雜誌ー日本思想雜誌), *Shisō* (思想), No. 447 (September, 1961), 117–128. Honjō Eijirō (本庄榮治郎) takes a more traditional view of the Meirokusha as enlighteners in his excellent article "Meirokusha ni tsuite" (明六社について), *Nihon Gakushiin Kiyō* (日本學士院紀要), 26 (12 June 1968), 91–113. Yanagida Izumi (柳田泉) was especially concerned with the impact of the Meirokusha on literature and language in his *Meiji Shoki no Bungaku Shisō* (明治初期の文學思想) (2 vols.: Tokyo, 1965). In addition to the English biographies of Meirokusha members cited hereafter, the Meirokusha is treated in English in Kosaka Masaaki, *Japanese Thought in the Meiji Era* (Tokyo, 1958), translated by David Abosch, and in the somewhat disenchanted article by David J. Huish, "The Meirokusha: Some Grounds for Reassessment," *Harvard Journal of Asiatic Studies,* 32 (1972), 208–229. The *Meiroku Zasshi* is reprinted with occasional typographic errors in volume 18, *Zasshi Hen* (雜誌編) of the *Meiji Bunka*

Zenshū (明治文化全集), (24 vols.: Tokyo, 1928–1930) edited by Yoshino Sakuzō (吉野作造).

[2]The two most important sources on the origin of the Meirokusha are Nishimura Shigeki's memoirs *Ōjiroku* (往事錄), (Tokyo, 1905), pp. 65–66, and Mori Arinori's address on the first anniversary of the Meirokusha translated in Issue Thirty of the *Meiroku Zasshi,* pp. 364–375. The translation of the journal will be cited hereafter as *M.R.Z.* See p. xlix for a list of the Meirokusha members in May 1875.

[3]Regulations, 1874, Ōkubo, *Meiji Keimō Shisō Shū,* pp. 403–404.

[4]"Writing Japanese with the Western Alphabet," *M.R.Z.,* Issue One, p. 4.

[5]"Methods for Advancing Enlightenment," *M.R.Z.,* Issue Three, p. 38.

[6]Facts of publication are reproduced in Ōkubo, *Meiji Keimō Shisō Shū,* p. 406.

[7]See especially *M.R.Z.,* Issue One, p. 8 and Issue Seven (May, 1874), p. 97. A decade later, Kanda Kōhei spoke out eloquently in favor of a common written and spoken form in Japanese in response to the more academic approach by Nishimura Shigeki (Yamamoto Masahide [山本正秀], *Kindai Buntai Hassei no Shiteki Kenkyū* [近代文體發生の史的研究], [Tokyo, 1965], pp. 331–335).

[8]Katō, "Church and State in America," *M.R.Z.,* Issue Thirteen, p. 165; Mitsukuri Rinshō, "The Interrelation of Freedom of Peoples and Climates of Regions," *M.R.Z.,* Issue Five, p. 66.

[9]For Fukuzawa's account of the episode, see Ishikawa Kammei (石河幹明), *Fukuzawa Yukichi Den* (福澤諭吉傳), (4 vols.: Tokyo, 1932), II, 209–210.

[10]Ivan Hall, *Mori Arinori* (Cambridge, 1971), pp. 189–195.

[11]Ōkubo, *Meiji Keimō Shisō Shū,* pp. 408–409; Hall, *Mori Arinori,* pp. 238–239.

[12]Revised regulations in Ōkubo, *Meiji Keimo Shisō Shū,* pp. 404–405.

[13]Kiyooka Eichi, trans. *The Autobiography of Fukuzawa Yukichi* (New York, 1966), p. 100.

[14]The *Minkan Zasshi* is reproduced in the *Meiji Bunka Zenshū,* XVIII, 269–321.

[15]Fukuzawa Yukichi, *The Encouragement of Learning,* trans. David D. Dilworth and Umeyo Hirano (Tokyo, 1969), pp. 21–28.

[16]The standard biography of Fukuzawa is that by Ishikawa Kammei previously cited. Fukuzawa's complete works are assembled in a second edition of his *Zenshū* (Keiō Gijuku Hensan [慶應義塾編纂], *Fukuzawa Yukichi Zenshū* [福澤諭吉全集], [21 vols.: Tokyo, 1958–1964]). Carmen Blacker presents a synthesis of Fukuzawa's ideas in *The Japanese Enlightenment: A Study of the Writings of Fukuzawa Yukichi* (Cambridge, 1964), while Albert Craig discusses the changes in Fukuzawa's outlook through his life in "Fukuzawa Yukichi: The Philosophical Foundations of Meiji Nationalism," in *Political Development in Modern Japan,* ed. Robert E. Ward (Princeton, 1968), pp. 99–148. In addition to the English translations of Fukuzawa's *Autobiography* and *The Encouragement of Learning* cited above, his *An Outline of a Theory of Civilization* (*Bummeiron no Gairyaku,* [文明論之概略]) has been rendered into English by David A. Dilworth and D. Cameron Hurst (Tokyo, 1973). Important articles on Fukuzawa's philosophy and relating Fukuzawa's thought to the Japanese tradition of practical studies by Maruyama Masao (丸山眞男) are "Fukuzawa Yukichi ni okeru Jitsugaku no Tenkai," (福澤諭吉に於ける實學の展開), *Tōyō Bunka Kenkyū* (東洋文化研究), No. 3 (March, 1947), pp. 1–19, and "Fukuzawa Yukichi no Tetsugaku—Toku ni sono Jiji Hihan to no Kanren" (福澤諭吉の哲學ーとくにその時事批判との關連), *Kokka Gakkai Zasshi* (國家學會雜誌), 61 (September 1947).

[17]The most detailed biography of Mori Arinori is that by Ivan Hall previously cited. The leading Japanese authority on Mori is Hayashi Takeji (林竹二), whose numerous articles are listed in Hall's bibliography. For many years, the standard bio-

graphy of Mori in Japanese was that by Kimura Tadashi (木村匡), *Mori Sensei Den* (森先生傳) (Tokyo, 1897), which may be supplemented by two brief interpretations: Ōkubo Toshiaki (大久保利謙), *Mori Arinori* (森有禮) (Tokyo, 1944) and Harada Minoru (原田實), *Mori Arinori* (森有禮) (Tokyo, 1966). Mori's writings have been assembled by Ōkubo in the *Mori Arinori Zenshū* (森有禮全集) (3 vols.: Tokyo, 1972).

[18]Nishi's life and thought is most fully treated in English by Thomas R. H. Havens in *Nishi Amane and Modern Japanese Thought* (Cambridge, 1970), which provides a far more complete appreciation of Nishi the man than does Mori Ōgai (森鷗外) in *Nishi Amane Den* (西周傳), reprinted in *Ōgai Zenshū* (鷗外全集) (Tokyo, 1963), XI, 1–110. Nishi's philosophical writings are also discussed by Asō Yoshiteru in his previously cited *Kinsei Nihon Tetsugaku Shi* and by Kuwaki Genyoku (桑木嚴翼), in *Nishi Amane no Hyakuichi Shinron* (西周の百一新論) (Tokyo, 1940); his contributions to law, by Richard H. Minear in "Nishi Amane and the Reception of Western Law," *Monumenta Nipponica*, 28 (Summer, 1973), 151–175. Ōkubo Toshiaki has assembled Nishi's writings in *Nishi Amane Zenshū* (西周全集), (4 vols.: Tokyo, 1945–1966).

[19]Ōkubo, *Meiji Keimō Shisō Shū*, p. 442.

[20]The principal sources on Tsuda Mamichi are his biography by Tsuda Michiharu (津田道治), *Tsuda Mamichi* (津田眞道) (Tokyo, 1940) and Ōkubo Toshiaki's reviews of Tsuda's writings, "Tsuda Mamichi ni tsuite" (津田眞道について), *Teikoku Gakushiin Kiji* (帝國學士院紀事) (November 1944, March 1946, March 1949), 489–520, 17–47, 47–79.

[21]*Rikken Seitai Ryaku* (立憲政體略) (1868); *Shinsei Taii* (眞政太意) (1871); *Kokutai Shinron* (國體新論) (1874). Katō also authored a tract in the form of a dialogue that developed the advantages of opening Japan to foreign trade, *Kōeki Mondō* (交易問答) (1869).

[22]David Abosch, "Katō Hiroyuki and the Introduction of German Political Thought in Modern Japan" (Ph. D. dissertation, University of California, Berkeley, 1964), p. 454.

[23]Aside from David Abosch's study cited above, the most important sources on Katō are his autobiography, *Katō Hiroyuki Jijoden* (加藤弘之自敍傳) (Tokyo, 1915) and monographs by Tabata Shinobu (田畑忍), *Katō Hiroyuki no Kokka Shisō* (加藤弘之の國家思想) (Tokyo, 1939) and *Katō Hiroyuki* (加藤弘之) in the *Jimbutsu Sōsho* (人物叢書) series (Tokyo, 1959).

[24]*Nōshōben* reproduced in Ōkubo, *Meiji Keimō Shisō Shū*, p. 199.

[25]Proposals quoted in ibid., p. 209.

[26]Kanda's son, Kanda Naibu (神田乃武), prepared a short biography, *Kanda Kōhei Ryakuden* (神田孝平略傳) (Tokyo, 1900) and collected Kōhei's most significant writings in *Tangai Ikō* (淡崖遺稿) (Tokyo, 1900).

[27]Request to study abroad, Ōkubo, *Meiji Keimō Shisō Shū*, p. 279.

[28]Memorial printed in ibid., p. 281.

[29]The old standard biography of Nakamura by Ishii Tamiji (石井民司), *Jijoteki Jimbutsu Tenkei Nakamura Masanao Den* (自助的人物典型中村正直傳) (Tokyo, 1907) may be supplemented by the more popular Takahashi Masao (高橋昌郎), *Nakamura Keiu* (中村敬宇) (Tokyo, 1966) in the *Jimbutsu Sōsho* series.

[30]In addition to his autobiography, *Ōjiroku*, previously noted, there is an official biography of Nishimura prepared by the Nishimura Sensei Denki Hensan Kai (西村先生傳記編纂會), *Hakuō Nishimura Shigeki Den* (泊翁西村茂樹傳) (2 vols.: Tokyo, 1933), and a collection of Nishimura's works by the society he helped found, the Nihon Kōdō Kai (日本弘道會), and entitled *Hakuō Sōsho* (泊翁叢書) (Tokyo, 1908). For an excellent introduction to Nishimura in English, see Donald H. Shiveley,

"Nishimura Shigeki: A Confucian View of Modernization," in *Changing Japanese Attitudes Toward Modernization*, ed. Marius B. Jansen (Princeton, 1965), pp. 193–241.

[31]A helpful review to Sakatani Shiroshi's life may be found in the biography of his son, Sakatani Yoshio: Ko Sakatani Shishaku Kinen Jigyō Kai (故阪谷子爵記念事業會), *Sakatani Yoshio* (阪谷芳男) (Tokyo, 1951), pp. 3–53. Sakatani Yoshio collected his father's writings in Chinese style (*kanbun*) in *Rōro Zenshū* (朗廬全集) (Tokyo, 1922).

[32]For Sugi Kōji, there is Sugi's autobiography, *Sugi Kōji Jijoden* (杉亨二自敍傳) (Tokyo, 1915); a collection of Sugi's speeches edited by the Meirokusha secretary Sera Taichi (世良太一), Sera Taichi Hen (世良太一編), *Sugi Sensei Kōen Shū* (杉先生講演集) (Tokyo, 1902); and a recent semipopular biography by Kaji Shigeo (加地成雄), *Sugi Kōji Den* (杉亨二傳) (Tokyo, 1960).

[33]Ōtsuki Fumihiko (大槻文彥), *Mitsukuri Rinshō Kun Den* (箕作麟祥君傳) (Tokyo, 1907).

[34]There is a brief account of Tsuda Sen by Tomabeji Kazuo (苫米地一男) in the *Meiji Bunka Zenshū*, XXIV, 18–19. Short biographies of other Meirokusha members may be found in Heibonsha (平凡社), *Dai Jimmei Jiten* (大人名事典) (10 vols.: Tokyo, 1953–1955).

[35]Inouye Kazuo (井上和雄), "Mizuhoya Usaburō" (みづほ屋卯三郎), *Shinkyū Jidai* (新舊時代), 1 (May, June, and August 1928), 49–54, 51–57, 49–56.

[36]Memorial on the establishment of a representative assembly, 17 January 1874, Reply by Gotō and Soejima to Katō, 20 February 1874, Walter W. McLaren, editor, "Japanese Government Documents," *Transactions of the Asiatic Society of Japan*, 1st series, 42 (1914), 426–432, 440–448; Shimbun Shūsei Meiji Hennen Shi Hensan Kai (新聞集成明治編年史編纂會), *Shimbun Shūsei Meiji Hennen Shi* (新聞集成明治編年史) (15 vols.: Tokyo, 1934–1936), II, 117–118, 131–133. The memorialists were Soejima Taneomi (副島種臣), Gotō Shōjirō (後藤象二郎), Itagaki Taisuke (板垣退助), Etō Shimpei (江藤新平), Yuri Kimimasa (由利公正), Okamoto Kenzaburō (岡本健三郎), Furusawa Urō (古澤迂郎), and Komuro Nobuo (小室信夫).

[37]I believe that Mitsukuri Rinshō's attitude toward a popularly elected assembly may be conjectured from the last sentence in his second article on "Liberty", in *M.R.Z.*, Issue Fourteen (July 1874), p. 180, and his other writings and translations.

[38]Response by Katō Hiroyuki, 26 January 1874, McLaren, "Japanese Government Documents," pp. 433–439; *Shimbun Shūsei Meiji Hennen Shi*, II, 118–120.

[39]"An Abridged Translation from Bluntschli . . . ," *M.R.Z.*, Issue Four, pp. 47–49.

[40]"Refuting the Joint Statement of the Former Ministers," *M.R.Z.*, Issue Three, pp. 40–43; "An All Inclusive Parliament," Issue Twenty-Nine (February, 1874), pp. 352–355; Havens, *Nishi Amane*, pp. 60–64, 183–190.

[41]"Criticism of the Memorial on the Establishment of a Popularly Elected Assembly," *M.R.Z.*, Issue Three, pp. 32–34.

[42]"Reform of National Finance," *M.R.Z.*, Issue Seventeen (September 1874), pp. 213–218; "The Time for a Popularly Elected Assembly Is Not Yet," *M.R.Z.*, Issue Nineteen (October 1874), pp. 240–241.

[43]"On Government, Part Three," *M.R.Z.*, Issue Twelve (June 1874), pp. 155–159; "Minsen Giin Ron" (民選議院論) printed in Tsuda Michiharu, *Tsuda Mamichi*, pp. 185–188.

[44]"Should We Not Determine the Political Structure before Introducing a Popularly Elected Assembly?" *M.R.Z.*, Issue Thirteen (June 1874), pp. 169–175; "On the Irregular Route to a Popularly Elected Assembly: Parts One and Two," *M.R.Z.*, Issues Twenty-Seven and Twenty-Eight (February 1875), pp. 333–345.

[45]Nishimura, *Ōjiroku*, pp. 157–163.

[46]"Three Types of Political System: Part One and Conclusion," *M.R.Z.*, Issue Twenty-Eight (February 1875), pp. 346–350.

[47]Memorial to *Sain*, March 1874, Matsudaira Naosuke, editor (松平直亮編), *Nishimura Shigeki Sensei Ronsetsu Shū* (西村茂樹先生論說集) (1894,) pp. 91–93.

[48]"On Changing the Character of the People," *M.R.Z.*, Issue Thirty (February 1875), pp. 372–374.

[49]*Minsen Giin Ronkō* reproduced in Ōkubo, *Meiji Keimō Shisō Shū*, pp. 289–290.

[50]Report from the *Chōya Shimbun*, 7 May 1875, *Fukuzawa Yukichi Zenshū*, XXI, 296–299.

[51]"Kokken Kabun," reprinted in *Meiji Bunka Zenshū*, XVIII, 523–538.

[52]*Meiji Bunka Zenshū*, V, 17–19.

[53]"On Freedom of the Press," *M.R.Z.*, Issue Six, pp. 72–73; "On the Press," *M.R.Z.*, Issue Twenty (November 1874), pp. 250–252.

[54]"Speech . . . on the First Anniversary of the Meirokusha," *M.R.Z.*, Issue Thirty (February 1875), pp. 367–368.

[55]Press law, 28 June 1875, McLaren, "Japanese Government Documents," pp. 539–543; *Shimbun Jōrei* (新聞條例) and *Zambō Ritsu* (讒謗律), 28 June 1875, *Shimbun Shūsei Meiji Hennen Shi*, II, 343–344.

[56]Report with Fukuzawa's statement from the *Yūbin Hōchi Shimbun* (郵便報知新聞), 4 September 1875, reprinted in Ōkubo, *Meiji Keimō Shisō Shū*, pp. 409–411; Hall, *Mori Arinori*, pp. 242–245.

[57]Ōkubo Toshiaki (大久保利謙), "Meirokusha no Kaisan" (明六社の解散), *Nihon Rekishi* (日本歴史), No. 9 (January 1966), 46–48.

[58]Shimizu Renrō (清水連郎), "Mizuhoya Usaburō no Koto" (瑞穂屋卯三郎のこと), *Shinkyū Jidai* (新舊時代), 1 (December 1925), pp. 44–45.

[59]On Fukuzawa, the Meirokusha members, and the founding of the Tokyo Academy, see especially Ōkubo Toshiaki, "Fukuzawa Yukichi to Meiji Shoki no Gakkai—toku ni Meirokusha to Tokyo Gakushiin o Chūshin to shite" (福澤諭吉と明治初期の學界—とくに明六社と東京學士會院を中心として), *Shigaku* (史學), XXVII, 116–160.

[60]Honjō, "Meiroku Zasshi ni tsuite," p. 111.

MEIROKUSHA MEMBERS, MAY 1875

Hatakeyama Yoshinari, 畠山義成	
Nishi Amane, 西周	Director
Nishimura Shigeki, 西村茂樹	Director
Ōtsuki Fumihiko, 大槻文彦	
Katō Hiroyuki, 加藤弘之	
Tanaka Fujimaro, 田中不二麿	
Tsuda Mamichi, 津田眞道	Director
Tsuda Sen, 津田仙	
Nakamura Masanao, 中村正直	
Tsuji Shinji, 辻新次	
Kuki Ryūichi, 九鬼隆一	
Fukuzawa Yukichi, 福澤諭吉	Director
Furukawa Masao, 古川正雄	
Akiyama Kōtarō, 秋山恆太郎	
Asai Harubumi, 淺井晴文	
Sakatani Shiroshi, 阪谷素	
Mitsukuri Shūhei, 箕作秋坪	Director
Shimizu Usaburō, 清水卯三郎	Treasurer
Hida Shōsaku, 肥田昭作	
Mori Arinori, 森有禮	Director
Sera Taichi, 世良太一	Secretary
Sugi Kōji, 杉亨二	
Kanda Kōhei, 神田孝平	Corresponding Member
Tomita Tetsunosuke, 富田銕(鐵)之助	Corresponding Member
Takagi Saburō, 高木三郎	Corresponding Member
[William E.] Griffis,	Corresponding Member
Kashiwabara Takaaki, 柏原孝章	Corresponding Member

Former Member

Mitsukuri Rinshō, 箕作麟祥

MEIROKU ZASSHI

Writing Japanese with the Western Alphabet[1]

Nishi Amane

My colleagues and I have often drawn comparisons with the various countries of Europe when a few of us have discussed from time to time such matters as the rise and fall of states and the evidences of merit in government. Envying their civilization and mourning our own unenlightenment, we have suffered unbearable sorrow, having finally concluded that our people seem indeed to be incorrigibly ignorant. Since the Restoration, men of talent have emerged in large numbers, and all areas [of government] have been revitalized. From the highest offices in the capital to the sixty-odd prefectures, everything is already different from Old Japan. The government's fine policies and good works are also beyond enumeration.

Yet if one looks carefully from a different point of view, all is still confused and imperfect. The fine policies notwithstanding, the people remain unenlightened as before, and there have been numerous cases in which the profit from the truly good works has not compensated for the injury. This is because, however grand the external structure may be, the time since the Restoration has been too short for its inner spirit to prevail. It is like clothing a monkey or adorning a charwoman with a dancing costume. The intentions of the high, therefore, do not penetrate to the low, while the feelings of the low fail to reach the high. The situation is like a man whose entire body is paralyzed. Thus, even though one or two wise men of heroic proportions want to encourage and stimulate change, it seems that, having exhausted their strength, they will collapse, as their task is like waking a child from a fast sleep or helping a husband in a drunken stupor. This is precisely why even such outstanding leaders and promoters finally submit without revealing their true minds and with equivocation humbly accept the situation regardless of their real feelings.

According to my view, this is an evil prevalent throughout society, an evil attributable to the fact that, the wise being few and the ignorant many, the few have not the power to oppose the many. This is why I previously stated that the people seem indeed to be incorrigibly ignorant. This evil, in the final analysis, is not limited only to those who govern and carry out the laws. Today in society as well, we invariably confront this one insurmountable obstacle [of ignorance] first when we want to achieve something by mobilizing in the least the people's strength.

Yet it is naturally the responsibility of those in authority in good time to guide the people tenderly by the hand from ignorance to the level of enlightenment, just as one gently removes all the weeds without pulling up the seedlings. To do otherwise would seem to be truly a crime from the point of view of governing. Yet if the people in our society are deprived of happiness because of this failure by their leaders and if degradation becomes so extreme as to be incurable, this is not only the crime of the government. It is first of all a "social" crime of the people themselves. Should those who aspire in the least to intellectual leadership fail to assume the initiative in curing this ignorance, they are undeniably guilty of a social crime.

Herein, after all, lies the reason why Mori now wants to form this society for science, the arts, and letters. Science, the arts, and letters all destroy such ignorance. Since these are the tools for overcoming this great obstacle, I feel that there can be no better pursuits for the people themselves to follow if they want to destroy completely the forces of ignorance in society. Therefore, foolish incompetent that I may be, I wish to exert my best efforts and to join this society. I cannot but privately suspect that, even though we may take science, the arts, and letters as our objectives, our painstaking efforts will lead to nothing unless we have some project upon which to proceed. That is, by meeting together to sharpen our wits, now assiduously presenting our opinions and now raising questions, we companions naturally profit not a little from our discussions and study. Yet what I most fear is that, if we do not have a project to follow, we may be unable to achieve the great aim of destroying the strong forces of ignorance.

Despite the superficiality of my learning, therefore, I shall endeavor to startle my colleagues in this society by proposing a strange plan. This strange and startling proposal is indeed like throwing the jewel of Sui into the dark.[2] Yet I believe that, if the society adopts the project, we may hope that it will be the vanguard in the destruction of the forces of ignorance. If we now just consider the import of the words "science, the arts, and letters" in the motto of our society, what we call science and the arts emerge after letters exist. Without letters, how can there be science and the arts? The ancients also said that literature is the means for understanding the Way. In our letters at present, however, it is improper for us to write as we speak as well as improper to speak as we write since the grammars of speech and writing in our language are different.

After all, since men in society already recognize this to be the folly in our letters as well as their greatest obstacle, there have also been efforts to rectify this situation. Some propose that we reduce and fix the number of Chinese ideographs (*kanji*). Others would use only the Japanese syllabaries or *kana,* publish *kana* dictionaries, and prepare *kana* grammars. Even though there are still other suggestions, these are the influential two of recent days. It may be said that proposals to limit *kanji* are extremely biased. When cows, goats, foxes, and badgers drink together from one lake only to the limit of their stomachs' capacities, why should one regret the largeness of the lake? These men who urge the limitation of *kanji* would probably say: "There are few with stomachs as large as cows and goats and many with stomachs as small as foxes and badgers. Let us judge those with large stomachs in terms of those with small ones." These are like the men of small capacity in Europe who differ from those who, together with the various living languages, extend their competence to the dead languages of Latin, Greek, Hebrew, and Sanskrit.

Those who advocate using only *kana* seem to be extremely reasonable, but how can there be anything more inconvenient than the *kana* system in which vowels are linked with consonants? I would like to discuss this later in detail. I know that I definitely cannot agree with either of the above suggestions. The present trend to introduce the manifold ways of Europe is like a flood. There is no area to which we have not turned to adopt from them, be it clothing, food, drink, lodging, law, government, manners, and the hundred sciences, arts, and industries. Moreover, so-called mixed residence and Western religion are only a matter of time. In the long run, the introduction of Western religion and mixed residence by foreigners among Japanese is inevitable.

Now take the man who eats sweet potatoes. He can desist from eating if he has not yet started. But if he wants to stop in the midst of his enjoyment, how can he do so? Since the trend to import from the West is already so strong that we cannot leave three after taking seven out of ten, I think it best to adopt their entire alphabet. We first adopted Chinese writing and derived our literature entirely from China during the reigns of our early kings. Now when we are already importing literature from Europe in conformity with the trends of the times, why do we fail only to adopt their writing? In a country like China, the territory has long been broad, the people teeming, the national power firm, and letters flourishing. Should you trace these elements back to antiquity, her civilization was then not inferior to that of Europe. If China has been somewhat parochial, this is understandable. Why should she look elsewhere?

Referring historically to the civilization of a country like Japan and examining it in light of the people's character, however, she is strong at emulating others but weak at creating things herself, being expert at imitation. Thus to cite the example of past literature, we honored Hakushi [Po Chü-i][3] in the Middle Ages; [Hayashi] Razan[4] and [Yamazaki] Ansai[5] regarded the Sung Confucians as their teachers; Nakae [Tōju][6] and Kumazawa [Banzan][7] were rooted in [Wang] Yang-ming; Ken-en [Ogyū Sorai] looked to Wang [Shih-chên] and Li [P'an-lung];[8] and we have come more recently to emulate the Yüan brothers[9] and Chung [Hsing].[10]

Since we have not yet witnessed the appearance of an individual able to turn out new contrivances, it is needless to say that our new is their old. Being people of this type in a country like ours, why should we hesitate to adopt the strong points of others and make them our strong points? Indeed, rising above himself to follow others was the true virtue of the great Shun,[11] quickly submitting after recognizing justice was the great principle of Confucius' *teaching* [Jikun];[12] and only to derive pleasure from one's own achievements does not comport with superior wisdom. Then why should the Japanese now cling to their parochialism?

I would say that, even though our people themselves may not be creative, it is also true virtue to conform to the good after recognizing it and to adopt the strong points of others. Should I simply affirm this view, however, someone will refute me. While allowing that it is naturally fine to adopt the strong points of others and to employ their alphabet, he will question me regarding the fact that it will be extremely difficult suddenly to induce the nation to learn their letters. Or another may say: "It is indeed good to employ their alphabet, but there is ultimately nothing better than to introduce the use of English or French. It would also be appropriate to follow the example of Russian government officials who formerly all employed French but who are now inclined to use their own language."

I do not believe this to be true. After all, the language of a people is innate. It arises inalterably from the mutual association of the basic factors of race, climate, and environment. The sounds that we studied in China during antiquity lost their true quality over a long period of time until they became what is known as *Go-on* [Wu pronunciation].[13] We again studied Chinese phonetics during the Middle Ages, and these sounds also changed from the original to become *Kan-on* [Han pronunciation].[14] There have thus emerged two variant pronunciations that differ from the present *Tō-on* [T'ang pronunciation][15] and that have been transmitted until finally we are unable to do without them. Again, since the offices of the imperial court in antiquity employed the Han tongue (*Kan-go*),[16] their culture was restricted and could not spread through the land. This early Chinese (*Kan-go*) finally changed into *sōrōbun*[17] in which such words as *tatematsuru, itasu, tame,* and *gotoshi*[18] are used in Chinese order even though the language is Japanese. This transformation of *Kan-go* into *sōrōbun* should indeed be a warning to those who would destroy our innate tongue and adopt a foreign language.

I may then be asked, "If this is the case, then what about your proposal to adopt the Western alphabet?" My response is that I would only write Japanese with the Western alphabet and then read it in accordance with established rules of pronunciation. This is not something, however, that can be taught under compulsion or achieved by strict command. The reform will be accomplished through months and years of gradual learning, the few growing to the many and the small becoming the big. It will be impossible unless men of common purpose form a society and throw themselves into the project. This is why it is important to establish a society and why borrowing the prestige of my colleagues is essential for success. Someone may argue that matters are not changed unless there is sufficient profit and that methods are not reformed unless there have been grave injuries. Should you ask what, after all, are the advantages of writing Japanese with the Western alphabet? I would state them as follows:

First. We shall perfect Japanese grammar by adopting the Western alphabet.

Second. Manifestly, the reform will simplify the difficulties of embarking on study. At the beginning of their schooling, students will first become familiar with the Japanese language and with the names and principles of things generally. When they subsequently are able to enter foreign language study, these other languages no longer will appear strange since they are written in the same Western alphabet. Having become proficient in the distinctions between parts of speech and different pronunciations [in Japanese], learning foreign languages for students will be only a labor of memory.

Third. Since writing and speaking will follow the same rules, what is appropriate in writing will also be appropriate in speaking. That is, lectures, toasts, speeches before assemblies, and sermons by preachers may all then be recited as they are written and recorded as they are read.

Fourth. If they know the twenty-six letters of the "ABC's" and just learn pronunciation and spelling, even children will be able to read the writing of men, even the ignorant will be able to comprehend the works of gentlemen, and both children and the ignorant will be able to record their opinions themselves.

Fifth. There are numerous persons proficient in the Western mathematics that is currently being introduced. Along with this, these people have come to adopt and can appreciate the convenience of writing sideways [with the alphabet]. Furthermore, when the Finance and War Ministries and others have adopted "bookkeeping" methods, they have shifted wholly to the Western system of writing sideways.

Sixth. This method can be applied uniformly once it is established. Hepburn's dictionary[19] and the Japanese language society of the Frenchman Rosny have recently appeared.[20] But they have only transcribed today's vulgar tongue directly, without achieving complete perfection.

Seventh. Eventual adoption of the Western alphabet will greatly assist writers and translators.

Eighth. Once we introduce their letters, we can employ in its present form the printing machinery that has been invented in the West. There are no words to describe this convenience of printing that is entirely dependent upon their form of writing.

Ninth. Technical words in translations can be employed directly without translation, just as today we transcribe them phonetically with characters. We will also be able to use the original words for machines and celebrated products without being obliged to employ ideographic translation.

Tenth. If we adopt their system, all things of Europe will be entirely ours. Since grasping this strong point of theirs while destroying our current writing system is not to be compared with a trivial change in clothing, we can boast to the world that it is the beauty of our people's character thus to follow the good. This will suffice to leave them dumbstruck.

Given these ten advantages, why do we hesitate? Should I be asked if, after all, there will be no harm, I would reply:

The first alleged disadvantage is that the sellers of brushes and ink sticks will lose their businesses. There are very few of these shops, however, even in the urban centers. Moreover, they will have time to change their businesses since the adoption of Western letters will be gradual. Thus this problem really need not be considered.

Second of the supposed disadvantages is that we shall be forced to alter the manufacture of paper. There are already arrangements, however, to build a mill for producing Western-style paper, and we may presume that this industry will spread gradually through the country. Moreover, our paper being abundant, we can provide paper for the use of the world if we substitute glass for *shōji*.[21] Thus we shall convert a disadvantage into an advantage.

Third, it is said that scholars in Chinese and Japanese classical studies will become extremely angry and jealous if they hear of this idea. Looked at from the point of view of Japanese classical studies, however, our language study can only be established through the adoption of the Western alphabet. This should be a source for rejoicing rather than regret. Nay, whether writing is Chinese or Western is naturally of no consequence to us. Indeed, the Western alphabet, being phonetic, does not conflict with our language as do Chinese ideographs. Therefore, those in Japanese studies should really agree when they fully appreciate the convenience of the alphabet.

Chinese in Japan is like Latin in the West. Children will first learn Japanese and then be introduced to Chinese studies, which will be a discipline of the middle schools and above. This separation is self-evidently clear. The teachers of Chinese classical studies in the middle schools and above will resemble those of Greek and Latin in the West. Again, this is not something to be feared since the status of their studies will thereby be elevated. Only the village pedagogues, the teachers in the *terakoya,*[22] and petty officials will be extremely displeased if they hear of the change. Even so, they should understand that they will not suffer from the suddenness of the reform since it will not be ordered and since its gradual introduction will cause them no great hardship. Thus the three supposed injuries are not legitimate injuries, but the ten advantages are real benefits. How can one empty injury be matched against ten real benefits?

Someone may comment that, while the advantages of the alphabet are already manifest, we must consider the difficulties connected with its introduction. It is said that there are three difficulties, the first of which is grammatical. Who does not now want to establish Japanese grammar? Those in classical Japanese studies, however, do not understand what is suitable for actual usage as they only know the use of ancient literary styles. Among the forms in common usage, *sōrōbun* is different from what is spoken. Recently, in publications such as this journal, it has been fairly standard to write with a mixture of [Chinese ideographs] and the *katakana* syllabary. Even so, these publications have achieved no stylistic unity, as from time to time they mix Chinese and Japanese grammatical forms. Those opposed to the Japanese classical scholars, therefore, desire ultimately to write directly in today's vulgar tongue (*zokugo*)[23] and to abandon completely the system of postpositions. If this struggle between the Japanese classical scholars and their critics is not halted, how can grammar be established? This then is the first difficulty.

I would not say, however, that there are not means for bringing compromise between the two. Should you ask what these means might be, I would respond that we shall achieve a compromise by establishing rules for "spelling" and "pronunciation." Now, the frequent differences between spelling and pronunciation in English, after all, are as inevitable as in Japanese, and the differences between literary (*ga*)[24] and vulgar (*zoku*) Japanese, therefore, closely resemble those between English pronunciation and spelling. Let me take up a few examples:

Explanation of Table

The first line is the spelled (literary) form.

The second line is the pronounced (vulgar) form.

A dot (.) indicates letters that are not read.

A circumflex (^) indicates letters whose pronunciation is changed.

Italics indicate the words concerned.

Adjectives:

ikasama *omosirosi*
ikasama *omosiro.i*
kore wa *yorosisi*
kore wa *yorosi.i*
omorosiroki koto
omorosiro.i koto
utukusiki hana
utukusi.i hana
atuku naru
atu.u naru
samuku naru
samu.u naru

Note: In the last two examples, the pronunciation is from the Kyōto dialect. The pronunciation in Edo is the same as the written form.

Predicates used as modifiers:

kitai naru hito
kitai na..hito

fusigi naru koto
fusigi na.. koto

Note: *Naru* is a contraction of the particle *ni* and the verb *aru*. For the moment, let us regard this as a natural (*senten*) form.[25]

Pronouns:

kare
.are
idure
.dôre
iduko
.dôko

Postpositions:

kore *nite* yosi
kore *..d̂e* yo.i
sore *nitemo* yosi
sore *..d̂emo* yo.i

Verbs:

ima *kikam. yuwam.*
ima *kikaû yuwaû*
yume vo *mitari*
yume vo *mita..*
ima *ikitu*
ima *it̂ûtâ*
kiruru
kirêru
moyuru
moyêru
} There are many such as these.
nani nitemo kanitemo benkiyau vo
nan. . .d̂emo ka . . d̂emo benkiyau vo sezu ba narumazi
sezu ba naruma.i

In the above fashion, I hope generally to harmonize the quarrels between those advocating the literary and vulgar styles. In addition, however, there are indeed a great many instances in which compromise between the two styles has not been possible as there are forms that can be neither adopted nor rejected even though we desire to do so, such as the employment of *gozaru* for *aru,* the polite usage of *mosu* and *masu,* and a variety of other honorific expressions (*keigo*).[26] But if there is mutual conciliation between the advocates of the literary style and those favoring the vulgar style, the one refraining from common use of excessively elevated grammatical forms and the other giving full attention to the spoken language, endeavoring to speak as we are able to write, a natural style will become innate, and our language may reach European levels of refinement within a century. This is why I said that it is necessary to adopt the Western alphabet since our *kana,* in which vowels and consonants are linked, are inconvenient.

Second, there is the difficulty from the governmental point of view. Apart from the emperor, none in government are considering letters. Even though the situation may not be to our liking, all will be in vain if there is not governmental approval or should we once suffer a veto by the Ministry of Education. Since the lords and ministers of the present Restoration are all men who are directed toward change, however, we can ultimately secure their sanction once they understand from our moderate and reasonable representations that the reform will only benefit their country. Therefore, the second difficulty can also be eliminated.

Third is the difficulty of expense. This matter is not one, however, that requires extensive financing. The expenses necessary at the first stage comprise only three items: support for meetings (which we can provide ourselves), the salary for a secretary, and resources for publication. Once we have gotten under way, there will be expenses for printing dictionaries, grammars, and various other types of literature. As for methods to meet these expenses, once we have decided in the society to carry out the project, the present members will be designated charter members, and the members entering thereafter will each be charged a three-yen initiation fee. If we accumulate this money to serve as resources for a later day, we can just cover expenses by gathering Yen 3000 as the membership gradually increases to 1000.

Furthermore, when we have reached the point of publication, after having established the rules of grammar in our discussions, we shall distribute these rules in small pamphlets and oblige the new members to observe them. We shall allow the new members to raise questions about points that they may not understand. And if they have suggestions, they may submit these proposals for discussion and possible adoption by the charter members of the society. In their correspondence as well as in their discussions of science, the arts, and letters, the society's members necessarily should be proficient in using these rules. Of course, these practices need not be applied to writings and translations outside the society. In this fashion, the gradually expanding "circle" will broaden within three years to twenty or thirty thousand members, and we shall have gathered Yen 90,000 once the membership reaches 30,000. At this point, we shall be able to undertake all manner of activities, such as printing, writing, translating, and publishing a journal.

When organizing the society, however, it is most essential first to establish rules for determining its charter members and then, exerting ourselves energetically in the society's affairs, to conduct business privately, without pressing others into the directorate and especially rejecting immature scholars. After all, "curiosity" is a principal characteristic of man, and the more secrecy there is, the more this quality of curiosity is stimulated. Such being the case, we shall draw active members into the society once it is tightly formed.

There is still another advantage [to be derived from the society]. If we finally establish this society, its members should all be persons of active character directed toward Western ways, whether they are scholars in Chinese or Japanese classical studies or just ordinary men. There is a saying that the brave and the heroic attract men's minds. If we embrace the talented of the nation in one society and if we employ only good methods, we shall surely achieve full cooperation from those in "science," the "arts," "literature," and "morals." Only then shall we annihilate the obdurate armies of ignorance and ultimately be able to trumpet the fanfare of our civilization. As for the estimated time, we can establish rules [for Romanization] in one year, distribute them to the cities in two years, meet with first success in three years, and spread the rules through the nation in seven years. Finally in ten years, women and children will be reciting them, and students will begin their schooling with them.

Once we have removed the above three difficulties, one more will appear. Should you ask what this difficulty may be, I would respond that there will clearly be no profit redounding to the personal interest of those in the society who pursue the project. Probably, there will be only loss and no profit. Since their endeavors will be wholly on behalf of the people of the nation, the members will suffer in advance of the nation's suffering and enjoy only after the nation has enjoyed. Of course in the beginning, but also in the later stages, there will necessarily be times when the participants may not be entirely pleased or may become tired. My colleagues can only meet this difficulty by adhering to the four principles of patience, diligence, responsibility, and strenuous exertion. Of course, we can never accomplish anything if one of these is lacking in the least.

This then is what I earlier described as a strange and startling proposal. At first glance, it seems to be a plan that rashly runs with the times and leads the nation in the path of the West. Looked at more deliberately, it appears cold-hearted and heedlessly oblivious of the times. If we follow this project energetically, however, we can avoid falling into extreme hardships and difficulties. I have pondered the fact that the Europeans now lead the world. If one considers this from the point of view of reason, their race has achieved greatness by piling up the lesser results of their minute observations. They view even the vastness of the universe in terms of the falling apple. They guide legions by beginning with the training of but one soldier. They depend upon nothing more than the expanding power of steam to send ships across the four seas. Their transmission of electricity to the four continents is derived just from observing a humble kite. And similarly nothing has contributed more to their world preeminence in science, the arts, and letters than the twenty-six letters of the "ABCs." If my colleagues favor me by now agreeing with my views, they should start with the letter "A." The following is what I have already concluded to be the order for proceeding in the matter.

1. Determine the relationship between the "ABCs" and sounds in Japanese.

2. Establish rules for distinguishing the four voices in our phonetics.[27]

3. Create parts of speech after determining the nature of the language.

4. Determine what is inherent and what is extrinsic in the language.[28]

5. Decide the rules for spelling.

6. Decide the rules for pronunciation.
7. Decide the rules for inflection.
8. Decide the tenses and conjugations of verbs.
9. Decide the rules for employing the sounds of Chinese ideographs (*kanji*).
10. Decide the rules for employing Western words.

Such a matter as the usage of vulgar and literary forms can await resolution at a later date. Having set forth a few humble thoughts, I await the judgment of my friends. Even though I dare not hope for its adoption, I shall be happy should my plan receive my colleagues' kind consideration.

Why the Reform of Writing Should Depend on the Level of Enlightenment

Nishimura Shigeki

Upon carefully reading several times Nishi's discourse on the reform of writing, I have found that the refinement of his explanations leaves nothing to be desired. After all, should the project develop as he predicts, men of letters like ourselves will really derive utmost pleasure from the great advance in culture. The ignorant people of today, however, know nothing of scholarship, and they cannot be taught even the conventional characters without laboring over numerous explanations. Still more will we be adding difficulty to difficulty if we undertake to teach them a foreign script that resembles wriggling worms after abandoning the forty-eight symbols [*kana*] that until now have been the national writing. Whereas Nishi states that we shall destroy the people's ignorance by reforming their writing, I think that we cannot change writing until their ignorance has been destroyed. It is generally the case that wise men invariably judge matters by weighing the advantages and disadvantages. Since it would be superfluous for me to repeat the advantages that Nishi has already elucidated in detail, I would supplement where it seems that his discussion of the disadvantages is not yet fully developed.

In general, it is the nature of man to dislike jumbled complexity and to enjoy simple clarity. Now the writing is simple and the meaning clear when we write the ideograph for mountain (山) and river (川). But when one writes these words as *yama* and *kawa,* their appearance is somewhat unclear as the writing is rather complex. Again, the characters for river (川), hides (革), and side (側) may be understood at a glance, but it is extremely difficult to distinguish the meanings of these three words when they are transcribed as *kawa, kawa,* and *kawa.* This is the first disadvantage.

In antiquity, we were readily successful in adopting Chinese characters and discarding our ancient writing because our literature was then at an embryonic stage.[29] Even though we cannot now know the rough and simple script originally used in our country, the glittering and cultured writing of China, after all, was incomparably more convenient. This is probably why the intellectuals of that time quickly substituted Chinese for the ancient Japanese writing and the people of the entire country also readily altered their old usage.[30] The situation is entirely different today, however. Since we have used the language and writing of China together with our own for more than a thousand years, employing their characters is extremely convenient [at our present level of enlightenment]. To replace entirely the mixed system of *kanji* and *kana* with the Western alphabet will be far more difficult than discarding our ancient script. This is the second disadvantage.

At present, *kana* and *kanji* are invariably used in all communications ranging from edicts by the court to correspondence by the people, and they are invariably employed in all literature that expounds theory, instructs the people, records history, explains the arts, and the like. As men would be wholly unable to read materials from the past should they completely abandon *kana* and *kanji* for the Western alphabet (I refer only to those of shallow learning), the last two thousand years of Japanese and Chinese history would be as obscure as midnight. Furthermore, even though scholars would emerge to transcribe the histories of Japan and China in Western letters, this necessarily involves duplication of labor. This is the third disadvantage.

Even a child of three feet can understand how extremely difficult it would be to attempt the introduction of an entirely different and previously unknown method in defiance of these three disadvantages. If asked then whether we should ultimately refrain from reforming our writing, I would respond that, quite the contrary, the above disadvantages apply only to our ignorant countrymen of today. From the point of view of enlightened and cultured people, these three disadvantages are insufficient to count even as one disadvantage. When asked regarding the proper order for undertaking a reform in writing in our country at present, I would state that the urgent business of today is only to encourage as many people as possible to exert themselves in scholarship, whether in Chinese, Japanese, or Western studies. They will naturally understand the numerous deficiencies in our language and writing once they have exerted themselves in study. And the idea will surely emerge that we should try to reform our writing once its inadequacies are appreciated. If there then develops sentiment for adopting Western letters in place of *kana* and *kanji,* we should be able to achieve success as easily as a ship moves with the current. This is why I affirm that we cannot reform our writing system until we have destroyed the ignorance of the people. It is probably true, as Nishi says, that we shall advance in literature only after we have altered writing.

Nishi's opinions in regard to the society's regulations may also be quite appropriate. I hear in this connection that there is a draft by Mori. It is to be hoped that we can complete the regulations by bringing together the proposals of the two gentlemen and introducing amendments and compromises during discussions by the members. Generally speaking, men are without freedom once they are bound by regulations that are strictly established at the outset. On the other hand, if we fail to adopt a few regulations, the society's progress will be long delayed by backing and filling in repetitious discussions at each meeting. I hope that the members confer and agree on the following points:

1. The name of the society.
2. The number of members in the society.
3. The methods for electing new members to the society.
4. The admission fee to be charged new members.
5. The method for determining the president.
6. The time of meeting and the rules governing discussions.

7. The selection of secretary and a treasurer.
8. Methods for publishing the society's proceedings.

Ours is the first literary and scientific society to be established in the country. Moreover, the savants of the society are all celebrated figures in the land. Men all say that splendid discussions and immortal theories will surely emerge from this society. I pray that the honorable members may fulfill the expectations of discerning people by establishing a model for the nation and by opening the eyes of the ignorant with their elevated and penetrating opinions.

[1]Although Nishi was genuinely interested in language and coined many terms that have survived as common words in Japanese to the present day, this first essay is also significant as an opening appeal by one of Japan's foremost enlighteners for a campaign to destroy the dark forces of ignorance. But for Nishi's positive call, the inauguration of the *Meiroku Zasshi* would have been dominated by the negative responses of those Meirokusha members who rejected the plea by Fukuzawa Yukichi that they abandon government service and promote enlightenment in society as private individuals. Nishi had already predicted four years earlier that the Japanese would abandon the use of Chinese ideographs within fifty to sixty years. Apart from his proposal to shift to Western letters, linguists are especially interested in his recommendation that the Japanese abandon their highly artificial traditional literary forms and adopt common rules for writing and speaking. He may thus be regarded as an early advocate of what the Japanese call *gembun itchi,* 言文一致, a common written and spoken form.

[2]The jewel of Sui, *Sui chu,* 隋珠, refers to a splendid jewel that a grateful dragon is said to have bestowed on the Marquis of Sui in Chinese antiquity. In China and Japan, it was traditionally the most precious jewel in the world. Nishi is thus suggesting that his proposal may seem completely futile, like throwing away the most valuable treasure.

[3]Hakushi, 白氏, the Chinese poet Po Chü-i, 白居易, A.D. 772–846, was especially admired by aristocrats at the Japanese court during the Heian Period, 794–1160.

[4][Hayashi] Razan, 林羅山, 1583–1657, was the first of the great family of scholars who labored to establish the philosophy of Chu Hsi, 朱熹, and his Sung Dynasty school as the philosophical basis for the Tokugawa state.

[5][Yamazaki] Ansai, 山崎闇齋, 1618–1682, sought to combine the Chu Hsi tradition with the doctrines of Japan's native faith to form Suika Shintō, 垂下神道.

[6]Nakae [Tōju], 中江藤樹, 1608–1648, espoused the intuitional school of the sixteenth-century Chinese philosopher Wang Yang-ming, 王陽明, who stressed that the inner light should be man's guide in life.

[7][Kumazawa] Banzan, 熊澤蕃山, 1619–1691, sought to apply Wang Yang-ming's theories to statecraft.

[8]Ken-en, 蘐園, is a pen-name of Ogyū Sorai, 荻生徂徠, 1666–1728, the brilliant scholar who is generally classified as a member of the so-called Ancient School, Kogaku, 古學, of Confucian thought. Sorai was influenced by the archaistic literary styles

exemplified by the sixteenth-century Chinese scholars Wang Shih-chên, 王世貞, and Li P'an-lung, 李攀龍. Nishi and others of his generation were attracted by the pragmatic quality in Sorai's thought.

[9]Yüan Sung-tao, 袁宗道, Yüan Chung-tao, 袁中道, and Yüan Hung-tao, 袁宏道, were three famous brothers who sought to introduce vulgar styles in opposition to Wang Shih-chên and Li P'an-lung.

[10]Chung [Hsing], 鍾惺, a critic of the Yüan brothers who favored highly individual style.

[11]Shun, 舜, the Chinese legendary emperor traditionally regarded as one of the twenty-four examples of filial piety.

[12]Jikun, 尼訓.

[13]*Go-on*, 呉音.

[14]*Kan-on*, 漢音.

[15]*Tō-on*, 唐音.

[16]*Kan-go*, 漢語.

[17]*Sōrōbun*, 候文, the Japanese epistolary style.

[18]*Tatematsuru*, 奉ル; *itasu*, 致ス; *tame*, 爲メ; *gotoshi*, 如シ.

[19]Dr. J. C. Hepburn, the American missionary, brought out his first *Japanese and English Dictionary* in 1867. Hepburn's system of Romanization remains standard to the present day.

[20]Leon Rosny, a French orientalist and ethnologist who befriended Shimizu Usaburō and other young Japanese who visited the Paris Exposition in 1867–1868.

[21]*Shōji*, 障子, translucent sliding paper doors.

[22]*Terakoya*, 寺子屋, the so-called temple schools that were private schools for commoners during the Tokugawa Period.

[23]*Zokugo*, 俗語.

[24]*Gago*, 雅語.

[25]*Senten*, 先天. *Senten* in modern Japanese means "innate." I would suggest that Nishi regards *naru* as a genuine or innate Japanese form, as distinguished from the artificial styles of *sōrōbun*.

[26]*Keigo*, 敬語.

[27]*Waga on ni shisei no betsu ari, sono hō o sadamu*, 我音ニ四聲ノ別アリ其法ヲ定ム. The exact meaning of this phrase is unclear. The term *shisei*, four voices, is most commonly used to refer to the four tones in Chinese, wholly unrelated to Romanizing Japanese. Since Nishi uses *on* to refer to the three pronunciations of ideographs derivative from Chinese, the four voices may refer to *Go-on, Kan-on*, and *Tō-on* pronunciations derivative from China and a fourth, or Japanese, pronunciation, *Wa-on*, 和音.

[28]*Go ni zenten to kōten no betsu ari, kore o sadamu*. 語ニ前天ト後天トノ別アリ之ヲ定ム. Again, the meaning of this phrase is unclear. From his earlier discussion, I have concluded that Nishi here proposes to distinguish between inherent (*zenten*) Japanese forms and extrinsic (*kōten*) forms derived from China.

[29]Although Nishimura labored to spread information about Western history and ideas, this article is representative of the better known conservative side of his nature. By his own account, he was instrumental in preventing the Education Ministry from giving its support to those who would make speech and writing one (*gembun itchi*) shortly after he joined the ministry in 1873. While disapproving of the *gembun itchi* movement, however, Nishimura employed a simple, terse, and dignified style in which he avoided unusual ideographs.

[30]Nishimura presumably refers to the theory of Hirata Atsutane, 平田篤胤, scholar in Japanese national studies, that the Japanese had a crude writng system before they adopted Chinese ideographs.

Fukuzawa's discussion of the role of scholars has appeared in the fourth number of *Gakumon no Susume*[1] published by Keiō Gijuku.[2] The essay naturally should have been published in this magazine as it was prepared by the honorable gentleman for the society. Since it has already come out, however, we would refer our readers to the original without printing it here.

In Response to Fukuzawa

Katō Hiroyuki

In his article, my esteemed friend states that there should be a balance between internal cultivation (that is, administration by government officials) and external stimulation (stimulation of the government by the people). He seems to regard external stimulation as of especial importance, stating as follows:

> Among those in Western studies, there are some who read without understanding as well as some who understand principle without having the rectitude actually to put it into practice. Only knowing official matters without appreciating the private sector, they think that nothing can be accomplished unless it is by the government.

Even though my esteemed friend strongly deplores the presence in government of scholars in Western studies, I feel that it is especially urgent in times like these to have internal cultivation [within the government], notwithstanding the importance of both external stimulation [from the people] and internal cultivation [within the government]. It follows, therefore, that it is always appropriate for scholars in Western studies to serve the government if they are inclined to do so. My friend's discussion is "liberal," and "liberalism" is never inappropriate. The progress by various European countries in the modern world is naturally a triumph for "liberalism." Yet the state's power must ultimately be undermined if there is a great excess of "liberalism." A nation can never survive once the state power has been undermined. A gentleman by the name of Frantz states in his *Physiologie van Staaten*:[3]

> Even though the "Liberal" and "Communist" Parties are complete opposites, they are both wrong. This is because both parties fail to understand why state power and private power is separated. Since the "Liberal" Party desires energetically to expand the people's power and to reduce the power of the state, it assumes that such public services as education, communications, and the mails may well be privately controlled without government interference. The "Communist" Party, however, holds that the state itself should manage all agriculture, industry, and commerce, vigorously expanding the state power and reducing private power.

We must fear that we may finally err on the side of the "Liberal" Party's views if we stress external stimulation [by the people] while making light of internal stimulation [within the government]. Since both government and private affairs are important, therefore, I feel that it would be best for scholars in Western studies to avoid following one course, some going into government and others into private undertakings in line with their talents and training.

Criticism of the Essay on the Role of Scholars

Mori Arinori

The essay [by Fukuzawa] on establishing the power of the people is sufficient to move the reader, its meaning being clear and its logic well developed. I feel, however, that some aspects of his thought are immoderate.

First, Fukuzawa states, "A country in its entirety can only be successfully ordered if government and people stand side by side." What kind of reasoning is this? The people have military as well as civil obligations vital to the nation that they can never evade. There can be no doubt that the people should honor these obligations to the best of their abilities. Should you ask who the people are, the term signifies persons who possess rights associated with obligations and duties that involve responsibilities. Officials, aristocrats, and commoners, therefore, are all included in the people. No person listed in the land registers (*hanseki*)[4] of Japan can avoid classification as a Japanese national who must invariably shoulder the obligations [of a Japanese national]. Moreover, the government, being the government of all the people, is established by the people and for the people. And so, I neither understand the principle nor recognize the situation in which government and people stand side by side. There were absolute monarchs in the various countries of Europe who ruled as they pleased, since the royal authority was unlimited and since political rights were held by one family. From this, there arose discord and disturbances among the disaffected people so that limited monarchies or republics often have been finally established by restricting absolute power and by sharing political power widely. Nevertheless, I have never heard of an example or a theory in which government and people, standing side by side, stimulate and conciliate each other.

Second, it is Fukuzawa's view that "the progress of civilization in society should not depend alone upon the power of governments." It is impossible to regard the progress of civilization in society as the responsibility of government. After all, this responsibility lies with the people who understand and promote civilization. Persons who promote civilization should advance the public interest in society and exercise their responsibilities as people in conformity with their respective views because they understand their positions well and are accomplished in public affairs. It makes no difference whether they promote civilization as officials or as private persons. Fukuzawa's purpose in pointing out a course for men of the nation through his private endeavor should be esteemed as his purpose. It is also a pleasing purpose for the type of men who honor it. Nevertheless, Fukuzawa's purport has not escaped bias when he discusses public interest by comparing private with public service. Should we assume that public benefit from official service does not equal profit to society from private service, then profit to society will only arise after scholars have all departed from official life, leaving government entirely to the unlettered. I believe that this is not quite my honorable friend's thought. Presumably, his views on this question arise from a broad feeling of anxiety for the country. They would shine forth still more clearly if he omits his postscript.[5]

Criticism of the Essay on the Role of Scholars

Tsuda Mamichi

A nation may be compared to a person. To refer to the government as the life force and to the people as an external stimulus [as does Fukuzawa], however, seems a mistaken metaphor. Now if the people are likened to an external stimulus, this is comparing them with an entity outside the country. Nevertheless, the people, being people within the country, are factors within the country. Presumably, an external stimulus should be compared with foreign relations.

I feel that the government is like the spirit while the people are like the body. Just as a person is formed by uniting body and spirit, a nation is created by joining people and government. A body without a spirit is a corpse, and a disembodied spirit is not a man. Just so, people there may be, but without a government they do not constitute a country. Still less is a country composed of a government alone without people. Furthermore, even though it is thought that the body should follow directions from the spirit, such is not the case. There is a natural law that controls the body itself. If the body is forced artificially beyond this natural law, the spirit then will also tire, and the person will weaken and finally die. The body will become stronger and stronger if it is nurtured in accordance with the law of nature. Yet it is a fact extremely to be deplored that, under conditions existing in our country today, there are very few people of independent spirit. Not only are they very few. They are almost nonexistent.

From ancient days, the people have been forced by the tradition of unlimited monarchy to follow the government's decrees, however unreasonable they may have been. Men all assumed that it was as impossible to triumph over the land stewards as over crying children. To this extremely lamentable situation may be entirely attributed the failure of our country to expand its power. Therefore, I greatly hope that, by advocating ideas of liberty and independence to the limit of our strength, we shall implant a spirit of freedom in our people and teach them that they have a right to deny even unreasonableness in government decrees. Whether we are officials or private citizens, we should be able respectively to follow our professions and exert ourselves appropriately to this end. It is indeed an overstatement to say that this cannot be done unless we leave office for private life.

Criticism of the Essay on the Role of Scholars

Nishi Amane

[Fukuzawa's] main theme is indeed clear and forthright. Nevertheless, since I cannot but find fault with it, I am now setting forth my views as follows.

First. Taking as his theme at the outset that we should doubt and fear for the independence of the country, [Fukuzawa] concludes that scholars should support this independence [from outside the government] in private life. His admonitions on doubts and fears are drawn from generalities, as is his succeeding discussion on the national character. Nowhere, therefore, is his discussion based on actual facts. His statement that we should fear for the independence of the country is thus extremely ambiguous. And it is like trying to convert vapor into a solid to urge on such ambiguous grounds that all scholars be encouraged to resign from government so that they may exert themselves in private life. Although his views are not entirely without reason, are they not deceptive from the point of view of logic?

Second. I would affirm as clearly appropriate for our times his references to Japan's continuing tradition of autocratic government and to our ignorant people who, now as in the past, are powerless and without spirit. Yet, even should we desire to reform, we probably cannot achieve success with a single blow since these [evils] did not arise in a night and a day. In a country like ours, in which the original clan theocracy was followed by the Chinese imperial system and later by military rule, oppression and servility have been daily fare for 2500 years. Even though the Restoration strongly affirmed Western institutions, it was but seven years ago. Still more, the Restoration, having originated in *sonnō jōi*,[6] was carried out with oppression and servility to which the nation adapted as naturally as to rice and *takuan*.[7] While we may now want to press for quick success within a day, is this not like an over-hasty scheme to roast birds before they are caught? This condition is not peculiar to our country. In the area to the northeast of the Himalayas and the Pamirs, we have yet to see a people or a government throw off these traditions [of despotism and servility].

Third. [Fukuzawa] states that Japan has not yet equalled foreign lands in learning, commerce, and legislation and that, as even laymen recognize, our country quite clearly will lose its independence unless it excels in these three fields. This is true. Nevertheless, it is also futile to rail violently against this situation without considering its origin. Until seven or eight years ago, so-called scholarship was limited to the sphere of the *Four Books* and the *Five Classics*.[8] Moreover, even these Chinese classics were only toys. When debased, such studies ranked with tea ceremony and flower arrangement, and at their most exalted they were only comparable to the arts of the bow, horse, sword, and spear. Is it not impractical to raise our scholarship quickly to compete neck and neck with that of the West? Accordingly, it is my view that we should not claim that even our great scholars have penetrated the inner mysteries of so-called Western scholarship. What we call the elevation [of scholarship] will take generations, and the situation is exactly the same in law and business. Indeed, we still follow the traditions of T'ang and Ming in legal matters, only adopting trifling Western interpretations.[9] When will the day come when our judges and attorneys abandon the outmoded customs of the *kujikata tomeyaku*[10] and the *kujiyado*?[11] How can we compare them to Western levels in law?

Fourth. [Fukuzawa] says that students want to become officials once they have read a little in books, thus emulating the great men who have already acquired fame. It seems to me that he is unjust if one considers the reasons for what he says. The real reasons are that the students are absolutely without educational support, that they are searching for sustenance, and that there is demand [from the government] for persons who can read Western books. Furthermore, just recall the fact that intellectuals of the mid-Tokugawa Period, being considered mad and deranged, lived contentedly by themselves without participating in administration and without understanding affairs of the world. Men in public life were then commonly drawn from military and civil retainers. Now they are drawn from students. While this may be deplored as a bad practice, it seems to be a slight advance as compared with former times.

Fifth. I also think improper [Fukuzawa's] statement that it is already the fashion for scholars in Western studies [generally to adopt an attitude of fawning servility] when they publish newspapers or memorialize the government. Such flattery and servility may usually be traced to Shintō scholar-politicians. I feel that this is an entirely false charge when directed against those in Western studies.

Sixth. There is Fukuzawa's comparison of government to the life force within the human body and the people to an external stimulus. Notwithstanding the fact that his discussion of life force and external stimulus is the logical heart of his reasoning, I am obliged to take issue with this point. After all, it would be all right if the external stimulus were properly applied. One can only fear, however, that a still more grave illness will develop should the basically weak life force be excessively stimulated. For example, a man's weak eyes will be seriously injured if they are exposed to the excessively strong stimulation of light. All will be well if the external stimulation is applied gradually as the people advance toward enlightenment. But we probably shall not avoid excess if artificial stimulation is attempted. On the whole, such stimulation cannot be well applied by human artifice. Nor can anything be done about the results of stimulation once they have germinated.

It is, then, very fine when the public spirit is strong and when society is upright. But it is most unfortunate when disturbances ultimately erupt after the emergence of factionalism. Therefore, we must also reflect on the fact that England and America are countries in which stimulation is appropriate, while stimulation is somewhat unbalanced in France and Spain. Such things generally depend upon the current of the times and are not easily controlled by a single man or a single party. If one faction is established, a second must invariably emerge. What will be the end if factions successively proliferate one after another? There will be no limits to dissent and disruption in society brought on by these boastful braggarts who need not look far to learn the consequences of their behavior.

Assuming that the government is the life spirit, it is necessary for scholars to serve in the government since quinine must be administered to cause this life spirit to pulsate. And if we accept the people as the stimulus, it is also essential for scholars to function in private life since the stimulus must invariably be moderate. One-sided emphasis on private scholarship without nurturing this life spirit, however, is like a sickly person who catches a cold and fever after having been exposed to the elements. Will not his cold then develop into a fatal illness?

In sum, it is my opinion that, since men differ both in their abilities and their intentions, it is equally appropriate for even those in Western studies either to serve in government or to remain in private life. Being naturally aware that I am a person of no account who only provides minor bits of translation to the government, I have long respected my honorable friend's exalted spirit. I feel that I shall eventually follow his lead [by retiring to private life], although I have not yet been able resolutely and enthusiastically to do so.

[1]*Gakumon no Susume,* 學問ノ勸メ, or *An Encouragement of Learning,* was the famous series of seventeen essays that the great enlightener Fukuzawa Yukichi wrote during 1873–1875 for the edification of his countrymen. In the fourth essay that appeared in January 1874, Fukuzawa criticized those in Western studies who, like many in the Meirokusha, accepted office in the government. On the assumption that civilization could not be achieved by relying on the power of government alone, Fukuzawa urged that enlightenment would be best promoted among the traditionally subservient people if scholars devoted their energies to the private sector. The essay together with the responses in this journal clearly illustrate the deep cleavage between Fukuzawa, the private scholar, and the more government-oriented members of the Meirokusha. For a translation of Fukuzawa's essay, see David L. Dilworth and Umeyo Hirano, trans., *Fukuzawa Yukichi's "An Encouragement to Learning"* (Tokyo, 1969), pp. 20–28.

[2]*Keiō Gijuku,* 慶應義塾, the private school founded by Fukuzawa shortly before the Meiji Restoration that survives today as Keiō University.

[3]Katō here refers to Gustav Adolph Constantin Frantz, *Vorschule zur Physiologie der Staaten* (Berlin, 1857). In his *Kokutai Shinron,* 國體新論 (1875), Katō lists Frantz's *Die Naturlehre des Staats als Grundlage aller Staatswissenschaft* (Leipzig, 1870). Frantz advocated Christian pan-Germanism founded on liberalism and socialism. Katō's translation is noteworthy for what was probably the first printed reference in Japan to the Communist Party.

[4]*Hanseki,* 版籍, the registers of population and land that were returned to the emperor by the various feudal domains shortly after the Meiji Restoration of 1868, an action symbolic of the restoration of centralized authority and the end of feudalism.

[5]At the end of his essay, Fukuzawa appended an answer to anonymous questioners, at the conclusion of which he declared rather haughtily that he would not be friends with those who lived in luxury on excessive government stipends because they were unable to make their way in private life.

[6]*Sonnō jōi,* 尊王攘夷, "revere the emperor and expel the barbarians," the slogan of those who opposed the reopening of Japan after 1853.

[7]*Takuan,* 澤庵, pickled radish that was common fare of the Japanese people.

[8]The *Four Books* and the *Five Classics, Ssû Shu,* 四書, and *Wu Ching,* 五經, were the Confucian canons upon which traditional Chinese and Japanese education was based.

[9]The first criminal codes issued by the new Meiji government, the *Shinritsu Kōryō,* 新律綱領 (1870), and the *Kaitei Ritsurei,* 改定律例 (1873), were largely based on the Chinese codes of the Ming and the Ch'ing dynasties, 1368–1912.

[10]*Kujikata tomeyaku,* 公事方留役, refers to the traditional mediation proceedings under the *kujikata,* a compilation of decrees and precedents completed in 1742 for the information of magistrates and supreme court judges.

[11]*Kujiyado,* 公事宿, licensed inns where litigants stopped during the Edo Period, 1600–1868.

First Essay on Enlightenment[1]

Mori Arinori

Scholars are of the opinion that the course of world civilization since creation has never turned downward notwithstanding the rise and fall of nations. Judging from the evidence of the past, it is indeed true that there has generally been progress and change in man's means of support. Thus, in the beginning when men were savages, their means of support were hardly different from those of beasts. As they progressed, men learned hunting and fishing, observed changes in the seasons, understood techniques for sowing and harvesting, and then advanced sufficiently to appreciate how to conserve their labor by employing horses and oxen. These may be regarded as the means of support at the first stage of enlightenment. We may term half-enlightened those who have come to look upon the products of labor as private property, to see hard work as a source of happiness, to recognize the assignment of occupations as a requirement for community living, and to regard the expansion of social relations as a source of increased pleasure.

Many instances may be found in history of people who have stopped temporarily at this point of half-enlightenment. In the long run, this arises when men have become unable to stimulate their intellects, their thought being out of harmony with their feelings so that they are credulous, or misled, or boastful, or hesitant. Those who overcome these uncertainties and advance steadily against a myriad of difficulties will finally attain a brilliant level of talent and virtue, having understood the wonders of creation and the principles in things, encouraged brotherly love, and developed discrimination. These should be called men who have reached the level of enlightenment. Once national customs have achieved this level in some part, countries can construct machines, erect buildings, dig mines, build ships, open seaways, produce carriages, and improve highways. Thus will the thousand industries and ten thousand arts burst forth one after another. By these means, the virtues of social intercourse will spread through the liberal expansion of commerce, products will reach perfection as machines are increasingly refined, and men will ultimately appreciate the true value of civilization. I would say that only then can countries defend their prestige and enter the glorious realm [of enlightenment].

Words of Admonition

Nishimura Shigeki

I am deeply impressed and most fearful when I read the histories of Western countries. When Greece first arose in ancient times, her strong and brave people were filled with patriotism. They were consequently able to defeat their great enemy Persia, and their prestige spread in all directions. The country thereafter prospered, the knowledge of her people advanced day by day, and the refinement of their arts reached its zenith. From that time, however, the customs of the people deteriorated: luxury, greed, frivolity, and cunning were prevalent; the early spirit of bravery and strength was completely extinguished; and Greece was finally conquered by the Romans.

Since the rugged and sturdy Romans at first had a spirit that was bold and indomitable, they were able to expand their territory by conquering East and West so that the world was obliged to respect their authority reverently. After Rome's national power reached its zenith, her people achieved the level of enlightenment by competing for knowledge and perfecting their skills. From this time, however, the customs of the people disintegrated; their rugged and sturdy ways were replaced by the vices of lust, luxury, frivolity, and cunning; and Rome was finally destroyed by the various German tribesmen.

Looking at the causes, it is clear that ruggedness and bravery are medicines to strengthen countries, while luxury and frivolity are poisons that destroy countries. The customs of our people since antiquity have not been inferior to those of the Greeks and the Romans. Recently, there has been daily broadening of the people's knowledge and great advances in the arts and industries, but the people's traditional strong and sturdy spirit has [also] gradually declined so that their low ways now closely resemble those during the latter days of Greece and Rome. Is this not something to be feared? The arts and industries decorative during peace are not tools for supporting the nation. The independence of the nation can only be well maintained by the will and the conduct of the people. An ancient has said that Heaven's Law (*Tenri*)[2] and the greed of men are mutually contradictory. If one adds a share of luxury, then ruggedness will be reduced one measure; and honesty will be compromised to a corresponding degree if one adds a part of insincerity. Greedy ones, glaring with tigerlike voracity, are today crowding in around our country. What is a gentleman who fears for his country to do?

Criticism of the Memorial on Establishing a Popularly Elected Assembly[3]

Mori Arinori

It is, of course, a fact that general public discussion of the national government is evidence of the increasing prosperity of the people as well as of the actual independence of the country. In the *Nisshin Shinjishi*[4] of the 18th, there appeared a memorial to the *Sain*[5] by Soejima and eight others which, on its face, is a discussion of the establishment of a popularly elected assembly. Their arguments relate wholly to the national government, and their stated objectives are the independence of the country and the prosperity of the people. Since I feel that their intentions are still unclear and that their purport is disquieting, however, I shall now submit one or two criticisms.

First. The memorialists state:

Conditions have recently reached such a point that we cannot

> deny the evidence of breakdown arising from doubts between rulers and ruled and from agitation of the public mind. In the final analysis, this may be attributed to the fact that public opinion and public discussion have been muzzled throughout the country.

Without going into the correctness of this view and first assuming temporarily that such a situation actually exists, upon whom should be placed responsibility for stirring it up? Should it fall only on the present government officials? Are conditions today really so different from when the memorialists were officials? I hear privately that a majority of the group are those who pressed for an attack on Korea. I cannot fully credit their claim that there would have been no muzzling of public opinion and public discussion had their views been carried out. In the proclamation of last October,[6] the clauses relating to the press state:

> It is forbidden to bring injury to the nation by attacking the national structure (*kokutai*),[7] discussing national laws, or advocating and propagating foreign doctrines. . . . It is forbidden to include indiscriminate criticism when reporting such matters as laws and administration. . . . It is forbidden recklessly to cause injury to political principles by referring to religious principles.

These various regulations were promulgated when the memorialists were in office. At the beginning of the memorial, they affirm:

> Being our established beliefs, the opinions presented in the attached paper include convictions that we often incorporated in our memorials while serving the government.

It seems that the press regulations were promulgated at least with their grudging consent. And it is thus not entirely unreasonable to recognize that, along with the above press regulations, the memorialists, however reluctantly, have been themselves instrumental in muzzling public opinion and in contributing to the breakdown with the attendant doubts between rulers and ruled. Today's conditions, after all, have not been suddenly fomented by officials now in office.

Second. The memorialists state: "What is issued in the morning may be altered in the evening, policy decisions are made arbitrarily, and rewards and punishments follow personal prejudices." This was probably inserted by mistake. It is unthinkable that these words could come from such renowned persons of intelligence as the memorialists.

Third. What then is this institution known as a popularly elected assembly? Is it a body established by government order? Is it an assembly freely formed by the people after having been reported to the government? Or is it an organ founded by government permission? The memorialist's statement that "this proposal should be thoroughly discussed in official circles" conveys the sense that the government should establish a deliberative assembly on behalf of the people. If such, after all, be the case, then the new body will be entirely the government's assembly rather than an assembly of the people. Even the term "popularly elected" (*minsen*)[8] would probably signify assemblymen selected by the government from the people. Since the representatives will have been gathered together at the government's behest, when the government is displeased, they can also be dismissed at the government's discretion, notwithstanding the fact that they may constitute an established assembly. It is entirely clear and completely natural that the representatives under such circumstances not only will be unable to discuss political matters without reserve. They will also invariably obey the government. Being subservient to the government, their deliberations will naturally praise the government's conduct, and they will ultimately be criticized in society for being flatterers of the government.

The Final Instructions of King Peter of Russia[9]

Sugi Kōji

First. The Russian people should always be kept in the condition of a nation at war. This is to provide strong soldiers who will always be prepared for use in war. The people should not be allowed to rest until they have placed their finances in order, trained their army, and are ready for a good opportunity to attack. That is, they should prepare for war during peace and prepare for peace during war. These things should all be done because it is necessary more and more to increase the size and prosperity of Russia.

Second. As far as possible, generals should be brought from the powerful and prosperous European states during war. And foreign scholars should be invited during peace to teach our people the advantages enjoyed by other countries. Our national policies then will lack nothing.

Third. We should invariably intervene between the various European countries when disputes and incidents arise between them. Especially is it important to interfere in Germany's affairs since she is our neighbor.

Fourth. We should always promote disruption in Poland by agitating and creating jealousies among her people. We should buy the hearts of her influential leaders with money, control the election of her king in the diet, and assemble a pro-Russian party to which we should afford protection. We should despatch an army into Poland and keep it there until we have secured our objectives. When neighboring countries plan to intervene, we would satisfy them with slices of Poland and then await a later opportunity to regain the territory.

Fifth. Whenever there is anything to be seized in Sweden, we should take everything until we have finally occupied the entire country. Therefore, it is sound policy to break the alliance between Sweden and Denmark, cause them to separate, and excite their mutual jealousies.

Sixth. In Russian royal marriages, consorts shall be selected from the German royal houses. By thus increasing the number of related houses and uniting their interests with ours, we can cause Germany to follow our plans.

Seventh. Securing an alliance with England lies wholly in planning trade benefits. While our products are indispensable for the English navy, there are also things in the English navy essential to our navy. Thus we can exchange for English gold the lumber from our country that is required by England's navy. It is important that our seamen become skilled in the English naval arts and that our merchants become dextrous in their mercantile methods by constantly cultivating intimate relations with the seamen and merchants of England.

Eighth. Russia should continually expand her territory along the Eastern Sea [Baltic] to the north and the Black Sea to the south.

Ninth. We should strive to approach Constantinople and India. Since the party controlling Constantinople and India will be the true master of the world, no interruption should be permitted in our wars with Turkey and Persia. It is important to develop numerous shipyards in the Black Sea. Then expanding our power in the Black Sea and the Eastern Sea, extending our influence to the Persian Gulf through rapidly declining Persia, and laboring to restore the former eastern trade routes through Syria, we can reach the world treasure house of India. Once in India, we shall deprive England of her gold.

Tenth. We should pay careful attention to planning for an enduring alliance with Austria. While publicly supporting the chimera of German unity, we should secretly incite the rulers of the small states against Austria—sometimes inducing the small states to cooperate with us and sometimes protecting Austria. In this way, we shall hold Austria subdued in the palm of our hand.

Eleventh. The imperial house of Austria invariably assumes responsibility for throwing Turkey out of Europe, and Austria's jealousy will surely be aroused when we attack Constantinople. In such an event, we can overcome her jealousy by embroiling her with other European states or by giving her a slice of our occupied territory that we can later recover easily.

Twelfth. We should never fail to draw together the Greek Orthodox believers scattered through Hungary and southern Poland, and we can seize full control over them by appearing to be the rock of the church and by persuading them to accept us as protector. Thereby can we plant our party in enemy countries.

Thirteenth. After we overcome Sweden, destroy Persia, divide Poland, and take Turkey, we shall assemble our armies from the four quarters and have the Black and Eastern Seas defended by our ships. Then we should first approach Versailles (then the seat of the French government) and later Vienna with a plan for dividing the world and seizing supreme power between us. Also, we should follow an opportunistic path—negotiating with only one party and planning secretly. By thus satisfying the desires of either France or Austria for fame and prosperity can we bring one of them to adopt our views. Having first destroyed one with the help of the other, we may then pick a quarrel with the remaining party and eliminate it too. It cannot be doubted that we shall grasp the rewards of certain victory at this time since we shall already occupy the greater part of Europe as the master of the various countries of the East.

Fourteenth. Should by any remote chance neither France nor Austria enter our plot, we shall stir up a conflict between them and then wait until they have exhausted themselves in fighting. Seizing this opportunity, we can advance into Germany with our assembled army while our fleets sail forth, one from Archangel and the other from the Sea of Azov. Two transport groups carrying our Asian troops will be protected by our fleets in the Black and Eastern Seas. While we attack France simultaneously from the Atlantic and the Mediterranean from one side, we shall subdue Germany with our army from the other. We can tranquilize the remaining countries of Europe once France and Germany are conquered.

Comment: From the above article in which Peter speaks of using the Greek Church to establish friendly parties in enemy countries, it is clear that Russia regards the Greek Church as a tool for expansion. I have heard privately that the Greek Church has already entered our country. It is, of course, insignificant, but the danger arising from its long-term penetration cannot be expressed in words. What then are the means to protect this? I would say that we shall only overcome their Greek Church by being careful to broaden our knowledge, to follow the faith that we have selected from the good and flourishing religions in the world, and to halt the general proliferation of faiths.

Methods for Advancing Enlightenment[10]

Tsuda Mamichi

Nowadays, men talk of "enlightenment, enlightenment" whenever they open their mouths. For the reason that learning and religion are generally circulating through the country, the level of enlightenment is gradually changing, just as night gives way to day. In the final analysis, learning falls into two major categories. There are empty studies (*kyogaku*) that are devoted to such lofty doctrines as nonexistence and Nirvana [of Buddhism],[11] the theory of the five elements [of Sung Confucianism],[12] or intuitive knowledge and intuitive ability [of *Yōmeigaku*].[13] And there are practical studies (*jitsugaku*) that solely explain factual principles through actual observation and verification, such as astronomy, physics, chemistry, medicine, political economy, and philosophy of the modern West. We may call a society truly civilized when the reason of each individual has been illumined by the general circulation of practical studies through the land. Progress by the people as a whole to the area of civilization, however, cannot be expected for a very long time even in the various countries of the West. How much more is this the case in the regions of the South and Eastern Seas! Ah, when can our people reach the area of civilization? When I contemplate the matter, I am in despair. When asked then by what means we should promote education generally among the people who have not achieved civilization, I would say by religion. On the whole, the object of religion is to lead the unenlightened people so that they will advance along the good path.

Among the various religions of the world, two are practiced in our country: Shintō and Buddhism. Although the religions practiced abroad are innumerable, the most important are not many: Buddhism, Zoroastrianism, Islam, and Christianity. Of these, Christianity is the most fine. Christianity may in turn be divided into three sects: Greek, Roman, and Protestant, of which the Protestant is the most fine. Protestantism is further divided into factions, among them the Lutheran and the Calvinist. And within these, there is a split between the old and the new groups, of which the preponderantly liberal new elements come closest to civilized thinking.

Now, when religion spreads among the people, the pressure for the superior to overcome the inferior and for the new to win over the old is as steady as the flow of water. The examples of this tendency in the histories of the various foreign countries are beyond counting. Setting these aside for the moment, I would turn to our own land. Before the introduction of Chinese characters, our country was a Shintō theocracy in which administration and religious rites were one and men were confused with gods. Upon the introduction of the *Analects* and the *Thousand Character Classic* by Achiki,[14] Chinese writing spread with extreme rapidity in the court. Nakatomi Kamako and Moriya Ō-muraji[15] thereafter were helpless to halt the eastward flow of Buddhism even though they opposed it with all their might, and the religion was rapidly diffused through the country. When the Zen, Pure Land (Jōdo), and Lotus (Hōkke) Sects[16] subsequently emerged or were introduced, there were none who stopped them, although many tried to hurt them. In the recent past, the single sect of Catholicism alone has been successfully suppressed after the shogun's might with one blow exterminated thousands of lives at Shimabara.[17]

Still more recently, there were also efforts to crush Western scholarship when it was first introduced, but its circulation was speeded with the changed conditions in the country after the arrival of the American ships at Uraga.[18] And so we have finally reached the situation today in which men discuss enlightenment whenever they open their mouths. The persons who thus discuss enlightenment, however, do not exceed a few hundred scholars, officials, and newspaper editors. They thus really constitute only an infinitesimal fraction of our population of thirty million. In the final analysis, the people of our country, being men attached to customs of the past, are generally rude fellows misled by groundless theories of hades, paradise, cause and effect, reward and punishment, the five elements, and geomancy.[19] How can we call these people half-enlightened?

Judging from present conditions, it is clear as the reflection in a mirror that the Christian invasion of our country cannot be prevented as it is just like a rushing torrent. There can be nothing like another Shimabara.

There is no religion in the world today that promotes enlightenment as does Christianity. Nevertheless, since all Christianity is

not an unmixed blessing, the best way at present to promote enlightenment is to adopt the Christian ideas that are most liberal, most civilized, and most advanced. Now what if we should employ the best and most enlightened missionaries to guide our people openly, just as we are learning their arts and sciences from the numerous Westerners employed by the various ministries? I beg your comments on my proposal.

Refuting the Joint Statement by the Former Ministers

Nishi Amane

I have been unable to avoid some private doubts after reading the memorial to the *sain* in which the former ministers and other gentlemen propose a popularly elected assembly. Let me take up in sequence the gist of their arguments. The purport of their memorial seems to be as follows. Strengthening the government lies in uniting the minds of the people; establishing a popularly elected assembly will unite the minds of the people; and the way to introduce a popularly elected assembly is to adopt and apply the rules governing parliamentary proceedings in the West, just as we make use of steam trains and the telegraph, whose principles have been discovered in the West. The memorialists point out that the government really would be unable to undertake anything should it delay using steam trains and constructing telegraphs until we ourselves invent such things. Ah, how mistaken is their reasoning [when they thus treat physical and human laws in the same manner]!

In what disciplines and in what texts are such things as steamships and telegraphs taught and discussed in the West? We study them through physics, chemistry, and mechanics. Then can these disciplines be discussed in the same manner as politics, law, and religion? I have not heard that gravity follows a different law in England from in France or that the principles of electricity in America vary from those in Japan. Then why do political matters alone, on the contrary, not conform to universal principles? Why are not the parliaments of England and France regulated by the same law? And why do the political structures of England and America differ as does Heaven from earth? Now in trains and the like, only a few years will suffice to develop technical proficiency if we select talented students and have them trained in the West. Their success may be expected in due course if we provide them with capital and charge them with administrative responsibility. Can we then invariably hope for success in political matters if we follow a similar course? Now let me inquire further into the thinking of the memorialists.

If you try throwing a pebble into the air, it will rise toward the heavens according to the strength of your thrust. Even if the pebble rises to extreme heights, however, it will invariably fall, and its velocity will multiply while falling. Even a child of but three feet will not doubt this fact. If you now employ an indigent man with whom you have had no daily contact and provide him with one hundred yen with which to purchase goods thirty miles away, do you know that the man will invariably return with the goods, just as you expect the stone to fall from the heights? Now I have heard that, according to Western studies in government, a rule will only be successful if it is adapted to the area and the times after the level of public enlightenment has been clarified. Here is where the fundamental laws of the physical sciences and of government differ. The former ministers now want to treat the two as one. Is there, after all, such a study in the West?

The former ministers state that there is a universal principle of government that the people derive the rights to participate in, to know, and to sanction their government's affairs from their obligation to pay taxes. Is this principle then universal? The people may have the right to expect security in return for payment of taxes. The rights of participation and sanction, however, should only be determined when the nation establishes its political structure.

Now let me take up government as an entity that arises from a social contract. According to one version, the people say to the officials, "You shall rule us because we are supporting you by contributing half of our labor to your administration." Another type of social contract arises when the people say: "We shall subscribe half our labor for your support so that you may rule us. To prevent you from acting arbitrarily, however, we shall participate in formulating the laws by which you will govern us." Thus, while we may assume that government arises entirely from a social contract, as did Rousseau, the right to participate in government is not a right related to the payment of taxes. Indeed, the government of a country does not invariably arise from a contract. This is especially the case when historical traditions differ. While the memorialists state that they have inquired into the great principles of the universe, I do not yet know upon what discipline they base their contentions.

The former ministers further claim that establishment of a popularly elected assembly is the path for advancing the wisdom and scholarship of the people to the level of enlightenment. And they aver that their proposal will cause rights to be protected as well as induce a spirit of self-importance and self-respect, leading the people to share joys and fears with the entire country. Shall we secure protection of the so-called rights of the people from a popularly elected assembly or from the responsible administration of justice? The rights of the people can be absolutely protected if there is truly impartial administration of justice and if there is not government oppression. We should look to men of scholarship if we desire to acquire a spirit of self-importance and self-respect conducive to the common sharing of joys and fears with the entire country. Can we say that the true path for encouraging such scholarship lies in convening a popularly elected assembly without first having sought it [scholarship] through a program of education? Drawing a parallel with a theatrical performance, is drama studied before the curtain goes up or is the curtain raised before study? Ah, in the theater, the play will stop when the patrons cease coming after the opening of an unrehearsed performance, and there may be no harm even from a failure in the acting. Should we now treat the nation's political affairs like a stage performance?

I must grieve for the former ministers if their views are derived from their own experiences while still in office. It would be appropriate for them to criticize the reduction of imperial authority, the impetuous promulgation of numerous contradictory decrees, and the appearance of favoritism should the government fail to reform these evils after they have been out of office for a year.

Their attack on the government is no more than spitting in their own faces, however, since they departed from office only a few months ago. While I do not personally endorse the gentlemen's views, there is truth in their statement that political power at present rests neither in the throne above nor in the people below. It is also not unreasonable to desire a positive strengthening of political power by sharing this power with a deliberative assembly. In light of the times and of the present level of public enlightenment, however, it cannot yet be said that the memorialists are striking the right note when they suddenly desire a law for a Western-style lower house chosen by the people. I am not now presuming to discuss the merits of establishing a deliberative assembly. I am more especially concerned with the gross misrepresentations in their discussions. If the people of the nation are agitated by such misrepresentations and if we once mistakenly establish a deliberative assembly of false advocates, will not the country be endangered by the confusion in national affairs arising from the debates [in parliament] between such false advocates?

[1]This essay is especially important as an expression of Mori's commitment to the Western concept of progress, an idea to which he was probably first exposed when he studied in England in 1865–1868. The word here translated as enlightenment is *kaika,* 開化, which may also be rendered as civilization. Mori and others in the Meirokusha were committed to leading their half-enlightened or half-civilized compatriots to full civilization and enlightenment.

[2]*Tenri,* 天理.

[3]Although the Meirokusha was theoretically dedicated to the spread of enlightenment rather than to politics, its members were perhaps inevitably drawn into the early debates of the so-called people's rights movement (*jiyū minken undō,* 自由民権運動), that erupted in early 1874 after Soejima Taneomi, 副島種臣, Itagaki Taisuke, 板垣退助, Etō Shimpei, 江藤新平, and five other former members of the government submitted their famous memorial in which they called for the establishment of a popularly elected assembly (*minsen giin,* 民選議院). As their comments in this and later issues of the *Meiroku Zasshi* indicate, the Meirokusha members accepted the eventual establishment of an assembly as inevitable even though they generally held that the country was not yet ready for a genuine parliament. Their attitudes on this single issue have commonly been taken by scholars as a criterion by which the genuineness of their enlightenment may be measured. For further discussion of this point, see the introduction. The memorial is printed in the *Shimbun Shūsei Meiji Hennen Shi* 新聞集成明治編年史 (15 vols.: Tokyo, 1934–1936), II, 117–118. For an English transla-

tion, see W. W. McLaren, ''Japanese Government Documents,'' *Transactions of the Asiatic Society of Japan,* XLII, 426–432.

[4]*Nisshin Shinjishi,* 日新眞事誌, was a Tokyo newspaper founded by an Australian, J. R. Black, that could publish materials critical of the Japanese government since its owner as a foreigner was protected by his extraterritorial rights from prosecution under Japanese press laws.

[5]*Sain,* 左院, or the Left Chamber of the revived *Dajōkan,* 太政官, was established in 1873 to advise on legislation proposed by the government.

[6]For these press regulations, see McLaren, "Japanese Government Documents," pp. 53–537.

[7]*Kokutai,* 國體.

[8]*Minsen,* 民選.

[9]While this testament attributed to Tsar Peter the Great may be spurious, it naturally was widely noted by Russia's Asian neighbors. For an English translation, see Percy Sykes, *A History of Persia* (London, 1930), II, 244–246.

[10]Tsuda's essay on enlightenment is a classic statement by one of the early Meiji enlighteners in support of practical studies, *jitsugaku,* 實學, as distinguished from empty or useless studies, *kyogaku,* 虛學. The term *jitsugaku* had been used by Confucian scholars to refer to knowledge useful in helping man determine the moral path, and it went through successive changes in meaning before it was equated by Tsuda with Western empirical studies. It is noteworthy that Tsuda apparently did not include the ancient studies (*kogaku,* 古學) branch of Confucian scholarship in his definition of empty studies, perhaps because he approved the emphasis of the *kogaku* scholars on useful, empirical knowledge. His view of Protestant Christianity as the most progressive of religions doubtless reflects in part his study in Protestant Holland. For another statement on practical studies, see Fukuzawa Yukichi's first essay in *Gakumon no Susume,* 學問のすゝめ, the *Encouragement of Learning.*

[11]Non-existence and Nirvana, *kyomu jakumetsu,* 虛無寂滅.

[12]Five elements theory, *gogyō seiri,* 五行性理.

[13]Intuitive knowledge and intuitive ability, *ryōchi ryōnō,* 良知良能, refers to the introspective philosophy of Wang Yang-ming, 王陽明, and the philosophical school commonly known in Japan as *Yōmeigaku.*

[14]Achiki, 阿直岐, an envoy from the king of the Korean state of Kudara to the Emperor Ōjin, 應神. According to the *Kojiki,* 古事記, Achiki was followed by a second Korean named Wani, 王仁, who brought the *Analects* of *Confucius* (*Lun Yü,* 論語) and the *Ten Thousand Character Classic* (*Ch'ien Tzŭ Wen,* 千字文).

[15]Nakatomi Kamako, 中臣鎌子, was a minister who opposed Buddhism when it was first imported from Korea in about 552 A.D.; Moriya Ō-muraji, 守屋大連, –587 A.D., the chief of the Mononobe 物部 Clan, which was exterminated when it sought to halt the spread of Buddhism under the patronage of the Soga 蘇我 Clan.

[16]The Zen, 禪, Jōdo, 淨土, and Hokke, 法華, Sects emerged to importance with the rise of the military houses or *buke,* 武家, in the twelfth and thirteenth centuries.

[17]Shimabara, 島原, refers to the slaughter of a reputed 38,000 Christians who rebelled against the lord of Shimabara in 1637–1638.

[18]Uraga, 浦賀, i.e., the arrival of the American squadron under Commodore Matthew Calbraith Perry at Uraga in 1853.

[19]Hades, *jigoku,* 地獄; paradise, *gokuraku,* 極樂; cause and effect, *inga,* 因果; reward and punishment, *ōhō,* 應報; the five elements, *gōgyō,* 五行; and geomancy, *hōi,* 方位; all refer to Buddhist and Chinese beliefs that Tsuda identified with backward Asian superstitions.

The Interrelation between the Freedom of Peoples and the Climates of Regions[1]

Mitsukuri Rinshō

Just as the power of parents over children and that of husbands over wives naturally varies according to climate, the power of governments over peoples also differs according to climate. After all, people of hot areas are muscularly weak and faint-hearted, while those of cold areas have strength to accomplish great works as they are strong in body and mind and possess great endurance. Moreover, this distinction is not only something that can be clearly recognized between individual countries. It is also evident in the northern and southern regions of the same country. For example, the people of north China are more brave than those of the south, and the same situation obtains in Korea. This is why the people of the hot regions, being timid cowards, for the most part bow obediently to their rulers' despotic decrees, while the spirited people of cold regions are able to protect their liberties. Similarly, it was the natural course in the Americas for free peoples to be gathered in small villages in the cold regions of the north, while the old despotisms in countries like Mexico and Peru were normally in the hot lands close to the equator.

Considering the climates of Asia, the climate is extremely cold in the northern region that extends from 40° north latitude to the North Pole and from the Ural Mountains in the west to the Pacific in the east. Especially in Siberia, only shrubs and grasses grow sparsely because of the most extreme winters, and agriculture cannot be practiced, the industry of the Russian people notwithstanding. The inhabitants of Siberia are only primitive barbarians, and there are naturally no settlements that might be called cities. The reasons for the extreme cold in this area of Asia are the height of the land and the fact that the north winds are uninterrupted, since the mountain ranges gradually become lower as one moves from the south toward the north. In Europe, however, the cold is not extreme even in countries of the far north because the northern winds are broken by the high mountains of Norway and Lapland. Even in a place like Stockholm, at 61° north latitude, men can easily cultivate the soil and open silver mines.

Reflecting on these climatic patterns, the cold territories of Tartary and Siberia touch the hot regions of Turkey, Persia, and China since there is no temperate zone in Asia between the hot and cold areas. In Europe, on the other hand, there is a large temperate zone. Furthermore, although such countries as Sweden and Norway really differ greatly in climate from Italy and Spain, the weather of Europe only gradually becomes warmer as one moves from north to south, there being no change comparable to moving suddenly from the arctic to the tropics. Therefore, there is no great difference between the climates of countries that share borders. Looked at from this point of view, since the strong and industrious people of the cold areas of Asia are immediate neighbors of the weak and lethargic people of the hotlands, people from the cold regions are always conquering those from the hot, and there is an invariable tendency for the latter to be subdued and enslaved.

In Europe, however, it is extremely difficult for one country to conquer another with one blow since the strong border on the strong and since the power of each is relatively equal because of the gradual change in climate. This is the main reason for the weakness of Asia, whose peoples are inclined toward subservience, and the strength of Europe, where the peoples are habitually free. This theory may indeed contradict popular views today, but I cling to it firmly. Consider the fact that the peoples of Asia have not increased their liberties since antiquity, while liberties in Europe have finally become fully developed, notwithstanding temporary setbacks under particular circumstances.[2]

[Note by Mitsukuri. Aristotle, the great philosopher of Greece, said: "Although Asians on the whole are quick-witted and skilled in the arts, they dare not aspire to liberty, being habitually submissive because they lack spirit."]

What I have previously noted can all be proved historically. For instance, northerners conquered eleven out of thirteen times during which Asians subdued each other; southerners, only twice. From the rise and colonization of Europe by the Greeks and Phoenicians in antiquity to the present, however, the really great upheavals have been limited to but four: the Roman conquests, the incursions by the northern barbarians, Charlemagne's victories, and the Norman invasions. Even during these four times of great turmoil, there was relative stability in the balance of power between the European states. After all, when the Romans attacked Asia, they easily conquered since none dared to oppose them, but such was not the case when they subdued Europe. They were barely able to conquer the various European countries after several hard wars. The barbarians subsequently destroyed Rome, but not easily, and Charlemagne's victories as well as the Norman conquests were also extremely difficult. This demonstrates the fact that the differences in power between the European states since antiquity have always been small.

[Note by Mitsukuri. This is a translation and abridgment from the *Spirit of the Laws* by the French scholar Montesquieu. My subsequent translation will appear in the succeeding issue.]

An Abridged Translation from Bluntschli's "*Allgemeines Staatsrecht*" on the Inappropriateness of Establishing a Popularly Elected Assembly[3]

Katō Hiroyuki

Since the former ministers and others have come out in favor of establishing a popularly elected assembly, the reform parties in society have frequently supported the proposal and freely affirmed the validity of public discussion and public opinion without considering the times or the condition of the people. They assume that there is clearly no better means for promoting national tranquility than to expand public discussion. Therefore, I have made the following abridged translation that shows why it might be necessary to oppose public opinion even in modern enlightened Europe. In Bluntschli's *Allgemeines Staatsrecht*, it is stated:

It is extremely injurious to the nation when a minister loses the confidence of the majorities in both houses of parliament. This is because, under such circumstances, he will ultimately be unable to carry out even his programs for the public benefit since there is no hope for [parliamentary] approval. Therefore, there is no alternative but to dismiss a minister once he has incurred the ineradicable enmity of both houses. This point, however, has never been decided by law, and there have already been numerous instances in individual countries in which ministers, without regard to the enmity of the majorities, have resolutely remained in office for years with only minority support. In England, the authority and power of parliament is really surprising since parliament has exercised the legislative function from the olden days. (Note: The parliament in England holds full legislative powers as its authority flourishes.) Such a system actually contributes to tranquil rule in England while tranquil rule is almost invariably injured in other constitutional countries when parliamentary authority becomes so excessively strong. There is, consequently, an established tradition in England that a minister usually resigns his post if he suffers defeat in parliament. Even in England, however, several ministers in the past have firmly held power after they have incurred the enmity of the lower house. An example is the wise minister [William] Pitt (1750–1806). Why is it not disadvantageous for England to follow the custom by which a minister resigns from office whenever he is defeated in parliament, while such a practice can be extremely disadvantageous for the countries on the Continent? It is because there are many illustrious persons in England who enjoy the confidence of both the monarch and the people, and those endowed with great authority as the cornerstone of the nation are the aristocrats, the men of wealth, and the educated. These classes have no wish strongly to oppose the government by rashly fomenting trouble since the aristocrats fear for a decline in their forefather's reputation, the rich for a loss of their wealth, and the educated for an infringement of their principles. The countries of the Continent, however, have not yet achieved England's genuine tranquility. More especially, since the power of the common people in these countries is excessive, it is essential for the ministers to remain at their posts unperturbed by the opposition of the majorities in their houses of parliament.

For example, Graf Bismarck finally achieved the present strength of Prussia and restored the might of Germany because he resolutely remained in office even though he incurred the deep enmity of the diet during his early years. There is no purpose in discussing the minister who is unable firmly to hold office since he incurs the enmity of the majority from beginning to end. (This material appeared in my previous translation of the *Allgemeines Staatsrecht,* but the present translation includes a few additions and deletions. The earlier translation was based on the third edition of 1864; the present, on the fourth edition of 1868.)

I beg the readers to believe that this translation is in no sense an effort to deny the validity of public discussion and public opinion. I only desire to explain the error of recklessly trying to expand public discussion without reference to the times and the condition of the people.

The Frenchman Sully on Symptoms That Indicate National Decline[4]

Sugi Kōji

—— Levying of numerous taxes.
—— Monopolistic commercial practices. There is the greatest injury to commerce arising from monopolies over cereals.
—— Allowing trade, industry, and agriculture to be neglected.
—— Numerous expenditures in connection with tax collections.
—— Numerous unnecessary officials.
—— Excessive national expenditures.
—— Delayed justice as well as improper administration of justice.
—— Want of industry arising from idleness.
—— Luxury.
—— Useless expenditures.
—— Failure to defend against disturbing religious practices.
—— Numerous currency fluctuations.
—— Numerous wars.

—— Irresponsible conduct of government.
—— Opposition to the spread of knowledge.
—— Failure to reform continuing mistakes.
—— Other symptoms similar to the above.

Sully was a man of the 1600's who, as the chief minister of France, ruled his country well during exceedingly troubled times. In those days, such countries as England and Holland all introduced reforms in conformity with his advice. I am just recording these items in the society's minutes since I do not know whether our countrymen may regard them as hackneyed.

On Religion[5] Part One

Nishi Amane

Religion is established on faith, and faith is rooted in the area beyond human knowledge. Once something comes within the realm of human knowledge, its principle (*ri*)[6] is man's possession. Yet when man cannot understand something, he [can] only have faith in what he does not know by conjecturing from what he does know. The principles (*ri*) [governing the area of faith], therefore, do not lie within man's grasp. Thus, when common people deify trees, stones, insects, and beasts or when the eminent and erudite believe in Heaven (*Ten*),[7] Reason (*Ri*), or a Supreme Ruler (*Jōtei*),[8] they all believe without knowing. Although their beliefs are different, therefore, their act of faith is the same.

Moreover, what we call faith is something in the hearts of men. Even bold men, therefore, are unable to rob others of their faith, and even wise men are unable to impose their faith on others with argument. For this reason also, government should permit freedom of belief, and it can never cause men to believe this or to disbelieve that. Should you ask why, it is because those in government are invariably men. Being men, they believe in the unknown even though they are the eminent and the erudite who are infinitely superior to the vulgar commoners. Being men who do not know, the eminent and erudite in government clearly have no reason [*ri*] to cause other men to believe in what they themselves believe. And it is also clear that they have no right to force their faith on others just as they also have no reason to do so.

Someone may say, "Even though such may be the case, to abandon one's gods in favor of another's is to lose the substance of faith." I would respond that men should only believe in what they assume to be true since faith is without substance. When common people have faith in trees, stones, insects, and beasts, they also believe in what they think true. Men will abandon their faith once they in the least appreciate its falseness. Therefore, men only believe in what they assume to be true, as faith is without proved validity and without substance. How then can men be robbed of their faith on grounds of proved validity or substance?

Someone may then ask, "Even though such may be the case, what about a religion that interferes with the national structure (*kokutai*)?"[9] He may wonder whether a religion may eventually injure the national structure if, as previously stated, the government leaves religion to individual preference on the assumption that it has no power to affirm or deny faith. I would respond that the powers of government are really not in the same sphere as the path of religion. Therefore, men follow the secular law from birth to death on earth, and government only asks them to obey its legislation without inquiring into their consciences. What government should stress is the preservation of tranquil rule by gathering the people together, forming a state, and preventing the unjust from compromising the just. This is the area of the government's power as well as its obligation. How can it have time to inquire further?

Let us assume that the path of religion is entirely otherwise from that of government, that it extends retrospectively to the past and prospectively to the future without being limited to the present world, that it only inquires into the hearts of men without reference to their subservience before the law, and that its purpose is to gather converts together inquiring into their consciences, affirming the good, and reforming the evil in anticipation of the Judgment in the Hereafter. Then how can it invade the sphere of secular law and administration in this world? The areas of government and religion thus being entirely separate, how can there be anything injurious to government but beneficial to religion through the interference of one in the affairs of the other?

Nevertheless, there have been theocracies in the world, such as those of ancient Judea, Egypt, India, and modern Tibet, in which heroic men of old undertook to rule and exert religious authority by grasping political and religious power in one hand. This may indeed have been unavoidable in the old days, but there has been a tendency in later generations to reject these falsehoods and finally to destroy such old customs with the broadening of human wisdom. A government supported by religion, therefore, can only survive if the people are dull and backward like the Tibetans. Once there is the slightest appreciation among the people of their religion's falsehood, however, the country will surely suffer quick disaster. In antiquity, there was a king of a certain barbarian state who alone knew how to prophecy solar and lunar eclipses. This secret was transmitted by the royal house from generation to generation as a means of inducing popular respect and for spreading the royal authority. Thereafter, the people advanced in culture until they finally learned how to predict eclipses, and their dynasty ultimately lost its power. How can any regime avoid destruction and ruin if, rather than rely on what should be relied on, it relies on something the falseness of which it conceals? Thus the association between state and religion should be quickly severed when the government is in the least theocratic. Only thereby shall we prevent the evil in religion from injuring the state.

An Essay on Brick Construction

Nishi Amane

When traveling in Europe, I saw brick buildings five to six stories high and six hundred to a thousand feet wide. Moreover, they are so firm and strong that they cannot be rocked or bent, and they are formed on four sides by magnificent high brick walls. This method of construction has recently been used on the streets to the north of Shimbashi in buildings that are worth seeing even though they do not compare in strength and firmness with those of Europe.[10]

Ah, why is this type of skilled craftsmanship lacking only among political leaders? Bricks are fine and strong in character as well as square and upright in shape. Being fine and strong as well as square and upright, they are inflexible and unbending. And taking advantage of this shape and character, builders are able to achieve such heights by piling one brick on another. Now if builders produce bricks that are not entirely fine and strong as well as square and upright, and then arbitrarily try to pile one on another, depending mainly on the mortar's strength, the bricks will wear down and flake away, their shape will erode, their corners will disintegrate, and they will be progressively rounded. How can builders hope to construct high buildings with such materials?

When officials now injure the rights of individuals below with arbitrary oppression, those below are unable to protect their rights and finally become sycophants. Even though there may be some of strength and uprightness, these persons must invariably bow to the crowd once such compromising sycophancy in the least prevails. Similarly, how can builders preserve the sharp edges of a few square and upright bricks when they rub against rounded bricks? Indeed, if an official deals with his subordinates in a manner injurious to their independence and orders them temporarily to compromise their squareness and uprightness in conformity with his wishes, this is like the builder who, arbitrarily chipping and chiselling, forces the bricks to yield to his purposes without availing himself of the brick's original squareness and uprightness. How can he expect that his building of chipped and chiselled bricks will not be an area of disintegration and destruction in another day?

Fineness and strength as well as squareness and uprightness is the nature of bricks, and protecting human rights is the nature of man. Once their natures have been altered in the least by rounding off the bricks or by compromising sycophancy among men, there will be no room for the builder or the statesman to exercise their powers even though the builder exhausts his arts and the statesman fully exerts his talents. If the single fragile brick of a lofty wall falls out, the remaining fine and strong ones will also give way accordingly, and the entire wall will ultimately collapse.

The builder and the statesman, therefore, will be successful if the former does not trifle with the character of a single brick and if the latter does not make light of the rights of the common people. Especially is this the case in a country such as ours in which the bricks are basically fragile and the rights of the people are especially weak! Institutions were simple and the people high-spirited at the outset of the [Meiji] Restoration. By now, however, there has been a return of decadence to the arts of war and peace. Indeed, when everything is being changed down to the smallest detail, the evil of arbitrary oppression has inevitably emerged. This then is my essay on brick construction.

[1]Although trained in French, it appears that Mitsukuri translated this material from an English version of Book XVII of Montesquieu's *Spirit of the Laws*.

[2]Montesquieu did not go so far as to claim that the Europeans had fully achieved their liberties.

[3]Johann Kaspar Bluntschli, 1808–1881, Swiss-born professor of law and international relations. Katō's translation of Bluntschli's *Allgemeines Staatsrecht* was published in Tokyo in 1875 under the title *Kokuhō Hanron,* 國法汎論.

[4]Sully, Maximilen de Bethun, Duc de, 1560–1641, a statesman who served King Henry IV of France in many capacities.

[5]*Kyōmonron,* 教門論. In this and succeeding essays on religion, Nishi assumed a position, shared by other Japanese enlighteners, against the policy adopted by the Meiji government in its early years to unite government with the Shintō religion, a policy that was identified with the phrases *saisei itchi,* 祭政一致, and *seikyō itchi,* 政教一致, "the union of church and state." Without denying faith, Nishi's commitment to a strong state led him to urge the complete separation of church and state because he felt that faith in the unknown would be a very insecure foundation for any state or nation. His warning against accepting a sun myth similar to that of the vanished Inca Empire in his third essay would surely have been unacceptable in Japan twenty years later. Indeed, the articles by Kashiwabara Takaaki and Sakatani Shiroshi in this journal indicate that Nishi's views appeared radical to some of the Meirokusha.

[6]*Ri,* 理.

[7]*Ten,* 天.

[8]*Jōtei,* 上帝. From his later essays in this series, it is clear that Nishi here refers to the Supreme Ruler (*Jōtei*) in which he believed as distinguished from the traditional East Asian conceptions of Heaven (*Ten*) and Reason or Principle (*Ri*).

[9]*Kokutai,* 國體, the term generally translated as "national structure" that was associated with the unbroken line of Japanese sovereigns who claimed descent from the Sun Goddess. Nishi apparently would have shorn the term of much of its mystique by establishing the state on strictly secular foundations.

[10]After a great fire that destroyed the Ginza, 銀座, area of Tokyo in February 1872, the Japanese government undertook reconstruction in brick, completing work extending from Shimbashi, 新橋, to Kyōbashi, 京橋, in 1873. Although Nishi is apparently lamenting the declining caliber of government officials generally, without pointing to a specific failure, there was considerable controversy regarding the methods for financing the reconstruction.

In Opposition to Protective Tariffs[1]

Tsuda Mamichi

If one compares the recent imports and exports through the various ports of our country, the value of imports is said to have exceeded that of exports by about Yen 8,000,000 in 1872 and by about Yen 7,000,000 in 1873. If one adds to these sums about Yen 2,000,000 paid to foreign teachers by government and private bodies and some tens of thousands of yen in interest charges on the nation's foreign debt, our currency exports then will mount to Yen 100,000,000 in ten years. If such be the case, then our country's gold and silver will be completely exhausted within some ten-odd years. Patriots affirm that this bullion is the people's capital upon which the nation is based. And they wonder what will survive once they are thus impoverished. Ah, would there not be deep sorrow and great sights? It is thus essential to establish a protective policy, these patriots claim. Pointing to the wise men of earlier Europe who first controlled this injury with protective tariffs and to the present employment of protection by the United States, they aver that a similar protective tariff policy is the only means for sustaining our national destiny under present conditions.

I do not agree with these views. It is generally accepted among Western political economists that these tariffs, rather than provide protection, are bad measures injurious to the people generally. Someone may observe, however, that there are numerous expressions approving protective tariffs in America. In the final analysis the American production costs cannot yet be reduced to the level of the European because American industry is still meager and unskilled as compared with the sophistication of Europe. Therefore, the Americans protect their home industry by imposing high imports on goods shipped from abroad. Often the only objective of these tariffs is to encourage American industry, even though the people as a whole are necessarily injured. Now the levels of our arts, industries, and scholarship cannot yet be considered in the same breath with those of America. Still less can we compete with the various countries of Europe! It would be like pitting women and children against the strongest of men. This is why it is necessary for us to spend as much as Yen 2,000,000 on salaries for foreign teachers. Under such conditions, the protectionists would vainly follow American national policies. While the stupidity of their views is immediately obvious, I shall endeavor categorically to set forth my opinions as discussions of protective tariffs have yet to appear in public and because there are many radical people in society.

Our country cannot freely introduce protective tariffs since our tariffs are established by treaties of commerce with the foreign nations. This is the first reason why protective theories cannot be implemented.

While a heavy commodity like iron is costly to transport, the price of iron brought several thousand miles distant by sea from England is actually cheaper than our domestic iron. This may be attributed entirely to the technological backwardness of our iron mining and production. There is an old saying that wisdom and foolishness are three thousand miles apart. It is not alone in the iron industry that our country and Europe are three thousand miles apart. Our industries generally are similarly far behind. It is thus both rash and extremely thoughtless to assume that we can make our industries competitive with theirs by the single method of tariff protection. This is the second reason for not adopting protective tariffs.

In the past, foreign commodities desired by the people were little more than toys. Now there is generally compelling demand for articles ranging from clothing and household appliances to eating utensils. Even house construction in the cities is often shifting to foreign styles. We may indeed attempt to protect our industries by imposing heavy duties on essential imports such as woolens and blankets, but we have as yet no factories for producing these goods. This is the third reason for opposing protective tariffs.

Until ten years ago, the country resounded generally with anti-foreign sentiment. By now, however, the gap between our imports and exports has finally increased to several million yen each year, the people having suddenly become devoted to foreign commodities and attached to foreign customs generally. Even though this is due to the trends of the times, it is also because the gentlemen of the court are changing fashions and transforming the vulgar. By now suddenly taxing foreign commodities heavily, they would reduce imports and prevent satisfaction of popular demand. This is as absurd as taking with one hand and giving with the other, and it is the fourth reason for opposing protection.

Under existing conditions in the country, our people have only peeped through the outer gates to the wonders of the West, without yet entering the inner halls of enlightenment. In other words, they should be compared to small children entering primary school rather than to students of a university. Even if they were university students, since they have not yet graduated, they have been unable yet to reap profit [from their education], having only paid numerous school expenses from year to year. In the present situation, therefore, if we increase the knowledge of our people still more, we may then add still more to the imbalance between our imports and exports. How can we expect to reduce the discrepancy? This is the fifth reason for opposing protective tariffs.

There are those, however, who lament that, should we neglect the present situation, there will be no trace of gold or silver in the country ten-odd years hence. I would urge them not to grieve as I am completely certain that such will not come to pass. Even though at times we may not avoid fluctuations in the comparative rates of imports and exports, an excess in one will never destroy the equilibrium over the long run. This same principle operates during the seasons in which the equilibrium is never seriously upset even though we may not escape extremes in heat and cold or in winds and floods. This is a principle from which nature never deviates, namely, that the seasonal equilibrium is invariably maintained through recurring change. How then will the equilibrium be restored in the imbalance between exports and imports? I would respond that there are but two ways—through an increase in the level of exports or through a decrease in the number of imports. Now under recent conditions in our country, exports exceeded imports for several years after the opening of the ports, and imports exceeded exports for three or four years thereafter.

I would judge that exports should also exceed imports for some years to come. Exports and imports thus will never lose their equilibrium, as they circulate in accordance with the laws of nature, never ceasing recurrently to rise and fall. Such being the case, enlightenment will progress with advancing technology. I say that one should never worry groundlessly.

On Religion Part Two[2]

Nishi Amane

Even though the people are allowed to believe what they believe and to honor what they honor, what injury can befall temporal rule once government faces the people after severing its ties with religion, clarifying the great powers of governing, and establishing a just legal system? State and church were closely connected in Europe during the Middle Ages. Royal authority was then based on this connection and wars arose from it. Charlemagne secured the title of emperor after having been crowned by the pope, and the brave Henry IV was unable to recover his position even though, barefoot and kneeling, he begged the pope's mercy.[3] It can thus be said that extreme disturbances and widespread harm arose from such laws and institutions as excommunication (*kyōmon zekkō*)[4] and the inquisition (*kambō gamon*).[5] In modern times, men have finally appreciated these abuses and established complete separation of church and state. Thus Catholics have remained largely indifferent even though the pope has been deprived of his temporal power. Indeed, how can the temporal power be injured by religion when Jews line up with Catholics and Protestants in the nation to serve the royal cause?

Someone may then ask about the ways to separate the state from religion. I would respond that the government offices for supervising religions (*shikyō no gamon*)[6] should be allowed no more control over religion than is necessary to prevent religious disturbances. We need not bother to question whether people believe in foxes, badgers, Buddhas, or angels.[7] The fate of the various religions is entirely their responsibility, not ours. We are interested only in preventing injury by religion to temporal rule, protecting this principle strictly, and punishing those who transgress it. Nor is the state concerned with whether a certain religion is right or wrong. Thus government should not be prone to inquire into the good or evil within men's hearts since law by its nature regulates externals.

Now, if we want government in the least to control matters within the heart, orders sent to every household will invariably prove inadequate. Even with torture how can it accomplish anything against people who conform externally without following in their inner hearts? There is an old truism that the commander of great armies may be seized but that the most humble people cannot be deprived of their resolution. It is sufficient, therefore, if government offices for supervising religions prohibit only outward contradiction of the nation's temporal rule without regard to what the people believe in their hearts.

It is the obligation of a man from the day he crosses a nation's border to follow its government and to respect the king or emperor endowed with the powers of leadership. This applies all the more to people born and residing in a country. The obligation is absolutely clear regardless of whether it is written into the law. As men are held accountable for the slightest violation of the law, therefore, it is a fact that government may impose even the death penalty or exile without fear of consequences to itself. Even so, if the government wants to have the people believe in a king or an emperor as a god, as a source of truth, or as the creator, why should the nation do so? Kings and emperors are inescapably human, however highly honored they may be. Since they are no less human than others, their faith also arises in the area that they themselves do not comprehend.

Since the ruler has faith in what he himself does not know, why should the nation obey him in its inner heart if he tries to compel the people to believe in his faith? Still more, who will believe the ruler's falsehoods if he tries to compare himself with so-called gods and to equate his power with the Creator or with the Supreme Ultimate of all things? European monarchs as far as possible draw close to the people through such activities as reviewing cavalry, opening educational institutions, visiting hospitals, inspecting factories, and riding and hunting. But such conduct is not cause for the people to worship their rulers like the living Buddha of Tibet. Since it is really not right to want both fish and bear's palm,[8] it is sufficient for government offices when supervising religions only to regulate externals, leaving the people to believe as they please.

When asked about the method for regulating externals, I would respond that it is by establishing prohibitions. To cite a few examples, I feel that warlike debates between religious sects should be forbidden. This does not mean that discourses on the merits of religious principles are not to be allowed, but there should be punishment when words become abusive. Generally, those guilty of fomenting religious arguments should be punished for having started these arguments without regard to whether their views are right or wrong. We should prohibit the followers of different faiths from upsetting established rites when it is felt that such conduct is disturbing to manners and mores.

There should be punishment of those who interfere with freedom to change religion among the members of a sect who no longer believe its tenets. There should also be freedom for agnostics as well as those of pluralistic beliefs, and persons who oppose this should be punished. We should prohibit compulsion of nonbelievers and forced monetary donations for the reason that people live in the same village. We should outlaw the building of shrines and temples without official permission. We should forbid religious services outside churches and temples authorized by the government. Raising banners, ringing bells, and incanting prayers in public should be strictly forbidden except in the compounds of officially sanctioned churches and temples. Followers of various religions should not be allowed to conduct funeral services until they have passed through the gates of their cemeteries. While men should be allowed freedom to build altars and chapels and to conduct services according to their beliefs in their own homes, they should be strictly forbidden from building even small shrines outside their homes.

In general, religious gatherings of more than ten people in homes and outside officially sanctioned churches and temples should be barred. Religious assemblies in isolated mountains and forests should be generally forbidden. We should forbid absolutely and without question any religious practice likely to bewitch the eyes of men or to foment widespread disturbances by erecting roadside altars, wearing strange priestly vestments, and public movement of wood and stone images from distant places. Various sects should be encouraged as far as possible to honor their religious principles. The more important prohibitions should be collected in legal codes for the supervision of religions; the less important, in regulations established by the departments of public morals (*fūkenbu*)[9] charged with apprehending violations. It will suffice for the offices for supervising religions to exercise control [over the sects] and oversee suits.

We have no power to confer or to determine anything like theological ranks within the various religions. Such ecclesiastic ranking should be left to previously determined religious policy or to public election by church congregation since it is none of our concern. Thus, Amida, *Bosatsu, Nyorai* and the designations for holy men (*shōnin*), saints (*shōnin*), priests (*oshō*), and elders (*chōrō*) are only titles indicating virtue and scholarship that we naturally should not control.[10] If we try to equate these titles with military and government ranks, then we shall want to revive a previously separated connection between spiritual and temporal matters and once again make them one by equating god and man. Now if government has the power to select and promote religious teachers and to determine religious ranks, this amounts to adopting religion by the state. We shall then draw into one intimate family circle with government not only Shaka, Daruma, *yamabushi,* and blind priests (*kosō*) but also foxes (*kitsune*) and snakes (*daija*).[11] How strange this would be!

The Independence of the United States of North America[12]

Sugi Kōji

The English began colonizing North America during the time of Queen Elizabeth. Thereafter, the colonies gradually expanded as large numbers of Germans, French, and Dutch migrated from their home countries for religious reasons. The source of the country's prosperity lay in farming and breeding of livestock by the immigrants. These people were then all social equals without a powerful aristocracy. Only in the southern region was agriculture developed with the labor of black slaves. Moreover, communication was facilitated by waterways, the natural terrain, and the absence of injury from customs barriers. In law and religion, the people enjoyed religious freedom, and they nourished the spirit of liberty and stressed self-government in emulation of England. In 1755, the so-called Seven Years War broke out after England struggled with France over their colonial boundaries in North America. Even though England was not unreasonable when she desired to raise the money in the colonies to pay for the war, the English government of the royal party tried to impose its taxes arbitrarily, consulting parliament but not referring them to the colonies. The colonies, therefore, opposed this policy, basing their opposition on the English law that there should be no taxation without representation. An English government order in 1764, however, directed that heavy taxes be imposed on the previously untaxed colonial imports of sugar, coffee, and silk, the proceeds from which would be devoted toward defraying expenses for American defense.

Although the colonies complained that these taxes violated English law and injured their popular rights, England did not listen, and a subsequent decree of 1765 directed that all American merchants should use stamps. The greatly disturbed colonists thereupon denied the stamps everywhere and vowed to halt all imports of English goods if the stamp tax was not abolished. Bowing to the colonists, England revoked the stamp system, but she did not intend to abandon her earlier intention to impose taxes. Since England the following year placed a tax on all imports of tea, paper, paint, and glass, the merchants of Massachusetts unanimously declared in a congress at Boston that they would buy nothing imported from England. Moreover, they dispatched galloping messengers to report in all directions, and the people in their discussions were all of one mind and without dissent.

A large number of English factories, therefore, were suddenly depressed. Now the anger of the colonists was increasingly deepened by such arbitrary conduct on the part of the English government. After a change in the English government in 1770, the previous measures were revoked except for a five-pence tax on each pound of tea with which the government hoped to restore its earlier revenues. Recognizing this artifice, however, the colonists again stopped buying tea and resorted to secret purchases from Holland for the tea that they used. To end this secret trade, therefore, the English government ordered the East India Company to ship tea to America and to sell it at a low price. When the company's ships arrived in America thus loaded with tea, none of the various ports would buy the tea, and the vessels were ultimately obliged to return to England.

In Boston harbor, however, three ships were boarded at night by citizens who invaded the vessels' interior and threw into the sea all of the 342 boxes of tea in the cargo. This was 18 December 1773. A royalist prime minister, however, decided to suppress the movement by force without listening to the Elder Pitt. After he closed the port of Boston and destroyed the government of Massachusetts in 1774, all of the American states arose in opposition, and hostilities finally broke out between the two countries in 1775. The following year, representatives of the thirteen states, meeting in Philadelphia, swore from that time to dissolve their ties with England and to establish an independent country. The two countries fought until America was finally victorious after a period of eight years. England's colonial rule in America was ended by the peace negotiations at Paris in 1783, and the newly established independent nation emerged.

Comment by the translator [Sugi]: Each time I reach this section when reading Western history, I can only set the book down and sigh in despair. Ah, should not those who participate in the least in government reflect on the fact that losing the affection of the people and wronging the country by tyrannical oppression will lead to such an end!

The Interrelation between the Freedom of Peoples and the Climates of Regions (Continued)[13]

Mitsukuri Rinshō

The peoples of northern Europe conquered the European continent as free men, but the enslaved people of northern Asia conquered the Asian continent for their rulers. Now to cite an example, the Tartars have indeed established nations embracing southern Asia on several occasions, but they only spread the power of their rulers. These Tartar rulers first gain control over the fallen southerners and then concentrate the mobile armies of the north under their domination. The territory known today as Chinese Tartary, therefore, is ruled despotically by the Chinese emperor, being no different in appearance from China proper.

Moreover, if one refers to the materials in Chinese records that describe how Chinese emperors moved their people into Tartary, these Chinese for the most part became Tartars. But there was no change in their traditional Chinese attitudes of subservience and submission even though they came to regard China as an enemy. Also, when one looks at the Tartars who returned to their homeland having been expelled from the country [China] that they had previously conquered, these Tartars often carried back the subservient customs with which they had been infected in the southern area. Such reports are especially to be found in the Chinese histories.

Generally speaking, therefore, Asians are likely to be governed oppressively, but the spirit of Europeans is bravely to deny such practices and to throw off tyranny with all their might. And so, from antiquity what have been called punishments in Asia have been termed cruelty in Europe. The European "Goths" went so far as to establish constitutional government and the people's freedom when they conquered Rome, but the Asian Tartars introduced tyrannical rule everywhere after they destroyed the Greek Empire. Reflect on the fact that, even though the famous Rudbeck in his *Atlantica* applauds the virtues of Scandinavia, his great shortcoming is his failure to mention the most important fact that the Scandinavians surpass others since they were the source of modern European freedom. (Outside Europe, nations of free peoples are extremely rare.) Again, Jordanes pointed to northern Europe as the producer of various European peoples, but I would prefer to call these northern territories the factory for the tools that destroyed the chains enslaving southern Europe. In my opinion, the northern Europeans broke out of their countries to destroy tyranny and to liberate the enslaved peoples wherever they went. They led the people of the world to know that men are all born equal and that the distinctions between rulers and ruled do not go beyond what conduces to mutual well-being.

Even though Asian rulers since antiquity have dominated countless souls of the world in great states, only rarely have such large countries appeared in Europe. Now if one considers the reasons for this, Asia is, after all, an area of numerous vast expanses, and the regions into which it is divided by seas and mountains are far larger than those of Europe. More especially, since Asia's lands are also more southerly than those of Europe, its rivers dry up easily, its mountains accumulate little snow, and its natural boundaries are self-evidently few. Asian monarchs are thus unable to rule its vast territories unless they govern with autocratic regimes. Even though Asia may divide into numerous individual states, it will quickly reunite into one great land since geographic conditions really are not conducive to division.

This is why Asian peoples through history have failed to throw off their spirit of subservience. There is no spirit of freedom among Asians to be found in the historical sources, only a spirit of bravery among the subservient. In Europe, on the other hand, there are a great many natural boundaries, and the entire area is consequently divided to form numerous small and medium-sized states. Therefore, not only are its states easily maintained by legal means alone. When autocrats arbitrarily conduct despotic rule without reliance on law in Europe, their countries invariably decline until their national power is far below that of other states. This is why the peoples of Europe have always maintained a spirit of freedom and why it is extremely difficult for one part of the continent to conquer another with its power.

Africans are generally subservient as the African climate resembles that of the southern regions of Asia. It is impossible to pass clear judgment on America as Europeans in only a few years have moved into the territory, increasingly prospered, and finally established countries after pushing back the aborigines. In general, however, it may be said that America conforms most closely to my thesis if one judges from its early history.

On the basis of the major premise set forth in the above discussion, a ruler should give strict attention to selecting a favorable geographical position when he establishes his capital. In sum, while those who establish their capitals in southern regions generally fear the loss of their northern lands, it is not too difficult for rulers with capitals in the north to govern southern territories. Nevertheless, what I have indicated here is only a generalization that may, after all, be inappropriate for all times and places. Even as friction in a machine may on occasion prevent the actual operation of an engineering principle, it may also be impossible to avoid changing these views according to the circumstances.

Church and State in America[14]

Katō Hiroyuki, translator

Note by the translator [Katō]: This work by the American Mr. Thompson discusses why the separation and independence of church and state is assured under the American system by separating religious rites from government administration and by dissociating religion from government. Thompson also explains why this system is essential if one aspires generally to political peace in the nation and the enlightenment of men's intellects. This is already discussed fully in my translation of Bluntschli's *Allgemeines Staatsrecht*.[15] When observant persons read carefully these two works of exactly the same purport, they will appreciate why the union of religious rites and government administration as well as church and state in the various states of old Europe brought confusion to society and the suppression of human knowledge. They should also be able to understand why political peace and the enlightenment of men's intellects have greatly benefited since church and state in Europe and, of course, in America have recently become practically separate and independent through the final dissolution of their union. These are writings that persons concerned should surely read, and I am indeed anxious to translate Thompson's work quickly so that it may be shown to the informed persons in society. Since I have been prevented from finishing a translation of this material by my total preoccupation with the translation of the *Allgemeines Staatsrecht,* I hope to complete my translation of Thompson gradually, printing in this journal the few pages that I am able to translate for each of the Meirokusha's semi-monthly meetings.

First Section. Part One. Laws Relating to Church Matters and Constitutional Provisions Determining Matters of Religion in the United States.

In the Constitution of the United States, it is provided that there shall never be any consideration of religion when making appointments to public office in any part of the territory of the United States. (See Article VI, Section 3 of the Constitution.) The power to establish a state church or to interfere with religious liberty is even forbidden to the Congress (which may be translated as the legislative body [*rippōfu*][16] or the discussion chamber [*gi-jiin*].)[17] (See Amendment I to the Constitution.)

Part Two. The Right of Religious Liberty (as Distinguished from Toleration.)

The two articles of the Constitution cited above are extremely simple in style and economical in wording. Nevertheless, they actually embrace all matters relating to religious affairs from a constitutional point of view, and they are also sufficient to indicate that religious liberty is a basic right of the American people. The system by which the American people possess this basic right may be termed one of complete religious liberty and is not to be compared with toleration of various religions in a state where there is an established church. When officials are appointed in the United States, the government is never allowed to inquire into their religious beliefs. Nor may the government ever protect one church or injure another.

It is never appropriate to call toleration a system under which government is absolutely unrelated to religion or under which religions are completely equal. The word toleration derives from the fact that a nation permits public worship in other faiths without daring to prohibit them even though it especially honors a certain religion. Or it is based on the theory that a government holds legal power to determine church matters.

The word toleration really means to allow what one does not desire. Therefore, when speaking of religious toleration, this conveys the sense of invariably allowing faiths whose creeds and liturgies are not the same as those of the national church or that employ liturgies entirely contrary to those of the national church (the church that the nation as a whole honors). Looking at the matter in this light, toleration may be said to exist when a government, which actually stands above the church and holds the power to administer and control the church, abandons part of this power of its own accord.

Religious liberty, however, is quite the opposite of this, being a system in which there is complete freedom of both religious belief and practice for all men. After all, liberty of religious belief and practice can never depend upon sanction by government as it is inextricably linked with the free right of men to determine innately what is right and wrong (freedom to distinguish between right and wrong according to one's heaven-endowed conscience).

The English government's method may be taken as a good illustration of the principle of toleration. England has established as the national church what is known as the High Church (*Hoofu Kiruhe*),[18] but it also tolerates other churches even though it especially honors the High Church. In the past, however, very strict limitations were placed on the rights of subjects who were followers of the Catholic, Jewish, and other faiths. (Note: "Other faiths" refers only to Christian sects that differ in belief from the national church.) Only in modern times have these limitations been almost entirely removed. In Scotland, however, the Presbyterian Church is the established church, and the High Church is regarded as the dissenting church.

Since there has never been an established church in the United States, however, there are absolutely no churches of dissenting beliefs. Moreover, there has never been a church that has been regarded as the main church or the main sect. The principle of tolerating other churches and sects also has never existed since the various churches and sects generally enjoy complete equality before the law.

Liberty of public discussion, liberty of worship, and liberty in all other matters relating to religion are never privileges bestowed by government. They are truly rights that reside in the spirits and souls of men. Government, therefore, has an invariable obligation to refrain from injuring them. This then is a fundamental principle under the American Constitution.

A further translation will appear in the next issue.

[1]Since Japan was bound to extremely low tariffs on imports and exports by the tariff convention that she concluded with the United States, Great Britain, France, and the Netherlands in 1866, she was unable to raise her tariffs either to protect her new industries or to curtail the mounting imports that caused her to suffer serious adverse balances of trade. In this article and elsewhere in the *Meiroku Zasshi,* Tsuda stoutly opposes the protectionist views on trade that began to appear in Japan in the early 1870s. His liberal, anti-protectionist stance presumably was derived from his study in Holland under the eminent legal scholar Simon Vissering, who was a vigorous advocate of nineteenth-century liberal economics and supporter of the Anti-Corn Law movement in England. Unfortunately, Tsuda's notes on Vissering's lectures have apparently been lost.

[2]Continued from the previous issue.

[3]Nishi here refers to the famed pilgrimage by the Holy Roman Emperor Henry IV to humble himself before Pope Gregory VII at Canossa in January 1077.

[4]*Kyōmon zekkō*, ,教門絶交.

[5]*Kambō gamon,* 監謗衙門.

[6]*Shikyō no gamon,* 司教ノ衙門.

[7]Foxes, *kitsune,* 狐; badgers, *tanuki,* 狸; Buddhas, *Nyorai,* 如來; and angels, *tennin,* 天人.

[8]*Uo to yūshō to kana emu to hossu,* to desire both fish and bear's palm, 魚ト熊掌ト兼得ムト欲ス. This is drawn from the statement by Mencius that, athough he was especially fond of fish and bear's palm, he would take bear's palm and forego fish if he could not have both at the same time. The sage was warning against allowing a secondary desire prevent achievement of a primary objective.

[9]*Fūkenbu,* 風憲部.

[10]Amida, 阿彌陀; *Bosatsu,* 菩薩; *Nyorai,* 如來; *shōnin,* 聖人; *shōnin,* 上人; *oshō,* 和尙; *chōrō,* 長老.

[11]Shaka, 釋迦; Daruma, 達磨; *yamabushi,* 山伏; *kosō,* 瞽僧; *kitsune,* 狐; *daija,* 大蛇.

[12]In both this essay and his later discourse on the states of North and South America, Sugi has chosen themes that clearly suggest his support of the movement for a popularly elected assembly and at least tacit criticism of the government's restrictive measures. Agitators for the assembly, like proponents of parliaments everywhere, argued that there should be no taxation without representation.

[13]See Issue Four.

[14]From Joseph Parrish Thompson, *Kirche und Staat in den Vereinigten Staaten* (Berlin, 1873). Thompson was an American Congregational clergyman who became interested in the conflict between the German state and the Catholic Church when he was living in retirement in Berlin during Bismarck's *Kulturkampf*. His small booklet was entirely in line with the reasoning of the Japanese enlighteners who sought separation of church and state.

[15]Katō's translation of Bluntschli's *Allgemeines Staatsrecht* appeared in 1875 as *Kokuhō Hanron*, 國法汎論.

[16]*Rippōfu*, 立法府

[17]*Gijiin*, 議事院

[18]*Hoofu Kiruhe* is Katō's rendering of the German "*Hoche Kirche*."

On Desiring Freedom of the Press[1]

Tsuda Mamichi

Civilized peoples escape from the reins with which barbarian governments oppress men. The distinction between civilization and barbarism can only be viewed in terms of whether people have or have not freedom of speech and conduct. The souls of men are free in essence, and even the devil can never obstruct the freedom with which superior men calmly honor Heaven and contemplate good. Their speech and conduct, however, are sometimes suppressed arbitrarily and sometimes controlled by law. Arbitrary suppression is an attribute of ugly rule by barbarians and outside the present discussion. I would here undertake to consider briefly the control of speech and conduct by law. There are many despotic regimes in semi-civilized countries that resort to this practice, and one sometimes hears of such control even in countries reputed to be civilized.

The people of England and America, who really possess freedom of speech and conduct, are all the more prevented from obstructing the freedom of others because they attach so much importance to their own freedom. France and other countries have press laws that absolutely forbid publication of books without official permission. Rule by governments in a country like France has been extremely disturbed from the outset by popular tumult and by willful discussion among men out of office. Moreover, this unrest appears to be the principal reason for the successive overthrow of French governments, and the governments, sensing this threat, thus try to preserve tranquility by forcefully silencing the people. Even though Napoleon III seems to have been a person able successfully for a time to administer with cunning talent, his rule was ultimately overthrown, and he died in England after his plans failed, his strategems were exhausted, and he had fallen prisoner to Prussia. How can we think that his rule was successful?

In my opinion, the source of successive French upheavals lies in the silencing of the people and in the obstruction of freedom. Even though some say that the enlightenment of our countrymen has been considerably broadened, it is not one-tenth that of the French. Men out of office occasionally discuss, but they generally go no farther than to applaud and to associate with the sentiments of the court. How narrow this is! What trouble can it cause the court? The discussions by men out of office might indeed be as willful as those of the French, but the conduct of the court's affairs should be in the determined manner of Peter the Great of Russia or of Prince Bismarck of Prussia.

Why should such strong leadership fear the clamorous discussion of men out of office? It is appropriate to impose suitable punishment for such crimes recognized in law as slandering administration, making false accusations, and abusing others. Even though there be press regulations, how can censors examine in detail the millions of words printed each year? In reality, such measures seem futile and ineffective. What we beg of the court is that it broadly encourage a policy of unrestricted freedom and that it open the eyes of our countrymen still more by granting freedom of the press to all persons through the prompt promulgation of regulations whose truth, justice, and clarity are like the sun and the moon hanging in heaven. After all, this is the fastest way to advance civilization and enlightenment.

On Religion Part Three[2]

Nishi Amane

Should I be asked if I have not discussed enough the absolute separation of government and religion, I would respond that there are still one or two additional practices that we must certainly adopt. One of these is to destroy any evidence of association between government and religion by clarifying the fundamental upon which governing is established. That Japan shall be ruled by one dynasty is the glory of our national system that absolutely permits no compromise. Nevertheless, we must reflect on the fact that something like relying on a divine commission from a sun god smacks closely of the old dynasty of Peru. Furthermore, if the great rights of governing are exercized by the sovereign over the people by Heaven's Grace (*Tenshoku*),[3] these rights will be the same as those held by the rulers of all countries. Since it is artificial to try now to elevate the sovereign to the level of a god and since traditional Chinese terminology in foreign relations[4] is contrary to fact, we should conform to the above international usage [of ascribing the sovereign's governing powers to Heaven's Grace].

Continuing to the next point, according to Western practice, officials in charge of ceremonies arrange rituals, banquets, and audiences as court attendants; court ceremonies connected with rites at graves are generally regarded as the dynastic affairs of royalty; and honoring of dynastic divinities is entrusted to the descendants and unrelated to government. Such being the case, government itself is wholly charged with governing powers, and it also spreads education as a part of ruling. Thus the perception of men is daily advanced, and their faith becomes elevated naturally without government interference. Moving away from crude and vulgar addictions, they strive for a true faith of purity and abnegation. Why then should popular beliefs be upset by government regulation?

When asked how religion differs from education, I would respond that they really are as far apart as heaven and earth since the hundred arts and sciences civilize and enlighten the intellect, while religion is rooted in the area that does not reach the intellect and arises from faith. Faith itself, however, will become more elevated as education advances. Thus beliefs in foxes, snakes, goblins (*tengu*)[5] and the like will be proved false if we just further the study of zoology. Knowledge of electricity and the weather will clear up doubts leading to beliefs in the gods of thunder, lightening, wind, and rain. Beliefs in the pool of blood and the mountain of swords[6] will be exploded through the study of geology. And the falseness of beliefs in ancient legends will be naturally revealed by studying "paleontology" and by becoming acquainted with the "mythologies" of all countries.

Generally in such fashion will crude and vulgar beliefs be vanquished by enlightening and civilizing the intellect. Assuming that, such being the case, men will naturally achieve a faith of purity and abnegation without contradicting statecraft, why should they be constrained to believe with coercive power?

[I am unable to find fault with an essay of such sharp reasoning and clear meaning. It may be termed sufficient to remedy the malady of a united church and state. The phrase Heaven's Grace or *Tenshoku,* however, seems to contradict the present discussions of civilization and enlightenment since it is a semicivilized Chinese compound close to "theocracy." Katō Hiroyuki]

Church and State in America (Continued)[7]

Katō Hiroyuki, translator

Part Three. Religion and Law in the Various States. It is stipulated in the constitutions of several states that persons positively may not be appointed officials or bear witness in court unless they really believe in the existence of God and in rewards and punishments in the hereafter. These are only empty provisos that are absolutely never enforced, however. Moreover, the two states of North Carolina and Maryland have lately modified this restric tion, and other states have generally removed the stipulations requiring adherence to religion when they have revised their constitutions.

It is provided in the constitution of New Jersey that none of the religions in the state shall be especially honored. Along with this, it is stated that men may manage government affairs as officials regardless of their religious affiliations, that they will never be prevented by their religion from administering public matters entrusted to them, and that they will never be denied or accorded rights because of their religion. Although the constitutions of other states are not so clear, their intentions are absolutely the same.

There is not a single state that does not forbid the honoring of a particular religion as the state church. (This refers to a church honored especially by the state.) This prohibition is achieved by various methods—by clear injunctions in the state constitutions, by prohibition through enactment (laws of the legislatures), and by actual practice or tacit consent by the public. This tacit consent and actual practice, however, have already become de facto law.

Liberty of religion for individuals alone does not compose complete religious liberty. (Of course, even this liberty is not allowed to injure public peace and morals.) It can be said that complete religious liberty only truly exists after there is also established complete freedom from taxation for the support of another church.

Upon consulting the texts of the constitutions of the various states and of the laws derived therefrom, we can recognize that none of the states of the Union allow the following:

One. Promulgation of laws for an established church.

Two. Anything like compulsory taxation to defray expenditures for religious education.

Three. Compulsory participation in religious services and worship.

Four. Any limitation on freedom of worship according to a man's own individual conscience.

Five. Any limitation on the freedom of persons to discuss what they themselves approve in religion. (See *Constitutional Limitations* by Cooley.[8] The title refers to limiting the powers of governments with constitutions.)

The Fourteenth Amendment to the Constitution of the United States adopted after the Civil War (the recent war between the northern and southern sections of the United States) may be regarded as the provision that prohibits any questioning of religious affiliation when the states entrust their citizens with the conduct of public affairs. Implementation of this prohibition by "Congress" (the legislature of the United States) naturally arises from its power to regulate the state legislatures.

The amendment then declares: "The states shall not pass laws that intentionally injure the rights and privileges of the citizens of the United States." And it further states: "In the various elections (elections for the President and Vice President, for members of

'Congress,' or for various state executive and judicial officers), when male citizens of the United States who have reached twenty-one years of age are deprived of or limited in the right to voice opinions*[9] (excepting persons attached to revolutionary parties or guilty of other major offenses), then the representatives of each state will be reduced in proportion to the number of males over twenty-one years of age whose rights the state has obstructed.** (See Section 2 of Amendment XIV.)

Some may regard as arbitrary the power of the United States to prevent the various states from robbing a portion of their citizens of their rights since, after all, the powers of the United States are also invariably limited. Even so, a state has absolutely no power to prevent charges from being brought against it when it limits the rights of its citizens to express opinions.

The addition of this amendment was actually for the purpose of preventing the various states from arbitrarily restricting the slaves who had become liberated freemen. The intent of the provisions is so broad, however, that they have been interpreted as sufficient to protect the rights of citizens generally.

Stipulations such as the above provide a system that absolutely forbids the various states from enacting and enforcing laws that limit the rights and privileges of citizens of the United States, and they also provide a system under which official appointments and the exercise of official responsibility are completely unrelated to the religion of the individuals concerned. Since these two systems exist, the states naturally can never inquire into the religious affiliations of persons whom they designate as officials. If any state violates these principles, there is absolutely no doubt that the Supreme Court will invariably judge such action to be contrary to the Fourteenth Amendment and therefore completely invalid.

It is entirely unlikely that a dispute will arise from such conduct by the states, however. Still less can it be doubted that, even though some states still preserve systems for inquiring into the religious beliefs of those to whom they entrust public affairs, such practices will quickly be ended or completely fall into disuse.

After all, the people of the United States understand that a

*This refers to the right to express opinions by participating in electoral meetings.

**This is because the number of representatives should vary in accordance with the number of voters.

nation should not direct religious affairs, that it should not administer governmental and religious affairs together, and that it should concentrate on purely governmental affairs. In his book on *Civil Liberty* (meaning liberty of subjects), Lieber (born in Germany in 1800 and later moved to America) wrote:[10]

> The system that absolutely separates from government the bodies (meaning churches) that propagate and protect religion generally is truly the free system of America.

I shall publish more in the next issue.

Religion

Mori Arinori

While Tsuda holds that the soundest policy is to select the best religion in the world and establish it as our national church, Nishi believes that the meritorious plan is permanently to establish religious liberty and completely to separate church and state in accordance with the respective principles of religion and government. I feel that religious matters should be left to the individual preference of the people since the government's responsibility is only to protect human life and property. If there is physical injury to others arising from this policy, however, the government may properly control this injury by law. I have recently acquired several chapters from the sections on religion in the legal writings of the great legal scholars, Vattel and Phillimore, that relate to religious evils, popular rights, national systems, international relations, and the like. And I wish now to offer them as a basis for discussion of this important matter by my honorable colleagues. April 1, 1874.

Sections on Religion from Vattel's *Law of Nations* (*Bankoku Kōhō*, 萬國公法).[11] (Summary)

National Rights and National Duties.

Religion that abides in the hearts of men is indeed a spiritual matter, but it becomes the business of the state once it is publicly established in the open.

Religious liberty possessed by the people is only the right not to believe the religions they do not like and not to obey coercive official orders relating to religion. Men never have the right to disturb society by publicly conducting religion as they please (p. 56).

When all the people serve a god, then the nation must invariably honor him. To the nation alone belongs the right to select a religion and to establish laws for worshipping.

When the majority in the nation worships in a particular religion, it should then be adopted as the sole national faith.

Whether a national religion is newly adopted or changed falls entirely within the rights of the nation. This is not something to be undertaken by an individual on his own authority. Nor should individuals attempt to preach new religious doctrines. A person of dissenting beliefs should invariably present these to the national authorities and abide by their directives (p. 57).

The Rights and Duties of the Ruler.

Adoption of an established religion in a country where there is not yet a state faith may be accomplished when the ruler selects the religion that he feels in his heart to be most true and most good. It would be appropriate to call this a duty of the ruler. This is because the sovereign, after all, has the responsibility to plan what will conduce to the benefit of the people in all matters. His authority in this regard, however, does not include the right to oppress and compel the people.

Even though, as previously stated, the ruler does not possess the right to compel the people in religious matters, he must control with full power such obstructions to the national administration and destruction of morals as may arise (p. 57).

The ruler's power in religion extends to restraining disruptive injury arising from matters connected with the external manifestations of religion. When he undertakes to control such injury, however, he will limit himself only to pacifying disturbances without in the least using his authority to oppress. Moreover, the ruler may not force the people to worship against their will. Should he thus wrongfully exert his authority, the people will sink to falsehood and deception if they do not disobey and rise in rebellion.

The best way to prevent disturbances that arise from differences between religions is to tolerate completely and to allow free conduct of religions that do not obstruct the national administration or damage morals. There should be permitted no cruelty to men because of religious differences, and those who stir up men for religious reasons should be strictly punished. Then it will be the principal aim of all the differing religions in the country to live happily together and to lead together toward goodness and righteousness.

The relation between religion and society is important. The national authorities must have complete power to supervise religions and to regulate their preachers. Since the objective of the government in society is necessarily to preserve peace in the country, it is clearly appropriate that the ruler possess these powers over religion. Even though he may not desire them, he cannot give them up without the people's consent.

A country is not completely free and independent if it does not have power to control its religious affairs. Its sovereignty would then only be partial (p. 66).

The National Menace of Religious Disturbances.

Should a factional group strongly inspired by religion reach the point of disturbing the people by proclaiming false and injurious doctrines, where will the flood of disasters end? Foolish beliefs only give birth to false, obstinate, destructive, and cruel persons whose injury to society and disturbance of morals is really a hundred times more extreme than the evil of libertines. Since antiquity, there have often appeared tyrants in the world who have trampled on the laws of creation and oppressed the people on the pretext of earnestly glorifying the true God (p. 55).

If delusive and visionary ideas are circulated and if errors of belief are progressively deepened in countries whose people are immature and easily influenced, what will be the consequences? Men will all be unconcerned with worldly affairs, finally reaching the point of abandoning their livelihood.

Numerous priests in various countries depend for their offices on a foreign government (the papacy). This transgresses the inherent rights of the nation and contradicts public justice under law (p. 67).

(The following appears at the end of Vattel's description of the subordination of priests to papal control:)

> The priests are customarily careful in all matters not to give offense to the papacy, conducting their offices in a manner to secure its warm commendation. And the papacy supports its followers with all its powers, helps them by exerting its authority, and protects them by opposing their enemies. If there is a person who tries to limit their rights, the papacy forthwith protects its followers by opposing such limitation. In addition, it also customarily shelters them against the wrath of the ruler. In such manner, the papacy strengthens the allegiance of the priests and ultimately commands the support of large numbers of the subjects and high officials in other countries. Should we not say that this destroys the mores of society and shakes the foundations of government? How can enlightened monarchs in the world permit such religion? Such being the case, the expulsion of missionaries from China was also not unreasonable.

Regulations Relating to the Priesthood.

We may allow the priests to be honored. But they should not be given the slightest power, and they certainly should not be permitted to demand independent power. First, in their work, equally with other men, they should be absolutely subject to the government's authority and responsible to the government for their conduct. Second, the ruler should be careful to have preachers honored by the people and to assure to preachers the dignity that is essential in the practice of their professions as preachers. The wise Romans of antiquity selected high and important preachers from among the legislators without establishing a strange, long-sleeved priesthood and without recognizing a distinction between clergy and laity (p. 64).

Rights of Individuals.

As selection of a religion by an individual according to his own disposition is really an important and natural liberty, this is beyond the sphere of regulation by other men. Should authority intrude into this sphere, what kind of faith will an individual hold? It is the basic nature of human beings that they strive to ascertain the true God from the depths of their hearts and that they possess a desire to worship Him. Such being the case, men cannot be released from this desire even by mingling in society. Nor should they lose the freedom that is essential for the practice of their faith. This is a fundamental principle of man's basic nature that cannot be violated. We may really say that it is a disgrace to mankind that this truth must even now still be proved.

When an inconsiderable number of people believe in a religion different from the state religion and when the government does not permit freedom of religion within the nation, the dissenters should have the right to sell their property and migrate with their families and movable possessions. In the final analysis, even society and the power of national law can never violate the hearts of men. Men should invariably possess the right to leave the country if society and the law do not permit them to freely practice their faith and to defend the desire [to honor the true God] from which they cannot be freed (p. 57).

Government never has any duties in religious matters that relate to more than their external forms. The inner heart of religion is the concern of individuals themselves. None should be able to persecute or control the faith of an individual unless it disrupts and obstructs society. Nor should men be punished for developing their private opinions unless these opinions incite others and create factionalism. We may say that the policy of a ruler is truly unjust when he imposes such punishment (p. 58).

Discussions Relating to Religion from Phillimore's "International Law" [12] (Summary)

Shibata[13]

Cicero has observed that men alone among animals acknowledge the existence of God and that even rude barbarians, the rightness of their gods aside, invariably recognize the worship of gods (*International Law,* II, 321).

Since it is a fundamental of nature that man and religion are mutually joined together for the well-being of humanity, they must more or less follow the direction of men responsible for this well-being. Grotius, therefore, has clearly explained that the meritorious influence of religion on human relations is extremely large even though its original aim was principally to propagate the grace of God. Plato deeply appreciated its merits in this respect and pointed to religion as a protector of political power and a link with natural law (p. 322).

In April 1812, Lord Wellesley made the following statement in the House of Lords:[14]

> I venture to say that the condition of the national religion may impose on a state the irrefutable duty to proscribe other religions. This is not to say, however, that excessive cruelties should be practiced. The realm of religion is not limited to mutual sympathy between man and God. It is also an aid in opening avenues of human endeavor generally. Moreover, even though religion is derived from men's consciences, it eventually inculcates the great principles of human morality as the appropriate basis for the conduct of men. A state has the right to suppress other religions when this is ultimately in the interest of national tranquility (p. 322).

It is stated in the teachings of the church that men "should render unto Caesar what is Caesar's and unto God the things that are God's," that temporal offices are positions established by God, that human beings generally should obey not only because they fear punishment but because they follow their consciences, etc., etc. (p. 325).

Discussion of the Right to Intervene in Religious Affairs

Gibbon has stated that there must be deeper study of the facts of the Moslem wars of conquest.[15] In his view, we do not yet honor the admonition of the followers of Christianity that one should not touch lethal weapons except for clear cause, just reason, and under unavoidable circumstances.

The above is the view of a famous historian that relates to Christian religious conditions in Constantinople, and it is probably founded on truth (Phillimore, *International Law,* I, 516).

We should make a distinction, which is important in the conduct of affairs, between the rights of countries to intervene in the affairs of other countries on behalf of their co-religionists. First, there is the principle that it may be necessary for a Christian nation to intervene in the affairs of another Christian nation on behalf of a particular group of Christians whose sect is the same as that of the intervening nation but different from that of the nation of which they are subjects. Second, there is the principle that it may be necessary for a Christian state to intervene in the affairs of a non-Christian state on behalf of Christians generally or of a certain group of Christians (I, 517).

The particular principle of this type of intervention (as between Christian nations) is given specific force through its inclusion in important treaty agreements (I, 518).

Special attention should be given to the fact that intervention is generally sought by residents of the country (I, 519).

It is said that this principle of intervention must be still further expanded. Thus, it is contended that for international law to permit forceful intervention in a country that oppresses its people in religious matters would be the same as intervening in and punishing a country beset by unending confusion and bloodshed. These two theories naturally must be further studied.

It is really extremely dangerous to plan interventions of the above type as they disregard the sound policy that one does not intervene in the affairs of other countries (I, 520).

(Omission.) Therefore, in the opinion of the prudent and thorough Martens,[16] wars that have arisen for religious reasons or nominally religious reasons generally manifest the following four features: first, the reason for opening war with a foreign power is not wholly religious; second, the nation raises the religious issue when there is a concurrence between government and religion; third, religious concerns actually take second place to political considerations; and fourth, political factors often induce action that is contrary to religious interest.

Saint Priest,[17] the resident French ambassador to Turkey from 1768 to 1785, has discussed as follows the role of France as protector of the Catholic Church in the Orient:

> Now even though the kings of our country outwardly profess concern for faith and declare their aim to protect the Catholic Church in the East, this is really little more than a sham. Religious men who do not understand the situation, therefore, have been confused. Moreover, the sultans of Turkey have never dreamed of the rights claimed by the French kings to meddle in the religions of Turkish subjects. The Marquis de Bonnat, the former French ambassador, has stated in a memorandum that the Turks are as sensitive as other peoples on the point that the sovereign of another country should not be allowed to interfere in the religious affairs of their land, however friendly he may be. It is not difficult to understand that France deals with Turkey with no other feeling than friendly intimacy and thus is unable to impose obligations injurious to Turkey. My diplomatic instructions also particularly avoided matters that might excite Turkish suspicions and adopted an especially liberal interpretation toward the capitulations relating to religion.

There could be no more fair expression of the principles of international law in this matter than the above quotation (I, 520).

The various great Christian states along with Russia mediated the Greek war to pacify a struggle that both disturbed the peace and obstructed commerce. The mediation by the European states probably complied with a request from Greece (I, 528).

[1]Tsuda's strong defense of freedom of the press is presumed to be a protest against the Japanese government's press regulations of 19 October 1873 that prohibited newspapers from attacking the government or criticizing its laws. (For the text of these

regulations, see W. W. McLaren, ed., "Japanese Government Documents," *Transactions of the Asiatic Society of Japan*, XLII [1914], 534–535.) Tsuda's essay may also have been an indirect warning against still stricter press laws such as the measure promulgated in June 1875 that was the ostensible cause for halting publication of the *Meiroku Zasshi* a few months later.

[2]Continued from previous issue.

[3]*Tenshoku*, 天職.

[4]Nishi here refers to ceremonial correspondence of the *Hung Lu Bu*, 鴻臚部, presumably the *Hung Lu Ssŭ*, 鴻臚寺, an office in imperial China that dealt with the non-Chinese peoples of inner Asia. During their early history, the Japanese maintained similarly named offices, the *Kōrokan*, 鴻臚館, for the welcoming of foreign visitors at Kyōto, the neighboring port of Naniwa, and the Dazaifu in northern Kyūshū.

[5]*Tengu*, 天狗, long-nosed creatures of the mountains found extensively in Japanese lore.

[6]The pool of blood, *chi no ike*, 血ノ池, and the mountain of swords, *tsurugi no yama*, 劍ノ山, are areas in the Buddhist hell.

[7]Continuation from previous issue of Katō's translation from Joseph Parrish Thompson, *Kirche und Staat in den Vereinigten Staaten* (Berlin, 1873).

[8]Cooley, Thomas McIntyre, *A Treatise on Constitutional Limitations Which Rest Upon the Legislative Power of the States of the American Union* (Boston, 1868).

[9]For the English word "vote," Katō employed *hatsugen*, 發言, to speak, utter, open one's mouth, or voice opinions.

[10]Francis Lieber, 1800–1872, a political scientist and college professor who wrote *On Civil Liberty and Self Government* (2 vols.: Philadelphia, 1853).

[11]Vattel, Emeric D., *Droit des gens, ou principes de la loi naturelle appliqués à la conduite et aux affaires des nations et des soverains* (Neuchâtel, 1858).

[12]Phillimore, Robert, *Commentaries on International Law* (2nd ed., 3 vols.: New York, 1872–1873).

[13]Shibata's given name is not recorded in the text. He may well have been Shibata Masakichi, 柴田昌吉, a compiler of the important early English-Japanese dictionary entitled *An English and Japanese Dictionary*. . . (Tokyo, 1873).

[14]Wellesley, Richard Colley, Marquis of, 1760–1842.

[15]Phillimore's original was "holy war" rather than "Moslem wars of conquest," *Kaikyō seisen*, 回教征戰.

[16]Martens, George Friedrich von, 1756–1821.

[17]Saint Priest, Emanuel Guinnard, 1735–1821.

The Rights and Obligations of Independent Nations[1]

Mori Arinori

The rights of nations differ, as naturally do their obligations. States recognized as independent under [international] law are those that possess full power to govern themselves and to conclude treaties regardless of their strength and national polity. Such states are roughly of three types: completely independent, conditionally independent, and tributary independent. A completely independent state is one that has power to manage alone its domestic affairs and to conclude treaties freely with foreign countries. A conditionally independent state is one whose independence is protected by treaties with other states or a state that is restrained by treaties forced on it by foreign powers and that is subject to these treaty restrictions for a long term without power to abrogate them. Finally, a tributary independent state is one that pays tribute while actually retaining power independently to control its domestic affairs and to conclude treaties with foreign lands, notwithstanding its outward appearance of subservience.

The completely independent states in the world today include our empire in Asia; Russia, the Germanic Confederation,[2] Austria, Italy, France, Holland, Denmark, Sweden, Spain, and Portugal in Europe; Liberia in Africa and the United States as well as the various states of Central and South America. States with conditional independence are Turkey, Greece, Belgium, and Switzerland in Europe; and China, Siam, and Persia in Asia. Korea and Tibet in Asia, Serbia in Europe, and Morocco, Tripoli, and Tunis in Africa are tributary independent states.

There are certain states that are unable to conclude treaties directly with foreign countries even though they fully control their domestic affairs. These may be defined as states that have actual independence, [international] law notwithstanding. Such states that generally have power to freely establish and to operate their state institutions include the Ryūkyūs in Asia; Hungary, Montenegro, Moldavia, Walachia, and the German states in Europe; Egypt in Africa; and the individual states in the various confederations in America.

Our empire is an example of a completely independent state that has temporarily yielded a part of its national power to foreign countries. Our country really suffered numerous handicaps when it first began foreign intercourse. Acceding to the demands of foreigners, we yielded a part of our rights and obligations to protect and control foreigners in the land, to govern the open port areas, and to levy harbor dues, lighthouse duties, and tariffs on exports and imports. Some independent states, in order to promote their interests, enter into contracts by which they mutually divide and share their national rights. Such contracts may be dissolved at the convenience of one of the parties. If there is a time limit, then the contract period must be honored when one of the parties does not agree to its abrogation.

Treaties between conditionally independent states are fundamentally different. This is the situation of a state like neighboring China. Having finally begged for peace after being defeated in wars with the foreign powers, China initially concluded agreements without a time limit in which she sacrificed her national rights.[3] Even though she has subsequently desired to rectify these losses and to dissolve the treaties, she can do nothing unless the foreign powers accede to her requests. She suffers permanent bondage from these arrangements, and she is unable to freely exercise independent power.

Since countries like Belgium, Switzerland, and Greece are states guaranteed against aggression by treaties and alliances concluded at congresses of the great European powers, they always maintain neutrality and thence are able to protect their independence. Russia and Austria habitually want to annex Turkey, but Turkey is able to preserve her independence by securing the help of English and French power.

Some deny that our empire is completely independent. They say that, even though she may desire to do so, our country cannot actually exercise the rights of independence or meet her obligations since she is still bound by treaty limitations, without fixed laws, militarily weak, and culturally immature. Although these words are too absurd to deny, it may be entirely appropriate to expose their absurdity and thereby clarify the true condition of our national independence. Our country long maintained a seclusion policy being tranquilly content without any desire for foreign relations. Once American ships penetrated Edo Bay and demanded a treaty of intercourse, we acceded to their wishes and extended to them conveniences for coming and going to Japan. Thereafter, the English, Russians, Dutch, and French pressed into Japan one after the other, and we further concluded the treaties of commerce and friendship of 1858 (Ansei 3), which were for a ten-year period.

Japan subsequently agreed to all the requests of other powers, and the ten-year limit specified in the English and American treaties was extended to 1872 (Meiji 5).[4] These grants did not in the least arise from oppression by the foreign powers, as they were made by our country's free will. They are not the same as the arrangements with China and Turkey. Now that the term of the treaties is completed, they may naturally be abrogated by one of the contracting parties, or a revised treaty can be newly concluded after negotiation by the parties concerned. Even should there be no new treaties, there is international law by which we and they can increasingly broaden our relations and gradually improve the conveniences of trade. There are not a few examples among the various countries of Europe and America in which relations are perfected and trade developed without resort to treaties. Nor does it seem inappropriate for our country to emulate their example.

Since whether a country is culturally undeveloped and militarily weak is entirely the nation's domestic concern and unrelated to diplomacy, there is no need to answer for these factors abroad. It seems that we should give some attention to the criticism of our undetermined laws. Nevertheless, for our country to carry out its obligation to protect foreigners by formulating laws for their control will not be too difficult. While there may be numerous methods, there is probably none better than to compile completely practical and suitable new laws and to select judicial officials for their enforcement. Moreover, these laws should be fair and just, neither injuring the old customs of our country nor contradicting the statutes of foreign countries.

Military Obedience

Katō Hiroyuki

In enlightened and civilized countries, it is regarded as best and most important for military officials to earnestly obey their sovereigns' commands. Once this principle is strictly established, military officials only follow their master's orders in offense and defense, being absolutely prohibited from venturing to discuss the merits of war and peace. Of course, even civil officials may not presume to contradict their monarch's will. Rulers, however, are not permitted to govern arbitrarily as their power over civil officials is strictly limited, and civil officials are invariably called upon to discuss freely the merits of government measures.

The rights of civil officials vis-a-vis their rulers in this regard are far greater than those of the military, and obedience required of them is also far less strict. Still lighter is the obligation to obey their sovereigns on the part of the practically independent legislatures and judiciaries. Then why is it that military officials alone must be strictly obedient and that the authority of rulers over them is extremely broad? It is, after all, because military power, being violent and evil, should never be employed except in cases of real necessity. Allowing military officials to discuss independently the merits of war and peace and to wield their power freely is like giving an iron rod to the devil.[5] One then cannot but fear easy outbreak of unjust and ill-advised wars. This is why the authority of military officials is strictly controlled and why they are invariably obliged earnestly to obey royal commands.

In unenlightened countries, however, military officials are inclined to oppress their governments by usurping power to discuss the merits of war and peace without authority. As governments in such countries cringe before the power of the military and treat the military with extreme flattery, they rashly plan matters and ultimately mismanage national affairs. What a dreadful prospect! Responsible officials should well take warning. For a more detailed exposition on military obedience, I would refer readers to the section on the powers of supreme military command in my translation of *Allgemeines Staatsrecht*.[6]

Relying on Public Opinion Rather than on Government to Advance Civilization; Abridged Translation from Buckle's "*History of Civilization in England*"[7]

Mitsukuri Rinshō

Writers commonly state that progress among the civilized countries of Europe has depended on new restraints of law and on the elimination of injurious abuses by the wisdom of government. Such assertions are indeed numerous, but they prove to be untrustworthy and groundless fabrications once we consider them fully in the light of history. By way of explanation, let me first ask what kind of persons generally occupy high position, hold power, and are entrusted with governing the nation? Briefly, they are only men born in their country, trained in its writings, colored by its customs, permeated with its prejudices, and enveloped by its surroundings. We should reflect on the fact that, however wise and keen such men may be, they are the creatures of society rather than the creators of society.

The work of such men, therefore, is also the end result of civilization and progress, inadequate to serve as the generator of progress. As evidence of this, not one of the great national changes recorded in the whole of history has arisen from creative leadership among the governing authorities of the time. The fact that these reforms all necessarily arose from the pressure of public opinion should be sufficient to prove that the above discussion is not absurd.

To pursue this line of discussion further, once injurious abuses appear in the country, gentlemen of intelligence indeed stand forth among the people to discuss fearlessly and without equivocation the urgent necessity for reform to eliminate the abuses. Yet the government, being completely heedless of these outcries, accepts the ancient evils for some millenia of years until irrepressible public opinion boils over. The reform undertaken only thereafter is not achieved alone by the bigoted and dispirited government.

This is also invariably the case even with governments in the various enlightened countries that generally accept suggestions derived from the people after broad consultation and wise planning. Even though there may be authorities who boast that they have contributed to the nation by introducing reforms, most of them adopt views that were shaped some decades before they were born. Their achievements also do not generally go beyond clamorously raising their voices on behalf of the lessons previously imparted to them by their teachers. Those who themselves shoulder the burden of reform, after all, carry out their measures because they recognize that public opinion is overwhelming. They may be compared with the man who buoyantly floats with the current of flood waters whose destructive force he cannot oppose.

What should be admired in these reformers is only that they seize the opportunity to join decisively with public opinion and to actually carry out reforms of national importance at a time when many are opposed to these changes that clearly are already especially urgent. While there is not time to enumerate all of the examples to be found in the full sweep of the various national histories, let me take up a really notable case. None will dispute that the recent repeal of the corn laws (laws that forbade importation of grain from foreign countries except when domestic cereal prices were high) was an instance in which the people of present-day England recognized their interest, but men still do not clearly understand the means by which the reform was carried out.

Among those who have not read the history of the times carefully, there are inevitably some who would attribute the reform to the strength of parliament or of the Anti-Corn Law League (the society that agitated for repeal of the corn laws). Nevertheless, if one searches minutely into the origins of the reform, the first evidence probably appears in the eighteenth century. The injury arising from laws restricting grain imports was then generally recognized by political economists, and readers of their writings thereafter all necessarily recognized the justice of their arguments and the validity of their words. Reflect on the fact that the government, the parliament, and the league were ultimately all instruments moved by the force of public opinion, whose strength and magnitude was irresistible.

The repeal of the corn laws, therefore, was not for the benefit of one party or in the interest of another. Since repeal depended on the knowledge of the people, the laws' outcome conformed with a natural trend that followed the gradual progress of human knowledge. It was not that the league was not successful in spreading this knowledge or that the parliament was not successful in taking in and following this knowledge. In sum, however, their success depended on the progress of human knowledge, and it only slightly hastened a reform that had become inevitable. Moreover, the recent enactments of such measures as the Reform Bill (the proposal to reform the system for electing members of parliament) were by means no different from those described above. Therefore, I say that we shall cleanse old abuses and thereby advance civilization in the country by relying on public opinion rather than by relying on the power of government.

The Federated States of North and South America

Sugi Kōji

Although the rise and fall of nations seems to be determined by fate, their course generally depends on whether those guiding the people adopt appropriate methods. In the past, the colonies of North America revolted against England, and those of South America arose against Spain to establish their independence. Since the founding of these nations, the federated states of North America [the United States] have progressed day by day, but those of South America have successively fallen into disorder. When one asks the reason for this, it lies simply in whether governments respect the rights and liberties of the people.

As England from the outset honored the wishes of her colonists, accorded them religious freedom, and allowed them political liberty, the people already understand the principles of self-government. The colonists established their independence once the English king and his ministers resorted to oppression and lost popular support, and the subsequent stability of their country may be attributed to the fact that the people already individually understood their rights.

Such was not the case with Spain, which denied her colonists self-government. In addition to fettering his people's minds by driving them into the Roman Church that he honored, the Spanish monarch long drew his subjects' blood with his violent tyranny. Unable to bear this oppressive rule, the people established their independence. Internal griefs again arose, however, despite the departure of external troubles. The consequent disturbances in these countries may be ascribed to the fact that they were established without a common and single purpose since the poison of oppression had penetrated their bodies deeply, their rights had suffered, and men's minds were upset. Even such wise and noble men as Bolivar and San Martin were ultimately unable to unite their countries. In Mexico, for example, the form of government has been changed more than nine times, and there have been more than three hundred instances in which a party has been formed or destroyed.

After all, England was the one that encouraged luxuriant stems and branches by cultivating the roots. In the case of Spain, however, the stems and branches were weakened by failure to nourish the roots. How correct it is to state that England sowed good seeds in North America and that Spain planted bad seeds in South America!

On Torture[8] Part One

Tsuda Mamichi

No evil in the world is more wretched than torture, and no injury in history is more poisonous than torture. The injurious evil of the tyrannical and immoral Chieh and Chou cannot be compared with the wretched poison of torture.[9] Why is this so? It is because the evil of tyranny, after all, is the wicked action of but one man while the injury of torture embodies the bad conduct of unnumbered judicial officials extending over some tens of generations. How can the victims of such wretched poison as torture be compared with those only temporarily touched by the tyrannical rath of a Chieh or a Chou?

Crime is indeed evil, but it is only the work of an individual. Public procurators (*kenkan*)[10] arrest criminals with imperial writs, and judicial officers investigate them while brandishing the government's authority. Even if there is absolutely no use of torture, when legal officers are so completely superior to the accused, the accused humbly prostrate themselves before the authorities and present their cases with shaking hearts. There cannot be anything like the clarification found in civil suits in which plaintiffs and defendants both assert their rights, and it is often impossible to avoid false convictions. How much more are persons forced to submit to false conviction once torture is used!

Associate Justice Tamano[11] has explained that he too desires to destroy torture. Speaking of this injury, he states that, if inquiries are conducted under compulsion with the use of torture, conviction of even officials and generals will be easier than turning one's hand. Oh, how dreadful is the injury of torture! Therefore, when persons are once suspected by legal officers [and torture is used], there is a tendency for them invariably to admit the false charges even though they are not guilty. After all, such persons cannot endure the pain of torture. Ordinary people would rather die falsely charged than suffer torture. Ah, how wretched is the injury of torture!

The highest mountains in our world are the Himalayas in the center of Asia. To the south and west of these mountains are people of the Indo-German race, and one reaches Africa by crossing the sea to the west. To the north and east of these mountains are the Mongoloid and Chinese races. Across the sea to the east are the American aborigines, who are probably a branch of the Mongol race. There is now no torture in the countries of the German race, but the Mongol races generally have not yet escaped torture. Ah, what a great dividing barrier are the Himalayas! To think that there are such happy people as the Germans and such unhappy people as the Mongols among the men of the world!

I crossed the Indian Ocean in my youth. The Malayan inhabitants of the various islands of the Indies probably belong to a branch of the Mongol race. As subjects of England and Holland, they have escaped the evils of torture. The peoples of Africa belong to the so-called black race, but those governed by the European and American nations have also escaped torture. If asked whether these differences are caused by race, [I would] reply in the negative as they are determined by knowledge, civilization, and enlightenment.

Since there is nothing in world history to compare with its injury, cannot torture then be absolutely destroyed? I would respond that it is absolutely essential to abolish torture. If we do not abolish torture, we cannot eventually ride forth side by side with the various countries of Europe and America. If we do not abolish torture, we cannot conclude equal treaties with them. If we do not abolish torture, we cannot place under our laws the Europeans and Americans settled in our country. I shall discuss this further in a later issue.

Hiragana

Shimizu Usaburō[12]

Among the writers who have wanted to improve communication by reforming our script since the Meiji Restoration, some favor the use of *katakana* or *hiragana*;[13] some, a change to Western letters; some, the construction of a new written form; and some, the abandonment of our national language for English. And there are still those who would retain the traditional mixed Chinese-Japanese usage. While each will respond with their particular views when asked, it is impractical to adopt inconvenient means for communicating national matters, and employment of such impractical means is injurious to education.

To replace our national language with English, of course, is out of the question. Even though it may be practical to adopt the mixed Chinese-Japanese usage that has been employed since antiquity, how many people in the country read this script and how will they understand the *sōsho* and *gyōsho*[14] styles of writing, the existence of ideographic dictionaries notwithstanding? How many people are able to understand the public announcements that are loaded with *furigana*[15] and assisting words (*jogo*)?[16]

These deficiencies may indeed arise from inadequate instruction, but they are really to be attributed to the difficulty of learning. Moreover, there are instances when different characters may represent the same things such as 烟管 and 喜世留 for *kiseru* (pipe, tobacco), 硝子 and 玻璃 for *garasu* (glass), and 莫大小 and 目利安 for *meriyasu* (knitted fabrics), and 不二山 and 富士山 for Fujisan (Mt. Fuji). Then there are words that cannot be understood without consulting a dictionary, such as 長谷 (Hase), 愛宕 (Atago), 飛鳥 (Asuka), 日下 (Kusaka), 不入斗 (Iriyamazu), and 九十九 (*tsukumo,* ninety-nine). Or there are ideographic compounds that have two readings such as *nisshoku* and *jissoku* for 日蝕, *kōkō* and Honkon [Hong Kong] for 香港, *shōkai* and Sanhai [Shanghai] for 上海, *shiso* and *chiso* for 紫蘇, and *kombu* and *kobu* for 昆布. Finally, there are ideographic compounds that have several readings such as 清水, which may be read as Shimizu, Kiyomizu, or Saisui; and 神戸, which may be read as Kōbe, Kambe, Kando, or Kōdo. We may not know which sound to select even though it is proposed to compile new dictionaries.

It is impossible to read even ordinary materials without years of arduous study when new ideographic renderings are continually introduced as at present. Thus the mixed Chinese-Japanese script is not a convenient tool for daily usage except in education. Switching to foreign letters is like the clear inconvenience of substituting bread for rice or milk for bean paste, their superior nutritional qualities notwithstanding. Yet adopting Western letters is better than inventing an entirely new script. As sentences in letters reproduce speech forms with phonetic symbols, a phonetic script, after all, is the best instrument for daily memoranda that spread the arts, record promises, exchange communications, and note down matters past and present.

There naturally should be no departure from the spoken language. If the written form differs from the spoken language, reading the material will not produce feelings of joy, anger, sorrow, and happiness. And education loses its appeal when these emotions are not stimulated. Even women and children are readily moved to sorrow and laughter by reading such works as the *Inaka Genji,*[17] the *Jiraiya Monogatari,*[18] the *Hizakurige,*[19] the *Hasshōjin,*[20] the

Gidayūbon,[21] and the *jōruribon*[22] because they were written in language that is the same as the spoken tongue.

It is noteworthy, therefore, that the nations of Europe and America invariably prefer prose that is the same as the national tongue. While the Americans share the same language with the English, they have constructed their own characteristic prose form as well as revised reprints of English editions to conform with their national usage. We should also appreciate the efforts of the Chinese who, according to recent report, attach teachers of their national language to the students who are sent abroad for study.

Then why does our country alone follow other countries in its language? It is probably because patriotism is extremely undeveloped and because habits and customs cannot easily be changed. The responsibility of scholars and teachers, of course, is to spread learning broadly among the people by providing the nation with prose resembling speech that is both easy to read and easy to understand. We should reflect on the fact that scholars are extremely lax in their responsibilities when, ignoring this principle, they are inured to their studies and make boastful displays of strange characters and new words.

Since only a few know *katakana,* I urge that we employ only *hiragana*. The widespread use of *hiragana* may be seen by looking at signboards, door curtains (*noren*), petitions, and popular stories. This is the reasons for my counsel to gentlemen of like mind when I translated *Seimi no Kai* (*A Guide to Chemistry*).[23]

Nishimura takes exception to Nishi's proposal [that we adopt the Western alphabet] by asking about the confusion that may arise when *kawa* is substituted for the three characters 皮, 側, and 川. Meaning, however, never depends upon a single word as it is clarified in both writing and conversation by the context. Simple sentences and abbreviated words are easily communicated phonetically in telegrams. How much more so in writing and conversation!

There are also instances of one word with several meanings in English such as the use of "lot" for lottery, fate, a piece of land, or a number of people; "state" for a condition, a minister of state, or a nation; "tin" for tin, iron plates, or coinage; "branch" for a tree branch, a field of study, or a genealogical line; "arms" for human arms, fighting forces, and armor; "type" for moveable type, sign, or a variety of disease; and "lime" for limestone or birdlime. I understand that the same applies to Dutch and French. Since those languages are rarely misunderstood, why should even ours be misunderstood? Nishimura, after all, completely misses the mark when he fails to inquire into this. Generally speaking, man is the lord of creation because he possesses powers of thought and consideration. He can employ these powers to understand defaced writings and read ancient texts, and homonyms in writing and speech are still less a problem.

If asked why I do not use *hiragana* in this magazine, I would respond that my *hiragana* theory is only for the convenience of later generations. This article is prepared for the serious consideration of scholars. The circle of scholars in Chinese studies formerly regarded the West as barbarian and threw away, without consideration, even Western materials that had been translated into Japanese. They first recognized that these materials were not barbaric after they were imported in the form of Chinese translations. Only then did these scholars, in large numbers, finally change. On the whole, Confucian scholars only listen attentively to discussions on Chinese matters; merchants raise their ears when there is talk of profit; and artisans and farmers are all the same. I am writing here in this style only because men by their nature are habitually inclined toward what they have already learned. I have previously written in *hiragana* and explained its significance in the introduction to *Seimi no Kai*.

[1]Apart from explaining to his countrymen the status of independent states under Western international law, Mori is trying to establish the legal basis for Japan's quest for revision of the so-called unequal treaties of 1858 by which the Japanese promised the various Western powers the rights of extraterritoriality, conventional tariffs. and most-favored-nation treatment. His claim that Japan was somehow more completely independent than China was obviously derived as much from his pride as a Japanese as from any real difference between the treaties that the two Asian empires had concluded with the West. It also anticipates an assumption by Japanese later in the century that equality with the West implied superiority to China. Mori's threefold division of independent states was presumably drawn from Henry Wheaton, who classified sovereign states in three categories: completely sovereign, semi-sovereign, and tributary. Mori's conditionally sovereign state, *yakusoku dokuritsu no kuni* 約束獨立國, however, suggests more an independence defined by contractual arrangement

than does Wheaton's term "semi-sovereign." See Henry Wheaton, *Elements of International Law* (Boston, 1866), pp. 33–37.

[2]*Doitsu Rempō*, 獨逸聯邦. Mori's use of the term German Confederation indicates that he based his essay on a text that appeared before the founding of the German Empire in 1871.

[3]Actually, China's treaties with the United States and France in 1844 were subject to revision after twelve years; the Tientsin treaties of 1858, after ten years.

[4]Mori's statement notwithstanding, Japan based her claim for revision on her treaty with the United States in 1858 that provided for revision after 4 July 1872 should the government of either nation so desire. See W. G. Beasley, *Select Documents on Japanese Foreign Policy, 1853–1868* (London, 1955), p. 189.

[5]"To give an iron rod to the devil," *Oni ni kanabō o atau*, 鬼ニ金棒ヲ與フ, is a Japanese idiom that means adding strength to strength.

[6]See Katō's translation of J. K. Bluntschli's *Allgemeines Staatsrecht* entitled *Kokuhō Hanron*, 國法汎論 (Tokyo, 1875), Book VI, No. 2, pp. 54–61, chapter entitled *Heiba no Taiken*, 兵馬ノ大權.

[7]From Henry Thomas Buckle, *Introduction to the History of Civilization in England*, Chapter V, section on "Influence of government on the progress of society."

[8]Torture, *gōmon*, 拷問. Tsuda here is trying to mobilize enlightened opinion against the continued use of torture, which was authorized in the new codes of criminal procedure promulgated by the Japanese government in the early 1870s. Torture was then allowed when the criminal refused to confess notwithstanding clear evidence of his guilt. In 1876, however, the Council of State (*Dajōkan*, 太政官) adopted new regulations that allowed judgment of crimes based on evidence alone, and the stipulations providing for torture were officially rescinded in 1879.

[9]Chieh, 桀, and Chou Hsin, 紂辛. the last rulers respectively of the ancient Hsia, 夏, and Shang, 商, Dynasties, whose tyranny typified to Chinese and Japanese the ultimate in depraved cruelty.

[10]*Kenkan*, 檢官.

[11]Tamano Seiri, 玉乃世履, 1825–1886, sometime retainer of the Iwakura Clan, twice chief justice, minister of finance, and diet member during the Meiji Period.

[12]A commoner by origin, Shimizu Usaburō even before the Meiji Restoration was interested in reforming the Japanese language and shifting to transcription with the *hiragana* syllabary. Chosen to accompany the Japanese mission to the Paris Exposition of 1867, Shimizu helped Leon Rosny, the French orientalist, to publish one issue of a newspaper in *hiragana* entitled *Yo no Uwasa*. Upon his return to Japan in 1868 with Western printing and lithography machines and various other materials, Shimizu established a paper and printing establishment known as Mizuhoya, 瑞穗屋, where he printed works by Meirokusha members and materials in *hiragana*. In 1879–1880, he joined with the great dictionary compiler Ōtsuki Fumihiko, 大槻文彥, and others to establish the Kana no Kai(かなのくわい), a society dedicated to the promotion of writing with *hiragana*.

[13]*Katakana*, 片假名, and *hiragana*, 平假名, are the two Japanese syllabaries originally derived from Chinese ideographs that are employed in Japanese for phonetic transcription.

[14]*Sōsho*, 草書, and *gyōsho*, 行書, are, respectively, the cursive and semi-cursive styles of Japanese handwriting.

[15]*Furigana*, ふりがな(傍訓), are *kana* inscriptions written beside the Chinese ideographs to assist unlettered readers.

[16]*Jogo*, 助語, literally "assisting words," are words introduced into literary texts, sometimes derivative from Chinese and sometimes as decoration without meaning.

[17]*Inaka Genji* or "Rustic Genji," 田舎源氏, is a ninety volume collection of popular tales by Tanehiko Ryūtei (1783–1842), 種彦柳亭, that deal with a struggle between rival military houses in the fifteenth century.

[18]*Jiraiya Monogatari*, 自來也物語, are stories of a Robin Hood type who took from the rich to give to the poor.

[19]*Hizakurige*, 膝栗毛, of Jippensha Ikku (?-1831), 十返舎一九, is a humorous tale of travels by two commoners, Yajirōbei and Kitahachi, along the Tōkaidō and other highways of Tokugawa Japan.

[20]*Hanagoyomi Hasshōjin*, 花暦八笑人, story of the pranks and escapades of eight vagabonds.

[21]*Gidayūbon*, 義太夫本, ballads in the style of Takemoto Gidayū, 竹本義太夫, 1651–1714.

[22]*Jōruribon*, 浄瑠理本, a kind of ballad drama popular during the Tokugawa Period.

[23]*Seimi no Kai*, 舎密ノ階. For extensive quotations from Shimizu's *hiragana* introduction to this work in which he argues in favor of adoption of *hiragana* and a prose style close to speech, see Yamamoto Masahide, 山本正秀, *Kindai Buntai Hassei no Shiteki Kenkyū*, 近代文體發生の史的研究 (Tokyo, 1965), pp. 185–189.

On Official Insignia[1]

Tsuda Mamichi

There may be some doubt as to whether the ranking of officials and the wearing of official insignia were originally European or Asian customs. I have not heard that there ever existed in Europe systems comparable to the ten-odd ranks of officials in China and Japan. Nor in the wearing of official insignia have I heard that in Europe there has been distinction of official ranks by colors as in China and Japan. Among the military, however, there are extremely strict distinctions between ranks since military forces have the responsibility for meeting force with force and since military commands must be carried out just as the body follows the directives of the mind. Identifying insignia, therefore, are essential to make clear at a glance the distinction between senior and junior among the numerous grades and ranks into which the two principal categories of officer and commissioned personnel are divided.

Among diplomats, also, official insignia are used to distinguish ranks in which ambassadors represent monarchs; ministers, nations; and chargé d'affaires, foreign secretaries. There are also orders of knighthood in European countries. Generally speaking, sovereigns of the various nations head these orders that flatter those military men and even civil officials who aspire to fame by awarding various star-shaped decorations in recognition of exceptional merit and achievement. These orders actually arose during the crusades of the Middle Ages when knights and commoners secretly organized societies of military character in which the various ranks from the heads down were distinguished by decorations. They are a means by which kings and emperors in Europe even today assure the loyalty of their entourages.

The European knightly orders are more intelligent than the court ranks of China or the bestowal of vessels for the tea ceremony by Toyotomi Hideyoshi,[2] but they are never employed in America since it is the American democratic political tradition to appreciate real worth more than empty titles.

In the various countries of Europe and America today, all persons from kings to commoners wear the same formal dress in their capacities as civil officials. This is the semiformal dress (*shōreifuku*)[3] of Japan. The essentials of civil rule, after all, rest on morals that move men's consciences and laws that control their misdeeds. Western civil officials [do not fear disorder] in their ranks even though they avoid using clothing to distinguish between high and low because their civil rule differs from military administration in which the lower ranks, like horses or oxen in harness, are controlled by threatening authority. The university doctors and judicial ranks [in the West], however, wear a special type of clothing whose purport is analogous to the special clothing worn by the priests of Greece and Rome.

Given the modern methods of war, it is absolutely necessary that the military and naval uniforms in our country now be closely patterned after those of France and England. But uneducated that I am, I do not understand the basis for the full court dress (*taireifuku*)[4] of our civil officials. Its origin is indeed not so clear as when our ancient official robes were modelled on the systems of Sui and T'ang.[5] I have wondered whether this court dress is an adaptation of European military uniforms to the official ranks originally derived from Asian customs.

Now, the inconvenience of Chinese clothing is of the same order as their binding of ladies' feet. To honor the small feet of ladies is a custom of the five continents, but its abuse is extreme in the case of Chinese women. In general, Chinese women are all crippled and unable to walk alone because from childhood their feet are painfully bound and forcibly prevented from growing. The ancient ceremonial crowns, belts, and robes of China as well as our old official garments were certainly beautiful, but men could not don them unassisted by others. How can such clothing be called wise? When I accompanied Lord Date on the mission to China and we entered Peking from Tientsin,[6] Lord Date wore a *konōshi*[7] bestowed upon him by the emperor, and I was clothed in *eboshi*[8] and *hitatare*.[9] The Chinese from Prime Minister Li[10] down viewed our attire with extreme jealousy. Now in my opinion, Manchu robes far surpass in convenience Chinese clothing since the three dynasties.[11] Yet the Chinese still yearn for their old raiment. How stupid this is! Why have they not stopped even today from harboring a feeling of hatred for the change in clothing and hairdress forced upon them by the Aisin Gioro?[12]

Years ago while still young, I sailed to Europe by the Cape of Good Hope. My ship on the return trip stopped in Hong Kong. And when I visited the Dutch consulate, the consul was clothed in a gold embroidered uniform that closely resembled our present full court dress. In some wonder, I asked the reason since I had never seen such garments worn in Europe except by ambassadors, military officers, or members of the nobility such as dukes, counts, and viscounts. The consul smilingly replied that the barbarian peoples of Asia would not recognize the high station of the consul of Holland if he failed to wear such attire. I too smiled and then departed.

On Wives and Concubines[13] Part One

Mori Arinori

The relation between man and wife is the fundamental of human morals. The moral path will be achieved by establishing this fundamental, and the country will only be firmly based if the moral path is realized. When people marry, rights and obligations emerge between them so that neither can take advantage of the other. If you ask what these rights and obligations are, they may be described as the paths of mutual assistance and mutual protection. That is, the husband has the right to demand assistance from the wife while he shoulders the obligation to protect her. And, conversely, the wife has the right to demand protection from the husband while she bears the obligation to assist him. Unless the marriage is strictly according to these principles, it cannot be recognized as human marriage. Looking at marriage customs in our country today, the husband treats the wife as he pleases, and there is still no national legislation [protecting the wife] against arbitrary divorce by the husband simply because she does not please him. Since husbands and wives cannot mutually honor their rights and obligations and since, even though persons are husbands and wives in name, they are far from such in actuality, I would affirm that our country has not yet established the fundamental of human morals.

There have hitherto been a variety of marriage practices [in our country]. Persons married through the agency of a go-between (*nakōdo*)[14] are known as husband and wife, and the woman in such a union is recognized as the wife. The woman is called a concubine in a union not arranged by a go-between. Sometimes there may be one or even several concubines in addition to the wife, and sometimes a concubine may become the wife. Sometimes the wife and the concubines live in the same establishment. Sometimes they are separated, and the concubine is the favored one while the wife is neglected. Moreover, marriages are negotiated by the respective parents, it sometimes being only necessary to obtain their consent.

Taking a concubine is by arbitrary decision of the man and with acquiescence of the concubine's family. The arrangement, known as *ukedashi,*[15] is made by paying money to the family of the concubine. This means, in other words, that concubines are bought with money. Since concubines are generally *geisha*[16] and prostitutes patronized by rich men and nobles, many descendants in the rich and noble houses are the children of bought women. Even though the wife is superior to the concubine in households where they live together, there is commonly jealousy and hatred between them because the husband generally favors the concubine. Therefore, there are numerous instances when, the wife and the concubines being scattered in separate establishments, the husband repairs to the abode of the one with whom he is infatuated and wilfully resorts to scandalous conduct.

In extreme cases, those who take concubines boast of their affluence and are disdainful of those who abstain from the practice. The national law regards wives and concubines as equals and accords equal rights to their offspring. Thus, I have here explained that our country has not yet established the fundamental of human morality, and I hope later to discuss how this situation injures our customs and obstructs enlightenment.

On Education

Mitsukuri Shūhei

Our children will surely become ill and die if we fail to give attention to their care during childhood. Moreover, if we do not educate them thoughtfully, they will invariably grow up so bigoted and stupid that they will be unable to compete even among barbarians. These are truisms most easy to understand. When it comes to caring for children, there is a natural instinct among parents, regardless of wealth and sophistication, to feel that they must earnestly protect their young. Is it not really strange and regrettable, however, that there are not a few who without reflection ignore the factor of education?

From infancy until they are six or seven, children's minds are clean and without the slightest blemish while their characters are as pure and unadulterated as a perfect pearl. Since what then touches their eyes and ears, whether good or bad, makes a deep impression that will not be wiped out until death, this age provides the best opportunity for disciplining their natures and training them in deportment. They will become learned and virtuous if the training methods are appropriate, stupid and bigoted if the methods are bad. Just as a young tree once bent at planting cannot be straightened when it grows up, what deeply penetrates children's minds during this sensitive and keen period cannot be changed after they grow up, even though one may desire to do so. How can we avoid giving attention to this age that is the dividing point at which it is determined whether an individual throughout his life will be wise or stupid, good or bad?

The countries of Europe and America have naturally left nothing undone in establishing schools everywhere and developing every method for the education of their children. With the advance of modern culture, however, the theory is increasingly widespread that education in the home clearly surpasses that in the schools. The theory runs as follows: A family resembles a country, and for parents to educate their children is their clear responsibility from the point of view of natural ethics (*tendō jinri*).[17] Parents at home are able to guide children at any time during infancy when the young are most receptive. Teaching what they desire to teach and transmitting what they desire to transmit, the father by his strictness and the mother by her tenderness carry on together without the injury of outsiders disturbing and tempting the children. Once the children leave home, it will be impossible for them to avoid disturbing and tempting evils even though their education is in a place of upright customs. Since the affection of even good teachers and good friends naturally is vastly different from the guidance of parents, the home should be regarded as the best school and the parents as the best teachers for educating small children.

This principle applies, however, only to the comparatively wealthy middle and upper class families since there are few parents even in the enlightened countries, not to mention unenlightened countries, who train their children sufficiently at home. There are times when even such [advantaged] parents can only entrust the training of their children to others for the reason that they are prevented by their occupations from performing their family duties. Under present conditions in society, however, parents take for granted that their children should be entrusted to others, and they seem not to recognize that their children's education is their principal parental responsibility. The homes being without parental training, the children of the rich consequently become accustomed to arrogant and extravagant ways by associating only with ignorant and blind servants, while the children of the poor learn mean and dirty habits by mingling with ignorant and stupid children. How can these children avoid becoming ignorant and stupid when they thus waste their days in profitless and harmful activities?

When the children grow up ignorant and delinquent because their parents were prevented by their occupations from training them, not a few parents freely admonish the children or even go so far as to reproach the children's friends and teachers without recognizing that they, the parents, themselves are the guilty. While they may be extremely mistaken, however, they should not be harshly blamed. Should you ask why, it is because they do not know how to educate their children since they, after all, did not themselves receive training from their parents.

What then should we do about the situation? Needless to say, even though we want to halt the illness, the cure cannot be accomplished in a day when the disease has penetrated to the marrow of the bone. Therefore, I do not now suddenly hold the parents wholly responsible for the education of their children. If parents just recognize the training of their children to be their responsibility and if they attentively exhaust their powers to this end, then I hope that their children will also understand their responsibility to educate the succeeding generation and that this may ultimately become a family tradition and regional custom. What I desire still more deeply is only that, by actively establishing girls' schools and devoting our energies to educating girls, we may train these girls to understand how important it is for them to educate the children to whom they give birth.

Napoleon I once observed to the famous woman teacher Campan,[18] "Since all the old methods of education really seem to be worthy of respect, what do we lack for the good upbringing of the people?" When Campan replied "Mothers," the emperor exclaimed in surprise, "Ah, this is true! This single word suffices as the guiding principle of education." These are indeed meaningful words.

In a later number, I shall explain the necessity for girls' schools.

Speculators[19]

Sugi Kōji

False expectations arise when nations fall into economic difficulties and people are stupid. When King Louis XIV of France died leaving a debt of one billion livres (about Yen 600 million), this burden was placed on the people, and finances were extremely confused. Speculators then began to operate in France and spread to neighboring countries, bringing indescribable harm to the people. The Scotsman John Law, who had studied Italian banking methods, habitually dreamed of grand designs. Seeing France in extreme poverty, helplessly bewailing her misfortunes, Law thought that he would take advantage of the situation to devise a plot. Thus, he went to France and explained to the government that he had a method for paying off the national debt. If his method were followed, he [promised] to completely erase the debt within a few years. The government having acceded to his proposal, Law established a bank, promised those joining the company that he would increase their capital with expanding profits, and took in large amounts of treasure by exchanging the company's paper (*tegata*)[20] for gold and silver, which he spent as he collected. Thereupon, he announced that he had acquired a gold mine in Mississippi of French America and collected large sums of bullion after forming the Mississippi Company.

In England, a fellow by the name of [John] Blunt proposed to reap vast profits from the South Seas. Petitioning the government, he formed a company and collected large sums by exchanging paper for gold. Blunt's intent was the same as Law's even though their enterprises differed. Since they resorted to false schemes without any validity whatsoever, their notes ceased to circulate after their value suddenly collapsed, and untold numbers of people lost their wealth and fell into poverty.

Thus bank notes are only paper if they are not trusted. Since this is a law of nature, the injury of excessive bank notes is either a corresponding jump in commodity prices or total bankruptcy. These speculators ultimately brought unimagined harm to the people as they inversely mistook paper for the root and bullion for the branches, thereby opposing a law of nature. It was said that the face value of the South Sea Company's inconvertible paper was £300 million (about Yen 1.5 billion) while the French Mississippi Company's notes amounted to Livres 2 billion (or about Yen 1.2 billion). Because their proposals arose from false expectations, I would call these charlatans speculators. Are not speculators indeed to be feared!

On Religion Part Five[21]

Nishi Amane

Some have asked, "Having heard the decree that the people should not be compelled to believe,[22] will the government, with complete indifference, allow the people to believe as they please?"

My response would be as follows: As the relations between government and people are like those between parent and child, how can the government not want the people to turn toward good religion and to avoid superstition even though it does not have the right to compel them to believe? Faith is indeed rooted in what men cannot understand, but we should not deceive ourselves as to the depth and breadth of knowledge. Men of extensive knowledge, therefore, are elevated in their faith while those of deep knowledge are invariably broad in their faith.

Let me translate this into terms of measurement. Although wise men no less than fools are uncertain as to the full extent of the universe, measurements in miles are larger than those in rods and those in feet are longer than those counted in inches. Since human knowledge in the final analysis also follows this universal principle, we may assume that the faith of those of broad and extensive knowledge is far removed from that of the mean and narrow in view, even though the faith of the former is not always correct. Now take the common people who believe in foxes, badgers, snakes, and insects and the sages who believe in a Supreme King of Kings (*Jōtei Shusai*).[23] Even though both equally have faith in what they do not know, are not their beliefs farther apart than Heaven and earth?

Those who lead and assist society, therefore, should indeed not force others to believe, but they should espouse and affirm the beliefs of those who are most discriminating and most elevated in their wisdom. By so doing, they will freely establish what they believe without imposing any restrictions whatsoever. In this fashion, the wise will fully exert their powers of inducement and persuasion by making clear their faith, and the fanaticism and superstitions of the common people will thus also be entirely reformed through a gradual process of change. From the point of view of the art of governing, this is the way to deal with the people's faith. Should my interrogators then ask whether after all the wise in society have faith, I would respond that, since the common people have faith, how can we suppose that the wise are without faith?

Now it is entirely possible to discern with naked eyes that the heavens are high and that the sun, the moon, and the stars are distant. But with the invention of the telescope, we see what cannot be discerned with naked eyes, distinguishing near from far and understanding actual conditions. With the power of instruments, we can clearly establish the facts and understand the principles of such heavenly bodies as Orion, the Dipper, the Milky Way, the unformed nebula and the lately destroyed star Syrius, the fireball of the sun, and the mountains and rivers of the moon.

The same principle, after all, also applies to metaphysical wisdom. If man just studies the delicacy of human nature and penetrates the causes of being, he will be content to believe in a Supreme Being (*Shusai*) after he has employed this knowledge to conjecture the existence of the Creator. Once man believes in the Supreme Being, he knows the Lord's will to be infallible. The truth that commands unceasing awe and admiration and that is unembarrassed by inner impurity is derived from the great thinkers of all generations and is valid throughout the world. When it comes to religions, however, their rules of ethics and propriety as well as their forms of worship vary with individual sects. This is to be attributed wholly to the fact that such matters are left to individual preference.

On the Plurality of the Origin of Things

Tsuda Mamichi

Men have thought that there was but one source for all things. Such reasoning may have derived from the theory of Chinese scholars who have regarded Heaven as the source of the Way; or the Shintō scholars (*Kōgaku-sharyū*)[24] who said that all things were contrived by the Heavenly Deities (*Amatsu-kami*);[25] or the Western scholars who have attributed everything in the universe to the Creator. While it is easy to ascribe the origin of all things to the Heavenly Deities or the Creator, is it a fact that there were Heavenly Deities or a Creator? This is beyond the realm of human knowledge, and it is foolish to seriously discuss what is beyond knowledge. As Confucius said, the unknown should be left unknown.

Putting aside the Heavenly Deities and the Creator for the reason that they are in the realm of the unknown, the origins of things, the sources of all forms, are then by no means one. Indeed, they are invariably numerous. First to consider this world, the Chinese ascribed the source of all things to five basic elements (wood, fire, water, earth, and metal); the Indians, to five (air, wind, fire, water, and earth); and the ancient Europeans, to four (water, fire, earth, and air). They were all mistaken, however. Westerners have recently reported that they have determined through the science of chemistry that there are more than sixty basic elements.

It may be said that each of these basic elements is its unique source. Yet being basic elements, they are not all things. Only such rare substances as gold and silver appear in the form of basic elements.

Any number of substances are formed through the union of these sixty or more elements. When one discusses the origins of this world, therefore, they should never be reduced to less than sixty or more.

Setting aside material things and inquiring into the sources of our birth, we have two parents and four grandparents, and their forebears successively multiply back to the innumerable remote ancestors. We are composed of two factors, body and soul. While it is impossible to know the nature of the soul, the body is made up of numerous substances such as skin, flesh, bone, blood, hair, and nail which, when analyzed, are ultimately composed of many basic elements.

Again, should you inquire into the sources of water, it is mistaken to say that they are but one. Large rivers arise from many streams, and the sources of the lesser streams are hundreds of thousands of springs. When we look at the many branches that stem from the trunk of a tree, are we not mistaken to think of the trunk as the single source? The sources of trees and bushes are their roots, not their trunks, and each root is derived from any number of lesser roots. Therefore, the origins of trees and bushes are many, not one.

Thoughtful men do not doubt in the least that the origins of the universe are many, not just one. Shallow men may believe that fire power is the sole source of the trajectory of bullets, but the source is not fire power alone. The course of a bullet is determined by a combination of fire power, gravity, and resistance of the atmosphere.

Those who regard the ruler as the foundation of the nation are mistaken. Since the Chinese were correct when they observed at an early day that the people are the foundation of a nation, the foundation of a nation is the mass of its population. And since the people are the foundation of the nation, the ruler clearly came later. The people may be compared to the foundation of a house; the ruler to its ridgepole.

The majesty of the ruler is beyond dispute even though he appeared after the foundation. If one inquires into the order of appearance in this world, earth and stone, plants, animals, and finally man successively came into being. Man, the last of these, is the most noble and most spiritual. Then the ruler, who emerged last among men, is the most noble of men. Among the achievements of men generally, whether in science or in the arts, the most noble and most good are those developed last through the pooling of strengths and knowledge. Therefore, even as the son is more intelligent than the father, the younger brother superior to the elder brother, and the student ahead of the teacher, human wisdom progresses through the world. This does not mean, however, that from the point of view of ethics the son is nobler than the father, or that the younger brother is above the older brother, or that the student is higher than the teacher. One should never fall into such an error.

[1]Official insignia, *fukushō,* 服章. In 1872 the Japanese government ordered the abandonment of traditional dress by officials and the adoption of two styles of Western clothing, full ceremonial dress and ordinary formal dress. In this essay, Tsuda is disparaging the elaborate new uniforms, which symbolized to him lingering backwardness of the East rather than the enlightenment of the West.

[2]Toyotomi Hideyoshi, 豐臣秀吉, 1536–1596, sought to enhance his position as strong man of Japan through his patronage of the art of tea and lavish entertainments at the famed Palace of Pleasures. It is recorded that 360 persons attended his tea entertainment at Kitano, 北野, in 1587.

[3]*Shōreifuku,* 小禮服.

[4]*Taireifuku,* 大禮服.

[5]Sui, 隋, and T'ang, 唐. In the seventh century, the Japanese court emulated the courts of the Sui and T'ang dynasties in China by establishing ranks with corresponding caps of designated colors.

[6]Date [Munenari], 伊達宗城, 1817–1882. The former lord of Sendai, Date led the mission to Peking in 1871 that concluded the first treaty of commerce and friendship between Japan and China.

[7]*Konōshi,* 小直衣, a short jacket with broad sleeves and fitted collar.

[8]*Eboshi,* 烏帽子, a cap worn by Japanese court nobles.

[9]*Hitatare,* 直垂, a ceremonial robe.

[10]Li [Hung-chang], 李鴻章, 1822–1901, was actually governor-general of Chihli, 直隷, not prime minister.

[11]The term three dynasties, *sandai,* 三代, here refers to the Hsia, 夏, the Shang, 商, and the Chou, 周, dynasties, the three earliest Chinese dynasties whose traditional dates are 2205–265 B.C.

[12]Aisin Gioro 愛親覺羅, was the Manchu clan from which the last ruling house of China, the Ch'ing Dynasty, emerged. In addition to requiring all Chinese males to wear the queue, the Manchus strictly regulated the dress of their Chinese subjects in order to preserve the distinction between the Manchu and Chinese peoples.

[13]From the arrival of Japan's first embassy to the United States in 1860, Japanese visitors to the West were struck by the high status of Western women as compared with the subservience of Japanese women. This high status they recognized as a source of Western strength as well as a benefit to the women themselves. Of the early Meiji enlighteners, none acted more dramatically or wrote more eloquently than did Mori Arinori on behalf of enhancing the dignity of Japanese women. Mori's most important contribution to the *Meiroku Zasshi* is this series of articles on wives and concubines in which he attacks the traditional Japanese marriage and family practices that were uncivilized, at least from the Western point of view. Although Mori advocated more equitable relations between husbands and wives, however, he was not for equal rights for men and women. He was doubtless embarrassed when the Japanese government in 1870 accorded concubines legal status equal to that of wives. Concubines lost their legal status in 1882.

[14]*Nakōdo,* 媒(*bai*).

[15]*Ukedashi,* ウケダシ.

[16]*Geisha,* 藝者.

[17]*Tendō jinri,* 天道人理.

[18]Campan, Jeanne Louise Henriette, 1752–1822, the famed French educator who was appointed by Napoleon in 1807 to head a school for the daughters, sisters, and nieces of officers of the Legion of Honor.

[19]Speculators, *kūshō,* 空商.

[20]*Tegata,* 手形.

[21]Continued from Part Three in the sixth issue. There was evidently no Part Four.

[22]In 1873 the Japanese government quietly abandoned Japan's traditional vigorous suppression of Christianity when it removed the placards that had publicly denounced Christianity as an evil religion.

[23]*Jōtei Shusai,* 上帝主宰.

[24]*Kōgaku-sharyū,* 皇學者流.

[25]*Amatsu-kami,* 天神.

On Transportation[1]

Tsuda Mamichi

I began studying Western letters as a young man. Reading a biography of the great Tsar Peter of Russia, I learned what are regarded as his three major achievements: reform of the military system, establishment of schools, and the development of transportation. At the time, I thought that the development of transportation was of but trifling consequence to the country, and I wondered how it could be compared with reforming the military system and building schools. Only during adult years have I come to believe that transportation should certainly rank ahead of the military system and building schools.

Reforming the military system is for the purpose of strengthening the army; schools are established to spread knowledge; and transportation is developed to promote national prosperity. The *Kuan-tzu*[2] states that etiquette will be understood if food and clothing are sufficient, and the *Lun Yü*[3] observes that armies are sufficient when food is sufficient. Kuan Chung and Confucius thus already knew that national prosperity is the most important factor in governing, a principle that even adolescents today all appreciate. When it comes to developing transportation for the purpose of bringing prosperity to the country, however, even gentlemen in authority and elderly Confucian teachers may also have doubts. Let me undertake to discuss this matter.

What Heaven creates varies from area to area. It endows the mountains with minerals, forests, grasses, birds, and beasts; plants the fields with cereals and vegetables; and produces salt and fish in the sea. This is known even to women. Species of plants and animals, however, likewise vary according to the degrees of latitude. Even a wise person cannot induce equatorial plants and animals to thrive in the extreme north. Similarly in the temperate zone, if you plant *tachibana* from Kiangnan in Kiangpei, they will become *karatachi*.[4] It is impossible to plant Chinese and Japanese teas in England, Germany, and other countries even though one desires to do so. As for minerals, one should not try to find Chinese jade in Japan or American gold and silver mines in Europe.

It may generally be said of wealth in the world that there is nothing more important than putting to our use the products and riches that we have gathered from many lands. Men invariably mention London in England if they speak of wealth in the world today. It is just as if no place in the five continents were as wealthy as London. Should you ask the reason for this English prosperity, it is because England leads the countries of the world in transportation. While the convenience of English transportation naturally lies in the country's geographic position, it also derives from the fact that the people vie in the crafts and compete in diligence.

England is renowned in the world as the real leader in transport facilities because her ships are numerous and her railways are developed. This naturally arises from the enlightenment and diligence of the English people. Then why have the English been able thus at will to extend their mental powers? I would say that the reason is principally because the English government has given unrestricted freedom to the people.

Our empire, equally with China, depends on the five grains for the people's daily food.[5] Since rice is regarded as the best for eating, fluctuations in the price of rice, being related to the people's lives, are the greatest concern of administrative officials. There is wide variation in the average price of rice in the different districts, our country's small size notwithstanding. For example, the rice prices this year ranged from two yen per *koku*[6] to seven yen per *koku* according to district. This was caused by the inadequacy of our transportation facilities. Moreover, the price of rice in Tokyo recently rose suddenly until it reached eight or nine yen. When I asked about this in amazement, I was told that rice is more scarce than usual because its movement into the city has been unusually restricted. Upon inquiring further into the cause, I was informed that the government has borrowed our transport for military purposes in connection with the Taiwan Incident, with results that are just like blocking the rice transport route.[7]

There is so-called port blockade in modern warfare. The term refers to the complete cutting off of one's enemy from outside communication in which he is caused distress because our ships block his ports and prohibit the ships of others from entering. When our government recently sought offenders among the Taiwan aborigines, the result was actually like establishing a blockade of the port of our capital. Ah, are our government's deliberations after all wise or foolish? This is not the place for me to attempt such a discussion.

"Liberty"

Mitsukuri Rinshō

The translation of "liberty" is *jiyū*.[8] It means to accord to people the free exercise of their rights (*kenri*)[9] without restriction by others. To the liberty of the people may be traced the fact that the countries of Europe and America are today all enjoying perfection in government and expanding in national power. Those who desire to know its details may consult Nakamura's translation of Mill's *On Liberty*.[10] Without attempting an exhaustive discussion, therefore, I shall publish the following outline of the history of liberty from antiquity to the present.

"Liberty," that is *jiyū,* is derived from the Latin *libertas*. This *libertas* refers to the social station of free men as distinguished from that of slaves or *servitas*.[11] Roman law recognized two types of men in conformity with the major division in society, the *liberi* or free men and the *servi* or slaves. "Liberty," therefore, originally referred to the social status of free men as contrasted with that of slaves. There was also a similar usage in Greek in which the word for master, or *despotes,* indicated a free man, while the term for servant, *doulos,* pointed to a slave.

The word "liberty" was also used in Rome when referring to the right of freedom from a political point of view. This sense derived from the social status of free men who were not slaves. The people of a country are like servants enslaved by their masters when they are oppressed by their ruler. When people manage to escape from despotic government, they are said to have acquired "liberty" since they are like free men liberated from slavery. The Roman people, therefore, said that they had acquired "liberty" when they threw off the oppressive rule of tyrants. And even in Greece, the words *despotes* or master and *doulos* or slave were slightly altered to mean respectively monarch and subjects when used from a political point of view. The king of Persia, therefore, was a *despotes* or master, and his subject was invariably a *doulos* or slave.

The word "liberty" is thus used from a political point of view, and what is today called "political liberty" was originally derived from *libertas,* the social station that was not slavery. When men acquire liberty by changing their status from slavery in republics, they can become men who possess in their persons the rights of liberty from a political point of view, but this is impossible under monarchial despotisms. Even though slaves in despotic lands may acquire the status of freed men, therefore, they can only obediently honor, without daring to oppose such arbitrary edicts as their rulers may hand down.

In the previous discussion, [I] have generally referred to people free from oppression by monarchs and aristocrats when using the word "liberty" in the political sense, and I signified persons oppressed by monarchs and aristocrats when employing the word "slavery." Therefore, "liberty" cannot in the least be enjoyed by the people in their persons unless constitutional rule really prevails in the country. And even though a ruler may conduct benevolent government and caress his people under monarchial despotism, the people do not in the least enjoy political "liberty" since these favors are entirely dependent upon the monarch's will. Looking at liberty in this way, the people cannot have full political "liberty" when sovereignty is placed entirely in the hands of the monarch or aristocrats. Moreover, in the interest of liberty, it is urgent that all the people or, this failing, a majority of the people invariably participate in ruling the country.

Now, under monarchial despotism there are two types of monarchs who do not grant "political liberty" to the people. On the one hand, there are monarchs who, like those in oriental countries, are rulers by hereditary succession. On the other hand, there are rulers like Pisistratus in Athens and Polikrates on the island of Samos who destroyed constitutions and usurped power.

The Greeks clearly distinguished between these two types of monarchy even though both alike were autocratic and oppressed the people. It was established that the people should obey the hereditary monarchs or *basileis* in all matters. But it was held that the people need not invariably obey and even had the right to resist usurping rulers or *tyrannos*, however loving their rule might be. Greek historians, therefore, recognized as legitimate even enemies of Greece, such as King Darius of Persia, because they had long inherited their title, but they held rulers like Dionysius of Syracuse to be usurpers although they were Greeks.

On Religion Part Six[12]

Nishi Amane

When asked if I select my faith, I reply that I do. I select the truth. But since it is impossible to know in advance what is true, one should select what seems close to the truth. When I am asked whether there is then a method of selecting, I reply that there is. We should select what seems in our hearts to be true or close to the truth without being bound by custom, or glued to family tradition, or influenced by public opinion. Nor should we yield to the persuasions of other men or consider what is convenient or inconvenient in the matter. When asked how one determines in his heart what is true or close to the truth, I reply that this should naturally become apparent if one asks in his heart what are the great principles for conducting one's affairs and governing the body. I am only speaking for scholarly circles, however. This is not advice for superstitious commoners.

Then someone may wonder about the methods for searching in one's heart for the truth. When I ask him if he has ever done what he thought good in his heart or what he thought bad in his heart, he replies that he has. Asked how he feels after doing good, he replies that he is happy. And when I ask how he feels after doing something very bad, he answers that he feels agonized repentance.

I then ask who understands an individual's mind. I wonder if the monarch knows the subject's mind since the monarch is called the lord of his subject. And I wonder whether the father understands the child's mind since the father is called the lord of the child. My friend replies that no one understands these things.

I then ask, since no one understands these things, why my friend feels happy after doing good and repentant after doing bad. He replies that this is a matter of individual conscience (*sei*)[13] and depends upon no one else. I then ask who creates and who forms this thing called conscience. Since my friend is reared by his lord, is his conscience not created by his lord? Or is not his conscience formed by his father who gave him birth? My friend replies that one's conscience cannot be created by either king or father since it is naturally within the individual.

Since a person's conscience is thus within himself, I ask my friend if he does not become angry when he is injured by another. My friend responds that of course he becomes angry. If a person is angered because of injury to the interests of another, how much more is this the case if his own interests are hurt! I then ask why he should become angry. If it is held that the injury, being natural, arises from man's conscience, the deed, after all, originates in the individual's intrinsic inner nature even though it may be caused by a good or an evil conscience.

If one would allow men to follow their individual consciences, then thieves, violent people, and killers will say that they are only acting in accordance with their consciences. Since there is no means for knowing the individual minds of men, it would be necessary to accept their words. Then how, I would ask my friend, can we punish them and how can we execute them? My friend responds that he was mistaken. Man's conscience is Heaven Endowed (*Tembu*).[14] This Heaven-Endowed nature functions alike in all men. And we may become angry with as well as punish these criminals since they violate Heaven's Endowment. The ancients have said that the foundation of the Way (*Michi*)[15] is unchanging as it is derived from Heaven and that its substance cannot be dismembered as it is formed by Heaven. My friend reminds me that I have already said this, and I agree. It is quite close to the truth to assume that man's conscience is Heaven Endowed and not something that can be created by king or father.

Now while it is known that man's conscience, being Heaven Endowed, is not the property of king or father, [I wonder] if we do not know that man's external body, after all, is born of the father and reared by the king. My friend responds that it is correct that the child is born of the father and reared by the king. Then I ask whether one's external body is the possession of king and father since man's conscience alone is Heaven Endowed. If such be the case, then why cannot [my friend's] father choose between beauty and ugliness when creating his child? And why does not the king rear all men equally without allowing any distinction between rich and poor? My friend replies that man's body is also Heaven Endowed. Then I ask, if both body and conscience are bestowed by Heaven, is not Heaven the origin of man? Moreover, even the importance of king and father cannot be compared with Heaven. If this is the case, is not Heaven unique? My friend agrees, continuing to explain that, even though Heaven may be inscrutable, it is invariably infinite and without parallel. I state that this is rather close to the truth.

I then suggest that we shift the discussion to inquire into the meaning of the word Heaven (*Ten*).[16] Should my friend state that Heaven may simply refer to the clear blue sky as distinguished from earth, I would then respond that the clear blue sky is produced by light and air. Or should he affirm that the term Heaven signifies the sun, moon, and stars, then I would reply that these bodies are inanimate. If we point to them when speaking of Heaven, how can Heaven have will? And if Heaven is without will, then how can it endow my friend with body and conscience? My friend interjects that, since Heaven is Reason (*Ri*)[17] and Reason prevails, is it not also possible that there is a special Heaven that gives shape to all things? I answer that this is the erroneous path of the Sung Confucians. Once we are led astray down this path, even the thread of Ariadne[18] cannot save us.

Now, if my friend assumes that Heaven is Reason, it may then be asked if the evils of the world do not arise from Reason and are not accomplished by Reason. Reason then becomes a word comprehending both good and evil. Now if we take Heaven for Reason, does evil also become Heaven's Reason? I would also have my friend note that the Sung Confucians have referred to human desire in conjunction with Heaven's Reason. Why, I ask, is Heaven added to Reason in the term Heaven's Reason (*Tenri*)?[19] My friend responds that, if one speaks of Reason, one then points especially to good, which is nothing but Heaven's Reason. To this I counter by asking, what then is the significance of equating Heaven and Reason? If the two are the same, then are they interchangeable? My friend answers affirmatively.

Then I wonder, if we assume that Heaven and Reason are identical, is this to say that Heaven's Reason is Reason's Reason? Nay, Heaven and Reason, after all, are not the same, as Heaven indicates the source of Reason. Analogically speaking, Heaven is king, and the king's ordinances and edicts are Reason. Would it not be absurd to say that the edicts and ordinances are the king himself? It would be as mistaken as to refer to Heaven as Reason as to speak of edicts and ordinances as the king. After all, what we call Heaven is only a word indicating position to which there is no superior. This is like referring to the royal administration as the government and like honoring the monarch by calling him *denka*[20] without pointing to him directly.

Yet since the government is not the monarch, we speak of the man specifically as the emperor (*tei*)[21] since he is the government's sovereign. And to indicate the superiority of the heavenly over the human ruler, we call the former the Supreme Ruler (*Jōtei*).[22] We also call Him God (*Kami*)[23] because His virtue is inscrutable. Therefore, Heaven's Reason being God's Reason, the body and soul of man are entirely endowed by God. The slightest inner awareness will surely reflect His teachings as His commandments are deeply engraved in the hearts of man. If we just honor His commandments, we shall be happy for all time, not for this life alone. If we deviate in the slightest from His commandments, we shall suffer agony and punishment both in this life and later. Being lord of the universe and the most high of all things, man is able to share His mind, to know His conscience, and to surmise His Reason. Therefore, man is conscious of the causes for his own existence and follows God's way with respect, love, and trepidation. If this be not the case, how will man differ from the coral anthazoa even though he may live in a great hall or a brick mansion?

On Government[24] Part One

Tsuda Mamichi

A legacy from ancient times when men and gods, visibly and invisibly, were mutually interrelated is that the great affairs of state are rites and war. Rites are no longer state affairs in the various modern enlightened countries where religion and government are separated and festivals and government have different origins. How can they be called great affairs of state? Such being the case, then what should be regarded as the great affairs of state? These are such occasions as the enthronement, marriage, and funerals of monarchs, the opening of parliamentary sessions, exchanges of visits between sovereigns, and receptions of national envoys. Now as in the past, war is a great state affair. Enthronement of monarchs and their visits to each other are great state affairs in all nations alike. In the following, I shall now briefly explain the differences [in this regard] between ourselves and others.

The age of the gods before the founding of the Japanese Empire cannot be chronologically known. Because the unbroken line of emperors has continued for more than 2500 years since the calendar was clarified after the empire's founding, there are numerous instances in which national rites have been established custom without change since the age of the gods. And since this is the system in which church and state are united and in which festivals and governing are one, none of our national ceremonies are more important than religious festivals, and the several hundred festivals described on the front page of the new calendar are invariably great national affairs. Especially, such festivals as the *Daijō*,[25] the *Niiname*,[26] and the *Genshi*[27] as well as those commemorating the Emperors Jimmu and Kōmei are regarded as great ceremonies. There are no more important and magnificent normal rites in the country than these ceremonies conducted by the emperor himself, which are attended by hundreds of officials who respectfully purify themselves and are extremely dignified. No rites of this sort exist in the countries of Europe and America except Russia and Mongolia.

On the opening day of parliament in European countries,

several hundred members take their seats in formal clothing, and the monarch, wearing his coronation robes emblazoned with stars and medals, rides to meet them in a glassed coach drawn slowly by eight horses. Honor guards composed of battalions of infantry and cavalry in military formation protect the state coach from front and rear, while ministers of the government and princes and nobles of the court are stately and magnificent as they lead the procession or ride behind. On this occasion, the sovereign mounts the throne and himself proclaims the royal will.

This is their most magnificent ceremony of normal times since legislation is regarded in those countries as the most important national business. When the nation decides on new legislation, a draft may be proposed by a member of parliament or the sovereign may have a bill drawn up by the prime minister or by the official especially responsible. The bill only becomes law after the sovereign has consulted with the two houses of parliament in mutual exchanges between monarch and the people's representatives. The sovereign himself promulgates laws in the same manner as when our emperor intones Shintō prayers during our great national rites. The chief minister concerned, however, invariably assumes responsibility for signing his name at the end of the law.

In our country, an imperial rescript in vermillion letters is added at the beginning of a roll of one or two laws, but there is no signature by the sovereign. Foreigners have said that this system is most improper when judged from their point of view, and more recent laws and ordinances have been signed by the chancellor (*dajōdaijin*)[28] alone without, however, carrying the signature of the minister (*keiho*)[29] concerned with the law in question. In the final analysis, laws are promulgaged in our country without the imperial signature because legislative matters are not comparable in importance to rites.

When only the chancellor signs a law and the ministers concerned do not, does this mean that the chancellor alone is charged with the matter while other ministers escape their responsibilities? Ah, how difficult is the position of the chancellor! And how light are the responsibilies of the other ministers! Now in the various European countries, the signing ministers alone take charge of their business, and others escape responsibility. After all, criminal and civil law are the responsibility of the justice minister; revenue measures and the like, of the finance minister; and the basic laws, more especially of the prime minister. In the event of a miscarriage, the minister himself assumes his responsibility and resigns or takes the blame.

This is the point where our systems differ. The wisdom of our people, however, is increasing with the days and months and is not to be compared with the past. Men in the past only recognized that they should honor their forebears without appreciating that they should respect later generations, and they knew only our [country] but not other [countries]. Such is not the case today. In general, the persons are not few who recognize that sons and younger brothers excel their fathers and elder brothers and that our [country] is inferior to others. How can they not know that, once public opinion has changed in another day, a change in the political system will not be far away?

Once legislative business becomes the most important business of the nation, laws are invariably promulgated with the emperor's signature, and the ministers concerned assume their responsibilities; only then shall we naturally erase without exhausting debate the abuses, the excessive edicts, and the repeated changes in personnel that today well-nigh confuse the public mind.

[1]Dedicated as it was to the promotion of enlightenment and national strength, the Meiji government almost from its inception appreciated the importance of building a modern transportation system, a consequence of which was that approximately 33 percent of the state's investments were devoted to railway construction between 1870 and 1874. Thereafter, however, government funds were diverted to defense expenditures in connection with the flare-up between China and Japan over Taiwan, and the government's outlays for railways fell to 7.1 percent of its investments in 1875. While Tsuda in this essay deplores any downgrading of transportation to satisfy the transient requirements of national prestige, the railways in Japan proved so successful that railway construction continued unabated after 1875 with support from private capital. Unlike railways, demands of defense only encouraged the government to subsidize an expanding modern merchant marine.

[2]*Kuan-tzŭ*, 管子, a speculative work attributed to Kuan I-wu,管夷吾, otherwise Kuan Chung,管仲, a minister of the state of Ch'i,齊, in the seventh century B.C.

[3]*Lun Yü*, 論語, the *Analects* of Confucius.

[4]Tsuda here is employing an old Chinese adage warning against the futility of

trying to interfere with the laws of nature. Kiangnan, 江南, and Kiangpei, 江北, are the areas to the north and south of the Yangtze River, 長江. *Tachibana,* 橘, is a mandarin orange; *karatachi* 枳, a trifoliate orange.

[5]Five grains, *gokoku,* 五穀, i.e., rice, wheat, beans, and two types of millet (*awa,* 粟, and *kibi,* 黍). Another version would substitute barley for wheat.

[6]*Koku,* 石, 4.96 bushels.

[7]Tsuda here refers to the Japanese expedition to Taiwan in 1874 to punish aborigines who had massacred Ryūkyūan castaways on the island's southeast coast three years before.

[8]*Jiyū,* 自由.

[9]*Kenri,* 權利.

[10]Nakamura Masanao's translation of John Stuart Mill's *On Liberty* appeared in 1871 under the title of *Jiyū no Ri,* 自由ノ理, the "Principle of Liberty."

[11]*Servitas* should be *servitium.*

[12]Continued from the previous issue. In this essay, fully as important as Nishi's commitment as an enlightened scholar to faith in a Supreme Ruler or a Supreme Being is his employment of logical argument to refute Heaven (*Ten*) and Reason (*Ri*) that were at the heart of the Neo-Confucian tradition from which he had consciously broken. Nishi's denial of the Neo-Confucian concept of an all-embracing *Ri* is also implied in his famous division of scholarship into intellectual sciences (*shinrigaku*) and physical sciences (*butsurigaku*) in his fifth essay on knowledge in the twenty-fifth issue of this journal. For Nishi's opposition to Neo-Confucianism, see Thomas H. R. Havens, *Nishi Amane and Modern Japanese Thought* (Princeton, 1970), pp. 144ff.

[13]*Sei,* 性.

[14]*Tembu,* 天賦.

[15]*Michi,* or *Tao* in Chinese, 道.

[16]*Ten,* 天.

[17]*Ri,* 理.

[18]The thread given by Ariadne to Theseus that enabled him to escape from the labyrinth.

[19]*Tenri,* 天理.

[20]*Denka,* 殿下. An honorific form used for "imperial highness" that may be translated literally as "under the palace."

[21]*Tei,* 帝.

[22]*Jōtei,* 上帝.

[23]*Kami,* 神.

[24]In this his first essay on government, Tsuda joins Nishi Amane (see Nishi's essay on *Religion* in the third issue) and other Japanese enlighteners to urge the separation of church and state. Tsuda would also reconstitute the Japanese monarchy along lines of the more secularly oriented monarchies of the West in which legislation was the first order of business and government officials were individually responsible for their acts.

[25]*Daijōsai,* 大嘗祭, the great thanksgiving festival after the imperial enthronement.

[26]*Niinamesai,* 新嘗祭, an autumn festival in thanks to the gods for abundant harvests.

[27]*Genshisai,* 元始祭, the New Year's festival of the imperial court.

[28]*Dajōdaijin,* 太政大臣.

[29]*Keiho,* 卿輔.

On Torture Part Two[1]

Tsuda Mamichi

The independent states of Europe and America invariably conclude agreements on a reciprocal basis when establishing relations of commerce and friendship, and they are neither superior nor inferior to each other as their rights are the same. It is a matter of course that, when a national of one of their states goes to another, he is invariably protected by the laws of the other and abides by its directives. Under the treaties concluded between the Japanese Empire and the nations of the West, however, foreign violators of the law in our country cannot be punished under our national law. That is, the treaties do not establish equal rights between us, and it cannot be denied that our national structure is wholly uninjured. Then why can we not revise the treaties forthwith? It is because our criminal laws are not the same as theirs and more especially because our methods for administering criminal justice are clearly different from theirs.

Even though our criminal laws and theirs are not the same, the differences are not so great. It is only that their people have freedom, while ours have not escaped bondage. This is not limited only to the spheres of law and politics but extends also to the daily morals of the people. To cite examples from our respective criminal laws, the punishment in our country was formerly beheading for children who struck their parents and grandparents. But under the Revised Criminal Statutes (*Kaitei Ritsurei*),[2] the punishment is ten years, and the penalty for killing offspring is penal servitude. In the West, the former crime is punished with penal servitude or imprisonment; the latter, by death. In these cases, therefore, it should be possible to make our system of penalties identical with theirs by introducing slight modifications.

When it comes to methods for administering criminal justice, we clearly differ from them. For example, even if a crime has been committed, their judicial officers cannot arrest persons without evidence. With us, however, investigating officers are able to arrest immediately upon suspicion even if there is no evidence. Again, even if there is evidence of wrong, a crime cannot be punished in the West if it is not recognized in law. In our country, malpractices may be immediately punished even if they are not specified in law. In the West generally, evidence is heard by juries selected from the people, and judges cannot exact punishment under the criminal law on persons whose punishment has not been recommended by these juries in fair and frank judgments, the criminal laws notwithstanding. We have not yet established the jury system, however.

Moreover, they prosecute criminals under law without resorting to forced confessions if clear evidence is beyond doubt. This is why torture is completely unnecessary in the West. Torture is essential for us because it is our general practice that there can be no judgment against a criminal without his confession even though evidence of guilt is fully established. This becomes an abuse when, even without clear evidence, a person may be ultimately judged guilty after being forced into submission through the use of torture, and it becomes an injury when an innocent person is thus falsely convicted.

Since criminals generally are by nature wicked people who want to hide their crimes and escape punishment, a confession is extremely difficult to obtain even though desired. It is, after all, a common practice in all countries that even criminals escape or receive reduced punishment once they have confessed and repented. To reduce or waive punishment, therefore, is not unreasonable should the criminal confess and repent during questioning, and to pardon a person who returns to the righteous path through repenting and religious cleansing is a principle maintained by the various religions of the world. It is indisputable, however, that this principle cannot be adopted into national law. Then what is the sense of wanting to impose punishment on a criminal, having forced his confession and thereby treated him as though he had the nature of a virtuous person? This is the reason why people from the West of the Himalayas cannot submit to the laws of those to the East of the Himalayas.

It is well to punish when there is clear evidence of guilt. Once dead, the criminal will descend to hell or purgatory, and need not confess. Even though this may belong to the realm of religious conjecture, not to require confession also seems quite appropriate for adoption in the provisos for administering criminal justice, especially since this is already the prevailing practice in Europe and America.

There is also no great difference between our old methods of adjudication and the new methods of the West in so far as it is the prevailing practice in civil judgments to rely on evidence when determining right and wrong. Now will not the listener be confused as to what is right and wrong if he believes only the words of the defendants and the plaintiffs who try to hide their weaknesses when stating their cases, or of their lawyers who elaborate on their testimony? How can there be fair and impartial justice without reliance on evidence? Coming then to criminal law, how improper a custom it is absolutely to forbid punishment unless there is confession even though the evidence is completely clear! Will it not be impossible to conclude treaties on equal terms with the West and to govern the free people of foreign countries with our laws if this improper custom is perpetuated? Is not the impropriety of this custom also most extreme?

Should I be asked what can be done when, no confession being required, a case is decided entirely on erroneous evidence, I would respond that in Europe and America there is appeal under both criminal and civil law. If a criminal does not accept punishment after the decision is handed down, he can then appeal to a higher court within a certain time. This enables the criminal, as a guarantee against error by the judiciary, to secure rectification by judicial review when evidence is mistaken. We should thus eliminate torture if we desire to conclude equal treaties between our empire and the Western powers and to induce foreign nationals resident in our country to honor our laws. And we should first reform the laws for administering criminal justice if we desire to eliminate torture. After all, the countries of Europe and America all have what are known as codes of criminal procedure. Why should it now be difficult to establish suitable provisions governing the administration of criminal justice in our empire by drawing eclectically from Western law if we follow the methods that we employed when the Taihō Penal Code (*Taihō Ritsu*)[3] was modelled after the T'ang codes or when we established the Essentials of the New Penal Code (*Shinritsu Kōryō*)[4] in which we harmonized the Criminal Code (*Ritsurei*)[5] of the bakufu with the codes of the T'ang, Ming, and Ch'ing dynasties.

When I served as a justice official with Messrs. Matsumoto, Mizumoto, and Kiyooka,[6] we labored hard to draft a new penal code based on the French code. I later heard that this undertaking was halted after my retirement. Being clumsy and uninformed, I was not qualified for these duties, and there is no need to regret the project's halt.[7] The able legal experts in the *Sain*[8] and the *Meihōryō*[9] are not few, and I personally hope that these officials will devote their full energies quickly to drafting and submitting to the sovereign the most appropriate provisions for administering criminal justice in our country. I also beg His Majesty the Emperor decisively to end torture by special decree. What a magnificent and beautiful act this would be!

Some may argue as follows: We have already heard your view that, if we do not end torture, Western countries will not conclude equal treaties with us and that we shall be unable to place foreign residents under our law. Nevertheless, we cannot understand why Japan should not ultimately be able to ride side by side with the nations of Europe and America if torture is not destroyed. Our empire's ability to compete with Western countries wholly depends on the culture of the people and on the military power of the government, not on the ending of torture.

My reply is that it is indeed true that, if the culture of the people is really advanced, the bad practices of torture and the like surely will disappear completely from our empire. Even though we increase our military power several levels above the present, this will neither alter the barbarian nor bring culture. We may indeed want to ride side by side with the Western nations. But how can they permit this when we preserve without change such bad practices as torture?

I may also be asked about the man who by luck is able to escape punishment because the evidence alone is insufficient for sentencing him. When I asked European lawyers, they responded that not a single innocent man should be punished even though a hundred criminals may escape by chance. An old Chinese proverb states that it is better not to apply the law at all than to kill the innocent.

Ah, how chagrined I am to think that the Japanese of today are inferior to the Chinese of antiquity! Our country still has torture. But do you suppose that none escape justice by luck? This is indeed thoughtless.

The True Statesman

Sugi Kōji

If asked what a true statesman may be, I would respond as follows: A true statesman possesses innate talents and virtues that enable him during peace to plan for the increasing prosperity of the country and during adversity to restore peace and tranquility by healing injuries and by easing national calamities. This true statesman will accumulate training and expand in wisdom by observing foreign and domestic history in detail and by committing to memory the true record of his own country. In addition to ripening his knowledge in written materials, he will also verify on the basis of actual facts. Thereby will he acquire means for administering the country, for thoroughly understanding the true principles of society, for penetrating public feeling, and for acquiring facts.

While he will consider what conduces to public interest and what brings national advantage, he will learn public sentiment in other countries as well as the institutions by which this sentiment is controlled. And with this knowledge, he will determine the objectives that can lead to the peace, prosperity, and happiness of his own country. Establishing his methods for attaining these objectives and carrying them out, he will gain advantage for his country without public criticism or remonstrance. He will also conduct foreign affairs in consultation with the enlightened rulers and great ministers of the world, and he will plan benefits for our country based on the accumulated knowledge of the tastes and cherished views of foreign leaders.

After discerning the sentiments of foreign leaders who desire fame and seek prosperity, he will explode their designing ideas before they germinate. If he knows that he cannot oppose them with our power, he will then respond to them with strategy and blunt their thrusts with wisdom. Penetrating their future plans, he will cause them to flinch before the brilliance of his wisdom. Moreover, when establishing a policy, he will invariably anticipate what benefits will be derived from this policy after first appreciating what it can achieve.

In this way will the true statesman establish the national structure and promote the national destiny. And in this way will he oblige enemy countries always to fear his person and prevent them from cherishing designing thoughts. Without falling before their artifices, he will instead penetrate their calculations while hiding our secrets. What he achieves for us with his wisdom and skill will truly be like defending our country against hundreds of enemy arrows with an iron castle. The methods by which he carries out these arrangements will all contribute to the happiness of his countrymen.

In time of national crisis, the true statesman will reassure his countrymen with his words and strengthen their determination by his conduct. As the crisis increasingly deepens, he will appear like a Bodhisattva to his countrymen by employing all manner of defense techniques to prepare against foreign invasion and to heighten increasingly the nation's prestige. We may compare him to an experienced mariner who, upon meeting a great storm on an ocean crossing, cuts through the gales and high waters to bring his ship safely into port or calm waters. How difficult it is to be a true statesman!

An Outline of Western Culture

Nakamura Masanao[10]

When Greece and Rome were at their zenith, letters flourished as scholars and literary men emerged in great numbers. Very few of their writings have been preserved for later generations since there was then as yet no printing. But among their writings, "truth" and "science" appear here and there like twinkling stars, the great brilliance of whose light has remained bright through succeeding generations. Discussions by scholars of antiquity may seem useless at first glance since they were usually based on imagination. Nevertheless, it may be said that we have indirectly derived great benefit from them as they are the ultimate roots of modern scholarship.

During the twelfth century, studies of Roman law spread broadly through the world, expanded men's views, and strengthened their thought. Since people at that time still worshipped images and were in a dense fog, their theories on these legal studies were not yet firmly fixed. From these studies, however, the light of human wisdom appeared in the darkness, and humanistic and political studies gradually emerged. This was the source of "liberal politics"* and "pure ethics"** that have been taught in recent times.

It was indeed fortunate for later generations that [Hugo] Grotius began the study of "natural jurisprudence"*** as a separate discipline, a study that European scholars followed for a hundred and fifty years thereafter. The invention of printing in 1441 should really be regarded as the great dividing point between ancient and modern scholarship. Since we now read printed books from childhood, it is impossible for us to imagine how inconvenient it was to be without printing. From the introduction of printing, the people in European countries were able to easily read texts.

Such a person as [Martin] Luther consequently read the Bible with ripe understanding and knew that the teachings of the Roman Church were opposed to God's Truth so that he ultimately founded a sect known as the Church of the Reformation. Thereafter, the Bible was translated into the vernaculars of the various European countries, and the people gradually turned toward the Reformed Church as the power of the Roman popes declined more and more. The English Reformation began in 1547. From the Reformation, men were not only freed from oppression by others in religious matters. Since they sought to gain benefit by

*"Liberal politics" is politics that conforms to the public interest and promotes reciprocal benefits, being free from oppression by despotic law.

**"Pure ethics" teaches men to cultivate virtue not only through upright external conduct but also by being true in their hearts.

***Heaven's Law.

carrying old experience into new fields without being mired in the tracks of the ancients, there also emerged in philosophy such great heroic figures as Erasmus, Juan Luis Vives, and Sir Thomas More.[11] These men stand side by side with Luther as their scholarly perception was truly unequaled by that of their predecessors. Aristotelian philosophy from antiquity had been obstinately defended from generation to generation as immutable doctrine. Not only did Luther make light of Aristotle's teachings as being without benefit to Christianity. He even branded it as useless in "natural philosophy."*

The invention of printing was the beginning of the enlightenment of men's minds. In addition, learning was advanced by the fact that the vulgar people of Europe were able to enhance their spiritual power. This was partly attributable to the proliferation of wealth from flourishing trade and partly to the ability of men to satisfy their individual ambitions after the aristocrats lost their power to oppress. Having created an atmosphere conducive to broad scholarship and love of learning and having time for scholarship, men gradually encouraged useful studies and exploded false doctrines.

The emergence of truly practical studies after scholarship had changed and false theories had been exploded was rooted in the scholarly efforts of various talented men to know conditions as they are through the verification of actual facts, a method known as "experimental inquiry." Paracelsus was the founding father of this new type of scholarship that was beyond even the dreams of his predecessors.[12] Born in 1493, Paracelsus was hardly ten years younger than Luther. His scholarship, however, was still inadequate even though he carried out numerous tests in chemistry** and studied the varieties of stones, minerals, beasts, and plants. Only with the coming of Lord [Francis] Bacon were the foundations of experimental studies established.

Scholarship was also increasingly expanded by the discoveries of America and of the route around the Cape of Good Hope to India. As a consequence, northern peoples came to use the products from southern areas; southern countries imported the manufactures of the northerners; and the peoples of the West employed

* The study of the principles of the universe.

**The art of chemical analysis (*bunrijutsu*, 分離術).

cloth from the East for clothing. In addition, customs, theories, laws, diseases, medicines, virtues, and vices were mutually exchanged, contributed, and taught by peoples from the four quarters of the globe. All of this greatly illumined men's minds and greatly advanced their scholarship.

[Note. According to this essay, the sources for the advance of scholarship in the world were: first, the reading of religious materials and the rise of Protestantism that was only possible after the invention of printing; second, the emergence of numerous scholars once the common people gradually acquired liberty; third, the rise of experimental and empirical studies; and fourth, exchange and travel over the four seas. Human wisdom was thus greatly expanded as if it had been awakened from a dream.]

To be continued in the next issue.

A Certain Question

Sakatani Shiroshi

Even though Shiroshi is a fool, he despises secretiveness, egocentricity, and prejudice. He consequently admires men in European studies, notwithstanding the fact that he is too stupid to understand European languages, and he desires fairly to realize the unity of Chinese and Western scholarship. Having recently heard of the establishment of the Meirokusha, he was happy when he obtained permission to sit at the rear of the audience. While he has gained great profit therefrom, he also has had many questions that he fears would interrupt the discourse should he raise them one by one. Therefore, he will jot them down from time to time and beg elucidation. He would be extremely pleased if the honorable gentlemen do not hesitate to answer him freely.

For some years in the daily press there have appeared discussions by persons in the public as well as by the Education Ministry regarding reform of the Japanese language and writing. The question has lately been discussed in this society's journal by Messrs. Nishi, Nishimura, and Shimizu.[13] While I have been impressed by the depth of their thought and the reasonableness of their words whenever I have read their essays, their suggestions are extremely difficult to put into practice.

Even after a hundred years, the various countries with whom we have relations will preserve their identity, and it will be necessary to use the English and French languages with the English and the French, the Russian and the German languages with the Russians and the Germans, and the Chinese and Korean languages with the Chinese and Koreans. If we follow one, we shall run counter to the other. And if we accommodate one, we shall inconvenience another. The same may also be applied to foreign countries in their relations with Japan. We cannot avoid studying all these languages with utmost diligence since their use is already mandatory. Ah, why is it the practical way to employ different languages? How unfortunate it is that these differences consume so much time and seriously interfere with the spread of enlightenment to the five continents!

If you ask what should be done, the only solution is to make the languages of the world one. There is merit in agreement in the world as when men individually reach the same conclusions regarding right and wrong or profit and loss. There may also be merit in difference, however. Thus, utensils have different characteristics in conformity with their manifold uses, and one's relatives are never injuriously mistaken for another's because of their different countenances. When it comes to languages, there can only be profit in making one the different words and pronunciations employed by men. The convenience will really be great for scholarship and social intercourse.

There are now numerous impediments to carrying out such a program in our country alone. But by increasing the scope of the plan, we may well establish a harmonious program for all countries. Should you ask how the policy is to be established, I would respond that it will be realized only through discussion and decision by the various nations in accordance with universal principles. Still, even the enlightened nations of Europe and America have not yet developed this proposal as the problem is large and difficult.

Now let us suppose that the Meirokusha members assume the leadership with flags and drums. After discussing the rules and procedures at each meeting, we shall devise a basis for amalgamating the various languages by adopting the strong points of one and rejecting the shortcomings of another. What an unprecedented blessing it will be if, after consulting with foreign countries, we achieve through indefatigable effort the great benefit of a common world language! I have heard of a proposal by European philosophers to abolish war. Even though this would be an unprecedented achievement of greatest benefit to all countries, their proposal will probably end in futile discussion unless the various countries become sufficiently enlightened and sincere to deny completely their selfish independence.

Coming to language, a common tongue is only an advantage for all countries alike without regard to their wealth and power. It will also hasten the world toward enlightenment and make good the deficiencies of creation. These big words may indeed seem completely inappropriate since we have not reached this level of enlightenment, but the principle is correct. Are my colleagues not of a mind to begin?

I presume that carrying out this language reform will be most difficult for China. Nevertheless, there is good reason for the Chinese to accept the reform since they detest the numerous differences between the Manchu and Chinese tongues and since they have been still more vexed by language differences following their recent entry into Western studies. Thus I am of the opinion that once the distinction is first established between public and private usage, the individual states will employ the newly determined language in public usage while retaining their traditional languages for private usage. Books and mail will invariably conform with public usage, and private usage will dwindle as public usage becomes more prevalent. What then will be the consequence? Even though the language of public use is thus an amalgam of Russian and Chinese or of English and French and even though only the countries contributing to the new tongue will receive benefits in both public and private usage, the new public usage will arise from public discussion. And there will be no denying its success since the new usage will greatly benefit scholarship and intercourse in all lands.

[1]For Tsuda's previous article on torture, see Issue Seven. Whereas Tsuda earlier stressed the evil of torture from a humanitarian point of view, this article brings out still more clearly the fact that, so long as Japan retained torture, she could not expect to achieve equality with the West by recovering full judicial independence through the abolition of extraterritorial rights then held by Western nations. This mingling of idealism with very practical considerations was characteristic of much writing by the Japanese enlighteners. Tsuda's record demonstrates, however, that he was a genuine humanitarian even though he may have employed other arguments when trying to convince his countrymen.

[2]Revised Criminal Statutes, *Kaitei Ritsurei,* 改定律例, promulgated in 1873.

[3]The Taihō Penal Code, *Taihō Ritsu,* 太寶律, was adopted in 702, when Japan was introducing many institutions modelled after T'ang China.

[4]Essentials of the New Penal Code, *Shinritsu Kōryō,* 新律綱領, adopted in 1870.

[5]*Ritsurei,* 律例, regulations for criminal procedure issued in the mid-Edo Period.

[6]Matsumoto, 松本, Mizumoto, 水本, and Kiyooka, 清岡. Although the personal names of the three are not given, Tsuda may refer to Matsumoto Masatada, 松本正志, 1833–1891; and Kiyooka Takamoto, 清岡公張, 1841–1901.

[7]Tsuda resigned from the Justice Ministry because he could not agree with the hasty methods by which Justice Minister Etō Shimpei, 江藤新平, proposed to translate and adopt the French legal codes without regard to Japanese tradition.

[8]*Sain,* 左院, the Left Chamber of the Council of State, *Dajōkan,* 太政官, that reviewed legislation.

[9]*Meihōryō,* 明法寮, the Justice Ministry's Institute for Clarifying the Law.

[10]Although Nakamura is identified as the translator, the original source is not given. It is entirely likely that Nakamura selected an undistinguished work, perhaps a school text, that presented simply and clearly the information and ideas that he wanted to convey to his countrymen.

[11]Erasmus, Vives, and More were humanist scholars of the European Renaissance.

[12]Paracelsus, Theophrastus Bombast Hohenheim, 1493–1541, a renowned German physician.

[13]For the views of Nishi, Nishimura, and Shimizu on language and writing, see Issues One and Seven. Sakatani's proposal to contrive a new international language anticipated the invention of Esperanto by thirteen years. He was perhaps more ready than other Meirokusha members to consider adoption of an entirely new language because he employed Chinese rather than Japanese in his most important writing. Reflecting his training in Chinese studies, Sakatani in the *Meiroku Zasshi* used a difficult prose style heavily loaded with Chinese words that is unintelligible to most modern Japanese.

On Government Part Two[1]

Tsuda Mamichi

The world is like but one grain of rice in the great storehouse of the universe whose infinite reaches are unknown. Yet the proliferation of types of things, the manifold sources, and the variety of manifestations in the world are beyond enumeration and beyond description. Ordinary men, therefore, cannot but lament their own insignificance. Even so, physical and human affairs are invariably governed by laws. And these laws, being natural laws, are absolutely never controlled by man. They are called Heaven's Law (*Tenritsu*)[2] by Westerners and Heaven's Principle (*Tenri*)[3] by the Chinese.

Heaven's Law or Heaven's Principle refers to the systematic order in all things, as it is nothing more than the cause that determines the nature of things. A principle (*ri*)[4] most easy to recognize is that, once a ball is thrown into the air, it will invariably fall toward the earth. The law of gravity is somewhat difficult to understand, but still more difficult to fathom are the principles governing the flowering of plants, the formation of fruits, and the minds and movements of animals. Then when we observe the phenomenon of man, investigate his reason (*ri*), penetrate the causes of this life and the hereafter, search for the secrets of man's creation, and inquire into the principle governing his conscience, we have reached the principles most difficult to understand. Yet this is also no more than discovering Heaven's Law. Now regardless of the ease or difficulty with which man discovers Heaven's Law or Heaven's Principle, it is invariably the cause that determines the nature of things.

The instrument by which men gather together, protect each other, and hold land and property is called the nation. The nation establishes rules to preserve the peace and to prevent disturbance of the public order. Designated public law (*kokuhō*)[5] and civil law (*mimpō*),[6] these rules are man made and are not Heaven's Creation.

In ancient China, these rules were known as proprieties (*rei*).[7] Later generations referred to them with a variety of designations whose different terminology only indicated their classifications at different times.[8]

Even though public law and civil law are man made, they follow the nation's progress, vary with the enlightenment of the people, and arise from unavoidable conditions and the dictates of the times. This is almost in the same category as Heaven's Law that has been a compelling determinant through the ages. Human laws are invariably injurious if they do not arise from unavoidable dictates, and unchanging human laws have yet to be established since their value varies according to time and place. This is why Yao and Shun[9] invariably followed the middle path.

Institutions are simple and laws rough in uncivilized societies. As nations gradually advance, their laws become more detailed and their institutions more complex, and there are numerous reforms in which the old is thrown out and the new introduced. These reforms are beneficial to the nation and profitable for the people if they really arise from unavoidable conditions and the dictates of the times. If they do not, they are injurious. Great disturbances invariably occur if old customs are preserved unchanged despite unavoidable conditions and the dictates of the times. In old Germany, the disturbance of the Thirty Years War broke out when religious laws were not changed as they should have been. France suffered the overthrow of the monarchy and the execution of the king when secular laws were not reformed as they should have been. The bakufu finally lost power when it clung to old customs and abuses accumulated. But those who, yearning for foreign institutions and culture, destroy old customs suited to the people of the time will themselves be destroyed. The imperial authority was grabbed by the *bushi* after our emperors departed from the warlike traditions of the Divine Land to imitate the culture and institutions of the Sui and T'ang dynasties in China.[10] Ashikaga Yoshimasa and Ōuchi Yoshitaka invited the Ōnin War and the destruction of Yamaguchi by forgetting the prowess of their ancestors and delighting in the beauties of the delicate culture of the court.[11]

The recent Meiji Restoration has been a time of reform. Once the bakufu altered the policy of closed country, the opening of the two cities and the five ports,[12] the conclusion of treaties of commerce and friendship with the countries of Europe and America, and the former Tokugawa shogun's restitution of governing power to the emperor were changes arising from unavoidable conditions and the dictates of the times. The return of the feudal registers after the Restoration was part of the same movement to restore governing power to the emperor. Since then, there has been introduced local government in the course of which the feudal system has been completely destroyed, the domains (*han*) abolished, and the prefectures established.[13]

In the old days, emperors were like queen consorts since rule was conducted from behind the bamboo curtain. The unavoidable conditions and the dictates of the times were met, however, when this was completely changed so that the emperor himself appeared in the state council and himself attended to myriad matters. It is of the greatest importance that the emperor resolutely granted reforms that were really appropriate. After all, in his resolute reforms appropriate to the times lie the foundations for uniting the institutions and the hearts of the people in the entire nation and for enabling the country to stand side by side with the nations of Europe and America. His unprecedented decisions, of course, are to be praised. These together with his innumerable other wise acts are the source of the Restoration's success today.

The military institutions of the army and navy as well as the Education Ministry's school system are following Western practices for the most part. The Ministry of Public Works is establishing posts, telegraphs, railways, and lighthouses. The Foreign Office is sending ministers and consuls abroad. The Justice Ministry is gradually establishing courts in various parts of the country. And the Finance Ministry has created paper and metal currency. These measures have generally been absolutely necessary, although some were perhaps somewhat premature.

It is entirely appropriate to divide clearly the business of finance and home affairs. Even so, they have been unceasingly united and divided, the two having first been placed under the general supervision of the Accounting Bureau (*Kaikeikan*),[14] then divided between the Ministries for Finance (*Ōkura*) and Civil Affairs (*Mimbu*), and still later brought together in the Finance Ministry following the abolition of the Civil Affairs Ministry. Most recently, the Home *(Naimu)* Ministry has been established [for separate management of civil affairs].[15] Now religion and governing, which are separate in the West, are handled together in Asia, and the Chinese Board of Revenue *(Hu Bu)*[16] also manages financial and religious affairs together. In Europe and America, the judicial power stands side by side with the legislative and the executive to form the three powers of government. In Asia, however, justice and administration are both the business of regional offices. Moreover, just as bureaucratic offices are usually simple in early days and proliferate later, they are few in Asia and numerous in Europe. This proliferation is not especially desired in modern Europe, but it arises from the inescapable reason that government business is greatly augmented as civilization advances.

Under present conditions in our country, we have not yet achieved complete separation of the judiciary. Still less is this the case in home and financial affairs. That there has been no injury from administering these matters in one ministry arises from the fact that a change has not yet been dictated by the times. It may appear that there has been no injury even though the two are now separated. But there has been injury, the injury of numerous new public expenditures that, after all, are invariably followed by heavy additional taxation of the people. Our Asian sages of several thousand years ago said that the injury from heavy taxation should be more feared than robbery and far more dreaded than tigers and wolves. This is why the curtailment of superfluous officials has been highly regarded since antiquity. I would submit, therefore, that we should not divide offices and add functionaries unless these changes are dictated by the times. Should we not reflect on the admonition by the ancients that achieving one benefit does not compare with eliminating one injury?

Religious freedom is injured when [government] offices of religion determine religious regulations and appoint churchmen; the liberty of the people is compromised when law officers employ torture; freedom of the press is harmed when the Education Ministry establishes press regulations; and freedom of movement is obstructed when laws for the household registration of the population (*koseki*) are imposed.[17] I shall not prate further on these matters, however, as I have already discussed them generally and in some detail in previous issues.

Brick structures are being erected to the south of Kyōbashi[18] in Tokyo, and the main road is divided between horse and pedestrian paths quite in the manner of the great avenues of Paris. These are official works, however, that do not arise from exertions of the people. After all, why is it that the government is undertaking these great works and bestowing special favor on a ward of the capital with several millions in gold collected from people in the suburbs (*kyōgai*)? The people in the suburbs, of course, are under no such obligation, and the people of the said ward within the capital naturally possess no such special rights. Not only do they not possess these special rights. They do not now want them. Not only do they not want them. The streets are filled with the cries of the ward people bewailing their troubles. What is this if it is not "tyranny" arbitrarily imposed by the government without regard to the people's rights and obligations or to their interests?

Such works may be for beautification or to prevent fires. While they are attractive in appearance and while they may be a preventive against fire, however, they are only a great injustice since they do not arise from unavoidable conditions and the dictates of the times. The French people are trivial by nature and fond of useless beauty. Drawing on the sweat and blood of their entire country, they only adorn their capital and frequently suffer upheavals. The sober-minded English give their attention to fundamentals. London indeed may not be beautiful. But it has long escaped the devastation of war, and its prosperity is unexcelled in the five continents. We should reflect on which have suffered and which have profited.

On Wives and Concubines Part Two[19]

Mori Arinori

Honoring the blood line is the foundation upon which morality is customarily based in Western countries. This is not invariably the case in Asian lands, especially in our country where honoring the blood line is treated most lightly. Since husbands and wives in

Japan do not practice marriage morality and thus no longer understand ethics, I shall take up the making light of the blood line and refer to its evils. It is our national custom to regard family lineage as a type of asset. Under what is denominated as the *yōshi* [adoption] system, even a person from outside the family may be brought in and appointed family heir when there is no son to succeed. Moreover, if there are only daughters in the family, a man may be selected to marry a daughter and to continue the family line under the system of *mukoyōshi* [adopted son-in-law].

Since the connection between an adopted son-in-law and his parents-in-law is viewed as that of parent and child under our national law, there can be no distinction between the bonds linking parents-in-law and the adopted son-in-law and those between parents and child. Looked at from this point of view, marriage under the *mukoyōshi* system is equivalent to marriage between brother and sister. National law that permits marriage between brother and sister cannot yet be regarded as based on honoring ethics. There might be no objection to the *mukoyōshi* system if daughters were recognized as within the blood line and allowed to carry on the family line. Nevertheless, since the national law does not recognize the daughter as within the blood line [with the right to succeed], the *mukoyōshi* system, no less than the *yōshi* system, severs the family line.

Let me here point out an instance in which morality is not clear because the blood line is not honored. Even though the child of a concubine commonly is made heir to the house after the wife fails to give birth to a son, the wife continues in her previous station thereafter, and the concubine also placidly remains a concubine. The heir treats his real mother like a nurse and looks up to his father's unrelated wife as his mother. The mother whom he recognizes, however, is very different from a foster mother, the superficial similarity notwithstanding. Bereft of the loving admiration of her child at home and ignorant of the pleasures of normal social intercourse outside, the wife ultimately will fail to know human happiness. To adopt a child from outside the family may not be as shameful for the wife, but for her to be forced to recognize the son of her husband's concubine as her son is indeed cruel and unjust.

Unquestionably, the child of a concubine is unrelated to his father's wife since husband and wife are not blood relations, and the wife naturally is not happy to accept this unrelated son as her son. How much more reluctant will she be to accept under compulsion the child of a servant as her son! Once the national law permits the sons of concubines to succeed in the family line, we may mistakenly recognize as our child the unrelated child born by a servant or by a concubine as the result of some private affair, and there is absolutely no way under national law to prevent the succession of this unrelated child in the family line.

I have previously explained that marriage is only nominal and without reality if the rights and duties of husband and wife are not mutually honored. There also cannot be marriage in name if even children born out of wedlock are allowed to perpetuate the family line along with the wife's offspring. Such being the case, marriage in our country is without reality or name. Once marriage is without reality or name, how can there be substance in the relations between parents and children, brothers and sisters, and other members of the family?

An Outline of Western Culture (Continued)[20]

Nakamura Masanao

Close to a century after the invention of printing, Copernicus discovered the true principles behind the movement of the planets. And a few years later, there appeared the three precursors of Newton: Tycho Brahe, Keppler, and Galileo. Copernicus' views were often attacked since they were absolutely contrary to those of his predecessors and differed from those of his contemporaries. Until that time, Aristotle's views had been regarded as orthodox; anything opposed to Aristotle had been branded as heterodox; and disobedience against the orders of the Roman Church had been declared heretical.

It was generally assumed in the world until to Copernicus' time that the explanations of the ancients were definitive and that there was no need for modification by men of later generations. Keppler alone, however, defended the new Copernican views, holding Copernicus to have been a man of great wisdom and broad intellect who had set forth a most important theory. Thereafter, astronomy was fundamentally changed as men in the world gradually recognized the correctness of Copernicus' views. Not only was this beneficial to astronomy. In a variety of other sciences, men developed the habit of endeavoring to supplement the deficiencies of old laws and to acquire new insights. Later scholars recognized both that the laws of the Roman Church were inadequate for a foundation and that it was essential to revise and amend the views of the ancients as the latter were inadequate in conception and had not yet penetrated the whole truth. It may be said that this perception brought great benefits.

I have not yet gone into the history of the development of "metaphysics," "morals," and "politics." Little attention had been given to these three studies before they became genuine disciplines in the seventeenth century. There had already been extremely rapid progress in "mathematics," "astronomy," and "physics" during the previous sixteenth century. Before the great clarification of ethics after the Reformation, during the Temmon Period,[21] lectures on ethics had been mired in the Scriptures, and anything not explained by God's Revelations was rejected as heretical. Luther's friend Melancthon stated:

> Although we have long taken as law the Commandments by God to Moses that were carved on stone, I think it a grave error to regard these alone as the Lord's will. This is because men are born with consciences, as if God had carved good in their hearts with His own hand. The Commandments of the Lord, therefore, are the teachings that wise scholars have formulated and that are based on the sense of good and bad with which they are endowed. What should we think if men are mired in Commandments carved on stone and neglect those engraved in their hearts? Is this God's will?

These teachings by Melancthon came to be regarded as most important and most pure in the study of morals. For many years thereafter, however, it remained the fashion for theologians to cling to old ideas and to assert empty theories.

As the teachings of the Roman Church gradually declined after the Reformation and as [the Europeans] daily excluded the obstructions to the eyes and ears of the world as well as the things that contradict the justice in men's hearts and Divine Revelation, man's goodness and the Lord's Will were increasingly clarified. The great philosopher Locke stated:

> Truth is daily becoming more and more clear. It is as if the extremely dim and distant stars, which could not be distinguished in the vast darkness of antiquity, can daily be seen through a telescope with increasing clarity.

A Certain Question

Sakatani Shiroshi

In Mitsukuri's translation of Buckle's views on civilization that has appeared in this journal and in the *Shinjishi*,[22] I am deeply impressed by the great man's penetrating, firm, and unswerving justice. Nevertheless, in order to warn against the error of those who boast of worldly success and those who, in the words of the ancients, artificially stimulate the growth of seedlings, his teachings seem to rest on natural trends without regard to war and peace. But he fails to conclude with the thought that government, while recognizing these natural principles, should earnestly and diligently advance culture and promote peace without being boastfully arrogant or artificial. When it does not do these things, government may then lapse into a Zen-like trance on the assumption that it is futile to earnestly correct its rule. Apart from inducing the evil of boastful arrogance, will there then not also be injury to the trends of the times?

I have heard that a patient's recovery depends on his natural recuperative power rather than on medical care, the latter merely guiding and supplementing the former. This is a most appropriate and immutable theory. Yet a doctor is the enemy of the patient's recuperative power, and not a doctor, if he states that recovery should depend upon this power without operating when he should, without causing the patient to vomit when he should, and without administering medicine according to the required prescription. There are indeed many government officials who procrastinatingly espouse tranquility and indolently follow their private interests. Shōtoku Taishi[23] was an exalted example of such a person; Ōno Kurobei,[24] a low one; and the injury of Shaka's enlightened way was generally of this type.

Persons guilty of such conduct are not only enemies of Buckle. They are also enemies of the European concepts of diligence and accomplishment. As we have washed away the accumulated poisons and old abuses and daily introduced new remedies during the last five to six years, the country has come out of its coma with a marked drop in the fever of "typhoid" and "typhus." Nevertheless, there are still the evils of boastful arrogance along with such side effects of the drugs as weakness, dizziness, and headaches. The theories of Buckle for such ailments are indeed good medicine of great value. Yet there is a strong tendency among officials to be repelled by the side effects and to treat the leaves and the branches while ignoring the diseased roots. Failing to make use of public opinion on the pretext that society has not yet reached the level of enlightenment, they outwardly favor freedom of speech while privately opposing it.

The question of degree or level in matters is indeed important, and the reckless administering of even good medicine may kill a person whose illness has not yet developed to a serious degree. Even so, is not the doctor the enemy of Buckle when he allows the patient excessive freedom in such matters as rest, diet, and ventilation without appreciating the seriousness of the illness and when he assumes that it is best to administer no medicine because he mistakes the degree to which he should guide and supplement the natural recuperative power of the body? Yet the government will happily protest:

> It is the opinion of the great thinker Buckle that the progress of enlightenment depends upon public opinion rather than upon the government. In the translation, he states that persons of intelligence, spearheading the people, may indeed discuss unhesitatingly and without fear the urgency for reform and for

removing their evils but that even civilized governments, making light of old abuses and ignoring their critics, delay for centuries until public opinion irresistibly boils over.

If the government is bigoted to this extent, then the country will be exactly like the European nations that have awaited great upheavals before reforming and advancing toward enlightenment. This is like the doctor who claims that the best treatment is to await reforms by the successor after the sick parent has died. Where in the world does such reasoning prevail? In the discussions in the *Shinjishi*, some have held a popularly elected assembly to be premature but none have denied it. Even to an ill-informed underling like myself, it appears that the government regards the assembly as premature.

Yet to consider it premature is to desire it in the future. Waiting for the maturity of a later day will be long. And when the remedies of today are applied over a long period of time, will they be appropriate to the symptoms and will there be no regrets? Or should we discuss the treatment more fully? Public opinion seems to be vociferously unsettled and rebellious. Once we feel that the assembly is premature without wholly rejecting it, there is no reason to await death without discussing in detail the symptoms and the remedies [to be undertaken] during the long period before the level of enlightenment is fully achieved. How can the government's interpretation of Buckle be taken as his view? According to a statement by Sugi, a nation's rise or fall depends on whether the methods for guiding the people are appropriate during normal times, and this guidance is the responsibility of the government. This then is what must be added to Buckle's theory. I suggest that my friends respond as soon as possible.

[1]Continued from Issue Nine.
[2]Heaven's Law, *Tenritsu,* 天律.
[3]Heaven's Principle, *Tenri,* 天理.
[4]*Ri,* 理.
[5]Public law, *kokuhō,* 國法.
[6]Civil law, *mimpō,* 民法.
[7]*Rei,* 禮.

[8]Tsuda here lists the following traditional legal terms: *hō*, 法; *ritsu*, 律; *ten*, 典; *rei*, 令; *kyakushiki*, 格式; and *kisoku*, 規則.

[9]Yao, 堯, and Shun, 舜, model emperors of legendary Chinese history.

[10]*Bushi*, 武士, warrior or samurai. Tsuda here refers to the emergence of the samurai class that attended the breakdown of the national land system modelled after the Chinese land system of the Sui (隋) and T'ang (唐) dynasties in the seventh century.

[11]Ashikaga Yoshimasa, 足利義政, 1435–1490, the eighth shogun of the Ashikaga line, to whose patronage of the arts to the neglect of state affairs has been attributed the outbreak of the Ōnin (應仁) War, 1467–1477, that marked the end of real Ashikaga power; Ōuchi Yoshitaka, 大内義隆, 1507–1551, the lord of Yamaguchi (山口) to whose love of pleasure has been ascribed the ultimate destruction of the Ōuchi house.

[12]The two cities (*fu*, 府) of Ōsaka (大坂) and Edo (江戸) and the five ports (*kō*, 港) of Nagasaki (長崎), Hakodate (箱館), Yokohama (横濱), Niigata (新潟), and Hyōgo (兵庫) or Kōbe (神戸).

[13]*Han*, 藩. This refers to the abolition of the feudal domains in 1871 that enabled the Japanese government to establish prefectures with governors appointed by and responsible to Tokyo.

[14]Accounting Bureau, *Kaikeikan*, 會計官, an office established in 1868 within the *Dajōkan* (太政官), the new government of Meiji.

[15]Before the ministries of the new government were firmly established during the early Meiji Period, they were repeatedly united and divided as much to serve the political interests of individual leaders and their followings as to advance administrative efficiency. Thus when Saigō Takamori (西郷隆盛) moved to replace one of Ōkubo Toshimichi's (大久保利通) proteges, Ōkuma Shigenobu (大隈重信), as vice finance minister in 1871, Ōkubo caused the Civil Affairs Ministry (*Mimbushō*, 民部省) to be abolished, its duties shifted to the Finance Ministry (*Ōkurashō*, 大藏省), and himself named finance minister with Ōkuma as second in command. Ōkubo thus gathered under his control the business normally transacted by the finance, home, agriculture, commerce, and communications ministries. He retained his post as finance minister after he joined the Iwakura (岩倉) Mission that visited the West, 1871–1873. After his return to Japan, he became head of the new Home Ministry (*Naimushō*, 内務省) and thereafter the most powerful figure in the Japanese government. Ōkuma Shigenobu continued as finance minister until his dismissal from public office in 1881.

[16]*Hu Pu*, 戸部, the Board of Revenue, from the seventh century one of the six principal boards in the imperial Chinese government.

[17]*Koseki*, 戸籍. In 1871 the new government of Meiji promulgated a household registration law, which theoretically revived the institution of household registries that was first adopted in 646 A.D. at the time of the Great Reform. By the 1871 law, district officials were required to keep an accurate census according to households in which they registered all inhabitants, births and deaths, and arrivals and departures from their districts. See earlier issues of this journal for Tsuda's essays on torture, the separation of church and state, and freedom of the press.

[18]Kyōbashi, 京橋, a district in central Tokyo. After the great Tokyo fire of 1872, Yuri Kimimasa (由利公正), then governor of Tokyo, devised a plan to reconstruct the entire heart of the city with brick buildings in French fashion. A crisis broke out, however, when Yuri sought to divert funds originally collected for relief to his reconstruction project. Tsuda is here protesting against the diversion of donations collected from people in the suburbs (*kyōgai*, 京外) to an undertaking that was not really desired by those of the inner city. New buildings were constructed in the Ginza (銀座) area, but many remained unoccupied for some time because the Japanese were not

yet ready to accept Western-style structures. In other words, the undertaking was artificially contrived and thus did not arise from what Tsuda termed "unavoidable conditions and the dictates of the times."

[19]Continued from Issue Eight. Mori is here striking at the fundamentals of the traditional Japanese family system that placed greatest emphasis on assuring the succession of an able male as head of household even though it might be necessary to draw from outside the blood line to do so. Because providing for an able male household head was so supremely important, the institutions of adopted son (*yōshi,* 養子), adopted son-in-law (*mukoyōshi,* 壻養子), and concubines (*mekake,* 妾) assumed significance characteristically Japanese. It was extremely common at least down to 1945 for families to adopt males as presumptive heirs, or *yōshi.* In the case of an adopted son-in-law, a male would be adopted to succeed as household head when he married a daughter of the family. Household heads also often took concubines for the purpose of securing male heirs that their wives had failed to provide.

[20]Continued from Issue Ten.

[21]Temmon (天文) Period, 1532–1555.

[22][*Nisshin*] *Shinjishi,* 日新眞事誌, the prominent Tokyo newspaper. For Mitsukuri's translation of Buckle, see Issue Eleven of this journal.

[23]Shōtoku Taishi, 聖德太子, the imperial prince and devout Buddhist who served as regent for his aunt, the Empress Suiko (推古), from 592 until his death in 621. Sakatani has evidently allowed his aversion for Buddhism to hide Shōtoku Taishi's major contributions as an enlightened reformer who aimed to raise Japan to the level of Chinese civilization even as the enlighteners of the Meiji Period sought to overtake the West.

[24]Ōno Kurobei, 大野九郎兵衛. Senior retainer of the Akō (赤穗) domain, Ōno left Akō and vanished into obscurity after disagreeing with Ōishi Yoshio (大石良雄), the leader of the domain's famed vendetta of forty-seven *rōnin* (浪人).

On Religion Part Seven[1]

Nishi Amane

I have been asked, since I have already said that I honor and revere the Supreme Ruler (*Jōtei*)[2] in whose existence I have faith, whether there are any benefits and rewards to be derived from thus honoring Him? What need is there for a Supreme Ruler if man establishes definite ethical principles and follows this moral path steadfastly, firmly avoiding error? You may assume that man will then receive blessings if there is a Supreme Ruler and a Hereafter or that there is no harm in believing in them even if they do not exist. Is this not also an oversimplification? Is it far from superstitious blasphemy for men to talk glibly about a Supreme Ruler and to honor Him obediently when they cannot know of His Being? How does this differ from the veneration of foxes, badgers, trees, and stones by the common people?

I would reply that faith is the source of man's virtue and the foundation of all conduct, like the proverbial axle without which a carriage cannot move. Now is it not fine if man's nature is benevolent and loving? Yet if these qualities are not based on anything at all, the love of women and the benevolence of grandmothers will only suffice to injure the universal love and the universal benevolence. It is also extremely fine if man's nature is loyal and faithful. Yet if this loyalty and faithfulness is without any basis, we may reach the point where the loyalty of slaves and the faith of mistresses actually injure the true loyalty and the true faith. Finally, how splendid it is that men are by nature talented, wise, scholarly, and skilled! But if these qualities are not based on anything, talent will change to slyness, wisdom will become deception, and scholarship and skills will be the means for stimulating vice and guile.

You have also said that you do not believe in the Supreme Ruler because He cannot be known. Under such circumstances, men will be overcome by lust and disturbed by passions since their daily conduct will be plagued by half-belief and half-doubt, the existence of definite and unchanging ethical principles notwithstanding. How can even the wise then avoid being outwardly virtuous and inwardly evil if they cannot resolutely honor the Divine Commands that are engraved in their hearts?

Now who does not laugh with pity at the old men of the rice fields and the village girls who believe in images and pictures and whose trivial minds and superstitious faiths are really extremely vulgar and most irrational? Yet should you compare these people with those degraded youth who make light of goblins, deny gods, indulge in wine, women, and gambling, and are unrestrained except by their fears of the police, which would you regard as closest to humanity? Now if there are such differences between commoners who believe and who do not believe, how much more is this the case with philosophers? The faith of wise men is achieved by utmost mental endeavor and by understanding nature. Are not man's virtues, conduct, and methods for governing others and controlling himself all based upon faith?

Ah, what can we expect from the ignorant and impoverished masses in society? Gentlemen and scholars will be astounded and disdainful if they are shown the humble beliefs of these farm folk. But let us reflect what, after all, these fine gentlemen cultivate in their daily lives. They wallow in profits, are greedy for luxuries, follow whims, and covet power. Overflowing with delicacies and surrounded by beauties, they are escorted by clattering horsemen when they go out, and at home in glittering surroundings they inflate their egos and stimulate their spirits. Since these fellows, who take such conduct for their life work, are wholly bereft of faith and principles, are they so different from the village girls and old men in the fields? Ah, how impossible it is to hope that such gentlemen will promote civilization and enlightenment!

If the great men and leaders in society are shown these evils, will they not be sorely grieved? Yet upon reflection, how do these great leaders actually conduct themselves? They talk of loyalty and patriotism, of civilization and enlightenment, of advancing profit and excluding injury, and of enriching the country and strengthening the army. They say that they will induce their sovereign to be like Peter and Napoleon and their people to emulate the Americans, the English, and the French. They boast of surpassing the achievements of Li Hung-chang[3] and excelling the triumphs of Bismarck. And they speak of advancing to the four quarters and swallowing the world. How splendid are their loyalty and their determination!

Yet since they have neither clarified the moral path nor stand on principle, are they far removed from the aforementioned gentlemen and scholars? Ah, such people are still five hundred miles deep in a fog when it comes to the principles of having faith in Heaven and cultivating the person. They may indeed be talented, wise, scholarly, skilled, meritorious, accomplished, successful, and famous, but they are also dreaming their lives away. Once matters are decided and funeral dirges float over their coffins, mourners will recall the past. Upon considering deeply what the deceased planned and achieved so diligently through life, will they seem so different from the village girls and old men in the fields?

Faith, therefore, is the basis for all conduct and the human virtues as well as the foundation for ruling others and controlling oneself. Only after we have established the great principles of faith will we enjoy health and security of body as well as peace and strength in the country. Now the foundations for our national security are not yet established; our people have yet to achieve full enlightenment; and we still suffer the insults of foreign countries. Moreover, the real wealth of our country is daily diminishing while the customs of our people are daily becoming more frivolous. Having thus already wasted years of our lives, what will be the consequences during the years to come should we continue in this manner? How can we speak of independence once such frivolity prevails?

Heaven is to man as a gardener is to trees and shrubs. Heaven fertilizes what it has planted and throws away the withered. Heaven never saves rotten branches and dead roots. Nor does Heaven preserve worm-eaten limbs and twisted trunks. One day, Heaven instructed its gardener as follows:

> I do not like this garden that has gone to ruin. When cultivating the soil, please replace the old plants with new. I want to see a profusion of rare spring flowers and a garden filled with strange scents.

Ah, the prophecies of the rise and fall of empire were indeed widespread. Yet priests and elders failed to heed these words, and the people knew not the road to repentance. Let us take warning from the fate of Israel.

On Government Part Three[4]

Tsuda Mamichi

Since the publication of the memorial by former Councillor Soejima and others on a popularly elected assembly, the mutual attacks and refutations have been so exhaustive that the press seems just like a battleground. Subsequently, there has been the rescript convening an assembly of regional officials as well as talk of establishing a house of peers.[5]

Attributing the present prosperity and strength of the countries of Europe and America to the fact that various types of representatives prevent governmental despotism by their discussions of national policies, a certain person has suggested that our empire should establish three types of representatives[6] in imitation of the West. When he has asked how such a splendid undertaking for the country could fail to bring great happiness to the people and whether this reform is not required by what I have termed unavoidable conditions and the dictates of the times, I have humbly begged to differ. Please allow me to attempt an explanation of my views.

By gathering together and deliberating, the noble lords (*shinshin kazoku*)[7] hope to imitate the form of the English upper house, to assist the sovereign, and to bring a flood of benefits to the nation. Even though their inclinations may be fine and their intentions praiseworthy, I am not convinced that their proposal is valid. After all, whether parliamentarians benefit the country depends wholly on their understanding (*chishiki*).[8]

The noble lords are generally all former feudal domain rulers. Even though they listen to admonitions and are virtuous beyond other men, they are most deficient in understanding as they have generally grown up in the depths of their palaces and remain ignorant of actual conditions. It is indeed true that various lords have gradually become accustomed to low ways, stooped somewhat to cunning, or compromised their virtue since the abolition of the domains, but they are as deficient in understanding as before. What then will be the result for the nation should these men of deficient understanding gather together like ants for discussion? Such a plan can only be expected to lead to destruction. How can it be ascribed to what I call unavoidable conditions and the dictates of the times?

Instead, the noble lords should devote their full energies and wealth toward establishing schools for the nobility, employing great teachers, and educating their sons. There is no better undertaking for them than to train their sons in practical studies and to develop in them true understanding. When this is done, I especially hope that the nobles and gentlemen in the future will establish an upper house, rise to high councils, and sit in the cabinet. They will then be lofty pillars of the nation, contributing to its strength and prosperity and promoting its welfare, like the English aristocracy from which numerous famous prime ministers have emerged.

Now having already voluntarily returned their lands to the throne and introduced peaceful rule in the countries and prefectures throughout the country, the achievements of the former domain lords and princes are not insignificant. Therefore, they remain luminous gentlemen of good heart even though, without inquiring into current affairs, they only write, play music, and roam the mountains and streams. Still more will they be remembered if they plan benefits for a later day by educating their sons.

Regional officials govern their respective prefectures and conduct administration in place of the emperor. That is, they are the deputies (*daikan*)[9] of the emperor. Now they are being assembled as legislative representatives. But are they after all representatives of the emperor or representatives of the people? There is no more extreme misnomer or contradiction of fact [than to call these officials representatives of the people]. Emissaries sent to various countries are representatives of their nation's government and sovereign, but the present legislative representatives resemble emissaries recalled from their posts abroad and converted into representatives of the countries to which they have been despatched.

How in the world can there be such reasoning? Confucius said: "Speech is not appropriate when things are not called by the right names, and nothing is accomplished when speech is not appropriate"[10] I cannot yet believe that our country will profit from the establishment of an assembly of regional officials. How does it arise from what I have called unavoidable conditions and the dictates of the times?

Popularly elected legislators are really representatives of the people as they are elected by the people. It cannot be said that there are absolutely none among the thirty millions in our empire who possess sufficient understanding to participate in these elections. Yet it is important that the electors possess appropriate understanding. These people may indeed not handle national affairs directly. Since electing representatives constitutes participation in national affairs, however, the right to elect representatives is termed a political right of the people in the countries of Europe and America.

In their election laws, the common practice is generally to deny this political right to women, children, and incompetents as well as the ignorant, the illiterate, and others who are deficient in understanding. Therefore, they establish restrictions on who may vote rather than impose limitations on who may serve as representatives. Women, children, incompetents and the like, of course, are easily excluded. Yet since it is extremely difficult to determine literacy, special regulations are essential. In the West, the payment of a certain amount of taxes is generally taken as the standard for determining the electorate. Even though this is but a policy adopted out of necessity, I have not yet heard of a better system. Our country, therefore, should also adopt regulations resembling those of the West but adapted to our own customs and conditions.

Since in the past the former samurai (*shizoku*)[11] have mostly been literate while few commoners other than the wealthy could read, the electorate should now be determined as including all the nobility (*kazoku*)[12] and former samurai as well as the highest taxpayers among the commoners. Among the commoners, voters in the cities might be limited to persons who possess title deeds (*chiken*)[13] to property with value of at least 200 to 1000 yen, and the minimum for villagers might be placed at 50 to 100 yen. Of course, we shall also exclude women, children, and incompetents as well as those who have been sentenced to penal servitude or more serious punishment.

Persons selected in this fashion will be called primary electors (*shosenja*),[14] and these primary electors will elect from each hundred of their peers one person of discernment known as a principal elector (*honsenja*).[15] Then the principal electors will elect persons as representatives who, assembled in parliament, will be charged with discussing national affairs as representatives of the entire country.

We should permit election of representatives without distinction as to whether they are nobles, lords, former samurai, men of letters, rich farmers, merchants, the poor, students, or rustics. It should be our only objective that these persons possess sufficient insight to determine right from wrong in national affairs. But we should exclude those condemned to penal servitude or more serious punishment.

Sixty to one hundred representatives should be elected from our population of 30 million, that is, one from each 250 to 500 thousand persons. Representatives should be replaced after terms of four years. It is important to divide the representatives into right and left ranks [of equal size] and to change one half every two years. Thus if the left rank is elected this year, the right rank will be elected two years hence.

What I have set forth above is a broad outline. Beginning with the designation of the speaker of parliament, the rules in all their details may well be formed by modifying the election laws of European countries to suit the cultural level of our people. In advance of this, however, draft proposals should be drawn up by especially appointed officials.

Those elected in the above manner should fully understand that they conduct their business as the representatives of the Japanese people in the true and proper sense of the word. How can we doubt that there are men of suitable understanding to provide 60 to 120 legislators from a population of 30 million? After all, this is the reason for reaffirming the purport of the five-article oath that all matters shall be determined by public discussion.[16]

Legislation is the special responsibility and special right of the representatives. Nevertheless, whether the laws they discuss shall be promulgated in our empire is especially the imperial prerogative of His Majesty the Emperor and, in no sense, a right of the representatives.

The representatives should also possess the right to supervise the great affairs of state, starting with revenues and expenditures. Only thus will the people check governmental autocracy, oblige the government to administer reasonably, and prevent the government from obstructing the natural course of enlightenment. How can such benefits be called trivial? Moreover, as our people have been long subject to oppressive rule, their spirit of liberty has broken down. That the national prestige and vigor are not flourishing may be attributed to the fact that this spirit is the national vigor.

There is no better way to promote and enhance the national prestige and vigor at present than to encourage popular participation in national affairs. And there is nothing like introducing a popularly elected assembly to stimulate participation by the people in national affairs. Such being the case, it seems that we must acknowledge that this reform assuredly arises from unavoidable circumstances and the dictates of the times. After all, where else is public discussion and public opinion leading [than to participation by the people in national affairs through a popularly elected assembly]?

An Outline of Western Culture (Continued)[17]

Nakamura Masanao

Born ten years before Luther, Machiavelli established a separate school of thought and greatly injured government and morals. Because of him, genuine ethics and true statecraft were impeded. After all, for the reason that Machiavelli directed his attention exclusively to enhancing man's power without being concerned with advancing the popular intellect, his theories, when practiced in Italy, ultimately so destroyed manners and customs that killing, poisoning, injuring and other crimes reached an all-time high. True human morality being thus gradually destroyed, methods for safeguarding human intercourse were also injured. Moreover, the great principle of human duty was obscured by atheists and preachers of superstition who together blindly agitated men's minds.

Machiavelli's discussions of political systems failed to penetrate the fundamentals of politics as they only propounded theories based on past practices. Since they also neither conformed to unchanging and impartial principles nor were based on the natural essence of man's character, his writings are only of minor significance in apprising scholars of past opinion. Looked at from the viewpoint of political economists today, adoption of his views as norms is to be feared as seriously injurious to society.

Even though Machiavelli's theories flourished for a time, the European countries understood their falseness and ceased to accept them as gospel as the level of scholarship advanced. The theories of [David] Hume were especially significant in destroying Machiavelli's distorted views. (According to Machiavelli, despots should take their own interests as their objective and favor a population in which the ignorant are numerous and the learned few.) Hume stated as follows:

> There are now various forms of government in the world that are day by day and month by month advancing toward perfection. It may be said of the enlightened countries that the political structures are most developed when the government system is monarchial. In the republics of antiquity, it was observed that republics rule with laws of great fairness rather than with the edicts of men. The rulers of the various nations today do not issue proclamations at will even though they surpass the people in enlightenment. All conduct government according to established laws whose completeness and minuteness are surprising. After all, when it comes to the people's industries (lands, homes, and wealth upon which men depend for their lives), the rulers carefully protect these from harm. (Countries are not the enterprises of monarchs alone. Since the so-called nation, *tenka,* is the possession of the nation, *tenka no tenka,*[18] and not the property of a single man, it is the responsibility of the ruler to assure the peace and happiness of the people by protecting their industries, preventing crises, and developing programs for profit and public

welfare.) Rulers endeavor to protect the hundred branches of agriculture and industry, nurturing them as if they were the monarch's own body. It is expected that they will encourage learning and skills to flourish and prosper. Seated in their palaces, they are just like fathers to many children. There were four tyrants among the twelve emperors of ancient Rome. Today there is not one in a hundred rulers who employs his power arbitrarily to oppress the people.

As has been stated above, the rulers of antiquity exerted their authority arbitrarily; the people, being ignorant, accepted the rulers' domination; and national foundations were not established. Today's rulers have adopted a general manner in which they have become like fathers and mothers to their subjects, bring happiness to the people by satisfying popular aspirations, and enjoy peace together with the people. What is the reason for this? It is nothing more than the spread of knowledge to all classes since the invention of printing.

In "free states" (this refers to countries in which the people are able to express their will freely), the spirit and enlightenment of the people have been enhanced by developing the press as a "bulwark" (this means castle) against the oppression of rulers. Since the introduction of printing, it has been recognized that the basic foundations of nations rest on the enlightenment of the people's minds, the prosperity of their finance and industry, and their general satisfaction in mind and body. Never failing to appreciate this, kings plan for the lasting benefit of their countries as a whole rather than for their own personal benefit. Thus if the world hereafter moves steadily toward enlightenment and if the people increasingly enjoy the blessing of happiness, will not the results be truly beyond imagination?

After Machiavelli's distorted views were halted, there appeared in succession such "philosophical reformers" as Nizolius, Patricius, and Gentilis.[19] The writings of Gentilis were more accepted in England and Germany than in his native Italy, where they were not highly respected. Since Gentilis believed in reforming the Catholic Church, he was expelled by the Italians and fled to England, where he received an appointment to the law faculty at Oxford in 1587. His book entitled *De jure belli et pacis* [*sic*][20] is a work honored by scholars as it denied Machiavelli's ideas and established a model for rulers.

The great philosopher [Tomasso] Campanella appeared later in Italy. Leibnitz compared Campanella to [Francis] Bacon, and he considered brilliant the discussions by Hobbes on "morals" and by Descartes on "physics" (the study of the physical structure of all things in the universe). Not only did Leibnitz feel that Bacon and Campanella were as far superior to Descartes and Hobbes as Heaven is to earth, but he also held that Bacon and Campanella really established the most important foundations of scholarship. (See a later issue for an outline of Bacon's philosophy.)

Note by the translator [Nakamura]: Western languages possess the word "liberty" for which there is no equivalent in either Chinese or Japanese. [Robert] Morrison translated the word as *jishu no ri* (the principle of self rule);[21] [Wilhelm] Lobschied, as *nin-ikō no ken* (the power of voluntary action).[22] After all, this amounts to the power of men to do as they please. In Western countries, where "civil liberty" is assumed to be the foundation of enlightened rule, the term is defined as the power of the people not to be oppressed or controlled as long as they honor laws beneficial to the public and profitable to the community. If they speak of the term "religious liberty," therefore, they mean allowing men to follow the religion that they believe in their hearts to be good without being pressed or forcefully robbed of their persuasion by those above. In the West during the Middle Ages, rulers desired vigorously to compel the people to follow their [the rulers'] faith as they did not understand the truly correct way to govern, and there have been numerous instances until the recent past in which rulers have coerced men's minds by imposing strict prohibitions. Today, Europeans have acquired "liberty" and follow their hearts' desires since they have generally destroyed the customs of trifling with human freedoms. No longer silenced by useless restrictions, individuals may expand their aspirations and plan alike for public benefits. Men's hearts daily move toward good, and the custom has prevailed that the pen and the sword are equal.

[1]Continued from Issue Nine.

[2]*Jōtei,* 上帝.

[3]Li Hung-chang, 李鴻章, then governor-general of the province of Chihli (直隷) and the most prominent official of imperial China.

[4]Continued from Issue Ten.

[5]See Issue Three, footnote three, and the introduction for the Meirokusha and the memorial by Soejima Taneomi (副島種臣) and others calling for a popularly elected assembly. Doubtless in part responding to the demands for an assembly, the Japanese government in May 1874 published an imperial rescript directing the convening of an assembly of regional officials (*chihōkan kaigi,* 地方官會議) as representatives of the entire nation to advise on the determination of laws.

[6]It is unclear from the vague language whether Tsuda here refers to a specific individual. From the essay itself, it appears that the three types of representatives were those drawn from the nobility, appointed by the Government, and elected by the people.

[7]*Shinshin kazoku,* 縉紳華族.

[8]*Chishiki,* 智識.

[9]*Daikan,* 代官, the designation for the intendants of the Tokugawa *bakufu.*

[10]From book thirteen entitled Tzŭ-Lu (子路) of the *Analects* (*Lun Yü,* 論語) of Confucius.

[11]*Shizoku,* 士族.

[12]*Kazoku,* 華族, members of the old court aristocracy and former great feudal lords (*daimyō,* 大名).

[13]*Chiken,* 地券, title deeds confirming land ownership that were issued by the Meiji government after the abolition of feudalism.

[14]*Shosenja,* 初撰者

[15]*Honsenja,* 本撰者.

[16]Five Article Imperial Oath, *Gokajō no Goseimon,* 五箇條ノ御誓文, the declaration by the Meiji Emperor on 6 April 1868 that promised determination of all matters by open discussion.

[17]Continued from Issue Eleven.

[18]*Tenka no tenka,* 天下ノ天下.

[19]Mario Nizzoli, Francesco Patrizzi, and Alberico Gentili.

[20]Nakamura here mistakenly gives the title of a treatise by Hugo Grotius. Gentili wrote *De jure belli libri tres* and *De juri belli commentatio.*

[21]*Jishu no ri,* 自主ノ理. Robert Morrison was the first Protestant missionary to China dispatched by the London Missionary Society in 1807.

[22]*Nin-ikō no ken,* 任意行之權. [Wilhelm] Lobschied of the Rhenish Mission is remembered for the medical treatises that he prepared for the Chinese.

Church and State in America (Continuation from Number Six)[1]

Katō Hiroyuki, translator

Part Four. The Importance of Never Using Religion as a Tool for Covering Crime. (With Reference to Religion in General Rather Than a Particular Faith.)

It is recognized as a matter of course under the republican system in the United States that freedom of conscience is one of the rights invariably guaranteed to man. Nevertheless, no one disputes the fact that an individual is never allowed to cherish the hope that he may use his faith in a religion as a cover for his crimes. Should men be allowed ultimately to escape punishment because of religious freedom, there will then inevitably be such extreme cases as the fellows who, having fallen under the spell of false religion or being intoxicated by heresy, willfully injure the legal system of the country, or the Thuggs (an Indian religious sect) who freely make human sacrifices to gods, or the church officials who themselves revive laws for the persecution of nonbelievers with arbitrary cruelty.[2]

Even though free countries never decide that a religion shall or shall not be tolerated simply because it is a particular sect, governments must invariably have the right to forbid or to punish clear cases of injury to public order or opposition to public morals, notwithstanding the fact that the guilty persons may be acting in conformity with their religious principles. Examples of such injury are polygamy among the Mormons (a church in the United States), killing of their own daughters by the Chinese, and voluntary suicide by women in India. (According to custom in India, it is regarded as loyal for the wife to follow her husband in death by throwing herself on his funeral pyre.)

Therefore, it should be provided in law that the government has a special right to forbid any act injurious to national security even though such act may be allowed by religion. This should never be mistakenly regarded as a right that has been conceded by the church. (The Christian Church is implied here.) Generally speaking, the family is the foundation of the state, and true social intercourse really derives from the family. Furthermore, in the various Western countries, it is assumed that family relations are rooted in monogamous marriage. In the final analysis, this is why the civilization of the West clearly surpasses that of the Eastern lands.[3]

Even though marriage is a contract under civil law in the United States, the people generally regard it as a religious matter and are normally married by religious rites. Since the churches are allowed by law to perform marriages between members according to their own rites, their marriage services range from the simple rites of the "Quaker" sect (a Christian sect) to the extremely elaborate rites of the Catholics. Nevertheless, the stipulations that determine the validity of marriages are invariably established by civil law. Since civil law (not church law) establishes all the regulations essential for validating marriages as well as the provisos for the civil and religious officials who conduct marriages, even church officials are entrusted by law with the right to perform marriages. If they do not fully observe the marriage regulations established by law, they cannot be allowed to perform valid marriages.

In general, churchmen only perform marriages by authority of the government as this right is never derived from their proper churchly authority, and registry of marriages is entirely by government offices, never by church officials. Since there naturally is also complete freedom to seek marriage in a civil ceremony without resorting to a religious service, a marriage, of course, may not be invalidated just because a religious service has not been performed. The state also possesses the right to regulate the conditions of both divorce and marriage. With an eye to tranquility in social intercourse, it permits only monogamous marriage and holds the right to punish polygamy and adultery as major national crimes.

Whereas the religion of the Mormons permits one's husband to take several wives, the Free Lovers assert that to change spouses at will is one of man's inherent rights. (There has recently arisen a party in America that assumes that couples have complete freedom to change spouses at will in conformity with changing sentiments of husband and wife.) Nevertheless, the state invariably has the right to interfere and admonish as follows: "Marriage practices must always be controlled by law since the right or wrong of marriages invariably later affects the interests of society and since begetting of children begins with marriage."

Thus when a husband takes several wives or when free love is permitted, rearing the offspring will invariably become a public responsibility as the parents will be unable to raise their families. After all, this is why the evils of polygamy and free love cannot be allowed. Therefore, I would say that it is naturally important for government itself, in conformity with the logic of morals and utilizing its appropriate rights that relate to society, to establish laws prohibiting polygamy and free-mating even though the Mormons and the Free Lovers claim that these evil customs are sanctioned by the religions in which they believe.

I shall defer until later my discussion on why the government properly has an obligation to follow the moral path. It is my intention here only to prevent misunderstanding of religious freedom by discussing its true meaning. Even though it is important for government to be entirely separated from church affairs, it also should not disregard morality. Even though it is important for government always to recognize the right of religious freedom, it also must not tolerate immorality and wrong among its subjects. [To be continued in the next issue.]

Imagination (*Sōzō*)[4]

Tsuda Mamichi

Imagination is a succession of forms conceived by men during meditation that closely resembles a mirage. A mirage is without substance, but its vivid forms appear as a reflection in the atmospheric mirror. [Similarly], even though there is no actual trace of men or of the manifold things of the universe in our hearts, imagination is a clear reflection in our hearts, there being nothing that we cannot conceive during meditation. The Japanese word *omokage* is a synonym for *sōzō* or imagination. Some mistakenly think that *omoiyari* is the Japanese [*kun*][5] reading of the characters for *sōzō,* imagination. *Omoiyari,* however, had the meaning of casting out trouble [*haimon*][6] in ancient Japanese, and it has assumed the meaning of compassion [*jo*][7] in common speech.

Imagination is different from memory. Memory is not forgetting a previously noted experience. Imagination is contriving anew what has not yet been previously experienced. Since imagination is not without some connection to previous experience, however, it is naturally related to memory. The plays and novels by Japanese and Chinese usually arise from their authors' imaginations, and the verse by the most famous European poets also generally is all derived from imagination.

Events in the antiquities of various countries as transmitted by the ancients are a mixture of imagination and memory. The doings on the Plain of High Heaven [Takama-ga-hara],[8] in Hades [Yomi],[9] or at the Dragon King's Palace [Ryūgū][10] of Japan as well as the legends of Egypt, Greece, India, and Rome are all absurdities unworthy of belief because they arose from the imagination of the ancients. Did not Confucius decide to omit from his editing of the *Book of History* everything before T'ang and Yü because he saw no value in teaching myths?[11] This elder should be praised for the high level of his perception. The imaginations of Buddha and Christ happened to coincide in their respective comments on heaven and hell. It may be said that the views of Daruma and his followers were also elevated when they penetrated the truth with one stroke.[12]

Then did Confucius and Daruma wholly eschew imagination and are they to be compared with Lao Tzŭ's accomplished man who does not dream?[13] It may be replied that Confucius and Daruma were both men who employed their powers of imagination to a great extent. Confucius' commentaries on the *Book of Changes* and Daruma's enlightenment through meditation [*zazen kampō*][14] are all forms of broad imagination. It is only that their imagination was somewhat different and more elevated than that of the ancients. Even though there were distinctions in the degrees of profundity in the later Chinese studies on the natural principles of the five elements and the florid scholarship of rote memory,[15] they were generally not without imagination. The empiricism of the Ch'ing scholars and modern scientific research in the West employ only a minimum of imagination.[16] Yet in such matters as appreciating that the earth is oval or discovering new stars, scientific research generally only establishes Heaven's Laws after verification of what originally had been imagined.

What we refer to as the principles of morality or political economy largely arise from imagination. If conjectures on things are verified by experiment, these principles are then regarded as unchanging Laws of Heaven. But if conjectures are proved wrong by experiment, we know that principles diverge from facts. Verification, however, is easy in the natural sciences and difficult in the humanities. This is why metaphysical disciplines are so divided that they cannot reach conclusions. Even the self-evident principles governing such phenomena as comets and eclipses do not escape from unsupported hypotheses. How much more difficult it is to understand the humanities!

The black man cannot become white because he honors the black skin. We Japanese are indeed of the yellow race, but we enjoy the whiteness of skin rather than its yellowness. Since this is, after all, an innate character, it is instinctively our nature to enjoy Western styles. My theory should not be judged as wholly imaginary since our people, hardly ten years after the country abandoned its seclusion policies, crave all things Western from clothing and utensils to the institutions of civilization. There is absolutely no room for doubt regarding clothing and utensils, which are evident at a glance.

Our people, however, cannot easily investigate and understand the institutions of civilization that have been derived from interminable disputes through countless centuries of learning and experience. The Siamese do not know ice, and the men of inner Africa do not know white men. Even though their wise men chance to hear of and to imagine ice or white men, they are like the blind men who imagined the elephant.[17] Today's so-called enlightened scholars imagine liberty without knowing the price of liberty, and they freely discuss French codes, English law, and American government without studying law and political economy. In extreme cases, they would forthwith adopt a translation of the French Civil Code as the civil code of Japan. They are exactly like the Siamese who misunderstand ice or the Africans who imagine white men. How dangerous this is!

Should We Not First Determine the Political Structure before Introducing a Popularly Elected Assembly?

Sakatani Shiroshi

In the recent vigorous discussion about a popularly elected assembly, not one has wholly denied the system, the multiplicity of views notwithstanding. More particularly, there is general concensus that it would be premature to introduce such an assembly before we have reached the level of enlightenment. While I believe that it is indeed too early, to assume the time to be premature is to be waiting achievement of the level of enlightenment.

There are also things that must be done during the waiting period. One of these is education, but there is also the root of the undertaking. Failing to plant this root, the popularly elected assembly will be no more than leaves and branches. If you ask what the root is, I would suggest that it is establishing the objective of our political structure.[18] Judging from history, the political structures of nations have all emerged from their inborn natures. Yet the reform of political structures is generally produced by political disturbances, and political disturbances are by Heaven's Nature. It is man's responsibility to judiciously cultivate [*saisei hoshō*][19] Heaven's Nature. To leave political disturbances to Nature is like the mean man of trivial mind who nonchalantly plays on thin ice.

It is said that Washington and other statesmen labored seriously and diligently in numerous conferences before the formation of the United States. This is the common method of superior men as well as the source of the present expression of opinions on a popularly elected assembly. Personally, however, I doubt the utility of a popularly elected assembly before the political structure is determined. Then why is it that the polemicists have not one word for the political structure when they talk lightly of establishing a popularly elected assembly?

The popularly elected assembly is an instrument for joint rule by high and low (*jōge dōji*).[20] When the authors of the memorial on the popularly elected assembly[21] now want to establish such an assembly from above, what profit will arise therefrom if the structure for harmonious rule by high and low has not yet been determined? My scholarship is shallow. If a popularly elected assembly can be successfully introduced as a separate undertaking before we have established the structure for harmonious rule by high and low, then I have erred, I humbly apologize, and I shall welcome your instruction. If such is not the case and if the two are inseparable, then we had best first consider the establishment of the political structure for harmonious rule by high and low before we attempt to introduce a popularly elected assembly.

Or is it that the memorialists speak under the guise of a popularly elected assembly out of respect for the imperial household even though they intend to achieve harmonious rule by high and low? Such conduct is the flattering subservience of women that actually deceives the imperial family. If there is deception, then disrespect is extreme. We should adopt man's attitude of genuine respect. I am also generally of the opinion that we should now promote theories for determining the political structure of harmonious rule by high and low, a structure that will lead to what we earnestly desire: protection of the imperial line as well as the enlightenment, strength, and prosperity of the empire.

Men of the slightest learning all know that the national structure (*kokutai*)[22] of our country differs from those of other nations, as the hearts of Japanese have always been bound to the unbroken imperial line. Truly, if the just and upright savants of the United States and Sweden were reared in this country, there is clearly no doubt that, from the point of view of protecting the people, they would neither run counter to the natural, national structure nor establish a federal republic. The men who now desire to establish a popularly elected assembly as well as those who think the assembly premature without denying it also invariably aim only to protect the imperial line and to promote the prosperity and strength of the empire.

I need not discuss here the fact that the injury from changing dynasties and electing chiefs of state has already been pointed out by savants who were born in countries where such traditions prevail. Nevertheless, sovereigns change if the dynasty does not. And even though our dynasty, of course, has provided for the luminous transmission of imperial virtue, there have inherently been fluctuations in this imperial virtue over the centuries. In the old days, the domination of the Fujiwara and the hegemony of the military class both arose from these fluctuations.[23] Moreover, when a violent or dull sovereign emerged, the laws of his enlightened predecessors were completely destroyed. Even though a later enlightened ruler expended his strength in restoration, he would die of old age before he could attempt anything new. And if there were destruction under a succeeding stupid and unwise ruler, this was only trouble for an enlightened successor. When there are such fluctuations in imperial virtue, how can the country be strong and prosperous and how can rule be enlightened?

We should reflect on the fact that our country and China have experienced repeated political disturbances during their progress toward enlightenment. Even if a stupid sovereign appears where the dynasty is protected by harmonious rule by high and low, the former enlightenment only stagnates without regressing in the least. Moreover, when an enlightened monarch and ministers again emerge, time is not lost in unnecessary reconstruction, and civilization and enlightenment invariably advance by several degrees. This is a principle that has been recently exemplified by Prussia and that conforms to the course of Nature. Still more valid is the principle today when the times are different from the past!

It is the general situation today that greedy and avaricious powers are pressing on each other's borders, overcoming the weak and becoming intimate with the strong. One day, fellows like Masakado and Takauji[24] may emerge in foreign countries to take advantage of a moment when our country is weak. With what arguments will we then be able to dissuade them and with what policies will we then frustrate them? This is what we should really fear. At this time, when an enlightened sovereign reigns, when the high places are filled by the wise, and when unprecedented reforms are being carried out, why do we delay in establishing the objective of the political structure? Because we have not yet established this objective, the people are without principle and without faith in their leaders, while the leaders fail earnestly to discuss and repeatedly avoid decisions, the level of today's enlightenment notwithstanding.

To press for a popularly elected assembly under such conditions would be like firing without a target. Not only would the assembly be a waste like the late *shūgiin*.[25] It would probably generate destruction. Not only would there be the injury from the popularly elected assembly. Schools and the like that lead to civilization and enlightenment would become enterprises endangering the imperial line by promoting men's wisdom, advancing craftiness, and fomenting great disturbances.

As was clearly demonstrated by England in America, oppression of the people in different countries has been followed by disturbances. Judged from the point of view of later generations, it is extremely fine that the great disturbance in America was followed by good government. Should we then allow Nature to take its course without now doing anything? Is there anyone who wants a disturbance that is extremely injurious to the country? Enlightenment and progress without disturbance are fine achievements in the world and the great obligation of man.

Our country is only an island in the sea, its superlative beauty notwithstanding. If we reach the point of allowing Nature free course without exerting ourselves to the utmost, if the people conduct themselves wantonly without regulation, and if they are uncontrolled in body as well as neglectful of the spirit, will not our country, like Poland or Mongolia, surely suffer some unexpected disaster when the foreign powers seize this opportunity? Should such a fate by chance befall the country, we of today would never be able to atone to later generations for our criminal neglect of duty.

What then should we now determine to be the objective of our national structure? Some may say that what we really want is to add the strong points of Russia to our political system. This cannot be accomplished, however, as the times, the countries, the factors, and the trends differ. Since England is a country in which these differences are not so marked, we can only adopt the strong points of the English system of harmonious rule by high and low. Even so, the fundamental rights of liberty and the details of the arrangements naturally cannot be completely identical given the differences between the countries and the peoples.

It should be the grand objective of high and low only to adopt the good and fine points in which England excels. This policy was established at the beginning of the Restoration when [the Emperor] stated that "assemblies should be widely convoked and all matters decided by public opinion."[26] This is the objective of harmonious rule by high and low. Since the emperor's wishes have come to naught and since the results have been insignificant, however, all business is in confusion, and men generally have lost their principles. Now when discussion of a popularly elected assembly has appeared, yesterday's enlightened imperial rescript and today's agitation for the assembly unexpectedly point to the same end. This end is none other than harmonious rule by high and low.

Even at this level of natural development, some still admonish against giving offense while others say that we should be careful. How dangerous it is to allow Nature to take its course as if we were sitting in a tottering house without undertaking repairs! It may be asked from what the practice of harmonious rule by high and low will arise if it is not from a popularly elected assembly. My response would be that we should first lay the foundations before building the house. A popularly elected assembly being the pillars and the beams, how can we erect it without first establishing the foundations? Should it then be asked where we shall begin the foundations for the structure of harmonious rule by high and low, I would respond that we shall surely hit the mark if we patiently and unwaveringly aim at the target after establishing the objective.

Once we have clearly established the objective, its policies and good institutions will spontaneously arise from public discussion. Just to cite one or two examples, ministers should strictly observe methods of harmonious discussion without the petty foolishness of resigning or being dismissed if they disagree but once. They will perfect the objective of harmonious rule by high and low if they carry out appropriate policies upon which they have reached agreement after repeated discussions.

This objective of harmonious rule by high and low will also surely be perfected if the various ministries present their respective views without allowing factions within their ministries to put the public interest in second place. So that nothing will be carried out without discussion, there must be harmonious discussion between high and low among the ministries, within the ministries, and in especially established committees. There will then invariably be discussion if there is intent to act. If there are difficulties in executing policies that have been decided after discussion, persons responsible for carrying out these difficult policies will achieve the objective of harmonious rule by high and low by invariably reaching decisions after vigorous discussion.

Most officials, without exerting themselves to the utmost, only pay attention to their monthly stipends, being jealous and subject to flattery as well as delinquent and intemperate. Therefore, shunning trouble, despising the unlettered, and failing to make clear that all matters should be determined by public discussion, these high officials conduct affairs without earnestly and skillfully developing their own abilities and without understanding administration through broad consultation with their subordinates. Lesser officials are now enraged by their superior's contempt for them. Seeing the vacillations, the unfairness, and the partiality in his policies, they privately sneer at his foolishness, saying:

> The man becomes lower as the official rises. We stand below this foolish chief without being consulted by him. What concern is it of ours how he transacts business? We are content if only our salaries suffice to sustain us.

In extreme cases, out of anger or hate, they vent their discontent in inappropriate places, and the chief for his part calls his subordinates malcontents and brutes. We should appreciate that the common people will generally be still more extreme if the high and low officials thus diverge in different directions, being without principle in their hearts or assurance in their views.

How then shall we implant enlightened customs and how shall we achieve the reality of a popularly elected assembly? The evils have extended thus far because we have not made clear the objective of harmonious rule by high and low, having failed to establish the principle of deciding everything by public opinion. There is consequently nothing for us to do but to establish the design of harmonious rule by high and low, restore its benefits, and banish the above evils. If we solemnly establish this objective in actuality, then teaching in the schools will readily flourish, and an enlightened administration will function with increasing ease. In addition to this, if famous and promising gentlemen in the provinces are officially selected each year in accordance with public opinion and gathered in assemblies and if popular elections are thereafter gradually introduced, there will be indications of success in three years, small success in seven years, and the ultimate achievement of the so-called popularly elected assembly after but ten years.

Thus will we assure beyond doubt the everlasting rule of the imperial line, establish a really strong, prosperous, and enlightened country, and clarify the path for protecting the people. Even though these ill-conceived opinions of mine may disturb the government, there is an order that permits us to risk the government's displeasure.[27] If we hesitatingly fail to set things right, when shall we be free of anxiety? I would humbly beg my colleagues' opinions on when foolish Sakatani's objective will be achieved.

[1]Continuation of Katō's translation from Joseph Parrish Thompson, *Kirche und Staat in den Vereinigten Staaten* (Berlin, 1873).

[2]The original refers here to restoration of the Inquisition.

[3]Thompson made no reference to the superiority of Western over Eastern civilization.

[4]*Sōzō*, 想像.

[5]*Kun*, 訓.

[6]*Haimon*, 排悶.

[7]*Jo*, 恕.

[8]Takama-ga-hara, 高天原, the heavenly abode of deities in the Shintō (神道) faith.

[9]Yomi, 黄泉.

[10]Ryūgū, 龍宮, the undersea palace to which Urashima Tarō (浦島太郎) was conveyed by a tortoise, according to popular legend.

[11]T'ang, 唐, and Yü, 虞, refers to the times of the legendary emperors Yao (堯) and Shun (舜).

[12]Daruma, 達磨. Tsuda here refers to the enlightenment of Zen (禪) Buddhism. Daruma or Bodhidharma was the Indian holy man said to have brought Zen (Ch'an) teachings from India to China by sea in the sixth century.

[13]*Shijin yume naki mono*, 至人夢ナキ者. This is the man who, according to the tradition of the philosophers Lao Tzu (老子) and Chuang Tzu (莊子), does not dream because he is without irrelevant thoughts and involvements.

[14]*Zazen kampō*, 坐禪觀法.

[15]Natural principles of the five elements, *gogyō seiri*, 五行性理, i.e., Neo-Confucianism of the Chu Hsi School (*Shushi-gaku*, 朱子學).

[16]The Ch'ing (淸) empiricists studied the ancient Chinese texts with the inductive method and sought to base their conclusions on solid evidence.

[17]This is the Indian fable of a king who summoned several blind men to touch an elephant and tell him what it was. One blind man declared the elephant to be a wall after touching its side; the second thought it a giant snake after grasping its long nose; the third guessed it to be a snake or a rope after fingering its tail; and the fourth thought it just like the trunk of a tree after feeling its leg.

[18]Objective of the political structure, *seitai mokuteki*, 政體目的. It is unclear exactly what Sakatani meant by the objective of the political structure. Through his writings, however, he repeatedly affirms his devotion to Japan's unique, unbroken imperial line, and his essay on a popularly elected assembly in Issue Twenty-Eight suggests his objective to be protection of both the imperial line and the people through the timely adoption of harmonious rule by high and low, i.e., a limited monarchy including a deliberative assembly.

[19]*Saisei hoshō*, 裁成輔相, is a phrase derived from the *Book of Changes* (*I Ching*, 易經) that Sakatani employs repeatedly in his later essays in which he urges a course of moderate development in conformity with Nature.

[20]*Jōge dōji*, 上下同治, a phrase commonly used by writers of this period when discussing parliamentary government or limited monarchy.

[21]The memorial by Soejima Taneomi (副島種臣) and other former government members in February 1874 calling for the establishment of a popularly elected assembly.

[22]*Kokutai*, 國體.

[23]The Fujiwara (藤原) family emerged to dominate the throne in the Ninth Century and in turn lost power to the rising regional military houses (*buke*, 武家) during the twelfth century and after.

[24][Taira] Masakado, 平將門, and [Ashikaga] Takauji, 足利尊氏, traditionally regarded by the Japanese as infamous traitors. Masakado attempted unsuccessfully to establish an imperial government in eastern Japan in the early tenth century, and Takauji turned against Emperor Go-Daigo (後醍醐) after the Kemmu Restoration (Kemmu Chūkō, 建武中興) of 1333.

[25]*Shūgiin*, 集議院, a deliberative assembly established in 1869 that exerted little influence on national policies down to its abolition in 1873.

[26]A phrase drawn from the Five Article Imperial Oath (*Gokajō no Goseimon*, 五箇條ノ御誓文) of 6 April 1868.

[27]I am unable to identify the order here mentioned. Sakatani may refer to the above article in the Imperial Oath of 1868 that was re-affirmed in the imperial rescript of May 1874 calling together an assembly of regional officials.

Knowledge Part One[1]

Nishi Amane

Wisdom is an essential part of man's mind that is associated with volition and emotion. Moreover, since its position is highest and its influence strongest, wisdom at times establishes its control over the associated volition and emotion and then forces them into subservience. The kingdom of man's mind cannot enjoy peace if volition and emotion do not abide by wisdom's control and follow its orders. There is then insatiable pursuit of pleasure within the palace, and persons outside the dynasty like Wang Mang and Ts'ao Ts'ao arbitrarily exert their power.[2]

The uses of wisdom are extremely broad. Among the manifold matters in the world, human deportment, treatment of other men, the governing of nations, and the conquest of all lands within the four seas are invariably ascribed to wisdom. Alexander's appearance in Greece, Caesar's domination of Rome, Napoleon's reverberations through Europe, Genghiz Khan's terror in the northern desert, and the Taikō's rumblings in the Eastern Seas[3] all arose from their cerebrums. Reason is the enemy with which wisdom is incessantly fighting in the war called scholarship or research and learning. Therefore, when wisdom fights reason, captures a part of reason, and makes this captured reason its follower, this reason also ultimately serves wisdom under wisdom's control.

The war of wisdom is called scholarship; its ramparts, schools. Schools embrace the books, pictures, and equipment that are the essential tools with which wisdom attacks, captures, and presses reason into subservience, just as a military commander employs his warships and guns. In this unceasing war between wisdom and reason, wisdom daily assembles the elements of reason that it has captured and uses them for its own purposes. As the captures of reason increasingly mount, the generals of wisdom daily become more powerful.

At times, there are those among the enemy who falsely masquerade under the name of reason. Far from bringing profit, even though they be captured by wisdom, these fakers consume supplies and destroy courage. Therefore, when wisdom fights well, it first distinguishes between true and false and then prevents false reason from entering his ranks. If it captures reason in this manner, wisdom will expand its power by accumulating the captured elements of reason over a long period of time, an achievement still greater than the expansion of Ch'in over the six states of ancient China.[4] In addition, since knowledge is the area commanded by wisdom, knowledge cannot be gained without employing the tools of scholarship in an unremitting struggle of a hundred wars. And since those ranging from sages to lowly couples invariably possess this wisdom, none are without an area of knowledge at their command. It is only that the areas are not equal in size.

Now if we employ ordinary words to establish distinctions within wisdom, its nature is customarily of three types: talent (*sai*), ability (*nō*), and understanding (*shiki*).[5] Since talent pertains to the objective aspect of wisdom, it is concerned with particular skills in each area of knowledge. Therefore, even though there are differences in degree of talent, it is usually confined to particular spheres, such as the talent of painters, the talent of writers, or the talent of poets. Ability pertains to the subjective aspect of wisdom. Without necessarily extending to particulars, ability is something that covers types and classes, such as the ability of national officials or that of local officials.

Of the two, talent is most commonly associated with physical principles (*butsuri*), whereas ability usually relates to mental principles (*shinri*).[6] Nevertheless, men of the past did not understand the distinction between these principles (*ri*),[7] and they only used the terms instinctively. Understanding is different from talent and ability. Even though its fundamental essence is based upon wisdom, understanding, of course, cannot exist if it has not acquired command over a large territory after it has fought and subdued a large part of reason. It is not invariably necessary to cultivate talent and ability, as they are innate (*yasei*).[8] They become useful with only a little training. Just as great timbers sometimes appear in the wild (*yasei*), men who rose to the top like Genghiz Khan and the Taikō were examples of extraordinary innate genius.

Coming to understanding, even though understanding may be innate, it is for the most part like a plant reared by a gardener. Understanding in its essence combines the objective and subjective views and clarifies distinctly and delineates in detail the roots and branches of reason. Even though there are instances of innate understanding, therefore, it cannot finally be perfected without the assistance of cultivation. Yet understanding may be partly innate since cultivated people are not always endowed with it.

On the whole, even though the three qualities of talent, ability, and understanding may sometimes appear in one person, this is extremely rare. Moreover, they are always possessed in varying degrees. While they are possessed innately or cultivated to varying degrees in each individual, however, all are equally rooted in wisdom and can consequently profit from cultivation. Volition and emotion differ from understanding in that they seem not to profit from training.

If we consider the suitable application of talent, ability, and understanding, having discussed the fundamental nature of wisdom in mental philosophy, it was generally reasonable in antiquity to speak of naming sages to high rank and able men as administrators. Following this principle, let the wise men of understanding occupy high stations and decide the direction or administration after reflecting on the past and determining their country's future course. Having impartially decided initial methods according to the existing situation, they may successfully adjust their policies to changing circumstances. Then if the men of talent and ability diligently pursue their duties in obedience to the aims of their superiors, the tranquility of the country will be within grasp. Should this principle be contradicted, Heaven's Judgment will surely follow.

"Liberty" (Continued from Issue Nine)

Mitsukuri Rinshō

Men in Greece already practiced liberty in ancient times. In a country like Sparta, ruling power was held by a council of thirty representatives of the people and by five administrative officers called *ephors,* while the king's power was limited to just leading his soldiers. Nevertheless, if one considers conditions in Sparta at that time, it will be seen that private affairs and, naturally, public affairs were all determined by the government. Thus the government interfered in relations between husbands and wives as well as parents and children to regulate family affairs, divided the people into classes especially assigning their occupations, suppressed scholarship, restricted education so that it was directed toward the sole objective of preserving bodily strength, and passed strict laws for the suppression of luxury.

Since the state thus invariably interfered in all matters, the *ephors'* rule had as its fundamental purpose the administration of the state's affairs in accordance with the will of the people. From the point of view of individuals, however, the Spartan government was nothing more than tyranny. The people, therefore, were absolutely unable to have liberty as individuals even though they seemed to possess liberty as a group.

In Greece of that time, however, Athens differed from Sparta. The Athenians were the first to enjoy liberty as individuals. Judging from the oration in which Pericles mourned the Athenians who died for their country fighting the Persians, it seems that all citizens had the right to participate in government. They consequently followed their own volition when electing their representatives, managing their family matters, and providing their food, clothing, and tools.

As their attention was wholly turned toward learning and enlightenment during peace, the Athenians were not invariably required to regard military training and gymnastics as their prime undertaking. Reading what they liked as individuals and mutually exchanging opinions, they seem to have achieved complete liberty. In addition to being brave in spirit and quite willing to risk danger without thinking of themselves, therefore, the Athenians also surpassed their contemporaries in their pursuit of letters and of the arts and sciences.

Thus, even though Athens included slaves who, like living tools, were unable to enjoy any liberty, those who were once designated citizens were no different from European and American citizens of today in so far as they possessed equal rights and really defended their political liberty.

Rome, which arose after the fall of Greece, was indeed a republic in name, but its people could not really enjoy political liberty. When the government suppressed the rights of the people, it acted on behalf of the interests of the entire nation and invariably intervened in the private affairs of individual households. Thereby winning victory after victory in war after war, Rome quickly became extremely wealthy and powerful and built a state of unprecedented size.

While Rome indeed achieved success by expanding the power of the nation through the suppression of the rights of individuals, should we not deplore that it vainly expanded its authority by restricting the cherished aspirations of the people and by completely suppressing liberty? A succession of villainous generals and cunning rogues emerged meanwhile who regarded the people as rubbish and who sought to employ their authority to realize their ambitions. The national structure was finally converted into an empire, and the liberty of the people was thereby completely destroyed.

When the German barbarians invaded the empire, the Roman people for years had been suppressed by tyrannical rulers and grown effeminate from customs of decadence and subservience. Without heart to think of their country, the weakened people had not strength to oppose their enemies. The conditions in Rome having thus finally reached the point of collapse, the empire could no longer be held together. By the end of the 400s, the Roman Empire of the West was completely destroyed, and the Eastern Roman Empire barely survived at Constantinople.

The German barbarians, who swept across Europe and destroyed Rome, were indeed uncultured and unenlightened, but they were completely unwilling to be restricted or oppressed by their chiefs when they fought and hunted in their native mountains and marshes. Since they were individually endowed by nature with liberty, they later advanced gradually to the level of enlightenment. And they were able to preserve their liberty when they established states in France, Italy, Germany and England.

The feudal system of the Middle Ages later produced extreme injuries, and rival lords, asserting their authority in the four quarters, daily engaged in internecine warfare. But even then, when their lives were in danger, the people did not lose their fundamental liberty. By the 1200s, in northern Germany, the people of the city states known as "Hanseatic towns" had established city councils of their elected leaders and were joined together for the conduct of free governments. Then when the Eastern Roman Empire was destroyed in the 1400s, its eminent scholars were scattered through Europe, broadly spreading in the four directions the learning of ancient Greece and the ideas of liberty.

Europeans, therefore, habitually labored to maintain their rights of liberty without ever forgetting them. Once various territorial magnates who had gathered powerful armies were gradually destroyed and the feudal system had finally come to an end, however, kings and emperors of various countries again conducted absolute government. It may be said that despotism reached its peak in the late 1600s, when King Louis XIV of France, speaking of himself, stated, "I am the state." This injury reached such a point that, after the people could no longer endure mounting years of oppression, the Great French Revolution suddenly broke out in the late 1700s, and the people joined in proclaiming the principles of liberty.

The Americans were already supporting the rights of liberty, their country having turned against England and established an independent nation. Outside of England, however, few of the European peoples possess true liberty since their advocates of liberty have generally been too radical to complete their designs. Even so and in sum, once people have tasted and experienced liberty for a long time, their kings are unable to restore autocratic and despotic powers. Reflecting on current trends, therefore, since the various nations have severally reached the point of entrusting legislative power to representatives of the people in parliaments, this is sufficient to indicate that the powers of kings are gradually declining, while the people are moving toward the fullness of liberty.

The Advantages of Currency

Sugi Kōji

Wealth is generally not produced unless there are avenues of trade. A person may indeed trade the shoes he manufactures for food and other daily necessities. But if he cannot trade his shoes, he has no reason for manufacturing them, and he will consequently produce no wealth. The shoemaker's shoes only produce wealth and have utility for him if he exchanges them for what he needs. Yet barter is not easy since it is difficult for one person to quickly find another whose desires correspond with his needs.

Even though a fellow may want shoes, he cannot barter for them unless he has commodities desired by the shoemaker. Take the example of A who weaves cotton but lacks food. If B has food but does not desire cotton fabric, barter cannot then be carried out forthwith. Should B answer that he will exchange for a desk when A is obliged to ask him for what he will trade his food, A will then search for a person who will barter a desk for his fabric. Only after finding such person will A be able to satisfy the demands of three parties by trading the fabric for the desk and the desk for the food. Nevertheless, since A suffers loss of valuable time when he searches for a person who will exchange a desk for cotton fabric, barter is in fact an awkward operation.

Moreover, the greatest difficulty in bartering goods arises from the fact that they have different values. This difficulty may be avoided if trade is facilitated by dividing commodities into small units. It may be convenient for A to barter varying amounts of cotton if he regulates its value by altering the amount sold. If he wants to exchange an umbrella he manufactures for food, however, he cannot reduce the size of the umbrella to conform with the desired price. And he thus cannot avoid loss amounting to the difference between the values of one umbrella and the food if he makes the exchange. His only alternative is to refuse to exchange for the food he wants.

Such being the case, if we can always trade the goods we want to trade for what we demand regardless of the amount and if we are well informed on who desire the goods we produce, the difficulties in trading are invariably eased, and exchange is further convenienced. Since we convert gold and silver into currency to promote both these beneficial conditions, currency possesses five advantages as an essential commodity for carrying on trade.

One. Small pieces of gold and silver are rarely destroyed or reduced through use.

Two. Gold and silver are easily divisible, and they may be readily melted into lumps without reducing their value appreciably.

Three. Gold and silver are convenient for carrying, a reason why they are suitable for daily use.

Four. The value of gold and silver rarely changes whereas the value of other commodities fluctuates considerably. This is because gold and silver are extremely difficult to produce, circulate broadly, and are very convenient to transport. Thus even if production increases, [their value will change very little] because the metals will rapidly go into circulation and because the amount produced will still be small as compared with the amount in circulation.

With the passage of time, men have finally come to appreciate that these are the most important reasons for employing gold and silver in the world when trading commodities. Using gold and silver by common consent, people have adopted the custom of measuring commodities in terms of these metals and thereby easily establish the value of individual items.

Five. Since men understand the convenience of using gold and silver when trading commodities, the greatest hindrance to commerce has been eased. Men naturally assume the necessity for gold and silver to facilitate mutual exchange by providing a means for knowing the people who desire commodities. Thus has been established a profitable way for mutually conducting business in which men desiring our goods trade for them with money while we secure the goods we need with this money.

Tengu[9]

Tsuda Mamichi

If there are no *tengu* in the five continents of the human world, are there then *tengu* in the universe beyond the human world? Some say that there are also living creatures on various planets within the solar system that resemble animals on earth. Since this is the conjecture of modern European astronomers based on observations of phenomena, it is supported by extremely clear evidence that I cannot doubt. Nevertheless, I do not yet know of *tengu*. After all, only our ignorant people of Japan believe in *tengu* and insistently misrepresent that they are not false. *Tengu* are not discussed in India and China, still less in the countries of Europe and America. Even in ancient Japan talk of *tengu* was not yet heard. The word *tengu* dates from our empire's Middle Ages.

If one searches for the origin of *tengu* peculiar to Japan, there can be no doubt that they arose from the fabrications of magical priests. Probably, when priests spread the Buddhist Law through our empire during the Middle Ages, *tengu* were no more than instruments with which priests compelled belief in their doctrine by taking advantage of widespread nescience, representing their teachings as mysterious and intimidating the ignorant people. These priests, who were known in antiquity as distinguished priests (*meisō*)[10] and who are still called *Bosatsu,*[11] crossed marshes never before penetrated by man, climbed high mountains, and opened thickets to establish sanctuaries. Adopting *tengu* and devils as tutelary gods and thereby attracting the faith of the ignorant people, these priests themselves became founding saints of their holy mountain retreats (*kaizan shōnin*).[12] Invariably, therefore, the high peaks and famous mountains of our land are Buddhist centers. Even those mountains that had been called habitats of the gods before the introduction of Buddhism have all suffered from Buddhist encroachments. When such men as Genkū and Shinran[13] introduced new doctrines in later generations, people only followed conventional nomenclature when they referred to these priests as founding saints of the mountains (*kaizan shōnin*) even though they were not based in the mountains.

Wise and enlightened people should be taught by reason, but

those not yet enlightened are instructed sometimes by intimidation, sometimes by cajolery. This is the reason for theories of Heaven (*Gokuraku*) and Hell (*Jigoku*).[14] Since those who are not yet wise and enlightened, after all, are by force of circumstance generally first intimidated and then gradually led to good, we should not harshly blame the priests of ancient days even if they used *tengu,* gods, and devils. Unexplored high mountains and deep valleys abound in quiet mystic interior retreats thickly covered with *sugi*[15] and *hinoki*[16] that seem just like the habitats of ghosts and devils. Even brave men, therefore, find it difficult to avoid fears in such places unless they are scholars well versed in physical phenomena. How much more is this so with ignorant people! The sagely wise cringe from fear of thunder and eclipses even though the principles behind these phenomena have recently been explained. How much more is this so with the ignorant!

Thus the priests deceitfully won the faith and admiration of the ignorant by falsely boasting that with their occult powers they would drive away dragons and thunder, expel ghosts and devils, torment the gods of the mountains, and execrate devils. Such invariably were the methods of Ozunu,[17] Saichō,[18] Kūkai,[19] Nichiren,[20] and the others. The so-called *tengu* are generally transformed wandering priests or ascetics, the most famous examples of whom were the Abbot Jirōtarō,[21] Sanjakubō[22] and others from such places as Ei-zan, Kurama, Atago, Kompira, Ōmine, Mitake, Daisen, Myōgi, Akiba, and Nikkō.[23] When Shaka formulated the means to righteousness (*hōben*)[24] on Ryōjusen[25] three thousand years ago, how could he know that the *tengu* of Japan would be contrived by his followers? After all, the devils of India, the hermits of China, and our *tengu* are all of the same ilk. The only difference is that the hermit's purity is lovable, while the evil of *tengu* and devils is detestable.

Since such present-day pilgrimage brotherhoods as those of Fuji and Mitake[26] are societies of ignorant people that practice most low and cheap religions of fear, we really should not censure them deeply for honoring nonexistent *tengu*. It is only astonishing that scholars of broad view and many accomplishments fail to understand the falsity of *tengu* and wood spirits. What is still more surprising is that scholars in national studies (*kōgaku-sharyū*)[27] prattle about a world of *tengu* above the human world. Are the heirs of Ozunu and Kūkai still in the clouds a thousand years later?

One day, when I was speaking before a gathering in this manner, a friend arose and said:

> I should express pleasure since your explanation has swept away a delusion that has hovered over our country for a thousand years. Nevertheless there is still a type of boastful *tengu* wandering around among human beings. There are those who think that they themselves have entered the halls of learning without climbing to that high estate, those who pretend to be Bismarcks of Asia even though they do not possess the wisdom of a Li Hung-Chang,[28] and those who assume that they have already advanced rapidly to the area of enlightenment while they are still half enlightened. All these boasters are still a type of human *tengu*.

Everyone dispersed convulsed in laughter, and I have accordingly written on *tengu*.

[1]Of Nishi's contributions to the *Meiroku Zasshi*, none reflect his thought more clearly than his essays on "Knowledge" (*Chisetsu*, 知說), "Religion" (*Kyōmonron*, 教門論), and the "Three Human Treasures" (*Jinsei Sambōsetsu*, 人世三寶說). Students of Nishi see in his thought during the Meirokusha period the strong influence of two major Western thinkers, Auguste Comte and John Stuart Mill. Although it is unclear how much of Comte and Mill he read in the original and how much he derived from his teachers in Holland, his writings indicate that he knew of Comte's *Cours de philosophie positive* and Mill's *A System of Logic*. And while he was drawn to Mill's logic, like Comte he tried to devise a scheme for organizing the various branches of knowledge. Nishi's organization of knowledge, however, is wholly his own, not Comte's. Much of the material for his five essays on "Knowledge" is drawn from his lectures on the "Interrelation of the Hundred Sciences" (*Hyakugaku Renkan*, 百學連環). For a perceptive interpretation of Nishi's thought see Thomas H. R. Havens, *Nishi Amane and Modern Japanese Thought* (Princeton, 1970).

[2]Wang Mang, 王莽, and Ts'ao Ts'ao, 曹操, two Chinese ministers traditionally regarded as usurpers of imperial authority who lived respectively at the close of the Former Han (Ch'ien Han, 前漢) and the Later Han (Hou Han, 後漢) dynasties.

[3]Taikō, 太閤, the traditional identification for Toyotomi Hideyoshi (豐臣秀吉), the Japanese leader who dispatched armies to Korea in 1592 and in 1597.

[4]Ch'in, 秦, the state in northwest China that completed the unification of China in 221 B.C. after conquering the rival Chinese states one after another.

[5]*Sai,* 才; *nō,* 能; *shiki,* 識.

[6]*Butsuri,* 物理, and *shinri,* 心理.

[7]Here Nishi is denying the Confucian scholars who ascribed all things physical and metaphysical to a single Reason or Principle (*Ri*).

[8]*Yasei,* 野生.

[9]*Tengu,* 天狗 winged demons of the mountains often represented with long noses or beaks and said to live at the tops of giant cryptomeria. As a rational being attracted to materialism, Tsuda was repelled by popular belief in *tengu,* which symbolized for him the backwardness and superstition that he earnestly desired to destroy with enlightenment.

[10]*Meisō,* 名僧.

[11]Bosatsu, 菩薩, a Buddhist saint or *Bodhisattva.*

[12]*Kaizan shōnin,* 開山上人.

[13]Genkū (源空) or Hōnen Shōnin (法然上人), 1133–1212, and Shinran (親鸞), 1174–1268, were, respectively, founders of the two principal Pure Land sects, *Jōdo Shū* (浄土宗) and *Jōdo Shinshū* (浄土眞宗), that promised salvation through invocation of the name of the Amida Buddha.

[14]*Gokuraku,* 極樂, and *Jigoku,* 地獄.

[15]*Sugi,* 杉, cryptomeria.

[16]*Hinoki,* 檜, Japanese cypress.

[17][En no] Ozunu, 役小角, one of the earliest shamanistic Buddhists who came to be regarded as the founder of the tradition of wandering mountain priests or *yamabushi* (山伏).

[18]Saichō, 最澄, 767–822, the great teacher of Tendai (天台) Buddhism who started the complex of temples on Mount Hiei (比叡).

[19]Kūkai, 空海, 774–835, the gifted monk who introduced Shingon (眞言) Buddhism to Japan and founded the great Buddhist center on Mount Kōya (高野).

[20]Nichiren, 日蓮, 1222–1282, founder of the Hokke (法華) Sect based on the doctrines of the Lotus Sutra.

[21]Jirōtarō, 次郎太郎.

[22]Sanjakubō, 三尺坊.

[23][Hi]ei-zan, 比叡山; Kurama, 鞍馬; Atago, 愛宕; Kompira, 金毘羅; Ōmine, 大峯; Mitake (Ontake), 御嶽; Daisen, 大山; Myōgi, 妙義; Akiba, 秋葉; and Nikkō, 日光, are all holy mountain retreats.

[24]*Hōben,* 方便.

[25]*Ryōjusen,* 靈鷲山, Vulture Peak.

[26]Devotional associations (*kō,* 講) centering on the deities (*kami,* 神) believed to reside atop Mounts Fuji (富士) and Mitake (御嶽).

[27]*Kōgaku-sharyū,* 皇學者流, scholars in Japanese national studies.

[28]Li Hung Chang 李鴻章

On Wives and Concubines Part Three[1]

Mori Arinori

When righteousness does not prevail, the strong oppress the weak, and the smart deceive the stupid. In extreme cases, immorality becomes an amusement providing a source of livelihood as well as of pleasure. Among the customs common among barbarians, mistreatment of wives by their husbands is especially intolerable to witness.

Just relations between husband and wife are not in the least practiced under our national customs. In truth, the husband is entirely the master of the slave, and the wife is no different from a chattel. It is the wife's duty only to follow her husband's orders without questioning in the least the merit of his directives. From morning to evening, therefore, the wife obediently runs about serving her husband with body and soul almost like a spiritless machine. Furthermore, if she fails to meet her husband's wishes, he scolds, hits, curses, and kicks in a manner that is often really beyond description. Because of woman's fundamentally patient character, she has not yet come deeply to resent even such violent conduct by man. Yet the husband does not especially appreciate that his wife gives her body to him and protects her chastity with her life. How can we adequately describe a wife's anguish when her husband goes so far as willfully to indulge his carnal desires with wenches and concubines? Such conduct may indeed be termed cruel and unjust in the extreme. Undeniably, it would not be too harsh if such excesses by the husband were punished under the law as if they were murder. Even though some may argue that women may be regarded as beasts one level below human beings who can be used freely as men wish, it is pointless to dwell here on such barbaric attitudes.

When a marriage contract is concluded and the obligations therein are established, it is expected that the couple will not switch their affections to others in the least and that they will devotedly love and protect each other. If the husband goes so far as to destroy these bonds, to indulge in loose living with women, and to satisfy freely his sexual desires in the pleasure quarters, we should never complain of the failure by the wife to preserve her chastity as a sacrifice of marriage obligations. If it is assumed that the wife must invariably preserve her chastity even though her husband is unfaithful, then she should be completely devoted and truly sacrifice her body to him.

On the other hand, if the husband marries many females in the manner of farmyard animals, then how can he ever requite their devoted affection? Even though he may say that he repays their faithfulness with unbiased fairness, he will invariably respond with divided loyalty and coldness as he cannot really give them devoted affection. A husband is indeed immoral if he repays the devoted affection of his wife with coldness and divided loyalty. If a husband's improprieties are excused, he should then have no right to denounce his wife even should she fail to defend her chastity. Such an attitude conduces to the conclusion that it is appropriate to refrain from questioning either the man's correctness or the woman's constancy.

If we really want to achieve marriage worthy of the name, there is no better approach than to spread education generally and then await the time when women voluntarily protect their chastity. Such being the case, we must all endeavor industriously to bring about this condition of affairs. To preach this vainly without achieving actual results is not only useless verbiage. Such conduct generally obstructs the road to enlightenment and is indeed hateful.

Some say that, if we want to promote enlightenment by reforming marriage, we should strive for it naturally by first selecting the true religion and then spreading this truth broadly.[2] Or it is urged that there is no better way to exemplify genuine moral relations between husband and wife than to exhort the people to marry upright foreigners.[3] Such suggestions are indeed too fantastic to merit serious consideration, but they reflect a belief that our country, having not yet established marriage morals, ultimately will be unable to do so in the future. It is evident that our country lacks independent judgment if such suggestions are really valid. Rather than aspire for a culture arising from industrious endeavor in a nation deficient in judgment, these people come close to saying that there is no better way to invigorate our culture than to rely completely on the strengths of foreigners. Now should these words be heard by our countrymen who refer to their land as the divine or imperial country and who boast courage and judgment, how can they control their wrath?

An Outline of Western Culture (Continued from Issue Twelve)

Nakamura Masanao

In the sixteenth century, the French philosopher [Michel] L'Hôpital displayed talent and virtue as a judge. His discussions were magnanimous and clear when he directed his attention to religious liberty (the right of men to follow freely their own beliefs in religious matters.) [Jean] Bodin at this time was concerned with religious liberty as well as with civil liberty (the right for people to follow freely their own will without being oppressed). Bodin held that radical reform is a poor method for conducting government and brews injury for the nation. The reader may appreciate his general thoughts from the following outline that I have prepared of his writings:

> The more powerful a man is, the more important it is that he act with unbiased justice and moderately avoid extremes when dealing with the people. Especially will a ruler provoke great harm should he willfully attempt to promote rapid reforms among the people. Therefore, even when the authority of the bishop of Rome (the head of the Catholic Church) was broken at the Council of Basel (a place where the people conduct government by assembly,)[4] there was no desire suddenly to drive from their churches those monks and nuns who were attached to their old faith. An order was issued especially prohibiting the replacement of these nuns and monks after their death. There would surely have been violent disturbances

among the old believers had [the council] wanted completely to destroy or sweepingly to change their faith. It was indeed wise, therefore, that [the council] planned only gradually to reduce and naturally to destroy the old ways. As expected, the old beliefs thereafter were gradually extinguished, and their followers quickly turned to the new faith. Years later, however, a stubborn defender of the old faith was still able to live peacefully in his hermitage. The authorities did not interfere even though he did not change the old rules and former rites to which he had become accustomed. I would say that it was especially praiseworthy that he was not robbed of his faith.

When the new church was established in Switzerland,[5] its preachers were supported by offerings collected by government order. Nevertheless, persons who refused to follow the reformed faith were allowed to live in the churches of the old faith. Only after their death was it forbidden to select successors to fill their places. Presumably, such benevolent measures were adopted because some did not want to alter their old faith even after the reformed church was functioning and because others would have lost their means of support had the old faith been strictly forbidden.

There is no more serious crisis for a nation than that arising from a desire to change in a day the manners, customs, and laws of the people that have long existed.

The way to govern nations resembles the grand manner with which the Lord manages Creation. While it seems that all living things grow and flourish quite easily, they develop only gradually. For example, take growing trees that gradually germinate from seeds, slowly develop luxuriant foliage, and finally become giants reaching to the sky. Their extremely minute daily growth is hardly perceptible to the human eye. Never do they suddenly grow rapidly. Moreover, since the Lord God dislikes excessive pressure, he avoids sudden change and moderates the seasons by placing spring and autumn between summer and winter. If you look further at the methods of Creation, there is nothing that does not advance gradually and nothing that is not carried out with moderation. Then should not those who conduct government on behalf of Nature be guided by the example of Nature's work?

The famous Scottish scholar Buchanan[6] was born in 1506. At a time when studies of government were not yet defined, Buchanan stood against prevailing opinion. In regard to the unreasonably cruel punishment imposed on the assassin of King James I of Scotland, he observed:

> The killing of the Scottish king was a cruel act, but the punishment of the criminal was still more extreme in its cruelty. After all, when criminals are punished without mercy, the extreme cruelty only encourages crime without correcting the criminals. This is because people become accustomed to seeing cruelty if harsh punishments are often administered. Not only is the sense of fear then reduced. Inclinations to do wrong and to permit pain are also encouraged. The people will commit extreme crimes more and more, therefore, if the courts impose extreme punishments. And so it is entirely mistaken to attempt the prevention of crime with severe punishments.

Buchanan is honored as a penetrating scholar because his ideas in the sixteenth century resemble those of modern students of government.

To be continued in the next issue.

On the Taxing Power as the Public Business of High and Low

Sakatani Shiroshi

Morality (*toku*)[7] is the root; wealth (*zai*)[8] the branches. Morality is metaphysical, and it is practiced in accordance with wealth. Wealth is physical, and all things in the world depend upon it. Strength and prosperity, decline and destruction, peace and conflict depend on wealth, as do happiness and sorrow, anger and pleasure, security and peril, and life and death. Moreover, the desires of the world are attributable to wealth. These desires embrace public need and private greed. If public need is not oppressed by private greed, then private greed will be extinguished in the world, and there will be the great achievement of widespread plenty. This is what is called the root of morality.

Wealth is publicly possessed and privately possessed. Individuals and families possess the right of private wealth that should never be violated by other men. Anyone who violates this right is a robber. Public wealth is shared by the people. And it should never be violated by individuals or families as it belongs to the people by inherent right. Those who violate public wealth are also robbers.

Now, taxation is the most important element of wealth. When for the protection of the people men contribute their cherished goods that should never be violated by others, this wealth becomes public wealth. When wealth is still private, its owners have the right to determine how much should be contributed to the public. Even a monarch should not violate this right. Once the principle of public protection is clarified, the contributions of private wealth to meet public need should invariably be determined through broad public discussion. Any other method is extortionate robbery.

When public wealth is distributed, it becomes the private wealth of the imperial household when granted to the imperial household or the private wealth of officials when given to officials. If public wealth is given to laborers, merchants, and manufacturers, it also becomes their private wealth. Although private wealth naturally is solely the possession of its owners, the public possesses the right to determine distribution of public wealth before it becomes private. This also is a right that even a monarch should not violate.

Once the principle of public protection is clarified, the distribution of public wealth in accordance with public needs should be invariably determined through broad public discussion. Any other method would be extortionate robbery. While this principle is as clear as the sun and the moon, there has been a gradually increasing tendency to lose sight of it, and high and low fail to recognize that they have become robbers. The principle clearly remains valid although unrecognized. Since the principle remains, doubts have gradually emerged among the people, and rising doubts have brought unrest.

Reviewing the past, one may note wise rulers and ministers in antiquity who understood this principle well. Since men's intellects were uncultivated, the way for protecting private wealth was unknown. Rulers and teachers, therefore, caused the private wealth of individuals to be preserved by establishing methods for its protection and by teaching the principles for its cultivation.

In those days, the rights of wealth in the nation were held by the sovereign. But that these rights should be held by the sovereign was not the desire of enlightened rulers and ministers. Since this situation was inevitable, [these enlightened rulers] were not at peace for a moment, being troubled in their hearts and indefatigable in their labors. Often ordering the distribution of charity, they exhausted their hearts in assisting all those who had fallen into difficulty, such as widows, widowers, orphans, the solitary, and the disabled. And when they thought this insufficient, they would give up half the land tax. The people, therefore, did not doubt in the least their rulers' virtues, their adulation being like the love of a child for its mother. The people felt that, ignorant as they were, they would only bring harm if they themselves participated in affairs and that there was no better way to escape all harm than to entrust matters to the rulers.

This was the practice in antiquity. As there was an increasing tendency for the people to be inured to this tradition, they had no doubts as long as there was no great harm. When wicked rulers and immoral ministers emerged, their injuries daily increased, and it became impossible to protect even private wealth. Reflecting on this, the people wondered why the rulers should willfully practice deceitful extortion by grabbing their laboriously acquired private wealth, which should never be violated by others. Then wicked rulers, taking advantage of popular discontent, professed a policy of protection under the guise of benevolence. And the people switched allegiance to these wicked leaders on the assumption that they were right.

On the whole, this tendency prevailed alike in the various countries of Europe and Asia during the Middle Ages. In the enlightened countries of Europe and America at present, taxation is clearly the public business of high and low without reference to the capricious virtues of officials. Public need is clarified, and private greed is thwarted in broad public discussions among wise men who are selected to represent the people, and morality and wealth are thereby placed in correct relationship to each other as root and branches.

The instruments for broad public discussion are the so-called popularly elected assemblies. The fundamental of our national structure naturally is the uninterrupted line of emperors extending through ages eternal. But in our country as in foreign lands during the Middle Ages, doubts emerged among the people, numerous wars broke out, and wicked leaders jockeyed for power. Now, since the Restoration, the imperial government, having opened intercourse with Europe and America, is adopting their strong points, and the people also recognize taxation as a public matter.

It is naturally impossible to grant anything like a special remission of the land tax as in the past. Therefore, unless we take advantage of this opportunity to enhance the glory of our unbroken line of sovereigns by extinguishing the doubts of the people, by crushing the ambitions of wicked leaders, by recognizing that the virtue of rulers is not unfailing, and by honoring the views of the wise rulers and ministers of antiquity, I fear that it will be impossible to avoid the calamities and disturbances that would invite the appearance of a foreign threat comparable to that of a Masakado or a Takauji[9] in domestic affairs.

The purpose of the court is to encourage the strength and prosperity of the country and to enhance the imperial prestige. To make clear now the actual operation of taxation as public business will extinguish the people's doubts and induce them to honor the rulers with one heart. The people will then strive earnestly in the knowledge that even their private property cannot be protected if national power is not expanded. And with expanding maritime power and communications, we may confidently expect patriotism to increase daily and enlightenment to expand monthly.

Skilled management of wealth, therefore, will only arise when taxation is the public business of high and low. We should clearly reflect on the relative merits of the various countries of Europe, America, and Asia. We differ from them in that we reform before disturbances arise, whereas they reform after disturbances. The sovereign has justly divided his power and shared it with the people, and the sovereign power has naturally been strengthened now that the virtue of the monarch has been clarified. Why should we delay?

On Government Part Four[10]

Tsuda Mamichi

This country and China have inspecting and impeaching officials, among whom were the censors of the bakufu.[11] This type of functionary, however, is absent from the official lists of European and American countries. Yet if one considers their institutions carefully, one will find that they invariably provide for inspecting and impeaching functions in actuality. It is only that they are not so specified by name.

After all, surveillance of the merits of laws is by special right the duty of one or both houses of their legislatures; apprehension and prosecution of crimes is the function of procurators; correction of offenders caught in the act belongs to the police; and judgment of errors of public officials is the higher judiciary's responsibility. Nor are even the petty bureaucrats among the tax and other officials who manage money allowed to administer independently. These officials are invariably followed by an inspector so that everything is supervised down to the smallest detail. The level of receipts and expenditures established in the national accounts is what popularly elected assemblies especially control.

And since national budgets of this type are the aggregate of various lesser accounts, a person must first inquire into the minor accounts minutely, without the slightest error, should one desire to verify and investigate the correctness of the national budget. Legislators, however, cannot well supervise small budgetary details as they are busy discussing important matters of state. It is the common practice of other countries, therefore, to establish statistical bureaus under the direct control of the rulers. On behalf of the legislators, these bureaus investigate the figures for expenditures by various offices down to the minutest detail and then prepare completely accurate and clear tabulated reports which they present to the legislatures. Some say that the business of the statistical bureaus in other countries generally approximates the functions of the Audit Bureau (*Kensaryō*)[12] in our Finance Ministry. Their statistical bureaus, however, differ from our Audit Bureau as they are completely independent of the finance ministries and as their chiefs rank directly under the prime ministers.

This difference is the reason why they have more important functions in the nation than our Audit Bureau.

Should you refer to the Taihō Code,[13] you will not find anything resembling the Audit Bureau in the Finance Ministry. I shall leave it to my readers to determine whether there was anything resembling the Audit Bureau in the Board of Revenue (*Hu Pu*)[14] under the six codes of the T'ang Dynasty. The functions of the Audit Bureau clearly most resemble those of the Office for Examination of Accounts (*Kanjō Gimmi Yaku*)[15] in the old bakufu. The latter office was extremely beneficial when it was introduced upon the recommendation of Arai Hakuseki. Later, however, these examiners became no more than petty officials attached to the finance commissioners (*kanjō bugyō*), and they inquired only at the pleasure of the commissioners. The cause of this evil was simply that the examiners, being of low rank, lacked power to investigate the conduct of the finance commissioners.

Then will not the Audit Bureau repeat the error of its predecessors? For the preparation of current statistics, there should be established an independent statistical bureau directly under the Council of State (*Dajōkan*),[16] the regulations for this bureau to be determined after we have considered the rules for similar offices in the West. The various offices of the central government, the prefectures, the army and navy, the courts, the government schools, and the national banks should present detailed and complete reports to this bureau. After conducting minute investigations and revising inconsistencies in the figures, the bureau should present its clear and accurate tabulated report to the entire nation.

There is nothing finer than thus to clarify to all the people of our empire the fact that, while the imperial court, of course, is upright and enlightened, there is elsewhere no leakage of even the smallest sums into private pockets, as the officials are also all honorable and forthright. Only thereby can the government win the full confidence of the nation. Thus the source for increased national power is the concord in the people's hearts, and the source of concord in people's hearts lies in their faith in the government. I always say that we may expect our empire to be strong and prosperous only after there are no discrepancies in our national accounts. How can this invariable position of mine deceive the people?

[1]Continued from Issue Eleven.

[2]Mori presumably refers to those who, like Tsuda Mamichi in Issue Eight, recommended adoption of Christianty as a matter of policy.

[3]When Mori was serving as Japan's charge d'affaires in Washington, Tanaka Fujimaro (田中不二麿), then vice minister of education, reputedly advised the young Japanese diplomat to set his countrymen an example by himself taking a Western wife, a suggestion upon which Mori declined to act hastily. Kaneko Kentarō (金子堅太郎) also recalled a speech in which Mori recommended to Japanese students in New York that they take Western wives to improve the Japanese race. This essay would indicate, however, that Mori seriously entertained such an idea only briefly if at all.

[4]Nakamura refers to a national assembly at *Bashiru* (*Bashiru no kokkai*, バシルノ國會).

[5]The country is *Zuikoku*, Juikuo, (瑞國), which could refer to either Sweden (*Zuiten*, Juitien, 瑞典) or Switzerland (*Zuisei*, Juihsi, 瑞西).

[6]George Buchanan, 1506–1582, the Scottish humanist who held in his *Regni apud Scotos* that the people are the source of political power, that the king is bound by the terms under which power was first committed into his hands, and that it is lawful to resist tyrants.

[7]*Toku*, 德.

[8]*Zai*, 財.

[9][Taira] Masakado, 平將門, and [Ashikaga] Takauji, 足利尊氏, as usurpers of imperial authority were for Sakatani prime examples of wicked leadership.

[10]Continued from Issue Twelve.

[11]Tsuda refers to the *metsuke* (目付), the censors or intelligence officers of the Tokugawa bakufu (幕府).

[12]*Kensaryō*, 檢査寮, an office established in 1871 within the Finance Ministry (*Ōkurashō*, 大藏省) upon the recommendation of Itō Hirobumi (伊藤博文).

[13]*Taihō Ryō*, 大寶令, an administrative code promulgated in 702 A.D.

[14]*Hu Pu*, 戶部, one of the six principal boards in the Chinese state from the Sui (隋) and T'ang (唐) dynasties to the twentieth century.

[15]*Kanjō Gimmi Yaku*, 勘定吟味役, comptrollers of finance, first established in 1682 and revived in 1712 with higher rank by the famed Confucian scholar official Arai Hakuseki (新井白石), partially as a check on the powerful finance commissioners (*kanjō bugyō*, 勘定奉行).

[16]*Dajōkan*, 太政官. Although generally translated as Council of State, the term *Dajōkan* applied to the central imperial administration that was theoretically restored after 1868. The Japanese government in 1881 finally established an Audit Board (*Kaikei Kensa In*, 會計檢査院) as an agency directly under the *Dajōkan* and independent of the Finance Ministry in accordance with Tsuda's recommendation.

On Government Part Five[1]

Tsuda Mamichi

A title deed (*chiken*)[2] is a bond by which private ownership of land is established. Even as Confucius said that there is no better method than the method that avoids litigation,[3] these title deeds were not introduced for verification in the courts and are wholly sufficient to prevent litigation. As yet unknown in China and unused in Europe and America, the title deeds arise more especially from the recent decision of our gracious sovereign. Are there any among the people of the Great Japanese Empire who are not deeply moved by the broad and boundless grace of the emperor?

After all, under the old order in Japan, the country was the possession of one man and not that of the nation. It was the national law in our empire from the age of the gods that there should be absolutely no private land ownership by the people as the land of the eight provinces all belonged to the emperor. We cannot know accurately the details of conditions in antiquity, but land in early Japanese history was portioned out according to mouths under the *kubunden*[4] system. Even though the *kubunden* system came to an end when military men (*bujin*)[5] seized power after the decline of imperial authority, the people were as before prohibited from privately buying and selling land.

These restrictions fettered our people for more than three thousand years. At the time of the Meiji Restoration, the emperor, by a decision of unprecedented wisdom, removed these ancient and firm restrictions and gave the people freedom to buy and sell land. Since he permanently guaranteed private ownership by issuing title deeds as proof of the people's individual ownership of their lands, the nation has belonged to the nation and not to one man.

The title deeds are clear evidence that our august and gracious sovereign, who represents an unending line of rulers, does not claim the territory of Japan as his private property. What need is there for a humble subject like me fawningly to praise the emperor whose eternal virtue has never faded through the hundred generations of our pure history? His action is many times superior to the recent freeing of the slaves in Europe and America. We should just note that only since acquiring the title deeds have the people of the empire fully achieved the rights of freedom.

The countries of Europe and America possess the system of registry offices. When immovable property is mortgaged to cover a loan, the creditor and the land-owner record their respective undertakings in one of these offices as verification against error. Since Western countries do not possess the system of title deeds, this method is essential for guaranteeing mortgages.

But since we have the system of title deeds, a landowner can deposit his deed with his creditor when he mortgages his property to borrow money. Is there any better security for the creditor than possession of this title deed? Why is it necessary to record such a transaction at a registry office? In our country where there is already verification by the title deeds, however, the creditor loses the right to collect the collateral if the parties to the mortgage on the land have not applied for and received a guarantee from the local official when the loan is made.

Although it may be said that the degree of protection afforded our people far exceeds that accorded in the West, to be excessive is also like being inadequate, and excessively broad protection is completely in vain. After all, requiring a guarantee by local officials was really the most appropriate method before the establishment of title deeds. Yet such a guarantee is superfluous after the issuance of the title deeds, being no more than an instrument that unnecessarily confuses the people and robs them of their time. A Westerner once said, "Time is money." Why should we make light of robbing people of time? I have also heard a great merchant state:

> Gold and silver are to merchants what munitions and supplies are to armies. Poverty in munitions and supplies is an army's greatest secret during war, and poverty in gold and silver is a merchant's greatest secret when trading. Now merchants cringe inwardly before the requirement that they always apply publicly

to the local offices when they present their title deeds, borrow money, and raise capital.

Even though [I] do not know whether these words are after all correct, legislators should also certainly consider them. Indeed, that it is the imperial wish to energetically protect the liberties of the people is demonstrated just by issuing the title deeds [thus obviating any need] for resorting to further proof [such as the western practice of verification in registry offices]. How can legislators ignore this?

Since there are no title deeds for buildings, people require the protection of local officers when they lend money with these properties as security. Yet they actually do not have this protection. Buildings and land are equally immoveable property, and I do not understand why the protection for one is now deficient while that for the other is excessive.

Human Social Intercourse[6]

Sugi Kōji

According to Westerners, there were originally one man and one woman. Mingling, they gave birth to children, their children in turn begat grandchildren, and thus the generations were perpetuated. Authority at first was held by the father, but there were later differing degrees of authority after it was divided and shared according to age and capacity. The only basis for morality is good and evil. It is said that you will be judged by your deeds and that you will be esteemed and increasingly honored by society if you contribute greatly to its peace and prosperity. This, after all, is the source of man's authority. At first, men's desires were extremely limited because they did not look beyond themselves. Moreover, men's conduct was then extremely rough and coarse because there were no means for restraining them.

It is the nature of men to cater to each other's needs, mutually to help the weak and the lonely, to repay kindness, and to associate intimately with others with a spirit of self denial. Relatives at first drew together for mutual protection. Then, gradually expanding and dividing, a family produced branch families, branch families further divided to become numerous families, and numerous families proliferated to follow their respective lives.

Men in those days, being honest and straightforward, lived in peace and food was abundant. Even though as nomads they supported themselves by hunting and fishing, they were obliged by recurring shortages to move often and change their homelands. When men tired of nomadic life and their tribes became large, they recognized that hunting and fishing were insufficient to provide for their livelihood, finally settled on the land, cultivated the soil, and raised domestic animals.

Men being acquisitive by nature, farmers and ranchers inevitably desire bountiful harvests and multiplying herds. If men are plundered of their profits, who will then want diligently to promote their industries? Desiring tranquility in their callings and the protection of society, men established laws by mutual agreement that they individually followed as a duty. They also entered into agreements by which they established the right of private property, according the produce to the tillers and breeders in the fields as well as designating as proprietors the persons who first acquired the land. If there was injury by others to private ownership of lands and goods, men joined to carry out their obligations to protect [property] and to prevent [injury].

The strength of the individual was insufficient to completely prevent injury when men were still in a state of nature. Once there were established institutions for human social intercourse, however, people enhanced their power by relying on each other. When confronted by the tyranny of others, they sacrificed a part of liberty and thereby prevented injury, protected the public peace, and defended personal independence and liberty. Briefly, the reason for this is as follows. Since some want to force our submission by their oppression, we try to oppose this oppression by conforming to the authority of society and thus protect our independence by sacrificing a part of our liberty to society.

An Outline of Western Culture (Continued)[7]

Nakamura Masanao

Bacon

[Francis] Bacon, the father of experimental philosophy, was born in England toward the end of the sixteenth century. Bacon's viewpoint and knowledge were broad and precise since, in addition to being endowed with superior talent, he was able to exchange with great men throughout Europe because his father was one of Queen Elizabeth's chief ministers. Although he devoted much energy through his life to spiritual philosophy, he contributed to the progress of later generations in the material sciences, in which his successes were most spectacular.

Mushosōshi [Nakamura][8] would explain as follows:

> In Western theory, knowledge is divided into two major categories called "immaterial knowledge" and "material knowledge," in other words, abstract and concrete studies. Whereas literature, logic, religion, ethics, law, and politics belong to abstract studies, concrete studies include physics, engineering, chemistry, medicine, and agriculture. Even though the principles of religion had already been explained to the world by Luther, mental philosophy was not yet firmly established, being no more than mental imagination. Bacon's philosophy explained the principles of the human mind, but it also assumed the importance of actual verification without resorting to empty imagination. Since this view spread increasingly through the world, men undertook experimental studies of matter, and physics daily advanced toward enlightenment. As the study of physics became more refined, the work of the supreme Creator was increasingly apparent; men believed that the unseen, true God invariably controlled all things in Heaven and Earth, and they knew that they should hope for Heaven's bounty as well as Heaven's punishment. Such being the case, men's minds daily turned toward good and drew away from evil.

Mental philosophy before Bacon was only empty reasoning without verification. Bacon did not go further into such scholarly problems as to what the essence of the mind might be; whether the mind, being omnipresent, is without place; whether it could be broadened; or whether it is related to time or space. (Space refers to width and breadth; time to shortness and length.) In the final analysis, he avoided useless and unnecessary verbiage, observing:

> Since men have the power of reason (reason being the function of the mind) while animals have only basic drives (basic drives being functions of the body), men and animals are of distinctly different species. We should regard as mistaken the philosophers of antiquity who placed men's minds on a level above those of animals as if to distinguish between inferior and superior within the same species, just as the sun is superior to the stars and gold is above other metals.

Bacon also excelled in the study of logic. ("Logic" may be translated as the principle of lucidity or the study of rational intelligence.) Once, when discussing the importance of relating words to thought, he observed: "Men only think that reason controls words as their master, but I believe that words sometimes usurp reason." Along this line, Locke has an essay, much prized by scholars, in which he discussed the injuries to reasoning that arise because words are incomplete or misused. (Comment by Nakamura: Since words in the East and the West differ in essence, I shall abbreviate the discussion of words as it cannot be translated.)

In his discussion of ethics (the study of the way of man or morals), Bacon was not concerned with the ethical principles and objectives that were studied in England during the eighteenth century. Even though his discussions were based only on the actual conduct of affairs, his consideration of how human minds are moved by habits and customs was most important and a supplement to the undeveloped views of his predecessors.

Bacon was also well versed in statesmanship. An outline of his views is evident from the following quotation:

> It is essential for men who conduct government by law above all to understand and always to keep in mind for what objectives government is carried on and for what purposes laws are formulated. After all, their legal systems are all instruments for accomplishing their objectives. What is the ultimate objective toward which their legislation is directed? They want to make men happy. Then how will this objective be reached? First, it is essen-

tial to accord men "religious and pious education" (education that plants justice in men's hearts and encourages good conduct through faith in God and fear of Heaven's Way.) Second, it is essential to provide the people with training in "good morals" (good principles of human ethics.) Third, it is essential to make prudent military preparations and to preserve perfect calm among the people even when an enemy country invades from without. Fourth, it is essential to protect the people and to establish good laws in order to avoid daily violence, robbery, and killing. Fifth, it is essential to instill in the people a feeling of patriotism and to cause them to obey the government. Sixth, it is essential to provide for the prosperity and wealth of the people, to fill the public treasury, and to furnish essential relief. If men desire to establish a legal system to provide for the above, it is essential that they first consider the "social order,"* the order by which men mutually preserve an equilibrium in their vocations. Next it is essential for men to understand the benefits of human social intercourse. Then it is essential for them to know the justice and appropriateness of law. Still further, it is essential for them to appreciate the customs of the peoples of various countries. And finally, it is essential for them to understand the different political systems of other countries. If laws are established after these factors are understood, legislation will generally conform with justice and not contradict reason and feeling.

What is desired of legislators, therefore, is that they study two principles, "natural justice" (the sense of right and wrong found in the conscience) and "political expediency" (opportune means to be employed in legislation). In this way, legislators will be-

*(Comment by Nakamura: "Social order" may be translated as the order in the affairs of mutually intimate persons in the same pursuit, just as there is an order in the classes of men. After all, people are drawn together into pursuits, and things are divided into classifications. Farmers have relations with other farmers in which they endeavor to advance the prosperity of farming with pooled strength, united hearts, mutual intimacy, and common good will. In the hundred trades, all persons, equally participants in their enterprises, labor for the advancement of these enterprises with mutually intimate love. These persons, therefore, do not plan for individual profit; there is no hatred within the same profession; and there are no disputes within the same industry. Forming their respective associations and planning for common profit, they comprise "society." The social order, therefore, is the order and the equilibrium that arises from a balanced relationship between the military, farming, worker, merchant, cultural and other associations within the nation.)

come accomplished in formulating laws and ultimately able to supplement and improve these laws. I also beg the legislators always to remember in their inner hearts that they should bring happiness to the people.

The superiority of Bacon's talent and knowledge may be understood from the above extract. Yet his depth and his discrimination seems still more surprising if one reads the following discourse on new laws:

Clinging to old customs and past habits as well as confused change to new laws are equally injurious to the country. In reforming the old and adopting the new, nothing surpasses seasonal change. Indeed, men are thus naturally induced to change quietly and without raising a voice. If such be the case, can we not carry out natural change by imitating the seasons?

[I], Mushosōshi, would comment:

Of the eras of untrammeled tranquility during the Sung Dynasty, none compared with the reign of Jên Tsung.[9] We may appreciate the glories of Jên Tsung's rule by reading the following poem of Shao K'ang-chieh:[10]

> The streets are always crowded with those in
> luxurious attire,
> Everywhere are high buildings and the playing
> of musical instruments,
> Peace pervades the empire as the days are
> without incident,
> And birds and flowers are limitless, the sun
> being at its high.

If such was the case, how was it accomplished by Jên Tsung? According to a court historian, Jên Tsung supported the virtues expressed in the saying: "Honor Heaven and respect the people with humbleness and benevolence." That is, since he honored the Supreme Ruler (*Shang-ti*)[11] in High Heaven (*Huang T'ien*),[12] true merit was promoted by establishing the principle of moderation. And since he respected the farmers and the people, wise and loyal government was conducted with a deeply sympathetic heart. Thus did he ultimately achieve such tranquility. After Jên Tsung's death, the following poem was inscribed on his mausoleum:

> Farming and sericulture regularly advanced
> undisturbed from year to year,
> Frontier generals were without heroic
> achievements while officials failed to display
> talent,
> The forty-two years of his rule are like a dream.
> My tears are blown past his grave by a spring
> breeze.

Actually, when officials are inclined to display their talents, they invariably introduce useless reforms, indulge in untimely and confused changes, bring misfortune to the state, and promote destructive harm among the people. To say that officials failed to display their talents, therefore, was indeed to extol the emperor's virtue.

Coming to the reign of Shên Tsung,[13] when measures were energetically planned and when heroic achievements were sought night and day, however, men like Wang An-shih[14] carried out new laws and disturbed the world with alarms. Misfortunes and disorders arose daily therefrom, until finally the Sung Dynasty no longer exerted authority. Bacon's warning that confused changes by new laws grievously injures nations should truly be called a lesson for all times.

Resembling the above sentiments is Bacon's discussion at the beginning of his *De Augmentis Scientiarium*, which reads as follows:

> On the whole, it is invariably important to follow the customs of the land and to conform with the sentiments of the people when drawing up new laws and establishing new regulations. The great danger is that "literary men" (a translation for scholars or literati), without paying attention to this, one morning may suddenly practice in administration what they have been able to learn from the writings of the ancients.

I believe that these words are truly of utmost significance.

On Loving One's Enemies

Nishi Amane

Glanced at hastily, the phrase "You should love your enemy" may seem strange and surprising. Yet if you inquire deeply into its meaning, the statement entirely embraces the virtues of the Supreme Being's Infinite Love and Pure Goodness. Men desiring in the least to follow the Will of High Heaven should take this admonition as the highest and ultimate principle of morality. Let me try to explain this.

It is invariably appropriate to take as the norm in our daily lives the principle of Confucius that one should recompense virtue with virtue and hatred with sincerity. After all, the feelings of like and dislike as well as of love and hate arise from the nature of men's minds since it is entirely reasonable for them to seek redress when their rights are transgressed. Yet it is the fundamental essence of men's minds normally to be happy and cheerful, abnormally to be sad and pessimistic. Therefore, once men conform to principle when dealing with others and conducting business, they should be calm and warm hearted and never assume violence and immorality to be normal. Indeed, since men are inherently communal, they are invariably of loving nature when dealing with others. Hatred, therefore, arises from abnormality as love is the essence of the mind. Let me clarify this principle by drawing an analogy with great storms, furious rains, and dark clouds. Such conditions indeed have their essential roles as, of course, they invariably arise from nature, but clear and fair weather is normal. Since it may be assumed, therefore, that human nature is normally loving and abnormally hating, one should approach even an enemy in a normal rather than an abnormal state of mind. This is one reason for saying that you should love your enemy.

Let us look still further into the meaning of the word enemy. Since a so-called enemy is a being like ourselves, we should invariably love him as a fellow being even though it is hateful for him to be our enemy. And since the superior man hates the crime but not the criminal, we should confine our hatred only to the crime itself as distinguished from the person. Under international law relating to war, civilized countries have already ceased such practices as killing prisoners, using poisoned projectiles, and employing false deceptions with the purpose of annihilating the enemy. They stop [fighting] once the enemy's power is destroyed. There has recently been discussion of the abolition of capital punishment in Western countries, and some have provided for this reform in their statutes. Even those failing to do so have all reduced the instances of such punishment. After all, man has no right to kill his fellow men. It is only appropriate to attack the causes of crime. This is another reason for saying that you should love your enemy.

Let us now look still further into the meaning of the word enemy. A so-called enemy is our rival. To think of another as one's rival is to demean oneself. Once we surpass him to the least extent, we will pity his mean mind, having appreciated his reasons for being our enemy. Men themselves understand this quite well from their daily experiences. The attitude is like parents toward their naughty child or superior men toward mean people. Even if a person injures us by attacking as our enemy, we accept this calmly without desiring to retaliate if he is not our equal. Rather, I would welcome it. Also note that the gang leader who boasts of his chivalry in the streets does not bother to compete in trivial matters with his inferiors. The phenomenon of rage and anger is found mostly among women and mean people. This is a further reason for saying that you should love your enemy.

Let us look still further into the meaning of the word enemy. A so-called enemy is one deeply related to ourselves. Now there was no reason for men of the ancient states of Ch'in and Yüeh[15] or for Australians and Siberians to hate each other as enemies. The mutual animosity of England and France arises from the fact that each claims superiority over the other. England and America as well as Holland and Belgium are mutually antagonistic because they stem from the same source. To the same root may be attributed the mutual animosity between Denmark and Sweden as well as between Spain and Portugal. Thus also brothers mutually hate each other in their struggle for wealth; officials, in their quest for power; associates, in their ambition for business; scholars of the same field, in their search for principle; and merchants of the same trade, in their competition for profit. These fellows would invariably be intimate friends if they considered their relationships and their common origins. Therefore, there is no reason for us to hate a person unless there is a relationship in which we love him. And by the same token, the person whom one hates is a person whom one has reason for loving. It is really important for men to associate according to this principle. Once a person acquires the frankness and open-mindedness of a superior man or a virtuous man, he has the sensation of floating in the clouds. Why do we not exert ourselves to this end? "Love your enemy" is the essence of morals, but it is not the basis of law from a political point of view. After all, these two [politics and morals] are not mutually opposed only when they proceed parallel with each other. Scholars should not confuse them.

[1]Continued from the previous issue.

[2]Following the abolition of feudalism, the recognition of private property, and the ending of the ban on selling land, the Japanese government in 1872 introduced title deeds *chiken* (地券), as verification of land ownership and a convenience in assessing taxes under the new land tax of 1873. After 1874 these deeds carried the assessed valuation of the land upon which the new tax was based. As Tsuda claims, the title deeds were in theory gifts from the emperor who had nominally recovered control of the land when feudalism was abolished. Nevertheless, the deeds provoked loud protests from those who felt that the land had not been granted to the legitimate owners, and the attendant land tax was extremely unpopular among farmers who were forced to pay the new impersonal tax on the assessed value of the land that was not subject to reduction in event of crop failure, as were the feudal levies under the old regime.

[3]Tsuda here refers to Book XII of the *Analects* (*Lun Yü*, 論語) entitled *Yen Yüan* (顏淵) in which Confucius states that what is necessary is to cause people to have no litigations. This is the source of the Confucian theory that the sage prizes rule that is so uneventful as to cause no litigation.

[4]*Kubunden*, 口分田, the system of dividing rice land according to mouths that was introduced from China in the seventh century.

[5]*Bujin*, 武人.

[6]Apart from his initial attribute to Westerners, the source of Sugi's four essays on social intercourse, like his other historical writings, remains obscure. His essays probably paraphrase one or more Western texts that caught his eye. Sugi recalled in his memoirs that he had labored for two and a half years digesting a ten-volume Western history of the world while he was attached to Tokugawa bakufu's (幕府) Institute of Development (*Kaiseijo*, 開成所) prior to the Meiji Restoration.

[7]Continued from the previous issue.

[8]Mushosōshi, 無所争子, one of Nakamura's pen names.

[9]Jên Tsung, 仁宗, the temple name of the fourth Sung (宋) emperor, Chao Chên, 趙禎, 1010–1063.

[10]Shao K'ang-chieh, 邵康節, the canonical name of the scholar Shao Yung, 邵雍,

1011–1177, one of the precursors of Chu Hsi (朱熹) in the Neo-Confucian tradition.

[11]*Shang-ti*, 上帝.

[12]*Huang T'ien*, 皇天.

[13]Shên Tsung, 神宗, the temple name of the sixth Sung emperor, Chao Hsü, 趙頊, 1048–1085.

[14]Wang An-shih, 王安石, 1021–1086, the innovating statesman of the Sung Dynasty who was an anathema to the more conservative Neo-Confucians. Nakamura himself was one of the most precocious Japanese scholars in the Chu Hsi tradition and thence hostile to Wang An-shih.

[15]Ch'in, 秦, and Yüeh, 越, two feudal states of ancient China whose interests did not conflict because they were so far removed from each other, Ch'in being situated in northwest China, Yüeh in the lower Yangtze Valley.

Reform of National Finance[1]

Kanda Kōhei

Under our country's financial administration in the past, the government collected taxes seasonally by levying appropriate imposts on produce without regard to occupation, whether persons were samurai, farmers, artisans, or merchants. The total revenues collected were the income of the state, and various administrative expenditures were met by once more disbursing the revenues. Even though this is the traditional method for determining disbursements after estimating collections, it seems finally to have become injurious in recent times. First to speak in generalities, revenues were inadequate when numerous difficulties in national affairs required large expenditures, and they were excessive for the small expenditures necessary during untroubled times. The government also suspected leaks, naturally wore the expression of a tax collector, was exceedingly harsh in all matters, and could neither depend upon the people nor itself exercise responsibility. Numerous abuses arose from these evils. The government was unjust in its reasoning, resorting to such practices as arbitrarily changing taxes and pressing the people to the point of bankruptcy. And the people came to have almost no concern for the safety of the country as they thought that their obligations were all finished once they had paid the government's taxes and as administration had the appearance of business to be undertaken by the government. These various factors have all been sources for divisions between men and inability to strengthen the nation's foundations. It is urgent that we quickly reform.

The method for financial reform is as follows. First, we will establish the institution of a popularly elected assembly, then create a board of audit, and thereafter have the various ministries and offices prepare estimates for the coming year's expenditures. Once the level of expenditures has been approved during open debate in the popularly elected assembly, taxes will be collected by apportioning the tax burden through the country. After the funds have been used to meet the government's expenditures, the expenditures will be calculated and compared with the estimates, and the business will be completed once the popularly elected assembly has approved the revised statement of expenditures.

Going into detail, I shall not now undertake a superfluous discussion of a popularly elected assembly since this matter already has been clarified fairly well in public exchanges. I would only take up here the essence of the assembly's financial responsibility. The people will be the ones who employ the government to administer the country by providing for salaries and expenditures. The government, as the employee of the people, will carry on administration upon receipt of salaries and expenses. The popularly elected assembly will then be the means by which the people place orders with the government for its services during the coming year and the means by which the government presents its financial statement to the people for services rendered during the previous year.

Even though the sessions of the popularly elected assembly conduct the important business, the assembly cannot assume complete responsibility for investigating the statements of expenditures in detail since its members are so numerous and since they are dispersed from time to time. In this connection, a body of men shall be publicly selected to assume full responsibility for these [financial] matters, and this body will be regularly charged with the accounting business under the government. Designated the Audit Bureau (*Kaikei Kensa Kyoku*),[2] it will be like the people's accountants.

Now coming to the procedures for estimating government expenditures, the various ministries will first have their respective bureaus and the prefectures prepare detailed estimates of expenses. After these have been assembled into a volume for each ministry, they will be forwarded to the Audit Bureau. The Audit Bureau will then make comparisons with former years, investigate in detail the reasons for increases and decreases, and estimate the general level of expenditures by assembling the estimates of the various ministries. In addition to these estimates, the Audit Bureau will also prepare for consideration by the assembly a supplement regarding factors anticipated to redound to the national welfare.

Upon the convening of the assembly, its members will begin deliberations after having received the estimates of the various ministries and considered the prognostications of the Audit Bureau. They will question the various ministerial chiefs [on their estimates] article by article and determine the general level of expenditures for the coming year after deciding to add what should be added, to reduce what should be reduced, and to delete or insert what should be deleted and inserted.

After determining the general level of expenditures, there will be completed estimates of what should be collected by apportionment to various parts of the country. Since these estimates are the responsibility of the parliament, the assembly should adopt the rule that the Audit Bureau will prepare the draft proposal. First of all, the Audit Bureau will deduct from the general level of expenditures its estimates of fixed income from such sources as tariffs on exports and imports, the stamp tax,[3] harvests from government lands, and the profits [from such government enterprises] as minting, mining, posts, and railways. Next, it will further deduct from the general level of expenditures its estimated income from commercial taxes that apply to the nation as a whole and that can be altered at will, such as tonnage dues and taxes on saké and tobacco. It will then apportion the balance [of the estimated general expenditures] among the various prefectures according to their rank. The ranks of the prefectures should be determined in advance after comparing their populations, their acreage, and the value of their lands.

The tax burden on the individual prefectures will be the level assigned by parliament; this sum will be apportioned among the towns and villages by decision of the prefectural assemblies; the towns and villages will similarly allot taxes to the various households; and the tax apportionment registers compiled in the individual towns and villages will be the basis for tax collections.

Since individuals, after all, are naturally classed rich or poor according to the property, income, and other assets that they possess, their tax classifications will first be searched out and entered into tax registers that shall be the basis of tax apportionment. It should, of course, be clear that the ranks of the respective towns and villages will be determined by adding together the previously determined ranks of individual households and that the ranks of prefectures will be the sum of the ranks of their towns and villages.

In prefectures of limited agriculture and flourishing commerce, a previously determined tax on commerce shall be first deducted from the total prefectural assessment and the balance apportioned among the farmers. If commerce and agriculture flourish while industry is not yet developed in a prefecture, then industry should be encouraged by lightening its taxes and by increasing those of agriculture and commerce. The particulars should all be determined by the prefectural assemblies as well as by the town and village councils for their respective levels.

Taxes from households will be gathered in the towns and villages; those from towns and villages, in the prefectures; and those from the prefectures, in the Finance Ministry. The manifold government expenditures will be met through apportionment of funds to the various ministries by the Finance Ministry. The Finance Ministry should make all of its collections and disbursements with the estimates of the previous year as its guide. The year for final rendering of the accounts will be the year following that during which the expenditures have been made or the third year from the original estimates. Each ministry will then prepare vouchers covering its disbursements. And should there be any deviations from the estimates, these deviations should be reported to the Audit Bureau in a detailed statement indicating the amounts involved and the reasons therefore.

The completed accounts will invariably be considered during the annual sessions of parliament, and the senior officials concerned must explain clearly the reasons for discrepancies from the estimates. They cannot escape responsibility when they are unable to clarify and explain a deviation. This is called the responsibility of senior officials.

Since the people want to lighten taxes as far as possible, parliament will reduce expenditures to the lowest level possible and withhold approval [of outlays] that are not absolutely necessary. And since the government naturally should not accumulate reserves, it will require funds beyond those in the original estimates once an emergency arises. On such an occasion, the difficulty will be explained to a special session of the parliament, and the emergency will be met by issuing public bonds with parliamentary approval. Interest and annual payments on the bonds will be collected from the people by including these sums in the estimates of expenditures beginning with the year following.

There are both benefits and injuries in the system of national bonds. As previously explained, taxes can be reduced to a minimum by depending on bonds. In addition, persons who cannot speculate with their property, such as widows, orphans, officials, and priests, can derive safe income from the purchase of bonds, and the people can put their inactive savings to work in bonds. Such being the benefits of bonds, their injury arises when rulers, recklessly employing the nation's resources, use bonds to expand their power, to oppress the people, or to bring on the disaster of national destruction. In sum, we should adopt the principle that there will be no increase or decrease in the national bonds without parliamentary approval. If we follow this rule well, I hope that we may long reap their benefits and escape their injuries.

What I have discussed above is the main purport of what I have to say regarding the reform of financial administration. I personally believe that we can bring unlimited benefits to the country if we follow these methods quite closely. First of all, there will not be the evil of officials recklessly spending the nation's resources, and the people will not be obliged to pay taxes for undefined reasons. The nation's finances being completely clear, there will not be stored up any doubts between officials and people. Since officials and people will clearly state their minds to each other and since the affairs of the people will be freely entrusted to the people, it should be possible to reduce the hordes of officials.

Actually, hitherto there has been need for large numbers of functionaries in the provinces as well as for harsh officials in the government because there has been much doubt as to whether the people are evading taxation.

The great benefit of these methods to the country is that they will stimulate abundant concern for national affairs in the hearts of the people. This is because their successes and failures will be individually related to the people themselves. For example, whenever the people hear of an expedition or a project by the government, they will gather around and discuss whether the project this time has been approved by the parliament, whether the government is guilty of arbitrary conduct, whether the project is after all being carried out according to estimates, and who is responsible should there be great national loss because the project has not been carried out as expected. There will be much applause should the project go ahead more expeditiously than anticipated, and some will become heroes whose success will necessarily be praised. But if the government has not previously consulted the people, the people will ask why they have not been consulted and whether the government will escape public debate by failing to consult the people. Ultimately, they will argue vociferously that what the government arbitrarily decides should be the government's sole responsibility and that there is no reason for the people to be concerned as to whether the government succeeds or fails.

If it becomes the custom for the people to discuss national affairs of their own free will, they will gradually become enlightened, penetrate world conditions, appreciate urgent matters, produce talented persons of statesmanship, and advance the national destiny. The civilized countries have demonstrated this to be clearly beyond doubt.

I know of no other way to advance the national destiny.

Earthquakes

Tsuda Mamichi

Earthquakes are the most dreadful of natural calamities. Their shocks destroy mountains, divert rivers, cause landslides, knock down houses, uproot trees, kill animals, and injure men. Ah, there is nothing more cruel than the damage from earthquakes! Moreover, their principles are most difficult to understand. Taking them for the wrath of Heaven, men in antiquity feared them no less than eclipses and comets. Yet earthquakes are not attributable to the wrath of Heaven. Nor are they Heaven-sent calamities for the purpose of admonishing rulers. In the final analysis, earthquakes are really unavoidable phenomena dating from the formation of the earth by the Creator. That is, they were no more than the means by which the Creator endowed the earth with its present shape and gave birth to human beings.

Our earth was only a big ball of fire when it was still in chaos. After all, the earth is a satellite that has separated from the sun and that also has the nature of radiating heat in the four directions. The earth's crust was only formed as the hot air of the fire-ball's exterior moved heavenward, cool spots gradually appeared on its exterior, and matter was congealed into what is known as the granite stratum. Generally speaking, matter rises as vapor when it is extremely hot, and it condenses into liquid and congeals to become solid as it cools. This is the same as when water changes into steam or ice. Once the vapor surrounding the earth gathered together into darkening fogs and clouds, floods from torrential rains welled up to flow round the earth and form the seas. Just reflect how awesome it is that the floods of this time were more than a thousand times those in the days of Yao.[4] Furthermore, faults appeared here and there in the earth's crust, just as the earth is cracked by the scorching sun. Then the sea waters rushed through these fissures into the earth's heart and were suddenly transformed into boiling water and steam when they touched the fiery heat. Steam requires some seventeen hundred times more space and is several hundred thousand times more powerful than water. Yet this extraordinary power notwithstanding, its expansion was obstructed by the restriction of the earth's crust. For this reason, the steam became still more agitated, spread its power more vigorously, raised the earth to form mountains, violently blew off the mountain tops, and shook the heavens with thunder and lightening. The aweful dreadfulness of this phenomenon was more than a thousand times that of today's volcanic eruptions and earthquakes. Nor do we know how many myriads of times such great catastrophic phenomena were repeated or over how many millennia they were extended. Thus did the world achieve its form of the proverbial six seas, three mountains, and one plain.[5] (This proportion is erroneous. According to Westerners, the seas are three times the area of land.) This is an outline of the theory of earthquakes and volcanoes before the great flood, the details of which may be understood through the study of geology. The earthquakes and volcanoes of today are the aftermaths of these earlier catastrophes. Westerners compare volcanoes to the escape valves of boilers.

If there had not been these catastrophic phenomena in the world and all had followed the force of gravity, the earth's heart, body, and skin would have been completely round, even as Gautama said that the earth's heart was a core of gold encircled by fire; its skin and meat, encircling rings of earth and water; and its clothing, a ring of atmosphere. Had such been the case, the earth's surface would have been completely covered by water and thus invisible. As all living beings would have then been aquatic life, there could have been absolutely no flowers, trees, animals, and birds born in the atmosphere of today's earth. Still less could there have been men! Earthquakes thus were absolutely essential phenomena by which the Creator formed this earth, and the existence of human beings in the world is then the gift of earthquakes. It is said that the Creator's use of earthquakes may be compared with man's employment of gunpowder to construct roads, excavate mountains, and blow up rocks.

This scholar Tengaishi[6] has been asked whether the use of soldiers by rulers is not like the Creator's employment of earthquakes. If nations use soldiers to meet truly unavoidable conditions and for truly unavoidable reasons, then national calamities can be avoided, national prestige expanded, national power augmented, national boundaries extended, and national happiness greatly increased. If such indeed be the case, the large profit arising from employment of soldiers by the nation can be likened to the Creator's great achievement in forming the world through the use of earthquakes. Nevertheless, by spending thousands in lives and millions in treasure, nations ultimately fail to escape the grief of exhausting their national resources. That is, war has its advantages, but rulers and people must all labor diligently for decades before they can completely heel the wounds and fully restore all things to their former condition. How much more injurious it is to play inconsiderately with armies and sacrifice soldiers impulsively and rashly! It is extremely rare that wars do not topple countries and destroy lives. Are not the consequences of military destruction extremely to be dreaded? Moreover, earthquakes were the principal means for creating land for the support of man.

Even though soldiers are used in the national interest, do they produce land for the support of anything? Rivalry between the kingfisher and the clam brought profit to the fisherman. How do we not know that the struggle between the yellow dragons in the field will not benefit the sons of the white emperors?[7] Ah, even though Napoleon III was an unprecedented hero, he died an exile in London, having finally suffered defeat after he moved arbitrarily and dishonored the military. As this was his own doing, whom could he blame? The only sufferers are the thirty million Frenchmen who have not yet escaped the injurious consequences of his conduct. This is a case most worthy of reflection.

Knowledge Part Two[8]

Nishi Amane

Since I have previously discussed quantitatively the emergence of wisdom as an attribute of man, I shall here consider this factor qualitatively. It would seem that the good in wisdom is comprised of such factors as prudence, enlightenment, acuteness, and insight while the bad includes cunning, craftiness, wickedness, deception and the like. These are all positive elements of wisdom, however. Among the negative elements are foolishness, incapacity, dullness, imbecility, and stupidity. All of the above attributes refer to wisdom from a qualitative point of view. Should I be asked why there are men of extraordinary knowledge and limited knowledge since both are derived from wisdom that is God-given, I would respond that the man of limited knowledge is a person of ordinary capacity whose view is no more than average—like the person who stands in the midst of a crowd. Since the view of such an individual does not extend beyond those immediately around him, his conduct is confined to knocking down the person ahead, hitting the person to the left, pushing the person behind, and brushing the person to the right. More especially, he fails to sense that the movements of the crowd as a whole are general tendencies rather than the individual movements of his neighbor.

How can such general tendencies be controlled by the elbowing of individuals in the crowd? The man of extraordinary knowledge is the opposite of this. Like one on a high stage looking down on the multitudes, he views several tens of thousands from the summit and at the same time. His movements in all directions, therefore, are unimpeded, and his conduct appropriate.

This is only to speak of the breadth and narrowness of views, however. There is another source of extraordinary knowledge. Wisdom by its nature penetrates many things with a keenness that is like a piercing awl. Apart from those who are deficient in wisdom, all men are invariably equipped with the quality of keenness. There are indeed differences in the size and number of wrinkles in men's forebrains, but the differences are not as large as those between mountains and ant-hills. Then why are the uses of keenness as different as Heaven is from earth? The effectiveness of keenness, after all, depends on whether or not it is correctly used. The man of extraordinary knowledge relies on the keenness of the masses without depending on his own keenness. Without displaying his own keenness, he energetically employs his strength to combine the keenness of the masses. Keenness is like a needle that will pierce no more than thin cloth when used individually. If a few needles are now forged together into a sharp gimlet, they can then pierce a wood board or iron armor. After all, since the combined keenness of the masses is unbending and unbreakable, the man of extraordinary knowledge easily achieves his objective [by using this combined keenness] like an armor penetrating arrow. From antiquity, rulers at the beginning of each period of Chinese and Japanese history have all invariably obtained the great objects of their desires by controlling the people's knowledge. This was the only way for a ruler to govern justly by humbly facing southward without exerting himself.[9] Invariably adopting the merits of others from the time when they were farmers, artisans, and fishermen until they became emperor, [these rulers] were indeed men of extraordinary knowledge, humbly honoring the advice of others, seeking their opinions, and appreciating the voice of the common people. Even when the brave deceive the enemy, they invariably achieve their objectives by relying on these methods. It is said that soldiers grasp the hearts of their brave leaders.[10] These all being examples of extraordinary knowledge, persons of extraordinary knowledge thus unite the keenness of the people without depending upon their own individual keenness.

Yet someone may ask if, such being the case, knowledge in the world ends here. I would respond that, when society is civilized and the times enlightened, human knowledge far surpasses the extraordinary knowledge of an individual. This I would call systematically organized knowledge. Although systematically organized knowledge takes the same direction as extraordinary knowledge, it is organized from manifold elements both large and small with a structure based on firm foundations and strongly supported by beams and pillars. This level of knowledge is only fully achieved through the endeavors of large numbers of people from many lands over a long period of gradually accumulated experience. In the world since antiquity, only the civilized people of Europe have acquired this systematically organized knowledge, which is not to be compared with the knowledge that accidentally appears at a certain time or arises in a certain place. Having been organized from luxuriant human culture and the flourishing knowledge of large numbers, systematically organized knowledge is not to be compared with the knowledge that can be brought together by but one man. Modern European civilization has not produced such a succession of great rulers as Alexander, Caesar, and Napoleon. Yet the prosperity of Europe exceeds that of all earlier ages. Nor has modern European civilization given birth to a succession of scholars like Aristotle, Plato, Newton, and Galileo. Yet the refinement of modern European scholarship overwhelmingly surpasses that of former days.

How could such luminaries and heroes individually achieve so much? If one compares the range between limited knowledge and systematically organized knowledge to weaving, the limited knowledge of a single individual is like a thread; well-woven, extraordinary knowledge like a piece of cloth; and systematically organized knowledge like brocade. To draw an analogy with shelters, limited knowledge would be a pit dwelling or tree house capable of protecting but one body; extraordinary knowledge, a rather prettily constructed house; and systematically organized knowledge, a great hall. To compare with war, limited knowledge is the fighting power of just one strong man who defeats only a single enemy when he is victorious. Even though extraordinary knowledge is a knight who, with sword and lance, can build armies and organize camps, its chivalry and sagacity do not go beyond that of a Takeda, an Uesugi,[11] a Yü Ta-yu, or a Ch'i Chi-kuang.[12] Systematically organized knowledge masters the extreme delicacy of battleships as well as attains perfection in ramparts and barricades. Its soldiers include infantry, cavalry, artillery, and engineers. Uniting the four, it commands three armies as if they were one. How can this be accomplished without long, gradually accumulated experience? To compare knowledge with industry, limited knowledge is like the craftsman who produces household implements with knives and saws. Even though he is extremely dextrous, he does not turn out large quantities. Extraordinary knowledge produces things after gathering workers together. All complete their tasks well, be they sawyers, planers, iron smiths, copper smiths, painters, or common laborers. Systematically organized knowledge is like modern factories whose well arranged plants rain sawdust thick and fast as they manufacture commodities with one movement or one turn. Such is the difference between systematically organized knowledge and the two lesser types of knowledge. I shall endeavor to discuss in the next essay how scholarship and national policy arise from systematically organized knowledge.

Just as I finish this essay, men are preoccupied by their pain from a roasting fire. I was reminded of Chên Tê-hsiu and Wei Liao-wêng[13] who were regarded as imposters and brought no benefit to affairs when they discoursed on philosophy and the Confucian path. This abuse of misunderstanding reached an extreme when the great official Lu Hsiu-fu lectured on the *Great Learning* from Yai Shan.[14] Reflecting on this, I sobbed and cried. I could not resist attaching this to the end. August 1874.

[1]Kanda Kōhei was surely the most influential of the Meiroku group in the area of economics. His proposal in the deliberative assembly known as the *kōgisho* (公議所) in 1869 to abandon feudal land tenure and to establish a tax based on the assessed value of privately owned land anticipated the Japanese government's decision to adopt a national land tax in 1873. The concept that the state's revenues should be raised and

lowered to meet the exigencies of the moment was unknown to traditional Japan, where the rulers had claimed a fixed percentage of the estimated product of the land. In this essay, Kanda develops still further his view that the Japanese should establish a government fiscal system to provide revenues in conformity with changing needs in place of the traditional practice in which expenditures conformed with fixed income. Also noteworthy is his endorsement of an independent Audit Bureau similar to that favored by Tsuda Mamichi and his commitment to a national parliament and local assemblies. Kanda himself served prominently in Japan's early deliberative assemblies and established assemblies at the town and village level while serving as governor of Hyōgo (兵庫) Prefecture, 1871–1876.

[2]*Kaikei Kensa Kyoku,* 會計檢査局

[3]*Impyōzei,* 印票稅. In 1873 the Japanese government imposed a stamp tax (*inshizei,* 印紙稅) on various agreements, such as money exchanges, loans, land purchases, exchange receipts, etc.

[4]Yao, 堯, a Chinese legendary ruler. According to tradition, the flood waters were actually drained by Yü (禹) before he became ruler.

[5]Six seas, three mountains, and one plain, *rokkai sansan ippei,* 六海三山一平.

[6]Tengaishi, 天外子, one of Tsuda's pen names.

[7]Tsuda is presumably warning that Japan and China (the yellow dragons) would be outwitted by the West if they disputed over Formosa, even as in the old tale the kingfisher and the clam were caught by the fisherman when they were diverted by their differences.

[8]Continued from Issue Fourteen.

[9]In the section of the *Analects* (*Lun Yü,* 論語) entitled *Wei Ling Kung* (衞靈公), Confucius points to Shun (舜) as a ruler who occupied his southward-facing royal seat, governing without exerting himself.

[10]*Hei wa eiyū no kokoro o toru,* 兵ハ英雄ノ心ヲ攬ル.

[11]Takeda Shingen, 武田信玄, 1521–1573, and Uesugi Kenshin, 上杉謙信, 1530–1578, great lords of eastern Japan who fought each other for twenty years without decision.

[12]Yü Ta-yu, 俞大猷, -1573, and Ch'i Chi-kuang, 戚繼光, -1585, military commanders celebrated for their defense of the south China coasts against Japanese raiders.

[13]Chên Tê-hsiu, 眞德秀, 1178–1235, and Wei Liao-wêng, 魏了翁, 1178–1237, scholar officials of the Chu Hsi (朱熹) School who suffered degradation because of false charges brought against them.

[14]Lu Hsiu-fu, 陸秀夫, 1238–1279, the heroic official who jumped with the last child emperor of the Sung (宋) Dynasty into the sea after a brave defense of Yai Shan (崖山) on the South China coast against the Mongols during which he lectured unperturbed on the *Great Learning* (*Ta Hsüeh,* 大學).

The Western Movement of Western Enlightenment

Tsuda Mamichi

After Gautama arose and developed the Law, his teachings spread eastward through Tibet, Mongolia, Siberia, Manchuria, Siam, Annam, China, Chōsen, and finally reached Japan. This is called the eastward penetration of Buddhism. Its converts included more than half the people of Asia. The Confucian Way also came to our country through Korea while it was extending to Cochin, Annam, and Ryūkyū. Why was their course to the East and South? Islam emerged in Arabia. On the one hand, it moved to the West from Turkey along the northern coast of Africa, across the straits, and into Spain, where it fought with Christianity and from whence it retreated in defeat to defend North Africa. Conversely, Islam also moved eastward across Persia, entered India, and spread to the Indies. Western culture originated in India, and Christianity appeared in Asia Minor. Passing through Greece and Rome, this [Western culture] flowed to all the states of Europe. Then crossing the Atlantic, it spread over North and South America and from thence across the Pacific to China and Japan. Having the power in the near future to diffuse to all the countries of Asia, it surely will ultimately illuminate the five continents after encircling the globe and returning to its native lands in India and Asia Minor. It would seem that the eastern penetration should not differ from the western movement in the round world. If we just judge in terms of the principle of the globe's [western] movement, however, the western course is natural and regular while the eastern penetration is regressive. It is natural that the western movement gradually moves forward and spreads out while the eastern penetration is hesitant and faltering. Should you ask, however, why the orderly westward progress of Islam was crushed by Christianity, I would respond that the Moslem creed is inferior to the Christian.

Christianity first came to Japan and China from Portugal. Our country, however, strictly forbad the religion, and it could not be practiced in China. More recently, Western enlightenment has rapidly entered both this country and China since they opened their relations with Europe and America. Moreover, its introduction has depended for the most part on Americans. Even though European and American enlightenment, of course, are one and not two, European scholarship is extremely refined and deep while American culture is rough and shallow. It is the nature of man to move from rough to refined and from near to far. Since American writings are simple to read and since the explanations of Americans are easy to hear, Japanese and Chinese rely largely on Americans and American materials when they inquire into Western studies and when they listen to Western discourses. This, after all, is following the natural course of enlightenment. A certain person once commented to Mr. Satow,[1] the secretary of the English legation, "English studies are extremely active in Japan." But Mr. Satow responded shaking his head, "Nay, you should say American studies." I constantly repeat that Western enlightenment, progressively moving to the West, will finally encircle the entire world. I dare say that within ten years to a century the public will ultimately appreciate that my words are not false.

Governments That Trifle with Nations

Katō Hiroyuki

Whether a system is established that allows the people to participate in national affairs naturally should depend upon the breadth and depth of public enlightenment. Nevertheless, even in countries where the people have not yet achieved the level of enlightenment sufficient to justify establishment of such a [representative] system, governments really have no right arbitrarily to oppress the people by endeavoring willfully to keep national affairs secret. This is because the government's affairs are the people's affairs; the government's powers are the people's powers; the government's revenues are the people's revenues; and the people are the root while the government is the branches. If there is intent to neglect the root for the branches and to oppress the root with the branches, this will naturally invite alienation of the people and national destruction. How can we say that such a government respects the nation? When the great King Frederick assumed despotic power, this, after all, was because he felt in his heart that such conduct was unavoidable, never from his lust for power. How can it be said that he oppressed the root with the branches or that he neglected the root for the branches? Suppose, however, that there is a government that desires arbitrarily to oppress the people by endeavoring to prevent them from hearing of national affairs, pretending outwardly that it acts from necessity while it privately plots to oppress the root [the people]. I would say that such a government is one that trifles with the nation.

Human Social Intercourse Number Two[2]

Sugi Kōji

The determination of laws, rituals, institutions and the like is invariably through human social intercourse. Since a father will especially strive to have his son reared well if he knows the child to be his own son, the wife should be particular to prevent her husband from confusing their child with another's. This is the reason for establishing the institution of marriage in which the man takes one wife, the woman marries one husband, and husband and wife maintain loving relations. (To what estate will mankind finally fall if fathers do not recognize their sons and if wives mix up their sons.)

The mother's frailty is insufficient to rear her son without relying on the father's strength. The father is also inadequate to have his newborn infant raised without depending on the tender love and indefatigable labors of the mother. It is the mutual responsibility of the man and the woman, therefore, to undertake together the rearing of their children, having first made clear that they are husband and wife by going through a public [marriage] ceremony. Moreover, from the fact that these obligations continue without break, marriage promises become enduring, life-long decisions.

As the father defends his rights during his lifetime and prevents injuries that arise from fraternal quarrels among his children and as it is appropriate that the father's bequest should pass to the child who has helped him to increase the family property, there have finally been established rules for inheritance. These rules for inheritance, after all, produced one evil while remedying another since man, being imperfect, does not achieve perfection. When men came to own land privately, to cherish the right of private ownership, and to enjoy the right to transfer private property, there were a great many ordinary people in society who lost their possessions and could not meet their natural [familial] obligations. Men with private property became wealthier; those without, poorer. Accordingly, looked at from the poor man's point of view, the transfer of private property did not seem fairly based upon principle. Since the poor were doomed to death from cold and starvation, however, propertied persons assured their production by employing the unpropertied while the unpropertied acquired sustenance and avoided catastrophe by securing work from the propertied in accordance with Heaven's Will to prevent harm.

That rich and poor are thus unequal but mutually inseparable may be called the cornerstone upon which are laid the foundations of human social intercourse, as it is the one great principle by which industriousness is stimulated in the world generally. Who would be induced to work diligently on behalf of others if such were not the case? After all, but for this principle, the hundred arts, industries, agriculture, and studies ultimately would be completely destroyed without leaving a trace. There is no path for man to follow but to gain profit through his own industry. Yet mankind will only return to the level of barbarism if individuals construct their own homes, make their own clothes, and produce their own foods.

Several philosophers assert their theories of self-support and self-reliance as they desire to relieve poverty in the world by equalizing wealth. Even though they want to return man to barbarism, how can they assume that the barbarous conditions of the past were superior to the situation today? Even though, given the special benefits of natural growth, not a few may be helped if men are returned to such a state, will not the harm be far greater than the benefit? Especially in a densely populated area of humming industry, where men mutually benefit and nurture each other by trading and transporting products and property, the situation, of course, is completely opposite from the barbarism of these gentlemen philosophers.

According to another theory, great injury to mankind arises from the fact that the affluent and the needy are mutually separated, the rich becoming richer, and the poor poorer. Assuming this injury to be especially serious in the towns and villages, those of this persuasion hold that there is no other remedy than to [equalize wealth] by transferring the excess wealth of the rich to the poor or by restoring the old land laws under which rice paddies were divided to become the property of individuals. They believe these two solutions to be appropriate methods for equalizing the wealth of the rich and, consequently, the means for realizing the fundamentals of statesmanship. Those who advocate the said equal fields also anticipate that we shall then one day witness a competitive situation in which men work industriously like a hill of ants. After all, these matters are not things that cannot be carried out to the full. Why should they be impossible if they are undertaken with steadfast and indomitable resolution by an ever increasing number of influential men who do their part? Should there be agitated dissent, a word will suffice to bring acceptance. It will be explained that such measures are only for the sake of public tranquility. Generally speaking, there are numerous instances verified in history in which the world's affairs have undergone great revolutionary change.

Doubts on Cremation[3]

Sakatani Shiroshi

I read in a *kanabon*[4] the other day about a fellow who assumed the name of Jinshichi[5] after coming from Korea during the Bunroku-Keichō Periods.[6] The site of his home and the tombstone of his daughter Ise[7] are in Takata Gun[8] of Aki no Kuni[9] to the West of Yoshida Mikkaichi.[10] According to local lore, Ise died young, and the father performed rites before her tombstone each year on the anniversary of her death during which he repeatedly cried out in sorrow: "Baby Ise, why do you not return? This spring, there were neither blooming flowers nor singing birds." While sojourning in Tokyo, I suffered the loss of my eldest son from illness in August of last year. I was unbearably grieved when I chanced to read this story on about the anniversary of my son's death, and the sorrow in my heart was beyond compare when I visited my son's tombstone. In this connection, my querulous thoughts turned to conditions under the ground. I prefer cremation even though I naturally do not believe in Buddhism. Scholars in society may indeed stoutly declare that burning the bodies of the parents and brothers is an unbearable barbarian custom. Yet how can they endure without reflection the custom of putting these precious remains in the mud, placing a large stone atop them as if to assure pickling, allowing them gradually to decay, and consigning them to slow torment by earthworms? Especially in the mountains, they will be dug up and eaten by wolves. The rich and the noble adopt the foolish customs of burying their dead in stone coffins padded in vermillion and, in extreme cases, of putting in treasures that invite grave robbers. Once the land has become fields or is washed by floods with the passage of time, the bones may be disturbed by hoes or exposed in the sand. Those who follow such burial practices may be complacent because, like children who steal bells while covering their ears, they do not know and do not see what goes on under the ground. Yet I am the type who is extremely disturbed by what I neither see nor know. Moreover, I have heard that man's health is injured when fumes from decaying corpses mix with the air and contaminate the water. This is inconsiderate to the world. Should we permit the death of our parents and brothers to hurt others? Still less is it endurable either to throw bodies into valleys or to float them on rivers or the sea as in the old days. Once the spirit has ascended to Heaven, the remains should be carefully burnt to prevent decay and then buried in a small urn. I naturally honored the sincere intentions behind the recent prohibition of cremation by burying my son in a large urn boxed in thick boards that I had painted with pitch. But the experience weighs heavily on this parent's heart to the present day. Furthermore, since it was an emergency burial in summer by a humble family, I had to place my son in damp grounds of a neighboring temple, and I have not had means to rebury him although I have thought of doing so. Having thus been increasingly disturbed by this matter, I would only suggest how good it would be if people were just allowed freely to practice cremation as in the past. When I read in a recent newspaper of an eccentric American who willed that his remains be dissected for medical purposes and then converted into fertilizer after being burnt in gas, I felt that this man was not an eccentric but that I wished to follow his example. Yet this is impossible since such a practice cannot be undertaken by descendants unless it is willed by the deceased. In America, however, cremation has been discussed and widely carried out, and there have also been rather heated discussions of the practice in Europe. Indeed, it does not seem that human nature has been elevated by the cessation of cremation. Pondering further on the future, in addition to the fellow in America who was converted into fertilizer, there are some who keep remains in their homes on the assumption that cemetaries are not permanent. Since it is improper to encourage abuses by willfully clinging to false pretexts, rather than being forced to repeal the prohibition after the appearance of abuses, [the government] with foresight should admonish the people as follows:

> You shall be accorded freedom to cremate or to bury as in former times. Hereafter, you shall be permitted individual burial or common burial without being beguiled by false ideas. If bodies are cremated into ashes, only small burial grounds will suffice. If you are so anxious for permanent graves [as to bury in your homes], what provision will there be should the

family line be extinguished or should your homes suffer unavoidable destruction by fire or other disaster? Abandon such a foolish idea! Assuming that the soul returns to the earth, the earth is indeed the best place [for the dead]. If the remains are cremated, you will not experience the insufferable anxiety that the bones some day may be exposed in the fields, and you may be happy in the knowledge that the remains will become fertilizer should the urn break.

It will be beneficial for later generations and men will be happy if they are instructed in this sense. Of course, cremators and those employing them will not escape scandals arising from foolish customs. Even though I think that it would be well to move toward a strict system of protection, I am not memorializing the government since I do not know the inner intent behind the prohibition. While we should mutually respect the prohibition until it is altered, I cannot but feel like Jinshichi. Having written, I beg your opinions.

Feelings of Personal Obligation (*Jōjitsu*[11])

Nishi Amane

How can man be no more than wood and stone when he has feelings of personal obligation? If he has these feelings, are they rooted in human nature (*sei*)?[12] Are they the heirs of benevolence (*jintoku*)[13] and the cousins of duty (*giri*)?[14] Is what we call the warm heart of woman another term for feelings of personal obligation? Since man also possesses these feelings, how can they belong to woman alone? Was the emergence of feelings of personal obligation associated with the end of the bakufu as well as with the great virtues of the Restoration? Are they related to embezzlement and to concubines? If so, then do low men of dangerous character really have feelings of personal obligation? Since low men prostrate themselves before authority and associate with power in a double-faced manner, how can they have feelings of personal obligation? If they do, then do the villainous men who cheat really have feelings of personal obligation? There are cunning rulers who are extremely doubting, cruel, and narrow minded. How can they have feelings of personal obligation? If they do, then what about the unbending and tough samurai? Are these men of direct words and stout rejoinders who are unmoved by enemies from without and families from within not influenced by feelings of personal obligation? After all, these feelings of personal obligation are characteristic of our moralistic land. If I am successful while my old friend is ruined, I cannot avoid recommending him even though I know he is without ability. If a friend benefits me privately, then I cannot but promote him publicly. When children of old friends call themselves [my] followers and rely on my assistance because of my earlier private relations [with their parents], I must care for them out of consideration for the old days. If a high official introduces his aspiring follower and entrusts him to my care, I can only take up the fellow's cause even though I know him to be unworthy. There is also the person without means of support who is incapable but sincere. I cannot but feel compassion when he sets forth family considerations and asks my assistance. When my wife or concubine makes an entreaty in bed regarding a favor sought by another, I can only do as she asks even though I know its filthy nature. If asked whether these things are all expressions of feelings of personal obligation, I would respond that feelings of personal obligation are far more ramified than those indicated above. I have feelings of personal obligation for another, he has these feelings for a third, and the third has them for still others. Feelings of personal obligation are involved when there is mutual love and mutual hate. We are completely interlaced with feelings of personal obligation that seem to have no shred of reason to foreigners who view them from outside. Only when one is within and enters the organs can one understand the individual reasons for the interconnected veins of feelings of personal obligation. In giving them a name, they might be called feelings of personal obligation that cannot be described. I would say that, when one glances quickly at the phrase "feelings of personal obligation," it seems the opposite of cold heartedness. Yet when one considers the words seriously, they are then the antithesis of justice.

On Promoting Our National Music

Kanda Kōhei

Among the numerous areas that should be promoted and reformed in our country today are such performing arts as music, singing, and drama. These arts indeed do not seem to be urgent matters. Yet since they cannot be perfected quickly, we cannot expect full success in them unless we soon give them assistance.

After all, never has there been a country more unskilled in harmony than ours. To be sure, T'ang music was brought to Japan in ancient days, but only the notes and not the lyrics have been handed down. Probably although lyrics were introduced, they were quickly snuffed out because we neither understood the pronunciations nor appreciated the meanings.

Such forms as *shirabyōshi*[15] and *sarugaku*[16] came later. While these were indeed inadequate as music, they were clearly better suited to the people's feelings than T'ang music because they were contrived by our countrymen.

I would say that, as compared with antiquity, music has advanced considerably with the emergence of various types of folk music and the addition of musical instruments since the Keichō-Genna Eras.[17] Being rustic and obscene, however, this music was generally unsuited for the enjoyment of refined people. It is to be regretted that refined people consequently by now have practically abandoned all music as they are uninterested in T'ang music and *sarugaku* and as they find the low forms of popular music unendurable.

If we now want to promote music, we should first investigate the study of harmony, which is a separate discipline based on scientific studies. This study of harmony develops methods for constructing notes according to sound and playing melodies by reading notes. These methods are fairly well advanced in China and extremely refined in the countries of Europe and America. Only our country has not yet been introduced to them, and the way to redress our deficiency is now to study them.

We should naturally select the instruments best suited to our needs, be they Chinese, Japanese, or Western.

As for lyrics, those of foreign countries are not suited for our use.

Nor do those sung in our country seem appropriate. If necessary, we can take from Kanze, Hōshō, Takemoto, or Utazawa[18] and for the time follow the current tastes of the people, just making a few additions and reforming musical transcription.

Since the lyrics of our country are completely without rhymes, they are inadequate to move the listeners greatly. If our people listen from time to time to Chinese and European songs and are able to understand the refinements of their rhymes, it should not be impossible to imitate their ways and to construct new compositions in Japanese.

I have previously stated that there are none of the foreign arts that we should not adopt. Yet we should especially avoid using lyrical forms as they exist in foreign countries. This is why it is essential to have new compositions.

Drama must be reformed still more. Restraints must be imposed upon our plays of today, which often injure men's minds because they are excessively obscene, sad, deceitful, and frank.

Moreover, our actors do not sing in their performances. It seems more colorful to mix speech and song in the manner of actors in foreign lands.

The styles of *kyōgen*[19] from *sarugaku* and the popular farcical *kyōgen* are especially good. Now going one step farther, the public will also benefit a great deal if we warn against the evils of the times and if we insert sarcasm into the jokes without resorting to obscenities or disturbing the times.

I have heard that famous literary men in foreign countries send their lyrics to the theatres and have their plays performed. This may be called the elegant amusement of the literary world. The plans for our theatre then must be greatly expanded. It will be most splendid if we employ public and private funds to construct in every city large and magnificent public halls in accordance generally with the regulations for public parks and if these halls become places for public entertainment where all persons, from emperor to commoners, enjoy the performances equally together.

In sum, there is nothing better than enjoying music with the public. How can we avoid encouraging music if we just reform it in accordance with the level of popular taste? It is only essential that we have the earnest guidance and correction of talented, ambitious, and influential persons.

Note: *Sumō*[20] is inescapably an ugly, barbarian custom notwithstanding its popularity among large numbers of our countrymen. That is, men should pit wisdom against wisdom since using strength against strength is the way of beasts. It is not becoming demeanor for men to enjoy watching other men perform like beasts. *Sumō*'s destruction should be gradually achieved since its followers will be enraged if it is suddenly prohibited.

[1]Satow, Ernest Mason, 1843–1929, interpreter and secretary to the British legation in Tokyo.

[2]Continued from Issue Sixteen.

[3]Sakatani is here protesting against the order by the Japanese government in 1873 prohibiting cremation, a directive that was apparently issued out of sensitivity for Western opinion. The order was rescinded two years later.

[4]*Kanabon,* 假名本, a book written in popular style with one of the Japanese syllabaries rather than with Chinese ideographs.

[5]Jinshichi, 甚七.

[6]Bunroku (文祿) and Keichō (慶長) Periods, 1592–1595 and 1596–1615, respectively.

[7]Ise, 伊勢.

[8]Takata Gun, 高田郡.

[9]Aki no Kuni, 安藝ノ國, the present Hiroshima (廣島) Prefecture.

[10]Yoshida Mikkaichi, 吉田三日市.

[11]*Jōjitsu,* 情實. Although *jōjitsu* might be more strictly translated as "personal feelings," Nishi clearly had in mind the infinite variety of status and societal obligations characteristically found among the Japanese and today identified as *ninjō* (人情), a sense of compassion coupled with obligation and duty arising from personal connections that he clearly deplored when it contributed to unsavory conduct or the condoning of unsavory conduct. Ivan P. Hall states, "*Jōjitsu* referred to sentiment, particularly to sentimental considerations, special connections, and favoritism in the conduct of public affairs, and evoked the entire cosmos of personalism in which Japanese social and political relations traditionally had been grounded." See I. P. Hall, *Mori Arinori* (Cambridge, Mass., 1973), pp. 270–271.

[12]*Sei,* 性.

[13]*Jintoku,* 仁德.

[14]*Giri,* 義理.

[15]*Shirabyōshi,* 白拍子, a female dancer of medieval times, robed in white and wearing a sword and man's headgear.

[16]*Sarugaku,* 猿樂, prototype of the farcical *kyōgen* (狂言) and classical *nō* (能) drama.

[17]Keichō-Genna (慶長元和) Eras, 1597-1615 and 1615–1634, respectively.

[18]Kanze (觀世) and Hōshō (寶生) are schools of *nō* drama; Takemoto Gidayū (竹本義太夫), 1651–1714, was the originator of the Gidayū form of ballad drama; and Utazawa refers to a school of vocal music founded by the first Utazawa Yamato-no-daijō (哥澤大和大掾).

[19]*Kyōgen,* 狂言, comic interludes performed between *nō* plays.

[20]*Sumō,* 角力, traditional Japanese wrestling.

Secrets

Nishi Amane

If men are presented with such a title as *Secrets* without even discussing the contents, their "curiosity" will be stirred so that they want to see, to hear, and to know the secrets. Bragging of secrets inevitably stimulates a response like scratching an itch or soothing a pain. Even though they know at first glance that the matter is not worthy of their attention, it is the fundamental nature of men, if they are not fools or self-abandoned, to be unable to set a secret aside once it has attracted their attention. Actually, therefore, the word *secret* strongly stimulates man's curiosity and all the more draws his attention. The ancients already practiced this trick. Mysterious formulas have been transmitted by families in medicine, and the arts of sword and spear have been handed down secretly. There have been exclusive melodies in music, private arts in *waka,*[1] and secret papers as well as secret traditions on the arts of defense in military strategy. In such manner have men made their hidden mysteries and utmost secrets the tools of monopolies. I have heard of an instance in the Confucian school of [Yamazaki] Ansai[2] in which tuition of one hundred rolls of silk was demanded for instruction on the section entitled *Yü Tien* in the *Lun Yü.*[3] After all, [the monopolist] only fears that such matters will be regarded as commonplace and that the value arising from their scarce preciousness will be reduced should their secrets be made public. Valueless objects, therefore, are made precious by the methods [of the monopolist] who prevents people from easily knowing or inquiring into [his wares] by carefully wrapping them up. With the progress of society toward enlightenment, however, such shady practices are generally being destroyed as men's wisdom daily increases. Had the Western arts of photography and electro-magnetism been kept secret, how astonishing they would seem to men! Westerners, however, have not the slightest regret that the principles and laws behind these techniques have been clarified and written down and spread through the world. Even ignorant people are able to understand and share these things. Once society is directed toward enlightenment in this manner, the esoteric law of Shingon[4] as well as the rites of the mountain priests (*Shugen Goma*)[5] will lose their significance and thereafter cease.

I would like to discuss a question regarding which I am myself puzzled—why there are still secret matters in political affairs. Even when society has reached the level of civilization and enlightenment, there are ultimately three types of secret that should be preserved. First, there are "moral" secrets. Just as men are admonished that obscene words should not be uttered, it has been human nature common the world over since antiquity that to cover ugliness and to hide filth is a cardinal rule of etiquette. Not only is this the case with savages. It is also the nature of birds and beasts such as cats that try to cover their dung by clawing the earth and dogs that endeavor to hide their urine by digging the sandy soil. Moral secrets, therefore, are indeed unavoidable. Second, there are secrets relating to military affairs. The plans of military headquarters should not be leaked, even as the proverb warns that, since wars are destructive and armies are instruments of murder, they naturally should not be discussed in a normal way. It was also said in antiquity that injury arises when military secrets are not kept. Military secrets are thus unavoidable. Then there is a third type of unavoidable secrets, secrets relating to "policy." Since the broad plans of the throne and the deeply laid schemes in the corridors are fundamentals of governing, they should never be handled in a deceptive manner. It is important that these matters be made known publicly and that the people be obliged invariably to obey them forthrightly. Only in foreign relations are there matters that should never be made public. Since such instruments as secret alliances are allowed under international law, policy secrets are also unavoidable. Even in civilized and enlightened societies, secrets of these three types can never be eliminated, or they cannot be dispensed with suddenly.

Aside from the above three, there is another type of secret, the so-called political secret. These secrets transmit the wiles of forebears in the manner of the previously mentioned medical and technical secrets. During the decline of the late bakufu, its leaders conducted arbitrary government while enjoying luxurious lives. They explained their conduct by saying that affairs are not esteemed if they are not private, that they have no weight if they are not secret, and that the country would be destroyed if their secrets lost value. The entire nation, therefore, was ignorant of the circumstances when the government suddenly fell. This was because understanding was prevented by a block in communication since rulers and ruled both held their secrets. The reforms of the Restoration have greatly changed these old secretive ways. Institutions are explained; regulations are published; all the people are enlightened together; edicts are daily issued; and the nation clearly understands the imperial intentions. When the nation thus reverently understands the imperial wishes, how can it fail to prosper? Sometimes there is still darkness and obscurity, however. In such a matter as the punitive expedition to Formosa, the nation today is only beginning to appreciate that we were obliged to chastise the Formosan aborigines and that China was iniquitous since the island had not belonged to her. Ah, was this then a policy secret? At any rate, rather than plan the great affairs of the nation arbitrarily and privately, it is far better for leaders to win widespread "sympathy" by taking the public into their confidence.[6]

The Time for a Popularly Elected Assembly Is Not Yet[7]

Kanda Kōhei

How can a popularly elected assembly be easily established? It will never be established until the time has come. And even when the time has come, it will never be a time of rejoicing.

Now the season for establishing a popularly elected assembly will be the time when the national structure is changed from autocratic despotism (*kunshu senken*)[8] to rule shared by monarch and people (*kummin bunken*).[9] This time is unlikely to be one of protest from the people since they will acquire rights. But even this cannot be stated definitely. It also cannot yet be known whether the court will graciously concede since it will give up half its power.

Even though the matter may be greatly expedited if the court graciously concedes, I doubt that such [an attitude] can be expected. When it is possible to recall power that had earlier been granted to appease the popular mind, such a grant, after all, cannot yet be called conclusive. If the ruler does not willingly concede, still less will the people be able to act whatever their aspirations may be. Considering the meekness of our people, it is also impossible for them to go as far as foreigners who have imposed contracts on their courts after raising armies and fighting victoriously.

Generally speaking, popularly elected assemblies are not established while the ruler is wise, while the country is not pressed by foreign enemies, while foreigners lend money, while paper currency circulates, and while the people acquiesce in increased taxes. Yet the world is a living organism, and its affairs cannot always be settled by the above means. Sometime in the future, the people will not acquiesce in increased taxes, the circulation of paper money will halt, foreigners will not lend money, enemy countries will arise to threaten from the outside, and the ruler by chance may not be wise. What shall we do if such should come to pass? The country will then invariably be destroyed if a popularly elected assembly is not established, and a popularly elected assembly will surely arise if the country is not destroyed. This is when I would say that the time has come. Yet it is not a time greatly to be desired. Therefore, I say that, even though the time comes, it will never be a time for rejoicing.

Honoring Differences

Sakatani Shiroshi

In general, affinity between things arises from their peculiarly analogous natures while distinction between things may be attributed to their peculiarly different natures. When the power of attraction is generated by the analogous natures of things, they draw together and congeal to become one. This is the function of conformity. Once things have become one, their different natures generate opposing power, and their component parts reveal their strengths by struggling against each other and dividing. This is the function of difference. While things are formed by drawing together such individual ingredients as water, fire, earth, wood, metal, bone, stone and leather, these ingredients separately rub and polish each other to develop tools and uses. These functions of conformity and difference are found throughout nature.

Now even though the function of conformity is naturally essential, the function of difference is also extremely important if one ponders the process of conformity. Upon examination all matter will be found to be composed of more than sixty different elements that are joined together in particular proportions. Nor will there be found in the universe any mountains, rivers, and other phenomena that are exactly the same. The manifold differences between all things extend even to those of the same species, such as plum trees and pines. Although there are similar persons among the billions of men and women in the world, none really have the same appearance or the same character. The dissimilarities between men's minds is like those between their faces. The function of similarity and affinity on earth arises from the fact that the universe fully tolerates its opposing forces without daring to employ them arbitrarily. This is why the greatness of the universe can be preserved forever. Men will only be successful in their enterprises if they tolerantly respect each other's differences. By means of their differences, teachers and students as well as good friends cultivate each other and develop their intellects and proficiencies. Just as a jewel must be polished with another stone, [these people] cultivate each other and strengthen their mental and physical powers by enduring the trials and hardships arising from their differences. Even books cannot be revised if we do not possess different versions. Is not the function of difference important?

I have heard that in European religion during the Middle Ages different opinions arose and vied with each other while debates were pressed. The great merit of this cultivation was that spirits were stimulated and famous teachers emerged in profusion. As theories were settled and dogmatism prevailed, submissive views daily spread, the power of opposition became thin, the spirit of discord slackened, and the emergence of famous teachers gradually diminished. Devoted disciples, regretting this, then artificially contrived differing opinions and stimulated their wits. We should understand that differences should be honored, and conformity disdained.

Government represents the universe, and its responsibilities for education and protection are large beyond compare with those of religion. This indeed is why government should tolerate and honor differences. Foreign countries stimulate each other with their differing customs and secular teachings (*seikyō*),[10] subordinate officials mutually cultivate each other with their differing opinions; and the common people improve each other with their differing expressions. The development of their just and appropriate measures and the promotion of high national prestige have all arisen from mutual cultivation through competing differences. If governments and high officials with courageous spirit disdain and reject subservient flatterers who conform while encouraging the power to oppose and if governments and high officials honor and respect those who cultivate each other with their differences while encouraging the power of fraternal attraction, then differences within the country will all harmoniously coalesce just as the sixty odd different elements mix with each other. Then may we expect with confidence the emergence of a [national] entity that is matchless in its strength and prosperity. If we honor differences and use them properly, even the unfeeling trees and stones will all serve our purposes. How much more so with feeling human beings! Rejecting and disdaining differences only resembles the former savage policy of expelling barbarians. How will governing of the nation be advanced [except by honoring differences]? Moreover, it is man's nature to rejoice in the realization of his designs. When neither government nor high officials accept one word of dissent, who will be content with the patronage of superior authority even though he daily receives large gratuities? Being flabby in spirit and disobedient in heart, officials just look after their private interests.

Since antiquity, failure to encourage officials has generally been the source of national destruction. To this may be attributed the rise or fall of Yao and Shun,[11] Chieh and Chou,[12] Ch'in Shih Huang-ti and Han Kao Tsu.[13] Even such great heroes as Oda Nobunaga and Toyotomi Hideyoshi were ultimately destroyed. But Tokugawa Ieyasu adopted the opinions of the common people, saying that the merit of their remonstrances surpassed that of the greatest military feat. Profiting from honoring their differences, Ieyasu successfully opened up new ways.[14] Such cases are unmistakable evidence from Japanese and Chinese history that should still cause men to reflect. Tsar Peter of Russia lost several wars against Sweden, but he observed, "I shall be instructed by their victories." We should appreciate the habitual frame of mind of such a man who respected the differences of even his powerful enemy. While he made mistakes, therefore, Peter achieved great success by adopting the differences of England, France and other countries. Napoleon III of France at first pretended for a time to honor difference. Becoming emperor, however, he sought to compel men to conform to his will by despotic means and by sagacity, and he fell prisoner after suffering defeat eighteen years later. We should clearly reflect on the attitudes of these two emperors toward difference and conformity.

Some who now favor a popularly elected assembly say that it is premature, but they neglect to discuss the methods for dealing with this prematurity. Some affirm that we should await the course of nature. To wait for nature, however, is only to postpone the assembly until after a great disturbance. These people all honor difference in name but detest it in actuality. Agitators among the public are vigorously trying to establish an assembly and to destroy the government without regard to the fundamentals of the political structure. If we do not prevent such from coming to pass, these lovers of turmoil will brew a disturbance comparable to the time of the French King Louis XVI. They are not persons who cooperate in a calm manner. If the opinions of others differ slightly from theirs, they quickly become angry and abusive. Selfishly employing their powers of attraction toward conformity, equally with the conservatives they abhor and dislike difference. What kind of assembly can be established when there are such inconsistencies and restraints arising from their personal loves and hates? Even if an assembly is established, conduct and discussions will be contradictory, and these fellows will only engage endlessly in futile and shameless recrimination. Measures and discussions in society today are all of such futile nature. It is quite understandable that there are numerous autocratic controls. What I fear is that the power of the opposition will furiously mount like a stopped-up water course. Breaking through banks and overflowing dikes, the water will carry everything before it in all directions until it reaches what vacillating people call the natural flood level.

It may be asked then, why did not China flourish during the Sung Dynasty when exchanges of differing opinions were most extreme? This was because, apart from Wang An-shih who blocked enlightenment by favoring conformity with his own views, the obstinate and intractable leaders of Sung were neither clearly just nor deeply attached to difference. This was exemplified when the virtuous Master Ssŭ-ma [Kuang] was cheated by the fellow Ts'ai Ch'ing.[15] The Master Ssŭ-ma was a true gentleman and scholar, but he did not know how to determine the affairs of the empire by public discussion. His labors and anxieties were only his tribulations as a single individual. Master Ssŭ-ma may indeed be excused, but what succour can result even from numerous discussions when mean men like crafty foxes clamorously grasp national power? Even so, Sung China, her weakness notwithstanding, was not then destroyed by a single defeat. It was because of numerous discussions that she defended the southern bank of the Yangtze. Sung's weakness would surely have been completely overcome and her mean leaders overthrown had these discussions been still more extensive. Rather than blame the multiplicity of discussions in Sung China, therefore, we should only regret that they were not more numerous. Should I be asked if war should be favored since it is a difference, I would respond that difference arises from conformity while conformity produces difference. The ultimate in conformity invariably breeds difference, disturbance, and war. And the ultimate in difference invariably brings conformity, peace, and harmony. Men fight because they are not at peace. This is why they search for a balance and achieve peace. This opinion, however, only concerns the course of nature. Once we have suffered defeat and destruction, our confusion will only promote rule by others. It is for men to make use of Creation by judicious cultivation (*saisei hoshō*).[16] War should be studied but not favored. Men promote nature by judicious cultivation. They are not men who attain ultimate conformity if they try to make others conform to themselves and if they love war and disturbance in violation of judicious cultivation. Since I have recently been impressed by reading Nishi's essay on loving one's enemy, I am circulating this for your criticism.

Human Social Intercourse Part Three[17]

Sugi Kōji

If there are suits and litigation, there must then invariably be justice. Moreover, those administering justice, being persons esteemed in society for their virtuous conduct, should have power to exercise their enlightenment on behalf of justice and to impose their judgments of right and wrong on wrong-doers. This is why judicial officers have been publicly established in society

Since hearing accusations and looking into criminal cases is extremely complicated, it was essential to establish a regular order in trials and to handle these according to common precedents. By such means were deceit punished, license prevented, and superfluous litigation avoided. This is why law codes were established. Ultimately, however, the great principles of these codes were successively abused, litigation stagnated, truth was sometimes lost in a bog of precedents, and miscarriage of justice sometimes arose from technicalities.

On the whole, instruments of threat and intimidation were introduced to correct conduct and enhance virtue in society because mean men could not be moved in their hearts simply by the example of rather exalted morality. This was the reason for introducing corporal punishments whose severity differed according to the injury incurred on human beings by the criminal.

Belief in God is an innate quality peculiar to men that moves them in their souls to develop the will for virtuous conduct. Moreover, since religion is the greatest power for correcting wrong, a group of teachers emerged to propagate it publicly in society. Now in religious matters, the level of belief depends upon the level of the believer's thought and wisdom. Since mean and rough people are extremely low in their thought and, therefore, weak and ignorant in their minds, they are without self-reliance, vainly praying to God to make good their deficiencies. The teachers of religion also fell into heresy since they were not illumined by the Reason of Divine Revelation. Becoming arrogant, they put their interests first, misled low men of trivial faith, and destroyed good and virtue. Thereby did heretical and deceptive ways gradually and spontaneously flourish. Moreover, in countries where despotism prevailed, false religion was the national religion, and its followers were honored persons. Troubles arose one after another from their errors of belief. Their teachings upset human enterprise as they mistook right from wrong and failed to discern the facts of our relations to things. Endeavoring to replace the affairs of the human world with those of the other world, they misled society along the heretical path of devils and witches, as if society were condemned to a dream shrouded in mist. At times, these teachers of religion, organizing themselves into factions, were intolerant of each other. Or, being fond of wealth and enjoying fame, they hoped to convert others with their superstitions and arrogantly employed military power. Matters of custom, education, and etiquette were generally all invariably dependent upon religious principles. Then when men believed in the things that they individually honored and as they moved into the region of superstition, honoring only ancient beliefs and destroying human ethics, divergent ideas flourished increasingly while religious tenets were more and more separated.

When mutual strife and discord arose from diversity of religious opinions, the light of truth began somewhat to flicker, sound scholarship consequently flourished, human feelings were renewed, human intercourse extended from near to far, and the status of human beings continually changed. Men's moral studies became increasingly refined and their knowledge, increasingly well rounded since they then wanted to promote what they should undertake, to exert themselves in what they could do well, to finish what they should aim at, and to gain what should be hoped for. Moreover, there were also numerous cases in which the area of scholarship was greatly broadened, the principles of the ancients became generally known to the world, scholars discovered still more new principles, and the foundations were laid for later study. Being unable to learn everything with their limited capacities, individuals studied the particular fields into which they divided knowledge. Yet scholars sometimes did not escape bias as the path of scholarship is long and deep with branches that have no single conclusion. In the name of scholarship and religion, men studied without reflecting and led the ignorant with their biased views until they finally provoked a crisis in society.

[1]*Waka,* 和歌, a thirty-one syllable Japanese verse form.

[2][Yamazaki] Ansai, 山崎闇齋, 1618–1682, a scholar in the Neo-Confucian tradition.

[3]*Yü Tien,* 與點, a famous section of the *Analects* (*Lun Yü,* 論語) entitled *Hsien Chin* (先進).

[4]Shingon, 眞言, esoteric Buddhism introduced to Japan in the early eighth century by the celebrated monk Kūkai (空海).

[5]*Shugen Goma,* 修験護摩. *Goma* is a holy fire of invocation in which cedar sticks are burned on an altar by the followers of Shugen-dō (修験道), wandering ascetics of the mountains.

[6]Nishi here is criticizing the government's handling of the expedition to chastize the Formosan aborigines who had murdered fifty-four Ryūkyū islanders stranded on Formosa's southern coast. Although Formosa then belonged to China, the Peking government disclaimed responsibility for the aborigines. The Japanese expedition was organized without notifying China and sailed from Nagasaki on 27 April 1874 without authority from the government in Tokyo. In addition to provoking a major crisis with China, the expedition was severely criticized by those Japanese who felt that their country was not yet ready to embark on foreign adventures. At the time of Nishi's writing, Ōkubo Toshimichi (大久保利通) was negotiating a settlement with the Chinese in Peking.

[7]Kanda in this essay is lamenting the crisis that would be the occasion for establishing a popularly elected assembly, not the assembly itself. His conduct and his other writings clearly indicate that he fully subscribed to the idea of a popularly elected assembly to be established at the appropriate time.

[8]*Kunshu senken,* 君主專權.

[9]*Kummin bunken,* 君民分權.

[10]*Seikyō,* 政教. For Sakatani's discussion of *seikyō*, secular teachings, as distinguished from religious teachings (*hōkyō,* 法教), see his essays on secular teachings in Issues Twenty-Two and Twenty-Five.

[11]Yao, 堯, and Shun, 舜, legendary Chinese model emperors.

[12]Chieh, 桀, and Chou Hsin, 紂辛, traditionally regarded by the Chinese as wicked rulers whose misdeeds brought the fall of the Hsia (夏) and the Shang (商) dynasties, respectively.

[13]Ch'in Shih Huang Ti, 秦始皇帝, and Han Kao Tsu, 漢高祖, the founders of the Ch'in and the Han dynasties in 221 B.C. and 206 B.C, respectively. Ch'in Shih Huang Ti was always excoriated by Confucian scholars because of his efforts to suppress their thought and destroy the Confucian canon. He ordered destruction of the books upon the recommendation of Li Ssŭ (李斯), his chief minister who brought the fall of the Ch'in shortly after the emperor's death. Han Kao Tsu, a practical farmer by origin, established the succeeding Han Dynasty that lasted with one significant break for about four centuries.

[14]Oda Nobunaga, 織田信長, Toyotomi Hideyoshi, 豐臣秀吉, and Tokugawa Ieyasu, 德川家康, the three outstanding leaders who together and in succession restored order in Japan between 1560–1615. Ieyasu outlived Nobunaga and Hideyoshi to lay the foundations for his family's two hundred and fifty years of supremacy in Japan.

[15]Ssŭ-ma [Kuang], 司馬光, and Ts'ai Ching, 蔡京. Ts'ai Ching, 1046–1126 A.D., was a disciple of the innovative minister Wang An-shih (王安石) who sought to disgrace the great historian Ssŭ-ma Kuang and other conservatives by having their names engraved on a stone tablet as traitors.

[16]*Saisei hoshō*, 裁成輔相, the Chinese phrase that Sakatani repeatedly employed to express his desire to encourage ordered progress.

[17]Continued from previous issue.

On the Press[1]

Tsuda Mamichi

As I have previously indicated in my discussion of freedom of the press, I hope that there will be no restraints from the government's side on the ability of men to write freely and to print what they want to say. After all, our time is the crucial period when the culture of our Japanese Empire is truly moving toward enlightenment, like the season when the foliage of plants and trees reaches effulgence or the period in the life of a man when he matures in intellectual power. Having lovingly reared and protected it, we must only avoid injury to its growth and development, allowing it to follow its natural course without interference or oppression from one side.

Since our government has permitted the publication of newspapers, several tens of journals have collected and printed anything in the least novel, odd, amusing, or new, ranging from government announcements to local matters, articles by writers, and foreign news. It should also be observed that the press has been truly significant in broadening the outlook of men as well as in advancing civilization and enlightenment. Moreover, to the press offices should be ascribed the nurturing of the roots of the nation's strength and prosperity.

About half of the local reports, however, relate to robberies and adultery. In the final analysis, since these reports naturally only record the facts as they exist under actual conditions, they are never fabrications or misrepresentations, and I do not doubt their truth. Now if one just reviews the poems and tales indigenous to our country, the poems are generally love poems, and the tales mostly pornographic affairs. Are not the lewd customs of our empire especially extreme? It may be retorted that the enlightenment of our country is in its youth, the age when men are beginning to develop their intellects, that is, the age of emerging lust and the age of sensitivity. Just to judge by comparing our poetry with that of China, enlightenment in our national ways has not yet reached the elegance of civilization. Even though it is reasonable that there naturally should be numerous expressions of affection between sexes, lust is what is admonished in young men, and, of course, it must be strictly forbidden in the nation. This is why, when we recently revised the stipulations regarding adultery under Japanese law, the provisions [against adultery] were extremely numerous as compared with those in European and American countries. While adulterous practices outwardly are strictly forbidden, however, it is privately admonished that such conduct is not to be exposed. For example, it is the universal practice that adultery by the wife is only referred to the law after it has been reported by the husband. Yet if one peruses the papers of our country, they often expose adultery before it has been revealed and investigated by the police. In extreme cases, they later apologize for their erroneous reports [of adultery]. It is beyond dispute that the individual suffers great harm from the disclosure of his private affairs. This is also contrary to the intent of the law. Especially unbearable is the fact that children are allowed to read these reports. Is the great injury thus incurred by the press against their morals, after all, different from that derived from the printing of lewd stories in indecent novels? It is also beyond dispute that, in addition to contradicting the purpose behind the permission by the government to publish newspapers, [these stories] are actually contrary to the aim of the press offices to advance civilization and enlightenment. How can the editors themselves fail to recognize this? While they intone "civilization and enlightenment" when they open their mouths, we may infer from just such conduct that they are themselves not endowed with views that are civilized and enlightened.

It is really bad that the press often reports a man's past crimes. That we humans generally shrink from raking up past crimes is human nature and rightly moral. The punishment of crimes is the responsibility of government. Yet there are examples under the law when punishment for an old crime is reduced or waived. Now is it not completely unendurable for the press to print and noise abroad the old crimes of others? Whenever they receive letters from spiteful persons, it would be well for the newspapers carefully to exercise reasonable discretion. I just hope that the editors will hear and be influenced by what I have written.

On Wives and Concubines Part Four[2]

Mori Arinori

Once a woman takes a husband and manages a household, her responsibilities are not light. Moreover, it may also be said that her obligations are really heavy and difficult when she becomes a mother and instructs her children. Thus a mother should invariably preserve her bodily strength since, if she is weak, she cannot well rear and protect the children who are completely dependent on her. Her nature should also be invariably fair and her disposition invariably pure. If she is not fair by nature, she cannot command obedience and respect when she manages her children. As children respond to their mother just like a reflection in a mirror, if the mother's disposition is not pure, then the children, reflecting this, also cannot be pure. If we desire children of fine character and disposition, therefore, then their mother by all means should also attain similar perfection. As honesty is the source of trust and as children depend entirely on their mother with sincere trust, how can she preserve their confidence if she is not honest? Ultimately, if there is deceit between mother and children, the children will grow up to cheat others and to injure the world. This is to be deeply pondered. The mother also should invariably have high ideals. Without high ideals, how can she encourage her children to render great services for the promotion of culture through great and righteous undertakings? Woman are by nature rich in sympathy and deeply loving. If they have not studied in their younger years, however, they often drown their children in love without understanding the means for employing their loving power in rearing their offspring. Women, therefore, should fully perceive the way to use their wealth in love after first acquiring the essentials of scholarship and the physical laws and broadening the bounds of their wisdom. If they do this, their deep love will mount more and more, and the benefits derived therefrom will be increasingly large. Ah, the duties of women are so difficult and their responsibilities so heavy! It is common practice, however, for men to use women as playthings, to gain pleasure from indulging licentiously and inconsiderately in saké, lewdness, music, and songs, and to refrain from mingling with women unless they share in these pleasures. It is not idle slander that in the eyes of foreigners ours is the most immoral country in the world.

Doubts on Fox Stories

Sakatani Shiroshi

The wiliness of foxes (*kitsune*)[3] is the same in East and West. Especially in Japan and China, however, have there been stories of people possessed by foxes and have all persons alike since antiquity taken foxes for ghostly apparitions. Opinions recently received from Europe make clear that these things may all be attributed to a type of mental derangement. Yet possessed persons so act and rant like foxes and badgers (*tanuki*)[4] that even scholars cannot explain their abnormality. Conjecturing on their origin, since fox and badger stories in Japan and China appeared during ignorant times of earliest antiquity, these beasts have been considered devils or gods, and warnings of their coming have been deeply planted as eradicable impressions on men's minds from childhood. Once a person's spirit becomes troubled, therefore, these deeply implanted impressions compete with each other, and nurses make a great fuss when treating supposed demention by foxes and badgers. Given such fake treatment, how can the patient avoid suffering from delusions of foxes and badgers? It is entirely reasonable for women to be deceived by kites and crows and for vulgar people, through ignorance or because of greed, to be misled and mocked by the craft of foxes and badgers. Further, people respond to these taunts in accordance with the deeply implanted impressions in their heads, and there are naturally times when they suffer hallucinations from which they cannot easily be persuaded by words.

Among the victims of these previously implanted impressions are timid people who, treading on rotten rope at night, mistake it for a snake and who see the shadows of bamboos as ghosts, defeated soldiers who take the whistling of the wind and the crane's cry for the enemy, the leader who, misled by lesser men, doubts the difficulties of his faithful retainer and believes him disloyal, and the suspicious person who, having lost something, takes his honest old neighbor for a thief. Viewing the matter in light of these examples, we can understand that such predilections and consequent daily habits should be moderated by education.

According to *Soi-seishi*[5] the dogs of Hokkaidō[6] are wise while the men are foolish, that the men of Honshū[7] are wise while the dogs are foolish, and that both men and dogs are wise in the West. It would seem from this same source that the wisdom of men generally depends on enlightenment while that of dogs arises from the earth's ether. While the craftiness of foxes in East and West is universal, *Soi-seishi* hears that the foxes of Hokkaidō are more foolish than those of Honshū. It may be that in Hokkaidō, where nature favors eccentricity, the earth's ether has caused the foxes to exchange a little of their sense with the dogs. If this is the case, then did the earth's ether cause the foolish dogs of Honshū to trade a little of their sense with the foxes? Again, how can we know that the minds of Japanese and Chinese are not impressed by the craft of foxes that is twice that of Western foxes. A similar case, after all, is the fact that Europeans have not been able to erase the expedients of religion that have been impressed on their minds. In short, how can we speak of ghosts when we are moving toward the world of enlightenment? All superstitions will disappear when Heaven's Way (*Tennen no Michi*)[8] and Nature's Reason (*Shizen no Ri*)[9] actually prevail and when men are strong and enlightened in body and mind. The impression of outmoded customs on men's minds should indeed be fully erased. Yet some people are impressing a form of new abuse on men's minds while searching for a short cut by avoiding the main road in their desire to erase the marks of outmoded customs. This is exchanging one fox for another. Is this still greater injury not to be regretted?

On the Broad Meaning of Foxes

Sakatani Shiroshi

I have previously discussed the fact that people are not possessed by foxes. Even if a man should be possessed by a fox, its seriousness only suffices for an evening's conversation over tea. There are other addictions that are really far more injurious than being possessed by foxes. If you ask what they are, one is opium smoking, which stupifies and debilitates men, and even reaches the point of causing a great war. Men know well the injury of opium without being able to stop it. The Chinese alone, however, are especially possessed by this evil. Another addiction is liquor. There are many varieties of liquor, but their poison is the same. Men of good sense have rebuked drinking since antiquity, and an American prohibitionist party is trying to stop it without in the least being able to reduce its charm. Yet partaking of liquor is not so all pervasive. There is also lust. Since women are beings endowed with wit and compassion, even brave warriors are fascinated by them. Clear examples are Cleopatra of Egypt who possessed two brave Romans, the captivation of Han Kao Tsu by the Empress Lü and T'ang Kao Tsung by the Empress Wu,[10] and the spells under which Yoritomo and Hideyoshi were held by Masako and Yodogimi.[11] In addition, women often destroy morality, carry on like beasts, and upset mind, body, family, and country. If such be not the case, keeping one concubine spreads scandal for a time. How dreadful is the power of women! Even so, women do not all exert such power of attraction since the beautiful are few while the ugly are many.

The hard, feelingless, inorganic metals of gold and silver alone dazzle the eyes of men with the brilliance of their color so that human beings throughout the world generally are somnolent under their spell—be the persons noble or vulgar, men or women, old or young. Money, of course, can neither be eaten when we are hungry nor worn when we are cold, but we quickly become cold and hungry if we are without it for only a day. Addiction to drink and lust are also encouraged by money. It is for the sake of money that scholars follow their studies, that officials are energetic in their duties, that merchants and artisans exhaust their powers, and that the humane are called humane or the unmerciful unmerciful. The crimes of robbery, murder, and deceit as well as strife among heroes and gallants who forget morality on the battlefield, sacrifice their lives, and devote themselves to strategy day and night—all these are induced by the spell of money. Moreover, while money did not exist in antiquity, it has gradually increased during later generations, and its impression on men's minds has become more and more extreme with advancing enlightenment. Even should we suppose that foxes really possess men's minds, can their spell be one ten-thousandth that of money?

Money's miraculous power is indeed beyond imagination. Yet when one ponders the matter deeply, it is not that money bewitches men with its wisdom. They only bewitch themselves with their desire for money. The fault lies in human desire, not in money. The benefits of money are also incomparably great since money serves the world by circulating, mixing together, and substituting for all things. Then shall we destroy desire? I would say no. Man will be destroyed if we destroy the desires that are a part of him. Men should only control the excess of their desire. If men are ultimately unable to control excess desire, this will be because their hearts, being without restraint, have lost their balance. Religion and law can exert control by establishing restraints, but they cannot prevent disturbances because they cannot assure a balance. Whether in republics or monarchies, leaders in actual practice should cause the people of the nation to enjoy the rights of freedom, liberty, and justice in accordance with their social status and the trends of the times. Only if they thus nurture and control all matters according to the workings of nature will the withered not complain and the fallen not be angry. Only thereby will they with certainty heighten courage by establishing mental restraints, extinguish private desire through the cultivation of superior talent, and protect individuals by establishing a balance between them.

Nevertheless, persons who can fully realize such ideals are Washingtons who appear only once in a thousand years. Such ideals are also difficult to attain in republics. But they alone should be our objective even though they may be difficult to attain. Since fairness and justice in the world are always directed toward these ideals, we can only expect the emergence of a great man [like Washington] if, without going to extremes, we gradually extinguish unseemly impressions from our heads and firmly defend this objective with fairness and justice. Especially to be regretted are leaders who rely on their own meagre talents, regard others as fools, and think of themselves as brave men. Themselves first falling under the spell of money, losing their objectives, and being unrestrained in their hearts, such leaders promote their own views, dislike the words of others, and mislead their subordinates with bribes if they do not take bribes themselves. They are always truckling to the feelings of others and changing their plans. Adorning themselves with deceptions and spreading their craftiness, they feel self-satisfied. They appear like gold narcissuses in gold hats and gold garments, but they are only foxes and badgers in disguise. It is clear from the past that such persons are fomenters of great disturbances in society who one day will be roasted like foxes by public wrath. The tricks of these human foxes and badgers really surpass the spells of opium, drink, and women. And their injury exceeds that of gold and silver. Thieving merchants of the towns and robbers of the highways are only small foxes and small badgers who vend lies and sell deceit. Are they thus degraded because they have learned a little [craftiness] from big foxes and old badgers?

Knowledge Part Three[12]

Nishi Amane

I shall now undertake to discuss how scholarship emerged with the development of systematically organized knowledge. As cultures in the world advance toward enlightenment, what we call scholarship emerges to organize all human matters by deepening the foundations of culture. In Eastern Asia, medicine, agriculture, and commerce stem from Shên Nung,[13] music had Nü Wa as its foundress,[14] astronomy was devised with the instruments of Shun,[15] geography and the art of ruling were introduced in Yü Kung,[16] Hou Chi was the father of gardening,[17] penal law is ascribed to Kao Yao,[18] K'uei was the originator of education,[19] and we honor Fu Yueh and I Yin in politics,[20] and thereafter came the men of Chou. How glorious were the men of Chou![21] The culture of the majority of the yellow race to the East of the Himalayas entirely depended for its origin on the Chou people, and Confucius and Mencius were thus their diapers. To the West of the Himalayas, astronomy arose in Chaldea, the study of language and phonetics was founded by the followers of ancient Brahman,* men honor Moses, Solon, and Lycurgus for law, Homer and David were the progenitors of poetry, and the Arabs originated algebra.

These studies flourished exceedingly in Greece and Alexandria, and Westerners do not doubt that their culture was germinated in ancient Athens. After all, without regard to country, once people have adopted writing after abandoning ropes as a means of communication, culture invariably arises and scholarship consequently also begins more or less to take shape. Indeed, ancient Egypt, having previously developed hieroglyphics, already possessed an orderly culture four thousand years ago. Ancient Mexico also possessed symbol writing, and Alexander Humbolt, putting together the ancient Mexican calendar from old stone inscriptions, judged extremely delicate the Aztec calendar that was based on a year of eighteen months of twenty days. Thus throughout the world, scholarship dates from antiquity. Yet when one compares [ancient scholarship] with that of modern Europe, they are as different as Heaven from earth. Moreover, when speaking of flourishing studies, I am not referring [only] to the mastery of individual disciplines through deep inquiry. I refer to the great task of gathering together the numerous sciences and various arts into systematically organized [knowledge]. This has only been taking shape in the nineteenth century, having been completely absent from the world in the past. As I now desire to discuss the reasons for systematically organized scholarship, I shall first take up the meaning of the two elements in the compound word *gakujutsu*,[22] scholarship, before continuing with the main discussion.

The elements *gaku* and *jutsu*, science and the arts, are indeed

*Before Aristotle, the Brahmans as well as the Buddhists of India also transmitted "logic" under the name *Nyaga*. See the discussion on the origin of logic and philosophy by the Frenchman [Pierre] Gassendi published in 1658.

well known to the world. But discussing them precisely, science is rooted in the faculty of wisdom and belongs to the sphere of illumination. The arts belong to the sphere of conduct, and they pertain to behaving according to the principles that are known. They follow an order of mutual relation in which science comes first, the arts later. Take the man who tries to catch a chicken. Once he hears the chicken's cluck, sees its form, and finds exactly where it is, he can follow the chicken with his feet and catch it easily with his hands. Knowledge, therefore, comes first; conduct later. Now applying this distinction between knowledge [science] and conduct [the arts] to the human body, the five senses of seeing, hearing, smelling, tasting, and feeling are all agents for wisdom that gather reports from outside and convey them to wisdom.

Then there are hands, feet, and the organs of speech that, as agents of volition, communicate or act outside the body in accordance with orders from within. If there are no reports from the outside, therefore, there can be no execution of orders from the inside. The reason for this is easily understood by judging in terms of science and the arts, and we can readily appreciate the essence of science and the arts if we discuss them on the basis of the principle in the above discussion. While the essence of science is knowing the truth, there are truths that we know innately even though we do not know them as facts from our experience.

Now, to speak of truth, we know that each fact and thing is invariably one, that one entity will invariably become two if it is bisected, but that one cannot be bisected to secure three, four, or five even though we may desire to do so. Even though this is speaking numerically, we humans already know by applying this principle generally that truth is invariably one, not two. We define investigation as the search for an understanding of truth, relying on this innate knowledge that truth is invariably one. It is beyond debate, therefore, that science rests on investigation. There are various methods of investigation, and we must first invariably determine these methods since random study cannot establish truth. The methods of investigation in the modern West are three in number: observation, experience, and proof. Even though it may be impossible to employ proof at certain times and under certain circumstances, there can be no investigation without the first two of the three: observation and experience. I want to continue this discussion, but I shall defer until later as time is running out.

[1]For Tsuda's previous essay on freedom of the press, see Issue Eleven of this journal.

[2]For part three of this series, see Issue Fifteen.

[3]*Kitsune,* 狐. Foxes (*kitsune*) in Japanese folklore are animals greatly to be feared for their tricky malevolence but also to be honored as the messengers of Inari (稲荷), the guardian deity of the rice crop. Whereas in Japan as in the West foxes are associated with wiliness, Japanese foxes, on occasion, may serve as protectors of children or take the guise of a loyal wife. In Japan foxes are also said to have the power to convert into human or other forms as well as enter the bodies of human beings. Possession by foxes (*kitsune tsuki,* 狐つき) is here disparaged by the Confucian rationalist Sakatani even as an enlightener like Tsuda Mamichi deplored beliefs in *tengu* (天狗). In the succeeding essay on foxes, Sakatani, the moralist, denounces the manifold evidences of deception and possession in contemporary Japanese society, which appear to him no different from possession by foxes.

[4]*Tanuki,* 狸. Badgers (*tanuki*), like foxes, are animals about whom there are infinite tales in Japanese folklore. Often linked with foxes in the word *kori* (狐狸), which is composed of the ideographs for fox and badger, *tanuki* are generally playful and amusing rogues innocent of the malevolent trickery of foxes. They are often represented with large stomachs and scrota that they are said to resound like drums, and they may on occasion transfix human beings. Like fox tales, badger stories were sources of derision among Japanese enlighteners who would banish superstition from their people.

[5]*Soi-seishi,* 素位醒史. I interpret this term to be one of Sakatani's pen-names.

[6]Hokkaidō, 北海道.

[7]Honshū, 本州.

[8]*Tennen no Michi,* 天然ノ道.

[9]*Shizen no Ri,* 自然ノ理.

[10]The Empresses Lü (呂后) and Wu (武則天) were both extremely able women who themselves assumed ruling powers after the deaths of their imperial husbands, Han Kao Tsu (漢高祖) and T'ang Kao Tsung (唐高宗).

[11]Commonly known as the nun *shōgun* (*ama shōgun,* 尼將軍), Masako (政子) was a masterful woman who struggled to assure the succession of her sons against the designs of her own family after the death of her husband, the *shōgun* Minamoto Yoritomo (源頼朝) in 1198. Four hundred years later, Yodogimi (淀君) strove vainly to secure the rights of her son Hideyori (秀頼) against the plots of Tokugawa Ieyasu (德川家康) after the death of her husband, Toyotomi Hideyoshi (豊臣秀吉).

[12]Continued from Issue Seventeen.

[13]Shên Nung, 神農, the legendary Chinese ruler, known as the Divine Husbandman, who reputedly first taught his people agriculture.

[14]Nü Wa, 女媧, is also said to have established rules governing relations between the sexes.

[15]Nishi here refers to the Hsüan Chi Yü Hung (璿璣玉衡), ancient astronomical instruments used during the days of the legendary emperor Shun (舜).

[16]Yü Kung, 禹貢, or the "Tribute of Yü" is a section in the *Book of History, Shu Ching,* 書經.

[17]Hou Chi, 后稷, earth god and agriculture minister during the reign of the legendary Huang Ti (皇帝).

[18]Kao Yao, 皋陶, is said to have been charged by Shun with the control of barbarous tribes, criminals, and insurgents.

[19]K'uei, 夔, one of Shun's nine ministers who was charged with the direction of music.

[20]Fu Yüeh, 傳說, and I Yin, 伊尹, were famous ministers of the semi-legendary Shang (商) Dynasty.

[21]Chou, 周.

[22]*Gakujutsu,* 學術.

A Speech on the Peace Negotiations Relating to the Formosa Expedition[1] (November 16, 1874)

Fukuzawa Yukichi

There are no limits to degradation when one looks down and no limits to ambition when one looks up. Although we should not forget the proverb that we should know what is enough when considering individual private interests, we should not be satisfied in the least when dealing with the great plans for national enlightenment. The section in the present peace settlement by which China, through the diligence of our government, is obliged to pay an indemnity of Tls. 500,000 should be a matter for congratulations on behalf of our country. To judge from the course of the Formosa expedition from the day of its departure to the present, China has been wholly defeated while we have been completely victorious. Is there anyone who is not exultant after comparing our situation today with that of the Chinese? I also am one of the exulting.

Yet we must ponder the fact that we cannot judge the outcome of the affair from the indemnity alone since the incident has deep roots in the past and will have further repercussions in the future. It is indeed clear that the causes of the present incident long antedate the sending of the expedition. I shall not discuss the inner causes since these are not matters that can be known to the people. Nor do we know its repercussions hereafter since we are not gods. How could a humble person like me speculate on such things?

I shall consequently discuss the situation on the very day that I received the telegram announcing peace. Even though the present arrangement is between China and Japan, its effects concern certain other parties. If you ask who these parties may be, they are the countries of the West. After all, Westerners were not directly involved in the discussions of peace and war (assuming that at the time there was no advice and discussion by foreigners intervening between the governments of the two countries), but they were concerned from the commercial point of view. Japan as well as China both undertook military preparations after the dispatch of the expedition, and their expeditures for the purchase of warships and arms were extremely large. Moreover, since the warships and arms were all bought from merchants of the Western powers, the Westerners were the venders while Japan and China were the customers. Therefore, even though Japan and China were the two parties directly concerned with making war and peace in the present instance, we must speak of the interests of three parties after including the Western countries as participants in the buying and selling of supplies.

Given the interests of the three parties, we should invariably line the three up side by side and distinguish between their profits and losses when we consider the facts of the matter. Possessing the wealth of the eighteen provinces and relying on the vastness of more than four hundred prefectures, China was so hesitating and vacillating as to be unable to determine matters of peace and war. By spending vast sums on useless military preparations and finally paying 500,000 in gold to the Japan that she had privately regarded as her slave for years, China implicitly compensated for her crime and completely exhausted her wealth and dignity. To suffer such loss without any gain should be considered total bankruptcy of policy.

Although Japan is one-twentieth the size of China, strength should not be discussed in terms of territorial extent. Since Japan never wavered once she decided on war and since she fully maintained her dignity as an independent nation without shedding a drop of blood, her prestige naturally cannot be discussed in the same breath with that of China. Yet when one considers from the financial point of view, can she cover all her military expenditures with the indemnity thus acquired? Probably, the sum will be far from adequate. Added to this is the fact that, when making military preparations, everything ranging from ships and guns to uniforms, shoes, and caps was invariably of foreign manufacture. Even though men in Western countries may not relish war, it is proverbial that their manufacturers and workers watch for war as they enjoy the industrial prosperity derived from war preparations. A country like Japan, however, cannot even sell a grass sandal (*waraji*)[2] for such an expedition. Since the greater part of our military expenditures only went to assist the commerce and industry of Western countries, it cannot be said that, financially speaking, [our] gains sufficed to cover [our] losses. The Western merchants were the ones who from beginning to end only profited without suffering loss. Simultaneously receiving orders from Japan and China and elatedly selling antiquated guns and warships, they were able to secure greedily millions in profits. Even though we do not know what may have been the blunders of our government in its purchases, we can well imagine the situation in China. The craftiness of Westerners should be feared even during peace. Still more during the flurry of purchasing at the outbreak of war, how could there be time to inspect their goods and question their prices? Being able to take advantage of our difficulties, the venders immediately had their own way just as the proprietor can freely set his prices when a father takes his beloved child into a toy shop. Assuming that the commissions averaged thirty percent of the approximately Yen 3,000,000 estimated value of the goods contracted for and sold to Japan and China at this time, their profit was Yen 900,000, far larger than the indemnity obtained by our country.

Thus as I have said, there are no limits to degradation if one looks downward, and China is truly to be pitied if one considers her situation. Had our recent fame been won in a man-to-man struggle, this would indeed be a time for unqualified satisfaction. When one considers from the point of view of the great plans for enlightening the country, however, we cannot yet be satisfied. This is an example of the fact that, when one looks up, ambition has no bounds. Westerners should be regarded as persons who pile profit on profit, seizing temporary profit after observing the disputes of others from the sidelines and then gaining profit as usual from normal trade when the disputes are amicably settled. Formerly, at the time of the Napoleonic Wars after the United States had acquired independence, the American republic, while observing neutrality, really gained great profits by encouraging its domestic industries and exporting its goods to Europe. Even though conditions then were different from now, the two cases closely resemble each other in the sense that profit was acquired from the exigencies of other countries. When one conjectures on the inner thoughts of Westerners, is it not indeed mortifying to think that hereafter they will always be praying for the outbreak of disturbances between Asian countries?

At any rate, even if Japan hereafter cannot make temporary profits from the disturbances in Western countries, we want to take care that we do not afford profits to them from Asian disturbances. It might indeed be different if we were in a world in which we could fight with swords, spears, and armor produced in our land. When we import instruments of war from the West, however, apart from victory or defeat, we should invariably consider the costs in money.

Now we should not speak only of monetary considerations, since wars are related to national prestige and lead to the rise and fall of national power. Thus it may be that, only by changing the spirit of the people through this victory over China, will we strengthen the foundations of our "nationality" (*kokutai*)[3] by clarifying the distinction between foreign and domestic. The fullness of this national power may reach the area of our relations with the Western nations. For example, the time is also soon coming for entering important negotiations for revision of the treaties during which our Japanese government will try to gain control over arrangements for the protective tariff as well as the governance over the residential settlements, assuming for ourselves both the rights of taxation and full judicial powers. It may be that, as a consequence of our strengthened nationality, we shall then stand equal with the nations of the West without in the least falling into their debt. We would no longer have reason for regret if, in addition, we are able to carry through fair and just negotiations on a give-and-take basis, as we have done with China. If there is expectation that we shall really achieve this vigour, we shall have nothing to regret and nothing to review. Why should we then enter into trivial monetary considerations? The people of Japan should then applaud with joy.

Being dissatisfied with present conditions and hopeful for the prosperity of the nation when I contemplate the future, the above is a discussion of my unbounded expectations. Yet not being divine, I do not know the future. This is all the more so since these matters also cannot be achieved unless they are undertaken gradually. We can only await the progress of men's minds. After all, our present difficulties lie in foreign affairs, and our principal antagonists are implicitly the Western nations. Moreover, they are commercial enemies rather than military enemies, enemies endowed with intellectual power rather than military power. Victory in this war of wisdom depends solely on the future efforts of our people.

The Three Sages

Tsuda Mamichi

Arising from Brahmanism, Buddhism underwent a definitive metamorphosis with the coming of Shaka; Christianity emerged from Judaism and underwent a definitive metamorphosis with the coming of Christ; and the Confucian Way (*Jusha no Michi*)[4] was handed down through many generations from Yao, Shun, Yü, T'ang, Wên, Wu, and Chou Kung[5] before it underwent a definitive metamorphosis with the coming of Confucius. The three sages achieved their great reforms after gathering together the teachings of thousands of wise men who had preceded them. Even though the wise and enlightened men have not been few during the several thousand years since the three, there have been absolutely none who have further modified their definitive teachings. Why, after all, should their teachings remain definitive hereafter? [I] Tengaishi[6] would observe that even the words of the sages, when viewed from the present, are at times hypothetical and imperfect, as truths have been defined by the great expansion of knowledge since their time. This is because the physical laws were then still unclear. Yet when it comes to the great principles of morality, the teachings of the three sages were positive, unshakable, and as indestructible as Heaven and earth. Should you ask the reason for this, I would say that it is because, when Buddha taught compassion, Confucius human heartedness, and Christ love, they made these virtues the foundations of their morality.[7] It is not that the wise men before the three sages were wholly igonorant of the virtues of compassion, human heartedness, and love. Still they had not yet made these virtues the cardinal principles of morality. After all, although the virtue of the Creator is indeed broad and unlimited, these words alone can express the great principle of His virtue in a single term. Filial piety, brotherly love, faithfulness, wisdom, bravery, and truth are indeed all essential to morality, but it would be mistaken to make them morality's cardinal principle. The three sages—Shaka, Confucius, and Christ—are incomparable because they made compassion, human heartedness, and love their cardinal virtues and thus were best able to embody the sentiment of the Creator's Original Love. This is why the three sages were the three sages and also why their ways have been transmitted through the generations without necessity for change. Even though the words compassion, human heartedness, and love are different, their meaning is the same. This is why they all express the virtue of the Creator's loving care for living things.

When Shaka said "Only I alone should be honored in the universe," he, after all, wanted himself to replace the Creator after robbing Him of His achievements. Christ called himself the Son of God and wanted to love God along with men. Confucius, being himself a man, wanted to honor Heaven and to treat men with human heartedness. The approaches to truth by the three sages thus differed from each other. [I], Tengai, would observe that, since men are all descended from divinity, we can only conclude that men alone should be honored in the universe. Being all brothers from the same womb, the billions of people born in this world should individually devote their bodies and souls to loving and nurturing each other. If they are completely of this persuasion, then I predict that they will forthwith conform to the Will of God, the Creator, and themselves be able to achieve the heavens of Christ and Shaka and the contentment of Confucius.

Human Social Intercourse Part Four[8]

Sugi Kōji

If the people enjoy peace and prosperity and the ruler consequently possesses authority, then ruler and people can mutually endeavor to support the nation by preserving their national essence (*kokutai*). After observing the tendency for weak countries to be overwhelmed by a single defeat from a foreign enemy, they prevented attacks from neighboring nations by establishing means for defense. This was the source of armaments. Moreover, because of long uncontrolled armed upheavals, men customarily established armies and developed military facilities. Then since obedience is honored for soldiers and since soldiers are generally inured to restraints and restrictions, there has been also an invariable tendency for their spirit of freedom to diminish and their patriotism to dim. When soldiers were primarily responsible for defending the people, they promoted their leaders and demeaned the people until they themselves finally became a type of special caste within the country. Relying on their superior strength, they inflated their egos and regarded the people as enemies. Soldiers also were often tools used by powerful men to serve their evil designs. It has been the clear record of history that, once their military evils pervade customs generally, the nation will ultimately be reduced to slavery.

Human beings established tax laws since financial resources are essential for their conduct of state business. Laws for the collection of taxes generally determine the levels of expenditures appropriate for the national business and assess these sums on individuals. Moreover, it is essential that these laws oblige men to pay equally and impartially in accordance with the [estimated] comparative magnitude of their wealth.

Taxes are the share of an individual's wealth that he contributes in order to protect the remainder of his wealth. This then is the essence of tax laws. Now in human social intercourse, men cultivate an innate morality in which they strive mutually to carry out their appropriate responsibilities. Thus it is the responsibility of civil officials to protect the lives of the people, to avoid injuring individual dignity, and to maintain private ownership; the responsibility of military men to prevent national calamities and to defend against foreign invasions with their lives; and the responsibility of religious teachers to encourage men to meet their obligations and to promote their virtues with teaching. In a word, leaders in social intercourse should invariably assume their responsibilities by individually honoring their duties and by carrying out their functions. It is morally inappropriate, however, for public leaders to indulge in useless luxury because they make light of human social intercourse. Is it not outlandish for these individuals to satisfy themselves with huge incomes sufficient to feed and clothe a hundred to a thousand households? Now such conduct is indeed criminal and shameful.

Female Decorations

Sakatani Shiroshi

There is much debate over whether numerous differing individual customs are right or wrong. Yet millions of people throughout the world since antiquity have all sensed no wrong in the fact that women make decoration their principal purpose. This seems wrong if one considers it in the least rationally and from the standpoint of human sentiment. There cannot now be hasty reform, but we must begin a judicious discussion. We call barbaric what has substance without polish and frivolous what is polished but without substance. If something is frivolous, it is held to be irrational and therefore barbaric. And enlightenment is said to embrace appropriate amounts of polish and substance. This applies to human beings without regard to sex. Just as Nature endowed men with beards and denied them to women, each sex has its particular decorations. By judicious cultivation (*saisei hoshō*),[9] human beings take advantage of decoration to enhance their respectability. Men, therefore, adorn their bodies with male decorations; women with female decorations. Men should not be without adornment, and women should not adorn themselves to excess. For what reason then do women take decoration as their principal purpose? Moreover, that women are expected to take decoration as their principal purpose has been the source of female vice throughout history as well as the reason for the obscenity and temptation that corrupt men's minds and ruin families and nations. As lust is common to human beings of all times and all nations, can there be anyone born with "passion" but innocent of lust? Virtuous conduct and scholarship are what people should take as their principal aims, be they male or female. Adorning the body is just one part of virtuous conduct, and decorations are improper for both men and women if they do not conform to virtuous conduct. Sexual desire is a fact of Nature (*Tenri*),[10] as a consequence of which men and women mate and marry.

Then why do women alone take decoration as their principal purpose? Moreover, adornments are considered beautiful according to custom, and what is beautiful to one may seem ugly to another because of their differing national customs. It is established by common custom that the unadorned loveliness of lotus on autumn waters is thought beautiful by all, and similarly the natural ugliness of withered willows and lotus, even though decorated, is thought ugly by all. Views on beauty and ugliness do not depend on decoration. Yet it is observed that women take decoration as their principal purpose by excessively adorning themselves, by disguising their ugliness, and by falsifying their beauty. Is not this "passion" of lust hateful? Should man try to act in opposition to birds whose male decorations exceed female? The adornments of birds were produced by Nature while those of women are artificial.

Nature distinguished between men and women, and their decorations should be appropriate to their respective sex without exceeding moderation. By disturbing Nature and resorting to extreme artifice, people encourage human greed, destroy moral principles, and thus promote beastly conduct. For women to take decoration as their principal purpose is to invite these evils. There are numerous instances in which women uselessly waste time on ornamentation, and their expenditures often cause lustful and foolish men to sacrifice their wealth. According to an American newspaper, the fine quality laces commonly used by English noblewomen and produced by some 135,000 Belgian workers range in price from three thousand to ten thousand francs a pound. We cannot know the numbers of workers producing ladies' decorations in Japan as there are as yet no indices. But the larger of the numerous firms seen in the streets of Tokyo sometimes employ some tens of persons in big buildings. We may also appreciate their prosperity from the extremely high cost of a coral hairpin or a tortoise comb. These all are only lewd and tempting bobbles that disturb customs. Truly to be deplored is the useless and injurious expenditure of such large amounts of human energy and money.

Three oddities in appearance among the women of the world are the bound feet of China, the contracted waists of the West, and the wide *obi* of Japan. Although different in appearance, the three derive equally from the idea that decoration is woman's principal purpose. Chinese and Japanese love their tempting concubines and torture their hard-working wives while European men and women enjoy equal rights. This phrase, equal rights for men and women (*danjo dōken*),[11] however, may ultimately produce the unseemly spectacle of men led around by the nose and reduced to drudging slavery by their wives. But for the moment setting aside conditions abroad, female virtue in our empire has long been at a low ebb. When men recently altered their hairdress, however, women tried to return to ancient fashions by introducing sweeping changes, abandoning their useless coiffeurs, and allowing their bobbed hair to hang down. I believe that adoption of a new hair style under proper guidance will enhance women's spirit and promote their virtue. If we destroy ornamentation that departs from moderation, extinguish "passion" that leads to harlotry, stress virtuous conduct and studies, and prize respectability, there may appear a faction of moral strength such as exists in America. An army of Amazons will emerge during a national emergency while enterprises for education and enlightened achievement (*kaibutsu seimu*)[12] will daily become more fine and monthly more widespread during peace. Women are the cause of many fashions in the world. If they are as upright as I wish them to be, they will stimulate the appearance in rapid succession of such men as Kikkawa Motoharu[13] and Tachibana Tōko[14] of Japan as well as King Chuang of Ch'u,[15] King Wei of Ch-i,[16] Liang Hung,[17] and Chu-ko Liang of China.[18] Our national industries will then be completely changed to produce useful commodities.

If one consults a doctor, he may explain:

> Hairpins, combs, wigs, and topknots follow tastes of the times and competitive fashions. Whereas the head suffers great injury from incessant attacks when pressed down and bound by hair

oils, glues, and cosmetics like muddy roads or a mess of food, the [simplified] customs of today are good for both health and spirit.

I feel that this is a propitious time for change. When I have asked in puzzlement why the order has been issued strictly prohibiting the new women's hair style, some attribute it to the fact that women take decoration as their principal purpose.[19] Others blame lustful officials who fear a coming shortage of tempting concubines. I thought the order surely arose from the government's deep commitment to moral ways, but I was proved wrong. Then I conjectured that, since all things necessarily include evil, how much more is this the case with innovations! The present is a time of manifold changes. [The government] often prevents an injury that may arise from a change without, however, abandoning the reform itself. Why only in the case of ladies' coiffeurs does it try to halt a reform because of a trifle, like the person who would break up a feast on the pretext that he had choked but once on the food?

In general, we stimulate the courage of the people by giving them independence and liberty in most matters, and we also may well accord independence and liberty to women in hairdressing. There are justice and injustice in independence as well as fairness and unfairness in liberty. While we should naturally protect against and prohibit injustice and unfairness, is the cutting of women's hair really unfair and unjust? Since it is neither unfair nor unjust, how absurd it is to encourage men and to prevent women from cutting their hair! If there is unalterable objection to a change in women's hairdress, then let us just construct a cap for the protection of their heads upon which we shall place sidelocks, topknots, and ornamental hairpins so as to make a wig. Women will be encouraged to wear this only when out-of-doors among people and to conserve their health by taking it off at home. This suggestion is only to meet an unavoidable situation. There is nothing better than to beautify women's customs by allowing them liberty in [hairdress] and thereby to encourage the nation's [useful] industry and commerce. We should indeed prevent the bad habit of dyeing teeth,[20] but some censure only the dyeing of teeth without looking into their hair. Do those who hate dyeing of teeth only passionately love beautiful white teeth without relying on ideas of just and fair independence?

[1]Fukuzawa's speech was prompted by the agreement concluded by Ōkubo Toshimichi (大久保利通) with the Chinese in Peking on 31 October 1874 that resolved the crisis between China and Japan arising from the Japanese expedition to chastise the Formosan aborigines who had killed fifty-four Ryūkyū islanders shipwrecked on Formosa's southern coast in 1871. By the accord, China recognized that Japan's punitive action had been appropriate and undertook to pay Tls. 500,000 indemnification, including Tls. 100,000 in relief for the families of the victims and Tls. 400,000 to compensate Japan for her expenditures. Although Fukuzawa, like Nishi Amane, held that it was the Westerners who profited from discord between Japan and China, the Peking agreement greatly enhanced Japan's claims to sovereignty over the Ryūkyū Islands. The accord was hailed in Japan at the time, and the Meiji Emperor rewarded Ōkubo with a gift of Yen 10,000.

[2]*Waraji* 草鞋, traditional Japanese straw sandals thonged between the big and other toes.

[3]*Kokutai,* 國體. "Nationality" is Fukuzawa's translation for *kokutai,* which is commonly rendered today as "national structure" or "national polity."

[4]*Jusha no Michi,* 儒者ノ道

[5]Yao, 堯; Shun, 舜; Yü, 禹; T'ang, 湯; Wên, 文; and Wu, 武 were all legendary Chinese emperors and kings. Chou Kung (周公) or the Duke of Chou was the younger brother of King Wu and renowned as a paragon of statesmanship.

[6]Tengaishi, 天外子, one of Tsuda's pen-names.

[7]Compassion, (*tz'ŭpêi,* 慈悲); human heartedness (*jên,* 仁); and love (*ai,* 愛).

[8]Continued from Issue Nineteen.

[9]*Saisei hoshō,* 裁成輔相.

[10]*Tenri,* 天理.

[11]*Danjo dōken,* 男女同權.

[12]*Kaibutsu seimu,* 開物成務.

[13]Kikkawa Motoharu, 吉川元春, 1530–1586, a samurai famed for his chivalry who fought to defend the domain of the Mōri (毛利) family.

[14]Tachibana Muneshige (Tōko), 立花宗茂 (統虎), 1567–1642, lord of Yanagawa (柳川) in Chikugo (筑後) who served both Toyotomi Hideyoshi (豐臣秀吉) and Tokugawa Ieyasu (德川家康).

[15]King Chuang (莊) of Ch'u (楚), died in 591 B.C., one of the five hegemon kings of the Spring and Autumn (Ch'un Ch'iu, 春秋) Period.

[16]King Wei (威) of Ch'i (齊), died in 320 B.C., fourth king of Ch'i.

[17]Liang Hung, 梁鴻, first century A.D., a scholar famous for having taken a strong, loyal, but ugly wife.

[18]Chu-ko Liang, 諸葛亮, 181–234 A.D., an ingenious warrior who resorted to numerous strategems to defend the state of Shu (蜀) during the Three Kingdoms (San Kuo, 三國) Period.

[19]In 1871 a women's hairdressing society was established that encouraged Japanese ladies to adopt simple coiffures along Western lines in place of elaborate traditional

hair styles that required the use of heavy glues and cumbersome ornaments. When the ladies began emulating the men by cutting their hair and allowing it to hang freely, however, the shocked government forbad the new fashion. Opposed to excessive decoration that might encourage vice, the moralist Sakatani here argues that ladies should be allowed freedom of hairdress in their homes while conceding that it might be appropriate to have them wear wigs outside.

[20]It was considered proper in pre-modern Japan for married women to blacken their teeth. In 1868, however, the government decreed that ladies need no longer blacken their teeth or shave their eyebrows, and the empress five years later provided a model for society by appearing with white teeth and natural eyebrows.

Knowledge Part Four[1]

Nishi Amane

Having already discussed the methods of scientific research, I would like now to consider the use of the deductive and inductive methods in investigation, which is of greatest importance to modern scholarship.[2] The difference between the two methods is like that between the scion of a rich house who spends wealth and the poor fellow who accumulates it. The deductive method may be compared to the rich man who, having determined that he possesses a million *ryō*[3] in gold, divides it and applies it to various expenditures. It is to apply deductively in a thousand ways a fundamental principle that one has determined *a priori* to be best and highest. Therefore, the end may indeed be appropriate if the principle is best, but the consequences of even the slightest error will spread far. Similarly, the rich man may quickly end in bankruptcy if he erroneously employs even a million *ryō* in a mistaken way. On the other hand, the inductive method ultimately achieves consistent truth by gathering minor facts together, just as the poor fellow finally amasses a great fortune by piling up *sen*[4] day by day and month by month. In this way, there is naturally no reason for error, and the inductive method discovers truth just as even a poor man may acquire a fortune.

What we call science (*gaku*)[5] is the pattern that emerges by inducing consistent truth from facts and by clarifying the process for attaining this truth. What we call the arts (*jutsu*)[6] are the means for usefully employing in manifold areas of human life the truth that has been previously revealed by science. The purpose of science, therefore, is only to search for the truth generally without consideration for its value to mankind. The arts then follow this truth and employ it to direct mortals toward profit and away from harm. For example, the detailed components of water are never visible to the naked eye. Nor is it possible to know water's structure even by using a delicate microscope. If we observe water in terms of its properties, however, we recognize its ability to move downward cohesively as well as to form rounded drops. We may also know its cohesive rounded shape from the proof of dropping it on a tray. If we thus inquire for the principles of water consistent with its properties by [employing] the three methods of observation, experience, and proof, we can surmise that this rounded quality of water occurs between the points when it vaporizes from heating and when it freezes into ice. Once we appreciate that water is extremely delicate and rounded, we also know its inevitable quality of flowing downward. This [scientific] knowledge, however, is unrelated to the benefits or injuries to be derived from water's downward flowing nature. Yet when this scientific knowledge is employed in hydrodynamics (the water principle art), water's flowing quality can serve a hundred uses by moving water wheels, and its pressure can vigorously produce fountains by harnessing its power. There is not time to enumerate all the other benefits to mankind that can be derived from using these qualities of water.

Science, therefore, possesses the ability to expand man's wisdom; the arts, to increase his capacity. Even though the purposes of science and the arts thus differ, however, they are so mutually intertwined in the natural sciences as to be practically indistinguishable. For example, chemistry is not a study that can be clear ly divided even though we may refer generally to analytical chemistry as a science or to synthetic chemistry as an art. As there is not time to discuss this here in detail, it is sufficient only to clarify the reasons for the interrelation between these sciences and arts.

I should just add a few words in an effort to explain the reason for systematically organizing the hundred sciences and the arts generally. Even though science and the arts in Europe are far more flourishing than ever before, they are today not yet established from the point of view of coordinated unity. In his classification of the various sciences, Auguste Comte devised a scheme of five sciences ranging from simple to complex. His [work] may be regarded as exhaustive as his reasoning was most delicate, and his discernment extremely acute. It is not easy, however, for a beginning scholar quickly to grasp his discussion as it reaches an extremely high level. Therefore, I shall now just try to outline the various studies by arranging them according to their mutual interrelationships. Naturally, this is not what in Europe would be called an established theory as it is only drawn from my mind. If we want to classify the hundred sciences and arts and indicate their essential qualities, however, there will be no means for beginning unless we divide them into major categories. For the moment, therefore, I shall assume three principal categories: common sciences, physical sciences, and intellectual sciences, and I hope to follow this order in the next essay. Even though I have established only major categories, I have necessarily appended special studies to the division of common sciences.[7] This is only for convenience of classification, and I beg your indulgence.

The Distinction between Husbands and Wives (*Fūfu Yūbetsu*)[8]

Tsuda Mamichi

The distinction between husband and wife has been faithfully and unquestioningly honored by billions of people in East Asia through the four thousand years since the command by Shun to Hsieh, as a consequence of which it became one of the five relationships to be taught and spread abroad. I myself have skeptically been unable to believe this [teaching] from an early age. When I questioned Confucian scholars after failing to resolve my doubts for some ten years, one responded: "There is a distinction between the spheres of the husband outside [the home] and the wife inside [the home], and husband and wife will mutually respect each other's sphere once they honor this distinction." Still another explained, "We do not confuse our husbands and wives with those of others, having established a distinction between their spouses and ours."

Yet why is this teaching of Shun so important today since adultery is punished by law and since even barbarian countries invariably hold that husbands and wives, once married, do not mix partners? Even though Yao[9] and Shun were great sages, Shun complacently knew no shame when he took two of Yao's women as his wives. Indeed, how can we doubt that in those days husbands and wives were mixed as morals were then not yet clarified? Such being the case, the latter explanation seems appropriate. Yet I wonder whether the followers of Confucius, Mencius, and the Sung scholars[10] earnestly believe in antiquity without altering their views in these modern times when the gradual progress of enlightenment has already established the distinction between husbands and wives and when there is no fear for confusion between theirs and ours.

Only a few years ago, when I was ordered on a mission to China, did I first understand that the phrase "distinction between husbands and wives" does not refer to distinguishing our spouses from those of others.[11] Rather, it has the meaning that husband and wife mutually respect each other's areas, as the spheres of the husband outside [the home] and the wife inside [the home] are distinct. When I passed through the crowded intersections of Shanghai, Tientsin, and Peking, the jams were even more confused than those I had seen even in London and Paris. Yet, I saw not a single Chinese wife on the streets. Nor did I see females sitting in the shops. After all, the wives have never had contacts with outsiders, as they are shut up in their domestic quarters by the strict segregation of the sexes. Apart from China, the countries of the western regions [of Asia] all adhere to this custom. It is said that the custom also prevails in Turkey, since the Turks are Tartars.

Now why is it that the sages thus strictly delimited the husbands' and the wives' areas by perfecting the distinction between the husband's sphere without and the wives' sphere within? I would observe that the Creator's virtue of nurturing love extends to men, beasts, trees, and grasses. Being abundant, it is never insufficient; and being universal, it is never inadequate. There is no doubt that it promotes the luxuriant propagation of birds, beasts, plants, and trees. The source for luxuriant propagation by man is rooted in the feeling of mutual love between men and women. If matters are left in the least to blind passion, how will men differ from beasts and how will there be distinction between husbands and wives? The sages invariably sought to control excess passion when they systematized the proprieties and introduced law. The reasons behind the strict marriage codes and the fears of overpopulation among Western philosophers do not differ greatly in their intent from the reasons of Chinese sages for strictly delimiting the spheres of the husband without and the wife within. Yet the Chinese way of demeaning womanhood, regarding their wives as maid servants and confining them to their chambers, was no different from incarcerating them in prison. This injury should also be termed extreme. Confucius, Mencius, and the Sung scholars were men of great discernment, but the Chinese ultimately failed to consider this cruelty. This is the injury arising from the blind faith of the Chinese in the past.

On Secular Ethical Teachings (*Seikyō*)[12] Part One

Sakatani Shiroshi

Principles invariably control all things, just as do the masters of households and the trunks of trees. There could be no uprightness but for controlling principles (*shu*).[13] What is the most important principle that should control all men in the world throughout their lives? There are two moral ways extending through history and spreading through the universe—the good and the evil. Evil cannot be the controlling principle of things as it is only what is not good. Assuming the controlling principle to be warmth, then evil is like cold that is produced as warmth decreases. Just as the atmosphere of the earth is useless if there is no warmth, morality would be completely destroyed if good were not the controlling principle. This would be "barbarism." Such being the case, only good determines man's course as the controlling principle through history the world over. Nations are founded on men, and good alone is a nation's *raison d'être.* The establishment of this good, moreover, lies exclusively in deep faith, and secular and religious ethical teachings alone will ultimately achieve firm and immovable faith by causing the people to believe deeply. After all, since nations arise after men have gathered together, the uprightness of nations is contingent on the uprightness of men. Since men are governed by their minds, the uprightness of men depends on the uprightness of their minds. Perplexity and confusion easily upset the nerves since the mind, as the source of consciousness, responds to many things and possesses numerous functions.

When direction and objectives are not clarified by establishing a controlling principle in the mind, therefore, all will become foxes, badgers, witches, and ghosts. Being completely confused and upset, a man's mind will then finally sink to the level of beasts. Even though a controlling principle may be established and direction may be clear, men are like boats drifting out of control or leaves waving in the breeze when they are without deep faith in principles and direction. But they can stand complacently even in fire and water if their faith is deep. Take the patient afflicted by a serious disease. If he has complete faith in his doctor, he will believe in the medicine even until death. Without such faith, however, he will die in bewilderment after having changed doctors and medicines night and day. Then even the patient's recovery would only be by chance. This is because the doctor, being the master [controlling principle] of the patient's mind, is not helpful unless he inspires faith. The power of armies during the great European wars has also been increased several times because they possessed fine doctors as well as renowned generals [who inspired faith]. Now if you want to set out for a certain place but lack faith in the road, indecision will prevent you from advancing a single step even though you stand all day before the gate. Once he just determines the target accurately and possesses deep faith, even a dull person will never fire to the south or the west the bullet that should be discharged to the east. With proper training, such a person will invariably hit the target.

In the words of an ancient, there will be no vacillation if the mind is endowed with a controlling principle. Confucius said that people without faith are not upright.[14] This is also why the ten thousand religions with all their differences invariably give first place to faith. Whether a man has direction or not, therefore, how can his manifold activities be upright in life if his faith is shallow? This great fundamental [regarding faith] is valid for all persons in all places throughout the world. Since it is invariable, all must conform to it. Neither men nor nations, therefore, are worthy of the name if they reject this great fundamental of faith. Families as well as nations without faith are invariably disturbed. If the billions of men in the world are diverse in mind, there will be neither harmony in republics nor agreement in parliaments. And there will naturally be disintegration and collapse just as matter breaks down into more than sixty elements. If you ask the reason for this, it is because evil flourishes when good does not prevail. Should "conscience," which derives from the justice of Heaven's Reason (*Tenri*),[15] be extinguished, then "passion," which arises from private greed, will abound.

What then unites the myriad minds of men by shutting out private greed and by encouraging deep faith after the good of Heaven's Reason has been adopted as the controlling principle? I say that it is only secular ethical teachings. But there are also religious ethical teachings for the occasions when secular ethical teachings should not be trusted. By such ethical teachings is the controlling principle established in men's minds. Whether their guidance and protection is by conduct or by words, secular teachings and religious teachings all only take good as their controlling principle and only encourage men to believe in good. In sum, good is their sole objective. Further, even though methods for teaching good proliferate into many branches, we cannot doubt their clear origin in good if we conjecture their logic. In a later issue, I shall point to the evidences of this in the histories of the East and the West and then ask for your comments.

An Outline of the New Chemistry[16]

Shimizu Usaburō

Western scholars form societies according to their individual disciplines in which the study of others supplements what one does not know, while one's own study completes what others do not know. By thus mutually exchanging through shared discussions do they establish their theories. Such is also the case with chemistry. When chemical compounds bearing such names as potassium sulphate, potassium iodate, and sodium carbonate were imported in recent years, I thought them to be Latin and wondered why their names reversed [the order of our usage]. Only later, after acquiring new materials, did I appreciate that there has been a great change in the study of chemistry. That I was slow in understanding these things arose from my failure to join the European chemical societies. Generally, there is a separate society for each branch of scholarship, and a person cannot acquire their discoveries and new principles if he does not search for explanations by entering the societies.

Now we shall see the outline of this great change in chemistry by explaining this reversal of names. What is ultimately most important in electricity in chemistry is that the 64 (or 63 or 65) elements, being all endowed with electricity, are invariably distinguished as to whether they are negative or positive. Given the distinction between positive and negative [elements], compounds arise when the positive associates with the negative or the negative joins the positive. Even though these are ordinary compounds, their names vary

The Negative Pole

—

oxygen	tantalum	uranium	aluminum
sulphur	columbium	bismuth	erbium
nitrogen	titanium	tin	yttrium
fluorine	silicon	indium	glucinum
chlorine	hydrogen	lead	magnesium
iodine	gold	cadmium	calcium
selenium	osmium	thallium	strontium
phosphorous	iridium	cobalt	barium
arsenic	platinum	nickel	lithium
chromium	radium	iron	sodium
vanadium	ruthenium	zinc	potassium
molybdenum	palladium	manganese	rubidium
tungsten	mercury	lanthanum	caesium
boron	silver	didymium	
carbon	copper	cerium	
antimony		zirconium	
thorium			

+

The Positive Pole

according to the numbers of positive and negative elements, just as oxidized iron is called rust or colcothar depending on the quantity of oxygen it contains. Since iron is positive in relation to oxygen, however, we must invariably speak of the compound as iron oxide in modern chemistry. The order of the elements is as in the chart [on the previous page].

In the chart, oxygen is the negative pole; caesium the positive pole. The atoms above an atom are negative (to that atom); those below, positive. For example, caesium is positive in relation to rubidium and those above while oxygen is negative as against sulphur and those below. Potassium, therefore, is positive to iodine, and iodine is negative to potassium. Such compounds as sodium chloride and aurum chloride all depend upon the principle by which the mutually opposed positive and negative [are united]. Since hydrogen is also positive in relation to sulphur, hydrogen in sulphuric acid is the base, and the compound is called hydrogen sulphide. Such compounds as those of hydrogen and chlorine as well as hydrogen and nitrogen also all follow the same principle. Moreover, this atomic theory is as clear as the details in the palm of one's hand. Ah, but the full maturity of chemistry is also not yet visible in its entirety! I am just setting this down for the information of my colleagues who do not yet know these developments.

An Entreaty Regarding the Convertibility of Paper Money (The First of Four Essays on Currency)[17]

Kanda Kōhei

It seems that our system of paper money is not yet operating perfectly. Since I personally fear that what does not operate well today will be a source of weakness tomorrow, I shall set forth my admittedly inadequate views in an effort to prepare a plan for consideration of men with perception. If you ask what is this thing that is not operating perfectly, I would reply that I refer to the inconvertibility [of our paper currency]. Since paper money is in essence no more than paper whatever its form or name may be, there is no reason for it to circulate in the same manner as gold and silver. Numerous countries throughout history have possessed paper currency systems, however. That these currencies attained circulation after gaining the same trust as gold and silver was only because they were freely exchangeable at all times for specie. Our country's recent paper currency alone from the beginning has not been exchanged for specie. Since this paper currency is not exchangeable for specie, it is now circulating more than should be expected. This may be explained by the fact that the authorities introduced the paper by strict government order at a time when the people suffered from debased metal currency. It is not that the authorities do not know that inconvertible paper currency is unreasonable. They have dared to carry out [the note issues] in the full knowledge that they do not conform with reason. The practice has been a necessary expedient to meet chaotic times. Once the critical period ends, it will be appropriate [for the authorities] quickly to abandon such expediency in favor of normal practices and to establish the principle of paper money convertible [to specie]. Up to now, there has been no such convertibility. Not only has there been no such convertibility. The authorities have taken advantage of the dullness of the people to accelerate increasingly the issuance of excessive amounts of paper currency for the support of various unnecessary public works. I must say that they have gone one step beyond the bounds of propriety.

In sum, the authorities cannot achieve the road to normalcy by relying on the fact that currency now circulates without obstruction. If we reflect carefully on the situation since the circulation of debased currency, it may be compared to villagers who withdraw temporarily to a lake of ice after being attacked by robbers. Having become confident after spending more than a day of anxiety on the ice without going through, they not only fail to return to the land, they move farther and farther out on the ice. If there is no convertibility between paper and specie and if paper is indefinitely circulated as though it were hard currency, it will be natural for hard currency increasingly to leave the country. This is like the villagers who, saying that being on the ice is the same as being on the land, do not in the least reflect on the fact that strangers have seized and occupied their homes on the land. Moreover, we cannot fight foreign countries so long as we have not developed a good [convertible] system of paper currency in the country. This is because, apart from victory or defeat, a foreign war would provoke domestic disturbances arising from a halt in the circulation of paper currency. Therefore, we are unable to fight foreign nations since we fear internal disturbances, and we necessarily suffer the contempt of foreign nations since we are unable to fight. This is like the people on the ice who, being unable to fight those on the land, inevitably are forced to endure the latter's insults.

There may be a number of other difficulties associated with paper currency. In most instances, it would be completely appropriate to compare them to the people on the ice. In sum, as I have said, even though paper currency now circulates freely, there will surely arise some obstruction sooner or later since the present course is by no means normal. Probably paper currency will ultimately be destroyed at this later point since there will be nothing for which it can be exchanged once hard currency has been completely exported. I beg rulers and ruled to think earnestly on this and now give it still greater attention. We should quickly establish currency convertibility before hard currency is completely exhausted. Thereby shall we prevent in advance a terrible disaster that would suddenly visit complete destruction on the savings that our thirty million countrymen have labored for centuries to accumulate. I suffer unendurable fear when I contemplate such a disaster. Daring to present my comments for the consideration of the men with perception, I would be most happy if they would favor me with their thoughts.

[1]Continued from Issue Twenty.

[2]Nishi here employs the terms *en-eki no hō* (演繹ノ法) and *kinō no hō* (歸納ノ法) in their modern usage as the deductive method and the inductive method, respectively.

[3]*Ryō*, 兩, a unit of gold equal to one *yen* (圓) in the early Meiji Period.

[4]*Sen*, 錢, one hundredth of a *yen*.

[5]*Gaku*, 學.

[6]*Jutsu*, 術.

[7]In his consideration of the common sciences in his fifth essay on "Knowledge," Nishi also discussed poetry and philosophy even though he did not think that they should be classified among the common sciences.

[8]*Fūfu yūbetsu*, 夫婦有別, is a phrase from the *Book of Mencius*. According to Mencius, the legendary Emperor Shun (舜) enjoined his minister of instruction, Hsieh (契) that husband and wife should have their separate spheres, which is the source of the Chinese tradition that the wife's sphere is within, and the husband's outside the home.

[9]Yao, 堯.

[10]Tsuda uses the term Ch'êng Chu (程朱), which refers to four scholars of the Sung Neo-Confucian School: Ch'êng Hao (程顥), Ch'êng Hsiang (程珦), Ch'êng I (程頤), and Chu Hsi (朱熹).

[11]Tsuda was a member of the Japanese mission led by Date Munenari (伊達宗城) to Peking in 1871, which concluded the first treaty of commerce and friendship between China and Japan.

[12]*Seikyō*, 政教. In this essay as well as in its sequel in Issue Twenty-Five, Sakatani is both protesting against those enlighteners who avidly sought Western material culture to the neglect of ethics and commenting at least indirectly on Nishi Amane's essays on religion (*Kyōmonron*, 教門論). Along with others deeply trained in the Confucian tradition, such as Nishimura Shigeki and Nakamura Masanao, Sakatani deplored what he regarded as the tendency of his age to slight the moral instruction that he held to be within the secular realm and not pertaining solely to religion. Thus, he points to the broad meaning of the ideograph for *kyō* or *oshie* (教), which embraced both secular ethical teachings (*seikyō*, 政教) and religious ethical teachings (*hōkyō*, 法教 or *shūkyō no oshie*, 宗教ノ教). Whereas Nishi employed *kyō* in the narrower religious sense when he argued for separation of church and state in his essays on religion (*kyōmon*, 教門), Sakatani held that those in government should not neglect their responsibilities in the area of secular ethical teaching. He anticipated the strong movement thereafter to restore ethical content to Japanese education.

[13]*Shu*, 主.

[14]*Tami ni shin naki* (*wa*) *tatazu*, 民ニ信ナキハ立タズ.

[15]*Tenri*, 天理.

[16]Western chemistry was still in its rudimentary stages in Japan at the time of this essay. The first treatise on Western chemistry to appear in the country was a translation by Udagawa Yōan (宇田川榕庵) of William Henry's *Epitomy of Chemistry*, which came out in 1839 under the title *Seimi Kaisō* (舎密開宗). The Tokugawa bakufu (德川幕府) in 1865 invited W. K. Gratama from Holland to begin instruction in chemistry at its Western studies institute, the *Kaiseijo* (開成所), and the first well-equipped chemistry laboratory was opened at the revived *Kaiseijo* in 1874. Shimizu himself was author of an introduction to chemistry entitled *Seimi no Kai* (舎密ノ階).

[17]In this and his later articles on currency, Kanda is warning of dangers ahead should Japan fail to adopt corrective policies that would place her currency on a sound basis. The new government of Meiji had sought to establish an orderly currency by introducing the yen in place of the variety of currencies that had circulated before 1868, but it was also forced by its inadequate revenues to resort to deficit financing, largely through the issuance of inconvertible notes. While Kanda observed correctly that the notes thus far had introduced no serious inconvenience, they ultimately contributed to serious inflation when they reached more than Yen 165 millions after the Satsuma (薩摩) Rebellion of 1877. As Kanda indicates in his later articles, Japan's currency situation was rendered still more precarious during the 1870's by the export of specie to pay for her regular unfavorable trade balances and for various enlightenment projects. His advice was finally adopted after Matsukata Masayoshi (松方正義) became finance minister in 1881 and embarked on financial retrenchment based on the assumption that Japan's inconvertible paper was the most important single factor contributing to her loss of specie.

Travel by Foreigners within the Country (*Naichi Ryokō*)[1]
Speech on November 16

Nishi Amane

When the subject of travel by foreigners within the country is brought up and I am asked about its merits, I wonder how best to respond. The situation is the same as when Mr. Parkes[2] brought pumpkins from his country and invited us to try them since they were tasty and healthful. Just as we did not know before eating them whether these admittedly rare fruit were flavorous or good for our stomachs, it is a fact that we do not know whether allowing foreigners to travel within the country will be beneficial.

Be that as it may, there is nothing that we can do once we are upset in our stomachs from eating the pumpkins. We may say that we should not have eaten them after having become ill, but it will be too late to repent. We must know, therefore, whether the pumpkins are delicious and whether they are poisonous to the stomach before eating them.

In the case of pumpkins, we can know whether they will taste good and whether they are poisonous by cutting them open and judging from the look of the meat and by breaking down the component parts through scientific analysis. Such is not the case with allowing foreigners to travel in the country.

While the methods of analysis in the two cases may indeed differ, it is quite true that we will not know the effects of either if we do not submit them to some method of analysis.

Thus I would say that we must search for a method of analysis. Since we know that we cannot carry out a chemical analysis, we must attempt a logical analysis [when dealing with travel by foreigners within the country].

Now let us assume that we will clearly understand such a problem as travel by foreigners within the country only after practicing a method of logical analysis. Should one inquire into the best ways for conducting such logical analysis, the methods are two.

One is by the deductive method; the other, by the inductive method. Let us begin first with the deductive method.

If we speak then of deductive analysis, its method is to explain step by step to the end on the basis of an assumed principle. Since travel by foreigners within the country is part of the larger whole [of foreign relations], we must search for the whole by conjecturing from its parts.

Our analysis, therefore, must follow the method of determining the whole by conjecturing from its parts just as one traces the orbits of planets in astronomy.

Now the so-called evening star may be seen in the West at sunset and to the East at sunrise. Since it is seen only when the sun rises and sets, it is visible for no more than a short span of twenty-four to twenty-five minutes. Be it in the East or in the West during these twenty-four to twenty-five minutes, however, we may understand that the star describes a curve when it then moves across several of the 360 degrees into which the heavens are divided. However short the described curve may be, it is certainly a curve. Inquiring into the reason, since it is an axiom of geometry that a straight line will continue straight forever, if you extend a curved line, it will invariably return to its starting point however large may be the circle. Even if the course is not a true circle, it eventually will invariably form a rounded shape. If we assume that the evening star describes a curve according to this principle as it moves through the heavens, we can determine the size of its entire orbit after measuring its curve. Similarly, the problem of travel by foreigners within the country is part of a larger whole. However large may be the orbit [of opening friendly foreign relations], we will invariably determine this whole by conjecturing from the curve of this segment [i.e., travel by foreigners in the country].

Now in this fashion, assuming the fact of travel by foreigners within the country to be the segment of a curve, breaking relations with and expelling foreigners is the antithesis of opening the country to travel, just as a straight line is the complete opposite of a curve. Looking at the matter from this point of view, travel within the country by foreigners is a curve and not a straight line. If we trace from where this curve begins to where it ends, we will know that travel by foreigners within the country is a curved segment of the circle [of opening friendly foreign intercourse], since the curve will describe the opening of friendly foreign relations, which is fundamentally the opposite of breaking relations with foreigners. Of course, when it comes to the whole of opening friendly foreign intercourse, there are also other segments in addition to travel by foreigners within the country. The various factors comprising segments within the orbit of opening friendly foreign relations include first, the successive opening of the five ports under the treaties of commerce and friendship; second, the gradual extension since their establishment of the residential concessions in Tokyo and Ōsaka; third, travel by foreigners within the country; and fifth [*sic*], mixed residence (*zakkyo*)[3] [by foreigners among Japanese in the interior]. Because, however they are viewed, these factors are all absolutely opposed to breaking of relations with and expelling foreigners and because travel by foreigners within the country is one part of the whole [orbit] of opening friendly foreign relations, it is clear that we must permit such internal travel if we have concern for opening friendly foreign relations.

Now if we consider the direction of political affairs, even laymen can appreciate that we have taken the course of opening friendly foreign relations. If we now say that we will not permit internal travel by foreigners, this is like sailing from Hachijōjima[4] toward the Bering Straits when our intended course is toward Australia.

When I speak in this manner, however, everyone will say that they can understand without academic explanations or deductive astronomy that allowing travel by foreigners within the country is part of the current policy of opening friendly foreign intercourse. But they will point out that things are not so simple as I say since there are various related considerations. The opinion will emerge that, while permission will indeed be granted in due course, it should not be given prematurely before the people of the interior have become somewhat more enlightened.

I have an argument, however, for those who say that it is too early. The residential concessions in Tokyo and Osaka were established in the days of the old bakufu before the course had been determined. The seven years since the Restoration is a period during which even the body of our nation is said to have completely changed from its bones. If [my critics] state that there has been no step forward since the bakufu, it would seem useless to claim that a course had been decided with the Restoration. I would ask, therefore, if they still insist that it is too early.

If you look carefully at my previously expressed opinions, however, they are indeed academic [in flavor]. Since the arguments affirming the necessity for allowing internal travel by foreigners are derived from the *a priori* ideal of opening friendly foreign intercourse, it cannot be helped even though they may be criticized as impractical.

Without being academic then, let us try to discuss by the inductive method that touches more closely our interests. Only insofar as I take up and enumerate some of the factors and differentiate between the benefits and injuries am I speaking in a manner like the inductive method.

Thus, when we consider how best to proceed with a discussion by the inductive method, we must first take up and enumerate the benefits and injuries that will arise from allowing travel by foreigners in the interior.

When we take up and enumerate these advantages and disadvantages, however, there is no way to compare them one by one as they are not of the same species. From the point of view of "logic," it is inappropriate to follow the mathematical method of making exact calculations by establishing 100 as the sum of the benefits and injuries and then showing that injuries total 12 while the benefits reach 88. Therefore, let me first assume the benefits of internal travel to be "positive," and the injuries "negative."

If we then eliminate and separate the positive factors, we shall know the number of injuries by counting up the remaining negative injuries. We shall then investigate to determine whether the injuries are wholly incurable or whether they can be prevented after the adoption of remedies. If they can be wholly prevented, their negative and injurious factors will be entirely changed in character, and the computation will be reduced to positive factors. On the other hand, the real injuries will be those that we have determined can be neither cured nor prevented by any means. It may be concluded that we should not adopt the policy if the injuries outweigh the benefits.

Should you then ask how many injuries will attend travel by foreigners within the country, they may be enumerated as follows:

1. Foreigners will probably carry on trade if they come in.
2. They will probably enter places that should not be entered.
3. It will be difficult to accord them protection.
4. We will be troubled when we do not understand their languages.
5. We will be troubled by the dogs that accompany them.
6. We will be troubled when incidents come up.
7. There may still be violent men, as in the recent incident relating to the German consul at Hakodate.[5]

First, foreigners will be guilty of misdemeanors should they carry on trade after it has been forbidden by proclamation at home and abroad. As for entering forbidden areas, the second injury, there are no areas in the land that should not be entered. In all countries, however, it is a misdemeanor alike for foreigners and natives without permission to enter government offices and fortresses (such as do not now exist in Japan). As for number three, which concerns protection, foreigners and Japanese will be treated in the same way since, even under the government order of this spring, foreigners are allowed to move without attendants. Fourth, it is not our business whether foreigners are accompanied by interpreters or not. It is their concern if they are hindered for want of understanding. Fifth concerns dogs accompanying foreigners. To be sure, since dogs are without reason, disputes may easily arise when their dogs fight [with ours], but we can forbid dogs to foreigners. Sixth, there is the matter of incidents. As proposed by the foreigners, these may generally be handled satisfactorily by depositing [security] money with their consuls, by making applications [in advance of travel], or by entrusting to judgment by the foreign ministers such disputes as may arise. Complaints arising from incidents are indeed important, however, and it is said that, whatever the trouble may be, the dumb and stupid Japanese will be tripped again and again by foreigners. Yet just as when one teaches *shōgi*[6] to children, the Japanese at first will not by any means be equal to their foreign teachers. This being the case, the students will eventually become the equal of the masters if we begin with the purpose of training them from the pawn up. Travel by foreigners in the interior being like elementary *shōgi* to children, no more than fifty to a hundred of our people will be deceived by foreigners from year to year even if such travel be allowed.

Then, there remains the matter of killing in the final, seventh point. As the author of the *Gaikō Shōgen*[7] said, since the government formerly assumed the mask of honoring the emperor and expelling the barbarians, we may still be troubled by the remaining actors from the old play. There is the precedent of the Hakodate affair, however, and life is dear to all men. If the government's course is unchanging and if it is completely sincere in opening friendly relations, then it will not matter even if there are two or three more incidents of this type. It will be all right if the prefectural governors apprehend and surrender the criminals with determination. Again, if the government is staunch in its sincerity to open friendly foreign relations, it will be all right when our government warns that foreigners travel at their own risk since there are people like Indians in the mountains who are reckless of life. Therefore, we have means somehow to prevent the seventh injury. If in addition we enter into treaties containing detailed stipulations covering everything that we may think important in this connection, the negative factors will be extinguished and disappear. Since there clearly remain only positive benefits, therefore, it is also reasonable to say that allowing [foreigners to travel within the country] is good even when judged by the inductive method.

There may be some, however, who are still dissatisfied with my discussion of the last two injuries. If they say that, even though my arguments sound logical, they cannot be trusted because they are the logic of an academic, then I have a number of "modifications." As I stated at the beginning when speaking of the orbit of opening friendly foreign relations, the curved segments comprising this orbit are not limited to that of travel by foreigners within the country. However you divide these curved segments, whether in halves, quarters, or eighths, they will never be a straight line as they are by their nature curves.

If we thus recognize travel by foreigners within the country as part of the orbit of opening friendly foreign relations, therefore, it may quite appropriately be introduced little by little. There are a number of different ways to carry out such a program. Dividing the curve into two or three, we might allow foreigners to travel on the Tōkaidō this year, on the Sanyō[dō] next year, and on the Tōsandō the following year.[8] The curve of travel by foreigners within the country is not alone in the orbit of opening friendly foreign relations. Turning to the previously mentioned curve of mixed residence (*zakkyo*) by foreigners among Japanese, here again we could broaden the areas of intermingling first from the Tsukiji district[9] of Tokyo to the old boundaries of Edo, thereafter to the two provinces of Musashi and Sagami,[10] and still later to the Tōkaidō.

Thus, without refusing the foreigners altogether, it would be well to seize this opportunity to permit a little travel. Even though the course to Australia points toward no-mans-land, it is better to steer toward the Ryūkyūs [from Hachijōjima] than to head toward the Bering Strait.

Some may say that our judicial power, having entirely different "jurisdiction," does not extend to foreigners, that we have not the power to modify the tariff, and that foreigners are crafty and dictatorial. Yet it may be concluded that we cannot oppose foreigners by force if we do not establish our national independence after introducing necessary reform.

But what will the authorities say if I speak in this fashion? They will say, "You should be quiet. Even though you speak reasonably, the matter is outside the area of your responsibility." Then, being at a loss, I shall come down from the platform.

Regrets on the Exports of Specie
(The Second of Four Essays on Currency)[11]

Kanda Kōhei

Exports of specie from our country, very large since the opening of the ports, have been most extreme recently. Generally speaking, these exports may be attributed to six causes: first, the unbalance between exports and imports; second, expenditures by students studying abroad; third, salaries given to foreign advisors; fourth, expenditures by Japanese missions abroad; fifth, payments on the national debt; and sixth, outlays for purchasing [foreign] commodities. The imports during these years were large; the exports, small; and the excess of the value of imports over that of exports thus represents [the amount] of specie exported. According to the foreign trade statistics for 1873, this reached the startlingly large sum of 8,036,153 yen, 22 sen, 6 rin. I have not yet been able to learn the figures for years before and after 1873, but I would surmise that they probably fluctuate above and below this figure. According to the revised figures for 1872, the expenses of private and government scholars studying abroad reached about Yen 500,000, and we may surmise the sums for other years.

It is stated in the same report that the salaries just for foreign advisors employed by the government amounted to one million yen in round numbers, and we may conjecture that they are increasing more and more even though we do not yet have the sums for other years. The amount would be still further augmented if one adds to it the salaries of foreigners employed privately. The expenses for Japanese missions abroad are those for maintaining ministers and consuls in foreign countries. According to the estimates for 1874, this amount appears to be Yen 363,235, and this seems to be progressively increasing. The annual instalments and interest on foreign indebtedness, amounting to Yen 3,570,203, remains about the same from year to year. While the figures for the above five items naturally fluctuate each year, we may conclude that their total cannot be less than Yen 10,000,000. The total figures for expenditures on [foreign] commodity purchases cannot be known precisely since there is no official record. There is not time to enumerate all the imports, which include guns, ships, shoes, woolens, iron rails, electric wire, spinning machinery, weaving equipment, minting machines, iron manufacturing equipment, mining equipment, tools for making paper, school materials, and medical supplies.

Aside from the above, there are extraordinary expenditures such as Yen 1,500,000 on the Shimonoseki indemnity,[12] Yen 2,000,000 for the special mission,[13] Yen 1,000,000 for the exposition in Austria (these last two are rumor),[14] and the expenses for the mission to China.[15] Should you inquire into them in still greater detail, this type of expenditure would be found to be extremely large. While we refer to them as extraordinary expenditures, specie is exported annually for these purposes as a regular practice. Since there are no means for calculating the total of these extraordinary expenditures, this is left to the conjecture of individuals. I have only confidence to state here that they must reach surprisingly large sums. There are only two sources for increasing the country's specie, the maritime customs and mining. According to the estimates for 1874, these two together amounted to only Yen 2,013,672, or Yen 1,716,915 from customs and Yen 296,757 from mining. I know of no other means for significantly increasing specie. Considering the matter carefully, even though we do not know the amount of specie we had in the past, it is certainly the case that our original wealth in specie has already been reduced by more than half since there has long been an excess of exports over imports of precious metals. Indeed, the present rate of specie exports is yearly increasing, and we must thus unavoidably exhaust our entire supply in the near future. We just cannot know the exact year when the supply will be exhausted since we cannot establish precisely our earlier holdings. Ah, is not such a future to be regretted?

An Outline of Western Culture (Continued)[16]

Nakamura Masanao

Approving the legislation of King Henry VII of England, [Francis] Bacon said that the laws established by the king were planned for the happiness of later generations as they were profound and neither crude nor rashly devised. It is necessary to distinguish between the profound and the crude. It is profound for a legislator to do nothing that will startle the senses of the people or quickly alter their long-standing customs even though he expects really to achieve his objectives and to realize full success. And it is profound to change normally over a long period of time by gradually carrying things out in a natural order and by strictly adhering to the natural spirit of the times.

This is the meaning of harmony (*yung*)[17] in troubled times as described in the *Yao Tien*.[18] If there is harmony of this type, the minds of the people will remain undisturbed while their customs are changed. But if a ruler establishes crude laws intending to carry out reforms hastily, he will only disturb the minds of the people. Ultimately failing to reform customs, he will be unable to achieve his objective.

The historian [David] Hume observed that, while Bacon's expositions on political institutions were deeply discriminating in purport, he fell into error when discussing commercial matters. Bacon wanted to control with laws and regulations the trade and commerce that originally had followed a natural course and been left to free conduct by the people. The laws of Henry VII were indeed generally just, but they were inappropriate when applied to trade. There were at that time laws that prevented the sale of horses abroad, established prices for hats and wool blankets, and determined the wages of laborers. These are matters that should be left to the free will of the people and the natural course of trade. In addition, Bacon heartily approved the land regulations of Henry's time. Yet looked at from the point of view of the present, these measures injured rather than encouraged agricultural efficiency. As might be expected, frequently enacted laws were completely ineffective to prevent the farm population from diminishing during the succeeding one hundred and fifty years. In the long run, farmers will exert their strength competitively in production if they quickly sell out the products of their diligent cultivation. Then why should there be fears for a declining farm population? To let nature take its course, therefore, is good medicine to eliminate paupery and the high road to national prosperity.

As Hume points out, Bacon's views on the political economy of nations should be called narrow as well as erroneous. Bacon was indeed a famous philosopher and wise minister, but he subscribed to the erroneous views of two hundred years ago. In this respect, it can be appreciated that the English people of today clearly surpass their predecessors in the profundity of their knowledge generally and in the just enlightenment with which they discuss legislative matters. Theories such as those of Hume have delineated the main principles of economics and have been adopted by public opinion of the English nation.

[1]Travel [by foreigners] within the country, *naichi ryokō*, 内地旅行. While Japan after 1872 sought a revision of the so-called unequal treaties to secure for herself full

judicial and fiscal independence through the elimination of extraterritoriality and the conventional tariff, foreigners in Japan agitated for an easing of their confinement to the seven cities that had been opened to foreign residence and trade. Thus, in 1873 the Western ministers proposed to the Japanese government a system whereby foreigners would be allowed to travel in the interior with passports issued by Japan through the ministers and consuls of the treaty powers. Under this system, a foreigner traveling under Japanese passport would subscribe $200 security and undertake to obey local Japanese laws and regulations. If apprehended violating these laws, he would be conveyed forthwith to the nearest treaty port for trial by the consul of his nationality. The Japanese government was naturally unwilling to grant to foreigners privileges that might imply foreign extraterritorial rights throughout the country. Nevertheless, Nishi Amane here takes the enlightened position that allowing foreigners to travel in the interior is the natural sequel to the earlier decision to reopen the country. Nishi also employs the issue of extending foreign travel rights as a pretext for demonstrating to his people the use of deductive and inductive reasoning.

[2]Sir Harry Parkes, British minister to Japan, 1865–1883.

[3]*Zakkyo,* 雜居.

[4]Hachijōjima, 八丈島, an island off the east coast of the Izu (伊豆) Peninsula that is a convenient landfall for mariners approaching Tokyo Bay.

[5]Nishi here refers to the assassination of M. L. Haber, the acting German consul at Hakodate (箱館), by a fanatic samurai named Tazaki Hidekichi (田崎秀吉). Tazaki was quickly brought to trial, deprived of his rank, and beheaded.

[6]*Shōgi,* 將棋, Japanese chess.

[7]*Gaikō Shōgen,* 外交小言.

[8]The Tōkaidō (東海道), Sanyōdō (山陽道), and Tōsandō (東山道) are three major routes that have linked the regions of Japan since antiquity.

[9]Tsukiji, 築地, the district of Edo (江戶) adjacent to the water that was first reserved for foreign residence.

[10]Musashi, 武藏, and Sagami, 相模.

[11]Continued from the previous issue.

[12]The Shimonoseki (下關) indemnity was the $3,000,000 indemnity imposed by the Western powers after Chōshū (長州) attempted to close the Shimonoseki Straits by force in 1863.

[13]The mission to the West led by Iwakura Tomomi (岩倉具視) in 1871–1873 that sought revision of the unequal treaties.

[14]The Vienna Exposition of 1873.

[15]The mission to China led by Ōkubo Toshimichi (大久保利通), which negotiated a settlement of the Formosa dispute in 1874.

[16]Continued from Issue Sixteen.

[17]*Yung,* 雍.

[18]*Yao Tien,* 堯典, or *Canon of Yao,* is a section of the *Book of History* (*Shu Ching,* 書經) that relates to the legendary Chinese Emperor Yao.

Travel by Foreigners within the Country

Tsuda Mamichi

The provisions that we desire most to revise in the treaties are those that would secure for us the two rights of judicial and tax independence.[1] Unless a country possesses both these rights in their entirety, its independence is necessarily prejudiced. Yet under the present conditions in our country, we are not yet able to exert the rights even though we may agitate vigorously for them. I believe that some years will be required before our country can gain the two rights completely.

What foreigners very much want is to secure freedom to travel inside the country. Our government, however, is unwilling to grant this [right] for the reasons that our people have not yet attained enlightenment and more especially because it fears the many ruffians in the remote corners of the land may provoke outbreaks, resulting in killing and injury [of foreigners]. Still another reason is probably grounded in a protective sense, the anxiety that our ignorant countrymen will suffer injury from cunning foreigners.

Being opposed to these fears, however, it is my view that we may properly and decisively allow foreigners to travel within the country. After all, what our people at present are poor in is knowledge, and what they lack is enlightenment. Even though knowledge and enlightenment should be gradually advanced primarily through education, they naturally cannot be well attained in a day or a night through education in the schools. Now the peoples of Europe and America have achieved their levels of knowledge and enlightenment for no other reason than that their world-wide commerce has been a vehicle for their enrichment in training and experience. It may be said, therefore, that men increase their knowledge by training and advance their enlightenment by intercourse. Reflecting on this, the very best policies at present to increase the knowledge and advance the enlightenment of our countrymen are to encourage them to travel abroad in large numbers, to increase their training, and to broaden their intercourse.

Nevertheless, we can only refer to these things theoretically as they cannot actually be carried out. This is because we do not have the huge sums necessary to promote foreign travel by large numbers of our people. Moreover, even though our merchants all now enjoy complete freedom to send ships abroad, to travel on the packetboats of foreign countries, to voyage to other lands, and to carry on trade, they are so poor in knowledge and financial resources that they cannot yet easily undertake these activities. Therefore, we may now well hope for travel by foreigners within the country. Quickly granting their requests, we should steadily advance the enlightenment and knowledge of the people of our empire generally through training and contact with foreigners. The benefits of experience and training, after all, are expressed in the proverbs "One hundred reports do not equal a single glimpse" and "There is no learning equal to experience."

Nevertheless, as I have previously stated, there is deep fear in official quarters that our ignorant countrymen will be injured and robbed of their profits by cunning foreigners. This may indeed be true. Yet if the people do not once confront such problems, they will not have the opportunity to dispel [their] ignorance and advance in knowledge. Now even though the untold wealth spent by the Europeans on the Crusades is beyond imagination, these movements were the means for bringing the peoples of the East and the West into mutual contact, and what the Europeans purchased was learning and knowledge. It is said that, even though the Europeans temporarily suffered extreme exhaustion, their numerous later benefits were actually more than sufficient to redeem their expenditures. Moreover, if you reflect on conditions in our country just a decade or so ago, there were then only people who regarded the opening of the ports and the development of foreign trade as an unprecedented calamity for the country. This produced extreme proposals for closing the ports and much talk of expelling the barbarians. As foreign intercourse is natural, however, it could not be denied by the power of reason. Inevitably, the old government ultimately opened the ports, and we have finally reached the present situation. Now, reflecting on this [trend], the advantages and disadvantages are quite clear without awaiting further elucidation.

At present, our people are gradually witnessing the first steps toward enlightenment and generally understand the benefits of Western studies. They have come to know that it is essential to train the intellect as well as to stimulate industry. If you ask the source of this [appreciation], it is the result of only some ten years of foreign intercourse. Now looking back to a decade ago, the persons who regarded Western studies as superior to ours numbered no more than a dozen or so doctors and students of military affairs. Still less were there then as yet any who recognized merit in Western law or who understood such things as civilization and enlightenment or liberty and independence. After a lapse of no more than a few years, we have reached the point when, if even young students open their mouths, they chant such phrases as liberty and independence or civilization and enlightenment. How can it be denied that this is great progress? Furthermore, how can the source of this great progress be other than the opening of the ports and foreign intercourse?

The current debate over [allowing] travel by foreigners within the country is generally the same as that over the opening the ports a decade ago. Even learned men ten years ago did not appreciate the present benefits to be derived from opening the ports. At present even learned men probably do not yet comprehend the benefits to be derived ten years hence from opening the country to foreign travelers. Yet by contemplating the benefits that have arisen from opening the ports, I appreciate those that will result from opening the country to travel. The general increase in the enlightenment and knowledge of our people in the ten years following the unrestricted opening of the country to travel should be almost beyond our imagination. After all, whereas the effects arising from ten years of open ports were limited to increasing the knowledge and enlightenment of the middle classes and above, those from travel by foreigners within the country during the next ten years should be to increase the knowledge and enlightenment of the middle classes and below. Are not these benefits extremely large?

According to my estimate of the matter, in resolutely opening the country to travel by foreigners lies the achievement for the empire of a position of unrestricted independence in the world through the acquisition of the two rights of fiscal and judicial independence that, of course, we deeply desire. Now at the time of the old bakufu, there was deep concern that, if the ports were suddenly opened, insoluble problems would arise from a succession of murderous attacks on foreigners by stalwarts of the anti-foreign (*jōi*)[2] party. Looking at the matter from the present [situation], there were no grounds for such serious fears even though the ports were finally opened under the irresistible pressure from the ministers of the foreign powers. I certainly do not question that their arguments naturally arise from a true spirit of patriotism, but those who now state belligerently that travel by foreigners within the country should never be allowed until we have recovered the twin rights of judicial and fiscal independence fall into the same error as those of the former day who, gnashing their teeth, hoped to close the ports. How can we call wise such futile discussion of what cannot be practiced? I just hope that, even as Yü[3] controlled the flood waters, we shall leave everything to the course of nature, move safely from government by palace camarilla to general public knowledge and enlightenment, and avoid an upset in the path of moderation.

On Reforming Trade[4] (December 16, 1874)

Sugi Kōji

Desiring to support our national sovereignty as time already presses for revising the treaties between Japan and the foreign powers, Nishi and Tsuda have both discussed the question of whether foreigners [should be allowed] to travel within the country.[5] I too regret the decline in our country's trade, and I am presenting my views here as I hope to remedy this situation.

Trade has generally become the way of human life without which there can be no rest for a moment, and there should be no upset in the balance between profit and loss. Once we fail [to preserve this balance], we shall forthwith reach the point from which national decline cannot be prevented. I shall discuss this in terms of what I know. Men differ in skills and in training, and the skilled easily control the unskilled while the trained readily overcome the untrained. This applies in all matters, but it is especially pronounced in trade. There have been manifold changes in the conditions in our country since the opening of the ports. Should you ask the reasons for these [changes], [I would respond] that there have invariably been strong currents as well as agents. The strong currents are the streams of world trade, and the agents are the science and technology that promote trade. When the foreign powers asked for trade sometime ago, we tried to resist them with our native produce. But the more we resisted the stronger they became. And our country gradually declined and became weakened as it was unable to compete with its divided power. Reflecting on the matter, even though it wanted to do so, our country could not suddenly concentrate its divided power to resist their great strength. Tracing further to the roots, therefore, it is essential to search for the agents for the rise in the strong current [of their trade]. We have searched. And the more we searched, the more numerous the agents became until finally we could not search farther. Once we recognized that our industrial power was inadequate, we then studied the science and technology of the West, and it was clear that we could not forthwith compete with them since we were then untrained.

Then what steps are appropriate in the case of trade? I would respond that there is nothing better than to increase gradually our industrial power by temporarily adopting protective measures. Some say that, if we adopt such protection, we shall violate the just principles of trade, limit the rights of the people, move progressively toward incompetence, and greatly accelerate injuries. I would respond that the adoption of protective measures will only increase our production and stimulate our industrial power. I always fear their talk of limiting the people's rights and violating justice. Like the smokers of opium, are not my critics extremely thoughtless? Now let me illustrate by taking up the levying of tariffs. From what country did we secure the cotton for our clothing before the opening of our ports? It was not from China, or Korea, or the Ryūkyūs, or Holland but entirely from the agricultural production of our country. Last year, the value of imported calicoes and cotton thread amounted to about 7,300,000, yen and the amount for the previous year was nearly the same. Since the level of cotton imports represents failure of our national production, upon what can we base our country, which from antiquity has traditionally honored agriculture?

Moreover, there is not time to enumerate all the figures for our exports of gold and silver and for our imports of such commodities as woolens, sugar, iron, and glass. Yet I would not today revive the former protective measures by which Western countries sought to control imports by imposing taxes on all imports. I am not [such a complete] protectionist. Selecting only two or three commodities for which we spend most on imports and that are retarding our domestic production, we shall stimulate the productive power of our country by forbidding their importation or by levying heavy duties on them. For example, since the fields in which our country is both skilled and trained are limited to the sphere of agriculture, we might protect domestic cottons and stimulate their production by levying tariffs on various types of cottons.

Since imported calicoes are cheap while domestic cottons are expensive, some may argue that it is also extremely injurious and not the way to rule the country [for us] to oblige the people to buy expensive domestic stuffs and to abandon cheaper foreign goods. Denying this, I would explain that the benefits will not be limited to cottons alone if we plan to ameliorate the depression in national production and circulate within the country the Yen 7,300,000 saved by halting cotton imports. Such being the case, the people will be able to buy cheaper cottons as prices go down with increased domestic production. We may then state that [such protection] is imposing taxes for the benefit of the people themselves.

Some may argue that, while there is logic in protecting cotton, this cannot protect the producers of sugar and iron, as only the workers in the cotton industry will benefit. According to this view, it is unjust to extend greater protection to one group than another among the people of the same nation, and the injuries from such excessive partiality cannot be few.

My response is that there has not yet been an instance in the world of profit alone without injury since there is invariably injury when there is profit. If we follow a course in which the profits are numerous and the injuries few, the minor injuries then will be ameliorated. Now from the historical point of view, the Englishman [Oliver] Cromwell and the Frenchman [Jean Baptiste] Colbert were extraordinary men and the fathers of protection. It cannot be said that the present wealth of England and the prosperity of France are not also their achievements. It was not that there were no injuries from the operation of protection in England and France but only that Cromwell and Colbert recognized the large profits to be derived therefrom. I have heard that of old in our country Arai Hakuseki saved some hundreds of thousands of pounds of copper by establishing controls over exports. It is probably a fact that, but for Arai Hakuseki,[6] the production of our copper mines would have been exhausted by unlimited exports over the last hundred and some tens of years. There is not sufficient praise for his consideration of later generations.

It may then be asked, since Colbert and Cromwell were men of two centuries ago, why should we follow their antiquated policies under the different conditions of today, suffer the abuses of corn laws and navigation acts, and bequeath later injuries?

To this I would respond that, as previously explained, men differ in their skills and training. Let us consider for a moment the condition of our nation's agriculture, crafts, and trade. It is my opinion that our country is accomplished first in agriculture and next in crafts but that we are untrained, incompetent, and therefore most clumsy in trade. I still do not know which would be superior if we competed with the skills of the West in agriculture, the industry in which we are most accomplished, but I can appreciate [the superiority] of the West in the civil, military, and technical arts that are now all taught in our country by Westerners. From the time long ago when they invented the compass, Westerners have discovered America by sailing West, passed India by sailing to the East, and pressed to the five continents invariably carrying on trade wherever they went. Even though it may be said that they were then trained in commerce, there is all the difference in the world between the changed face of modern Western states as compared with those of former times. Arguments favoring protection, however, have been unceasing during the last two centuries. I understand that currently in America political economists support these [protectionist] theories and that the government also is actually practicing them. This perhaps is because America still suffers from the aftermath of her internal disturbance [the Civil War] or because, being still young, her industrial power has not yet reached the English and French levels. There also, the advocates of free trade point out the injuries of protection by explaining free trade's advantages, and the proponents of protection uphold its advantages by discoursing on the differences between training and skills. When France some years ago introduced protection for her iron mining and iron tool industries, the free trade advocates held that agriculture was injured by this protection of iron.

France also has established protection for sugar. Advocates of protection explain that imports of foreign sugar have finally been crushed by protecting French sugar and by increasing domestic production. The diverse attitudes of the people toward protection, after all, depend solely upon when it is carried out. I believe that people of increasingly ripe training and steadily advancing skills welcome free trade and dislike protection because this protection then prevents them from freely carrying on their business. Again, people whose training is not yet ripe and whose skills are not yet advanced dislike free trade and welcome protection. This is because they must be protected until they are mature, just as are children by their parents and students by their teachers.

In the long run, the most exhaustive legislation will only invite injury unless there has been a clear appreciation of the people's feelings and the actual situation. Why should we fear harm if we introduce protective measures after careful consideration and in light of a thorough understanding of domestic and foreign conditions? I also have a proposal should we fail to decide on the merits of protection because of its adverse critics. We should summon from abroad the outstanding scholars who are familiar with the details of free trade as well as those versed in protection, select from ministers and lesser officials the men who have labored on these matters, and choose a number of our farmers, manufacturers, and merchants who are accomplished leaders and outstanding in their industries. Entrusted with complete responsibility and meeting together, the conferees will fully apprise the foreign scholars of the conditions within our country and undertake fair and open discussions. Having clarified the advantages and disadvantages of protection and decided its merits, they may appropriately announce to the world at large a reform in the trade of our country.

I know of no other policies than the above two that will prevent a decline in our country's trade. It is just like sitting ourselves on a volcano if we placidly remain content without considering foreign and domestic trends and if, as in the past, we sanction such free trade practices as depending upon imports from foreign lands, avoiding regulation of our purchases, and failing to consider imports and exports. Is this not dangerous? I do not hear at this time anyone who assumes responsibility for great national plans by raising even a finger in support of our country's commerce. It is unendurable to witness the disgraceful behavior of those who labor industriously for petty immediate gains or those who avariciously engage in sharp practices. Even though I have lampooned these people in my previous essay on speculators,[7] they seem neither to have heard nor to have understood. How extremely deplorable it is that, in addition to promoting their speculation and inviting their own destruction, they have robbed the respectable people throughout the country of their courage, increased the hardships of the poor, and finally induced our government to repeat the blunders of the former French government. I believe that we would now witness true free trade without the injury of reckless imports and exports in our country if, when the Americans first asked for trade arrangements, a man like Arai Hakuseki had considered foreign and domestic trends, introduced protective measures, imposed tariffs strictly, preserved a balanced trade, and planned thereby for the gradual progress of the country. This is why I say that we must have a balanced trade. It is indeed regrettable that the bakufu officials of that time did not appreciate this and were aimlessly controlled by the foreign nations. How can we regard as trivial the crimes of these officials whose injuries persist to the present? A guest may comment that, if we ask a person familiar with those times to discuss this problem, he will state that all the people of the nation were guilty, not just the bakufu officials.

[1]Tsuda here refers to the Japanese desire to revise their treaties with the West, thus eliminating extraterritoriality and securing tariff autonomy. Unlike those Japanese who regarded the opening of Japan to travel by foreigners as a threat, Tsuda sees such a move as a positive benefit that would hasten Japan's progress toward civilization and enlightenment and thence the revision of the treaties that all Japanese desired. Tsuda thus stands firmly with his good friend Nishi Amane in this controversy and in opposition to the most renowned of Meiji enlighteners, Fukuzawa Yukichi. For Fukuzawa's views, see Issue Twenty-Six..

[2]*Jōi*, 攘夷, or "expel the barbarians," the phrase identified with the critics of the Tokugawa bakufu (徳川幕府) who opposed the reopening of Japan after 1853.

[3]Yü, 禹, the ancient Chinese ruler reputed in legend to have introduced dikes to control the flood waters.

[4]Although Sugi denies that he is a complete protectionist, his article reflects the disenchantment with Western free trade principles that appeared in Japan during the early Meiji Period as the country regularly experienced adverse balances of trade and her native industries were hard pressed by foreign competition. The Japanese were probably first introduced to the arguments for protective tariffs by Kanda Kōhei's translation of William Ellis' *Outlines of Social Economy*, which appeared in 1867 under the title of *Keizai Shōgaku* (經濟小學). Ellis himself was an advocate of free trade, however. Four years later, Wakayama Giichi (若山儀一) brought out the first protectionist treatise in Japanese. Entitled *Hogozeisetsu* (保護稅說), "An Explanation of Protective Tariffs," the work presented the thought of the American protectionist Henry Charles Carey. The rising sentiment for protection was naturally fuel for those who called for restoration to Japan of full tariff autonomy.

[5]The views of Nishi Amane and Tsuda Mamichi on the issue of mixed residence appear in Issues Twenty-Three and Twenty-Four, respectively.

[6]Since the famed scholar-official Arai Hakuseki (新井白石) likened a nation's metals to the bones of the human body that could not be replaced, he deplored foreign trade in which the Japanese exported gold, silver, and copper through the Dutch and Chinese at Nagasaki (長崎). Acting on his advice, the Tokugawa bakufu in 1715 adopted strict regulations limiting exports of copper and silver and the numbers of Dutch and Chinese ships allowed to enter Nagasaki each year.

[7]For Sugi's essay on speculators, see Issue Eight.

MEIROKU ZASSHI Issue Twenty-Five December 1874

Knowledge Part Five[1]

Nishi Amane

Among the hundred sciences generally, those of literature, mathematics, history, and geography are the four that I would call common sciences. These four sciences explain and describe the intellectual (*shinri*) and physical (*butsuri*)[2] sciences without wholly belonging to either of these latter major categories. Even though mathematics and literature are rooted in the intellectual sciences and even though history and geography by their nature embrace both the intellectual and physical sciences, it is after all best to group [the four] together under common sciences. What we here refer to as literature generally includes scholarship in spoken and written languages. Following the European classification, literature may be broken down into "grammar" and "rhetoric." Grammar is an art that invariably governs all speech and writing since it determines the rules whereby statements are constructed by piling up the smallest elements in human speech.

Grammar in turn may be divided into four: "orthography," which discusses vocal sounds and their related phonetic symbols; "etymology," which deals with derivation and modification of words; "syntax," which concerns putting words together in sentences; and "prosody," which treats of tempo in speech and tones in reading aloud. Rhetoric is also called "eloquence" or "oratory." Even though the three are different in name, they are actually the same except that eloquence relates to talent. Oratory and rhetoric follow the same rules, their different names notwithstanding. It is only that oratory is spoken and that rhetoric is written. Rhetoric is subdivided into demonstrative, deliberative, and judicious. Demonstrative rhetoric consists of expressions of praise and censure of contemporary matters in words of applause, sorrow, and criticism. Deliberative rhetoric lays down exhortations and admonitions for the future in the words of moral discourses and all manner of instructive essays. Judicious rhetoric is used in stating accusations and defense concerning past events for the most part in words of appeal and judgment. Rhetoric is used in parliaments, public halls, courts, and lectures. However, these two forms, namely, grammar and rhetoric, establish rules exclusively for prose, and there is a separate rhyming form called poetry.

Prose is further divided into two types: expository prose, which generally advances "understanding," and argumentative prose, which is based upon "reason" and which is really rooted in "logic" even though it borrows rhetorical embellishments. Poetry is a form that especially stirs emotions and develops imaginative powers. It may be classified in lesser types all of which are formed of verses that have "rhymes," "meters," "stanzas," and "strophes." Epics such as the tales of the Heike[3] recount the heroic deeds of the ancients; lyrics sing the feelings of individuals in the manner of the *kotouta*;[4] ballads like the *hauta*[5] express the feelings of the country people; hymns such as the *wasan*[6] praise the virtues of deities; and dramas, for example *jōruri*,[7] make known feelings through vocal exchange. These dramas are also performed in the theatre as "comedies" and "tragedies." In the final analysis, the merits of poetry are not small since it is an instrument for elevating men's hearts and for beautifying customs.

Poetry and prose together are called literature, and upon literature invariably depends all manner of things in the world ranging from political and scholarly matters at the top to the mundane affairs of the people at the bottom. Writers invariably compose fables and romances when they vie with each other and compete for kudos on the literary stage. In Europe generally, men engaged in scholarship without exception study the languages of several countries. Thus the English study French and German; and the French learn English, German, or Italian. Europeans also regard as living languages the modern languages of various countries that are used in speech, but they designate as dead languages those unspoken tongues that survive in historical records. In addition to one or two modern languages, European scholars invariably train in the dead languages of Greek and Latin. Since European scholarship originated in Greece, was transmitted to Rome, and thereafter reached its recent flourishing condition, men invariably return to Greek and Latin when tracing back to its origins. This is similar to the situation in our country as a consequence of which we are invariably plagued by misunderstanding if we do not master Chinese ideographs. Western theologians also study Hebrew in order to master the original texts of the Old Testament and because their religious founder (*kyōso*)[8] emerged in Palestine.

The study of linguistics has recently become flourishing. In the beginning, men believed in the legend of the tower of Babel and assumed Hebrew to be the mother tongue of languages. Only since men have generally acknowledged their error with the emergence of "comparative philology" have they clarified the origin of Indo-German and understood that the mother tongue of the various European languages was Sanskrit (the language of ancient Indian holy literature). Furthermore, Hebrew together with Persian and Arabic constitute a separate family of Semitic languages. Originating in India, European languages ultimately divided into two. The South European languages spread from Greece to Italy, Spain, and finally France, while the North European languages, moving directly across the Black Sea from Asia Minor, spread to Germany and ended in England. Except for the Mongol languages of Turkish and Magyar, which came later, the origin of the European languages in India is proved absolutely beyond doubt even though the Scandinavian languages, which spread to the Northwest in antiquity, have been mixed with Mongol tongues. Comparative philologists hold that the Chinese and Japanese, languages had different origins even though there is no question that, when judged by skin color and physique, the Japanese equally with the Chinese and the Koreans, belong to what Westerners call the Mongol race. This theory is most doubtful, but I shall not discuss the matter here since it relates to the fundamental principles of "ethnology." Poetry and philology, indeed, should not be included in the category of common science as they are entirely separate disciplines, but I have for convenience taken them up in this essay since they are related to grammar and rhetoric.

More on Secular Ethical Teachings (*Seikyō*)[9]

Sakatani Shiroshi

When I recently sought to clarify questions on secular ethical teachings, I took up the objective that should be the controlling principle of men's hearts, and I was about to consider the changes in secular ethical teachings through history. However, I shall first mention a preliminary matter that urgently requires elucidation.

In the words of the great European philosophers, power without benevolence and love hastens a nation's decline, and wisdom without virtuous conduct leads to national calamity. They also say that, since the conduct of the people is the source of all matters relating to the nation, national conditions reflect whether conduct is good or bad. And they state that the prestige of a nation as well as the merits of its products, artisans, and merchants depend in large part on uprightness and honesty, as they cannot be based alone on sagacity and courage. These three statements seem to agree completely with the words of the wise men of ancient China and Japan. Such being the case, they clearly contain the essentials of government, morality (*jindō*),[10] and Heaven's Reason (*Tenri*).[11] Persons well informed on these principles, however, not only often fail to honor them, as they believe them to be stupid, but they also regard as stupid those who discuss the principles. Being exactly like the deranged person who mistakes the crooked for the straight road, however, they are really the ones who should be considered stupid. Therefore, I have submitted these three statements preliminary to the elucidation that I shall hereafter undertake.

It is unnecessary to discuss the outcome of the recent peace negotiations between China and Japan, as this is a matter of the past. The results were generally for the benefit of the people and favorable to both countries, and, needless to say, they more especially reflect the prestige of our country and the achievements of our ambassador.[12] There is the saying, however, "Let the victor look to the laces of his helmet." It is indeed important to prepare carefully for the future without indulging in useless self-congratulation. When the negotiations were underway, I discussed later arrangements, but there is still one more matter of importance.

Recently, when I have seen discussions in the press ranging from foreign affairs to reforming the national structure, selecting human talent, colonization, and redemption of the debt, there have been many matters that seem individually urgent. They also contained sources for rejoicing and celebration on behalf of the country, but the principles of the previously cited three statements are indispensable for the successful handling of these matters.

When one closely observes how conduct and customs reflect the national conditions, should they be regarded as upright and honest or frivolous and shallow? Even should we now secure an indemnity of Tls. 10,000,000 and even should all matters ranging from treaty relations to [reforming] the national structure progress entirely as we intend, I am anxious whether, as previously noted, we are hastening the nation's decline and heading toward national calamity since our achievements, like flowers without roots or streams without springs, are no more than temporary surface decorations when conduct and customs are bad. Now when we consider the source of conduct and customs of a nation, they invariably arise from the conduct and customs of the leaders who provide protection, whether the nation be a republic, a limited monarchy, or an autocracy. Even in a republic, leaders are naturally models for the people since they are regarded as good teachers once they are entrusted with protection after their election.

In limited monarchies, where ruling power is shared by high and low (*jōge dōji*),[13] this inclination is still more pronounced. And in autocracies, civilization as well as enlightenment arise entirely from the autocrat's protective measures since the people completely accept his rule as an absolute model. This being the case, if models and norms are twisted, the lower classes lose the important factor of faith, being in doubt and without established objectives. Being especially inclined to imitate false teachers from the upper classes, the lower then conform completely to the twisted path and become egocentric. It is, therefore, extremely unreasonable for the rulers to criticize the ruled (who encourage and remonstrate with each other) for being unenlightened and for failing to appreciate freedom and liberty. Such an attitude is exactly like a crooked measure criticizing the crookedness of paper, and patriots, therefore, should blame the rulers for degradation of conduct and customs. While it is appropriate to blame those in high position more than those in low, the upper should never blame the lower.

In this connection, there is a certain theory that the enlightened countries of Europe and America hold it to be quite natural for governments to be separated from ethical teachings (*oshie*) and for those who govern to be wholly unconnected with ethical teachings (*oshie*).[14] This theory arose from the injury produced by the confusion of secular ethical teachings (*seikyō no oshie*)[15] and religious ethical teachings (*shūkyō no oshie*).[16] Western countries do not in fact hold that government may unjustly oppress without relation to ethical teachings or that protecting leaders may act wrongly without concern for ethical teachings. In the area of ethical teachings generally, nothing contributes to the ethical teachings of a nation more than protective government. This is because such protective government is clear and concrete as well as close to the lives of men. Therefore, while the modern enlightened regimes of Europe and America refrain from employing ethical (*oshie*) terminology in order to avoid becoming mixed with religion (*hōkyō*),[17] they harmonize benevolent government with the principles of nature and have become truly ethical (*oshie*) in the wholly secular realm.

Our country is also learning this principle. Having fallen into serious misunderstanding because of differences between our language and those of the West, however, our leaders freely assume that conduct is unimportant if only they just develop a strict legal system. Since a legal system is a tool that, however good it may be, is useless if the employing hand is bad, even the so-called civilized nations of Europe are invariably disturbed when [their] protecting leaders are bad, and [their] disturbances are attributable to governments devoid of ethical teachings. If our leaders ignore customs and conduct without considering this and conceitedly boast of their grand strategy and great legislation, they will be like those who make dolls without souls or those who cause drunkards to perform religious services. If such be the case, what will be the national conditions in our country? Should we then think of the foundation of our national conditions [manners and customs] as that of Europe and America or that described by the accomplished men[18] of Chinese antiquity?

The advocates of civilization and enlightenment are like the free living retainers of great lords (*daimyō*)[19] except that they are no longer subject to the loss of status or domicilary confinement as they have been rid of supervision by censors (*metsuke*)[20] and gate-keepers (*momban*).[21] Mistaking license for liberty and freedom, they are like the fake students of medicine and Chinese studies who receive money. Will this not lead, after all, to destruction of honor that is of first importance for the people? Should the government, from its loathing of such ways, fall into errors of officialism and protocol by rapidly issuing unnecessary regulations, will this not lead to the practices of the *hatamoto* and the *gokenin*[22] of the bakufu who destroyed themselves [spiritually] on the inside while they decorated themselves on the outside and who left undone all that ought to have been done? There are also those who destroy both their spirit and their vigour by money-changing, trading, and conspiring with merchants under cover of official power, by fabricating names, by borrowing designations from Europe and America, by devoting their energies to the ways of commerce, and by promoting pernicious and evil practices. Are these not ways that will bring misery to the country? In such a case, even wise men will be influenced by the times and think that it is best to delay rather than uselessly face the rage [of the government] by administering bitter medicine.

Are conditions today such that all now are frustrated in spirit, do not exert themselves with energy, and only place emphasis on external appearances while they avoid immediate matters? If these customs and conditions are promoted, will we suffer the fate of the Greeks and the Romans? The heroism and bravery of the ancient Greeks changed after victory into shallow cunning, and Greece was destroyed. Simplicity and valor waxed in Rome, but Rome fell before the German tribes after she became vapid and demoralized following her rise to power. Even in Europe, government invariably fails to conform to law when the conduct and customs of the rulers are bad. How much more so in despotic, tradition-bound countries! Laws [in such countries] are only for the punishment of common people, while the rulers all escape without reproof even for such crimes as neglect of duty, infamy, deception, and irregularities. Even though I do not know whether it is the intent of the rulers that punishment shall not apply to them, laws are not established in this fashion. Such conditions only cause the enraged lower classes to lose faith in their rulers, and despotism becomes the model.

How can we then lead the people to civilization and enlightenment and establish [our country's] prestige among the nations? How can we then lay foundations immovable as a mountain in which we honor honest and upright customs, fully develop the merits of our products, merchants, and artisans, promote flourishing exports, bring prosperity to the country, and strengthen military discipline? If our country is not prosperous, when shall we extinguish the debts that troubled such peerless heroes as Washington and Wellington even more than the fury of a powerful enemy? We shall probably provoke a serious crisis if we boast of the freedom and independence of our country before establishing our national power and before extinguishing the national debt. Therefore, moved by insatiable ambition, I hope that [our rulers], without losing the opportunity arising from today's good fortune, will cultivate customs and conduct with great courage when chastising China and Korea. While the achievement of our returning ambassador is indeed immense, my thought arises from truly compelling patriotism. We should reflect that the fame of Hosokawa Yoriyuki has been transmitted through history because, even as he indefatigably assisted Ashikaga Yoshimitsu, Yoriyuki took as his controlling principle the strict regulation of customs and conduct in the shogun's court.[23] Still more should today's magnificent rulers be encouraged diligently to exert themselves.

Mysteries

Tsuda Mamichi

Probably because statesmanship gains no benefit from mysteries, [extraordinary] powers, disturbances, and spiritual beings, Confucius taught exclusively the science of governing without ever referring to such phantoms. I shall endeavor to discuss this by taking up the word "mysteries" (*kai*).[24] First of all, since the relation of mysteries to the human mind is really not insignificant, it should be conceded that understanding them is also not [just] a minor supplement to statesmanship.

Mysteries are what cannot be discerned by the human intellect. That they were numerous in antiquity and few in recent times is proof that recent generations are finally moving toward civilization. Even though it is said that the world at last has become civilized, if you look at the matter closely, there are naturally still many phenomena in the world the reasons for which are not yet clear. If there is anything that touches our senses whose principles are in the least unclear, hardly ever is it without mystery. Then why should we not discuss mysteries?

Although men take as a matter of course the heavenly movements to which they have become accustomed, these movements become mysteries if they are not explained by astronomy. Why should mysteries be limited only to eclipses and comets? If we become familiar in the least with astronomy, eclipses and comets are all natural phenomena and never mysterious. Yet the appearance of a mirage of two suns rising simultaneously seems mysterious, notwithstanding the fact that the principle of reflection in the atmosphere is like an image in a mirror or in the water. Men in the mountains take their own shadows for ghosts and the echoes of their own voices for gods of the valleys (*kokushin*).[25] Still such phenomena in reality are shadows and echoes that also are not mysteries once they are clarified by physics.

There are [really] no mysteries in the world. Mysteries only arise when we do not clearly understand the phenomena that we see. If upon looking at ourselves we do not completely penetrate the principles behind the complex structure and skills of human beings, the reasons for sense and movement are really beyond imagination. Even though the study of physiology has been greatly developed in recent years, how can we deny the mystery of the soul whose true character is still clouded in obscurity? Materialist scholars, however, regard mental qualities as a function of the brain and expect to explain the soul by physical laws when the study of the brain is advanced and clarified beyond the area of doubt. Only then will there finally be no mysteries in the world.

Those who discuss mysteries are noisily numerous, as are those who believe in mysteries. After all, the main source of belief in mysteries are the conjectures on immortality and on transmigration of the soul. How can we doubt the existence of ghosts and ogres if the soul is immortal? And how can we doubt possession by foxes and disguise as badgers if we believe in transmigration of the soul? Nevertheless, once these beliefs arose from the conjectures of early holy men, the apparitions that the vulgar persons in society sometimes said they saw and heard derived from nervous derangement or credulousness.

Men's beliefs in the supernatural are impressed on their minds from childhood. People who meet goblins (*tengu*)[26] and disguised foxes when they penetrate high mountains and deep valleys or who witness ghosts and Jack-o'-lanterns in cemeteries at night are upset in their minds and disturbed in their souls. This mental state emerges from momentary derangement, that is, from momentary trance. There are never goblins and ghosts in the world.

Sleepwalkers and the deranged, being both mentally ill, suffer impairment of the normal functioning and rapport between their brains and nerves. In their minds appear the abnormalities of mingling demons, shadows, thousands of ghosts, and tens of thousands of witches. It is stated in the *Great Learning* (*Ta Hsüeh*)[27] that, when man has no mind, he cannot see even if he looks or hear even if he listens. A person disturbed in the mind, on the other hand, sees what he does not see and hears what he does not hear. Actually, he sees and hears what he imagines in his mind just as one sees and hears in a dream. To be more specific, he reflects on the retina of his eye and constructs an image of what his inner heart imagines, and he sees various types of apparitions that have been impressed on his inner heart. This is why insane people see devils and ghosts. The source of their difficulty lies in a disturbance of the rapport between the mind and the nerves.

If a nation is compared to a person, the ruler is the brain, and the hundreds of officials are the five nerve senses and one hundred organs. Once the rapport between the brain and the nerves is disturbed, the five senses and hundred organs mistake their functions. This is called insanity. When women, priests, and eunuchs make light of official power or when government orders are inappropriate and the hundreds of officials mistake their functions, the great ministers being domineering and the military oppressive, how does the disturbance to the national structure (*kokutai*)[28] and the national illness differ from the diseases of insanity and sleep-walking? Such a country should be called a nation bewitched (*kaikoku*).[29] Why do we make light of the relation of mysteries to the nation? I have thus constructed this exposition on mysteries.

[1]Continued from Issue Twenty-Two.

[2]*Shinri*, 心理, and *butsuri*, 物理.

[3]*Heike* [*Monogatari*], 平家物語, [*Tales of the*] *Heike*, the famous medieval war tale that recounts the fall of the Taira (Hei) family.

[4]*Kotouta*, 琴歌, songs accompanied by the *koto*, Japanese harp.

[5]*Hauta*, 端唄, a short popular song.

[6]*Wasan*, 和讃, hymns in praise of a Buddha or a bodhisattva.

[7]*Jōruri*, 浄瑠璃, plays written for the puppet theater.

[8]*Kyōso*, 教祖. Nishi may refer to Christ.

[9]*Seikyō*, 政教. Continued from Issue Twenty-Two.

[10]*Jindō*, 人道.

[11]*Tenri*, 天理.

[12]Sakatani refers to the negotiations in Peking by Ōkubo Toshimichi (大久保利通) that settled the Formosa question.

[13]*Jōge dōji*, 上下同治.

[14]*Oshie*, 教.

[15]*Seikyō no oshie*, 政教ノ教.

[16]*Shūkyō no oshie*, 宗教ノ教.

[17]*Hōkyō*, 法教.

[18]Sakatani here refers to eight accomplished men (pa ta, 八達) during the era of the ancient Chinese states of Wei, 魏, Chin, 晉, Ch'i, 齊, and Liang,梁.

[19]*Daimyō*, 大名.

[20]*Metsuke*, 目付, censors of the Tokugawa bakufu.

[21]*Momban*, 門番.

[22]*Hatamoto*, 旗本, and *gokenin*, 御家人, were samurai retainers of the Tokugawa bakufu. The *gokenin* were of lower rank than the *hatamoto* and did not have the right of audience with the shogun (將軍).

[23]Hosokawa Yoriyuki, 細川頼之, and Ashikaga Yoshimitsu, 足利義滿. As senior administrator and regent during the early years of the third Ashikaga Shogun Yoshimitsu from 1368 to 1379, Hosokawa Yoriyuki followed policies that greatly enhanced the power of the Ashikaga family.

[24]*Kai*, 怪. In the Seventh Book, Chapter XX of the Analects (Lun Yü, 論語), it is stated that Confucius did not discuss mysteries (kuai, 怪), [extraordinary] powers (li, 力), disturbances (lun, 亂), and spiritual beings (shên, 神).

[25]*Kokushin*, 谷神.

[26]*Tengu*, 天狗, long-nosed creatures of the mountains.

[27]*Ta Hsüeh*, 大學.

[28]*Kokutai*, 國體.

[29]*Kaikoku*, 怪國.

Refuting Nishi's Discussion on Travel by Foreigners in the Country

Fukuzawa Yukichi

After hearing Nishi's speech on travel by foreigners in the country, I also published my views in the sixth issue of the *Minkan Zasshi*.[1] This publication, however, was not particularly directed against Nishi's views. Having later seen the text of Nishi's speech in the *Meiroku Zasshi*, I feel increasingly that we differ in our points of view, and thus I would now refute his opinions as follows.

Opening of the country to travel by foreigners is the broadening of foreign intercourse as it has been to the present, not a fresh beginning of something unprecedented. After the opening of the ports, foreigners were allowed to travel ten *ri* in all directions from the treaty ports, and to increase this ten *ri* to as much as one hundred *ri* or two hundred *ri* hereafter cannot be called a new departure.[2] Nishi is in error when he compares allowing internal travel by foreigners with the introduction by Minister Parkes of a pumpkin, for the pumpkin was introduced by the American Commodore Perry, not by the English Minister Parkes. In the Kaei Period, it became the official duty of Abe Ise no Kami to examine whether the [pumpkin's] taste was good or bad. Yet neither Ise nor Kami nor, of course, anyone else in Japan at that time appraised the pumpkin. Fearing the military power of the huckster [Perry], the Japanese were forced to eat the pumpkin without discussing its taste. Thus my honorable friend's theory seems to miss the mark.[3]

Since the Kaei Period, we have been eating the pumpkins that are bought and sold through high-pressure salesmanship. Even though the pumpkins are not of a poisonous nature, the Japanese began to suffer diarrhea since the vegetable did not agree with their constitutions. Gradually becoming weaker, the entire country has developed a condition in which it suffers from a loss of financial strength. The pumpkin, therefore, was Perry's produce, not Parkes' gift. Perry's produce, however, has been used within the ten *ri* radius while Parkes would spread its consumption to the entire country. It is not that the Japanese do not know the pumpkin's taste. Having eaten it, they are suffering from diarrhea. It is clear from previous experiments that their lives will be endangered by the pumpkins if, not satisfied with only eating them, they over-indulge in them. Therefore, is it not too late for Nishi now to begin his analysis?

Let us borrow Nishi's "logic" and use the deductive method. We can invariably determine the entire circle by looking at part of the curve even though that part is extremely small. This is the principle that we can seek the whole by deducing from a part, just as we can know the size of a tea cup by deducing from a fragment that we possess. Taking up our trade with foreigners, our losses become their gains since our people do not equal theirs in intellectual power (*chiryoku*).[4] Our nation's trade and commerce thus being a source of loss to us, I must say that there is great danger that this commerce will destroy our country if the intellectual power of our people remains as at present. How can we know the reason for this? By the deductive method, we may describe the full circle of destruction if we inquire into the whole future course by deducing from the segment of the destructive curve that extends from the opening of the ports to the present. That is, even as the increase in the foreign debt appears like part of the movement of the evening star, trade by borrowing capital from foreigners may be compared to the fragment of the tea cup. The course of the evening star must form a circle, and the entire shape of the tea cup must be a hollowed tea cup. According to my "logic," as the foreign debt of 200,000 may reach 50,000,000, [their] lending of capital is the first sign that [foreigners] are buying the immovable assets [Japan]. While our national wealth has really been reduced by previous foreign intercourse, however, it is now intended to broaden this intercourse by allowing foreigners to travel within the country. Deducing from one segment of destruction, thus to broaden foreign intercourse is no more than to push along the path that will lead to the full circle of destruction. This is because travel by foreigners within the country (*naichi ryokō*)[5] is preparation for mixed residence (*zakkyo*);[6] mixed residence is a convenience for trade; and trade is the source of destruction.

Again, in Nishi's opinion, allowing travel by foreigners [in Japan] cannot be called premature. He says that, during the seven years already passed since the Restoration, men, even physiologically, have fundamentally changed from the bones of their bodies and that it is indeed a fact that the enlightenment of society has invariably progressed during the subsequent days and months. Otherwise, he says, it would be futile to speak of having decided a new course with the Restoration. I must also doubt this theory. Now what was the Restoration? It was only replacing the signboard of the bakufu shop with the shop curtains (*noren*)[7] of the imperial household. If you compare the present councillors with the elder ministers of old, there is only the difference of three hairs. They are equally no more than men produced in Japan since the Tempō Era.[8] The government was established by assembling officials under these councillors. And even though the government has adopted the opening of friendly foreign relations as its course, this is only the policy of the governing party, not that of the people. Since the people were no more than powerless and unfeeling pebbles under the autocratic bakufu, they could not have either course or direction up to the present.

There has been a renewal of the bone structure during the last seven years, but the people's spirit undoubtedly remains as before. Even though Nishi seems to think that the Restoration has brought great results, I take a somewhat different view. I do not think that the Restoration, which only slightly altered the front part of the government store, has produced results that have changed the minds of the people one iota. Having determined the course of the people's minds and discerned the distinction between foreign and domestic, it has been impossible in just seven years to catch up with the foreigners in trade or public affairs. When discussing matters relating to the interests of the entire country in foreign intercourse, therefore, we must establish our theories on the assumption that the people remain unchanged from the people who were transferred from the bakufu [to the new government].

Since the people are essentially the same as before and since the effects of the Restoration have not yet penetrated to the bottom of their minds, we must say that it is really premature to allow travel by foreigners within the country. Here I would like to switch from the "logic" of the evening star to that of woman. It is clear from the time of birth that woman's nature is to marry. Every moment of her maturing period is inevitably a segment of the period of her marriage. Nevertheless, whether marriage is harmful or beneficial to the individual is related to age. Should we say that it is beneficial for a daughter of twelve or thirteen years if her parents arrange for her to marry Musashibō Benkei[9] and cause them to enter into mixed residence (*zakkyo*) on the assumption that it is woman's nature to marry? I must say that it is unreasonable and immoral to press the daughter, whatever the tricks of "logic." Since this daughter is in no sense a barren woman, it is not that she dislikes marriage. She only pleads to wait a little for the appropriate time. Nishi, upon hearing the daughter's plaint, would scold: "You are a freak who does not understand the way of women. Unless you experience the course of things, you will not become familiar with them. You shall marry either Musashibō or Kumasaka no Chōhan[10] at once." Is this not an embarrassing situation from the daughter's point of view?

While the above is rough, it is my deductive "logic." Hereafter, I shall comment on Nishi's inductive reasoning. Enumerating items that may become injuries, he states that, since there are means for their prevention, only "positive" advantages will remain. He does indeed indicate means for preventing all seven injuries, but I am extremely uncertain as to whether these means can actually be put into operation.

First, Nishi assumes that trade matters are prevented by proclamation at home and abroad. Although Nishi essentially agrees with me when he also clearly points out that inland trade [by foreigners] is injurious to the country, does he really think that it can be halted by prohibitions? Up to the present, the government's skills have been inadequate even to prevent hunting by foreigners. All the more, with what kind of directives can the government prohibit and halt trade, which is directly concerned with profits and losses? It is impossible to credit his views until we see his proof. Nishi also says that we should introduce measures for dealing with such infractions of prohibitions as may arise. What then will these measures be? In public litigation involving foreign countries up to now, the Justice Ministry has also been vexed, and the Japanese people have sustained loss in seven to eight out of ten cases. If foreign intercourse becomes more vexing as the area open to foreign travel is broadened hereafter, the number will probably increase to seventy or eighty out of a hundred. According to my way of thinking, if we are to lose, it is best to limit the losses to seven or eight. I certainly do not relish increasing the number to seventy or eighty. Between seven or eight and seventy and eighty, the difference is sixty-three to seventy-two. Anyone knowing simple mathematics cannot misunderstand these figures.

Even though Nishi's Number Two is to the effect that there are no places where a man should not enter, he should not enter the house of another unless he is led, and he should not transit roads marked "no thoroughfare." Nishi indeed explains that it is equally wrong for foreigners or Japanese to violate these regulations, but only to state the offense is not a means for preventing it. Even though by the above inductive "logic" Nishi may say that disadvantage will be converted into advantage if we are able completely to prevent these injuries, the disadvantage remains without the slightest change toward advantage since the offense is not prevented just by saying now that it is an offense.

As for the matter of protection under Number Three, there is no point in taking this up since there are currently no violent persons. Such matters are not worthy of our attention. In regard to Number Four, relating to difficulty of communication, there would arise misunderstandings from inconvenience in translation, and we cannot say that this is the concern of foreigners alone. Fifth, we naturally need not be concerned with regulations to prevent foreigners from being accompanied by dogs. Whether they are accompanied by dogs or tigers is optional. According to my way of thinking, we really should be far more concerned if foreigners import rabbits and exchange them for money than if they are accompanied by dogs. Under Number Six, Nishi states that disputes generally will be settled early by mutual agreement. Even though Nishi appears only to fear bodily injury, I have already spoken of difficulties arising from litigations with foreigners. These may be appreciated from experience since the Kaei Period. What I regret is not limited only to injury of persons. I am also anxious regarding injury to the independence of the country. As for Number Seven, murder, I do not particularly differ with Nishi that this should be handled by surrendering the criminal.

As indicated above, it seems that even Nishi really has no means for preventing injuries under points one to seven. The kernel of his argument is only in the method by which he would try to stop and prevent injuries by depending upon "stipulations" that he describes in the last part. At this point, Nishi's opinion differs entirely from mine. It is my belief that, if these stipulations were useful, there would be no anxiety from the outset. Unpleasant though it may be, we must reflect on the saying, "Power is right." Please see the sixth issue of the *Minkan Zasshi* for details on this.

Finally, even though we may be fundamentally of the same opinion regarding flexible measures, we should not lose our ultimate objective by altering the gist of the operation and following convenience. That is, even though the ship is directed in the same course, we should not expect that it will invariably advance forward if we select a flexible path. Properly included in this flexible policy may be cases when advance is good, or stopping is good, or times when retreating is also proper. The entire circle of the course of events cannot be determined in one or even several years. Under existing conditions, there are quite properly no obstructions in our present intercourse with foreign countries. Even though we may think that it would be convenient by retreating a little to distinguish still more clearly between domestic and foreign affairs and to establish special laws governing such matters as foreign and domestic loans and currency, there are no means to accomplish this since the government is without authority and the people are without intellectual power. Such conditions being irrevocable, there can be no other expedient than to wait for the season when we can act. Even though we wait for this season, we should not be fearful if we do not alter the course of the ship.

On the Trade Balance[11]

Tsuda Mamichi

If you refer to the balance between exports and imports during the scant ten odd years since the ports of our empire were opened to trade, exports greatly exceeded imports at first; then there was almost an equilibrium between the two, both having increased together as trade gradually flourished; but recently imports have greatly surpassed exports. According to trade tabulations for 1873, the difference then exceeded Yen 8 millions, and the comparative levels were probably about the same in 1872. Patriotic gentlemen fear that our empire's ready cash (*genkin*)[12] will ultimately be completely exported.

Although I have explained in an earlier essay opposing protective tariffs that we need not worry deeply about the imbalance, I desire here to point out in a few words a situation that should actually be cause for rejoicing. I shall be able to clarify that the situation does not warrant such anxiety when, once having inquired into the actual cases, it is finally known what the source of this great difference between exports and imports is. The various patriotic gentlemen, without perceiving this factor, vainly hold that the imbalance may long continue after they have observed today's spectacle. It is understandable that they have not escaped from their anxieties.

If you then inquire into what after all is the source of this imbalance, we find it is rooted in our innate nature. We possess minds that, by their characteristic innate nature, love novelty and enjoy colorful display. These minds are thus the real cause for the imbalance in trade. After all, these mental characteristics are really the great gift of the Creator as they are the reason why our productive power is encouraged and human happiness is enhanced. That our people fortunately have such minds is the reason why they are different from the savages of Africa and the Americas. Moreover, these minds are especially numerous among the various ministers who determine policy and administer the laws. Such minds are the cause behind the development of a variety of new projects for railways, telegraphs, lighthouses, arsenals, mints, shipbuilding, and the like. They are also the origin of undertakings by the various ministries and prefectures to build stone bridge, highway, and gas light facilities one after the other. And they are the source of the rules regarding ordinary, formal, and military dress for civil and military officials; the uniforms of soldiers and policemen; and the use by our thirty million people of formal dress in imitation of that manufactured abroad. As the lower classes invariably wax enthusiastic over what their rulers admire, the people in our empire are coming on the whole gradually to admire foreign ways, to wear foreign caps and clothes, and to construct foreign houses. Almost all the homes have come to depend upon foreign imports for household appliances ranging from such items as glass, mirrors, pictures, chairs, and tables to cakes, wines, and other edibles. Such are the reasons why the excess of imports over exports has reached the large sum of Yen 8 million each year.

Moreover, is it not because of the vigorous activity of our people, whose temperament is to love tricks and enjoy colorful display, that their productive capacity generally has greatly increased the output of thread, tea, and other commodities as compared with the old days? Yet since today's especially large gap between exports and imports upsets the natural equilibrium and since the large quantities of foreign imports exceeds the consuming power of our people, the popular demand for these commodities does not equal the level [of imports]. This is the reason why the prices of foreign goods have greatly declined so that they sometimes are below their original costs. I believe that the balance between imports and exports will surely be restored in a year like the present 1875. Or the deficits of previous years will be somewhat made up by an excess of exports over the level of imports, and thus the imbalance will necessarily be averaged out. After all, commerce cannot be carried on if in the long run an equilibrium is not achieved between imports and exports. This is like the principle of the winds and the tides. Now advancing and now receding, sometimes moving from the East and sometimes from the West, the winds and tides ultimately achieve an equilibrium. I say, therefore, that the gap between imports and exports does not warrant the serious anxieties provoked in the minds of the patriots.

As I have previously explained quite fully why it is wrong to try to restore the trade balance with protective tariffs, I shall not again go into this matter here. Moreover, the specie that we export without recovering is for such items as foreign advisers, educating students abroad, and foreign purchases. Are these expenses not truly indispensable if our empire desires in the least to achieve the objectives of progress and enlightenment? After all, as these expenses are like tuition for a child's elementary school, they will be a source for the supply of productive capital in a later day. Even though it is said that the losses are obviously not small, are the expenses not really essential if we compare them with future benefits? The losses from such expenses as those for the special embassy abroad,[13] the Austrian exhibition,[14] and the difficulty with China[15] will never be redeemed, and they are great losses for our empire. In addition, even though it is said that these payments were also related to really unavoidable outlays, the losses would not have been so excessive had the responsible ministers paid strict attention from the outset. It would be well if we would only pay attention to this clear warning in the future. It is, of course, beyond dispute, however, that expenses for such items as railway construction should gradually increase with the passage of time and never be reduced. I only say that we shall profit if we eliminate the numerous losses connected with such an item as ceremonial dress for civil officials.

Misgivings on the Outcome of Paper Currency
(The Third of Four Essays on Currency)[16]

Kanda Kōhei

I have been asked whether, once specie has been completely exhausted, there will occur an interruption [in the circulation of paper currency] since there seems to be no inconvenience in the circulation of paper at present. My response is that the occurrence of interruptions should not await the complete exhaustion of hard currency. Of course, with its gradual decline in value, paper money will cease to circulate as at present. I would clarify my views by propounding a certain hypothesis. After all, will not interruptions invariably appear at the open ports? Since foreigners at the open ports are unwilling to accept paper money, it will be impossible to buy foreign goods if there is no specie. Some discrepancy between paper money and specie, therefore, will emerge as the demand for specie increases. This discrepancy between the value of paper and specie is a symptom of the falling value of paper and the first stage in the so-called interruption. Even though the difference between the two currencies at first will be almost invisible, as it will be small and appear only at the treaty ports, it will later spread gradually in all directions, become large, and eventually become evident to the public.

In the early stages, the government will exert its momentary authority, strictly forbidding any discrepancy between paper and specie and executing those transgressing its prohibition. Yet the government itself before long will destroy the system and ultimately be unable to enforce its regulations. This is for no other reason than that the need of the government for specie will become still more pressing than the need of the people. After all, since the demand by the people for hard currency arises from their desire to purchase foreign goods, these purchases may be stopped temporarily at will, naturally without any great harm. The demands by the government for specie are quite different. They arise from salaries to foreign advisors, expenses for legations and consulates, the support of Japanese students abroad, costs for purchases, and payments of interest and annual installments on foreign loans. We may thus appreciate the urgency of the government's quest for hard currency since it cannot suddenly halt its extremely large specie payments even if it desires to do so.

Under such circumstances, we cannot know what policy will emerge from the government's search for specie. Nevertheless, since the government could not go so far as to seize the private property of the people, it would have no other alternative but to force specie out by resorting to numerous secret gratuities (*aikin*).[17] Therefore, I say that, even though the government at first strictly prohibits a discrepancy between hard and paper currency, it will itself eventually destroy the system. Yet since the demand for hard currency will become still more urgent with its increasing scarcity, the government will finally be unable to acquire specie even though it resorts to numerous secret gratuities. Under such circumstances, there will be persons who advocate still more drastic policies. Some will say that, since specie is the public treasure of the nation and since the private hoarders of specie obstruct national currency circulation, [the government] should relieve the hardships of the good people by strictly punishing these treacherous persons and thus causing specie to circulate. Some will also say that, as persons possessing golden baubles at this time wantonly indulge in private extravagance without reflecting on the fate of the nation, we may well oblige the individual owners of these gold and silver trinkets to present the trinkets to the mint in return for appropriate indemnification. And some will suggest that we should halt the present tax arrangements for a time, decide an appropriate market value for such items as silk, seeds, paper, tea, rice, barley, and various other grains, copper, tin, coal, etc., and allow these to be used for tax payments—without, however, imposing this rule on those who will desire to pay in specie.

When a discrepancy emerges for the first time between the value of paper money and specie, the public will just regard this as a rise in the price of gold without yet realizing that it is a fall in the value of paper money. They will only appreciate that the value of paper money has fallen after there has been a general rise in the prices of rice and cereals, property, and all other commodities. Then perceptive persons will quickly anticipate their opportunity, bury what gold and silver they have, purchase land, cereals, clothing, implements and other items with their paper money, and follow various other means to unload their paper as energetically as possible. Should such become the general practice in society, the value of declining paper will increasingly fall, and the rising commodity prices will increasingly rise until the price of rice will mount from Yen 1000 to Yen 10,000 per koku. Since paper currency will then be absolutely worthless, how can this be other than a major interruption [in currency circulation]? Nevertheless, this is entirely a momentary flight of my imagination, naturally not something developed from positive proof. I shall be happy if men of intelligence sympathize with what I have in mind.

[1]Fukuzawa is here responding to the speech by Nishi Amane that appears in Issue Twenty-Three. In his earlier article in the *Minkan Zasshi* (民間雑誌) on why travel and mixed residence by foreigners should not be allowed in Japan, Fukuzawa held that such travel and mixed residence would increase foreign trade and that foreign trade had only brought loss and no gain to the Japanese since the reopening of the country. Arguing that trade should be discouraged until the Japanese were ready to deal effectively with foreigners, Fukuzawa urged that Japan should first promote the intellectual vigor of her people by introducing them to civilization before she sought broader foreign contacts. He opposed opening the country to travel and mixed residence until the Japanese people were sufficiently advanced to control the foreigners in

their midst. For a reprint of Fukuzawa's *Minkan Zasshi* article, see the *Meiji Bunka Zenshū* (明治文化全集), *Zasshi Hen* (雑誌篇), pp. 291–295.

[2] *Ri*, 里, a Japanese measure equal to 2.44 miles.

[3] Abe Ise no Kami, 阿部伊勢守. Abe Masahiro (阿部正弘), the lord of Ise, was senior minister of the Tokugawa bakufu when Commodore Perry arrived in Japan in 1853 or the sixth year of the Kaei (嘉永) Period. Sir Harry Parkes took up residence in Japan as British minister in 1865.

[4] *Chiryoku*, 智力.

[5] *Naichi ryokō*, 内地旅行.

[6] *Zakkyo*, 雑居.

[7] *Noren*, 暖簾, the short curtains that traditionally hang across the doorways of Japanese shops.

[8] *Tempō* (天保) Era, 1830–1844, the period during which many of the early Meiji leaders were born.

[9] Musashibō Benkei, 武藏坊辨慶, d. 1189, the large, stout-hearted hero renowned as the loyal follower of the gallant Minamoto Yoshitsune (源義經).

[10] Kumasaka no Chōhan, 熊阪長範, a former thief who, like Benkei, is said to have become a follower of Minamoto Yoshitsune.

[11] While the optimistic Tsuda is here responding particularly to Kanda Kōhei's "Regrets on the Export of Specie" in Issue Twenty-Three, he seems also to be taking issue with Fukuzawa Yukichi, who would separate foreign trade from civilization and enlightenment and who deplored the dispirited nature of the Japanese people. For Tsuda's more general arguments against tariff protection, see his article in Issue Five entitled "In Opposition to Protective Tariffs."

[12] *Genkin*, 見金(現金).

[13] The mission led by Iwakura Tomomi (岩倉具視) to the West, 1871–1873.

[14] The Vienna Exposition of 1873.

[15] The dispute with China in 1874 that was occasioned by the Japanese expedition to chastise aborigines in southern Formosa.

[16] For the previous number in this series, see Issue Twenty-Three.

[17] *Aikin*, 間金.

MEIROKU ZASSHI Issue Twenty-Seven February 1875

On Wives and Concubines Part Five[1]

Mori Arinori

In the past, the difference between the designations of wife (*tsuma*)[2] and concubine (*mekake*)[3] has related only to the fact that, when they first entered the family, the former depended upon a formal arrangement by a go-between and the latter did not. Yet there has seemed to be no real difference between the two since they have appeared equal in the eyes of the law. There is thus really no necessity to discuss the difference in their designations. From the very beginning, when I have expressed myself on these matters and frequently sought the opinions of my colleagues in the society, I have been prompted especially by the feeling that the evils in the customs relating to wives and concubines should be extensively reformed. Now having considered a little the various marriage laws that are in operation in foreign countries, I would here propose steps to provide future marriage laws in our country. I respectfully beg your comments on my draft articles.[4]

Proposed Marriage Regulations

Section I. The Marriage Contract

Article One. In the consummation of a marriage, it is necessary to have the mutual agreement of both parties concerned. Furthermore, an appropriate legal ceremony must be carried out, and the mutual rights and obligations of husband and wife must be previously understood.

Article Two. Even though the rights and obligations between the husband and wife should generally depend on past custom, should the couple make written promises as the consequence of discussion at the time of marriage, they shall completely abide by this written contract.

Article Three. Men over twenty-five and women over twenty, individually and according to their own will, may consummate and enter into a marriage contract except under special circumstances provided by national law.

Article Four. Marriages may all be declared void if either party is not of age, is ill, or has signed a contract under force or through misrepresentation.

Article Five. Marriages between parents and children, grandparents and grandchildren, brothers and sisters, as well as uncles or aunts and nephews or nieces entirely violate morality. Such marriages, therefore, cannot be contracted or entered into from the outset.

Article Six. Except under the following conditions, neither husband or wife during life shall enter into a second marriage contract since such contracts are contrary to morality:

1. The previous marriage has already been dissolved.
2. The existence of the previous husband or wife has been unknown for a period of five years.

Article Seven. If either party entering the marriage did not know that the other was guilty of a crime, it is not invariably necessary to preserve the marriage contract. Moreover, once the marriage is consummated, should either party have intimate relations with a third person or should either suffer unbearably immoral treatment from the other, the [injured party] may bring suit before an official, receive a monetary settlement, and secure a divorce. The amount of the monetary settlement shall not exceed two-thirds of the property of the other party.

Article Eight. Those to be married must invariably ask validation by an official in the presence of a witness. Further, at the time of validation, the following information must be presented in writing.

1. The fact that the request for marriage arises from their mutual desires and is approved without doubt by both parties.
2. The address, names, and families of the two parties.
3. When the man is not yet twenty-five and the woman is not yet twenty, there should be written permission from their parents or their guardians.

Article Nine. Regardless of the region in which conclusion of the marriage is sought, the request for marriage validation shall be submitted to the local official in charge of marriages. (The ward chief may also serve in this capacity.)

Article Ten. At the time when public validation is granted, the couple shall be obliged to swear to an oath before the marriage official and in the presence of a witness. The official himself shall record this fact on the validating document and himself affix his signature and official title; the document shall be reproduced in triplicate; and copies shall be given to each party in the marriage as well as deposited in the marriage office.

[My] divorce law proposal will await the next issue.

The Irregular Route to a Popularly Elected Assembly

Speech on January 16, 1875[5]

Sakatani Shiroshi

While an introduction may be unnecessary, I shall speak a little about myself since this is my first appearance. I am an honest, dark-skinned dullard by the name of Sakatani Shiroshi. I have only dabbled a little in Chinese studies without reading any Western books at all. I have read but a hundredth of the translations of foreign books, and I have heard the discussions of my colleagues in this society from time to time. Having suffered pain in my teeth from the prime of life, I have lost them all, and it is difficult for me to speak clearly. I am so bold as to ask that you give me your attention because I believe that there is only one truth, even though the customs of Japan, China, and the West differ, because I want to hear your opinions, and because this is an opportunity for training myself. Therefore, I beg you hereafter fully to give me your opinions. Since I do not read Western writings, I ask your indulgence should my words be halting and inappropriate.

Now, while it is improper for a person in my position to speak, to do so on behalf of the country is in a way a duty. I speak first from my desire to obtain your views so that we can establish our objective. My purport follows the line that, to carry out the currently circulating theories regarding a popularly elected assembly, we should introduce the institution gradually by adopting the irregular approach of an officially selected assembly. Just as there are regular and irregular approaches to learning, this is like developing Western studies in our country by an irregular path.

Generally, if we want to accomplish anything, our efforts will be in vain unless we consider fundamentals, since foundations otherwise will not be established. National structures and customs differ, just as all things ranging from great rivers and mountains to small trees and grasses individually differ. To introduce Western parliamentary forms directly into our country, therefore, is like making our shoes according to the measurements of another's feet in accordance with the "deductive" method.[6] Such an approach would only bring injury and destruction to the country. Among the major differences between our country and foreign countries, there is first the difference between a monarchy and republics, but our monarchy also differs from theirs. Those who think it best not to speak of our emperor system actually mistake the "deductive" for the "inductive" method and would make rivers and mountains one. Since they do not distinguish between Japan and foreign countries, I hold that it is necessary to discuss [the Japanese monarchy] in order to establish our objective.

Monarchies as well as republics are all naturally formed and differ as do the mountains and rivers of England from the mountains and rivers of America. It is entirely mistaken, therefore, to condemn others in terms of our standards or to ape their standards. Of Europe, it may be said that all nations individually have their own natural systems. [Their rulers emerge] from election, hereditary succession, and individual arrogation of power while their dynasties customarily change from time to time under the hereditary system. It was probably wrong for countries like America and Switzerland even briefly to have had rulers like the first Napoleon of France or the kings of England as they are not essentially monarchial. France and Spain are not yet settled, but one may judge from their national tendencies that they are naturally suited to republicanism.

Our country is indeed called a monarchy, but we should refer to it as a permanently continuing monarchy rather than as a monarchy that was proclaimed. Its rationale differs from that of the vender of dolls' heads at a circus who walks around calling out, "Heads! Heads!" Fortunately, like people born with their heads attached, our country has been ruled by a single line from the beginning. Such a theory may savour of the myths of the Plain of High Heaven,[7] but this is really an actual fact [regarding our imperial line].

Some say, however, that there is no reason for honoring a person simply because of his birth; that we should not honor the emperor although we are thankful to God, the Creator; that republics conform to Heaven's Law (*Tenri*)[8] and human reason (*jinri*);[9] and that power will not expand except under a republican system. They talk as though the emperor were an obstruction, being pusillanimously fearful that they may be criticized for failing truly to understand Europe and America if they do not speak out boldly from self-centered "passion." Their biased views violate the true Heavenly Way (*Tendō*)[10] and human reason as they contradict the fair and objective views of the great thinkers of America and Switzerland who, aside from being teachers of republicanism, stress popular feelings and social conditions and explain that elected leaders are more injurious than hereditary sovereigns. If such biased views spread in a small country like Japan, if the traditional strength of the people's minds is destroyed, and if shallow customs flourish, we will sink to complete "barbarism." When such parties emerge and encourage liberty and freedom fashioned from "passion," the strength of the people's minds will be upset, great quarrels will become civil wars, their expenditures will all pile up debts, properties will be completely mortgaged, and the people will surely become just like slaves. At this point, whatever the "state" and whoever the "people," the great principle of "sovereignty" will be completely destroyed, and the country inured to slavery will become a truly enslaved country.

However I think on this, I am filled with innumerable regrets. Is there no desire to take vengeance on these false prophets? However one looks at the matter, we must honor and protect our imperial line in order to defend our Japan. Should carefully selected savants from America and Switzerland be asked to discuss this, I believe that they will come to no other conclusion. You are naturally well aware of this. Since this is a confused period in international relations, however, it is important that we hoist up this basic objective [to defend the imperial line]. Still more is this the case with such a matter as a popularly elected assembly that is unprecedented in our history. If we do not stand firm on this matter [of the imperial line], a small crack will open into a chasm thousands of miles in breadth, and Japan will be destroyed. Therefore, I am first undertaking this clarification.

From here, then, I shall speak of a popularly elected assembly. When asked what is most important for defense of the imperial line, my response is one word—sincerity (*makoto*).[11] I would further say that sincerity is achieved by honesty but that unbending honesty alone is not enough. Honesty is like water that finds its own level, invariably moving from its source to the sea without being frustrated however winding the course. Since this analogy is twisted, I shall try to clarify its logic by taking up the opposite of honesty. The opposite of honesty is that pernicious thing called flattery. Of course, it is unnecessary to discuss those who mean to flatter and deceive their superiors. In countries where subservient customs prevail, however, many resort to flattery, taking it for honesty. Since antiquity, what brought misfortune to the imperial line and the extinction of patriotism in times bereft of courage and greatness were always subservient customs of flattery that are the opposite of honesty. In the West during the 1660s and 1670s, Louis XIV of France said, "I am the state, and I hold unlimited power." Such foolish Chinese scholars of antiquity as Shên [Pu-hai] and Han [Fei-tzu][12] stated that the people will become the ruler's fetters unless he governs them arbitrarily. When it is assumed that the emperors exert their powers with complete license, then men like Ashikaga Takauji[13] and Taira Masakado[14] will arise as agents of the people's will. Are such fearful conditions to be still more common in the future?

It is indeed said that the nation is the sovereign's nation (*tenshi no tenka*),[15] but this means that the sovereign cannot govern his own possession arbitrarily even though he may treat the property of others as he pleases. The nation being Heaven's creation, it is still less possible for the emperor, who is the child and representative of Heaven, to betray Heaven's Way and human reason by acting with arbitrary "liberty." If you inquire as to the obligations and duties of the divine ruler, they are only to protect the people. Should he incline toward oppression by deviating even slightly from this course of protection, the emperor then becomes only a watchman, having failed to honor his obligations and duties.

It is honest, therefore, to regard "protection" of the people as "protection" of the imperial line so that the emperor may carry out his duties without sinking to the level of a watchman. It is flattery to adopt the opposite line, and ourselves become watchmen. Flattery paves the way for a really enslaved Japan and weakens the imperial line by excessive favoritism. Along with this, such foolish flatterers destroy themselves by destroying their own protection. For instance, take the sick family head who does not care for himself on the assumption that he has "liberty" to treat his body as he pleases since it is his own body. Should his doctor and family think it "kind" and the path of social intercourse to permit him his "liberty," their failure to perform the duties of doctor and family would be unenlightened "barbarism."

Putting aside the vicissitudes of the past for a moment, the "liberty" of the people today is daily encouraged by the imperial edict directing that everything should be decided by public discussion.[16] Such being the case, the rights and duties of the sovereign as well as the people and the "politics" of government officials may be appreciated, while conditions in Europe and America are clarified. At this time, when persons of the slightest scholarship and intellect nearly all understand the elements of "civilization," there will be confusion if officials adorn themselves with trifles and cast aside the great principles of the political structure by adopting secretive poses. To protect the people by taking "autocracy" [?][17] as the great principle is the same as overindulging the patient. Since to overindulge the imperial line is to overindulge the people while to overindulge the people is to overindulge the imperial line, it is really sincere "kindness" not to permit overindulgence even for a moment.

Taxation, civil law, travel, and mixed residence by foreigners within the country, the judicial system, determination of the imperial succession, and the monetary problems that are Kanda's concern are all pressing matters. When affairs are determined by secret oppression from above without establishing great principles and without clarifying the political structure, even wise and famous persons will not understand the laws, however good they may be. Everyone will mistrust, hate, and doubt as false the unexpected proclamations that startle them like a shining object in the dark, and profits will all be seized by foreigners once the public mind is confused. Thereafter, there will be nothing but fury and disorder.

Coming to the present situation, important foreign and domestic questions will not be decided in the "state" unless there is public discussion and decision by representatives of the people, unless the meaning of these discussions is fully appreciated throughout the country, unless high and low are led fully to understand that national affairs are their obligations and on their behalf, and unless established laws are not arbitrarily revised even by the most powerful. Spirit and courage arise especially from responsiblity, and the feeling of responsibility emerges more from wealth than from scholarship. Since even foolish people understand the significance of money, the spirit of even those addicted to servility will be so moved that they cannot remain silent when we clarify the principle that the sovereign and the people are mutually responsbile for taxation and expenditures, the determination of which is the main responsibility of the parliament. None in the world are uninfluenced by wealth, the lower classes all become servile when economic power is held by the upper, and honesty yields to flattery when obsequiousness prevails.

In short, can flattery lead elsewhere but to disturbance? There may be anxious people who argue that business will not be transacted when a parliament is established and who regard the advocates of a parliament as inveterate complainers. Such people may anticipate that there will be no preventing the appearance of claims one after another from commoners (*shomin*)[18] who refuse to pay taxes, from former samurai (*shizoku*)[19] who would increase their stipends, and from nobles (*kazoku*)[20] who would long delay a reduction in their allowances. What foolishness! Can anything be accomplished if these anxious persons of such mean character thus fail to understand the public mind and public morality? All are in doubt and resort to arguments since the upper classes conduct business in secret without establishing a parliament. But if men are publicly responsible, there will be no discussion that is not open and fair. Moreover, whether affairs are expedited depends on the merits of parliamentary proceedings as truth is clarified to the extent that there is free discussion.

I am not proposing now to advance such disorderly parliamentary proceedings as emerged from the French Revolution at the end of the eighteenth century. It cannot be determined whether the French legislative proceedings of that time embraced the radical ideas that were advocated by the "local folk." If you just look at them, [you will observe] that disturbances since antiquity have all arisen from the fact that opinions of others were regarded as ignorant, foolish, troublesome, or obstructive. Some rather encourage partisanship by writing that popularly elected assemblies are the vehicles of radicals, but I hold a different view. If the Emperor Go-Daigo at the beginning of the Kemmu Restoration had proclaimed that everything should be determined by public discussion and if there had been a parliament from which he could draw opinions, I believe that the enlightenment of Japan would have preceded that of the West as there would have been no wars between the Northern and Southern dynasties, [Ashikaga] Takauji would have been silenced, and the bakufu extinguished.[21] Since I do not believe that it is in the least too early [to introduce a parliament], I hold that we can deal with radicalism and gradualism in due course while settling parliamentary formalities after the assembly has been established.

Looking into the matter further, taxes, as I have observed, should be the public business of high and low.[22] Under our political system heretofore, measures for relief were entirely the responsibility of the rulers. Since taxes were always to be as low as possible, this meant that rulers would labor for the people's protection without food and without clothing. Such practices are indeed inappropriate today. There was a measure of power and prosperity during periods of sage kings and wise rulers. But since the power and prosperity of one generation would be destroyed during its successor, a still later generation of wise leaders would only exhaust their energies in repairing the damage. There is no expectation that power and prosperity will become great when alternate periods of destruction and repair thus succeed each other. It may be thought that this is the real reason why our country and China, their early enlightenment notwithstanding, later lagged behind the enlightened countries [of the West]. Therefore, however I consider the matter, I conclude that it is "patriotism" and "loyalty" based upon true honesty to urge the early establishment of a popularly elected assembly and that this is also an undertaking for the protection of the imperial line and the people together. (To be continued in the next issue.)

[1]See Issue Twenty for Part Four.

[2]*Tsuma*, 妻.

[3]*Mekake*, 妾.

[4]Mori himself undertook to practice what he preached when on 6 February 1875 he and his bride, Hirose Otsune (廣瀨阿常), signed a marriage contract in a ceremony before the governor of Tokyo, Ōkubo Ichiō (大久保一翁), with Fukuzawa Yukichi serving as witness. The marriage ended in divorce in 1886.

[5]See Issue Thirteen for Sakatani's previous article on a popularly elected assembly.

[6]Although Sakatani transcribed "induction" and "deduction" in the *katakana* syllabary, he clearly did not understand the terms.

[7]Plain of High Heaven (Takama-ga-hara, 高天原), the abode of the ancestress of the Japanese emperors, the Sun Goddess Amaterasu-ō-mikami (天照大御神).

[8]*Tenri*, 天理.

[9]*Jinri*, 人理.

[10]*Tendō*, 天道.

[11]*Makoto*, 誠.

[12]Shên [Pu-hai], 申不害, –337 B.C., and Han [Fei-tzu], 韓非子, –257 B.C., were Chinese legalist scholars.

[13]Ashikaga Takauji, 足利尊氏, 1305–1358, the founder of the Ashikaga line of shoguns who was denounced by traditional Japanese historians because he defied the imperial line that they regarded as legitimate.

[14]Taira Masakado, 平將門, –940, the leader of an unsuccessful revolt in eastern Japan during which he called himself the new emperor.

[15]*Tenshi no tenka*, 天子ノ天下.

[16]Sakatani here quotes the first article of the five-article imperial oath of 1868 (*Gokajō no Goseimon*, 五箇條ノ御誓文).

[17]Whereas Sakatani evidently intended "autocracy," his transcription in the *katakana* syllabary most closely resembles "orthodoxy."

[18]*Shomin*, 庶民.

[19]*Shizoku*, 士族.

[20]*Kazoku*, 華族.

[21]Sakatani here criticizes the efforts by the Emperor Go-Daigo (後醍醐) to restore the imperial supremacy at the time of the Kemmu Restoration *(Kemmu Gochūkō*, 建武御中興) of 1333. His efforts were undone when Ashikaga Takauji attempted to establish the so-called northern line of emperors, and Japan from 1336 was torn by fifty-six years of internecine wars between the Northern and Southern Dynasties (*Nambokuchō no Ran*, 南北朝の亂).

[22]See Sakatani's article in Issue Fifteen entitled "On the Taxing Power as the Public Business of High and Low."

MEIROKU ZASSHI Issue Twenty-Eight February 1875

The Irregular Route to a Popularly Elected Assembly
(Continuation from the Previous Issue)

Sakatani Shiroshi

As I previously stated when I urged early establishment of a popularly elected assembly, national customs differ even though the shape of parliaments may be the same. It is imperative, therefore, that we make the shoes to fit our own feet. The present discussions of popular elections, however, only contain eloquent verbiage without clarifying the actual situation. Indeed, there is a tendency not to start anything unless it has been recklessly espoused. Clever people may intend lightheartedly to conceive a plan appropriate for the moment. But when it comes to such a major undertaking as a popularly elected assembly, far from lightheartedly conceiving a plan, even great statesmen must indeed labor hard after the crisis has broken. This may be understood by just looking at Washington's trials. The fellows Mitani [Sankurō] and Ōno [Zensuke] intended to conduct their business lightheartedly, but they failed even though their enterprises were small.[1]

A popularly elected assembly is not to be treated opportunistically. More especially, since there has long been an increasing tendency for the upper classes to strengthen their oppressive control, such an assembly cannot be successful unless it serves the purposes of the rulers. Legislative systems independently established by the prefectures are without prospect of actually functioning if the superior central authorities have not yet made up their minds. It may be better to establish such impotent assemblies than not to create any whatsoever. Generally, however, such assemblies, being financial burdens on the people and without any real power, will become either enemies of the prefectural authorities or nests of scoundrels who pander to the whims of governors and councillors. Proposals for these assemblies may indeed be forwarded to the capital after having been approved by the prefectural authorities. If they do not suit the convenience of the central government, however, they will be shelved unless there are protests. The [local] spirit having been broken, the assemblies will be no more than cartoons and empty talk. At the village level, there have been gatherings for discussion by the mutual aid associations (*kumiai*),[2] and the *nembutsukō*[3] as well as the *Myokenkō*[4] have also discussed practical matters. In a repressive society, however, these meetings generally are only ratifying bodies. They may petition from time to time, but rejection of their petitions breeds talk of rebellion.

In sum, we will inevitably invite outbreaks and confusion if we now strongly stress the [political] aspects of assemblies. Such an approach would be valid if our objective were to establish a popularly elected assembly after having strengthened the people's rights and overthrown the government. But as I have previously stated, we would probably then promote [political] discussion that would enslave the country. The lower classes may indeed try to rise up with all their might without considering the above, but they will be obliged to stop once the leaders by a single order state that such action is strictly forbidden, shall not be practiced, and therefore shall not be discussed. If they do not stop, they will inevitably collide with the government. Since the government at the present time cannot be indifferent, saying that the assembly is too early but that nature will be allowed to take its course, it will inevitably start poking about at various minor details. This being the case, traditions of three thousand years, following the trends of the times, will suddenly collapse on every side, and [the rabble] will strike out blindly and recklessly after observing that the government is allowing nature to run its course. Revolution will follow since the government cannot suffer such blows. We may then advance to the level of civilization and enlightenment after a popularly elected assembly has arisen naturally.

But it is a regrettable fact that the peerless imperial line would be endangered. Moreover, unlike France and other countries, [Japan] is a small nation inhabited by narrow-minded people. We have forgotten "patriotism" and "sympathy" because we are moved by "ambition" not to concede what arises from fraternal quarreling. Yielding to the flattery of foreign countries, we freely buy their machines and ammunition, mortgaging our property without regard to the future until we shall finally reach the point of quarreling over whether to retain the monarchy. Foreigners will then say: "If you disturb the land that you have mortgaged, its value will go down. You should do your quarreling elsewhere. While you are away, we [shall take possession] and toss parched beans at you."

Japan will then be like a vagabond or a slave. All those fellows who hereafter plan rebellion so that they may expand their liberty to become shogun, president, or emperor, are fools who will become debt-ridden and homeless slaves, as indicated above. Our country since the opening of foreign intercourse has been like the family of which each of you is a member, and those who swagger about doing as they individually please are all inviting eviction. Once we have lost this home, we shall not find a place to enter our name, however hard we may search the household registers [*koseki*].[5] In our country, therefore, the upper classes must surely prepare the way for a popularly elected assembly. In all matters, as with the "education" of children, the early habits are most important. The successive assassinations in Russia and the continuing sentiment for monarchy even in enlightened countries like France that are trying to establish republics are [all remnants of habits from early days], like the restricting of waists by Western women, foot binding among the Chinese, and the tying of *obi* in Japan. Since it is difficult to eradicate such habits that have early saturated the mind, judicious and extended training also is the path of "protection."

Without hastening or delaying at the present juncture, therefore, the pivot by which we move from autocracy to harmonious rule [by limited monarchy] is extremely important. Our country is different from Europe and America where popularly elected assemblies were established after the overthrow of governments by the assertion of popular rights and where justifying theories relating to harmonious rule by high and low [limited monarchy] were only subsequently contrived.[6] We have the incomparable imperial line, as I have already stated. There were indeed people in the neighborhood of Azuma who indulged in the foolish habit of speaking scornfully of the emperor as *tenkō* or *kinkō*.[7] But since the imperial system, after all, has saturated even their minds, [our] country would sink to the aforementioned condition of slavery without it. Thus the tendency today and [our] proper obligation is invariably to affirm harmonious rule by high and low [limited monarchy] and thereby protect the people as well as the imperial line.

I believe that it is most important to arrange all matters in an orderly manner conducive to achieving this objective of harmonious rule by high and low by abandoning vacillating permissiveness, avoiding cheap tricks, putting an end to radical ideas that brew trouble, and setting aside violent means. It is thus best to begin with an officially selected assembly when establishing a popularly elected assembly. As for the matter of popular elections, the people are all completely impractical, untrained, and inclined only to argument. They are all unreasonable "local folk" whose aimless discussions are no more than a big noise and a complete waste. It is foolish to wait for nature [to run its course without undertaking a cure] on the ground that the sufferer from hunger or cold has not yet starved or frozen, but it is also foolish to give him hastily a feast or to bring him close to a great fire. He will become strong with surprising rapidity if, after diagnosis, he is slowly fed rice gruel or placed before a gentle fire. Therefore, since the most direct way is actually to start as soon as possible along the irregular path that leads to the regular path, it is best to create an officially selected assembly immediately after we have established harmonious rule by high and low [limited monarchy] as our objective. Members will be selected by the government according to (their) reputation from the numerous distinguished scholars currently in public service and from the talented persons gathered in Tokyo.

I believe that persons chosen will include many colleagues at this meeting. There are also numerous renowned and influential persons who should be selected regardless of whether they belong to a society. From persons in the provinces who are members of societies or who hold themselves apart without competing in public, the government will carefully select a few persons from each region (*dō*)[8] based upon of their scholarly and civic attainments. The government will augment their ample stipends annually, and it will increase the number selected as the people become accustomed to deliberation and legislation and with advancing enlightenment that accompanies teaching in the schools. After deciding the rules for parliamentary procedure, secret oppression will be eliminated by harmonizing administration with legislative discussion. Thereafter, arrangements for taxation, laws, foreign relations, and currency can in due order be discussed, approved, promulgated, and put into operation.

In the prefectures (*ken*),[9] prefectural and ward assemblies will promulgate the particular laws that they have adopted in accordance with local interests. The wisest persons in the localities, such as those from the middle and lower schools, will also be selected and sent to Tokyo [for training]. When appointing them to office, we shall also establish an official system for selecting personnel. As trained persons from the regions increase, we shall reduce the number of those who are both administrators and legislators and eventually establish laws for popular elections.

If we advance matters gradually and without interruption in the manner of growing trees and grasses as the wise Frenchman [Jean] Bodin advocated, we will establish a truly natural and regularly elected assembly within ten to thirteen years that conforms to the fine customs of our country and that corresponds with the true legislative principles of England and America. I have my own opinions on the matter of expense, believing that we can easily meet any that may arise. Once established, the principle of equal rights [limited monarchy] can never be altered even though the government may issue a thousand edicts disapproving the course upon which we have embarked. We shall by this means alone establish the "state's sovereignty," having escaped the misuse of "folk" violence. I believe that we should cut short the various "ambitions" of different classes and pursue this objective of harmonious rule by high and low [limited monarchy] as soon as possible. Realization of this objective, however, lies in courageous decision by the upper classes. If this courageous decision is not made, therefore, the trend hereafter will be toward violent popular elections and enslavement [of the country]. What "protection" will there then be for the imperial line and the people? Even though I exert myself to the utmost of my capacity, I am filled with unbearable anxiety when I ponder the hardships for the thirty million Japanese as well as my own hardships [should we fail]. Therefore, I have expressed my opinions while regretting that my long speech has delayed the business of this meeting.

Three Types of Political System Part One

Nishimura Shigeki

It is the common opinion in the world that the three types of political system (*seitai*)[10] are autocracies (*jinkun dokusai*),[11] constitutional monarchies (*kummin dōji*),[12] and democratic republics (*heimin kyōwa*).[13] I would propose three types of rule as a different approach: traditional rule (*inshū seiji*),[14] traditional rule mixed with reason (*inshū dōri kongō seiji*),[15] and rule by reason (*dōri seiji*).[16]

First, Traditional Rule. Traditional rule, regardless of the political system, generally takes the political system at the founding of the country as best, and it is conducted solely according to tradition without in the least considering whether this is good or bad. Now when one refers to condition at the founding of countries, men were ignorant and unenlightened in ancient times, like beasts being without etiquette and social intercourse. Finally, strong and courageous men emerged among them, subdued their people with power, and enforced order in their regions. There were many persons of this type at the founding of Babylon, Egypt, and the various countries of Europe and Asia. [I] would take this as the first type [of traditional rule]. People in ancient times also formed villages and delimited their own boundaries. When men of intellect emerged, the people of the villages established intimate relations with each other by drawing their communities together and entering into alliances in order to promote the security of the whole. An example of this is the twelve towns of Greece that joined together to rule the country. This may be taken as the second type [of traditional rule]. In antiquity, the inhabitants of an entire village might be drawn wholly from one family. As in the case of the founding of Israel, the members of a family would join together, select a chief, and obey his orders like the commands of a monarch. This may be taken as the third type [of traditional rule]. The first type was the origin of autocracy; the second, of republican rule; and the third, of tribal rule. The latter two, however, were both early destroyed, and only the first has persisted from the beginning to the present. Traditional rule, therefore, may be regarded today as another word for autocracy.

Second, Traditional Rule Mixed with Reason. Countries in

which today traditional rule mixed with reason functions were formerly all governed only by traditional rule. Once the people became quite enlightened, however, they recognized that traditional rule was not advantageous to the country and employed force or persuasion to reform their political system. The people determined their political systems half according to tradition and half according to reason in conformity with the level of their enlightenment and the virtue of their customs. There are numerous countries in Europe where these mixed systems operate. Being mixtures of the tradition of autocracy and the reason of democratic republics, they are called joint rule by monarch and people or limited monarchies (*seigen aru kunshu seiji*).[17] Constitutional monarchies, therefore, may also be called traditional rule mixed with reason.

Third, Rule by Reason. As the countries where this political system prevails were founded most recently, their people were already enlightened. Even though this was a time when older countries were establishing mixed rule, it was unnecessary for the new countries to follow this practice since they were without old customs. Since these new countries established their political systems only after consulting reason, they were able to introduce rule by pure reason. If you consider the matter from the point of view of reason, there may be no more perfect system than that of democratic republics. The political system of a democratic republic, therefore, may also be called rule by reason. Even in some new countries, however, there are instances, such as Greece and Belgium in which mixing with traditional rule could not be avoided because of conditions at the time of their founding. Even though new countries may not invariably establish rule by reason, therefore, I have not yet heard of an old country in which rule by reason has prevailed from antiquity.

We may refer to traditional rule as the system of high antiquity since it arose in ancient times, to mixed rule as the early modern political system since it appeared in the early modern period, and to rule by reason as the modern political system since it developed in modern times. (Even though Switzerland was established during the Middle Ages, it would not be misleading to refer to her as modern since she emerged much later than Germany, France, and England.) Now why does the political system of high antiquity to this day still stand majestically side by side with the early modern and modern systems although it should already have been destroyed? To draw an analogy with the soil, a substance like granite, the foundation of the earth, often appears as an outcropping from the earth in the modern world even though it is the oldest substance in the world. Even though political systems are of three types —ancient, early modern, and modern, they stand together in the world of today just as granite, ore, and soil appear together on the earth's surface of today.

Looked at from the above point of view, traditional rule seems to be a system of ignorance; mixed rule, a system in which ignorance and wisdom are combined; and rule by reason, purely a system of wisdom. How strange it is, however, that countries under traditional rule may enjoy peace and tranquility while those governed by the rule of reason sometimes cannot prevent upheavals!

Three Types of Political System (Conclusion)

Nishimura Shigeki

Generally, it is invariably necessary to distinguish between reason and practice when discussing governmental rule. When discussing rule from the point of view of reason, we can understand without question that rule by reason should be regarded as the very best. But when discussing rule from the point of view of practice, mixed rule at times surpasses rule by reason. Should you ask why, it is because the rule of a country should generally conform to the level of the people's enlightenment. A country's political system will govern if it conforms to the level of enlightenment of its people, but it will not govern if it does not so conform. When the conduct of traditional rule brings peace to the country, its people have not yet developed wisdom and are thus suited to this political system. When the conduct of mixed rule brings prosperity to a country, its people have already greatly developed their wisdom and are thus suited to this mixed political system. If rule by reason does not bring greater happiness to the people than mixed rule, the people are then not suited to rule by reason even though their wisdom is greatly developed.

It seems that the peoples of the various countries of Europe and America have now reached the highest level of enlightenment. Then why are they not suited to rule by reason? Rule by reason is the finest and the best of political systems, and those suited to this political system invariably must be the finest and the best people. Should you ask what kind of people are the finest and the best, I would reply that people are the finest and the best if they are of the type who, being deeply patriotic, completely shoulder their responsibilities and being neither envious nor haughty, loyally help each other and mix together with a spirit of justice. There may indeed be a large number of people of this type in the various countries of Europe and America, but I would not yet say that these nations are all of this character through and through. Since these countries are not entirely composed of people of such a high level, they cannot really be suited to rule by reason. I think, therefore, that rule by reason is the rule for future generations, not the rule for today. Yet I also cannot guarantee that the people of the world, after all, will really become the finest and the best by some future generation.

Countries at peace under traditional rule are analogous to weak people. As long as they do not face any attacks from the outside or the boiling up of internal poison, they think themselves healthy simply because they are not ill. Nevertheless, if you compare them with truly healthy men, you will recognize them to be sickly just by glancing at their pale complexions and their frail bodies. Even when they suffer from no particular illness, they cannot work like really healthy people. How many avoid death from exhaustion or prostration once they face internal or external illness? After all, the reason why people contented with traditional rule usually appear weak is because they are generally without a spirit of independence and are placidly subservient to autocratic government.

If you consider the matter from the point of view of reason, rule by reason may be taken for the highest form. But if you consider from the point of view of practice, rule by reason and mixed rule are both of the highest order without distinction as to inferiority or superiority. Without doubt, traditional rule belongs to the lowest order, whether it is considered from the point of view of practice or of reason.

Then what about Russia, which has become a powerful nation under autocratic government? It is said that the strength of Russia depends entirely upon the fact that her rulers are men of great ability. There are sometimes men in this world who are strong in body but poor in hygiene. If you ask what they rely upon, it is only the strength of their natural endowments. Affairs in Russia are no different. Yet Russia has suffered no decline in her prestige, as she has been favored by a succession of really able rulers. It may be observed that a country would be in extremely sore straits to defend herself with traditional rule if her rulers were not as able as those of Russia and if her people were not as sagacious as the English and French.

But should countries under traditional rule quickly reform their political systems to mixed rule or rule by reason? I would say that they should not. Just as there are cases when mixed rule should not be changed to rule by reason, so there are cases when traditional rule should not be changed to mixed rule. When a regime preserves its national security through the conduct of traditional rule, the enlightenment of the people is still appropriate to such a political system. When there is an abrupt change to a different political system at such a time, national disturbances are the more likely to arise as ignorant people will not understand the reasons for the change and rogues will take advantage of the ignorant to plot mischief. Nevertheless, if the wisdom of the people has gradually developed and there are signs of dissatisfaction with traditional rule, this political system should be quickly changed for another. The wisdom of the people should not be fettered by the bigotry of tradition. If the people are oppressed by the old methods of tradition when the rulers do not appreciate that the people are already enlightened, we should expect domestic disturbances before long, just as when Charles I governed the English and the Hapsburgs [?][18] ruled the Swiss. Nevertheless, it is impossible to anticipate whether national happiness will arise from these disturbances. (January 16, 1875)

[1]Mitani Sankurō, 三谷三九郎, and Ono Zensuke, 小野善助, were merchants from the Tokugawa Period who failed after they had overextended their commitments during early Meiji.

[2]*Kumiai*, 組合, assemblies of village headmen called to meet with the lords' intendants (*daikan*, 代官). While village assemblies in Tokugawa Japan functioned as organs of self-government, they were also means for extending authority downward from the great lords into the villages. Decisions usually represented a concensus reached among village leaders.

[3]*Nembutsukō*, 念佛講, societies organized by practitioners of *nembutsu*, invocation of the name of the Amida Buddha.

[4]*Myōkenkō*, 妙見講, societies formed of the followers of the Nichiren (日蓮) Sect who believed in the bodhisattva Myōken. Myōken is venerated as a protector of one's country and granter of long life.

[5]*Koseki*, 戸籍.

[6]Sakatani here uses two contemporary terms for limited monarchy: *Jōge dōji* (上下同治) and *kummin dōken* (君民同權).

[7]Azuma, 吾妻, refers to eastern Japan, the center of Tokugawa power. Hence it was the followers of the Tokugawa who called the emperor *tenkō* (天公), heavenly lord, and *kinkō* (禁公), the lord of the forbidden interior (*kinchū*, 禁中), the imperial palace.

[8]*Dō*, 道.

[9]*Ken*, 縣.

[10]*Seitai*, 政體.

[11]*Jinkun dokusai*, 人君獨裁.

[12]*Kummin dōji*, 君民同治.

[13]*Heimin kyōwa*, 平民共和.

[14]*Inshū seiji*, 因襲政治.

[15]*Inshū dōri kongō seiji*, 因襲道理混合政治.

[16]*Dōri seiji*, 道理政治.

[17]*Seigen aru kunshu seiji*, 制限アル君主政治.

[18]Hapsburg (?), 亞伯勒.

On an All-Inclusive Parliament

Nishi Amane

It is not yet known what will be the end of the discussion relating to a popularly elected assembly that has emerged in society, but the talk is sufficient to indicate the direction of public concern. After all, since a popularly elected assembly embraces the great principles of statecraft and the foundations for governing in modern European political economy, who does not earnestly desire the establishment of such an assembly in our country? This sentiment is only to be expected. How much more so is it the case with those who have engaged in European studies for even a short time! It should be understood that no one absolutely rejects an assembly.* It is only that the discussions of a popularly elected assembly are somewhat contradictory since we cannot suddenly establish such a body in this half-enlightened country.

Even though there has been vigorous discussion since the introduction of the parliamentary issue, however, there has always been a considerable area of agreement regarding the methods for establishing a popularly elected assembly. The plans embrace four main types of assemblies. The first provides for an assembly of prefectural governors. Such an assembly was called together by the government last fall, but it failed after confronting various national problems. The second type is an officially selected assembly or an assembly of imperial appointees. Probably, there have been supporters of this type despite the comparative indifference of the press to it. Third are prefectural (*ken*)[1] assemblies which, I hear, have been established here and there. And fourth are assemblies for large and small urban districts (*ku*)[2] that arise

*This is also why I stated that it is not unreasonable to share power by establishing a deliberative assembly in the latter part of my article in the third issue of the *Meiroku Zasshi* in which I refuted the arguments of the former ministers.

from a desire to begin with the smaller units. These four are all on the route that leads to a genuine popularly elected assembly, like bows and arrows with which it is hoped to hit the great target.

What I here call an all-inclusive assembly is a scheme directed toward a genuine popularly elected assembly through the amalgamation and full implementation of these four methods. If you ask regarding this plan, I would respond that the foundation should be the assembly of prefectural governors previously called together by the government. To have the prefectural governors represent the will of the people as legislators may smack of having the rulers and the people represented by the same persons. Yet after all, there are probably none who know better the feelings of the people in the prefectures than the governors. These prefectural governors, therefore, will form the main part of the assembly. There will also be officially appointed legislators working with the governors in the assembly.

The prefectural governors are indeed quite familiar with the conditions of the people under their administration, but they are probably in the dark on such matters as the great plans of state and foreign relations. Therefore, intermixed with the prefectural governors will be men carefully selected by the government on grounds of scholarship and moral influence. These officially selected members will be of two types. One type will be selected wholly on the basis of their moral influence and scholarship, while the other will be drawn from those within various ministries who are informed on the purport of ministerial business and who are thus qualified to represent the interests of their ministries. After all, even though men of scholarship and moral influence are broadly familiar with the problems of the country, they inevitably suffer from the malady of bias since they are somewhat prejudiced from the point of view of scholarship. [Inclusion of members selected from within the government] is thus to avoid the danger of failing to take into account the details relating to the business of various ministries. By forming a deliberative assembly composed of prefectural governors and government-selected legislators and by allowing the present *sain*[3] to serve as an upper house,* we shall temporarily establish a legislative organ resembling a parliament of two houses.

*Some of the previously mentioned government-selected representatives from the ministries could be sent to the upper house.

On the other hand, there will also be convoked assemblies in the prefectures as well as in the large and small urban districts (*ku*), which district assemblies should be responsible for discussing business relating solely to their localities and for establishing the methods for election and nomination.

If you ask about these matters, I would respond that assemblies in the small districts will nominate persons renowned for their ideas who will be raised to the assemblies of the large districts; nominees from large district [assemblies] will be elevated to the prefectural assemblies; and outstanding nominees from the prefectural assemblies will be raised to the national assembly to replace the prefectural governors. All of this business should generally be carried out in accordance with the stipulations in the election laws that establish length of terms, age limits, and the dates for elections. Such is my plan for an all-inclusive assembly. Should you ask if the emperor then will share some of his autocratic powers with this legislative assembly, I would respond, "Never." This is because we are now establishing the bow and arrows but not the target. Therefore, not only does the emperor retain completely the prerogatives to adjourn and dissolve the assembly, but also the government should have the power to reject at will the measures it disapproves even though they have been passed by the deliberative assembly.

Should you ask, if such be the case, then what benefits will arise from establishing a deliberative assembly, I would answer that, rather than direct benefits, we should look for the indirect effects arising from the assembly as a catalyst. Yet the direct benefits will ultimately not be few if we establish such a deliberative assembly. Should you inquire regarding the direct benefits, I would respond that it cannot be said that even such a deliberative assembly will provide no counsel to the government. Should the government desire to know broadly what public opinion may be on a matter, it will have an instrument for quickly acquiring such information. After all, just this benefit will never be small. Nor can it be said that there will not be some extension of popular rights [by the assembly]. The government is an institution to which the people look for protection; it is not the enemy of the people. That is, government officials and legislators are all men in the same boat [with the people]. If discussions by legislators really hit the mark, why should there be fear that they will not be taken up by government? Still less should there be anxiety at a time like the present when an enlightened ruler and loyal subjects are bound together, when ministers are loyal and wise, and when the government of these men is the source of civilization. Once public attitudes are known, is there any reason for government not to adopt them?

Should you then ask what then may be the indirect effects of a deliberative assembly as a catalyst, I would respond that, under these circumstances, the first result will be that men will invigorate each other, stimulate their "ambitions," and ultimately encourage a feeling that government and people stand side by side. Such being the case, the second result will be that we shall ultimately be able to discern fairly the course of public opinion in national affairs. From this, there will follow the third result. That is, the methods of debate will be gradually developed, a parliamentary system will naturally take shape, and we shall ultimately pave the way for achieving a genuine popularly elected assembly in another day. From this, there will follow the fourth result when men of scholarship and ability improve each other in the same chamber. Recognizing each other by face and understanding each other's minds, they will come spontaneously to pool their knowledge. From this will arise the fifth result that people in the nation will eventually understand what they should honor and take as models. These then are the [indirect] results of a deliberative assembly as a catalyst. If in this fashion we establish a true popularly elected assembly some years hence, we can say that we have really moved through all the stages leading to a parliament. These are my opinions on an all-inclusive assembly.

[Criticism by Mori Arinori: It seems to be the sense of Nishi's essay that we shall advance toward true popular elections by temporarily establishing a deliberative assembly of government appointees. What about the fact that he appears thus far not to have clarified the distinction between an all-inclusive assembly and an assembly of government appointees?]

On Free Trade

Nishimura Shigeki

In this discussion of free trade, I would like to consider its injuries. If you should ask what country is injured by free trade, I would respond that it is our Japanese Empire that is being injured.

Generally, the most refined discussions in the world do not depart from strict truth (*shikin no ri*).[4] When there is departure from strict truth, the discussion is invariably unsound. Even unlettered barbarians know well the strict truth that men should exhaust themselves in serving their parents filially. Even wise men who emerge to discuss the way to honor parents cannot, after all, go beyond filial piety. Mere stripling students often speak of the strict truth that one should prevent the reckless export of hard money when encouraging national prosperity. Even wise men who emerge to discuss political economic theory cannot, after all, assume the reckless export of hard money to be tolerable.

Advocates of free trade generally seem to have come to think that our country should adopt this policy after they have seen the prosperity in England, where free trade is practiced. Should you compare the trading position of our country with that of England, however, there is not the slightest similarity. England herself readily opened up trade, but our country opened trade under irresistible pressure from the Americans. Whereas the English people are good at figures and technically skilled, our people are deficient at figures and technically unskilled. England has no uncultivated land, as she has labored to develop her soil; and she has no waste manpower as her people are industrious. There is much untapped wealth in the undeveloped soil of our country, and there is much wasted manpower among our idle people. When England opened up free trade, she alone was accomplished in trade and industry while other countries were all unskilled. But when our country opened up free trade, we alone were unskilled in trade and industry while others were all skilled. When one considers these factors comparatively, it should be self-evident that our country should not carry on free trade.

Even a country like England, initially following the "mercantile system," prevented the reckless export of hard curency and stimulated her national industries by levying heavy import duties and by granting bounties on exports. In the late 1700's, Adam Smith for the first time discussed the demerits of the "mercantile system," explained the benefits of free trade, and finally led his country to change to free trade principles. Nevertheless, as I look at the matter, England's prosperity should be attributed to the fact that she encouraged her industries and prevented reckless exports of hard currency by initially following "mercantile" theories. By the late 1700's, English industry was extremely prosperous, and there was no wastage of manpower and land. Thereafter, it seems that she broadened the sphere of her trade through the adoption of free trade principles and thereby finally achieved the present level of prosperity. I know that Adam Smith would never have asserted free trade principles had he been born three or four hundred years earlier.

The Americans are resolutely carrying out a protective tariff policy, saying that they levy heavy duties on foreign imports in order to stimulate their national industry. If we now compare the trade positions of our country and America, the two are identical in that they opened up trade later than other countries. They are also alike in not having developed the resources of their soils. Even though our people are far behind the Americans in figures, the Americans also resemble us in being far below the Europeans in industry. Their only point of difference is that they voluntarily opened trade while we were forced to do so. I beg the gentlemen of perception to consider whether our commercial principles should emulate those of England, which differs from our country on four counts, or those of America, which differs from our country on one out of four counts.

My previous discussion, however, has been limited to the advantages and disadvantages from a theoretical point of view. The situation is still more extreme if you take up the profits and losses in light of actual experience. As is generally known to the public, we annually suffer losses from trade amounting to Yen 7,000,000. In industry, our workers fear that someday they will lose their jobs. If our annual loss in money continues to be as extreme as now and if the workers in industries (especially such industries as cotton, sugar, and iron) are reduced with passing years, how will our people survive and by what means will the nation maintain itself? This is really like sitting on tinder.

If we were only beginning to open free trade today, it might be that the advantages and disadvantages or profits and losses from free trade and protection would not be clear. We have already intimately tasted the injuries of free trade during the more than ten years since the opening of trade. As with the introduction of a strange, unnamed fruit from foreign lands, there could be none who knew the taste or the nature when it was first introduced. Even though we have suffered from extreme poisoning, having already eaten the fruit for years, some still stubbornly ignore the facts and state that the food is not injurious. I cannot understand the minds of such people.

Men's bodies become ill when there is not a balance between blood and muscles. A medical man is called a good doctor if he restores equilibrium to the body by treating it with medicine after making a diagnosis. Now how can we regard as a good doctor the physician who, having seen the disequilibrium in the body, administers no medicine at all and advises the patient to await a natural recovery? How can the doctor make amends to the patient if the sick man should finally die after his body has become progressively weakened without recovering equilibrium? How can those responsible for protection of the country not employ medicine for correcting the abnormality?

I earnestly beg that, having now an opportunity to correct the trade policies, we adopt protective tariffs in emulation of the American methods, on the one hand to prevent the reckless export of hard currency and on the other to stimulate industrial progress. (I shall discuss elsewhere why a protective tariff alone is insufficient to encourage industry.) Even though this reasoning is extremely shallow, perhaps the thought of perceptive men will not greatly differ.

Nevertheless, if we reach the point some years hence where the trade and industry of our people both surpass that of foreigners and where there is no wastage of our human and soil resources, the time will perhaps have come when we too may well adopt free trade. This is what I earnestly hope our people will achieve. (February 1, 1875.)

Doubts on Nishi's Discussion on Religion
Part One[5]

Kashiwabara Takaaki

[When I recently read Nishi's discussions on religion, I found his writing to be apt and his meaning profound. Rereading his essays several times, I was not a little enlightened. Moreover, since the purport of his arguments differs greatly from traditional views, I personally feel that we probably shall not penetrate the direction of his true thought unless we wash out prejudice from our minds. My bigotry notwithstanding, I dare to question Nishi after explaining why his ideas are difficult to understand. How happy I would be if he would honor me with further elucidation!]

We generally first win the faith of men before spreading religion and undertaking government. Having won their faith, the government's orders will be carried out, and religion will be established. If faith does not yet exist, governmental orders will not be carried out, and admonitions cannot be observed. Even though the paths for winning faith are not the same, they are one insofar as they ultimately banish men's doubts. Once men no longer doubt, they can be induced to walk on fire and water or to worship trees and stones. After all, the difficulty is not in believing but in leading others to believe. In other words, some people acquire faith by means of virtue, and some sell faith by trickery. There are none who believe without knowing first what they believe. Faith begins only when men have finally resolved their doubts, having come to know what is credible after seeing with their eyes, hearing with their ears, and conjecturing with their minds. The European who first sailed to India explained to an Indian king that there were winter days in his homeland during which the water froze like crystal or mirror, becoming hard as stone. Thinking that he had been deceived, the king had the European executed.. It was in a way rather natural for the king to have killed the European since he had not previously seen, heard, or known of ice. If a person does not himself understand after reflection, therefore, by what means can he have faith? And how can a person well induce others to have faith if he himself is without faith?

Among the ancients, there were not a few who demonstrated

faith by sacrificing their lives. Even so, if you look for evidence of their success, they seem just like men who had faith from the beginning without having known. Such persons unconsciously comply with the doctrines of the Lord (*Tei*).[6] This is called blind faith. Once man embraces blind faith, there are no means by which others can move him. Even so, rooted in their hearts, some have deep faith, some shallow faith. Those of deep faith are difficult to move, and those of shallow faith easy to shake. If you shake the person who is difficult to move, his roots will spread more and more even though his trunk and branches break. Even a powerful man ultimately cannot uproot such faith. If you first select the weak people and exterminate their faith, however, the person of deep faith also will not invariably be able to stand alone, and his vigor [of faith] ultimately will naturally collapse. After all, Buddha destroyed Brahmanism, Luther renewed Christianity, and Buddhist monks also successfully introduced their faith in our country. If you look at the matter in light of their examples, why cannot men's faith be changed?

The various countries of the West, being completely free of savage religions, may allow men to believe as they please. Moreover, since Western men are deep in their knowledge and broad in their scholarship, how can they believe in such things as trees, stones, insects, and beasts? It is unbearable for me to say that such is not the case in our country, where there are many foolish men and women who are addicted to and confused by savage religions. Moreover, why should not our government investigate these practices? I hear that rulers of countries are like the parents of a family and that all within the four seas are brothers. These persons who conduct government like parents and brothers hold beliefs that are naturally different from the views of the foolish people. If they indifferently see children and younger brothers addicted to savage religion without attempting to save them, however, how can they be regarded as parents and elder brothers?

How can similarly indifferent rulers be regarded as protectors of the people? And how will they escape censure for being unsympathetic and inhuman? Nishi says that "men should only believe in what they assume to be true since faith is without substance." This is like having a blind man select colors. Once you allow foolish people to believe what they respectively assume to be true, they will eventually worship Waraji Daiō.[7] This is the way indifferently to forsake man. Nishi also says, "When common people believe in stones, trees, insects, and beasts, they also believe in what they think is true." Ah, what kind of talk is this? If stones, trees, insects, and beasts are true, then why do we fear Heaven, why do we honor God (*Jōtei*),[8] and of what use is religion? The fundamental principle of religion is to search for truth by frustrating evil, rejecting lewdness, and casting out heresy. Nishi also observes:

> The powers of government are not in the same sphere as the way of religion. . . . What government should stress is preservation of tranquil rule by gathering people together, forming a state, and preventing evil from compromising good. . . . The sphere of religion is entirely otherwise from that of government. . . . The spheres of government and religion being entirely separate, how can there be anything injurious to government but beneficial to religion through the interference of one in the affairs of the other?

Reading thus far in Nishi's essay, I recognized that it was extremely difficult for me to understand him. This was because I did not yet know whether, when speaking of religion, Nishi meant true religion or savage religion.

Let me now just take up the example of the Christian religion. There are Ten Commandments in Christianity, of which the first three describe the way to honor God. The Fourth Commandment states, "Honor thy father and thy mother." This means that one should honor alike those ranging from kings and officials to parents and teachers. The Fifth Commandment affirms, "Thou shalt not kill." This generally admonishes against injuring or hurting men through vengeance or abuse. The Sixth is, "Thou shalt not commit adultery," and the Seventh states, "Thou shalt not steal." The latter admonishes generally against stealing other men's goods and unjust action. The Eighth, "Thou shalt not bear false witness," generally prohibits the blackening of men's reputations as well as misrepresenting other men. The Ninth, "Thou shalt not desire another's wife," would halt carnal desire. And the Tenth, "Thou shalt not envy another's property," admonishes against a covetous heart.

Violation of any of the above seven commandments is invariably sufficient to incur punishment by the government. The way of religion only refrains from establishing the details of penal law. Moreover, its punishments are more severe than those of government. Good men receive the rewards of Heaven, and bad men receive the punishments of Hell, which are more severe than the five punishments of government. If men observe these commandments completely, why cannot they entirely set aside even the five punishments?[9] If there is the least violation of these principles, how can government successfully preserve its tranquil rule by gathering people together, forming a state, and preventing evil from compromising good? From this point of view, how can it be said that the spheres of government and religion are separate? Again, how can it be said that they are not mutually interrelated? The law cannot function if government is without principle, and the people will not submit to government if they are without religion. Men should never be without religion even for a day. Living luxuriously without religion is close [to the level] of beasts. Religion has the same end as government.

I have heard that monarchs of enlightened countries invariably call upon ministers of religion to officiate on great ceremonial occasions. This is for the reasons that they honor Heaven and have faith in the people. Is not religion important to government? If the principles of religion are not upright, however, their injury to government is also not small. This is why men should not be permitted to believe as they please. If religion is completely upright and true, men's faith will increasingly deepen as they become enlightened and their faith will be increasingly essential in their conduct of government. If religion is false, how can it be sufficient to win the faith of an enlightened people? The so-called theocracies are really not religious but tricks to deceive foolish people. Is it not appropriate that barbarian kings ultimately meet their destruction if they try to control the masses with a false religion?

[1]*Ken*, 縣.

[2]*Ku*, 區. In 1874 Tokyo was divided into eleven large urban districts or wards (*daiku*, 大區), which in turn were subdivided into 103 small urban districts (*shōku*,

小區). This system continued until 1878, when the city was reorganized into 15 *ku.*

[3]*Sain,* 左院, the left chamber, an appointive body established by the Meiji government to advise on legislation.

[4]*Shikin no ri,* 至近ノ理.

[5]This essay is directed particularly at Nishi Amane's first essay "On Religion," which appears in Issue Four.

[6]*Tei,* 帝. Kashiwabara is here drawing from the seventh poem on King Wên (Wên Wang, 文王) entitled *Huang I* (皇矣) in the *Book of Poetry* (Shin Ching, 詩經).

[7]Waraji Daiō, 草鞋大王, Great Straw-Sandaled King, a guardian figure (niō, 仁王) at the entrances of Japanese temples on which the people hang straw sandals in veneration.

[8]*Jōtei,* 上帝.

[9]Five punishments, *wu hsing,* 五刑. The five punishments in ancient China were tattooing, cutting off the nose, cutting off a limb, castration for men or confinement for women, and beheading. Later in Japan they were flogging, beating, imprisonment, exile, and death.

MEIROKU ZASSHI Issue Thirty February 1875

Speech in Connection with New Elections of Officials on the First Anniversary of the Meirokusha

Mori Arinori

Being the first anniversary of the founding of the Meirokusha, today, February 1, 1875, is the occasion for again electing the society's officials. I shall, therefore, first outline the history of the society, extend felicitations for its prosperity, and thank the honorable members for their kind friendship and cordial fellowship. In addition, since I am about to relinquish responsibility as president of the society, I shall just express a few thoughts in regard to its future activities and respectfully beg your comments.

I planned establishment of the society upon my return from America in the seventh month of the sixth year of Meiji. As my friends were graciously quick to accede [to my proposals], we began consideration of the society's regulations after three or four meetings. But the discussions were so protracted that we only reached agreement in February 1874. As it had previously been our intention to elect Fukuzawa Yukichi as the society's president, Nishimura Shigeki and I were entrusted by the society with the task of conveying our request. But since Fukuzawa emphatically declined, the society turned to me, and I humbly accepted, daring not to decline. The society also gave to Shimizu Usaburō and Sera Taiichi, respectively, the responsibilities of treasurer and secretary. The energetic endeavors of these two gentlemen are now warmly appreciated by the society's members, and I believe that I speak for every member when I extend our thanks to them.

The charter members of the society were ten in number: Nishimura Shigeki, Tsuda Mamichi, Nishi Amane, Nakamura Masanao, Katō Hiroyuki, Mitsukuri Shūhei, Fukuzawa Yukichi, Sugi Kōji, Mitsukuri Rinshō, and Mori Arinori. Among these, Mitsukuri Rinshō was forced to leave the society for reasons of health. I would say that the loss of this gentleman of broad views is truly a misfortune for the society. I entertain no doubt that all members join with me in hoping for the time when he has sufficiently recovered to rejoin us. Since its founding, the society's membership has increased to a total of thirty by the admission of five more regular members, five corresponding members, and ten members temporarily resident in Tokyo. In addition, an uncounted number of persons, with the society's permission, have come irregularly to the meetings as guests. Nevertheless, it is impossible to estimate the hundreds who will come during the months ahead—given the recent trend toward larger meetings. Even though this may truly enhance the prestige of the society, we must adopt regulatory measures to deal with the consequent congestion and the additional expense to the society. I think that we should provide for these expenses by establishing a rule for the selling of tickets to guest members and that we can also escape the bother of congestion by marking these tickets with numbers that will determine the seating arrangements. Thereby shall we increase the society's happiness since the guests will be able upon buying tickets to attend the meetings as they please while the society will also be assisted in the transaction of its expanding affairs.

Publication of the *Meiroku Zasshi* began in February of last year. There were at first two numbers each month, but this was increased to three numbers in November. Last year, there were published twenty-five issues totalling 105,984 copies. 80,127 of these were sold, that is, an average of more than 3,205 copies of each issue. For details, I defer to the report of Sera.

The management of the society's accounts appears in detail in Shimizu's account book. In order to verify the accounts, Tsuda Sen and Sugi Kōji are entrusted with auditing the books. I hope that the two gentlemen can show the true condition of the accounts by their detailed investigation. Now according to Shimizu's accounts, the society's revenues reached a total of Yen 717, Sen 65, Rin 7 including Yen 632, Sen 82, Rin 5 income from the sale of the first nineteen issues of the *zasshi*;* Yen 81, Sen 50 in contributions from the members; and Yen 3, Sen 33, Rin 2 interest arising from the previous two.** The total expenditures were Yen

*According to Sera's *zasshi* statement, the amount was Yen 641, Sen 15. The difference seems to arise from a deduction from the total given Shimizu of the amount advanced for the society's use by *Hōchisha*.[1]

**See the society's account book for slight variations in the interest rate.

262, Sen 17, Rin 6, including Yen 214, Sen 84 for food; Yen 5, Sen 60, Rin 8, for miscellaneous expenditures; Yen 21, Sen 72, Rin 8, charges for official seal of approval (*ken-inryō*);[2] and Yen 20 in gratuities to the secretary and the accountant for the period from last December to this January. The difference between receipts and expenditures, that is, the society's balance, amounts to Yen 455, Sen 46, Rin 6. Since the amount yet to be received from the sales of *zasshi* numbers twenty to twenty-five is expected to be Yen 180, the total income from the *zasshi* for last year should reach more than Yen 810.

It has been decided that one-half the income from sales of the *zasshi* since last November would be saved by the society and that the other half would be distributed to the journal's contributors. The use of the society's savings, however, has not yet been determined. At the present rate of more than fifty yen a month (the amount remaining after paying the authors), the savings should reach more than Yen 600 a year. Even though we are naturally unable to predict in advance, it would be quite appropriate to expect a continuation of the trends of the previous year. Since, as previously explained, the use of the more than Yen 600 savings has not yet been decided, I have seriously considered whether it would not be safest and most profitable to apply the savings to the construction of a large meeting hall for the society. Let me now try to outline my thinking.

One. Based on an estimate of Yen 50 per *tsubo*[3] for a building of about 70 *tsubo*, the total cost of the hall would be Yen 3,500. The interest on this sum at ten percent a year is Yen 350; the rent for 100 *tsubo* of land would be Yen 60 a year; and the expenditures for guards, lesser staff, and other items, Yen 190. Thus the total estimated expenditures would reach Yen 600, in other words, the amount to be realized by our society as savings.

Two. We should promise to pay the money lenders financing the construction several tens of yen each month (at ten percent of the construction cost). When we cannot remit these sums, we would cover them with the rights to publish (*zōhan no kenri*) the *zasshi*.[4]

Three. We should undertake to pay those subscribing the costs of construction half the profits realized when the hall is used by others than the Meirokusha.

Four. The building fund would be divided into shares, each share to be valued at Yen 100. There would be no limitation on whether the subscribing lenders are one or many. Naturally, it would be entirely proper for the Meirokusha likewise to be a shareholder.

Five. When the Meirokusha takes in as rent on the hall Yen 50 that can be applied each month on the society's expenditures, the entire amount realized from sale of the *zasshi* can be distributed among the authors.

The above is the gist of my thought on constructing the hall. Even though its purpose is chiefly to provide a meeting place for the Meirokusha, there will be times when the hall can be put to other uses, as the society only meets twice monthly and then not later than 4:00 or 5:00 o'clock. Since this is the case, not only will there be profit from the hall's rent. The hall can also provide a facility that will greatly conduce to the public good. For example, it would be used for all sorts of beneficial gatherings, such as concerts, church meetings, art exhibits, business conferences, lectures, and discussion groups.

Since adopting the rules for the society's lectures last winter, the group has gradually assumed the shape of a society. Nevertheless, we have not reached the point of criticizing and discussing what we have heard. In the final analysis, this may be attributed to the fact that we have not yet fully developed lecturing methods and that the listeners are unable to clearly understand material in which large numbers of *kanji* have been used. We should plan to make the meetings more enjoyable and more profitable by giving these matters a little thoughtful attention and by taking steps to remove the difficulties [to oral understanding].[5]

As is stated in the first article of our society's regulations, the topics to be discussed are those literary, technical, scientific, and philosophical and other matters wholly relating to education that are important for stimulating men's intellectual powers as well as for improving their conduct. It is also to be expected that, as these important matters were generally concerned with the future, they may touch areas offensive today. This is inevitable. It was not originally the intention at the founding of our society, however, that the discussions would relate to contemporary political matters. Since, in addition to involving labor without profit, [political discussions] might quite possibly also bring needless injury to the soceity, I am here just admonishing in advance out of consideration for the society's future. I beg your understanding in this matter.[6]

Bearing on the new election of a president for the society, I assume it to be the outgoing president's responsibility to nominate a successor and to refer the nomination to the society for approval.[7] It is a genuine pleasure to do so today. It has also been a source of really great satisfaction to me that I have invariably received your special trust and loyal support during my term. This I fully appreciate today, and I beg you once more to accept my warm thanks.

It is appropriate that the society's president be affable in personality as well as broadly conversant with affairs. Recognizing these qualities in the Honorable Mitsukuri Shūhei, I nominate him for the presidency during the coming year. I shall be very pleased if my fellow members confirm this nomination with their approval.

Men of Talent (*Jinzai*)[8]

Tsuda Mamichi

When Heaven produces men of talent, their talents differ according to region and wax and wane with the times. Talents that differ according to region are related entirely to the fact that the various races live in different habitats and under varying climatic conditions. The waxing and waning of talent according to the times refers to the clear distinction arising from the times between men of talent who emerge in the same region. This waxing and waning of talent is related for the most part to the quality of customs and the strength of government. Thus large numbers of men of talent emerged in ancient Asia, and the various countries of modern Europe are producing a profusion of men of talent. To be more specific, there were numerous men of talent in northwest China when the five emperors and three kings[9] arose, while men of talent have been rather more in southeast China in modern times. Men of talent flourished in Mongolia with the rise of Temüjin[10] and were produced in large numbers in Manchuria when the Manchu-Ch'ing[11] emerged. Men of talent gathered in Greece during its zenith, and appeared in full with the rise of Rome. With the rise of Europe, men of talent have been produced in abundance in Germany, France, England, and other countries. To refer to our Japanese history in detail, men of talent were produced in large numbers in Yamato after the capital was established at Kashiwara,[12] in Yamashiro following the movement of the capital to Heian,[13] in the Kantō during the successive rise of the houses of Genji, Hōjō, Nitta, and Ashikaga;[14] in Owari with the houses of Oda and Toyotomi;[15] in Mikawa with the emergence of the Tokugawa,[16] and recently in Satsuma, Chōshū, Tosa, and Hizen at the time of the Restoration.[17]

The causes for the emergence of men of talent naturally are multiple and difficult to understand fully. Men of old ascribed their emergence to fate. In my opinion, even though the reasons for the proliferation of men of talent are difficult to understand and naturally not to be summed up in one word, they embrace primarily whether men are able to develop their talents without being suppressed. That is, men of talent will appear to the extent that men develop their innate characters as well as the spirit of freedom, liberty, and independence. The present abundance of men of talent in Europe and America is to be attributed to no other source than the extensive development of this spirit of liberty. Since it is the custom in Asia for despotic rule to exploit the aptitudes of the people, the places where men of talent develop are the localities to which the ruler's power does not extend. This is why it was in the simple countryside and on the frontiers, rather than in the great capitals of fashion and culture, that extraordinary men since antiquity have suddenly arisen [in Asia].

Furthermore, when a hero rises up like a mountain, he inspires others and thereby encourages their talents. This is why numerous wise men appear in territories where illustrious lords arise, and it, after all, is also why Satsuma, Chōshū, Tosa, and Hizen recently have far surpassed the various other domains in producing large numbers of men of talent. Nevertheless, the men of talent in our present Japan were nurtured during the period of seclusion.

That is, they are only men of talent in the Japanese manner and cannot be called talented men of the world. Who does not hope that the men of talent emerging in our empire hereafter will have the talents of the universe without being confined alone to the talents of the Land of the Dragonflies?[18] If we want to produce men of universal talent in our eastern region, however, our people must nurture a spirit of liberty, freedom, and independence and expand the outlook of men. Very strict attention must be given to these principles when legislators frame new laws and administrators carry out the laws.

Doubts on Nishi's Discussion on Religion Part Two[19]

Kashiwabara Takaaki

It is the nature of things that they contain evil, a fact that even saints cannot prevent. Rome was restored by the power of religion, but it was also destroyed by religion. Probably those who were called kings in those days all grasped power in the name of humanity. Flattering the pope, such rulers finally reduced their people to misery with what should have helped the world [religion]. How extreme is the injury of religion! Once Luther arose by Heaven's Will, he destroyed this injury, and the power of the pope suddenly declined.

When one considers the source of such injury, it lies, after all, in man, not in religion. If one draws an analogy with statecraft, there were such kings as Chieh and Chou[20] after the sage kings. States establish kings to protect the people, and yet there was the violence of Chieh and Chou. Men establish religions to succor society, but Rome was not thereby saved from collapse. Even so, there must always be rulers, and there must always be religion. Religion then is an instrument for appealing to men's hearts. When the heart is upright, the individual is morally restrained. When the individuals are morally restrained, the family is well ordered. If the family is not well ordered, with what will the rights of independence be established? If there is no moral restraint, to what can we look for elevated conduct? If the mind is not upright, how can man observe national laws?

Nishi now places greater emphasis on external forms than on the inner heart. To draw an analogy with objects, the inner heart is the object, and the external form is the shadow. If the object is round, the shadow will also be round. And if the object is square, the shadow will also be square. Similarly, if the heart is upright, then conduct must also invariably be upright. It is said that the truth will invariably reveal itself on the outside when it is rooted on the inside. To condemn vainly the external form without in the least disciplining the heart is just like searching for a round shadow of a square object. Generally, when men indulge in the evil course, they covet worldly goods, yearn for lewdness, expect profit from windfalls, and forget their share of obligations. They are without the human compassion to make light of worldly goods and to honor justice as well as the decency to overcome lustful desire and control the body. During life, they are the slaves of carnal desire; at death, the sacrifices to the devil. When men are allowed to worship foxes, badgers, trees, and stones as they please, it is clear that their hearts follow the hearts of those they worship and that they do not know their final destination.

Furthermore, if we rely on external form, this will lead to killing without teaching. And even though the maximum penalty is imposed, it will be no more than one life. Even though it may be sufficient to execute the murderer of an individual, what punishment is appropriate for the murderer of myriads of people? Since you will take only one life even if you kill him, how can this be called justice? Therefore, it is an essential of government to put virtue before punishment, and the foundation of virtue lies in uniting men's hearts with religion. Since the enlightened ruler directs the hearts of the people toward one path, what he orders is carried out, and what he forbids is stopped. If the people are allowed to follow their own persuasions, the ruler's orders will not be carried out even though hundreds of punishments are daily administered. How then can he execute the entire people? Government, after all, is composed of men. Insofar as it is composed of men, how can its beliefs not be the same as those of the people? If the government, after all, believes in foxes, badgers, trees, and stones, it is indeed natural that such a government of foxes, badgers, trees, and stones should be obliged to rule over people who believe in foxes, badgers, trees, and stones.

On Changing the Character of the People

Speech of February 16, 1875

Nakamura Masanao

When we speak of the imperial renewal since 1868, to what does "renewal" refer? It probably refers to the abandonment of the old of the bakufu and the introduction of the new of imperial rule. If this is the case, "renewal" refers only to that of the political system, not a renewal of the people. The people are like water, while the political system is like a vessel into which one pours water. If you pour water into a round vessel, it becomes round; into a square vessel, square. The character of the water does not change even though the vessel is changed for another of different shape. The people, after all, remain as before even though the vessel into which they have been placed since 1868 may have a better shape than the old one.

They are the people rooted in servitude, the people who are arrogant toward their inferiors and flattering toward their superiors, the ignorant and uneducated people, the people who love saké and sex, the people who do not like reading, the people who do not reflect on their duties and who know not the laws of Heaven, the people of shallow wisdom and limited capacity, the people who avoid toil and do not endure hardships, the egocentric people who practice cheap tricks, the people without perseverance and diligence in character, the frivolous and shallow people who are without principles in their hearts, the people who like to rely on others as they are without a spirit of independence, the people who are poor in their powers of thought and perception, the people who know not the value of money, the people who break promises without honoring loyalty, the people who are unable to act together and have but a slim capacity for friendship, and the people who do not strive for new inventions. People are generally of such types even though there naturally are not a few who are able to escape from the above injuries.

If we desire to change the people's character and thereby encourage elevated conduct and virtuous feelings, we will accomplish absolutely nothing if we only reform the political structure, which is only changing round containers for hexagonal or octagonal vessels without altering the character of the water within. Rather than changing the political structure, therefore, we should aspire instead to change the character of the people, more and more rooting out the old habits and achieving "renewal" with each new day.

We should welcome as a good omen the recent public clamor for a popularly elected assembly. Such an assembly, of course, will undoubtedly contribute to a renewal of the public mind since it will develop the will to possess and to defend the country among the people themselves, change the attitudes of those who have relied on government officials, daily reduce the spirit of subservience, enable talented men to emerge from all quarters in large numbers, and gradually halt the evil of selecting leaders from a single source.

There is one point, however, to which we should here give our attention. Even though the rulers may share a part of the political power with the people through the establishment of a popularly elected assembly, since the people still remain as before, there will be no major effect in the direction of changing the people's character from the fact that only the political structure has been somewhat changed. Should you ask how to change the character of the people, there are but two approaches—through religious and moral education and through education in the arts and sciences. Through the mutual assistance of these two acting together, like the wheels of a cart or the wings of a bird, we shall guide human lives to happiness.

The arts and sciences alone may indeed be advanced to the sphere of utmost refinement, but we cannot thereby rectify the demoralization in customs when, as in ancient Greece and Egypt, enlightenment is limited to the material sphere. It may be said that we shall prepare the way for renewing the people's hearts only if, through the vigorous practice of religious and moral education, we cultivate the area to which the influence of the arts and the sciences does not extend. This is a fact known to all, neither highbrow nor novel. Nevertheless, even among scholars and teachers, there are some who, giving their attention wholly to the arts and sciences, put religion and morals aside, or abominate Western religion and morals. I am, therefore, calling this extremely ordinary and extremely common idea to the attention of my honored colleagues. If there is any other method to change the character of the people and to elevate them to the level of the most advanced peoples of Europe and America, I shall welcome your advice.

[1]Hōchisha, 報知社. The publisher of the *Yūbin Hōchi Shimbun* (郵便報知新聞), the Hōchisha also printed and distributed the *Meiroku Zasshi*.

[2]*Ken-inryō*, 檢印料. This was apparently a stamp that approved or licensed publication.

[3]*Tsubo*, 坪, about thirty-six square feet.

[4]*Zōhan no kenri*, 藏版ノ權利.

[5]Mori presumably is here criticizing such men as Sakatani Shiroshi, whose terse style was so loaded with unusual ideographs (Kanji, 漢字) and Chinese phrases that it could hardly have been understood unless seen.

[6]Mori is anticipating the censorship that would eventually bring the Meirokusha to halt publication of the *zasshi*.

[7]For the society's regulations, see Ōkubo Toshiaki (大久保利謙), ed., *Meiji Bungaku Zenshū* (明治文學全集), vol. II, *Meiji Keimō Shisō Shū* (明治啓蒙思想集) (Tokyo, 1967), pp. 403–405.

[8]*Jinzai*, 人材.

[9]Five emperors and three kings, *wu-ti san-wang*, 五帝三王. Tsuda refers to the ancient and legendary period of Chinese history, whose traditional dates are 2953 to 1122 B.C. The five emperors were Fu Hsi (伏羲), Shên Nung (神農), Huang Ti (黃帝), Yao (堯), and Shun (舜); the three kings were the founders of the first three royal dynasties: Kings Yü (禹) of Hsia (夏), T'ang (湯) of Shang (商), and Wên (文) and/or Wu (武) of Chou (周).

[10]Temüjin, 鐵木眞, Jenghiz Khan.

[11]Manchu-Ch'ing, 滿洲淸, the rulers of China from 1644 to 1912.

[12]Kashiwara (橿原) in Yamato (大和) was the palace of the first Japanese emperor, Jimmu (神武).

[13]Heian (平安) in Yamashiro (山城), the present Kyōto, was founded by Emperor Kammu (桓武) in 794 A.D.

[14]The military houses of Minamoto (源), Hōjō (北條), Nitta (新田), and Ashikaga (足利) all arose in the Kantō (關東) region of eastern Japan.

[15]Owari, 尾張, the home province of Oda Nobunaga (織田信長) and Toyotomi Hideyoshi (豐臣秀吉).

[16]Mikawa, 三河, the home province of Tokugawa Ieyasu (德川家康).

[17]Satsuma, 薩摩, Chōshū, 長州, Tosa, 土佐, and Hizen, 肥前 were the great exterior domains most influential in the events of the Meiji Restoration.

[18]Land of the Dragonflies, Akitsushima, 蜻蜓洲, a poetic name for Japan.

[19]Kashiwabara is here commenting on Nishi Amane's second article on religion that appears in Issue Five. See Issue Twenty-Nine for Kashiwabara's previous article in this series.

[20]Chieh, 桀, and Chou, 紂, the wicked kings blamed in tradition for the fall of the Hsia (夏) and the Shang (商) dynasties, respectively.

MEIROKU ZASSHI Issue Thirty-One March 1875

Abuses of Equal Rights for Men and Women

Katō Hiroyuki

As the true principles regarding married couples have been gradually clarified in public since the appearance of the discussion on equal rights for husbands and wives by Mori and Fukuzawa,[1] the ugly custom of keeping concubines promiscuously and the bad practice by which the husband holds his wife in contempt will gradually be destroyed, and we shall consequently reach the point where equality between husband and wife is truly observed. Are not the achievements of these two gentlemen indeed wonderful?

It is my opinion, however, that, even though the system of near equality between husband and wife in modern Europe conforms with Heaven's Reason, the rights of the wife seem rather to surpass those of the husband in present-day society. This evil, after all, arises from a misunderstanding of the principle of equal rights. There is not time to enumerate all the abuses, but the following are a few examples.

When husband and wife pass through a door, the wife goes first and the husband follows. When they are seated, the wife occupies the highest seat; the husband, the next best seat. When others call on the couple, they greet the wife before the husband. When they address the couple, they place the wife's name first, the husband's later. If men are seated with ladies, they are especially discreet in speech, and they do not smoke without first securing permission from the ladies. The extent of women's rights is really surprising. Although it appears that Westerners cannot actually understand the impropriety of their ways since they have been soaked in them for a long time, I must say that the customs are indeed strange from the point of view of East Asians. How can they be called equal rights of husband and wife? The other day, when I was smoking as I pleased among a large number of women in a certain person's house, a foreign guest said to me, "Since many of the ladies present do not enjoy smoking, I beg you to stop." Even though I of course knew the custom that forbids smoking in the presence of Western ladies, I dared not to follow it since it is completely unreasonable. Frankly speaking, I must say that the foreigner's words were indeed uncivil. The prohibition against smoking may indeed have arisen from their dislike of the custom, but it is my free right to smoke since I enjoy tobacco. If ladies do not like smoking, they may themselves leave their seats. It can never be right for them to obstruct a man's freedom for the reason that they themselves disapprove. Moreover, why should dislike of smoking be limited only to women? There are also men who dislike smoking. I must say that I really cannot understand why women alone forbid smoking while we smoke without asking men whether they like it or not. Furthermore, if the habit violated morals or if it injured another's health, then I too, naturally, would not smoke. Since it does not in the least injure another's health or violate human morality, what reason is there for discriminating between men and women when determining whether one smokes?

Although such a question is really a small matter, it clearly misrepresents the principle of equality between men and women, and it is also clearly an evil that has arisen from the infatuation with which men court the favor of women with flattery. It is an unbearable but natural outcome that in Europe one often hears of adulterous scandals even about women reputed to be noble ladies. How dreadful this is! At present, when we are putting into practice in our country the principle of equal rights for men and women, we shall finally reach the point at which we are unable to control the injury of excessive women's rights if men of intelligence, fully recognizing this danger, do not prevent it in advance. What do my friends make of this?

Abuses of Equal Rights for Men and Women

Part Two, March 1, 1875

Katō Hiroyuki

Some gentlemen have said: "We found extremely mistaken your discussion of the abuses of equal rights for men and women. You said that Westerners, misunderstanding the principle of equal rights, have come to venerate women and finally to allow them excessively great power. After all, however, what you take for veneration by Westerners of women is never veneration. It is helping women. These practices arise from the fact that women can never be secure without the help of men since women in general, in addition to being weak in body, are by nature reserved. We beg you, therefore, seriously to consider how inappropriate it was for you recklessly to criticize Western customs without recognizing this principle."

Looked at from my point of view, the wisdom of my critics notwithstanding, they have so long soaked in Western customs that they no longer recognize the bad customs of the West, having accepted the evil together with the good. Let us consider, for example, the view of my critics that what appears to be veneration of women by men is not venerating women but helping them. After all, the distinction between helping and venerating is self-evident. How can they interpret as helping the practices of forbidding smoking before ladies, of calling the wife's name before the husband's, of seating the wife above the husband, and of greeting the wife before the husband? I must say, to regard the above practices as helping women really represents extreme inability to understand. If it is the opinion of my critics that in order for men to help women, men must follow even the above-described conduct that is practically the same as veneration, however, I have a further point to make.

Why is helping the weak wholly confined only to man's relations to woman? The government's relations to the people and the relations of parents to children all involve helping persons because of their weakness. (Even though the principles in the relations of government to people and parents to children are, of course, not the same, they are essentially similar in the sense that government and parents, respectively, protect their people and children for the reason that the recipients of their protection are unable to protect themselves.) If it is necessary to adopt such practices resembling veneration when helping the weak, the government must take a humble place while elevating the people to the highest level, and the parents must place their children in seats of honor while they themselves occupy lesser seats. Since such is never the case even in the West, however, why do these bad customs of veneration exist only in relations between men and women? (Since government exists for the people who are its masters, it seems that, as a fundamental principle, the people should take the upper place, and the government the lower place. Nevertheless, it is important that the government invariably occupy the upper position since it must grasp the power to protect the people. Governments, therefore, always rank above the people even in republican countries.) This is why I shall never concede to my critics' theory. How can it not be said that the [theory] is an abuse arising from amorous passion in which men court the favor of women with flattery? What do my critics have to say?

Government and Ethics Are Not Separate Paths[2]

Speech on March 1, 1875[2]

Nishimura Shigeki

Confucian scholars of China mourned the separation of scholarship and governing into two paths. I think it unnecessary to regret deeply the separation of scholarship and governing. What is to be regretted is the separation of ethics and governing into two paths. In the *Great Learning*[3] is explained the logical sequence of disciplining the individual person, managing the household, ruling the country, and keeping peace in the world, and Mencius also observed that the family is the foundation of the nation and that the individual person is the foundation of the family.[4]

There is not time to enumerate the other instances in which ethics have been regarded as the foundation of the country. When men in our country honored the ways of Confucius and Mencius, those who upheld these teachings and undertook to rule the country invariably thought that they should cultivate ethics. (Although, actually, there were exceptions.) Since the Restoration, scholarly styles have already changed. Just as when the sun has already set but the moon has not yet arisen, the Way of Confucius and Mencius has already declined, but the philosophy of the West has not yet entered. Thus the fellows devoted to the utilitarian (*kōri*)[5] in society assume the Way of Confucius and Mencius to be stupid and desist from practicing the arts of sincerity and ethics. They are above the common people in their social status but below the common people in their conduct. Is this not a situation extremely to be regretted? Even though we endeavor now to admonish these fellows with the Way of Confucius and Mencius, our words are in vain, since they scornfully reject the Confucian Way. Therefore, I would submit the following, which is based on the opinions of Western *savants* that the paths of ethics and governing the country are not two.

Even though it is impossible to count all the things in the universe, looked at simply, they fall into but three classifications: animal, plant, and mineral. These three all exist in the world under the governance of the Supreme Ruler (*Jōtei*).[6] Furthermore, the principles by which the Supreme Ruler governs these three classifications are no more than three: form, life, and sensitivity. Minerals have only form; plants have form and life but not sensitivity; and animals alone possess all three qualities. Viewed in this way, it is clear that the Supreme Ruler exerted greater effort on behalf of animals than on the other two classifications.

There are two types of animals: men and beasts. The reason for differentiating men from beasts is not just because of their shapes. All animals are endowed with one or both of two types of instinct—animal and rational. All naturally have the animal instinct whether they be men or beasts. The rational instinct is found only in men and never in beasts. Viewed in this light, it is clear that the Supreme Ruler gave more loving attention to men than to other animals. The animal instinct, or what Confucian scholars call the desire for things, is divided into greed and sensual desire. The rational instinct is proverbially known as Heaven's Reason (*Tenri*),[7] and its principal component is called conscience. Men can distinguish between the desire for things and Heaven's Reason by relying on the power of conscience.

To cultivate ethics, to manage the family, to rule the country, and to keep peace in the world are all matters of the rational world and not of the animal world (or the world of beasts). Generally, a superior man or a sage is one who habitually overcomes the animal instinct by strengthening the power of the rational instinct.

Lesser men or ordinary men, those we call near beasts, are men in whom the strong animal instinct habitually dominates the rational instinct. It is evident, therefore, that he who cultivates ethics well is also able to govern the country well. This is because ethics and governing the country are both matters of the rational world. Persons unable to cultivate ethics, as they are controlled by the desire for things, also quite manifestly cannot govern the country. This is because governing the country and ethics are not matters of the world of beasts. You can see that my words are not false from the fact that the American doctor [Francis Wayland?][8] said that ethics is the foundation of just government. And the English scholar [Jeremy] Bentham observed that what is good from the point of view of governing is not bad from the point of view of ethics. Ethics and government are, after all, both practiced with the power of the rational instinct. The two, therefore, are not separate branches as they are completely alike in what they hold good and bad. If men say that they trust to the animal instinct when cultivating morals and the rational instinct when conducting government, they cannot successfully conduct affairs unless they are half man and half horse or endowed with the bodies of men and the heads of cows.

In recent times, there have been some among the nobles and high officials who, because of their loose morals, have been scoffed by men of intelligence. Nevertheless, these exalted persons themselves presumably say that those who accomplish great things by establishing great enterprises have not the patience to observe various trifles. Why do they not know that what they violate is not so trifling and what they accomplish is not really so great? The English Doctor Thomas Brown observed, "One does not become brave by conquering the enemy. Only after a man has subdued his own passions can he be called a truly brave person."[9] Even though the great in troubled times will on occasion overlook their own conduct when discussing their achievements, they should also subdue their passions if they are to be judged by the standards of superior men. Still more in times of peace when we are trying to correct customs and to clarify the proprieties, why should we not pass judgment on the type of person who is a high official in his station and a vulgar commoner in his conduct?

Why do people of intelligence in society discuss without stopping man's private conduct although private conduct does not extend its injuries or benefits to other men as it is confined to the individual? It is because nobles and high officials are models for the people. Did not the ancients say that what the upper fancy, the lower invariably love still more? Since the king of Wu[10] prized swordsmanship, there were many in the land who killed men. When the tastes of officials and aristocrats are in the least incorrect, then the customs of the people are servile and ugly beyond endurance. Whether countries are judged barbarian or enlightened depends on the people's customs. The customs of the people conform to the conduct of those in high position, and the standing of the nation is determined in accordance with the customs of the people. Such being the case, why should not the upper classes cultivate their morals?

Today, wise persons in the upper classes, detesting barbarism, have a deep craving for civilization. They establish excessively detailed regulations for the correction of customs and the proprieties, and they punish all manner of things such as baring the legs and urinating in public. Thinking such rude conduct close to barbarism, they especially fail to understand that the rude conduct of officials and nobles is still more barbaric than urinating in public. As they condemn the trivial while abandoning the important, I suspect they mistake the means for the end, the light for the weighty. When government officials and nobles do not finally improve their personal conduct, the country cannot be called civilized even though it is prosperous, its army is strong, and it flaunts its superiority abroad. How much more is this the case when the country is not yet prosperous and its army, not yet strong!

I earnestly beg the high officials and nobles hereafter to quickly reform their conduct and to become models for the nation in speech and norms for the nation in conduct being deeply conscious that ethics are the foundation for ruling the country. When people honor, respect, and love their fine teachers, when customs are consequently reformed and the proprieties observed, and when the light of civilization radiates in the four directions, how can this represent only the glory of individual persons? The happiness of the country also can be no more than this.

Doubts on Nishi's Discussion on Religion Part Three[11]

Kashiwabara Takaaki

If you look at ancient history, there are many preposterous things that one must doubt. Yet there is also nothing that we can do about this several thousand years later. The ancient legends of the West also often contain matters that must be doubted. Among these is the story of Noah, who escaped the great flood after constructing an ark and loading it with his family as well as a pair of each bird and beast. Even though to this day we do not know the size of the boat or the number of passengers, how could they all be loaded aboard the boat since the number of beasts would exceed several hundred millions?

Among the beasts, also, there would be wild and vicious animals. The meat-eating animals could not be raised on grasses. Several might indeed be fed by killing one, but one couple would thereby be sacrificed. How much more would have been the loss if several head were killed just to feed one animal! Upon becoming hungry, the animals would surely have eaten each other up. How can we say that the tigers of antiquity were like today's cats or that the earliest bears were like today's dogs? If the wild beasts and poisonous snakes were allowed to fight on the boat, how could man avoid suffering from this catastrophe? And how can we believe the story that Noah's ship drifted ashore on Ararat after a long period of several months? There is also the case of our unbroken imperial line that is coeval with Heaven and earth. When one looks from the point of view of today at the story of the descent of the Heavenly grandson (*Tenson*)[12] as recorded in the histories of antiquity, it seems extremely doubtful. Yet that men of antiquity did not doubt this story may be ascribed to the fact that it was still possible in their day to verify with proof.

Recently, I have been able to resolve these doubts to a great extent by comparing this story with foreign histories. For example, there is the account of the ancestors of the ancient kings of Peru who also emerged from the sun. It is certainly a fact that one of our imperial princes in antiquity, having drifted as a castaway, was finally established as king there, after having been washed up on its shores. If you now observe the clothing of the Peruvian king, his chest was decorated with a chrysanthemum. (See page 90 of the geography by the American [Samuel Augustus] Mitchel published in 1863.)[13] Moreover, it is said that the grammar of their language closely resembles that of ours. There is also the symbol of a chrysanthemum adorning the forehead of the queen of Hawaii. (See the picture on page 464 of the book on regional customs by the Dutch author [Auguste Wahlen?][14] and printed in 1855.)

When asked to discuss these accounts, scholars in national studies (*kōkokugakusha*)[15] will surely say that castaways drifting abroad from our country in antiquity established countries in foreign regions. Yet how can a dynasty establish a religion in this manner? The Peruvian kings have already been destroyed by Spain. Of all the countries established by the descendants of Heaven, our empire alone survives to this day as an independent state among the nations of the world. How can we avoid reflecting on the example of Peru? Even if a person should actually descend from Heaven today, how could men regard him as the Son of God if his words and his conduct were not holy? Still less would we accept the descendants of a person whom men had not actually seen come down from Heaven. This is why all men, whether commoner or Son of Heaven, must invariably have religion.

We have had a religion since antiquity that is called the religion of Heavenly Nature (*Tennen*).[16] Its principles cause men naturally to return to the character of the original essence, that is, the unity of the sincere heart. Nevertheless, human affairs gradually became more complex with the unfolding of history, and the religion of Heavenly Nature was inadequate to correct evil. Thereupon, Confucian teachings (*meikyō*)[17] were spread and practiced, but this Chinese thought also was still inadequate to move the ignorant people. The religion of Shaka was then added, and the superstitious worship of insects, beasts, trees, and stones, in the meantime, emerged in confusion. Looking at the record from the point of view of today, why is it that some hold that it would have been best had there been no religion from the beginning? It is, after all, because men's minds have been confused by the profusion of religions. At this point, the ills of religion are indeed many. There will be untold harm to government in the near future if we do not at this time spread a new religion and remedy ancient evils. Yet the damage may also be large if the remedial religion is not appropriate.

It is said that the nation should select the best religion, or that it should let the people worship as they please, or that it should eclectically take from various religions what comports with national customs. These proposals are all oversimplifications. High-toned speeches cannot enter humble ears, and superior teachings are inadequate to lead mediocre men. What the superior man believes is doubted by the inferior, and what satisfies an old woman is ridiculed by youth. People who indulge in the new detest the old, and those who admire the old suspect the strange. The differences between men's minds are like those between their faces. If there are no accomplished leaders, therefore, a religion will not be practiced even though it is true in principle, and theories will not be believed, notwithstanding their reasonableness. Ah, the real difficulty in faith is the difficulty in causing others to believe. Is not describing the way of religion quite beyond the power of language?

The Equal Numbers of Men and Women[18]

Fukuzawa Yukichi

One does not know who is right in the recent noisy discussion of equal rights for men and women. Now when a person discusses anything, he will not grasp the matter unless he first closely examines its character. Therefore, we should take up even this discussion of equal rights for men and women only after we have first considered the nature of men and women and become well informed on what rights are. If to the contrary we set forth our opinions at will according to our individual viewpoints, conjecturing on the nature of men and women and speculating on the word "right," we shall be reduced to limitless futile argument. When equal seating for men and women is taken up, for example, giving precedence in seating to ladies is veneration for those who call it veneration and helping for those who call it helping. Even though some may not become angry when they think of the practice as helping, they may also gnash their teeth if they regard it as completely dedicated, sincere veneration.

Since public discussion has generally sunk to this level, rather than become embroiled in a noisy discussion of the merits of equal rights, I would direct attention only to an aspect that anyone can easily understand after we have taken up a simple point that is close at hand. This simple point is neither religious nor theoretical but rather a mathematical computation on the *soroban*[19] of the equal number of men and women that anyone can readily grasp.

First, since the number of men and women in the world are roughly equal, the calculation will show that one man should marry one woman. If, contrary to this, an excessive number of women is taken into one house, there must be scarcity in another. If the phrase "eight suitors for one daughter" on the *iroha* card[20] is unfair, it is also unreasonable for one man to take eight concubines. Today, setting aside the difficult discussion of equal rights, I only say that for one man to take several wives is not right as it does not conform to computations on the *soroban*. We may then take this as the first step toward equal rights and decide to postpone other discussion of the matter until scholarship has progressed. If anyone feels that even this theory is too advanced, we shall tacitly allow him to keep concubines or take *geisha*. But these practices must be hidden from others as private affairs. Hiding from others is the beginning of shame, and being ashamed naturally is the beginning of voluntary abstention. Once we thus introduce the first step toward equal rights, the present futile arguments somehow can also be resolved in a few years.

[1]*Fūfu dōken*, 夫婦同權, equal rights for men and women. The term *fūfu* may be construed as either husbands and wives or men and women, depending on the context. Katō here refers to Mori Arinori's articles "On Wives and Concubines" in this journal and to Fukuzawa Yukichi's eighth essay in his *Gakumon no Susume* (學問のすゝめ), *The Encouragement of Learning*, that appeared in April 1874. Whereas Katō makes fun of what he chooses to regard as subservience by Western men toward women as evidenced in their daily civilities, Mori and Fukuzawa were concerned to assure wives

basic dignity in their marital relations. Fukuzawa held that taking more than one wife violates the laws of nature, that even a lofty mansion is no more than a beast's hut if it is a house of one father and many mothers, and that failure to provide an heir should not be regarded as unfilial. The last point was directed against those who argued that a man should be allowed to take a concubine that he might secure an heir and thus fulfill what Mencius held to be the prime duty of a filial son. For an English translation of Fukuzawa's article, see David A. Dilworth and Umeyo Hirano, trs., *Fukuzawa Yukichi's Encouragement of Learning* (Tokyo, 1969), pp. 49–55.

[2]Although Nishimura actively engaged in writing and translation on behalf of enlightenment, he was more interested in the ethical (*shūshin,* 修身) and moral (*dōtoku,* 道德) aspects of Western culture, deplored the absence from the new Japanese education of training in the traditional virtues of loyalty, filial piety, human-heartedness, and justice (*chū kō jin gi,* 忠孝仁義), and rejected Western utilitarian individualism as an invitation to selfishness and licence. This essay epitomizes clearly Nishimura's desire to draw from the West as well as the East in his campaign to revive the teaching of ethics. In 1876 Nishimura joined with Sakatani Shiroshi and others to organize the Tōkyō Shūshin Gakusha (東京修身學社, Tokyo Scholars in Ethics) and thereafter emerged as one of the most active spokesmen for expanding the moral and ethical content in Japanese education, including the teaching of loyalty to the nation and the imperial line.

[3]*The Great Learning,* or *Ta Hsüeh,* 大學. Nishimura here refers to the famous statement in the *Ta Hsüeh* that families are regulated if persons are cultivated, that states are well ruled if families are regulated, and that that the world will be at peace if states are well ruled.

[4]This is from Book IV of the *Book of Mencius,* which states that the foundation of the world is the state; the foundation of the state, the family; and the foundation of the family, the person.

[5]*Kōri,* 功利.

[6]*Jōtei,* 上帝.

[7]*Tenri,* 天理.

[8]The phonetic original of this name is or "ayman." It seems entirely likely that Nishimura intended to refer to Francis Wayland, whose writings were popular among the early Meiji enlighteners.

[9]Thomas Brown, 1830–1897, a Scottish philosopher.

[10]Wu, 吳.

[11]Kashiwabara is presumably commenting on Nishi Amane's third article "On Religion" that appears in Issue Six. Part Two of this series appears in Issue Thirty.

[12]Tenson, 天孫.

[13][Samuel August] Mitchel, 1792–1868, a successful author of geography textbooks.

[14]The phonetic original is ム.イ.ハンオーヘン or "mu.ee. hanōhen." It is tempting to think that Kashiwabara refers to a Dutch edition of a work by the Belgian Auguste Wahlen (1785–1850) entitled *Moeurs, usages et costumes de tous les peoples du monde . . .* (4 vols.: Brussels, 1843–1844). See vol. IV, page 168 of this work for a picture of the queen of the Sandwich Islands who sports a decoration that could be taken for a chrysanthemum.

[15]*Kōkokugakusha,* 皇國學者.

[16]*Tennen,* 天然.

[17]*Meikyō,* 名教.

[18]In this essay on the equal numbers of men and women (*danjo dōsū,* 男女同數), Fukuzawa is responding to Katō Hiroyuki on the equal rights of men and women

(*fūfu dōken*). Here as in *Gakumon no Susume* Fukuzawa insists that monogamy is clearly appropriate since the number of men and women in the world is roughly equal.

[19]*Soroban*, 十露盤, the Japanese abacus.

[20]*Iroha* cards, playing cards for a game based on the Japanese *hiragana* syllabary.

National Character

Nishi Amane

I have seen the words "Asiatic luxury" and "Asiatic despotism" from time to time when reading in European histories. As these writings refer to Asia to the West of the Indus, they naturally do not extend to the East of the Himalayas. Yet such customs generally prevail to the East of the Dardenelles. The area to the East of the Himalayas, however, is rendered still more conspicuous by the fact that its people are also of a different race. In addition, since this area is divided into a number of large and small countries, the characters of its peoples also necessarily differ. Yet, generally speaking, despotism flourishes [in these lands], and it has been the character of their peoples under despotism to emulate the rule of Ch'in,[1] in which rulers were honored while the people were held in contempt.

Turning more especially to our country of Japan, despotism here has been even more extreme than in China, the people regarding themselves as slaves since they have honored an unbroken line of sovereigns from the founding of the country by Jimmu Tennō[2] 2535 years ago. Still more, having fallen under the domination of military lords and changed to feudal institutions during the Middle Ages, the nation was completely under camp government for almost 700 years. Retainers had their retainers, and slaves their slaves. The swaggering *bushi*[3] cut down farmers, artisans, and merchants at will, and governmental directives were no more than military orders. How could the spirit of the people be other than servile?

Even though since the Restoration and the abolition of the domains (*haihan*)[4] we have fundamentally changed this system and thereby paved the way for modern institutions, the time is still short. The government's rule is indeed magnanimous and public opinion honors liberty, but the spirit of the people remains as before without being restored to its original vigour. Such being the case, we cannot expect sudden change if we consider it from a historical point of view. This is because there is clearly no hope of reforming the old, and the young have only changed on the surface.

Nay, this [subservient] character should not be attributed to the government alone. This character has also had two other sources of stimulation: one is the school of the Kōmonkō,[5] which moved away from the *Spring and Autumn* [*Annals*] of Confucius, and the other is the *Gyojū Gaigen*,[6] in which Motoori Norinaga went beyond the studies of *waka* by Keichū Ajari[7] of Naniwa.[8] Therefore, the inability of our people to cast off their servility arises on the one hand historically from their political past and on the other hand, sad to say, from "philosophical contemplation." How can we suddenly change this subservience that has soaked into the people's minds until it sticks to them like hard glue? Now if you would have me label this character of our people to regard themselves as slaves since they have accepted oppression and have been unable to cast off servility, I would call it [their] "political" and "moral" character.

There is also what may be called "geographical" character. Although it has been impossible definitely to establish by verification whether this character should be ascribed to geography, I shall temporarily call it "geographical" since its source is not immediately clear. Now, generally, when discussing the temperament of our people, we may speak of their loyal faithfulness and simple directness. I feel that, because of their loyal faithfulness, there has been very little cruelty in our history as compared with China (aside from such cases as the family feuds within the Genji).[9] And because of this simple directness, as compared with China, there have been few cases in history like the fellow Ashikaga Yoshiakira.[10] Even though it cannot be said that these two qualities will invariably be found in individuals, these fine traits generally appear when one discusses the temperament of the people and the customs of the land. Motoori Norinaga wrote:

> Should anyone ask about the Japanese spirit,
> It is the wild cherry blossoms glowing in the morning sun.[11]

This poem may indeed be said to describe our people well as it epitomizes our national character that arises from the quality of simple directness.

Loyal faithfulness and simple directness are indeed fine virtues, but there are occasions when they are extremely injurious. Just to illustrate, the opposite of loyal faithfulness is cruelty. Writing loyal faithfulness and cruelty on parallel lines and adding to them, respectively, the two words stupidity and sagacity, we shall be inclined to associate stupidity with loyal faithfulness and sagacity with cruelty. Although loyal faithfulness may be a fine trait, therefore, it will not escape the fault of stupidity if scholarship is not prized. Again, the opposite of simple directness is bigoted deviousness (a term uncommon in Japanese). If you write "simple directness" on parallel lines with "bigoted deviousness," then add to each, respectively, the words "easily loses" and "loses with difficulty," and finally complete each line with "rights," there emerges the sense that "simple directness" by its nature possesses the fault of "easily losing rights."

The modern national character of the Japanese was formed by the mutual blending of these geographic traits [of loyal faithfulness and simple directness] with the previously discussed political and moral character [of despotism and servility].

It may be said that the national character is best and most convenient for despotic government when despotic government is above while the people are below, when the people regard themselves as slaves while honoring despotic government, and when the people conduct themselves with simple directness and carry out their affairs with loyal faithfulness. Samurai may then undertake vengeance on behalf of a family from whom his ancestors received benefits three generations before and chivalrously die in battle. Or the people may say [in helplessness] that crying babies and land stewards (*jitō*)[12] are creatures beyond their control or that lords and parents are by their nature unreasonable. After all, however, even though the full achievement of the great work of the Restoration may be ascribed to the sage virtues of the emperor, it was also greatly assisted by this national character of the people who, so to speak, bowed their heads to the ground in subservience even to the point of breaking their horns.[13]

Therefore, these national customs and public temperament

indeed produce a character that is ideal for despotic government. But this national character produces people described by Fukuzawa as without spirit and without power at a time when a world is emerging in which we are opening foreign relations, in which we are loosening the binding ropes within the country, and in which intellect is stronger than force. Still more will this [subservient] character be a principal hindrance when we reach the day when we want to establish a popularly elected assembly.

If we compare this national character to the human body, it is without bodily health, like the luxuriously clad child who has been brought up in the depths of a palace. All might be very well could the child remain permanently within the confines of his palace. But we should not expect much from a fellow of such weak body now that he has sacrificed his family stipend and moves into a world in which he would take up a plough and grasp a spade. Therefore, his natural health must be restored by feeding him a great amount of meat until his muscles stand out from his limbs.

Now this character is indeed as I have described above. Speaking generally, Chuang Tzŭ told of how Chaos (*Konton*), being a fellow without apertures [for seeing, hearing, eating, and the like], was bored with holes (and died on the seventh day).[14] Nevertheless, it is my view that, if we are to develop our natural health, we should introduce legal studies. I have strong opinions on the matter, but I shall defer until a later day a more extended discussion of the methods for introducing law.

On Concubines March 1, 1875

Sakatani Shiroshi

In my speech on February 1, I was guilty of unclear reasoning as I filled in at a moment's notice and spoke without even a draft in response to an urgent plea from the society. I am, therefore, following up my previous statement with an amplification of views.

The wise men of Japan, China, and the West are agreed in

holding that marriage is the foundation from which the fine qualities of nations emerge since it is the basis of morality and the source of propriety as well as the institution upon which the conduct of the people rests. Even though secular ethical teachings (*seikyō*)[15] are the source of the morals of marriage, the damage to customs from the concubine system is great, and the vice of concubines is rife in modern society. I am not resorting to idle theory apart from human feelings. Yet some will smile without becoming angry and think me impractical and unenlightened when I discuss concubines. Extreme persons claim boastfully and without shame that they are emulating Western ways when they ride with their concubines in the same carriage shoulder to shoulder and hand in hand, or when they walk with these ladies down the main streets in broad daylight.

Ah, how can the concubine system be attributed to the West? It is false to the West to ascribe such ugly and barbaric conduct to Western tutelage. Fortunately, however, distinguished scholars in Western studies are advocating reform [in this area]. Mori's discourses on wives and concubines are clear and just, while Fukuzawa is equally instructive to society when he felicitously calls even a lofty mansion the hut of beasts [if it is a house of but one father and many mothers].[16] Both gentlemen have washed out the eyes and ears of the pseudo-enlightened and left them speechless.

Evil customs are extremely difficult to change, however. Moreover, there are also conservatives who deliberately misrepresent the evil customs of China, or who force their views on others by taking shelter behind the name of our emperor. It is really extremely regrettable that such views should be encouraged today when men are almost without principle and when the evil of illicit intercourse gushes forth like a dirty wave to enter the sea of tacit acceptance. There is no need to say that the views of the conservatives arise from "passion" and sink to barbarism, but their comment on the [in]equality of desire is not without reason.

Men are naturally strong and weak, just as they are wise and ignorant. A weak person is troubled by just one mate, while a strong person is not satisfied with many men or many women. When the lust of heroes and that of men who live to eighty or ninety arises from their healthy spirit, inequality [in sexual desire] is natural, just as the price of shoes varies according to size. It is also true, however, that there can be no allowance for such natural differences when monogamy is invariably practiced. The middle and lower classes of Europe and America are still barbaric since they are so ugly as tacitly to accept sexual immorality. It is naturally a fine custom that their unmarried girls abstain from sexual intercourse because they fear that they may otherwise be unable to marry. But Japan and China are one with the West insofar as they praise virgins and think non-abstainers ugly. While agreeing with the West, it seems that we should strictly forbid promiscuous social intercourse by law, especially among officials, while leaving to an individual's free discretion according to his custom whether he takes a concubine. Then may we direct people toward the virtue of monogamy as society becomes enlightened. Such great barbarism as the practice of free love among the Mormons will certainly be abandoned.

When husband and wife enjoy equal rights, it would seem that the wife should also have the right to take additional mates if her husband keeps concubines. A woman is also a person. Women are by nature strong and weak, some being able to live without husbands all their lives, while others are not satisfied with several men. Morality is destroyed when men and women alike become so lustfully dissipated that they are no more than beasts. Thus the advocates of equal rights for men and women promote the establishment of morality by employing these rights to impose mutual restraints. Yet men stand above women, and husbands are above wives. Women are weak; men strong. The husband deals with the outside world while the wife manages domestic matters. Such occasional exceptions as the Queen of England notwithstanding, it is generally the invariable custom throughout the five continents that men are above women. The true principle of equal rights, therefore, appears to be limited only to the prevention of sexual license by establishing mutual restraints in the bedchamber.

The press has recently recorded such cases of extreme "barbarism" as the Tartar husband who boasts several wives, the marriages in remote districts of Russia at which the bride gives the groom a whip and resigns her life to him, and the light treatment of divorce in Italy. Such excesses may indeed be unworthy of discussion, but we should certainly keep them in mind. Our country, no less than China, honors the rights of males. From antiquity, however, we have had numerous Amazons who have regarded their husbands as slaves. Take the common custom in the back streets of Tokyo for the wives to dominate their husbands. After all, when a husband sells all his wife's clothing and hair ornaments in barbaric fashion, the wife, her "spirit" aroused by rage, will secure her retribution by going so far as to lead her husband around by the nose while vigorously upbraiding him. This is an example of flourishing women's rights. Of course, it is bad if the wife is oppressed by the husband's excessive rights, but it is far worse for the husband to be oppressed by the wife's excessive rights, even though the lower classes may temporarily profit from such practices.

What we should honor are the enlightened ideas of Europe and America according to which husband and wife equally love and help each other. Even though the European and American customs contain the reasonable intention that the weak female shall be protected by the strong male like a child, however, I must deplore the prevailing ugly way in which their men have practically all become slaves to women. This is exactly the same as the ugly situation in which wives are oppressed by the husband's rights in China and Japan. Looked at reasonably, even though it is naturally proper for the strong man to protect the woman, it is also right for the woman obediently to serve the man.

The words equal rights, therefore, should not establish equality in life generally, although they may provide equality in the bedchamber. If today we establish this equality between the sexes in all aspects of life, we shall reach the point where the men will strive to oppress the women while the women attempt to oppress the men. In America, women's parties have gained the right to agitate for prohibition of drinking by men. Even though their intentions may be fine, how are their acts fine? How is such conduct for the benefit of those [women] who should obediently receive protection? Such women probably resemble the wives in the back streets of Tokyo. In sum, the word "rights" includes evil. There is a tendency for the advocacy of rights to generate opposing power. This was never the intention of the wise men of Europe and America, and the translation [of the word "right" as *ken*][17] is not appropriate. Instead, it would be well to speak of preserving the spheres of men and women (*danjo shubun*)[18] or of the harmonious bodies of husband and wife (*fūfu dōtai*).[19] Further, from the point of view of rights, the man should stand slightly above the woman, just as elder brother takes precedence before younger brother. We naturally cannot discuss as typical a case such as England in which the husband's rights are necessarily inferior to those of the wife, who is queen and empress. Such a situation thus should not be regarded as the normal shape of things.

I have thought that the concubine system should be changed but that it should not be changed suddenly. Justification for change naturally lies in men's hearts and customs of our nation. Now it will not be impossible to change if we just direct our eyes to these factors and pay attention to law and enlightenment. If we superficially inveigh against concubines, others will find reason for opposing us. How much more will this be the case if we arbitrarily try to introduce foreign customs! I have said that change is only possible if it conforms with the men's hearts and customs [of the nation]. Setting aside the ancient days for the moment and coming to the Middle Ages when the imperial house had declined, the palaces in Kyōto were for the most part like aristocratic brothels, and there was ultimately no apparent shame in recording their loose morals in literature, especially in the poetry anthologies compiled by imperial command. Yet such conduct was not yet condoned in moral discussions. Of course, it was barbaric that emperors, shoguns, and great lords showed no moderation in the keeping of concubines more recently in Tokugawa times. Nevertheless, while even rich merchants and persons of high station below the great lords kept concubines, none approved the practice. All privately reviled the keeping of concubines, and none approved in their inner hearts. That people often stole out and resorted to intimate relations in secret was because they were themselves all ashamed.

Recently, the dissolute customs of former domain (*han*)[20] retainers and of those who had served the bakufu[21] as well as the knavish ways of students have been freed from supervision by *metsuke*[22] and by feudal gatemen. Even great nobles and officials love prostitutes and take them as wives and concubines with complete freedom and independence (*jishu jiyū*).[23] These men really cast out shame when their extreme loose living is carried to the point of breaking with their self-sacrificing wives and native hearths. Yet they boast openly that such are the ways of freedom and independence that prevail in the enlightened West. Only the ruling classes fail to condemn such conduct, however. And these men [of the ruling classes], in their inner hearts, do not want their sons to behave in this manner. Foreigners, without waiting for my enlightened colleagues to move, have vigorously attacked the taking of concubines by others although they themselves may resort to the practice. Almost without exception, none approve concubinage, and they relish Mori's views on wives and concubines as well as Fukuzawa's reference to animal huts.

It is in such times as these that customs [of concubinage] are broken down. Moreover, not only is the institution not approved in men's hearts, but it is also censured and scorned. And those who criticize all hope that successive attacks will correct the evil practice. Is not the means for change inseparably tied to the mind through men's hearts and customs? Why then cannot we change and forbid concubinage when men's hearts and customs are so fine? Moreover, why do I think that we cannot change suddenly? There are now no thieves who themselves approve of robbery, but there are many robbers in the land. Sexual lust and the desire for property are the same [in this regard]. If we try to change them, we will naturally achieve fine manners and customs only through guidance by religion and government. We cannot lightly and rashly look for a hasty ending of the concubine system. Without looking for a quick end of concubines, we must instead reform today's barbaric customs that encourage and promote the evil.

It is religious morality (*kyōhō*)[24] that unites men's hearts and frees them from sin. Nevertheless, religious morality in our country cannot be relied upon in the least since it is extremely degenerate, especially in the matter of wives and concubines. European religious morality possesses many fine points, but it is not quickly accepted by our countrymen. Even acceptance of their religious morality would also produce new evils, as customs are not quickly changed. Moreover, we should not depend solely on their religious morality in our country since it has eliminated neither adultery nor robbery in their countries.

Then what shall we do? Religious morality is to correct men's hearts. In the present concubine system, what should be corrected is men's conduct and deportment, since their hearts are as I have described. Correction of conduct is the responsibility of secular morality (*seihō*)[25] and encouraging the practice of secular morality depends on the conduct of the officials who practice it. This being the case, the present evil customs must surely be the responsibility of the upper classes. The conduct of the upper classes is like the wind; that of the lower, like grass. Grass invariably bends with the wind. Since this tendency is especially extreme in autocracies, we shall establish strict secular morality extending from ministers and nobles down. Promiscuous taking of concubines will be prohibited, no more than one being allowed if the practice continues. Wives will be given liberty to complain when maids are involved, and morals will be amended to increase wives' rights. Further, concubines will invariably be taxed heavily, and scandalous behavior by nobles and high officials will be more severely punished than commoners under the established law. Thereafter, we shall reflect on conditions past and present and draw from the strong points of China, Europe, and America to establish definite marriage rites after open discussion. Even though these are my humble proposals, I believe them to be appropriate.

Those who cite the emperor's example as support for concubines do not speak from their true hearts. Such people are indeed only trying to disguise their misconduct by borrowing sanction [from the emperor's conduct], but they entirely misunderstand the actual situation. The significance of our imperial line is unique in the nation. The imperial line should not be considered a norm since the imperial clan must be perpetuated by allowing concubines, even though we strictly limit their number that there be no injury to the sovereign's body. We certainly need not consider such large numbers as were provided by the ancient Chinese (which exceeded the "Mormons"), but in Europe the marriages of monarchs differ from those that commonly arise from the mutual love and mutual intimacy between man and woman. Thus rulers are naturally in a different position from the people. Even though women may be heads of households in Europe and America, it is the common practice [there] for the male to possess superior rights over the female and for the woman to accept her husband as the family head when she marries. Only in the case of a female monarch does the male consort not become family head or ruler upon marriage. This is the greatest distinction between monarch and commoner.

Thus, even though we one day achieve the fine custom in which there is not one concubine in the country, this will not apply to the emperor. How much less does it apply today! To have taken this matter up was extremely disrespectful. I can only be excused by the fact that people are not informed on the actual nature [of the imperial line]. As I have recently been extremely busy, I have had no time for detailed thought. Perhaps my colleagues will overlook the coarseness of my expression and grasp my intentions with a friendly spirit.

[I appear in the essays of Katō and others to be the pioneer in advocating equal rights for men and women. In my earlier essays on wives and concubines, I indeed said that husbands and wives should be honored without distinction as they are on the same level. I absolutely did not touch on equal rights, however. Accordingly, I am just clarifying this point here with an amendment as I fear that the public may interpret as equal rights what I have said about being on the same level. Mori Arinori]

[1]Ch in, 秦, the Chinese state founded on Legalist (*Fa Chia,* 法家) theory, which completed the unification of China in 221 B.C.

[2]Jimmu Tennō, 神武天皇.

[3]*Bushi,* 武士, the warrior class. By the right of *kirisute gomen* (切捨御免), *bushi* could use their swords on commoners at will. The right was abolished in 1871.

[4]*Haihan,* 廢藩, the abolition of the feudal domains (*han*) in 1871.

[5]Kōmonkō, 黄門公, the school established by Tokugawa Mitsukuni (德川光圀), 1628–1700, the lord of Mito (水戶), who stressed the virtue of loyalty in relations between ruler and subject.

[6]*Gyojū Gaigen,* also pronounced *Karaosame no Uretamigoto,* 馭戎慨言, was completed in 1777 by Motoori Norinaga (本居宣長), the great scholar in Japanese national studies (*kokugaku,* 國學). Dealing with intercourse between Japan, China, and Korea before 1600, it is a work in which Motoori sets forth most clearly his views on the superiority of Japan's indigenous ancient way (*inishie no michi,* 古道).

[7]Keichū Ajari, 契沖沙黎(阿闍梨), 1640–1701, a Buddhist priest whose pioneering studies of ancient Japanese literature, including the thirty-one syllable poems known as *waka* (和歌), greatly influenced Motoori Norinaga.

[8]Naniwa, 浪華.

[9]Genji, 源氏, the Minamoto family. Nishi here refers to the feuds within the Minamoto family during its rise to power in the late twelfth century.

[10]Ashikaga Yoshiakira, 足利義詮, 1330–1368, the second of the Ashikaga line of shoguns, who has been especially reviled by traditional Japanese historians for his alleged mistreatment of the imperial family.

[11]A poem that Motoori Norinaga wrote on a portrait that he had painted of himself. See Matsumoto Shigeru, *Motoori Norinaga, 1730–1804* (Cambridge, 1970), p. 1690.

[12]*Jitō*, 地頭, officers established during the early middle ages to oversee the administrations of manorial estates.

[13]Break horns, *tsuno o kuzusu*, 角ヲ崩ス, a phrase from the comic play *Dontarō* (鈍太郎).

[14]According to the famous story by Chuang Tzŭ (莊子), the Taoist philosopher of the fourth and third centuries B.C., King Fuss of the Northern Seas and King Fret of the Southern Seas occasionally met in the land of Chaos, the ruler of the central region. Observing that, unlike other beings, Chaos possessed no apertures for seeing, hearing, eating, and the like, Fuss and Fret decided to try boring holes into him. Each day they bored a hole into Chaos until he died on the seventh day. The word for chaos (*konton*, 混沌) also refers to the period in human affairs when men were still unenlightened and uneducated. Nishi, of course, was committed to the idea that men and society could and should be actively improved, an outlook that was alien to Chuang Tzŭ's thought. For Chuang Tzŭ's story, see Arthur Waley's *Three Ways of Thought in Ancient China* (Garden City, 1956), pp. 66–67.

[15]For Sakatani's discussions on secular ethical teachings (*seikyō*, 政教), see Issues Twenty-Two and Twenty-Five.

[16]On this reference to Fukuzawa, see footnote one of the previous issue.

[17]*Ken*, 權, includes a strong sense of power that is not so commonly associated with the English word "right."

[18]*Danjo shubun*, 男女守分. This phrase is very close to *fūfu yūbetsu* (夫婦有別) of Mencius, which Tsuda Mamichi criticized in his article of that name in Issue Twenty-Two.

[19]*Fūfu dōtai*, 夫婦同體.

[20]*Han*, 藩.

[21]*Bakufu*, 幕府.

[22]*Metsuke*, 目付, censors.

[23]*Jishu jiyū*, 自主自由.

[24]*Kyōhō*, 教法.

[25]*Seihō*, 政法. The term *hō* (法) may also be translated as "law." Whether it is taken to mean morality or law, Sakatani clearly did not contemplate depriving concubines of all recognition under the law.

Creating Good Mothers Speech on March 16, 1875

Nakamura Masanao

When I previously discussed reforming the character of the people,[1] I explained that we cannot renew the minds of the people and raise them to a high level unless we rely on the two main divisions of education. One is "religious" and "moral" education; the other, education in "science" and the "arts." Even though both are invariably essential, the former is the root; the latter, the branches. It cannot be said that we are late if we introduce education in science and the arts to children at five or six years, when their mental powers are gradually beginning to develop. Prenatal education is most essential in moral and religious training. Then if the kind words, good conduct, and superb example [of the mother] continuously saturates the child's eyes and ears and envelops his body, he will unconsciously and unwittingly acquire ingrown moral and religious principles before his intellect gradually begins to develop. Take the strength of the body, for example. If the mother is strong in body during pregnancy, her offspring will invariably be strong (providing the child receives proper rearing after birth). If prenatal nourishment is inadequate, any amount of care and skilled medical treatment can only promote normal growth without adding anything special [to make up the inherent deficiencies]. Judging from the experience of the body, this principle surely cannot be doubted. The psychological effects are still more surprising once this principle is applied to the mind and the spirit. After all, the spiritual and mental goodness of the child will generally reflect that of the mother. Even later tastes and habits of the child often resemble those of the mother.

Thus we must invariably have fine mothers if we want effectively to advance the people to the area of enlightenment and to alter their customs and conditions for the good. If the mothers are superb, they can have superb children, and Japan can become a splendid country in later generations. We can then have people trained in religious and moral education as well as in the sciences and arts whose intellects are advanced, whose minds are elevated, and whose conduct is high. Not having had adequate prenatal educational nourishment, I am at middle age unable sufficiently to realize my ambitions, only sadly languishing in shabby quarters [Japan] and envying the enlightenment of Europe and America. I have a deep, irrepressible desire that later generations shall be reared by fine mothers.

Now to develop fine mothers, there is nothing better than to educate daughters. Let us take the case of a woman endowed with moral and religious education who is married and gives birth to a child. The child during his mother's pregnancy will have been filled with a stout spirit and strong morals and breathed the atmosphere of pious virtue. Having basked in the sun of Divine Providence (*Tendō*),[2] his eyes and ears will be the gates to wisdom; and his inner heart will penetrate his still unformed, delicate body. It is then not excessive even to say that the foundations for his virtues of bravery, endurance, and perseverance of a later day were laid while he was still playing in his cradle and receiving his mother's milk. To fear harm from equal rights for men and women is no more than to fear that the uneducated woman will sit on her husband. This anxiety would not exist if women honored Divine Providence, respected noble sentiments, admired the arts, appreciated science, and helped their husbands, and if husbands and wives mutually loved and respected each other.

Aside from the matter of equal rights, the training of men and women should be equal and not of two types. If we desire to preserve an extremely high and extremely pure level among human beings as a whole, we should accord both men and women the same type of upbringing and enable them to progress equally. Pure-hearted women should invariably go side by side with pure-hearted men. Of course, men and women should observe virtuous principles equally and without distinction. Love is the most important of the many human virtues. To quote the famous words of the poet [Robert] Browning, "True love surpasses knowledge." It may also be said that, if you look at men in the world generally, the man of surpassing wisdom is the man whose sincere love is most deep while the man of deep love is the man of deep wisdom.

A wife possessed of a feeling of deep love will bring her husband ease and happiness and encourage him to exert himself in enterprises useful to the country. Not only in the West but even in China wise men recognize this fact. There is the chapter on *Ch'ien K'un* at the front of the *Book of Changes*[3] and the poem entitled *Kuan Chü* at the beginning of the *Book of Songs*.[4]

It has also been said that the uprightness of men and women is the great principle of the universe. A man like King Wên, who received prenatal training from his mother, T'ai Jên, was later wise in conduct and enjoyed the benefits of his wife's assistance.[5] The scholars of China, however, have not seriously considered these facts and only honor men's rights. I have recently come to recognize this as a great error. Some men of the present generation say that women will be conceited if they are allowed to read. Whether a woman is conceited or not may be related to education. I am not sure what may be the outcome should the education of women be limited to the arts and material matters. Will they become conceited if they are given training in morals and religion? Even in the West, there is an interesting idea that the arts should follow virtue in the training of women. When the English poet [Robert] Burns discussed the elements of a good wife, he divided her character into ten parts. Burns rated affectionate (that is, loving) character at four parts, sound opinions at two parts, and intellect at one part. He valued beauty (beauty of face and elegance of appearance) at one part. Together, these amount to eight parts, and the remaining two parts he accorded to the wife's property, her social contacts, and her superiority in education and the arts. He recommended that men divide these last attributes according to their own views while giving attention to one consideration. That is, none of these lesser factors are adequate individually to comprise ten percent of the whole.[6] Actually, as expressed in Burns' words, women place primary emphasis on affectionate disposition. Furthermore, their affectionate dispositions are entirely based upon or arise from love. It is said that the loving are invariably genial, that the genial are invariably happy, and that the happy are invariably beautiful. Intellect can be developed and great things accomplished as a consequence of the virtues born of love. To produce fine children by having mothers of affectionate disposition should be an easier undertaking than what I have previously described as reforming the present character of the people. How shall we acquire such mothers who virtuously practice prenatal training? I have just taken up the first steps in this small essay, and I hope that my readers will give the problem their serious consideration.

An Essay on *Zoku*[7] Speech on March 16

Nishimura Shigeki

The word *zoku* is given the meaning of robbery in the *Kuang Yün*, the *Chi Yün*, and the *Yün Hui*.[8] In the *Yü P'ien*,[9] it is to threaten men, and *zoku* refers to killing men[10] in the commentary on the *Book of History*. In the commentary on the *Tso Chuan*, *zoku* is injury.[11] While the meaning of the word *zoku* was generally of this nature, the Chinese of later generations have used *zoku* to indicate an enemy of the Son of Heaven. Even if the person is not an enemy of the Son of Heaven, the Chinese may call him *zoku* when he opposes the cause they themselves hold just. For example, in the *Hou Ch'u Shih Piao*, it is said that *zoku* and the Han were incompatible.[12]

In the *Nihon Shoki*,[13] *zoku* combined with *ryo*,[14] or captive, is read *ata*. *Ata* has the meaning of *ataru*, and it refers to all those who are one's contenders. The combination of *zoku* and *ro* in Chinese would form a boastful word that suggests esteeming oneself and despising others. Since there was probably no word in Chinese that corresponded to the Japanese *ata*, the combination of the two borrowed characters of *zoku* and *ro* really did not have the true meaning of the word *ata* even though we contrived to use them as such. We can understand this when we read the ideographs 强盗海賊 (*gōtō kaizoku*) for robbers and pirates in the *Wamyōshō*[15] without their Japanese readings. In the *Heike Monogatari* and the *Taiheiki*[16] and elsewhere, the person who contends against the emperor is called an enemy of the dynasty, or *chōteki*.[17] Even though the word is an unnatural combination of ideographs, we can say that it is rather close to the meaning. In later generations, we have generally referred to the enemies of sovereigns as *zoku* In a work like the *Nihon Gaishi,*[18] *zoku* is used to designate those who were never called by that name in the original documents. This probably was because the author [Rai Sanyō] did not himself know that he was following the false custom of China.

Zoku is not a word that points to the enemy of the emperor as it means to rob or to injure others. Generally to call the enemies of the emperor *zoku* is a mean usage that arises from excessively honoring the emperor, a practice in despotic lands. Our people scoff at the arrogance and self-complaisance of the Chinese. It is strange, however, that, so far as the word *zoku* is concerned, we have adopted the erroneous usage of the Chinese without correcting it.

The majority of our people think that they are following correct usage when they refer to the enemies of the dynasty as *zoku*, but I feel that they are thereby effacing the word's true meaning. It can be said that we are entirely following correct usage when we refer to a dog as a dog or a cat as a cat. How can we say that we are accurate if we refer to a dog as a cat? If we now call *zoku* a person who has not committed the act of *zoku*, how is this any different from calling a dog a cat?

Nevertheless, it should not be said that the enemies of the Son of Heaven are never *zoku*, robbers. There are some who should and some who should not be called *zoku*. Such persons as those who want to compete with the emperor for power, to halt tyranny, to relieve the ruler's suffering, or to oppose the government because of different views all should not be called *zoku*. But we should call *zoku* those who steal men's property, kill innocent persons, or bring injury to the people. Therefore, there are persons who should be called *zoku* among those who are enemies of sovereigns as well as among those who assist rulers.

The rebellion by America against England and the more recent rebellion by the South against the North in the United States were examples, respectively, of opposition to a ruler and to a government. Should our people be obliged to record these episodes they would surely refer to the American rebels as *zoku*. In the histories of England, however, the American rebels are called Americans, and the rebel states of the South are called Confederates in

American history. ("Confederate" has the meaning of associate. Since the southern states were associated against the government and called themselves Confederates, the term "Confederate" was adopted forthwith.) These designations are not only fair-minded. They are also true to the facts.

To refer to the enemies of the dynasty as *zoku* is just like calling foreign countries barbaric. Both practices stem from narrow-mindedness. Until ten years ago, we referred to foreign countries as the English or the American barbarians. But as there has been a complete change, we have come today to speak of them as the civilized countries of Europe and America or as the enlightened Western countries. Then why do we still refer in our writings to the enemies of the dynasty as *zoku*? After all, should we now refer to foreign countries as barbarians, one cannot guess what disturbances might arise in our relations or what injury might befall the country. The end of the word barbarian as a designation for foreign countries has indeed partly depended on the growing enlightenment of the people, but it seems to have been determined principally by our relations with other countries. Coming to the enemies of the dynasty, even such words as *zoku*, robber, and *tō*,[19] thief, can be wilfully used as their designations since the former generation [of rebels] is already dead and since the present generation has completely surrendered to the government. Nevertheless, when we ponder this situation with detachment and a calm heart, eliminate narrow views of the past, and consider these matters in terms of principles of universal justice, it seems really quite inappropriate to apply the word *zoku* to an enemy of the dynasty. Probably, if future historians pay attention to this and refrain from substituting *zoku* for the enemy of the dynasty, it may be said that the wisdom of our countrymen has thereby been advanced one step.

On Sunday Speech on March 16

Kashiwabara Takaaki

A strange day, whose name has not yet been fixed, has appeared since the Restoration. It has been called *Dondaku,* or *Sontoku,* or

Dondei,[20] which designations all signify Sunday by approximating the Western pronunciation. For the reason that Sunday comes at the beginning of each seven-day week, there are invariably fifty Sundays in each year. People ranging from gentlemen scholars to young students and enlightened persons assume it to be a day for enjoying the flowers and willows of the pleasure quarters. In the brothels and the saké shops, therefore, the day resembles the festival days of the past. Christians from of old have honored this day as the Day of the Resurrection of their church's founder. Yet the name arose from the fact that it was the day upon which "heathens" worshiped the sun as a god. The Jews also took this day as their day of worship. Since a certain Greek emperor in antiquity proclaimed that it should be for worshiping the gods, the day has finally become a holiday for the people of the world generally. It is said that sentiment opposing this trend has recently become strong. Looked at from the point of view of the believers, it is quite appropriate that they honor Heaven and conduct themselves circumspectly on this day. Nevertheless, I have not yet heard that the day should be one for excessive debauchery.

Our people, however, mistake the meaning of Sunday, and not a few go to the extreme of regarding Sunday as a day for excess and dissipation. One day, seeing my children and students abandon their studies and work, I asked the reason. And they all replied that they acted thus because the day was Sunday. I wonder if our people are only a few miles behind those of the West in conduct and scholarship. Even if we now cause the people to run day and night, we shall not overtake the West in less than a few decades. If such is the case, how much longer will it take if they waste a day each week? After all, the gentlemen scholars have already won fame and success, and enlightened persons may well be confident of themselves. Young students, however, look to the future for accomplishment. Why should they imitate the gentlemen scholars and enlightened persons by indulging themselves and dissipating on Sunday? Counting up by years, these Sundays will number 50 in one year, 500 in ten years, 1000 in twenty years, and 1500 in thirty years. This then becomes a total of four years and one month of days and nights. Is this period not sufficient for even a student of modest capacity to accomplish something if he uses the time in study? Feeling as I do, I have contrived an essay on Sunday.

Notes on Curing the Currency Disease
(Fourth of Four Essays on Currency)[21]

Kanda Kōhei

A grave crisis impends if the value of paper money falls with the decrease in specie. Should you ask the best way to avoid this national disaster, I would respond that there is no magic formula. Indeed, we can only halt the export of specie and reduce the amount of paper money. After all, when we want to stop exports of specie, we must as far as possible halt expenditures for the employment of foreign advisers, sending scholars abroad, maintaining legations and consulates, purchasing ships, weapons, and machinery, building railways and telegraphs, opening mines and industries, and sending abroad special missions and exhibitions. We may not end all of these expenditures, but we must reduce them as far as possible. Even if we do not cease the outlays now, we shall ultimately be forced to do so once our specie is exhausted.

When we decide on a program after fully appreciating this situation, we should be able to prevent the excessively large annual exports of specie. If we are to curtail the exports of specie induced by trade, we must discuss methods for restricting these exports after determining their cause. Specie is sent abroad because of temporary disturbances to commodity prices, because of hasty [programs] for enlightenment, and because it is driven out by paper. There is no other way to prevent paper from driving out specie than to reduce the amount of paper money. Exports of specie on behalf of hasty enlightenment will be halted only by substituting moderate reform for hasty change. From the point of view of orthodox theory, it is not invariably necessary to limit exports of specie arising from a temporary disturbance in commodity prices because the time will soon come when it will return. Nevertheless, there is no better way to ameliorate such a distressed time than to curtail exports of specie by temporarily removing duties on exports. After all, exports of commodities should increase if duties on exports are removed, and exports of specie should decrease when commodity exports increase. This is also a way to encourage national production.

When it comes to methods for restricting paper money, we shall stress utmost frugality in government. There is no question about eliminating wasteful expenditures on supernumeraries and nonessential construction. Even important military and naval expenditures should be stopped for a time when such curtailment is clearly warranted. Practicing frugality with one mind, we should burn the surplus paper currency that we have collected. This is the principle behind the sound and appropriate maxim that a person is rewarded in proportion to his efforts. Any other expedient is probably bad. Anything like buying up paper at a low price after waiting for it to depreciate is an extremely bad policy as it is the same as depreciating and taking the people's wealth.

We can thus annually reduce the amount of currency on the market when we redeem paper currency by the above methods at an annual rate of several millions of yen. When we annually reduce the amount of currency, commodity prices should also go down correspondingly. Exports of goods should increase as their prices depreciate. And specie should return to the country after the value of expanding exports exceeds that of imports. We shall ultimately reach the point at which there is practically an equilibrium between specie and paper if for some time the tendency continues without change to import specie as the amount of paper is reduced. Once this equilibrium is achieved, we should halt redemption of paper and establish a convertible reserve of specie. This reserve need not be large. Once the equilibrium is reached, we can operate with a reserve of specie one third the amount of paper in circulation.

At the same time that we introduce exchanging [paper for specie], we should permit the establishment of different values for paper and bullion. So long as this is not allowed, it cannot be said that we have yet excluded the injury of paper money.

What we should especially note is the outbreak of war with a foreign power. It is customary for paper currency to depreciate markedly during foreign wars. Since there is no way that this can be prevented by government order, even more than military expenditures, provision must be made for reserves of convertible specie when a country intends to make war. If war breaks out without such preparation, there may be extraordinary convulsions consequent to the depreciation of paper currency. This is why paper currency is extremely injurious so far as promoting national prestige is concerned.

We should not hastily contract foreign debts since their repayment entails large exports of specie. And since loans would also extend over set periods, we had best defer [such loans] until we have stabilized the paper currency. In sum, if we have already settled on the essential principles and also if deep in our hearts we deplore the injury of foreign indebtedness, there should be numerous expedient measures for coping with the times.

Some may say that, while the above proposals seem appropriate for managing our national finances, they only fear that the progress of enlightenment will be interrupted if we halt various construction projects and cease employing foreign advisors. I would respond that we shall not have true enlightenment unless we control our national finances. Indeed, we must first put our finances in order if we want true enlightenment. This is especially the case when enlightenment does not always require expenditures. While reforming our currency, it would be well only to encourage nonmaterial enlightenment that involves no expense.

Someone may then observe that enlightenment and progress will not be hindered even if we stop for the moment. "But what about the still more serious breakdown that might arise in the area of foreign relations?" he may ask. I would reply that we should, of course, decide which is the more important after comparing the seriousness of an interruption to foreign relations with a breakdown in the currency.

Nevertheless, there is a point that should be here especially considered. A country's currency is like blood in the body. Its interruption should be termed extremely serious, being really sufficient to destroy the country. When one considers recent trends in public opinion, it does not reflect the fact that we are often spending huge sums to erect major industries that could even be halted without great damage. It seems recklessly to make light of national finance by thoughtlessly manufacturing paper money and exporting specie. How greatly mistaken are these views! If men do not abandon such mistaken ideas, I think that, rather than being beneficial, even drawing comparisons will only increase the error of reckless spending.

Generally speaking, controlling currency at present is like controlling a disease. A patient can only hope for recovery if he completely avoids indulging his selfish desires, gives up fame and fortune, stops work, cuts off relations with others, and devotes his entire attention to recovery. However, what if he should say that he has no time for recuperation as he has urgent business that is still more important than his illness? I feel myself that he will finally reach a point from which he cannot recover, after he has progressively aggravated the disease by repeatedly neglecting medical treatment. Ah, should we not concentrate our entire attention on the remedies now that the currency disease has already become deep-seated?

[1]Nakamura refers to his article "On Changing the Character of the People" in Issue Thirty.

[2]*Tendō*, 天道.

[3]The section on *Ch'ien K'un* (乾坤) in the *Book of Changes* (*I Ching*, 易經) deals with the second of the sixty-four hexagrams, the second line of which is presumed to concern a young man who achieves happiness after postponing marriage ten years.

[4]The poem entitled *Kuan chü* (關雎), the first poem in the *Book of Poetry* (*Shih Ching*, 詩經), is about a young gentleman searching for a modest, retiring, and virtuous maiden.

[5]T'ai Jên (太任), the mother of King Wên (文) of Chou (周). Since she looked at nothing evil with her eyes, heard nothing salacious with her ears, and uttered nothing sinful with her mouth during pregnancy, T'ai Jên reputedly was able to teach her son while he was still in her womb.

[6]For the original, see Burns to Alexander Cunningham, 10 September 1792, *The Complete Works of Robert Burns* (6 vols: Philadelphia, 1909), IV, 309.

[7]*Zoku*, 賊. During the early Meiji Period, it was common in the press and public announcements to refer to the followers of the defeated Tokugawa (德川) by the humiliating epithet *zoku* or "robber." Although Nishimura quickly acquired fame and position in the new era, he had himself been a senior adviser to one of the leading retainers of the Tokugawa. His essay, therefore, is an appeal to the Japanese to adopt a more civil attitude toward those who had honorably opposed the imperial forces and lost.

[8]*Kuang Yün*, 廣韻, *Chi Yün*, 集韻, and *Yün Hui*, 韻會, are three famous Chinese dictionaries organized by homophones.

[9]*Yü P'ien*, 玉篇, an ideographic dictionary compiled in the sixth century.

[10]The commentary by K'ung An-kuo (孔安国) on the *Shun Tien* (舜典) section of the *Book of History* (*Shu Ching*, 書經).

[11]The commentary by Tu Yü (杜預) on the *Tso Ch'uan* (左傳), a history of the Chinese feudal period said to have been completed in about 300 B.C.

[12]*Hou Ch'u Shih Piao*, 後出師表, a famous memorial by Chu-ko Liang (諸葛亮), the

clever general who fought for the so-called Lesser Han (漢) Dynasty that ruled the state of Shu (蜀) during the Three Kingdoms (*San Kuo,* 三國) Period of Chinese history.

[13]*Nihon Shoki,* 日本書紀, official Japanese history completed in 720 A.D.

[14]*Ryo,* 虜.

[15]*Wamyōshō,* 和名鈔, is the abbreviated name for the *Wamyō Ruijushō* (和名類聚鈔), a Chinese-Japanese lexicon compiled by Minamoto Shitagō, 源順, 911–983 A.D.

[16]*Heike Monogatari,* 平家物語, and *Taiheiki,* 太平記, two historical tales dealing with the Taira (平) house in the twelfth century.

[17]*Chōteki,* 朝敵

[18]*Nihon Gaishi,* 日本外史, of Rai Sanyō (頼山陽), 1780–1832, is a history of the military houses (*buke,* 武家) to about 1600.

[19]*Tō,* 盗.

[20]*Dondaku,* 曇濁; *Sontoku,* 損徳; *Dondei,* 呑泥. The first two versions of Sunday were apparently renderings of the Dutch *Zonday.*

[21]Continued from Issue Twenty-Six.

Conjectures on an Imaginary Closed Country

Speech on March 16, 1875

Sugi Kōji

Currency is one of the many things in the world that are always doubtful and difficult to understand. Such being the case, I shall now undertake to speculate on monetary practices.

There is a story that iron coins were minted in place of silver and gold in ancient Greece. This was a scheme that arose in the patriotic heart of the famous Spartan legislator Lycurgus, who wanted somehow to defend his country. Lycurgus first gave attention to the fact that, without strong mothers, the country could not survive for want of strong descendants. He also divided the land among the people. And since circulation of gold and silver would encourage effeminacy by permitting license, he stressed simplicity and took steps to replace gold and silver with iron coinage as a device to assure austerity (*fujiyū*).[1] As Sparta's gold and silver were consequently soon scattered to the four quarters, ships from neighboring countries naturally ceased to enter her ports while merchants also gave up coming in disgust. Sparta's coins were eventually ridiculed as worthless iron in neighboring countries. Since Lycurgus' objectives were far-reaching, he was unmoved by the hardest of conditions. And since he had in mind only the permanency of the state, the people necessarily labored under increasingly frugal circumstances to produce for themselves everything ranging from food and drink to housing and clothing. It is said that former effete ways were finally replaced by courageous practices through the gradual development of an enterprising spirit among the people and that thanks to the iron coins robbery disappeared from Sparta.

Lycurgus also established a public assembly in which men and women were gathered in large numbers to vie with each other in strength and to test their courage. Therefore, even women, quickly transformed by the valor of men, learned the military arts and finally developed strength comparable to men. There were none in neighboring lands who compared in the martial arts with the offspring raised by these powerful women. Sparta was acclaimed the most powerful of countries, and her soldiers have been praised through later generations. Frederick II of Prussia was a man who changed the military institutions of Europe, but once, when hard pressed in battle, he grieved, "If only I had Spartan soldiers." During the five hundred years when the Spartans preserved the laws of Lycurgus, the entire country emphasized rude customs, honored bravery, lived in houses of straw, walked the roads barefoot, was habitually content with mean clothing and poor food, and was completely devoid of civilization and enlightenment. How could the Spartans have endured such privations!

A wise man named Solon emerged in the neighboring state of Athens who adopted entirely different methods from Sparta when establishing laws. Since he governed the country by following nature's course, he naturally minted gold money and promoted trade. And since he established colonies at more than eighty points from the Black Sea to the Mediterranean, commodity circulation was also widespread. The fame of his currency has been perpetuated in books to the present day. The extraordinary measures of Lycurgus were the opposite of the normal principles followed by Solon. Thereafter, from Roman days until our own times, there has been no trace of iron currency [in the West]. After all, it is known that human wisdom has become enlightened and followed the course of nature. Only in our Japan during the old bakufu were iron coins minted.[2] Irrespective of who contrived it, the system injured the country as its intent was not patriotic. At the time of the opening of the ports, foreigners saw advantage in the fact that copper and iron coins then circulated at the same value, and it is not known how many millions in copper coins they bought up and carried away. The effects are still evident in conditions today. It is fortunate, however, that the sums did not reach such extreme amounts as to cause uprisings among the people.

Again, there was the famous autocratic king, Louis XIV, who loved armies, indulged excessively in luxuries, and himself commonly boasted, *"L'état c'est moi"* (The nation is my possession). France was extremely impoverished after this king's death, but a clever man appeared in society when the country had sunk to such extremity that there seemed nothing to do but to cry. A Scotsman named John Law, taking advantage of the poverty in France, held that a country would always be prosperous if it only had money. Therefore, he advised the government that it could achieve prosperity if it managed to circulate paper as money. Thereupon, the government issued paper money. Even though Frenchmen were bewitched by its convenience, honored it more than gold currency for a time, and circulated it in large quantities, [the new money] was really a contrivance to deceive men and contrary to nature. Before many years had lapsed, therefore, the notes ceased to circulate, and millions of yen in paper were ultimately destroyed like rubbish. The consequent national disorders provoked the greatest confusion, and the government dispatched troops to subdue the difficulties in a cruel action. Fleeing in secrecy, Law hid in Geneva and finally died of hunger.

To my way of thinking, this paper money was one of the disastrous causes of the unprecedented French Revolution of 1789 in which the king and queen were executed. Properly speaking, gold and silver in the mountains, like salt in the sea, are not man-made. Since neither can be produced by human power, therefore, they seem to be substances bestowed by the Creator upon men with the injunction that they live in harmony with each other. In daily buying and selling, gold and silver are circulated as mediums of exchange with which the quality and quantity of goods are naturally calculated in terms of gold yen. Equally in the West and the East, therefore, gold and silver always command the confidence of men in the world. In their mutual theological disputes, the followers of religion formerly fought each other over what [they thought] right and wrong. Even though their enmity became so extreme that they fought each other without regard to life, I have not heard of instances in which men of different faiths have disputed the value of gold and silver, all having had faith in the metals regardless of their religion. Since the world generally follows the same principles [in regard to metal currency] and since it is the experience of men over several thousands of years that gold and silver circulate as mediums of exchange, my conclusions are clearly not unreasonable.

I heard as a child that the Taikō Hideyoshi[3] was able to draw large quantities of gold from China by encouraging trade with the

Chinese. It is said that more than half the gold coins of the Keichō Period[4] were also produced from this source. Deeply reflecting on the aftermath of military destruction that attended the hundred years of disturbances after the Ōnin Period,[5] Hideyoshi must have acquired a deep appreciation of these monetary principles.

It is rumored that close to Yen 100,000,000 of paper notes have recently been printed in our country. This averages three yen per head if you divide the Yen 100,000,000 among our estimated 30 million people without excluding a man, woman, or child. It may be that this large sum is beyond the resources of Japan. Then how should we truly value each note of paper currency? It may be thought that, since the bills can be freely printed according to man's whim, their value will be freely determined in the marketplace. If paper money circulates through the world in fixed denominations without being redeemed, it is put on the same level as bullion. I am extremely doubtful as to whether this will promote a spirit of freedom among the people or lead again to austerity.

In ancient times, after Chao Kao[6] brought a deer to the son of the Ch'in emperor and falsely represented it as a horse, the minister was executed and the country ultimately destroyed. Having been handed down through the generations as a joke, the word *baka*[7] composed of the ideographs for horse and deer still means "fool" today. I think that there is no room for wonder that men like Chao Kao and [John] Law were ultimately destroyed since they really acted in violation of [monetary] principles.

Because I have cited such historic examples in connection with the civilized society of our country of today, my hearers may become angry and criticize my remarks as inappropriate. Yet I have not willingly uttered improper words. I really have something to say. The movement of our society is faster than a team of four horses. There has been an unprecedented change in domestic conditions as we have moved from a closed country to expelling the barbarians, from expelling the barbarians to opening the ports, and from feudalism to the system of counties and prefectures. [The last twenty years] seem to have exceeded a century. It seems that since the opening of the ports those who honor the country and revere the emperor have exported hundreds of millions in gold and silver, the exact figures for which are probably beyond reckoning. Moreover, we know that, when bullion exports are large and domestic production is small, bullion will stop flowing once it is exhausted and that this will be a time of popular unrest. Foreigners will also gain no profit from trade if only paper money remains after domestic gold and silver is finally exhausted. Having neither acquired land nor sought Japanese nationality, foreign merchants will have no other recourse but to withdraw gradually and cease sending ships. Then our country will naturally enter a state of seclusion, the public will gradually confront frugal conditions, and this austerity will become increasingly extreme as the present generation gives way to the next. Once this juncture has been reached, we cannot know whether the theories of Communism espoused in France will begin to penetrate the country or whether we may establish a type of great power by moving toward the still more harsh ways of Sparta. Even though the course of history may not be predicted, I believe such to be the situation, having pondered the future toward which we are now moving. This is not a known future derived from the past. I am simply conjecturing on an imaginary closed country.

An Appendix to Four Essays on the Currency[8]

Kanda Kōhei

When I wrote four essays on the currency prospects, there were not a few instances in which I suffered criticism from correspondents in public. Among them, I recall some that were indeed praiseworthy and others that were absolutely wrong in their prognoses. My meaning may not yet be entirely clear since my power of expression is inadequate. Thinking that further explanation may now help to improve public opinion, I am presenting the following ill-considered thoughts.

One critic holds that the paper currency system in Japan is the same as those in the United States and Italy. I am completely unfamiliar with the Italian system, and I do not even know the American system well. Judging from a few reports on the latter and conjecturing the rest, however, I feel that the American system is entirely different from that of Japan. First, since I hear that the laws of the United States are as a rule determined during legislative debates in a body known as a national assembly, I believe that currency regulations also must invariably be considered [by that body]. If such after all be the case, the people of the entire country are all guarantors of the paper currency, and the assets of the entire country are all collateral for the notes. Who will deny the justice of this system? The paper currency in our country is different, however. The ambiguity of our system arises from the fact that it is arbitrarily decided and secretly carried out by one or two officers. Even those in important positions in the government offices and ministries are for the most part not consulted. Still less do the people of the nation deliberate currency matters. This is the most important difference between their system and ours.

Second, as paper currency in the United States was only issued during the war, I understand that none has been printed since the war. Such is not the case in Japan, where a very large amount of currency has been printed since the war. Paper currency in 1868 was definitely limited to 32.5 million *ryō*; about 3 million yen in paper notes were issued by 1871 in return for deposits of old gold and silver; bonds of the Hokkaidō Colonization Bureau (*Kaitakushi*)[9] amounted to 2.5 million yen by 1872; and, according to recent hearsay, total note issues already far exceed 100 million yen. One has no way of knowing where this will end.

Third, the United States does not prohibit fluctuations in the value of paper money. It is said that the value of $100 in paper is a little over $70 in hard currency. For this reason, there is no damage from exports of specie, and the country should suffer no loss. Our country does not permit establishment of a market price for our paper currency, and this error has led to exports of specie. Given such differences between the paper currency systems in our country and the United States, I think that it would be wrong to uphold the perfection of our paper currency by citing the example of the United States.

A critic states that there will be no interruption in the circulation of paper currency even during a foreign war if our country makes it legal tender, causes it to be circulated by law, and by these means has established commodity prices. According to my way of thinking, there then should be no interruption in circulation during peace if there is none during war. That is, there will ultimately be no time when circulation is obstructed. If such after all be the case, then why have not all countries of all ages rushed as fast as possible to establish this legal tender? And why do they make such a big fuss to laboriously establish hard currencies? If war breaks out with a foreign country after we have depended upon and trusted the opinions of this gentleman, I do not guar antee that the country will not fall into a perilous abyss.

Since I doubt the sufficiency of my explanation, that the export of specie is attributable to the failure to convert paper money into specie, I would discuss the problem as follows. The export of specie arises from inadequate exports of goods; inadequate exports of goods arise from high commodity prices; high commodity prices arise from a surplus of money; a money surplus arises when paper money is not converted into specie; and specie exports arise, therefore, from a failure to convert paper. Take the example of two men, A and B. A has Yen 100; B is empty-handed. Now when B borrows the money by subscribing to a note that states that he will make repayment upon request, B possesses Yen 100 in hard currency, and A holds Yen 100 as a note. Yet the two possess between them Yen 100 as before. If we assume that the note can circulate equally with specie without being redeemed, however, the note is converted into legal tender, and the property held by the two men then amounts to Yen 200, the sum of the legal tender and the specie. Please note that they hold Yen 200 if the legal tender is not redeemed and Yen 100 if it is redeemed. This is why I have said that a surplus of money arises when paper money is not converted. The price of commodities varies with the amount of currency. For example, if there are 100 items and yen 100, the price of one item will be one yen. If the currency is now increased to Yen 200, however, the price of one item should also increase to two yen. This is what I previously referred to as the high commodity price that arises from a surplus of money. In addition, there should be no necessity to discuss in detail the principle that commodity exports decrease with rising commodity prices while specie exports increase if commodity exports decrease.

A critic also states that the outflow of specie would not be halted even if paper currency is actually converted. This states only half the case. Foreigners, of course, generally dislike paper currency, and it is natural, therefore, that they invariably take hard currency for their salaries and to cover the difference between exports and imports. Nevertheless, if specie is freely exported for these purposes, the domestic specie will decrease, and its value will increase. Commodity prices will go down as its value increases. If commodity prices go down, exports will increase. And since these increased commodity exports will stimulate imports of specie equal to the specie that had been previously exported, the result will be the same as if there had been no exports of specie in the first place. On the other hand, there is a contrary line of reasoning as follows. When paper is not converted, the value of specie will not increase even though its quantity is reduced. Commodity prices will not fall since the value of specie does not rise, and there will be no increase of commodity exports since the value of commodities has not fallen. Commodity exports failing to increase, therefore, specie will be constantly exported, and it will not return to the country for a long time.

Another critic asks why the United States is not troubled by specie exports even though its paper currency is not converted. I would respond that this arises from the fact that trading in paper is permitted. Since it is possible to change paper into hard money at any time if trading in paper is permitted, the situation is no different from conversion. Now to be more precise, the value of specie will increase if large amounts are exported. If the value of specie increases, no injury to normal conditions of circulation will develop since the [values] of commodities and paper currency will depreciate together.

Still another critic observes that, by resorting to the means of redeeming the paper through flotation of public bonds, we shall establish a policy for converting to specie. This idea is extremely sophisticated. Without expressing myself for the moment on this point, I would just ask one question. Will the paper currency not be reissued once it has been redeemed? Were the paper to be reissued, the damage would be far more serious. What does my critic think of this? (A response to No. 885 of the *Nichi Nichi Shimbun.*)[10]

Another comments that I, in my list of sorrows on the export of specie, was guilty of omission when I stated that mining and customs duties are the only two ways for bringing in specie. He asks if the large expenditures by foreigners employed within the country are not also a means by which specie is recovered. I would respond that I am pleased to recognize his words as correct. (An answer to an anonymous correspondent.)

In addition to the above criticisms, I have often heard people say that the exports of specie are not enough to worry about. These seem to be people who speak without reflecting on the disease of paper money. If only there were not this disease of paper money, they would be quite correct since, as previously stated, specie would be returned to the country once it had been exported. Nevertheless, I am worried because, for the sole reason that we suffer from the disease of paper money, specie is only departing without returning and is unlikely to return hereafter. I beg my critics to reconsider.

Desire[11]

Tsuda Mamichi

As our most important innate quality, desire is the basis of human existence. How could the human race reproduce itself if we lacked desire as part of our nature? Had men lacked desire, then the human race would long since have become extinct. Food, drink, and sex are the major urges of living things in general. They are not confined to men alone. How could we live for even a day if we lack the desire for food and drink? Without the sexual desire how would we produce descendants? Not to speak of multiply! Someone may respond: "Even though we lack the attribute of desire, the Creator endowed us with wisdom. Wisdom is the attribute with which man understands the reasons for all things. Since we are endowed with wisdom, we clearly understand that we shall quickly die unless we eat and drink. Even though desire is lacking from the human attributes, therefore, we can know by exercising wisdom that we must eat and drink." This, however, is forcing what one's nature does not desire, like the sick man who compels himself to eat. If such were the case, how difficult human life would be! Yet there would be no alternative but to live in such fashion. When it comes to sexual desire, how can its lack be made up by the efforts of wisdom? I say, therefore, that desire is undoubtedly the Creator's great gift as it is the means by which He brings pleasure and comfort to our lives and by which He bestows great blessings on men.

The basic cravings for food, drink, and sex are human desires arising naturally from man's innate character. There are also desires born of wisdom and customs, however. Men poor in wisdom and customs may indeed be without desires, but those rich in wisdom and customs cannot lack compelling desires even for a moment. Since these desires are as strong as natural desires, the desires of enlightened peoples are larger and more numerous than those of barbarians. For example, [enlightened people] smoke tobacco and enjoy music and poetry.

Such are the reasons why desire is so important for us human beings. Buddha, however, regarded worldly passions as criminal, and Confucian scholars held human desires to be injurious. How are we to regard those who teach that man should endeavor to abandon desire? These thinkers vainly looked at the injuries of desire without considering its benefits. After all, men will reach the point of killing their innate consciences and destroying the true character of morality if, without consideration, they indulge only in the desires of the world, are addicted to avarice, descend to miserliness, and know not when they are sated in an orgy. It is impossible to assess the injury by these people to morality. This is the purport of the Buddhist and Confucian teachings that man should endeavor to abandon worldly passions and overcome human desires. Even though their intentions were good, their teachings unavoidably compromised moderation. How amusing it was when Buddha went so far as to shut out sexual craving and fasted.

Now the right of liberty is our inherent human right that is most honored by the various civilized countries. It is wrong, however, for men in the least to injure the liberty of others by abusively asserting their own rights. This misuse of liberty, therefore, is called arbitrariness. Have not all East Asians traditionally regarded freedom as a vice because they have seen only its misuse without recognizing its benefits? They have thus ultimately destroyed the true meaning of liberty, and slavish and mean customs have emerged among the people generally. Even though ambition for profit is an inherent quality that conduces to increasing human physical well-being, its abuse as avarice and greed should indeed be abhored. The teachings of the Confucians, however, only preached human-heartedness without investigating studies of political economy. That the East Asian countries have all been impoverished without achieving prosperity and that their people generally lack bodily welfare may be attributed to the fact that the Confucian teachings were without validity.

We may also scoff at the scholars of the Chu Hsi school who adopted the view that human desire and Heaven's Reason were mutually incompatible. How can they say that human desire is contrary to Heaven's Reason? Wishing to penetrate the nature of things, admiring the new, relishing liberty, wanting happiness, and other desires are all most fine human aspirations. Are they not essentials of human nature? After all, they are all factors that contribute to our human progress.

Western scholars have analyzed human nature to determine three qualities: wisdom, passion, and will. Wisdom is for knowing; passion, for desiring; and will, for acting. According to my way of thinking, it is bad for passion to overcome wisdom and good for wisdom to overcome passion. Thus when scholars investigate things to determine knowledge in the hundred arts and sciences, their efforts are invariably for the purpose of advancing this wisdom. There is the common saying that doctors fail to heal and scholars misbehave because they have not yet cultivated wisdom. Even so, I must add that the means for controlling passion are essential to morality since it is most difficult for us to attain enlightened wisdom.

[1]*Fujiyū*, 不自由.

[2]Between 1736 and 1774 and again after 1835, the Tokugawa bakufu (德川幕府) responded to the public demand for increased coinage by ordering the issuance of iron coins to supplement the existing copper coins.

[3]The appelation Taikō (太閤), retired regent, is the popular designation for Toyotomi Hideyoshi, (豐臣秀吉), 1536–1598. Japan's supply of gold in the late sixteenth

century was dramatically increased by both expanded domestic production and importations from China.

[4]Keichō, 慶長, the period from 1596 to 1615.

[5]The Ōnin (應仁) War, 1467–1477, was followed by approximately a century of civil wars.

[6]Chao Kao, 趙高, a notorious eunuch of the Ch'in (秦) Dynasty who was assassinated in 207 B.C.

[7]*Baka,* 馬鹿.

[8]Continued from the previous issue.

[9]*Kaitakushi,* 開拓使, an agency charged with the development of Hokkaidō (北海道) from 1869 to 1881.

[10]*Nichi Nichi Shimbun,* 日日新聞, a prominent Tokyo newspaper.

[11]Desire, *Jōyoku,* 情欲.

China Should Not Be Despised[1]

Nakamura Masanao

As may be seen by referring to history, China has produced numerous outstanding men, turning out sages, superior men, and heroes one after another. Should you desire their names recited in their entirety, they could not be exhausted even if you relieve me with an assistant. This is the first reason why China should not be despised. China can probably take first place in the East in the abundance of her writings. Furthermore, being tasteful, her prose can readily convey men's intentions. And having strict grammatical rules, it is also convenient for translating foreign materials. Even in daily communications, we must invariably use Chinese words when dealing with important matters. The Chinese seem to have a particular genius for contriving ideographs. As their own writing possesses some grace, they do not easily change to horizontal script or yearn for Western literary styles. Yet since China is a country skilled in letters, young Chinese studying abroad may emerge one after another within a few years to advance their [Western] studies to a high level. This is the second reason why China should not be despised.

Being now under a Tartar house, even the public-spirited men of China are disinclined to exert their natural vigor, and her people are seemingly in a drugged condition unable to move their arms and feet. If they throw off the poison of the Tartar drug and awake from their stupor, however, a Han Kao Tsu may emerge from the village headmen of Ssŭ Shui[2] or a Ming T'ai Tsu may come forth from the monks of Huang-chüeh Ssŭ.[3] In troubled times, a Hsiao Ho[4] may emerge from the lower officialdom or a Fan K'uai[5] from among the dog butchers. Or there may appear suddenly from among the peasants, beggars, or horse-traders in the town markets a civil official like Liu Ch'êng-i[6] or military officers like Hsü Ta[7] and Ch'ang Yü-ch'un,[8] who climbed the dragon's scales and mounted the wings of the phoenix.[9] How do we know that there is not a Han Kao Tsu or a Ming T'ai Tsu among the beggars to be seen in Shanghai today? How do we know that there is not a Hsiao, a Ts'ao, a Liu, or a Hsü[10] of another day among the children peddling in today's Tientsin? If from among the leading families of China Proper that bear the name of Li or Liu[11] there emerges a great hero who destroys the Manchu-Ch'ing Dynasty and who by resolute decree directs the use of the arts and sciences of Europe and America, he can quickly introduce steamships, trains, telegraph, fortifications, and warships the great distances between the eighteen provinces and the two capitals notwithstanding. Moreover, we will face an extremely serious situation should [China] then establish a popularly elected assembly and attempt to avenge the shame of defeat.[12] This is the third reason why China should not be despised.

That China produces many raw materials is entirely natural since she is a large country. Even in manufactures, however, her exports to Japan of ink, paper, and books alone have been extremely large for more than a century. Maki Ryōko[13] states that it should be appreciated that the Japanese calligraphers never equal those of China for no other reason than that Japanese craftsmen are clumsy at producing writing brushes. The Chinese in ancient times made useful skills of mathematics and astronomy in which they were extremely proficient. Our country employed Chinese texts on medicine and horticulture until twenty years ago. In addition, this country has not matched China in the large number of useful instruments that the Chinese have invented. In the words of an English friend, "The Chinese people are good, but their government is bad." If the above statement proves correct, once her government is reformed, China will necessarily progress since her people are really of a good type. This is the fourth reason why China should not be despised.

I hear that the following story is included in a textbook for instructing children in Russian:

> When a child uttered words abusive of China, his father admonished him as follows: "Rather than despised, China should be honored as a nation that has taught our country. That is to say, there are many matters in which our forefathers derived

> benefit from China as she was ahead of our country in developing the arts and sciences. Even though she is now asleep, China should not be despised since, once awake, she will become a dreadful enemy."

The Russians are indeed far-sighted. For young people to be inclined from childhood to despise something after observing it to be inferior to themselves is the root of superficiality. Petty superficiality may ruin a family; gross superficiality may destroy a nation. Furthermore, only to slander a country recklessly for her faults without recognizing her merits will cause her to be angry and us to be negligent. This is the height of foolishness. Since even a country like Russia, which surpasses China in many respects, thus admonishes [respect for China], should our country look down on her when we are brothers of equal power? This is the fifth reason why China should not be despised.

At the time of the recent incident between China and Japan, Li Hung-chang[14] judged that, should war break out, England and France could compel an armistice and that his shame would be still more extreme if an armistice were forced by other nations. Thus for the large country to submit to the small country and to reach a settlement by means of an indemnity was sufficient to indicate the virtue of Li's broad-mindedness and good judgment. Again, our country employed a number of foreigners at its headquarters without relying on its own people alone. It is indeed not known whether Li was assisted by Thomas Wade,[15] the English minister. But we naturally cannot guess the real reason why Li decisively departed from the tradition of viewing Japan as barbarian and treated the Japanese with utmost politeness. This is the sixth reason why China should not be despised.

Enlightenment in our country is now being fostered by foreigners rather than advanced by our own efforts. The situation is one in which, rather than using foreigners, we are being used by them. We have reached the point where [officials] within the various ministries are shifting their burdens to foreigners hired at exorbitant salaries. We cannot know whether the Chinese will cease admiring the foreigners once China has been induced to study Europe and America and surpassed the West in knowledge. If we disparage China, feeling that we have acquired a part of Western culture, we shall be scorned by intellectuals as this is just like the person who looks down on a man in rags after donning beautiful clothes borrowed from another. This is the seventh reason why China should not be despised. As the old proverb goes, "An individual should clean away the snow from before his own gate before he inquires into the frost on his neighbor's roof." We shall not have much time to reflect on others if we hereafter assiduously cultivate ourselves by devoting our attention to our nation's affairs and appreciating its inadequacies. Still less will we presume to despise other countries!

Descending from Heaven   Speech on April 1, 1875

Sakatani Shiroshi

There are no heights and depths in the world. What is high for others may be low for us. Once persons exist, however, there are families and nations into which these persons were born and reside. Looked at in relation to their nation and family, these individuals are separated into high and low and into insiders and outsiders. Once these distinctions are clarified, there then naturally emerges a difference in outlook between the exalted and the humble views. Yet if it is assumed that there is no mutual relationship between these points of view, those [persons] who regard matters from an elevated point of view will be prejudiced in the lofty direction, and those who look at matters from a humble view will be inclined toward the lowly position. The high and low being isolated, Heaven's Reason (*Tenri*) and the Human Way (*Jindō*)[16] both suffer. When looking down from an elevated position, affairs of the universe seem to be entirely encompassed by Heaven's Reason and Nature (*Shizen*)[17] without room for human contributions. On the other hand, when one looks up from the humble position, it seems that Heaven is only concerned with Heaven and unrelated to human beings. From this lower view, it appears that matters of the universe are wholly human and wholly contrived and that nothing depends on Nature or on Heaven's Reason.

Yet the fundamentals of Heaven's Reason and the Human Way are one, and the two function by mutually assisting each other. To allow Nature to take its course, therefore, is like growing the five grains without fertilizing or weeding. And to allow human artifice free course is like trying to elongate the grains with one's hands because they are not growing fast enough. Both methods are injurious. Therefore, human artifice should be judiciously cultivated (*saisei hoshō*)[18] in accordance with the logic of Heaven's Reason and Nature. It is invariably biased to incline in one direction or another. Even though Tsuda Sen appears artificially to stretch young plants by bending their branches to produce a profusion of fruit and flowers,[19] he is developing the art of judicious cultivation by guiding his plants according to the nature of their life. Discussion of world matters and the conduct of human affairs should indeed be in this manner. Then we shall really establish methods of enlightened achievement (*kaibutsu seimu*).[20] We must seriously consider the fact, however, that there have often been persons during all ages who, for their own ulterior reasons, have inclined to the high or to the low.

If one inclines to the view of an outsider who looks down from above, he will be dazzled by the grandeur of Heaven, and he will feel that all human contrivances are complete foolishness, disturbing to mind and injurious to body. He will also think that affairs of the world should be left solely to Nature. The Enlightenment of *Zen*[21] and the Way (*Tao*) of Lao Tzŭ and Chuang Tzŭ[22] arose in large part from this type of thought. Their virtue is that they try to depart from worldly lust and to put into practice a true morality that relies upon a higher justice. Even so, their vice is that they bestow their love equally, making no distinction between their own fathers and the fathers of others, good and bad, right and wrong, sweet and putrid. Being egotistical libertines, they fall into despair. Such people eventually are undisturbed even by the destruction of family and nation, believing this to be natural. Mencius detested despair. And in Western literature as well it is said that God helps those who help themselves and that God will do nothing for those who give up in despair.

There are also those who, while not despairing, lose their judgment as they are blinded by the fashions and affairs of the boundless world. Tiring of homeland and family where Heaven gave them birth and losing their spirit of patriotism, these people reject their origins and completely become the slaves to other countries. They imitate every foreign way like monkeys. Despised even by country women, they are like the fool who thinks healthy women deformed after falling in love with a noseless syphilitic. Such persons may reach the point of thinking foreign excreta elegant even though it stinks and foreign clothing beautiful even though it is tattered. When students learn from a teacher, they stress the cultivation of their individual intellects according to their own dispositions. What is the consequence, however, when students gather to learn the errors and bad habits of this or that teacher? It is always slavish and barbaric to invite derision by imitating others. There are numerous cases of country bumpkins who come to the city, are captivated by the gay quarters, forget their training and abandon their heritage, enter brothels to become pimps and panders, and boast of themselves as enlightened men of the world. These are all injuries that arise from aimlessly making no distinctions.

If men only look up from below without escaping inner bias, they neither appreciate the beauties of the outside nor understand the vastness of reason, they honor their own fathers and their own lords without recognizing the fathers and lords of others in the world, and they do not yearn for progress as they are bound by old customs. Such self-centered people also sink into despair. The ancient Chinese assumed that their country, as the especial charge of Heaven, was alone nurtured by Heaven. In old Japan, the people also thought foreign countries barbarian or they assumed that the world had been entirely created by their nation's ancestors. Even though feelings of respect and love of country may be deep, they contradict Heaven's Reason and the Human Way when they are narrow and bigoted. Such narrow and bigoted adulation of country rather contributes to disparagement and abomination of the country [by the people] and to derision by the world. In former days, the followers of great lords would hold that the capital was in desolation when their lord was in his domain. And there are also the foolish sons of rich and noble houses who think that their father takes the highest seat wherever he goes. Such people are indeed beyond benefit of education. They are all narrow bigots who compromise the value of making distinctions.

As it may be bad either to make distinctions or not to make distinctions, therefore, we should incline neither to the high nor to the low. If you ask how we should accomplish this, I feel that we as individuals should first regard the world impartially from above with the feeling of having ascended to Heaven. While making clear the distinctions between various things and countries as we do with the stars, we shall understand that all things, large or small, have shape and principles individual to themselves without distinctions in rank whether they be our country and parents or their countries and parents. And we shall also understand that we cannot artificially influence the endowments of Nature, as some things possess strength and others weakness, while some are confused even as others are well ordered. Thereafter, entrusting to the Will of "God" or Heaven, we should view matters after descending to the countries in which we were born.

Now looking at this country after descending from Heaven, the country of my birth is Japan, and we should love Japan. The sovereign is the ruler of our Japan, not the ruler of England, or Russia, or Prussia, or Austria. We were given birth by our parents in our Japan and not of Swiss, American, Italian, or French parents. After ruler and parents, there are elder brothers and seniors, the friends with whom we consort, and the wives and children with whom we share burdens. None of these are foreigners. Still further distinguishing matters within the country, there are clear distinctions between our possessions and those of others and between our relatives and those of others. There will be confusion if we attempt to mix these things and partiality if we do not conform to principle once the distinctions are made. In this manner, having first been rooted in Heaven's Reason by looking out from above, we shall then promote enterprises for enlightened achievement, prevent calamities, avoid hardships, and deal with the Human Way in the particular countries below to which we have individually brought Reason from Heaven. In this manner also, protection of peace and happiness will be advanced day by day and month by month like the gradual growth of pines and oaks or like the strengthening and nourishing [of bodies] by catering to the five tastes. Of course, there are often exceptional times and unusual circumstances when it is impossible to realize these intentions and this Way. But they are exceptional and not the rule. To incline either to the high or to the low by losing the norm in time of emergency is just like going mad under the influence of evil spirits. We can only then return to normalcy by protecting and healing.

Thus viewed, we should not honor the fathers of others equally with our own even though we also should not injure their fathers on account of ours. And while consideration for our ruler should not lead us to hurt the rulers of foreign countries, we also should not honor foreign rulers as we do our own. Honoring becomes flattery if we honor obsequiously by looking up from below without looking down from above in accordance with universal principle. This is the same as killing one's beloved child by allowing him to overeat. Honoring in accordance with universal principle is no more than to search collectively for security and happiness and to promote the path of protection common to all men. We should not concede anything on this point. This is avoiding bias by looking from both high and low, judicious cultivation of Heaven's Reason, and the fair conduct of human affairs. To deride England, Russia, Prussia, and Austria by comparing them with America and Switzerland, therefore, is to adopt a biased view without looking down from above. It is similarly biased to criticize Japan by comparing her with America, Switzerland, England, Russia, Prussia, and Austria.

What we should deride is that we cannot claim one discovery as an enlightened achievement of our country. That we have made no discoveries may be attributed to the fact that we have not put into practice these universal principles because methods for guiding human affairs are mired at the lower level. That is, we should establish the foundations for a type of individual identity by looking broadly at the affairs of the European and American states and by investigating their true principles after casting aside their superficialities. Mill has said that the foundation of a powerful state is a public mind that loathes peace and loves struggle. And Confucius has stated that there is no repose when Heaven's Will is strong and when superior men are independent. With what shall we establish the foundations for a strong country and with what shall we achieve discoveries if men's minds are not strong in spirit, if they are content in idleness and peace, and if they are not prepared for an emergency?

To establish one's liberty and freedom arises from the lower view since it concerns the individual. And to refrain from mutually obstructing intercourse arises from an elevated view being concerned with all men. The Human Way is based on the mutual association of these two views. Pursuing this line of reasoning, these two views are found in families, in villages and counties, in prefectures, in boards and ministries, and also in the entire nation. From antiquity, our country has desisted from intercourse with foreign nations as it has inclined toward freedom and independence. Recently, we have finally opened the country and understood the importance of intercourse. Yet [this open view] has not yet been adopted by our individuals, families, counties, prefectures, boards, and ministries. Intercourse between high and low has been so extremely obstructed that we seem to be mutually suppressed by so-called "despotism." While officials and people outwardly have intercourse, they have actually established their selfish views for oppressing each other. This is interjecting "despotism" or old-fashioned "barbarism" into fraternal relations. In this manner, while we study Europe and America, we are actually only importing their vices, especially imitating their superficialities and losing our original character.

How then can we acquire their truths and merits? There is no doubt that there is no preventing the constant changes in our country's course, which is like that of a ship dangerously adrift in wind and waves. Further, when one considers the prefectural level, the people are indeed ignorant, but they are generally only people who honor their rulers obediently and are easily moved by old traditions of humbleness. Prefectural officials should govern effortlessly if they are upright in mind and conduct, put aside selfish concern for personal and family freedom, clarify the principles of intercourse, honor their responsibility to protect, and promote men's wisdom by their unperturbable management [of affairs]. What difficulties can then arise?

However, take the example of the officials who cherish particular prejudices in their hearts, who suppress the equal rights of the people by means of petty class distinctions, and who disparage the principle of cooperation between high and low by distinguishing between their own interests and those of the people. In extreme cases, such men cater to their private whims, take as personal councillors the subordinates and cunning fellows by whose fraud they have been led astray, resort to secrecy in numerous matters, encourage concealment in conduct, and mislead the people by deceit. Then when their rule fails, these officials blame the ignorance of the people without accusing themselves and attribute troubles to the people while relying on the press to spread their own fame. How can such conduct be described?

Reflecting on the ministries and councils in this light, by what means shall we establish the path of intercourse if officials expand their own independent interests, if under the pretext of enlightenment they destroy the ancient sentiments that serve their country, if like mice they all bow humbly before foreign countries while disparaging our countrymen, and if they pretend friendship toward foreigners while hating foreigners in their hearts? By what means will a nation assure its freedom and independence if it has not established the path of intercourse? Moreover, taxation and finance are the foundation of the state and the public business of the nation. But discussion of such important matters will never be conducted if they are always postponed, if they are handled secretly, and if there are attempts to smooth over intercourse both within and without by employing empty rights and futile laws. Then even leaders of brave and noble appearance, being quavering abroad and fearful at home, can only be mouselike in their inner hearts, and the people below them will be without direction and undecided in their minds. [With such officials and such people], is there no danger that the whole country will finally expend its resources, exhaust its power, and actually become enslaved?

To establish rights of freedom and independence, therefore, we should first clarify the harmonious principles of intercourse by observing the world from above. Then after descending from Heaven to stand in our respective lands, we should make clear what should be protected of our own and what should not be injured of our substance in conformity with [what we observe] to be appropriate to the conditions and tendencies in our country, families, prefectures, councils, and ministries. Only by thus avoiding confusion and bigoted bias, by appreciating the principles governing Heaven and man above and below, and by expending our mental power in judicious cultivation can we expect the natural achievement [of the rights of freedom and independence]. This is the fundamental basis upon which affairs are conducted and enterprises are established in scholarship, in governing, and among human beings generally.

Distinguishing the Equal Rights of Husbands and Wives

Tsuda Mamichi

Why is it that the phrase "the equal rights of husbands and wives" (*fūfu dōken*),[23] having recently come into circulation, is scattered through the press as well as mistakenly uttered by accomplished gentlemen? Now "the equal rights of men and women" (*danjo dōken*)[24] are words that previously have been intoned quite often in the countries of Europe and America, and they correspond exactly to the position of Western men and women from the point of view of civil rights (*minken*).[25] For example, there is absolutely no discrimination or differentiation between the rights of men and women when one consults the stipulations in Western civil codes that establish personal rights, property rights, and the rights and duties of contract. Yet there are naturally distinctions between the public rights of men and women that relate to national political affairs. After all, women are unable to share these public rights as they have been customarily monopolized by men. This is for the reason that women have not yet participated in the three great rights of legislation, justice, and administration. Even though there have been suggestions that women should also share in these public rights, this has not yet actually been practiced.

On the other hand, there has been absolutely no provision even in civil law for what might be called "the equal rights of husbands and wives." This is because the husband is the person who controls the family's affairs as head of the household. A woman possessed of a husband, being a wife, is not allowed by civil law to manage the family's affairs except under extraordinary circumstances. Not only this, a wife also has not the right to manage even her private property, and a woman possessed of a husband does not have the right to institute civil suits in her own name. These are areas in which the provisions of Western civil codes differentiate between the rights of husbands and wives. This ought to be entirely understandable from one reading of the writings of Westerners on civil law. I am incredulous, therefore, when I hear references from time to time to "the equal rights of husbands and wives."

Even though husbands and wives do not possess the same rights under the law, they are naturally equal without distinction as to high or low in their traditional marital intercourse. After all, none doubt that husbands and wives should employ the proprieties of equals as was indeed the case in our ancient Japanese customs. Asians, however, debased womanhood to such an extreme degree that they do not enjoy what is called equal rights of men and women even under civil law. Especially, there is the evil among the Chinese in which wives, like criminals, are all shut up in their courtyards and forbidden any contact with outsiders. This is an extremely outrageous custom. Without appreciating this [great evil], gentlemen in society vainly discuss the minor abuse in which the frailty of wives is protected under Western custom. I also fail to understand the reason for this. How do [these gentlemen] hope to overtake the far higher level of European and American civilization and enlightenment? After all, this not being their intent, they have finally fallen to the evil of capricious progress. Let us reflect what in the final analysis will be their situation if they are moved to attempt the establishment of a popularly elected assembly? Undoubtedly, uneducated and unskilled fellows, with tumultuous clamor, will want to do things that have not yet been done in the countries of Europe and America. How will this achieve happiness for the people and the nation? As the proverb goes, "Superficial tactics are the source of great wounds." I would just say that superficial enlightenment is the cause of rebellion. Should we not be prudent? As I fear that I have reached the point of redundancy in elucidating the error of "equal rights of husbands and wives," I beg your kind indulgence.

[1]Before he gained his reputation as one of the enlighteners of the early Meiji Period, Nakamura had demonstrated remarkable brilliance at the *Shōheikō* (昌平黌), the prestigious Confucian college whose thought was in the Chu Hsi (朱熹) tradition. Being deeply rooted in Chinese studies, Nakamura naturally deplored the inclination

among his people to look down on China because Japan was more rapidly adopting at least the more superficial trappings of the West and had won an indemnity of Tls. 500,000 from China in the recent negotiations over the Formosa incident.

[2]Han Kao Tsu, 漢高祖, was the farmer Liu Pang (劉邦) and headman of the village of Ssŭ Shui (泗水) before he emerged to found the Han Dynasty in 202 B.C.

[3]Ming T'ai Tsu, 明太祖, the founder of the Ming Dynasty, started as the impoverished Chu Yüan-chang (朱元璋), who sought support by entering the temple named Huang-chüeh Ssŭ (皇覺寺).

[4]Hsiao Ho, 蕭何, d. 193 B.C., a humble official who arose with Liu Pang to become chief minister of the Han Dynasty.

[5]Fan K'uai, 樊噲, d. 189 B.C., a dog butcher who joined fortune with Liu Pang, the founder of the Han Dynasty.

[6]Liu Ch'êng-i, 劉誠意, a polite designation for Liu Chi (劉基), 1311–1375, an official who helped Chu Yüan-chang establish the Ming Dynasty.

[7]Hsü Ta, 徐達, 1329–1383, a commander who fought with Chu Yüan-chang to expel the Mongols from China.

[8]Ch'ang Yü-ch'un, 常遇春, 1330–1369, a bandit who joined with Chu Yüan-chang to win victories for the Ming.

[9]To climb the dragon's scales and mount the wings of the pheonix, *ryōrin o yoji hōyoku ni tsuku,* 龍鱗ヲ攀ジ鳳翼ニ附ク, a phrase meaning to rise to the greatest height.

[10]In addition to Hsiao Ho, Liu Cheng-i, and Hsü Ta previously noted, Nakamura here refers to Ts'ao Ts'an, 曹參, d. 190 B.C., who continued the work of Hsiao Ho in helping Liu Pang establish the Han dynasty.

[11]Li, 李, and Liu, 劉, were the family names of the T'ang (唐) and Han (漢) dynasties, respectively.

[12]Nakamura here refers to the shame of Kueichi (會稽), a battle in which King Kou Chien (勾踐) of Yüeh (越) was disastrously defeated by King Fu Ch'a (夫差) of Wu (呉). Years later, Kou Chien avenged the shame of his defeat by destroying his rival.

[13]Maki Ryōko, 卷菱湖, 1777–1843, a famous Japanese calligrapher.

[14]Li Hung-chang, 李鴻章, the governor-general of Chihli (直隸). It appears that the Japanese representative in the negotiations, Ōkubo Toshimichi (大久保利通), dealt with the *Tsungli Yamen* (總理衙門), the Chinese foreign office, rather than with Li Hung-chang.

[15]Sir Thomas Francis Wade, the British minister in Peking, served as mediator in bringing the settlement.

[16]*Tenri,* 天理, and *Jindō,* 人道.

[17]*Shizen,* 自然.

[18]*Saisei hoshō,* 裁成輔相.

[19]Tsuda Sen, 津田仙, the agricultural expert among the Meirokusha. See Issue Forty-One.

[20]*Kaibutsu seimu,* 開物成務.

[21]*Zen,* 禪.

[22]As a Confucian scholar, Sakatani could have no sympathy for the mystical *Tao* (道) of Lao Tzŭ (老子) and Chuang Tzŭ (莊子), even as the Taoists held Confucian ethics in contempt.

[23]*Fūfu dōken,* 夫婦同權. This article should be read as a response to Katō Hiroyuki's views on *fūfu dōken* in Issue Thirty-One and an amplification of Tsuda's own essay on the distinction between husbands and wives (*fūfu yūbetsu,* 夫婦有別) in Issue Twenty-Three. Whereas Tsuda rejects the teaching by Mencius that the spheres of husband

and wife are separate as well as the claim by Katō that the social civilities in the West point to the superiority of Western women over men, he also affirms that wives and women even in the West do not enjoy full equality with husbands and men. Essentially, he seems to agree with Mori Arinori that husbands and wives should be equal in their marital intercourse.

[24]*Danjo dōken,* 男女同權.

[25]*Minken,* 民權.

MEIROKU ZASSHI Issue Thirty-Six May 1875

Descending from Heaven (Concluded)[1]

Sakatani Shiroshi

Let us consider the meaning of exalted and humble views from the standpoint of nations. Since nations individually possess distinctive environmental conditions, their governments are also different, and they employ appropriate human contrivances to adjust to the differences in Heaven's Reason (*Tenri*)[2] and Nature (*Shizen*).[3] This conduct arises from the humble view. Turning to relations between countries, these relations are established by mutual discussion and conducted by methods of human contrivance in accordance with the harmonious combination of Heaven's Reason and Nature. This arises from the elevated view. International relations are universal; the law of individual nations, domestic. International and domestic are not mutually contradictory, external and internal being distinct. They have their individual spheres, being divided but not separated and associated but not mixed. Matters should generally be determined in this sense. A nation will not establish its independence if, aimlessly and in confusion, it is the slave of foreign countries. But if a nation clings to old traditions without knowing that they should be changed or if, desiring change, it fails to adopt the appropriate path of change, international relations will be injured, and the nation also will not survive.

The human races are divided into yellow, white, and black. When one looks down from above, the black race today is inferior to the yellow while the yellow is inferior to the white. This is discussing from the point of view of Nature. When a man takes the humble view after entering one of the races, however, he should not sink into despair because he realizes that the races are not equal. Nor should he despise other races because he is biased and self-centered. Men should only exert their respective spirits and mental powers in an enlightened way. Surprisingly enough, the late developers among things generally are the good and the beautiful. How do we know that the yellow and the black races may not one day surpass the white? This is also the virtue of judicious cultivation and simultaneously looking from above and below.

According to the wise men of Europe and America, enlightenment and popularly elected assemblies are all born of wars and disturbances. Our country today must properly appreciate the significance of their views. After all, having surveyed the entire history of the West, these thinkers take the exalted viewpoint and discuss the tendencies of Nature. They admonish against the short-tempered and impetuous people who destroy things, bring on disaster, and obstruct enlightenment by arbitrarily pushing ahead as they please. They show that we should be like Heaven, which awaits the germination of enlightenment while constantly nourishing the trees and plants without forcing their growth.

Those who oppose the course of Nature because they misunderstand this principle will struggle in vain, however patriotic or international they may be. This will also lead them to treat in the same manner their fathers and the fathers of others, their wives and the wives of others, their possessions and the possessions of others, the important and the unimportant. Ultimately, they will make no distinction between life and death, good and evil, and right and wrong. At best, their misunderstanding is like the unrealistic idealism of pseudo-Zen; at worst, they sink to the level of today's superficial enlightenment. Inclined to snatch at temporary pleasures and momentary splendors, they completely halt enlightened achievement (*kaibutsu seimu*).[4] Desisting from enlightened achievement may be all right for Zen sages, but men during their lives, however idle they may be, must somehow satisfy their desires for eating, drinking, resting, rising, gambling, and buying women. However enlightened a person may be, therefore, he cannot just idly sit doing nothing. Those who say that the times are not ripe or that it is too early, therefore, recklessly court destruction. Even though I do not know whether enlightenment is hastened by destructive disorder, such [heedless conduct] is certainly foolish. Wise men of old, therefore, having investigated high and low and considered principles from humble and exalted viewpoints, said, "We shall do our best and leave the rest to Providence (*Temmei*)."[5]

Being the best way to harmonize Heaven's Reason and the Human Way (*Jindō*),[6] the civilized countries of Europe and America of late have often conformed to this principle. I regret that China and Japan cannot await Providence, as there have been numerous occasions when they have not done their utmost in human affairs.

Unless they stimulate their spirits, men will not do their utmost while waiting for Providence. Even though our countrymen are of the yellow race, there were many in the Genki and Tenshō Periods[7] whose simple frugality, persevering endurance, brave spirits, and fearlessness in the face of death remain luminous to the present day. Nevertheless, the spirit of those days, born of the martial arts (*budō*),[8] was not based on enlightened achievement or on judicious cultivation (*saisei hoshō*).[9] When one considers those noble spirits, therefore, even though they were not inferior to Washington and Nelson, they only fought vainly in battle without benefiting the world. We shall nurture the spirit of scholarship if we aim to benefit society through enlightenment and enlightened achievement.

Public opinion throughout the world, whether from exalted or humble view, has always agreed on the importance of scholarship. Unprejudiced by old customs of individual countries and a destroyer of bias, this scholarship should be spread through education in accordance with its true and just principles based on exalted and humble viewpoints. Furthermore, when we are now opening the country, there is no doubt that honor ranks second only to scholarship as a stimulant of the spirit. The knights of Genki and Tenshō prized honor more than life. In order now to encourage honor based upon enlightened achievement, to promote accomplishment by suppressing vanity, and to stimulate talented spirit, we should clarify the right of popular election, the rewards of government, and the methods for licensing the press. These are also essential human contrivances as they are the means for uniting the hearts of men of exalted and humble view in their respective countries. There is still another major factor that unites the hearts of men and that can lay the foundations for our country's strength and prosperity by encouraging a spirit of responsibility and by stirring the entire nation. I would call this factor wealth (*zaihō*).[10]

From the humble and exalted poirts of view, there are no perceptive creatures in the universe that do not have desires. Only by relying on these desires are these beings led and disciplined. When Confucian scholarship assumed that men would be happy if they studied, it relied on the desire among men to search for happiness. When Mencius condemned profit and explained human-heartedness, the true benefits of security and happiness arose from the operation of human-heartedness. The heavens and hells of various religions, of course, tempt men by appealing to their desires. And governments, whether they be despotisms or republics, depend most upon these desires when they protect the people and aim at prosperity and strength. That they protect security and happiness alike by making these desires public is the great principle of governing and [social] intercourse.

There are three factors that assure security and happiness among men: food, clothing, and housing. Moreover, wealth, being exchangeable for commodities, flows like water to produce these three essentials to security and happiness. This is indeed why the desires of the world all come down to wealth, like the flowing of all the streams into the sea. Furthermore, although there are differences in the amount of wealth possessed, it moves here and circulates there, and people without distinction as to race, class, or affluence make use of it according to their station. If you survey history from the exalted and the humble points of view, money in the hands of the public is also like water. Honor in the final analysis lies in protecting and increasing this wealth for the benefit of the people. It is also the function of scholarship, in sum, to study the means for bringing security and happiness to the people by arranging and augmenting wealth. Therefore, there is not a person in the world who does not desire wealth, and wise men from antiquity have prized it most highly.

We call benevolent those rulers who employ wealth publicly and tyrants those rulers who keep wealth to themselves. To its public nature may be attributed peace in the universe and plenty in all things. But because of its private nature, blood flows and nations are subverted. In cases of extreme desire for wealth, men brave fire and water and do not fear for their lives. They are peaceful in mind if they possess wealth but starved in spirit without it. In extreme cases, they reach the point of violently committing robbery. In truth, wealth more than anything else feeds the spirit; feeding the spirit stimulates desire; and what stimulates desire is what stirs the nerves of the nation. If we conduct government openly, if we make completely clear the actual revenues and expenditures that relate to taxation, currency, and the public debt, and if we administer these by relying on public opinion, men will all then understand that they are individually responsible for protecting and increasing wealth, as it is public. Without concern for their lives once they have assumed responsibility, their spirits will naturally be stimulated, their wisdom naturally broadened, and their abilities naturally enhanced so that they will regard the country as the roof or storehouse for their wealth and their patriotism will become immeasurably strong.

In this way will men invariably cause the country as a whole to flourish and prosper by dredging waterways, cutting through mountains, and building railways, steamships, and factories. Moreover, since these undertakings depend upon scholarship and enterprise, men will prize their studies and labor hard any prohibitions notwithstanding. If the government deals with wealth arbitrarily and thus destroys the fair principle by which people and officials view things together from above and below, if the people are not consulted when the government levies taxes, prints or mints money, or contracts with foreign countries for large loans and purchases, and if the government goes to the extreme of not allowing the people to know the reasons for allocating public expenditures, how will such conduct by the government differ from that of the shōgun[11] who arbitrarily wielded his power to restrict the freedom of the Son of Heaven without allowing the sovereign to know or to participate in affairs? This principle is the same whether applied to aristocrats or commoners. Nay, still more is it applicable when the Son of Heaven is the receiver and the people are the payers! When property owners pay taxes without knowing why, they are pure slaves even though they are property owners. Since slaves are confused in spirit and completely ignorant of the direction of public affairs, it is natural that, like monkeys or rats, they will seek momentary profit by fraudulence and deceit. By what means will their minds be united and their spiritual courage stimulated?

The government may say, "You are under obligation to pay taxes when funds are inadequate for protection." Or it may say, "You should reform your mean minds, develop your spirit, and honor your duties to the nation." Such statements are like parents who press education on their children without providing the children with funds for their schooling. [Unlike taxes that are derived from the people's property], however, these school expenses are not provided from the children's property, and it may thus not be unreasonable for the parents not to provide the funds.[12] National finances, however, come from the people's property. How is it reasonable for the people's spirit to be nurtured by the expenditure of their property? Someone may say that we shall force the people to act by reducing them to extremity, just as Greece arose to strength by impoverishing the people. I would respond that countries like Greece were uncommon even in antiquity. I fear that today such hardships would produce a truly enslaved country. Another may say that, as disturbance is the foundation of enlightenment, it would be well to hasten disturbances by conducting still more despotic government. I would reply that this may be reasonable from an exalted position. When [men] look at matters from both the humble and the exalted viewpoints, however, how can there be such foolish talk?

Observing from the exalted and the humble points of view, there is one strange fact. As their peoples were generally ignorant and bigoted, all the enlightened countries of Europe and America, no less than those of Asia, were slaves to religion at the beginning. Even though "Protestant" teachings have recently spread and are gradually turning to the right course, they too are all based on the supernatural ideas of antiquity. Moreover, the church that defended these old traditions still flourishes.[13] Even though kings and emperors today no longer kiss the toes of popes, there are those who honor that religion without grudging their lives and without regard for parents, sons, brothers, or friends. Really popular are the slavish ways that this religion impresses on men's minds. It is truly strange and incredible that such things exist in civilized countries known for their spiritual courage and majesty.

Nevertheless, philosophers since antiquity have often denied these strange ideas. Frederick II of Prussia opposed the deceptions of religion with the assistance of the French philosopher Voltaire; Gibbon observed that the various religious principles are believed by the people, are regarded as deceptions by scholars, and are opportunistically used by politicians as instruments to control the people; Buckle held that enlightenment improves religious principles but that religious principles do not advance enlightenment; the great English scholar [Matthew] Tindale vigorously discussed the injuries of religion to scholarship; and other scholars have been largely in accord with these views. Thus, philosophers for the most part seem to regret these slavish customs of religions.

Is it good for the middle classes and above to be slaves to reason while the lower classes are slaves to religion? Since there are also large numbers of philosophers in the middle and upper classes who explain the merits of religion, is it good for all classes to be slaves of religion? There are various kinds of religion. While we may allow the people freedom of religious belief, by what religion would it be well for the converts to be enslaved? Our country, like Europe and America, has ceased the custom of basing political power on divine teachings (*shinkyō*).[14] Even so, the monarchs of the West respectively honor individual religions while allowing people other faiths. When establishing objectives for the people, should our [Japanese emperor] establish divine teachings outside and separate from the political power? There are already a number of Buddhist sects in our country. And even though Protestantism may be fine under present conditions, there is an increasing tendency to introduce a multiplicity of Western sects.

Although it recognizes that religion should be left to the people, the government should take precautionary measures to avoid the injuries of religion and to prevent religious disturbances, and it should quickly adopt laws to prevent the stirring up of great injuries consequent to the destruction of secular power [by religion]. Yet being inured to tranquility, it has failed to establish these protections. To call this negligence is not far from correct. If a variety of sects increasingly compete with each other, we will first suffer their injuries without experiencing their advantages. Should our country await the emergence of a Bismarck or a despotic Oda Nobunaga?[15]

Even though men may be accorded freedom of religious belief, how will the ignorant people know what they should believe? If the government opposes Western religion after the people have been converted, the people will defect to the foreign powers, and the disturbance will invariably be extreme. If the government tries to prevent conversions in advance, this will be like trying to halt with an embankment the flow of a river that cannot be stopped. Mean and slavish customs are characteristic of our people, and to be enslaved by Buddhism is also characteristic of our people. Still more, to be enslaved by Western religion is adding slavery to slavery, a servitude not to be desired. We should not leave the matter to nature and allow the people, who by custom are idle and narrow, to have this enslavement by religion impressed on their minds. Nor should we abandon the path of judicious cultivation of Heaven's Reason and the Human Way from both the humble and exalted points of view. I respectfully beg your comments.

An Explanation of Twelve Western Words Part One

Speech on April 16

Nishimura Shigeki

European and American studies in recent years have spread so broadly in our country that even children in the villages have come to use Western words. Since we cannot prevent some harm to scholarship once our usage departs from the original meaning of Western words, however, I shall analyze twelve selected Western words now most commonly employed by our people and thereby inform those who do not now read Western materials.

An Explanation of "Civilization"[16]

Bummei kaika is the translation of the English word "civilization." The Chinese have translated "civilization" in the sense of advancing toward propriety. Should we translate the word into our vulgar tongue, we would speak of the improvement of human character. It is said that "civilization" was originally derived from the Latin word *civis*. *Civis* conveys the sense of people living in cities. Should you inquire why a word meaning city dwellers changed to refer to the improvement of human character, it apparently was because, as compared with those in the country, city dwellers generally were more learned, more advanced in manner, and more refined in conduct.

Now to take up and analyze the word "civilization," what comes to mind is only the character of the people and mankind's social intercourse, never the wealth, ability, and power of the people. In the words of the renowned English scholar Mill, "Civilization" is the opposite of "savagery" when one speaks from the point of view of man's conduct as an individual or from the point of view of group relations. According to the French scholar Guizot, civilization in its original meaning had the sense of progress and development, and we should, therefore, speak of civilization by referring to the advance of group relations and individual human conduct together until they reach the level of perfection. When it refers to the conduct of man as an individual, civilization includes the idea of progress and development of knowledge, behavior, benevolence, brotherly love, ability, and taste. In the view of these two scholars, civilization's form appears on two paths: one is through the course of group relations, and the other through the conduct of man as an individual. To further clarify its meaning, civilization refers to the peace and happiness gained by both man as an individual and society as a whole as they gradually advanced in dignity.

We cannot speak of civilization unless there is parallel advance in the dignity of both social intercourse as a whole and man as an individual. Even though the nation as a whole moves toward prosperity, when the wisdom of the people has not advanced in the least, their prosperity is not to be trusted as its source is extremely unclear. Thus although civilization applies to social intercourse as a whole as well as to man as an individual, its essence, being the elevation of individual dignity, extends by inference to the whole of social intercourse.

Then by what method should we be able to elevate the dignity of the individual? There is no other way to achieve this than by good education. The best tool for advancing civilization is derived from a combination of two elements: the spread of knowledge among the people and the cultivation of good conduct. Without these two elements combined together, civilization must halt forthwith. Even though there may be the outward appearance of a full flow from the point of view of social intercourse, like a stream of water, civilization will drop off before long if it is deprived of its sources, education and good conduct. Being efficacious for good social intercourse among men, education is the factor that promotes morality, broadens knowledge, and increases the happiness of the people in its group. Education at its inception, therefore, arises from good social intercourse. Still more, nothing else can compete with the power of education in its effectiveness as the very best method for advancing the level of popular enlightenment and for bringing the conditions of social intercourse increasingly to perfection.

The concept of what is called the advanced level of human social intercourse or the elevated character of the individual must vary according to country. People in European countries assume that the conditions of social intercourse in their countries are the most civilized, and they regard as barbarians or half-civilized the peoples of other lands the roots of whose social intercourse are not the same as the European. After all, what will be the result if we look at the matter objectively? If we want to judge fairly, it is necessary to know the true meaning of the word "civilization." It may be that, in the long run, the above explanations of civilization [by Mill and Guizot] will not prove erroneous. If we assume that they, after all, convey the true meaning of civilization, then there is no doubt that the most civilized people in the world are the Europeans or those who migrated from Europe.

If you inquire into the fundamental roots of the Europeans and those who have migrated from Europe, their civilization ultimately arose from two elements. The first was the doctrine of Christianity; the second, the conditions of social intercourse in Rome at its zenith. Thereafter, with the introduction of legal systems of land registry in various countries, conditions of social intercourse advanced still another step ahead with really noteworthy results. Since the roots of social intercourse in India, China, and Arabia are entirely different from those of Europe, it is quite reasonable for the shape of their civilizations to be very different from that of the Europeans.

When one reads the history of man from furthest antiquity to the present, it seems clear that civilization has advanced step by step. Its progress, however, has not always been at the same rate. Having stopped at a given point, it may remain quite stationary or thereafter retreat. Or it may rest for a moment in order later to progress greatly. Looking at ancient history, there was invariably a conspicuous state in any given period, such as Rome, Greece, or the Frankish Empire. The level of civilization in these countries was closely related to the progress of civilization in the world. Rising one after another in this fashion, these great states during their flourishing periods always generated progress by steering the course of civilization in advance of the world. But when their time was up, their power greatly declined, and their progress gradually came to an end. If one country stopped progressing, however, another arose to become the leader of nations and to advance the course of civilization. This periodic rise and fall of states was sometimes a regional, sometimes a continental, and sometimes a world-wide phenomenon. I shall refrain here from reviewing the complex course of the rise and fall of states within each region and continent. If you review the path of rise and decline throughout the world, the areas that have advanced civilization after achieving prosperity at a particular time were Africa in ancient times, then Asia, and now, similarly, Europe. (I shall omit Japan, leaving the affairs of our country for a separate discussion.) In the future, America may come next and thereafter Australia. This is not my conjecture. I am only elaborating views drawn from the words of Western intellectuals.

[1]Continued from the previous issue.

[2]*Tenri*, 天理.

[3]*Shizen*, 自然.

[4]*Kaibutsu seimu*, 開物成務.

[5]*Temmei*, 天命.

[6]*Jindō*, 人道.

[7]Genki (元亀) and Tenshō (天正) Periods, 1570–1592, the eras when Japan was being reunited under the leadership of Oda Nobunaga (織田信長) and Toyotomi Hideyoshi (豐臣秀吉).

[8]*Budō*, 武道.

[9]*Saisei hoshō*, 裁成輔相.

[10]*Zaihō*, 財法.

[11]*Shōgun*, 將軍. Whereas in theory the shogun held powers mandated to them by the

emperor, they actually ruled without regard to the emperor during most of the Tokugawa Period.

[12]In this rather obscure statement, Sakatani means to compare government to parents, people to children.

[13]Sakatani is here referring to the Catholic Church.

[14]*Shinkyō*, 神教, i.e., the teachings of Shintō (神道).

[15]Even as Bismarck struck at the Catholic Church in the *Kulturkampf,* Oda Nobunaga (織田信長) destroyed the political power of the Buddhist Church in Japan.

[16]Civilization, *bummei kaika,* 文明開化. Nishimura's essay is splendid evidence of the commitment of the Meiji enlighteners to the Western concept of progress.

An Explanation of "Liberty" and "Freedom" (Second of a Series of Expositions on Foreign Words) Speech on May 1[1]

Nishimura Shigeki

Jishu and *jiyū*[2] are translations of the English words "liberty" and "freedom." "Liberty" is derived from the Latin *libertas;* freedom from the Teutonic word *Freiheit.* Under Roman law, there was a clear distinction between slaves and those who were self-supporting. *Liberi* was used to designate the condition of persons who were self-supporting; *servi,* that of slaves. In its original sense, therefore, the word liberty in Rome referred only to the condition of people who were self-supporting. Nevertheless, by a change in connotation, it came to be used in a political sense. It is recorded in Livy's history of Rome that the Roman people only acquired "liberty" after opposing the tyrant Tarquinius.[3] This meaning of "liberty" referred to whether the entire country was in a state of bondage or of freedom, as distinguished from the earlier sense that indicated the condition of persons who were slaves or self-supporting. When a country was under the oppressive rule of a tyrant, it was said to be in bondage. But it was said to have gained liberty once it escaped this oppression.

Greece possessed the words *despotes* and *doulos. Despotes* had the meaning of masters; *doulos,* of slaves. Even though these Greek words are antonyms, it is said that they cannot convey the same sense as the Latin *liberi* and *servi.*

Such generally was the usage of the words liberty and freedom in antiquity. In more recent times, liberty and freedom have been divided into two types. One is natural liberty or personal liberty; the other, liberty from the point of view of social intercourse or political liberty. Since the bodies of human beings may be regarded as small universes, what we call natural liberty is the means by which an individual can acquire everything he wants or manage his affairs to his full satisfaction. Natural liberty is the power of human beings to do according to their wishes anything they deem appropriate unless it is forbidden by natural law. Having been bestowed on mankind by the Supreme Ruler, natural liberty is an innate right possessed at birth. Be that as it may, not being able to function independently in society, human beings should invariably conduct their lives by mingling and associating with each other. Since others, like ourselves, possess liberty, men must perfect the morality of social intercourse by mutually sacrificing a part of their liberty once they associate and mingle with each other.

Even though social liberty, of course, is [in essence] identical with natural [personal] liberty, when we refer to social liberty, we mean individual liberty operating within an appropriate area after it has been subjected to minor restrictions in order to assure the security and happiness of society as a whole. If an individual obstructs the liberty of others by exerting his liberty at will, his willfulness must be controlled by law. Even though these laws slightly restrict the liberty of the individual, they are regarded as increasing social liberty since they actually broaden the liberty of the people. Social liberty, therefore, is something acquired by appropriate law. As the old adage correctly states, "There is no liberty in a land without law."

Social liberty is also called political liberty. Political liberty, the antonym of political bondage, denotes full protection of one's person and property without injury from tyranny by rulers or ministers. Political bondage refers to the situation of men who cannot protect their persons or property as they are habitually oppressed by the tyranny of rulers or ministers. When the government, without reason, fervently controls the ideas of the people according to its own whims, this also should be called tyranny. But when the government, without good reason or willful intent, promulgates laws restricting the persons and property of the people, this is properly termed obstructing the liberty of the people.

Then what is this thing that should be called social or political liberty? And by what means can this liberty be obtained? These are the two questions that are important for understanding liberty. On the whole, England ranks first among the European countries where the people possess liberty, and the liberty of the English people is established by their national law. The rights of the people are divided into three under English law. The first, the right of men to protection of their bodies, is the right by which all Englishmen are assured against injury in their lives, bodily health, and dignity. The second, the liberty of the individual, is the right by which men may follow their own inclinations to do anything that is not forbidden by law. The third is the right of private property or to property that one holds by his own power (including inherited property and property received from others). This is the right by men to follow their own wishes without restriction by the government in using, receiving, or selling such property. There can never be great error if these stipulations in English law are taken as models for the liberties of the people.

The methods by which people acquire their liberty generally all resemble each other in the various countries of the West. As a rule, the rulers in each country are extremely few while the ruled are extremely numerous. When these many and few become equals in scholarship and knowledge, the many take governing power from the few until they are finally able to plan for the peace and prosperity of the entire country as a whole. Under such circumstances, the people of the entire country can fully receive the benefits of their liberty. From the point of view of governmental structure, therefore, constitutional monarchies (*kummin dōji*)[4] and republics are the political forms under which people can have liberty while autocracies and aristocratic oligarchies are the political forms under which the people cannot have liberty. That is, the people cannot enjoy political liberty when a single ruler or a few ministers grasp power in the land. The political form in which there can be political liberty is the one in which the whole of society or a majority of society in the entire nation shares power.

Even among the enlightened nations of Europe, there are some, such as Russia and Prussia, in which the people do not have political liberty. In these countries, however, they have two explanations for denying political liberty. First, even though the people are already enlightened, as in Prussia, after the interests of the nation have been considered, liberty is denied on the assumption that the people of the entire country will actually benefit thereby. Second, as in Russia, it is held that liberty should not be allowed as the people are not yet enlightened. This is because political power must be shared with the entire country if the people are given liberty and a people as yet unenlightened cannot exercise or protect political power even though it may be given them. This being the case, this type of rule in such a country [as Russia] should also not be harshly censured. It is only that she must concede an inferior level of enlightenment as compared with England and America, where the people have acquired liberty.

Since my discussion has become tedious, I shall cease here even though there still remain [to be considered] religious liberty, freedom of the press, and other liberties.

Rewards and Punishments, Praise and Shame[5]

Nakamura Masanao

It is an entirely natural human sentiment for rewards and punishments to be sources of honor and disgrace while praise and shame produce joy and anger. If the rewards and punishments of royal law and the praise and shame of contemporary opinion move the hearts of men more and more to practice good and to repent evil, there is, of course, no doubt that such official and public recognition will benefit men's minds and social morality. (In addition, what are most to be desired and most to be feared are the rewards and punishments of the True God, which penetrate to the depths of men's minds and are all discerning. Nevertheless, I shall refrain from embarking here on a lengthy consideration of this question since it is not the focal point of this discussion.)

There are instances, however, when the rewards and punishments of royal law at times confuse love for hate and injure justice or when the praise and shame of contemporary opinion occasionally obscure the facts and upset right and wrong. When one reviews the course of history in the East and the West, therefore, not only were there times when honors and ranks were just not bestowed on those who are regarded today as great heroic figures. Often these illustrious persons were maligned, branded as criminals, thrown into prison, or executed. Or there are innumerable cases of such persons who, even though they escaped punishment by royal law, have departed from this world having been despised by the public and fallen into difficulty after wandering about without finding a livelihood. Looked at in this way, the rewards and punishments of royal law and the praise and shame of contemporary opinion are encouragement for the average and the superior, but they are inadequate to judge those in the first rank, namely, the great heroic figures. After all, in scholarship and discernment, the great heroic figures clearly surpass ordinary commoners and are beyond the sphere of usual customs. Their judgments of good and bad or of appropriateness and inappropriateness, therefore, are self-evidently no more harmonious with conventional opinion than is ice with charcoal, and doubt and suspicion of them by the public in extreme cases ends in their murder or exile.

Nevertheless, with the long passage of time, the fame of these great men becomes increasingly luminous, and their views and discernment spreads through the world so that they cannot be effaced by the ages. On the other hand, those who doubt and reject these great men vanish into thin air—be they kings, or great ministers, or commoners who once held power. When [these tarnished figures] happen to be transmitted in history, those who hear of their malodorous reputations hold their noses. Westerners call this the vengeance of history. This is something like the old tale of Confucius known to all in which the master recalled that, having been disgraced by Sung and persecuted by Ch'en and Ts'ai,[6] he was obliged to wander to the four directions without having time to settle down. Even though Chu Hsi today is honored by scholars with the appellation Chu Wên Kung,[7] he was viewed as a quack in his own time. Such a person as Su Tung-p'o[8] has indeed been praised by later generations for his prose and poetry, but he was taken by his contemporaries for a member of a treasonous faction.

It is said that a natural disaster destroyed the headstone of those who were regarded as traitors when it was erected by Ts'ai Ching[9] but that the marker thereafter was restored by their descendants who took it as an honor. When the rewards and punishments of royal law injure justice and the praise and shame of contemporary opinion mistake right for wrong, even the inscription of a name on a traitor's headstone may become an honor and not a shame. When the headstone of a traitor is taken for an honor, there is no guarantee that monuments to the meritorious will not become symbols of shame (when there has been the slightest favoritism or reckless conferment of awards). There are some who have achieved the prestige of knighthoods after taking thousands of lives and some who have received the death penalty after bequeathing benefits for a hundred generations.[10]

When matters come to such a pass, we may think that the rewards and punishments of mankind and those of Heaven are mutually opposed. Even in the West, Luther, who was a leader in the spread of the Reformation, opposed the Roman pope as a humble man, underwent manifold hardships, and endangered his life. Finally, today, his fame and glory is the envy of kings and ministers who cannot acquire it although during his lifetime he labored for a living cleaning clocks and engaging in gardening. It is also said that the conduct of the people in Germany today is Luther's work and not that of kings. How is the brilliance of such a great heroic figure enhanced by the rewards of kings?

Paul is a man honored in the countries where Christianity is practiced and whose writings are placed on a level with the Scriptures (*Keiten*).[11] During his life, however, he made tents for a living, initially scoffed at Christianity, and once converted suffered death on Christianity's behalf. How can such an extraordinary man be prevented from spreading his teachings by the punishments of royal law? Nevertheless, the new draws principles from the old, and the present patterns its affairs on the past. Even though we have not seen in recent times such great martyrdoms as the killing of saints, my translation of *Self Help*[12] contains numerous stories of those who were slandered and shamed when they introduced new laws, devised new instruments, and espoused new theories.

In sum, there have invariably been advocates in such fields as religion, ethics, political economy, philosophy, and medicine who today brought us great tangible and intangible benefits and blessings. When promoting their studies, they opposed the rulers and incurred the animosity of their generation, or they were slandered by the people and freely branded with such epithets as madman, idiot, and humbug. Holding independently to their beliefs and enduring any number of hardships, they were indifferent to human rewards and punishments as well as to the praise and shame of the multitudes. Ah, there is nothing so unreliable as opinion current at the time! And there is nothing more fugitive than immediate rewards! I am speaking to the young people and students of the world. If, having established firm resolve, they follow the line of their individual talents and study particular sciences or arts with all their hearts and without heeding praise and blame of the times, they may expect to become persons who perfect their own conduct and benefit their generation. If such, after all, be the case, they may even be able to wear on their ceremonial clothing the insignia and medals of rank bestowed during their own lifetime. Even though one may miss the rewards of royal law, one may be still more honored by later generations.

Some days ago, there was an imperial edict on ranks and decorations that naturally is a means for encouraging the contemporary generation. Yet how mistaken it is if a person thinks that there is no other praise and shame than that of royal law or contemporary opinion or if he gives special attention to the immediate rewards for his life's contributions, regarding them alone as the highest honors without realizing that there are posthumous honors as well as rewards and punishments of later generations! There may be men who contribute to national prosperity by faithfully following their occupations and who benefit others by living frugally, wearing rags, and eating humble fare in shabby shacks. Even though they are not honored by royal law, [these men] must exert their full energies since they can never doubt the invariable munificence of the emperor. An Englishman has said that a person will have happy dreams at night if he does his duty without violating his conscience. After all, a man should invariably look to his own conscience first for the rewards for his conduct.

On Whether Iron Mines Should Be Opened[13]

Kanda Kōhei

Should iron mines be opened with official support? Iron imports, which have been extremely large for some years, will continue hereafter gradually to increase, and the charges for transportation alone will be large. It is not that we do not produce iron in our country. Especially, since I also hear that we are deriving coal from places that are not far distant, it would seem economical for us to develop iron mines.

Someone may observe with an argument as follows that I know one without comprehending two. Since England has fully developed methods for extracting iron ore and has necessarily acquired all sorts of mining equipment, she produces enormous quantities of iron whose price is extremely cheap. We must now raise at least Yen 2–3 millions if we undertake to open iron mills in our country. And since the price of our iron will actually go up when this money is raised, [our product] will not be as cheap as imported English iron even after the transportation costs are saved.

I would beg to disagree. Our situation may be compared to that of a fellow who must buy mortar, pestle, and sieve to hull the large quantity of rice in his storehouse. My critic would say that the fellow had best buy only enough polished rice from a dealer to meet his daily needs since the price of his rice will actually become high when he buys the polishing equipment. This might be all right if his needs were limited to one or two *to*.[14] But it would be absurd for the fellow to allow his rice to rot in the storehouse while he purchases unlimited amounts of rice over an indefinite period of time. Even the most ignorant husband and the most foolish wife would never indulge in such an uneconomical practice. My critic, therefore, may indeed say that I know one without understanding two, but I believe that his views comprehend two without appreciating three.

There have long been rumors of a railway [to be built] between the western capital [Kyōto] and Tsuruga[15] and similar reports of a Tokyo-Utsunomiya line.[16] Both should be undertaken before long. I have recently heard that plans have been drawn up for a Tōkaidō line[17] as well as a line from Tokyo to Aomori[18] that I must say are magnificent. The railways will surely be extended to the Sanyō, San-in, Tōsan, Hokuriku, Nankai, Seikai, and Hokkai [routes][19] until we have spread a centralized network over the entire country. Should we also look to imports for all the iron products for these undertakings?

Steam engines contribute most to the prosperity of a nation. All the manifold industries today draw steam power from these engines that are almost invariably made of iron. In addition, the large number of iron bridges, iron fences, iron pipes, iron containers, iron plates, iron leaves, and iron tools are well nigh beyond counting. Once their use is known and they are no longer playthings, these iron products will all become essential forthwith. We should understand, in other words, that imports of iron products will increase day by day.

If they try to do so, [our] iron foundaries can turn out iron tools, but regrettably, they only use imported iron. This cannot be helped in a country without iron. But our country, fortunately, has iron mines as well as an established iron industry. Then why have we failed only to open up iron mines? I would suggest that such a situation cannot be regarded as well planned.

I understand that, according to a memorial by the war minister of last January, it is expected that coast defenses will be constructed the full length of the entire country. Even though we cannot know how these plans are to be carried out, large quantities of iron will also inevitably be required to equip such forts and batteries as may be built. Again, in the view of some, coast artillery alone is insufficient to defend the country. They hold that all the important points on the coast must be provided with warships, and that these warships will be inadequate if they are not ironclads. I think this opinion correct. Moreover, these various undertakings will all require iron. The War and Navy Ministries will surely have accurate information on whether, after all, we should take advantage of present low prices and use imported iron for such important military purposes.

This commentator would set forth the following predictions after reviewing all phases of the situation. I would say that the use of iron will gradually increase hereafter, and that there is absolutely no better way [to meet the demand for iron] than by opening iron mines. If they are ultimately to be opened, it is best to do so quickly. And if they are opened, numerous people will gain livelihoods in their vicinities. [Domestic iron] will indeed be higher than imported iron at first, but it will gradually become cheap thereafter. If we do not disregard the price and employ domestic iron in the sphere of military needs, we shall suffer disaster during wartime. If we do not grasp Heaven's endowment, there will surely be retribution. If we entrust development to the people, there will only be slow progress. The only appropriate policy is for the government to shoulder the burden of opening the mines as its obligation.

Upon the conclusion of my essay, a guest said that he thought a government order for the opening of iron mines actually had already been issued and that construction might now be underway. Should this prove to be true, I have nothing to say. I only pray that we shall be quickly successful in producing large quantities of iron and that we shall ultimately export our surplus. Nevertheless, as I cannot but doubt what the guest has said, I am sending this [essay] to the society for submission to criticism by the membership. Should the critics think my words without value, please throw them into a wastebasket.

[1]See the previous issue for Nishimura's first article in the series.

[2]*Jishu,* 自主, and *jiyū,* 自由.

[3]In his *Ab urbe condita libri,* Livy recounted the disintegration of Roman virtues that led to the overthrow of the Roman Republic.

[4]*Kummin dōji,* 君民同治.

[5]The occasion for Nakamura's essay was an imperial rescript issued on 10 April 1875 that announced eight orders of merit (*kuntō,* 勲等) with corresponding decorations (*shōhai,* 賞牌). Apart from warning that worldly rewards often escape the truly outstanding, Nakamura, like Nishimura Shigeki, may be expressing discontent that recognition would go to the government's friends. See Nishimura's essay entitled *Zoku* in Issue Thirty-Three.

[6]Sung, 宋, Ch'en, 陳, and Ts'ai, 蔡, were states that Confucius visited in his search for a model ruler.

[7]Chu Wên Kung, 朱文公, or the literary gentleman Chu. Having trained in the tradition of Chu Hsi (朱熹), Nakamura naturally loathed the great philosopher's political enemies who honored the innovator Wang An-shih (王安石).

[8]Su Tung-p'o, 蘇東坡, 1036–1101, the poet and bitter political enemy of Wang Anshih.

[9]Ts'ai Ching, 蔡京, 1046–1126, was a leading minister in the party of Wang Anshih who sought to avenge himself on his enemies by having their names carved on a tablet of traitors.

[10]Since Nakamura was a Christian, he may here refer to Christ.

[11]*Keiten,* 經典.

[12]Nakamura's translation of Samuel Smiles' *Self Help* appeared in 1871 under the title of *Saigoku Risshi Hen* (西國立志編).

[13]Although the Japanese government shared Kanda's estimate of the importance of developing iron mines, its major effort at the iron mines of Kamaishi (釜石) proved disastrous. It had already acquired the Kamaishi mines in 1873 and thereafter invested Yen 2,000,000 in their development. The project was abandoned in 1880

after operations were halted by technical difficulties, and the mines together with the expensive equipment were purchased four years later by a political entrepreneur named Tanaka Chōbei (田中長兵衛).

[14]*To*, 斗, a measure equal to approximately four gallons.

[15]Tsuruga, 敦賀. Work on the line from Kyōto to Tsuruga on the Sea of Japan was begun in 1875 and finished in 1884.

[16]Utsunomiya, 宇都宮.

[17]The Tōkaidō (東海道) line was completed in 1890.

[18]Aomori, 青森. The line from Tokyo to Aomori, the first Japanese railway built with private capital, was begun in 1881 and completed ten years later.

[19]Sanyō, 山陽, San-in, 山陰, Tōsan, 東山, Hokuriku, 北陸, Nankai, 南海, Seikai, 西海, and Hokkai, 北海, were all major regions or circuits (*dō*, 道) in old Japan.

The Three Human Treasures Part One[1]

Nishi Amane

Moral teachings in European philosophy have passed through various changes since antiquity without yet reaching a common path. Even though older theories* seem still to flourish, the emergence of "positivism" (*jitsuriha*)[2] of the Frenchman Auguste Comte appears greatly to have changed the world's outlook. And among the numerous theories of great thinkers that are ultimately based on positivism, John Stuart Mill's expansion of [Jeremy] Bentham's "utilitarianism"** (*rigaku*)[3] seems to be the most revolutionary from the point of view of modern morality.*** It is the purport of utilitarianism that the one great objective governing this human world seems to be the "most great happiness." Even though this theory may not be absolutely perfect, it is not to be lightly criticized by a lesser man of a later day since it is the established theory of great thinkers.****

What I would now discuss here are the means for attaining this general happiness on the assumption that it is the chief objective of mankind. Since general happiness then is a condition produced by the three human treasures, the three treasures should be called the second great objective, as they are not the final objective but rather the means and the media for reaching that objective, which is called the general happiness to the greatest extent. As the theory of the three treasures represents my personal views drawn from conjecture, however, it is not my aim to convey the thought of Western philosophers. I cannot guarantee whether, having established the three treasures as the second objective, they will

*Such as the idealism of Fichte, Schilling, and Hegel or Kant's theory of transcendental pure reason in the Koenigsberg philosophical school.

**An extension of the ancient Greek school of Epicurus.

***When I traveled in Holland ten years ago, [C.W.] Opzoomer, then the great philosopher in the land, seemed to honor Comte, Fourier, and Mill.

****I shall not discuss utilitarianism here, leaving it to Mill.

really lead to a state of general happiness from a moral point of view, or whether the great scholars would after all nod in approval should they be called from their graves and questioned. Nevertheless, recognizing my presumptuousness, I dare to ask my fellow members for their criticism.

Now the purport of what I say today is that there are three treasures in the human world and that, having taken these three treasures as his objective, man can devise means for governing himself and ruling others since he will conform to the dictates of morality if he honors the treasures well. Should you ask what these treasures are, they are health (*mame*), wisdom (*chie*), and wealth (*tomi*).*[4] In this moral treatise, therefore, I shall assume that honoring, valuing, desiring, seeking, and acquiring these three treasures will produce the means for achieving greatest happiness. But since conventional morality today regards humility, generosity, humbleness, modesty, unselfishness, and lack of desire as the first elementary principles, will there be anyone who does not scoff should he hear suddenly of these three treasures? Should morality be discussed in terms of the three treasures, men will think it the philosophy of gamblers and rickshawmen. This is because my critics will wonder how people will differ from gamblers and rickshawmen if they want strong arms, sharp intellects, and money. They will say that [such views] will create a den of greed and that the world will be led to thievery and robbery if greed is the objective of morality.

My view is different from this. I am of the opinion that achieving the three treasures in human affairs will not injure Heaven's endowment. It is completely natural for men to acquire and perfect the three treasures because they are the gifts of Heaven to man and the basis for the greatest happiness and health that we mortals receive from Heaven.

Although I am ignorant of the bliss in the Hereafter, such as Buddha, Confucius, and Christ taught, even these three holy men could not break away from these three objectives as the fundamentals for ordering life in this world. The validity of the three treasures is still more demonstrated by the fact that even stupid

*The word *tomi* [wealth] is rare in everyday usage. We may consider it temporarily as money and leave to the economists the distinction between money and wealth. In this study, however, the desire for money is conceived to be a part of morality.

couples can recognize them and that such people as gamblers, rickshawmen, servants, and chairbearers function within the limits of seeking them. It seems that such people as hermits, the followers of Zen,[5] as well as Lao Tzŭ and Chuang Tzŭ[6] are indeed searching elsewhere, having departed from the three treasures. But theirs are strange and heretical theories damaging to humanity. Even though there was not yet clarification of the three treasures in the paths advocated by Confucius and Mencius, their teachings are not practiced without the three treasures. As these three treasures are the three great essentials for achieving the greatest happiness among men generally, therefore, I also think that beauty and goodness among human beings ultimately will be advanced and clarified more and more if there is extreme vigour in searching for and perfecting the three treasures. As nothing in this life before the Hereafter can be accomplished without the three treasures, it is absolutely impossible either to govern oneself, to manage one's family, or to rule the nation without them.

Let me attempt an outline of my thoughts on the three treasures. Should you ask why I regard health to be a treasure, I would respond that the desire for life by all living beings is a fact observable to us today. Since this desire for life is an innate virtue, it is clear that preservation of life through the protection and improvement of health is man's first obligation to Heaven.

Should I be asked why I regard wisdom as a treasure, I would reply that the invariable desire by all living beings to surpass others is also a fact observable to us today as well as an innate virtue. Since man is a "rational being," however, he is not like the birds and beasts that try to excel others in bodily strength. Instead, he should endeavor to excel others with mental power.* Further, when individuals want to surpass each other with mental power, what other means is there than for them to advance their wisdom? To seek a broadening of wisdom, therefore, is the second obligation of man to Heaven.

[Finally], should I be asked why I consider wealth a treasure, I would reply that for all beings to acquire things for their use is also a fact observable to us today as well as an innate virtue. Even though birds and beasts are satisfied if only they possess enough

*It should be noted that even in war there has recently been more emphasis on mental power than on physical power.

food, the sources of man's manifold pleasures are not limited to one since he cannot survive for even a day without food, clothing, and lodging. Therefore, a variety of goods and property are necessary, and currency is essential to facilitate the apportionment, circulation, and accumulation of goods and property.* For all to desire an abundance of this wealth [in money] is thus the third obligation of man to Heaven.

Individuals, thus, should all energetically and assiduously exert their best efforts night and day to seek these three treasures as there is nothing more important for the individual than these three treasures as the norms of "conduct" and as the fundamentals of morality. There will be no time to escape the wrath of Heaven should men oppose these principles to the slightest extent. These then being Heaven's laws and Heaven's principles, they are factors that individuals must constantly honor and fear even as they dread Heaven's mandates and respect Heaven's authority.

Now are there any who make light of physical things? And are there any who willingly drink arsenic and tread on swords? Some, however, make light of spiritual matters. Be that as it may, retribution will immediately fall on the man who makes light of the three treasures to the slightest extent. Man will not suddenly reap punishment even if he transgresses a little the traditional rules of morality, such as humbleness, modesty, disinterestedness, and lack of desire. But how fearful he must be of the immediate retribution should he treat the three treasures lightly!

Let me undertake to outline my thought [on Heaven's retributions]. Should I be asked regarding the punishment for ignoring the first obligation [to guard health], I would reply that Heaven's retribution will immediately fall, should a person neglect the first obligation by indulging in private desires and by giving free rein to carnal drives without knowing how to discipline his body or how to protect his life. Such conduct at least will injure his health; at most, cost him his life. I would call this retribution disease. This, after all, is why sages from antiquity have earnestly and unceasingly exhorted and admonished against such behavior. Should you ask regarding the punishment for ignoring the second obligation [to promote wisdom], I would reply that Heaven's retribution

*This belongs to economic theory.

will fall immediately on the man who, in neglect of this obligation, does not like studying and asking questions, cannot turn to the good that he sees, cannot submit to the justice that he hears, enjoys himself arrogantly, or resigns himself in despair. Such a person will never be able to appreciate the joys in life. I would call this retribution ignorance. This, after all, is why wise men from antiquity have spared no efforts in training and guidance to promote scholarship and humility. [Finally], should you ask regarding the punishment for neglecting the third obligation [to seek wealth], I would reply that Heaven's retribution will immediately fall on the man who, neglecting this obligation, whimsically wastes his life by eschewing hard labor, avoiding serious endeavors, and idly indulging in pleasures. I would call this retribution poverty. Even the owner of great wealth in treasure will suddenly face starvation [if he thus ignores this treasure]. From ancient times, the sages have often touched on this point.*

Therefore, the great fundamentals of morality will [only] be established if individuals really honor these three treasures faithfully and avoid making light of Heaven's endowments. Thereby will they reach the level of greatest happiness. Nay, they can only hope for correct conduct and richness of mind after establishing these fundamentals. If they do not completely establish these three great fundamentals, men will meet unbearable embarrassment and daily frustrations even though they desire to be respectful in "conscience," to honor sincerity, to control themselves, and to abide by the proprieties. Indeed, retribution will fall on their backs if they in the least oppose these fundamentals. Binding and dragging us, the three [retributions] of illness, ignorance, and poverty will then despatch us to Hell. Since, among the retributions that fall upon individuals, there are none greater, none more important, and none more cruel than these three, we must energetically overcome them and thereby develop the great principles of morality. What else can there be than the three treasures as the keys to conduct and as principles for cultivating truth and for advancing morality among individuals?

Further, these being the principles by which individuals should

*The Confucian teaching that man should be satisfied with poverty only means that he should not indulge in ill-gained wealth. It does not admonish against earning money by hard work.

conduct themselves in [my] theory of morality, the principles for man's social intercourse (namely, the way men deal with their "fellow creatures") and the principles for governing men derived therefrom (namely, the way men assume responsibility once it has been entrusted by their fellow creatures) arise from nothing more than honoring these three treasures. This is a point that I shall take up in a later discussion. I indeed feel extreme shame and regret because, being weak in body, I have violated the first obligation; being biased and narrow in mind, I have violated the second obligation; and, having failed to provide sufficiently for my family, I have violated the third obligation.

Pivotal Times of Change Speech on May 1, 1875

Sakatani Shiroshi

There are pivots in the changes of things generally; just as last year came before this year, this year will become next year; spring becomes summer, summer, fall, and fall, winter. Even though these changes are all irrevocably the work of Providence (*Ten-un*)[7] and the trends of the times (*jisei*),[8] human power of judicious cultivation (*saisei hoshō*)[9] is also important as we move from one point to another. Nevertheless, the natural course of Providence cannot prevail, and arbitrariness may readily emerge if change is artificially contrived. Some people may then be influenced by old customs to regard vacillation as appropriate, while others may try violently to act with military force. Being like fitting a round peg into a square hole, such behavior will only produce confused disorder and lead to naught as it contradicts Providence and the trends of the times. We must be especially cautious at this time. The change of the Restoration was the greatest Heaven-sent opportunity in history. How really wonderful it is to reveal fresh glowing skin after washing away old sweat!

New injuries and great harm will again be incurred, however, if much is left undone during such a pivotal occasion. Our country is a house in which many persons are sheltered together. Year before last, even a humble person such as I feared for the destruction of the house when men's minds in the nation were misled by the agitation of great ministers.[10] I have discussed the fact that today's urgent business is to preserve harmonious government and to establish the structure of joint rule by high and low (*jōge dōji*)[11] before there are disturbances. And I have also explained that we should encourage a sense of responsibility through the whole country by referring to open discussion the taxes and finance that are the spiritual foundations of the nation. Some may say that I should confine myself to my own business. I am of the opinion that words labelling others' views as groundless fears are only slavish talk of "despotic" lands where the people do not assume responsibility on the ground that public matters are outside their concern. All persons, even beggars, should be concerned for their homeland during stirring times like these when the people's rights are cultivated and the challenging of traditional taboos is encouraged. When people are silent even though they are anxious in their hearts, they become flatterers, deceive, and forget their responsibilities. I think that this is a great crime.

Yet we cannot suddenly eliminate these old obsequious customs. The former ministers presented their memorial during a period of hesitation. While I certainly do not know their intentions when they thus addressed the *sain* at the beginning of February 1874,[12] they were not far from the facts. I subsequently joined the rear ranks of the Meirokusha, and the purport of my writings and criticisms have invariably drawn from the ideas in their memorial. I recognize, however, that a clumsy and circuitous fellow like me can only ventilate his sincere feelings. On April 14 of this year, an enlightened decree brilliantly perpetuated the Restoration Oath of 1868.[13] Directed toward establishing a constitutional system, this decree enjoins the people broadly to assist the throne while denying the ministers their private gains. This humble soul would deferentially await the achievements of the many wise men. Yet he cannot avoid passionate feelings of patriotism and deep anxiety. This is because the most noteworthy words in the edict warn against rash and sudden change as well as against clinging to past customs. The admonition has inevitably caused me deep concern at this pivotal time of unique opportunity [provided by the Meiji Restoration].

In the final analysis, it is the nature of things that there is momentum in movement and that calm is accompanied by inertia. A boat continues even after the oarsman stops rowing; a stopped cart hesitates even though the puller begins with full strength; breathing remains heavy after anger subsides; and eyes are still sleepy upon awakening. We call these phenomena momentum or inertia. Such momentum and inertia are most extreme in human feelings. Take saké for example. If one tries to halt drinking by degrees, one will ultimately fail as the disinclination to stop will be countered [by the phenomenon of momentum]. The habit can only be controlled by calm determination.

I need not speak of the beauties in the three thousand years of our national history. Mounting "despotism" and bigoted "ambition," however, have deeply penetrated and immobilized our minds, and sudden change is discouraged by the great mass of remaining inertia. Even men who want to reform the evils they recognize, therefore, are unwilling to go down among the people because they do not want first to sacrifice their privileges. They think that they will be despised if they descend, as their authority will not have been maintained. When undertaking changes in this frame of mind, they conduct affairs with their former oppressive power without being able to learn the fine points of the West. When they thus emphasize old customs and dominate the people, their inertia mires them to old ways and inures them to the past. Moreover, these leaders claim that the unenlightened people, obstinately clinging to the past, are too dispirited and listless to understand opposition to oppression. This type of leadership in the country promotes inertia. We should fear a slowing down at this time of pivotal change. There are also those who in general advance superficial features of Westernism one after another. Such people set aside what is privately inconvenient on the pretext that it is premature for our countrymen to learn the fundamental essence of the West, and they quickly carry out projects when these projects are handy as decorations, hasten their quest for power, and spread their fame. Their measures are like fitting a round peg in a square hole. If these fellows do not reflect that men's minds and customs are daily degenerating, the accelerating momentum will contribute to the rash and sudden change [against which the emperor warned]. They say, however: "Our conduct should be unfettered. Unenlightened persons who chatter incessantly only vainly protest their unrightness and make complaints. How are they worthy of our cooperation? We can only stimulate their knowledge through increased controls." These are people who defend the defects of accelerated momentum.

The people are comprised of high and low, and there is a large amount of both inertia and momentum among them. After all, as between high and low, which is most [plagued] by the inertia of those who are unenlightened and without spirit and by the momentum of those slaves to ambition who are wise to the ways of the West? Should we not reflect on the opium smoker in China, whose body will be damaged if he stops suddenly after the habit has already penetrated his brain? Yet if he tries to stop only indolently, he will die, though he changes the pretexts and methods of his smoking as he will take puff after puff until he finally stoops to theft.

Now let me just pose a few questions. Taxation and finance are the foundations of protection, being the nerves of the nation and the major items that should be shared publicly. As there have been established no clear and explicit public laws by which receipts are collected according to the amounts to be disbursed, however, finance is handled according to the old customs in which arbitrary expenditures are made from fixed requisitions. There are only private [financial] consultations inside the government without public discussions among those outside. If the spirit of responsibility is thus obstructed after the doubts of the people are stimulated, when will the inertia in the nation's nerves be ended? If we acknowledge the judicial power of foreigners and the maritime [conventional] tariff,[14] what can we do about the inertia in the national structure? The criminal code is a basic law. If we move rapidly to correct the offenses of the lower classes while, with inertia, we are perfunctory in dealing with the crimes of the upper classes, is this not the same as establishing law without putting it into practice?

I have recently heard of an incident relating to the Frenchman [Gustave] Boissonade,[15] who is employed as a lecturer on criminal law by the Justice Ministry. One day, upon hearing anguished cries from a torture chamber, Boissonade was greatly surprised and threatened with heated protests to halt his lectures for as long as torture continued. His passion and bravery are greatly to be admired. If we are unable completely to end torture, we cannot halt the inertia inherent in this condition. When promotions are often obtained by connections and obsequiousness, these practices encourage men to push their names to the fore whenever they accomplish anything and to embellish their reputations by undertaking spectacular public works. Such persons are narrow in their discussions and undertake reforms rashly. Officials and people are thus mutually deceptive and inconstant, trifles daily proliferate, and conduct and etiquette are rough. Relying on connections, graft, and silent usurpation, lower officials falsify accounts and flatter their superiors. As these are all old evils of the late bakufu, are we not encouraging inertia when we practice them now?

There are at present ranks in government and distinctions between classes. Such ranks encourage arrogant ways and only add useless complications. Regardless of whether peers, samurai, or the people are involved, these distinctions obstruct the progress of morality and destroy the means for communication between high and low. Such conditions may indeed be inevitable. But is not the present inertia also excessive in this respect? As taxes and finance have not yet been referred to public discussion, the people confuse public expenditures for their own property and are reduced to cunning by their extreme muddle-headedness. It is naturally appropriate to abolish controls on interest rates.[16] If we pay attention only to theory without heeding the evils, however, how shall we after all prevent injury and protect the people in conformity with the times?

Even civilized countries like France have established laws governing interest rates after discussing publicly the evils arising from absence of control. It is today a punishable crime in France when interest rates exceed five or six percent on public bonds and ten percent on private loans. After her recent great defeat, France rapidly paid off a huge indemnity, and her wealth is increasing still more. The people have recently been paying several times more in taxes than the officials have assessed. But even though the people thus habitually shoulder heavy responsibilities in public finance, there has been perfect confidence and mutual harmony between rich and poor because their financial measures contribute to protection. If such be not the case in Japan, how can we avoid the injuries arising from innumerable suits and bankruptcies, and the harm of falling victim to the momentum of financial profiteering after society has been confused by many superficial arguments in a multitude of tricky suits?

We unaccountably give profit to foreigners by failing to encourage maritime commerce, which is the foundation of English and French prosperity. In the development of Hokkaidō, wily officials and wicked persons are abusing the inhabitants.[17] Hurrying to levy taxes without long-range plans, they are inexorably heading toward destruction with their opportunistic attitude toward old customs. How much more is this the case in Karafuto![18] We should become champions of the nation by quickly establishing public laws for the election of a popularly elected assembly under the aegis of the throne. Vacillation and oppression, however, are daily stirring up anger, and the other agents of momentum and inertia cannot be counted.

What after all will come from this pivotal time of change, if we continue to suffer the twin ills of clinging to the past while we rashly introduce reforms? The people are responsible for failing to assist the throne, and the people naturally include high and low. Since the power of the people is now generally held by the upper classes, which is most to blame, the high or the low? I have heard that the English like neither to be controlled by other men nor to control other men. The Japanese, on the other hand, like to control other men and to be controlled by others. Their vices are that high and low flatter each other, oppress each other, imitate each other, bow to strength, scorn the weak, act violently if they are not shrinking, or are complacent with the domineering and frivolous manners of the Edokko.[19] Once enraged, such people are like mad rats. Otherwise, they are like mice—timid, suspicious of each other, and craven on the outside even as they are fearful on the in. Should we be the rotten rats who shrink, the poisonous rats who are violent, or change into good white mice?

We should really consider deeply this pivotal [time of] change. After all, the prevention of momentum and inertia lies in calm determination. To bravely punish anger, squelch desire, return to good, and correct errors are "morals" for the individual. Of still greater importance is the "moral" conduct of the nation by which the blessings of strength and prosperity are achieved through the elimination of private interest and the cleaning out of the inertia in old customs among harmonious leaders in government and energetic people below. I hope that we may assist the throne in the crisis of this pivotal time by prudent change, and that we shall observe "morals" conducive to courageously halting inertia and momentum in the nation, being united by "morals" that bravely exclude inertia and momentum among individuals through mutual stimulation among the people.

[1]Three Human Treasures, *Jinsei Sambō*, 人世三寶. Nishi's first four essays on the three human treasures were his most important philosophical contributions to the *Meiroku Zasshi*. They are also the essays in the journal that most clearly reflect the influence of John Stuart Mill's utilitarianism on Nishi's thought. Like Fukuzawa Yukichi, Nishi was convinced that Japan would only advance to the level of civilization if her feudal traditions of loyalty and subservience as well as the ethics of Chu Hsi (朱熹) Confucianism were replaced by a new morality that stressed individual initiative. To this end, he proposed as the ethical basis for society the individual pursuit of the three treasures of health, wealth, and wisdom. While his ideas of individual initiative and private gain may appear commonplace in the West, they were quite alien to the group-oriented society into which Nishi was born. For a fine explanation of the significance of Nishi's essays in Japan, see Thomas Havens, *Nishi Amane and Modern Japanese Thought* (Princeton, 1970), pp. 141–163. Nishi eventually completed eight essays in this series, but the Meirokusha halted publication of their journal before the final four could be printed. These last four may be found in the collection of Nishi's writings edited by Professor Ōkubo Toshiaki (大久保利謙), *Nishi Amane Zenshū*, 西周全集 (3 vols. plus one preliminary vol.: Tokyo, 1945–1966), I, 533–554.

[2]*Jitsuriha*, 實理派.

[3]*Rigaku*, 利學.

[4]For *mame*, *chie*, and *tomi*, Nishi also provides the ideographic synonyms *kenkō* (健康), *chishiki* (智識), and *fuyū*, (富有).

[5]*Zen*, 禪.

[6]Lao Tzŭ, 老子, and Chuang Tzŭ, 莊子. It is interesting to note that Nishi and Sakatani Shiroshi were united in their disparagement of Zen Buddhism and Taoism.

[7]*Ten-un*, 天運.

[8]*Jisei*, 時勢.

[9]*Saisei hoshō*, 裁成輔相.

[10]Sakatani refers to the division within the Japanese government over the Korean question that provoked Saigō Takamori (西郷隆盛), and Itagaki Taisuke (板垣退助), and others to resign.

[11]*Jōge dōji*, 上下同治. See especially Sakatani's articles in Issues Fifteen, Twenty-Seven, and Twenty-Eight.

[12]The memorial to the Left Chamber (*Sain*, 左院) in which Soejima Taneomi (副島種臣), Itagaki Taisuke, and others urged establishment of a popularly elected assembly.

[13]Sakatani refers to the imperial rescript of 14 April 1875 that ordered the establishment of the Senate (*Genrō-in,* 元老院), the Supreme Court (*Daishin-in,* 大審院), and an assembly of regional officials as steps toward the eventual creation of a constitutional system. See the *Shimbun Shūsei Meiji Hennen Shi,* 新聞集成明治編年史 (15 vols.: Tokyo, 1935), II, 307.

[14]Sakatani here refers to the rights of extraterritoriality and conventional tariff that were included in the so-called unequal treaties of 1858 and afterward between Japan and the West.

[15]Boissonade, Gustave Émile, 1825–1910, the French legal adviser who protested vigorously in both speech and writing against the use of torture in Japan.

[16]According to one estimate, rates charged by banks on loans during the years 1875–1884 averaged 15.09 percent. Fukuzawa Yukichi in 1875 stated that interest on short-term loans ranged between twenty and thirty percent when calculated on an annual basis.

[17]From its establishment in 1869 to its dissolution in 1882, the operations of the *Hokkaidō Kaitaku-shi* (北海道開拓使, the Hokkaidō Development Office) were the subject of recrimination and charges of malpractice.

[18]Japanese plans to open Karafuto (樺太), Sakhalin, were halted in 1875 when Japan ceded her interests in the island to Russia in exchange for the Russian Kuriles.

[19]Edokko, 江戸ッ子, natives of Edo.

The Three Human Treasures Part Two[1]

Nishi Amane

In my previous essay, I discussed the great principles by which individuals advance morality and cultivate virtue. Next there are the methods by which men mutually associate with their fellow creatures in accordance with the principles of social intercourse between individuals. In my moral theory, these methods lie in honoring the three great treasures and sharing them with others.

Now let me illustrate this thought in a summary outline. The first "rule" [for social intercourse between individuals] states, "Thou shalt not injure in the least the health of other men, and thou shalt promote the health of other men if this should be done with thy assistance." The second rule states, "Thou shalt not injure in the least the knowledge of other men,* and thou shalt promote the knowledge of other men if this should be done with your assistance." And the third rule states: "Thou shalt not injure in the least the property of others, and thou shalt promote the property of others if this should be done with thy assistance." If we really try hard to associate with others by honoring these three great rules, we shall attain so-called human-heartedness (*jin*)[2] and realize justice (*gi*).[3]

Let me endeavor to explain this thought by analyzing the above rules. When the conduct and affairs of individuals relate only to their own persons and not to others, it is sufficient for them solely to honor their own three treasures. Being completely one in mind, they do not distinguish between mine and thine. Once they enter into relations with fellow beings, however, they establish at this point a distinction between mine and thine, and their oneness of mind necessarily divides to become two. In such cases, the disease of bias is inevitable, as is the distinction between favoring oneself

*To injure the knowledge of other men is to deceive them, to hush them up, to slander them, to lie to them, and the like.

(mine) and neglecting others (thine). Yet this is only a distinction appearing in outward conduct. If you consider the minds of individuals, honoring the three treasures of others does not, of course, differ in the least [from honoring] our own three treasures. It is as evident as fire that the ancient sages for this reason admonished the world by proclaiming [their] great teachings. Christ said, "Thou shalt love others as thyself." And Confucius asserted, "[The virtuous man] helps others if he desires to help himself."[4] These are indeed splendid words for all times, upon which the wise men of succeeding generations have not been able to improve.

Even so, since there is a distinction between mine and thine, there must be an order of precedence by which men conduct their affairs. Now take the man who really loves others with utmost sincerity and benevolence. If he meets a sick man on the road, takes out medicine that he usually carries in his pocket, and suddenly thrusts the medicine into the sick man's mouth, however, will not the sick man take the loving individual for a madman? Not only will he call his benefactor a madman. He will also glare back in anger. Confucius said, "I dare not taste what I know not myself."[5] Since there is actually a distinction between mine and thine, therefore, there is necessarily an order in precedence when conducting affairs, the impartiality of men's minds notwithstanding.

And so, I first introduced my three rules with what I call their negative stipulations: "Thou shalt not injure the health of others, thou shalt not injure the knowledge of others, and thou shalt not injure the wealth of others." This is because they are all prohibitions and because they do not directly touch others, indicating, as they do, intent to control, to restrain, and to prevent oneself [from hurting] the three treasures of others. I would call positive stipulations the concluding phrases of the three rules that state, "Thou shalt promote . . . if it should be promoted." This is because they are positive precepts that permit men to assist, to encourage, and to affirm the three treasures of others. In this sense, the three negative stipulations constitute the area of morality that forms the basis of law, and the three positive stipulations become "moral obligations."

Let me undertake to discuss this further. Legal codes and systems are now beyond counting. In East Asian lands, legal codes have been gradually developed with the passage of time; the fairly well developed codes of T'ang were the basis for the ancient codes of our country, and there have also been the codes of Ming and Ch'ing.[6] Among the innumerable laws in the West, Roman law is especially honored, but there are also the Code Napoleon, English law, comparable laws currently in force in various other countries, and the codes in which religion and law are mutually related, such as Judaic law and the Koran. In sum, therefore, when these laws in the least regulate current human affairs, there are none that do not protect against injury to these three treasures. Their various stipulations, in short, actually should all lead only to this end.

To translate injury to the three treasures into legal terminology: injuring a man's life and health is called assault, injuring his knowledge, fraudulence, and taking his "property" [wealth], robbery. Even though the great crimes of the world seem manifold and without limit, they are all different forms of bodily assault, fraudulence, or robbery that injure the three treasures. Bodily assault, fraudulence, and robbery are also variant forms of the three retributions of disease, ignorance, and poverty that, when willfully perpetrated, [I] would call the three heinous crimes. Individuals in their conduct, therefore, honor their own three treasures, energetically avoid the three retributions, and firmly prevent the three heinous crimes of others. In the language of law, these are termed "rights" (*kenri*),[7] while to honor the three treasures of other men, to control our three heinous crimes, and to avoid violating the above rules are called "obligations" (*gimu*).[8] If men mutually affirm these rights and obligations and refrain from violating them in the least, the great principles of humanity will be established and the foundations of moral conduct laid.

We cannot yet say, however, that men have reached perfection. Achieving this perfection lies in preventing the three retributions from falling on others by honoring their three treasures. This is the greatest, highest, most beautiful, and most fine of human virtues, being the rule [of Christ] that man should love others as himself and [of Confucius] that man should help others if he desires to help himself. This virtue, after all, is rooted in human nature and arises from abundance of genuine feeling. When we see others afflicted by disease, death, ignorance, and poverty, therefore, we are sympathetically troubled in our hearts. This is sufficient to suggest that, since fellow creatures are really all of the same body as ourselves, we do not make any distinction between mine and thine when it comes to the enemies of the three treasures. From this [virtue of honoring the three treasures of others], there arises all virtuous conduct, such as sympathizing with the illness of others, extending condolences in the event of death, teaching those who are misled by ignorance, and assisting those who are oppressed by poverty. This virtuous conduct is what individuals take to be most important in their relations with others, as it is the factor that truly illuminates the three positive stipulations.

Be that as it may, why are the positive stipulations all written "hypothetically" by the insertion of "if"? This really indicates a distinction between mine and thine and reveals an order in which matters are taken up. "Should" is thus added to "if" to suggest that men are induced to act appropriately [on behalf of the three treasures] in compliance with the time and the place. Therefore, we should really pursue matters according to a definite order even though, having been led by our wholeheartedness, compassion, and anxiety to forget the distinction between mine and thine, we are taut as a bow string and sharp as a sword in honoring the three treasures of others and in preventing the three retributions from falling on others. These being moral obligations, they should not be confused with the previously mentioned rights and duties under the law. Nevertheless, moral obligations are fundamental principles of humanity, and honoring the three treasures lies in fulfilling man's moral obligations before which the various other rules are all subordinate, like the various stars that lose their light when the sun comes out. Thus when men confront adversity, suffer hardships of the times, and are truly oppressed by moral obligations, they meet their moral obligations by straining themselves on behalf of their fellow creatures without consideration for their lives. This is fulfilling one of the three treasures after casting aside another. Confucius said that [men of determination and virtue] sacrifice their lives to achieve virtuous compassion,[9] and the Holy Man of the West [Christ] exemplified this rule. How can there be anything more important than moral obligations? This is the key principle by which individuals have intercourse with their fellow creatures by honoring the three treasures. When an individual receives a commission from his fellow men and publicly exercises responsibility in their affairs, his path also will not go beyond honoring these three treasures. I shall discuss this more precisely later.

On the Divergent Interests of Governments and People
Speech on June 1

Nishimura Shigeki

Things are generally referred to as a whole or by their parts. Man is a whole, and his spirit and body are his parts. A nation is a whole, and its government and people are its parts. A man or a nation is a single entity when looked at from the point of view of the whole. Looked at from the point of view of their parts, they are two. Once they are divided into their two parts, there is an invariable tendency for the interests of each part to differ. Let me explain this in detail.

It is the merit of the human spirit that sages and superior men are produced and fame and wealth are acquired by individual exertion, by stimulation of thought, and by performing services. Yet from the point of view of the body, one must call such endeavors injurious if it is feared that, because of them, the man's health will be injured and his life shortened. To preserve one's health and longevity by moving the limbs and exercising the muscles without stimulating the intellect or employing the spirit is a benefit for the body. Yet from the spiritual point of view, it must be said that such activity is injurious if there is danger that it will ultimately produce stupid and foolish people without expanding knowledge and illuminating morals. How strange it is that, if you look at an individual as a whole, there is no reason for distinguishing between benefits and injuries since he is naturally one. Yet if you look at him from the point of view of his two parts, the benefit of one becomes the injury of the other as their interests are not mutually the same.

Such also is the case with nations. It is advantageous for the government when its power and authority flourishes, when the people regard this power with fear, when its orders are carried out, when its prohibitions are honored, and when there is absolutely no opposition in the nation to what the government desires to accomplish. From the people's point of view, however, one must term this [government authority] injurious if, because of it, men suffer restrictions, are subjected to repression, or are unable in the least to advance their rights. It is advantageous for the people if they expand their liberties, destroy their fetters, hold the power of taxation, and can raise or demote officials. Yet speaking for the government's position, such [popular rights] must be termed injurious if the authority of the government is consequently destroyed, the power of the ruler is reduced, and the government always fears conflicts with or interference by the people whenever it undertakes anything.

Now the people are taxpayers, and the government is the tax collector. Light taxes are an advantage for the taxpayer; heavy taxes, an advantage for the tax collector. Large tax collections are not advantageous for dictatorial governments alone. Even good governments never deplore the largeness of taxes. Nor are light taxes an advantage only for idle persons. Even good people never regret light taxes. Take the example of borrowers and lenders. It is to the advantage of borrowers to have low interest rates while high interest rates are advantageous to lenders. Even meritorious lenders favor high interest rates, and I have yet to hear of a lender who desires low interest rates. In marketing, sellers want high prices; buyers, low prices. I have not yet heard of even a superior person who wants to purchase at a high price and to sell at a low price.

Looked at in this light, to expect government to reduce taxes and administer benevolently is like expecting low prices from a seller or low interest rates from a lender. It is not natural to expect low prices and low interest rates from sellers and lenders since these are not in the least to their advantage. This is probably why since antiquity those administering oppressively have generally been numerous while those conducting benevolent rule have normally been few.

If this is the case, will governments never conduct benevolent administration if matters are left to nature? If the people want to acquire their rights, should they seize the rights forcefully with their own strength? And if they desire low taxes, can they only achieve their wish after threatening the government with [their] power?

A nation's affairs are generally composed of public and private interests. Serving the interest of others along with one's own interest is called public interest. Serving one's own interest without regard for injury to others is called private interest. Social intercourse is the inevitable path of human beings. When an individual enters into social intercourse, he should not injure the public interest of the people by claiming his private interest. Lenders, therefore, should consider the interest of borrowers; sellers, the interest of buyers. When this is not the case and an individual injures the public interest by pursuing his private interest, his presumed private interest actually may ultimately bring him injury rather than profit.

It thus seems that, since a person's body and that of another, of course, are clearly two, his interest is definitely not that of the other. Yet he will ultimately bring injury on himself if he simply serves his own interest without reflecting on the interests of others. A nation is no different from this. Even though it may be divided to distinguish government from people, it is fundamentally a whole entity, exactly like a man who consists of body and spirit. Once they are united in a whole entity, disadvantage for the people becomes disadvantage for the government, the interest of the government being the interest of the people. This may be compared to a man in whom a tired body is injurious to the spirit even as a weak spirit is injurious to the body.

Since I now speak in this fashion, is my previous explanation regarding advantage and injury to people and government absolutely wrong? I would respond that it is not. My earlier discussion is valid from the viewpoint of private interest; my later discussion, from the viewpoint of public interest.

What then are the public interests of the country? They are strength, prosperity, tranquility, and prestige. The people as well as the government must take these as their objectives. Even though it is to the government's interest to rule despotically and to levy taxes broadly, it should appropriately control its own desires, check its private interest, and thereby refrain from exercising such powers if their exercise injures the strength, prosperity, tranquility, and prestige of the nation. Even though it is in the people's interest to reduce taxes and to extend their rights, the people should appropriately control their own desires, check their private interests, and thereby refrain from exercising these rights if their exercise injures the strength, prosperity, tranquility, and prestige of the nation. When such is the case, the interests of high and low are one, and the entire country with united power can advance to a position of strength, prosperity, tranquility, and prestige without fear of rebellion by the people against the government and without danger of oppression of the people by the government.

In a half-civilized country, however, the government's authority is normally heavy, and its requisitions normally numerous. The position of the people is the opposite of this. If [we] try to establish a balance of national power, this cannot be truly achieved if both government and people retreat five steps, since the government's power normally amounts to eighty or ninety percent while the people's power does not exceed ten to twenty percent. Certainly, a balance can only be achieved if the government retreats two or three steps and the people advance eight or nine steps. This is why public-spirited men never cease to reiterate their support of the people's rights. After all, the people's rights, as the finest treasures inherent in the people, are not matters that should depend upon the generosity of the government. When we look at the present situation, it seems that the government, of course, already understands the public interest of the nation. If it understands the public interest well, the government will certainly not compete with the people over private interest. If the people want to establish an equilibrium in national power by energetically claiming their rights, there is no reason for the government absolutely to deny them. But we also cannot know whether the government will graciously concede them. If the people wait for the government to grant their rights by complacently placing their confidence in the government, it will be like waiting for the clearing of the Yellow River. The time will then never come when the government will concede. Let us strive! Let us strive!

An Outline of Western Culture[10]

Nakamura Masanao

Since [Francis] Bacon also compared the benefit from cultivating the intellect during childhood with the harvest invariably secured by the farmer from his spring ploughing, he discussed this theme under the title *Georgics of the Mind.* (The title suggests a song on the cultivation of mental fields. Bacon took the name from Virgil's poem entitled *Georgics* in which the Italian poet of antiquity depicts cultivation of the mind.) Using this metaphor, which conveys the sense of encouraging agriculture, Bacon wanted on the one hand to direct men's attention to opening up new fields and to promoting bountiful harvests and on the other hand to direct their view toward controlling the wildness of the mind and toward encouraging the germination of talent and virtue.

Fox observed that there was a surprising advance in the literary arts between 1588 and 1640 when [Richard] Hooker, [Walter] Raleigh, [Francis] Bacon, [Edmund] Spenser, [William] Shakespeare, and others adorned England with the beauties of their language and literature. After all, human ethics improved with the cultivation of language and literature since language and literature are tools for advancing morality. Even though the number of enlightened men was at first small, culture greatly progressed because these few encouraged enlightenment by themselves, thereby influencing others. Especially since they endeavored to bring together in one body the commonly used language and the ideas of the wise and the enlightened, they thereby enhanced men's natural power for enlightened understanding and enabled later generations to progress from a higher level of departure. The generation of their fathers had not yet reached this high level.

There were points on which Bacon and Raleigh resembled each other despite the considerable differences in their conduct and work. Both men fully exerted the power of their intellects and cast off the fetters of school and society (such as narrow-mindedness). Even the heroic figures of their day could not reach their level. It may be said that the great achievements of the two were to master the English language, to make it rich, diversified, and refined, and to reform the crudities in the vulgar tongue of the common people.

Hobbes

There was born in Malmesbury, England in 1588 a man named [Thomas] Hobbes, who founded a separate school of moral and political studies and whose thought is epitomized by his desire to return the powers of state to the sovereign. Celebrated men in moral and political studies of the eighteenth century one after the other refuted his ideas, and even today Hobbes' school is generally reviled in recent writings on the art of ruling. Nevertheless, I will here present an outline of Hobbes' views since they once influenced England.

Hobbes' thought ran as follows. Men in their original condition were without exception equal (that is, without distinction between exalted and vulgar), and the people before the appearance of rulers all equally enjoyed the right to divide and use the world's goods. Moreover, men without exception independently possessed their own individual characters. There inevitably emerged the practice by which men associated with others and formed groups to suit their convenience. In the long run, there was an invariable tendency for men to fight since they were all equal and possessed respectively their independent minds. How dangerous it was that they had no more than their own wisdom and their own strength upon which to depend when they sought security!

Hobbes drew from daily experience when he undertook to explain the origins of "society":

> Just reflect! Are there any who do not wear protective armor or desire to be accompanied by trusted companions when they travel? Are there any who do not want to lock their doors when they are asleep? Still more, are there any who do not use keys for chests even in their homes? And are there any who do not try to prove their innocence when they are falsely accused?

One of Hobbes' followers also spoke as follows in this regard:

> Just look at children. Are there any who do not dislike seeing men from strange countries or who are not afraid when they hear the unaccustomed sound of steps at night?

Hobbes further explained: Since there is an invariable tendency for men to fight if they are left to nature, it is essential to provide for peace and security by establishing law. If they desire this [peace], individuals should be satisfied to receive the advantages of secure protection together with all others in society in return for sacrificing their own individual rights. Therefore, a nation exists only after [the people] establish one man as their leader and give to him rights that should naturally be theirs. That is, one person drawn from the people of the nation unites their will and power to carry out policies for their protection. Moreover, the right to rule the country cannot later be withdrawn from the sovereign to whom it was originally entrusted. It should be impossible to punish the ruler even if his policies are inappropriate. Scholars should not be allowed individually to debate the determination of law since this belongs to the powers of government. When government determines right and wrong, the people should heed this decision, regarding it as the judgment from within their own individual hearts.

Hobbes also discussed the fact that the ruler alone should exercise authority. In his view, the people are like beasts that cannot be tamed, while the government is like a chain that serves as an instrument to prevent harm by the people. Hobbes' views were indeed biased. Yet many were converted to his thought since his was a time when the English King Charles II had secretly fled to France, when the people all disliked royal authority and harbored seditious thoughts, and when the country was disturbed. His fame thus loomed large in the world, and he was firmly established among the celebrated figures in philosophy.

[1]Continued from previous issue.

[2]*Jin*, 仁.

[3]*Gi*, 義.

[4][*Jinsha*] . . . *onore tassen to hosshite hito o tassu*, [仁者] . . . 己達セムト欲シテ人ヲ達ス. From the *Analects* (*Lun Yü*, 論語), Book VI, Chapt. XXVIII.

[5]*Kyū imada tassezu aete namezu*, 丘未ダ達セズ敢テ嘗メズ. From ibid., Book X, Chapt. XI.

[6]T'ang, 唐, Ming, 明, and Ch'ing, 清.

[7]*Kenri*, 權利.

[8]*Gimu*, 義務.

[9][*Shishi jinjin*] . . . *mi o koroshi motte jin o nasu*, [志士仁人]. . . .身ヲ殺シ以テ仁ヲ成ス From the *Analects* (*Lun Yü*, 論語), Book XV, Chapt. VIII.

[10]Continued from Issue Twenty-Three.

The Three Human Treasures Part Three[1]

Nishi Amane

In the last two parts, I discussed the fact that the great principles of morality in human life lie in honoring the three treasures, and I explained that we need no other principles to guide the main course of human relations and individual conduct. Continuing from here, I shall undertake to discuss the relation of the three treasures to the essentials for ruling the people. What is referred to here as governing the people is the method for conducting administration by distinguishing between rulers and subjects and establishing the nation. It is also the method for enhancing and increasing the happiness of our fellow creatures through the formation of what we call government.

There is, however, one matter that I should take up first—social life between human beings. This is because, looked at philosophically, fraternal social life is invariably mutually cultivated and an urgent necessity in the human world before government has yet been established. Now, fraternal social life is extremely broad and extremely active in the enlightened countries. Upon this active social life depends their strength and their prosperity, their peace and their turbulence, the emergence of industry and progress in scholarship. It may well be said that what men call government only presides impassively over the community.[2] That social intercourse flourishes to such an extent, of course, arises from the fact that secular teachings (*seikyō*)[3] are appropriate while enlightenment has been achieved. Yet when we consider its fundamental sources, social intercourse is rooted internally in the mental character of man and based externally on the character of human structure, that is, on natural reason. Since human beings evolved from monkeys and were born men, they have been inseparable from social life. Therefore, even the black men of Africa, the red men of the American mountains, the Mongol hordes, the Ainu, and the aborigines of Taiwan invariably and necessarily maintain social intercourse (albeit primitive) in their towns and hamlets that varies according to the nature of their societies. Even though their customs include such abuses as regarding neighboring villages with hostility, continually attacking each other, selling prisoners, and decorating skulls, such barbarian practices [indicate] only people who, being all men of limited and biased knowledge, have not yet been able to achieve perfection in their social life by expanding the character of their group life. (Recall that some ten years ago, this country also had laws for attacking the black ships.)[4]

Now if you compare these barbarian customs with the inclination of wise men in enlightened Western countries who desire forthwith to bring the whole world together in one society, they seem indeed as far apart as Heaven and earth. Yet if you consider their fundamental roots, they only differ in degree rather than in kind, like the difference between germinating sprouts and great pines of the mountains. Thus as it is an axiom that the social structure is inseparable from human life, it also cannot be doubted that this social structure is broadened and strengthened as culture becomes enlightened. Today the great emotions of society are "patriotism" and "nationalism." (For the moment, [I] shall leave to the imaginations of philosophers such ideals as Kant's "eternal peace" and "worldly republic.") Both indicate our human feelings in social intercourse, being called "nationalism" when they follow the times and "patriotism" when they oppose the times. They are like the feeling that a person has when, having been abroad for many years, he returns to his home and sees a great pine that he cherished first as a child. Why do we have this sentiment for unfeeling trees and stones? It is because the social emotions are firmly established in men's hearts. How much more is this the case with good friends and old acquaintances, and still more with relatives!

The path of social intercourse, therefore, is an urgent requirement of human life from which we cannot be separated for even a moment. Moreover, this path does not extend beyond honoring the aforementioned three treasures. After all, social intercourse is established and developed on the premise that honoring the three treasures is mutually associated from beginning to end with methods for mutually cultivating social life. I would like to discuss this in some detail.

Generally speaking, the desire for health is associated with the necessity for adequate supplies of such commodities as food, clothing, and shelter. Furthermore, these commodities can never be produced by individuals [alone] unless they are hermits inured to rustic life in nests and caves. This is why the social structure must be established with the inevitable division of labor. If a person wants to expand his wisdom, he cannot [alone] penetrate the principles behind all things during his lifetime. Nor can he invent one by one the commodities that he uses. This is why the social structure must be established with the inevitable development of scholarship. On the whole, if a person desires to increase as well as to improve and beautify his property, he cannot do so even though he wants [himself] to produce everything as well as improve and beautify everything. This is why social intercourse must be broadened as demands increase and as products multiply with the inevitable development of specialized industries and division of labor.

Therefore, it is a truism that, since honoring the three treasures is the foundation of social intercourse, the more the three treasures are honored, the more social intercourse expands and prospers. Such rude customs of barbarians as living in hovels, wearing rags, and eating and drinking coarsely arise from no other fact than that they do not yet honor health. That such people have yet to develop a system of recording with ropes, still less a writing technique, is for no other reason than that they still fail to honor knowledge. That they have no means for accumulating wealth or for gathering and distributing their accumulations by using currency is attributable to no other cause than that they have yet to reach the point of honoring their wealth.

Therefore, men inevitably develop the path of social intercourse if they in the least honor the three treasures. Why should men fear that social intercourse will not be broadened if they honor the three treasures more and more profoundly and if they promote them vigorously? After all, barbarians are barbarians because they are content with their meanness and waste Heaven's endowment. Now even among persons who are healthy throughout their lives, there are few who are not attended by mid-wives and obstetricians at birth. This is because it is essential to protect health. Once they reach adolescence, individuals inevitably learn their father's profession or another trade even though they may not be trained in scholarship. Or failing this, they invariably learn speech and manners. This is because the acquisition of knowledge is essential. Upon reaching maturity, men unavoidably live by their own labors by following such professions as agriculture, herding, carpentry, and trade. This is because the accumulation of wealth is also inevitable.

Thus from childhood to old age, the three treasures are the great principles of social intercourse from which men can invariably never escape. Furthermore, when a person contradicts this reasoning, makes light of the three treasures, and injures his health with illness, his wisdom with foolishness, and his wealth with idleness, he is then not rated as a human being but rejected from social intercourse. Such a person is called a beggar or an invalid. Even though he may not be guilty of a crime and even though his truly pitiable condition may arise from nature or fate, he cannot participate in regular social intercourse as he is deficient in the three treasures. If men truly honor the three treasures without any reservations, however, what will prevent them from being regular members of society even though they may differ in social station? For example, it is a matter of course that old men who repair pipes, young men who gather trash paper, common women who sell beans, and children who gather manure follow vulgar professions and are not elevated in their ways. And who is not impressed by the dignity of monarchs, the nobility of great ministers, and the prosperity of wealthy merchants and farmers? Yet if you look at them from the point of view of social intercourse, the former no less than the latter are individually members of society. Social intercourse is like a great hall in which kings and ministers are the beams and the commoners are the wedges and nails. If we assess their utility and their merit, they must all be counted even though they may differ in size.

Social intercourse, therefore, is like links in a chain or beads in a rosary. If you compare the individual links and beads, they are all equally parts of the chain or rosary even though they may vary in size. Just consider the injury to the chain or the rosary should one of its links or beads be defective. It is the nature of social intercourse, therefore, that, should a single individual in the least neglect or injure the three treasures, the bad consequences inevitably extends to the whole of social intercourse. Apart from beggars and invalids who cannot participate regularly in social intercourse, there is thus no one who does not occupy an appropriate position in social intercourse, and the three treasures of individual men, being invariably the same, never differ in significance.

In the "morality" of the three treasures, therefore, we uphold two fundamental principles as rules for social intercourse. The first is that the three treasures of men are equally precious without regard to men's differing social station. The second is that man is free and independent in all his conduct so long as he does not injure in the least these three treasures. These then are two fundamental principles found in Christianity as *"égalité et liberté."* The ethics of the three treasures cannot be established without relying on the principles of equality and liberty, notwithstanding the fact that the principles even today are unknown in East Asia. (While Buddha seems to have taught equality, the two principles belong to the lands to the west of the Himalayas.)

Should I then be asked if the preciousness of men's three treasures is always the same and never different, I would respond that there are absolutely no cases of difference. Whereupon it may be asked if there are absolutely no differences (*tōsai*)[5] in our honoring wisdom, ability, and wealth [among men]? To which I would respond that we respect men of wisdom and honor men of wealth for the very reason that there are absolutely no cases in which the preciousness of the three treasures of individuals differ. After all, the equal preciousness of the three treasures in individuals is like the "specific weights" in all matter. If there were exceptions to specific weights, what would be the standard for making comparisons? Now it is invariably the case that pure gold is nineteen times heavier than water (when measured by the same standard of weight), and we know that ten *sen* is ten times heavier than one *sen.*[6] If there were exceptions to specific weights, however, by what standards would we establish comparisons? Among men generally, therefore, the preciousness of the three treasures is invariably the same. Furthermore, just as ten *sen* is ten times heavier than one *sen,* there is a natural difference among men by which persons superior in strength, wisdom, and wealth increase their preciousness in proportion to the level of their superiority.

Now there are the caste systems of ancient Egypt as well as of India in which persons equally human are divided as if they have the different specific weights of gold, silver, copper and iron. But in addition to the caste systems, there are also customs of nepotism such as are often seen under despotic governments. These practices are all emphatically rejected by the morality of the three treasures in social intercourse. Since I have already spoken at length, I shall postpone for a later meeting discussion of still additional theories regarding the relation of the three treasures to social intercourse.

On Nurturing the Human Spirit Part One

Sakatani Shiroshi

The other day, I discussed the fact that two essentials for nurturing the spirit are expanding the intellect through cultivation of scholarship and encouraging responsibility through public management of finance. There is a matter, however, that I have considered still more fully. It is that, among the many sources of spiritual inferiority of China and Japan to the West, the most important is tools. If I take this line, the old teachers of religion and scholars in Chinese studies will surely revile me for stressing tools at the expense of morality (*michi*).[7] On the other hand, I value tools only because I esteem morality. That is, morality is abstract while machines are concrete, and the abstract cannot be achieved without reliance on the concrete. All the concrete, useful things ranging from houses, carts, and ships to foodstuffs, clothing, and arms are no more than tools. Loyal ministers and brave men all act on behalf of country, family, and friends with the assistance of tools. Drinking by drinkers, eating by eaters, and intercourse by farmers, artisans, and merchants in their respective occupations all depend on tools. But for good tools, their moral conduct would invariably be obstructed. A brave man will oppose his enemy with his bare hands, but he cannot succeed without tools. In the proverb, "Give an iron rod to a devil,"[8] the devil refers to an extremely strong person. Even an extremely strong person will be further strengthened if he acquires an iron rod. Without a rod, he will inevitably be frightened by the swords of children.

Normally, there are in society few brave men and many cowards as well as few skilled and many unskilled. With tools, however, the cowards can become brave, the unskilled, skilled. We should recognize that tools stimulate morality by encouraging the spirit and instilling bravery. Suppose the ships and arms of the West were transferred to China and Japan. Would not the strong and wealthy West necessarily take China and Japan as its guide? Now let us suppose that war breaks out. We would be entirely indebted to the West for arms and ammunition. But for the West, we would throw up our hands and die because we would have nothing upon which to depend. Fish depend on water for their exuberance; beasts, on the mountains for invigoration. Naturally, man's spirit flourishes once he has something to depend on. I hear that the military spirit is stirred in Western warfare by providing good doctors in addition to fine generals. Even timid women will walk on fire and water if they rely on the gods and Buddha. If we fail to develop tools, we shall ultimately be no more than slaves and children even though we sedulously study Western law, government, and religion.

When asked upon what we should depend to stimulate our spirit and establish our national power, some may respond, "Upon the teaching of morality." This is just like the teacher who told of the ants. Years ago, an old scholar in Chinese studies contrived a story about ants that ran as follows:

> One day, I sat by the roadside on the root of a pine tree and watched the coming and going of ants. Since they all courteously gave way to each other upon meeting, I knew that man also must be courteous.

An old farmer spoke up in derision:

> Without knowing a single character, I have understood since childhood that men must be courteous. How remarkable it is that you, a teacher, have only learned courtesy from the ants

> after years of study! I am happy and content to help others with the surplus from my plough. Even though you, sir, have read thousands of books, you have brought not one benefit to society with your futile unending discussions while you enjoy the food provided by others.

The words of the farmer are too harsh, but he could understand that his morality was supported with a tool [his plough]. As for the uses of tools in society, what a good man contrives poorly [without tools] is not as beneficial as what a wicked man contrives [well with tools].

Therefore, while the rise and fall of morality depends on whether the times are disturbed or not, tools are not thus related to the times. On occasion, the development of tools is only the more stimulated by disturbances. This may be why the enlightened states of the West greatly enhance their power by disturbance, while China and Japan are impoverished by disturbance. We should understand that concrete things expand the intellect and develop the spirit whereas empty theory is without profit.

Now tools have always been important even in China and Japan. Does their failure to develop tools arise from intellectual inferiority? It does not. China was ahead of the West in the invention of many tools. The English and the French have noted these Chinese inventions, and the Russians have feared them. The Chinese, however, have not improved their tools since the day of their invention. On the contrary, some have deteriorated or been abandoned. After some private reflection, I have concluded that this was because the Chinese study of matter (*kigaku*)[9] has not developed since it was halted at its inception. Tools arise from technology, and technology is born from skill and thought. Thought is most important in tools. Moreover, everything with form in this world is produced from matter. How can we exercise this thought and with what will we produce forms if we do not understand matter? I do not know, however, why China failed to develop the study of matter.

Modern theorists blame the backwardness of China on the fact that the Confucian Way made no provision for progress, and they explain that our country was also hurt thereby. Confucius, however, only discussed morality without going into the study of matter. Being concerned only with ethics and politics, his words did not embrace the study of matter, although they encouraged enlightenment and achievement. There were before Confucius no pioneers in the study of matter whose teachings his words could formulate and propagate. Westerners have noted that their religion obstructs science. In the early stages of Christianity, science certainly should have been hurt by revelations of divine power in which men were bewitched by miracles. Actually, however, [Western] science flourished. And also contrary to what one might expect, science did not arise after Confucius taught enlightenment and achievement. Is this not strange?

I have consequently pondered the reasons for this over and over again. The theories of the five elements (*wu hsing*)[10] were the cause of the injury in China. Confucius and Mencius rejected and ignored the theories of the five elements. The *Book of Changes* emphasized the *Yin* and the *Yang* that are traced to Fu Hsi.[11] Since the five elements arose from the Yin and the Yang, is Fu Hsi the source of the injury? In his day, however, there were marks of divination but no writing. The so-called Yin and Yang are only described in such terms as light and dark or male and female, and the words water, fire, metal, wood, and earth appear in the *Canon of Shun.*[12] This reference, however, explains the five elements in connection with agriculture and refers only to forms observed in daily usage. The theories of the five elements abound in the *Hung Fan.*[13] Since the terms for medicine by divination are traced to Shên Nung,[14] they also are of ancient origin. The art was increasingly widespread by the time of the *Tso Chuan,*[15] and its practitioners were all vulgarly superstitious. Even Confucius could not escape writing about superstitions relating to phoenixes, the gigantic horse of the Yellow River, and the hunted unicorn.[16] Mencius did not mention these matters at all. Yet these old customs were elaborated during the Warring States Period[17] and greatly expanded during Ch'in and Han,[18] so that only superstitions remained in the four hundred states of China. Consequently, there emerged the political school of Chia I,[19] whose poem on the long-eared owls was superstition. Tung Chung-shu, Liu Hsiang, and Yang Hsiung[20] were celebrated scholars, but they were superstitious people. Kuang Wu of the Later Han[21] was also a hero of great spirit, but his superstitions did not rise above the level of present-day elementary school children. The extreme of folly is reached in the "Records of the Five Elements" in the *History of the Former Han Dynasty,*[22] which occupies one fifth of one book.

How can we assign blame for the proliferation of superstitions thereafter? Looked at from this viewpoint, we can understand that the theory of the five elements closed men's minds without even permitting them to begin the analytical study of matter. For this reason, men only uselessly exhausted their spirits and labored in vain on superficialities even though there have been opportunities to introduce the conveniences of tools with changing times and changing conditions. This was not only applicable to tools. It extended to all activities. In sum, the result is aimless floundering that at most only invites laughter, like a blind man walking down a street or like pampered children who pay a charge of 100 *sen* with a ten *yen* piece because they have not learned the use of coins even though they know what they are. Thus, even though from antiquity we have not been poor in men of intellect and wit, these men were without the means to exert their power as they were like a person who tries to climb a roof without a ladder.

Newton discovered the force of gravitation after seeing an apple fall from a tree. Worcester apprehended the power of steam when he noticed the bobbing lid of a kettle. Galvani understood the electrical affinity of two metals upon observing the ability of two metals to move the thigh of a dead frog. And from these precursors came the later discoveries of Franklin and Watt that robbed nature of her secrets. These men were indeed outstanding geniuses even in the West, but they would not have been moved to new conceptions had there been no tradition for the study of matter. The falling apple and bobbing lid would then have fallen and bobbed unnoticed.

The Zen priest gains enlightenment from the moon and the rain; the calligrapher from fighting snakes and sword dancing; and the warrior from poetry, shells, and woodpeckers. The things they understand are different, but they arise alike from their daily habits. How can we know that China and Japan would not have discovered the uses of steam and electricity before the West if these two countries had developed the tradition of matter studies from antiquity and if they had been allowed from infancy fully to exercise their intellects within this tradition? Furthermore, the practical use of tools for the study of matter will not arise if minds are coarse, and they will not mature without patience. If man's mind is sharpened by patience, he will develop skills for all manner of purposes, and he will not, for want of full understanding, take up projects that are only superficially advantageous. Nor will he resort to rash and violent practices like a monkey. His bravery will increase day by day, and his spirit will expand month by month.

It is futile to blame the past for our failure to develop the study of matter. Now this study is fortunately introduced to us. What will we not attain if we learn from the past and give attention to the future? I hope that 100 Newtons and 1000 Watts will appear among us if we sedulously avoid the error of studying Western externals and if those responsible for education and protection keep this [study of matter] firmly in mind. If this be not the case and if we vainly discuss empty theories, inquire into false principles, and boast of superficial enlightenment, we shall be unable to fight, having become wholly dependent on foreigners for the tools necessary for even the slightest action. Even if we fight, we shall then not be able to preserve order because of our mounting debts. Even if we preserve order, we shall not be able to conduct trade and industry because matters will be largely like putting a round peg in a square hole. And even if we conduct trade and industry, our national power will daily decline. Ah, are my admonitions on Western studies like those in the teacher's story of the ants?

[1]Continued from previous issue.

[2]*Suikyō nammen,* 垂拱南面. Nishi here uses a phrase that refers to the Chinese ideal of the ruler who sits facing southward (*nammen*) placidly doing nothing, his arms folded (*kyō*) and his garments hanging serenely (*sui*).

[3]*Seikyō,* 政教. Although this term could be translated as politics (*sei*) and religion (*kyō*), I believe that Nishi intended to use it in the sense of Sakatani Shiroshi's essays on secular ethical teachings (*seikyō*) as a courteous recognition to a fellow member.

[4]As part of its exclusion policy, the Tokugawa bakufu (徳川幕府) in 1825 ordered that any foreign (black) ships approaching the Japanese coasts should be fired upon. The directive was modified in 1842 to allow assistance to foreign ships in need.

[5]*Tōsai,* 等殺. This word is apparently a contraction of two compounds, *tōdai* (等第) and *kōsai* (降殺).

[6]*Sen,* 錢, one-hundredth of a *yen*.

[7] *Michi,* 道.

[8] *Oni ni kanabō,* 鬼ニ金棒, a popular saying meaning "to add strength to the strong."

[9] *Kigaku,* 氣學

[10] *Wu hsing,* 五行. Sakatani in this essay is attacking the entire Chinese cosmological tradition identified with the five elements or powers (wood, fire, earth, metal, and water), theories of the positive *yang* (陽) and negative *yin* (陰), the sixty-four hexagrams, and the like. This was a tradition that linked the physical universe with the human virtues, the conduct of government, and a peaceful world. By separating Confucius from this tradition, Sakatani is able to advocate science in the Western sense without compromising his loyalty to the Chinese sage.

[11] Fu Hsi, 伏羲, the first of five legendary Chinese emperors, to whom was attributed invention of the eight trigrams that were incorporated in the *Book of Changes* (*I Ching,* 易經), the classic that treats the theories of *yin* and *yang.*

[12] The *Canon of Shun* (*Shun Tien* 舜典), a section of the *Book of History* (*Shu Ching,* 書經) that deals with the legendary emperor Shun.

[13] *Hung Fan,* 洪範, a section of the *Book of History* attributed to scholars of the *Yin-Yang* and Five Elements school.

[14] Shên Nung, 神農, second of the five legendary Chinese emperors and father of agriculture and medicine.

[15] *Tso Chuan,* 左傳, a history of the Spring and Autumn (Ch'un Ch'iu, 春秋) Period, 722–481 B.C.

[16] Sakatani here employs the Chinese phrases *fêng niao ho t'u* (鳳鳥河圖) and *huo lin* (獲麟). The first (*fêng niao ho t'u*) refers to Book IX, Chapter VIII of the *Analects* (*Lun Yü,* 論語) in which Confucius despairs for the future of his teachings since he has not been favored by two auspicious omens, a plan sent up by the river (*ho t'u*) or the coming of a pheonix (*Jêng niao*). The term *ho t'u* in turn points to the times of the first legendary emperor Fu Hsi, when an animal with the head of a dragon and the body of a horse arose from the Yellow River to reveal on his back the signs that led Fu Hsi to conceive the eight hexagrams. The term *huo lin* is derived from the section in the *Spring and Autumn Annals* (*Ch'un Ch'iu,* 春秋) dealing with the fourteenth year of Duke Ai (哀), in which there is a report of the capture of a unicorn during a winter hunt in the West. It is suspected that the passage may be the work of Confucius' disciples rather than by the master himself.

[17] Warring States (*Chan Kuo,* 戰國) Period, 479–221 B.C.

[18] Ch'in (秦) and Han (漢) dynasties, 221 B.C.–220 A.D.

[19] Chia I, 賈誼, poet and statesman, 201–169 B.C.

[20] Tung Chung-shu, 董仲舒, 179(?)–104(?) B.C., included yin-yang and Five Elements thought in the eclectic Confucianism that he developed to meet the needs of the new Han empire; Liu Hsiang, 劉向, 80–9 B.C., wrote an essay on the Five Elements; Yang Hsiung, 揚雄, 53 B.C.-18 A.D., reacted against yin-yang thought and favored a return to Confucian rationalism.

[21] Kuang Wu[Ti], 光武帝, the first emperor of the Later Han Dynasty, 25–56 A.D.

[22] "Records of the Five Elements," *Wu Hsing Chih,* 五行志, in the *History of the Former Han Dynasty, Chien Han Shu,* 前漢書. Materials for this section on the Five Elements were prepared by Liu Hsiang and his son, Liu Hsin (劉歆).

On the Death Penalty

Tsuda Mamichi

The death penalty as a punishment is like torture as a method for trying criminals. Having already discussed from time to time the fact that torture is injurious to justice,[1] I would now explain why the death penalty is not a punishment.

Punishments are for the purpose of correcting the misdeeds of men. What then is this correction? I would say that it is the proper objective of penal law to bring the criminal to repent, to regret his crime, and to return to the good path after he recognizes that he has sinned and that he should fear his sin. The objective of penal law should quite properly be of this nature. How can the punishment be corrective if the criminal's life is cut short by administration of the death penalty? Even though the man may be thus corrected, how can he return to the good path and how can he conduct himself uprightly in society once he is dead and his soul is no longer in his body? I would say, therefore, that the death penalty is not a punishment.

When we speak of legislation and the administration of justice, this refers to the adjudication by mortals of the laws that we have enacted. How can we say that it is appropriate for us willfully to promulgate and administer laws for killing people when we have not the power to give life? Since the death penalty is inescapably an act of violence, the penal statutes (*keiten*),[2] after all, exchange violence for violence when they state that the killer of a man shall die.

Some say that the death penalty corrects 10,000,000 with the punishment of one man. Now to administer the death penalty each year to an average of 1000 persons out of our national population of 30,000,000 is not insignificant. In the long run, has not the death penalty failed to correct after having been carried out over some hundreds of thousands of years? The combined population of the various countries of Europe and America is, of course, several times that of Japan. Yet only a few are executed each year in the West. Why are there only a few violent persons among them and many among us? After all, their penal laws are not the same as ours. Capital punishment is rare among them, and some [Western] countries have absolutely abolished the death penalty. These discrepancies are attributable only to the differing levels of enlightenment.

Revenge (*fukushū*)[3] is never good even though it has been so regarded since antiquity. On the contrary, it is a great evil. The nation today is not cruel when it applies murder laws to those guilty of revenge. Since revenge is really killing one's foe with a million strategems, we should not criticize the revision of the laws on revenge even though we cannot guarantee that, given our customs, the reform will not be opposed. I cannot understand, however, why we keep the death penalty while we quite properly forbid revenge in this day of civilization and enlightenment. To preserve the death penalty while forbidding revenge is like plying a convicted drunkard with liquor after having forbidden intoxicants.

It is sometimes stated that, as the principal purpose of punishment is to guard our fellow men in society against harm, we shall prevent such injury by killing the violent. These words are indeed reasonable, but persons desiring fully to achieve this objective should exclude the death penalty and look for other means. There is exile, but exile should not be practiced as it actually shifts the injury to other countries, just as Pai Kuei[4] perpetrated injury on a neighboring state by using it as an aqueduct when he controlled the waters [in his own state]. After all, only imprisonment and penal servitude are appropriate punishments that conform with the purpose [to prevent injury to our fellow men in society].

It is said in the *Shang Shu*[5] that the aim of punishment is that there shall be no punishment. This purpose may indeed be termed beautiful and good. Although it may be discussed theoretically, I do not know that it is yet within the realm of practicability. I thus aim to end the death penalty as a punishment. Even the civilized countries of Europe and America, however, have not yet completely ended the death penalty, notwithstanding a century of discussion to this end. How much less has this been possible in Eastern Asia! In the final analysis, I am only aiming at the future. When undertaking this exposition today, I would only say that, even though I know that I am myself premature, I want to disturb the slumber of our people in the manner of Beccaria.[6]

On a Method for Artificially Stimulating Flowering Grains

Tsuda Sen[7]

When I was a member of the mission dispatched to the opening of the Vienna Exhibition in 1873, I profited in a variety of ways from what I saw and heard. It was for me an unparalleled good fortune that I chanced to meet Daniel Hooibrenk, the great Dutch agricultural expert, who fortunately lived a few miles outside Vienna. Spotting me, Hooibrenk grasped my hand, greeted me like an old friend, and led me to his home. Thereafter, I was a guest in his home and received his instruction for half a year. It was his nature to love trees and grasses even more than he desired food and drink.

More than twenty years before, the Würzburger [Philipp Franz von] Siebold[8] had become a Hollander (for some reason), come to Nagasaki, and then carried plants of our country back to Europe. The present propagation of these plants in various Western countries is entirely of Hooibrenk's instigation, and the love and esteem by Westerners for our plants really originated with this scholar of truly distinguished attainments. Being especially fond of Japanese, Hooibrenk kindly cherished me and called me "dear son" of Japan. From morning to night, he kindly taught me the arts of cultivation, invariably lecturing to me courteously on the methods and principles of the tests and experiments that he carried out.

Since he hardly ever seemed tired, I was so extremely fortunate as to be able to inquire during a short period into the general scheme of the experiments that he had conducted over many years. The master was then already more than seventy years of age. Being still vigorous in body as well as able to hoe and carry baskets, he himself took pleasure from irrigating morning and night. He might be called a hale and hearty elder.

I have previously selected and outlined in my work entitled *Nōgyō Sanji* the three discoveries of Hooibrenk that have most benefited the world. On September 13 of last year in fields of Furukawa of the Azabu[9] district of Tokyo, I undertook to verify the third discovery embracing a method for artificially stimulating flowering rice plants. When I gathered the harvest on November 13 and compared it with ordinary fully matured rice, the experimental rice was of surprisingly high quality, the difference between the two types being on the order of that between the rice of Higo and Akita.[10] The figures for the amount of rice harvested are as follows:

Unhulled rice per tsubo	Artificially stimulated rice	Rice by the old method	Difference
	Experiment in Place A[11]		
Quantity	1 *shō*, 4 *gō*, 6 *shaku*	8 *gō*, 9 *shaku*	5 *gō*, 7 *shaku*
Weight	495 *momme*, 6 *bu*	281 *momme*, 3 *bu*, 4 *rin*	214 *momme*, 3 *bu*, 6 *rin*
	Experiment in Place B		
Quantity	1 *shō*, 8 *gō*, 3 *shaku*	1 *shō*, 4 *gō*, 3 *shaku*	4 *gō*
Weight	615 *momme*, 8 *bu*, 8 *rin*	413 *momme*, 2 *bu* 7 *rin*	202 *momme*, 6 *bu*, 1 *rin*
	Experiment in Place C		
Quantity	1 *shō*, 2 *gō*, 3 *shaku*	8 *gō*, 4 *shaku*	3 *gō*, 8 *shaku*
Weight	354 *momme*, 4 *bu*, 8 *rin*	248 *momme*, 2 *bu*	106 *momme*, 2 *bu*, 7 *rin*
	Average in Above Three Places		
Quantity	1 *shō*, 5 *gō*, 6 *sai* 6	1 *shō*, 5 *shaku*, 6 *sai* 6	4 *gō*, 5 *shaku*
Weight	488 *momme*, 7 *rin*, 3 *mō*	219 *momme*, 3 *rin*, 3 *mō*	169 *momme*, 3 *rin*, 9 *mō*

Quantity in Percentage: 42.58 percent advantage for artificially stimulated rice

Weight in Percentage: 55.19 percent advantage for artificially stimulated rice

Figures for Barley Harvested on 14 June of This Year in Asuka-yama-shita[12]

	Artificially stimulated barley	Barley by the old method	Difference	Percent advantage
First Experiment, Plot 52		Proprietor: Tobe Kisōji[13]		
Quantity per *tsubo*	7 *gō*, 4 *shaku*	5 *gō*, 1 *shaku*	2 *gō*, 3 *shaku*	45.098
Weight	241 *momme*	175 *momme*	66 *momme*	37.71
Second Experiment, Plot 47		Proprietor: Suzuki Yasuzaemon[14]		
A field one *jō* long by two *shaku* wide	2 *shō*, 5 *shaku*	7 *gō*, 3 *shaku*	3 *gō*, 2 *shaku*	43.83
	275 *momme*	203 *momme*	72 *momme*	35.46
Third Experiment, Plot 50		Proprietor: same		
Weight per 10 ears	7 *momme*	4 *momme*, 5 *bu*	2 *momme*, 5 *bu*	55.5
Fourth Experiment, Plot 30		Proprietor: Tobe Kisōji		
Quantity per *se*	2 *shō*, 9 *gō*, 6 *shaku*,	2 *shō*, 3 *gō*, 3 *shaku*,	6 *gō*, 3 *shaku*	27.038
Weight	820 *me*	650 *me* (*momme*)	170 *me*	26.15
Fifth Experiment, Plot 29		Proprietor: Tobe Yasōji[15]		
Weight per 10 ears high grade	16 *momme*, 6 *bu*, 5 *rin*	11 *momme*, 9 *bu*	4 *momme*, 7 *bu*, 5 *rin*	39.91

Average Increased Yield for Artificially Stimulated Grain

Quantity: 38.65 percent
Weight: 38.94 percent

As I have already indicated in my booklet entitled *Nōgyō Sanji*, the method of artificial stimulation is so extremely simple that, from the point of view of actual labor, it is even easier than removing weeds from the fields. The equipment is like the sacred rope (*shimenawa*)[16] that we customarily hang before entrances at New Year's. Fabricated of sheep's wool, I am reluctant to admit that it is today known as Tsuda's rope. All you have to do is to apply honey thinly to this rope and then brush it four or five times against the grain ears when they are about to flower. It would be quite easy for three people to apply this method to more than one *chō*[17] of rice fields a day. By this method, which might be called as simple as child's play, the proved increased production indicated in the above chart ranges from thirty to fifty percent. The increase is like expanding production without cost since it is achieved without additional expense or labor. Such being the case, it is no exaggeration to say that, without any especial effort, the method will produce harvests almost twice as large as before. If the farmers adopt this method, they will secure an additional year's income for every three years of tilling, the government will also collect taxes easily, and the people of the entire nation, whom we call our thirty-five million brothers, will for the most part escape starvation even though they experience a crop failure once every third year.

Ah, are not Hooibrenk's achievements surprising in the abundance of their benefits? Our government's present accumulated foreign and domestic debts of more than 31,200,000 in gold may in this way be fully absolved in less than three years. If the government encourages this method with complete earnestness, it will also have the means for carrying out effortlessly in some ten years any number of other undertakings such as a new imperial palace, buildings for the government ministries, stipends for the *kazoku* and *shizoku*,[18] and railways and telegraphs. Even so, thinking agriculture a mean affair, the government has not yet raised a finger in its behalf (except in Arakawa, Hamada, Meitō, Gifu, Miyagi,[19] and several other prefectures). Since the world is generally indifferent to the facts, I am obliged earnestly to beg the gentlemen of this society for their advice on the means for spreading this method among the farmers of our country.

On Nurturing the Human Spirit Part Two[20]

Sakatani Shiroshi

A certain ship ran into a hurricane. Among the passengers, the dancers danced; the musicians played; the acrobats performed;

the wrestlers contended; and the scholars lectured. If asked why they did so, they would have cited the old proverb that one is helped by his accomplishments. This is a common parable alluding to those who busy themselves with futile activities when facing an emergency in the manner of Lu Hsiu-fu who lectured on the *Great Learning* in a boat when Yai Shan fell at the end of the Sung Dynasty.[21] It is not right to disparage such conduct, which is like that of a Christian who recites the *Bible* while confronting death even though his difficulties are not eased thereby. This is because such people are of the type who remain steadfast at their daily tasks when there is nothing more to be done after they have individually exhausted their powers.

We should appreciate that their magnificent spirit is derived from their continuing activity. I am of the opinion, therefore, that men's spirits are powerfully nurtured if they are induced to devote their minds to their skills. This is also the case with letters. Still more are men greatly assisted to confront difficulty if their muscles are strengthened and their courage is stimulated by regular training in the military arts. Some may complain that my opinions approach "barbarism" at a time when we are putting swords aside, halting indiscriminate shooting, and restraining violence, but they are entirely wrong. While we should adopt the strong points of others when establishing the country, we should not lose our spirit. If we lose our spirit, we shall actually be injured by the strong points of others that we have grasped, as we shall be caught in conflicting interests and derided even by farm girls.

The military arts encourage bravery, and nothing is accomplished in the nation without bravery. Diligence and perseverance, of course, arise from bravery. How can a person do anything well in letters if he is not brave? Cultivation of bravery lies in the military arts. Our nation is quite like Germany insofar as our national traditions since antiquity have exalted honor and prized the military arts. The literary effeminacy of the court during the Middle Ages stemmed from the derision of the military by the upper classes, but the spirit of the *bushi*[22] remained vital. Even though there are numerous theories of Yamato Damashii,[23] they solely boast the spirit of the martial arts (*Budō*).[24] The martial arts flourished and spirits were brave during the Genki and Tenshō Periods.[25] Our spirit of courage was then no less vigorous than that of France or Germany, even though there may have been "barbarism" if we judge from the point of view of present-day enlightened scholarship. Becoming inured to peace and satisfied with trifles after the Kan-ei Period,[26] we deemed it proper to defend ourselves by cutting off foreign intercourse and to exclude the violent spirit of the warring states (*sengoku*)[27] as far as possible, not knowing that we could not nurture strength within if we did not have the vigor to move outward. We were so weakened by the delights of peace that the entire country was brought to complete confusion by the appearance of but one foreign ship off our shores.

During the Bunkyū and Keiō Periods,[28] we exerted ourselves strenuously against a sudden intrusion from abroad. Even though the sentiment for expelling the barbarians (*jōi*)[29] of those years arose from the stubborn views of bigots, it also contained the principles of *bushidō* that bravery emerges from fury and that human-heartedness is understood after observing wrong. Destructive violence and fanatical assassinations [then] reduced us practically to the level of wolves because we did not properly control this anti-foreign spirit.

Since Meiji,[30] we have abandoned the evil ways of barbarism and violence and adopted the civilized laws and customs of foreign countries. It is well that we have abolished the domains (*han*)[31] and deprived the samurai of their traditional [military] role. And it is also good that we have entrusted military affairs to the recently established army and navy, encouraged samurai to lay aside their swords, and forbidden indiscriminate shooting.[32] Nevertheless, the tendency to carry these things to extremes has completely swept the military arts from the land, and our domestic traditions of subservience have increasingly manifested their evils abroad. Whenever they have time, officials generally follow the mean practices of the lowest classes in the West—drinking, consorting with prostitutes, and exchanging obscenities so that high and low everywhere have sunk to frivolity and shallowness. Are those who go to such extremes not like a person who ceases eating having once choked on food or who blows on cold fish having once been burned by hot food? And are they not like the boisterous child who, because of his parents' admonitions, falls into irresolute depravity?

Man's spirit is strong if he has something to depend on. The broadening of intellectual horizons and felicitous adoption of tools are both major factors upon which man depends. Reliance on technical skills is also important. Still more do the military arts protect the body by preventing injury from outside! In German education, physical training is begun at eight years in the expectation that individuals will become sufficiently strong later to serve as soldiers. The Germans even instruct women in the martial arts and physical training so that they may serve in a national crisis. The ferocious German national character has not been weakened by flourishing scholarship. Having fought duels on a number of occasions, the wise Bismarck has finally attained true enlightenment without losing his characteristic bravery. Russia has been barbaric from of old. The Tsar Peter himself traveled to various countries and adopted their strong points. Yet he increasingly promoted the ferocious customs of his country, using them as a means for directing Russia toward civilization. This is because a student can be trained only after his fundamental character has been established and because bravery is the source of all achievement, even though it is not without evils. Meekness is encouraged by letters while bravery is nurtured by the military arts. Meekness without bravery leads only to defeat. How can such meekness alone suffice to advance civilization?

I have long been of the opinion that sexual love, love of money, love of country, and love of one's parents are all love. Only the uses of love differ. Robbery brought on by impoverishment and cruelty produced by angry ferocity both arise from courage. There are not two types of courage. When well employed, courage is a sublime and magnificent spirit that expands the national power. There are none in this world without ability, only those who lack courage. Should we not seriously reflect on the tendency during this pivotal time of change to bestow responsibility on weak persons who are without courage?

I would submit that the recent enlightened imperial edict proclaiming national military service is truly one of the fine acts of our time, providing one of the best systems of all times.[33] Nevertheless, the military classes, having been relieved of their normal occupations, forget that the military arts are the common obligation of the people, and the traditionally indolent masses do not fully understand their personal responsibility to defend the country. We have national military service in name, but high and low are actually conforming to placid new habits, and the bravery inherent in our country is about to be dissipated. Changing this whole trend naturally lies in promoting impartiality in government and wisdom in learning. While encouraging such government and education, we must also spread the glory of our national military service through the world by advancing the military arts along with letters. The measures for actually implementing national military service are not simple. Although I am not without opinions on the matter, I shall temporarily set it aside since it is not the concern of this essay.

What I would stress here is reviving the military arts. Of course, gymnastics are all right, but we have already attained proficiency in our traditional training in the use of swords, spears, cudgels, and *jūjutsu*.[34] Actually, it is only barbarism to reject these skills because they did not emerge in the West. There are now many from the former warrior classes who are expert in these arts. We should invite these former samurai into the lower and middle schools and into the police and the military where they should be encouraged to practice their skills energetically during their free time. If these former samurai pay particular attention to the lower and middle school students during their play hours, training them regularly and methodically in the warrior's arts, and putting them through mock military exercises with guns and cannon contrived of wood, customs of meekness and a spirit of bravery within a few years will naturally spread side by side. A tradition of national military service will then naturally take shape, and patriotic courage will daily prosper. During an emergency, we shall be able to call up quickly and direct [the people] toward the battlefield without waiting for training. If our spirit thus flourishes, Japan will advance to become an England or a France after thus exerting ourselves with this spirit [of bravery] of scholarship in the German manner. Will this not be the foundation for the one great civilized power in Eastern Asia? Some may still insist, however, that we should not adopt such "barbarism" tied to the past since the military arts are injurious to letters and the enemies of civilization. Ah, how shall I respond to this?

[1]See Issues Eight and Ten for Tsuda's essays on torture.
[2]*Keiten*, 刑典.

[3]*Fukushū*, 復讎. In opposing blood revenge, Tsuda is attacking an ancient and honorable tradition in Japan as exemplified in the vendetta of the forty-seven *rōnin* (浪人) made famous by the play *Chūshingura* (忠臣藏). Fukuzawa also vigorously denounced revenge and similar private acts outside the law in the sixth essay on the *Encouragement of Learning* (*Gakumon no Susume*, 學問のすゝめ) that appeared in February 1874. *Fukushū* had been forbidden by government order in early 1873.

[4]Pai Kuei 白圭, an official reproved by Mencius, 孟子, for protecting his own state from flooding by diverting the waters into neighboring states.

[5]*Shang Shu*, 尙書, or the *Book of History* (*Shu Ching*, 書經). The quotation is from the Counsels of the Great Yü (*Ta Yü Mo*, 大禹謨).

[6]Beccaria, Cesare, 1735–1794, advocated the abolition of the death penalty in his *Dei delitti e delle pene* (1764).

[7]Although Tsuda Sen is chiefly remembered today as the father of Tsuda Umeko (津田梅子), the founder of Tsuda College for Women, he was himself a prominent Christian convert and pioneer in improving agricultural methods. After returning from the Vienna Exposition of 1873, he founded a society for agricultural studies (*Nōgakusha*, 農學社) and opened a school for agriculture (*Nōgakkō*, 農學校) which published the agricultural journal *Nōgyō Zasshi* (農業雜誌). The *Nōgyō Sanji* (農業三事) mentioned in this article was a booklet published in 1874 that described three methods recommended by the Dutch agronomist Daniel Hooibrenk. In addition to the technique suggested in this article for improving the pollenization of grains, Tsuda described in his booklet a method for nourishing the branches of fruit trees by weighing them down toward the ground and a plan to enrich the soil by laying pipes four feet below the surface that would draw air into the soil from above. For the *Nōgyō Sanji*, see the *Meiji Bunka Zenshū* 明治文化全集 (24 vols.: Tokyo, 1928–1930), XXIV, 215–236.

[8]Siebold, Philipp Franz von, 1796–1866, the German scientist who gathered a great variety of natural specimens while residing at the Dutch factory in Japan, 1823–1830.

[9]Furukawa (古川) of Azabu (麻布).

[10]Higo, 肥後, and Akita, 秋田.

[11]Measures on chart. Area: *tsubo* (坪), 3.31 square meters; *se* (畝, 畦), 99.3 square meters; *jō* (丈), 3.03 meters; *shaku* (尺), 30.3 centimeters. Weight: *momme* (匁: *me*, 目), 3.75 grams; *bu* (分), 37.5 centigrams; *rin* (厘), 3.75 centigrams; *mō* (毛), 3.75 milligrams. Quantity: *shō* (升), 1.8 litres; *gō* (合), 0.18 litres; *shaku* (勺), 0.018 litres; *sai* (才), one cubic foot.

[12]Asukayama-shita, 飛鳥山下.

[13]Tobe Kisōji, 戸部喜想治.

[14]Suzuki Yasuzaemon, 鈴木安左衞門.

[15]Tobe Yasōji, 戸部彌想治.

[16]*Shimenawa*, 注連繩.

[17]*Chō*, 町, 2.45 acres.

[18]Stipends awarded the new *kazoku* (華族) and *shizoku* (士族) that replaced the older samurai and court ranks after 1869.

[19]Arakawa, 新川; Hamada, 濱田; Meitō, 名東; Gifu, 岐阜; Miyagi, 宮城.

[20]Continued from the previous issue.

[21]Lu Hsiu-fu, 陸秀夫, 1236–1239, the heroic minister of the Southern Sung (宋) Dynasty who calmly read the *Great Learning* (*Ta Hsüeh*, 大學) when the last Sung stronghold at Yaishan (崖山) was attacked by the Mongols. When Yaishan fell, Lu jumped into the sea with the last child emperor of Sung.

[22]Sakatani here refers to the rise of the military men (*bushi*, 武士) who seized power from the older court aristocracy (*kuge*, 公家) in the twelfth century and after.

[23]Yamato Damashii, 大和魂, the Japanese Spirit.

[24]*Budō*, 武道, martial arts.

[25]Genki (元龜) and Tenshō (天正) Periods, 1570–1591, the eras when Japan was once more reunited after a century of civil wars.

[26]Kan-ei (寛永) Period, 1624–1643, embracing most of the reign of the third Tokugawa shogun Iemitsu (家光), during which Japan adopted the policies of exclusion and seclusion.

[27]Warring states, *sengoku,* 戰國, the era of civil wars that lasted for more than a century after 1477 and during which the Japanese developed intercourse with China, Southeast Asia, and even Europe.

[28]Bunkyū (文久) and Keiō (慶應) Periods, 1861–1868, the last years of the Tokugawa bakufu (德川幕府).

[29]*Jōi,* 攘夷

[30]Meiji, 明治, 1868–1912.

[31]*Han,* 藩.

[32]Sakatani here refers to the efforts to eliminate the special prerequisites held by the samurai after the abolition of feudalism in 1871.

[33]National military conscription for males was proclaimed in January 1873.

[34]*Jūjutsu,* 柔術.

An Explanation of "Right" (Third of a Series of Expositions on Foreign Words)[1]

Nishimura Shigeki

Kenri[2] is the ideographic translation of the English word "right." Like the Latin word *jus*, "right" in its original Teutonic form conveyed the meaning of law and ability. Having completely lost its original legal meaning, the English word "right" has a number of meanings derivative from its sense of "ability."

The word "right" in its modern usage refers to a claim that has been accorded by law. It is also a word that may be construed to signify the power, through operation of the law, to declare guilty an assailant who has injured one's interests that have been established by law as just claims. The roots of what we call rights and the means for acquiring these rights are numerous—some being acquired naturally, some by mandate, and some by inheritance. All, however, are recognized by established legal opinion.

Rights and obligations are mutually interrelated. If one person enjoys a right, another is under obligation to that person. For example, one person is under obligation to refrain from entertaining designs on property that another has a right to own. Or children are under obligation to accord the respect that their parents have a right to receive.

Speaking of them generally, rights are as I have indicated above. But if they are described in particular, they may be broken down into eight types: natural rights, acquired rights, [alienable] rights that may be yielded to others, [inalienable] rights that may not be yielded to others, perfect rights, imperfect rights, rights of individuals, and general rights.

Natural rights are all the natural rights enjoyed by men generally such as those to life, limb, and liberty; to the product of their labor; and to light, water, and air that they share together. They are derived from the fact that human beings are rational animals endowed with life by Heaven. We refer to them as natural rights because human beings must invariably possess them in order to complete Heaven's Endowment.

Acquired rights are such rights as those relating to men's property and contracts or the rights of ruler over subject, general over private, and husband over wife. If there are people, there is invariably social intercourse that emerges naturally. Once it exists, social intercourse produces rights that must be added to natural rights. It is essential in social intercourse for retainers to honor lords, for privates to obey generals, and for people to protect their property as well as mutually to preserve their contracts. As the social status of rulers, generals, and husbands and wives was originally established by man, the various rights arising from social status are acquired rights, not natural rights. Yet [acquired rights] are honored equally with natural rights in human social intercourse. Men protect their lives, liberty, and property with the intellectual power that they have all received from the Creator inherently as human beings. Yet once the people of a country enter into social intercourse, they must yield to others the greater part of their individual rights. These are called rights that should be yielded to others. Should you ask to whom these rights are yielded, they are yielded up to law or to the sovereign power. The most important human rights are those of life, liberty, and property. If you ask why these rights are yielded so easily to law or to the sovereign power, transferring these rights from the people's own grasp is for the purpose of strengthening the security of their rights. Individuals may protect their rights with their own strength only when, because of a sudden incident or critical pressure, there is not time to work out arrangements under law. The rights of rulers over subjects, of husbands over wives, and of masters over servants are rights that are uniform throughout the country and that may not be yielded to others.

The term "perfect rights" refers to rights that individuals completely defend to the utmost with their intellectual power and that can be fully protected in social intercourse with the power of law. Imperfect rights are rights that cannot be fully asserted by the power of law or an individual's intellectual power. All rights to life, liberty, and property are perfect rights for the reason that, when they are injured or stolen by another, the injured party must be able to press his antagonist for indemnification or other satisfaction either with his own strength or by securing the transgressor's conviction through legal judgment. The dignity of woman is also a perfect right for the reason that she may kill her seducer if there is no other way for her to escape him.

When candidates are selected for office, they are first examined to determine if they have the essential ability and training. It is assumed that a person seeking an appointment has a right to the post if his ability and training conforms to the government's requirements. Yet this is an imperfect right since, when the government rejects a candidate and fails to employ his services, he can neither forcefully acquire the post with his own power nor satisfy his desire with the law's assistance. Again, the poor man in the Eastern house has the right to receive charity from the rich man in the Western house. Yet he cannot collect alms by compulsion should the rich man have no desire to give. Even though a benefactor has the right to receive recompense from the recipient of his favors, he cannot forcefully obtain his reward if such response is not forthcoming. A child also has the right to receive love and training from his parents while the parents have the right to filial love and support from the child. But neither can by their own power require the other to honor the obligations that either party may fail to perform. These then are all imperfect rights.

Rights of individuals are the special rights that individuals hold distinctly from other men because of their rank and station. They thus are the rights affixed in social intercourse such as those of rulers, masters, teachers, or husbands and wives. General rights are the rights belonging to human beings as a whole such as the right to derive foodstuffs from the flesh of animals or from plants of the earth. When human beings in general enjoy the right to eat the produce from the soil, men are guilty of reducing the common wealth bestowed by the Creator on mankind when their excessive sporting destroys a part of the rice fields. Following this line of reasoning, such measures as protecting the private rights of individuals with local regulations or legally permitting such practices as gambling are injurious to general rights. The English Doctor [William] Paley[3] states that matters pertaining to the public business as a rule should never be decided as the private affair of an individual.

Among the general rights, there is one called the right of necessity. This is the right to protect one's possessions by destroying the property of others. This right of necessity embraces such conduct as saving one's ship by throwing the cargo into the sea or preventing a fire from spreading by tearing down the house of a neighbor. Yet if one acts in this manner on such occasions, it is invariably appropriate to provide indemnification for the losses.

There is a second usage for the word right, that is, right when we speak of ethics. Although the ordinary word for right is defined by law and the term as applied in ethics is determined by the Will of the Supreme Being, the two naturally are not in conflict. The broad sphere of ethical rights, however, includes within its boundaries rights that are not described by law.

The Three Human Treasures Part Four[4]

Nishi Amane

In my previous discussion of the path of social intercourse, I clarified the fact that the source for the development and establishment of social intercourse is no more than the three treasures. Now as there are laws for the governance of all things, there are invariably principles for the maintenance of social intercourse once it is established. Once there are principles for the maintenance of social intercourse, it is necessary for us to have rules for their expression. The path of social intercourse first appears in towns and villages, and then spreads to prefectures and provinces, to nations, to regions, and finally to the entire world. The self-evident principle that this intercourse must invariably extend from smaller to larger units may be confirmed beyond doubt by referring to the histories of East and West.

I shall postpone consideration of this topic until a later day as it is a problem distinct from what I would discuss here. Now what I desire to discuss here is as follows. In social life that gradually expands and opens up in the above fashion, there are rules for social intercourse that individuals should adopt, and (as I have said before) it is naturally sufficient for individuals to honor the rules of the three treasures, however broad social intercourse may be, for the reason that the ethics by which man has intercourse with others is no more than honoring the three treasures. Even so, when we consider from the point of view of social intercourse itself, there are inevitably specific principles for the regulation of social intercourse and a specific rule that expresses these principles. Moreover, this rule is derived from two mutually opposed principles even as heterogeneity is converted into homogeneity in matters of character, antagonism into equilibrium in the realm of power, and fundamental opposites into a single reason in logic. This is like making fire and water one or like harmonizing charcoal and snow.

Now to define these opposite principles, one is the Christian point that "Man lives for others." (This is what I heard from a Protestant friend when I visited Holland, but I do not know to what denomination it belongs since I did not trace its origin at the time.) The other, which is the main theme of this discussion, is that man should energetically advance the three treasures by honoring his own three treasures. In other words, a person should continually plan for his own profit. Without going so far as the West, Mencius spoke exaggeratingly of Mo Tzŭ and Yang Tzŭ some 2300 years ago in our East Asia when he said that Yang Tzŭ would not pull out even a single hair to benefit the world while Mo Tzŭ would [rub his body smooth] for others without saving even a hair for himself.[5] It is thus clear that from Mencius' time there have been two moral extremes arising from these two mutually opposed paths that are identical with what I am discussing here. If we desire to apply these opposed theories to social intercourse, however, which would be the correct path to follow? Should men want to determine the path, they must invariably adopt what conforms to the truths suggested by the facts and by their experiences.

Now if we take up Yang Tzu's theory of selfishness and judge it factually, is there anything today that is only for the benefit of the individual himself? Would it not indeed be simple if individuals were [selfishly] satisfied with only enough food to fill their stomachs, clothing to cover their bodies, and housing to shelter their knees? Providing for one's descendants and for the happiness of one's family, however, must invariably be regarded as acting on behalf of others since such activity extends to matters outside one's body. Turning to the establishment of social intercourse and to methods for dividing labor, how much more is it a fact that all activities, whether in farming, manufacturing, and trade or in various other industries, are invariably on behalf of others! Now if one recalls from experience man's daily labors from morning to night, is there any time when man does things exclusively for his own benefit? Even though amusements are naturally for an individual's own enjoyment, what pleasure, after all, does a poet receive if he burns his poems without showing them to others or a lover of musical instruments secure from playing to himself within a temple kitchen? Such being the case even with pleasures, still more is it so with the profession that one takes up!

From these facts, it seems that men live for others as they are unable to adopt Yang Tzŭ's theories of complete egotism. If we judge Mo Tzŭ's theory of complete altruism in light of our actual experience, however, is there anything today that is entirely for the benefit of others? Apart from charity, a person serves his own interests even if he bows to the interests of others or plans profits for others. Who will stoop to labor for others if there is not the least profit for the individual himself? If one refers to man's own individual experience, there is no need for [further] proof that what moves man to pursue matters with all his soul, to anticipate the future, and to endure hardships is invariably the desire for fame if not for profit. The source of the three treasures, therefore, lies in promoting private interest without restricting this desire, and what conduces to this private interest is no more than the three treasures. Judged from these facts, therefore, Mo Tzŭ's theories of brotherly love seem to distort human nature.

Since the two theoretical extremes of Mo Tzŭ and Yang Tzŭ are thus completely antithetical, like charcoal and ice that will not mix, which shall we now judge good and which bad when applied to social intercourse? This is the purport of what I am discussing. And being a social question, it is the most difficult ethical problem to settle. Now it is not too difficult, however, to transform heterogeneity into homogeneity or to change antagonism into equilibrium. That is, we shall incorporate this into a rule stating that man ought to take public interest as the objective in human social intercourse. With this rule, we shall direct the two extremes of egotism and brotherly love toward the common public interest. Since there may be suspicion that I am inclining toward the school of Mo Tzŭ if I speak now of public interest, however, I would dispel such suspicion by formulating a proposition on the words "public interest," to wit, that public interest is the sum of private interest. To state it still more clearly, public interest is the aggregate of private interests. And to support this proposition factually, the public interest in the social intercourse of a village of 100 families embracing 500 persons invariably lies in the full satisfaction of all the private interests of the inhabitants.

Turning to the individual, let us take the old farmer who belongs to Yang Tzŭ's school of complete selfishness. What if he does amass wealth by laboring night and day and by taking private gain completely as his objective? Even though he may not want to share with his fellow men the wealth that he has exhausted his life's energies to amass, will not all his wealth inevitably go to society as a whole when he dies? Again, let us look at the old woman who is a follower of Mo Tzŭ's complete altruism. What if she does enjoy serving others and strives hard to bestow benefits throughout her life? Her unselfishness, after all, will have its private rewards as men will invariably try to recompense her in appreciation of her virtue. These facts establish the unity of the two mutually opposed extremes of Mo Tzŭ and Yang Tzŭ as the great rule for social intercourse. Borrowing a term from physics, I would call this phenomenon "polarization" [*sic*] or the complete unity of two opposite poles of interest, mine and thine. This is like producing darkness by bringing two lights together, silence by uniting two sounds, or flatness with two opposing waves. The objective of social intercourse, therefore, is public interest, and public interest is the aggregate of private interests. Moreover, private interest does not go beyond the three principles by which individuals strengthen their bodies, expand their wisdom, and accumulate wealth. Whereas what I define as private interest refers to individuals, public interest concerns social intercourse as a whole. Briefly, since both are no more than promoting the three treasures, man will begin by honoring his own three treasures if he desires in the least to cultivate morality.

On Destroying Prostitution

Tsuda Mamichi

If I take up such a matter as destroying prostitution, not only will people in general scoff at me, but so-called intellectuals and, of course, politicians will also smile at my ignorance of their current affairs. Nevertheless, I am undertaking this discussion here because, as hereafter explained, these thoughts on prostitution have been deeply impressed on my mind.

While on furlough this summer, I traveled to Matsushima in Mutsu.[6] Going by the Hama Kaidō and returning by the Ōshū Kaidō,[7] I took twenty days to cover the two hundred miles of the round trip. And among the innumerable inns at the tens of post stations that I passed, practically all were houses of prostitution except for those in Saitama Prefecture.[8] These establishments were especially numerous in the town of Kokubu in Sendai.[9] I understand that in former times prostitutes were strictly forbidden in the inns of Kokubu. Now, however, the inns are generally all houses of prostitution. At other post stations, there was formerly no prostitution at all at the inns known as Naniwakō,[10] but one now sees prostitution there from time to time. Moreover, the public thoughtlessly assumes that by such practices enlightenment today has been more and more advanced as compared with the past. How can we not say that the public has been misled? I am moved to express these thoughts on the matter for the reason that I deplore the ignorance of society.

Judging from present conditions, there is absolutely no doubt without relying on government statistics that, except in such prefectures as Gifu,[11] prostitution has greatly increased throughout the empire. Just considering conditions in our country from this point of view, it can only be said that the level of enlightenment as compared with the past has declined more and more. After all, these practices are only the spreading poison of the superficially enlightened. During times of cultural change like today, when we are generally throwing out the old and introducing the new in all spheres, it is inevitable and only natural that the superficially enlightened sometimes emerge. Now the obligation of scholars today is no more than to seek with their full strength to advance true enlightenment in society after rejecting the superficially enlightened.

There is really no doubt that prostitution demoralizes customs in society and greatly injures the upright conduct of men. Beyond description are the evils by which prostitution exhausts the people's wealth and weakens their physical strength. After all, nations are formed and established with the people as their support. The poverty of one man is then the poverty of the entire nation, and the weakness of one man is then the weakness of the entire nation. Now there are innumerable cases at present in which ignorant commoners destroy their homes by squandering their family fortunes on their addiction for prostitutes. Such people consequently contract syphilis and become debilitated in body and stupified in spirit. Ah, with such conditions existing today, by what means can the country escape poverty and by what means can the army avoid weakness? If prostitution is not now destroyed, how can there be no danger that even our splendid Japanese Empire, which has never suffered the derision of foreign powers for more than 2500 years, will not long maintain its independent national structure (*kokutai*)?[12] Now is the time when we must have relations with the so-called strong, prosperous, and civilized nations. Of course, it cannot be claimed that there is any similarity between today and former times when we had no relations with foreign countries and when we were able to preserve our national independence without effort. How can students of politics not be anxious in this regard?

I am elucidating in this way because [the problem of prostitution] in truth has made a compellingly urgent impression on my mind. Moreover, I anticipate that the public generally may only laugh scornfully and that even men of intellect may reject my views as empty theories easy to set forth but impossible to carry out. If such be the case, then it would be well for me just to remain silent. Yet when I previously advocated prohibition of human traffic, how could one believe that it would ultimately be achieved in society?[13] Indeed, within only a few years, the order was suddenly issued to free the prostitutes. Such having come to pass, I wonder if the time will not come when I shall be remembered for having shown in this essay the wisdom to see the future.

[1]Continued from Issue Thirty-Seven.

[2]*Kenri,* 權理

[3]Paley, William, 1743–1805, English divine, philosopher, and author of the *Principles of Moral Philosophy* (1785).

[4]Continued from Issue Forty.

[5]This famous story in which Mencius heaps scorn on the complete egoist Yang Tzŭ (楊子) and the complete altruist Mo Tzŭ (墨子) is from the *Book of Mencius,* Book VII, Part I, Chapter XXVI.

[6]Matsushima (松島) in Mutsu (陸奥), traditionally held to be one of the three most beautiful spots in Japan.

[7]Hama Kaidō (濱街道) and Ōshū Kaidō (奥州街道), two major roads leading from Edo to the North, the former generally following the east coast to Iwanuma (岩沼), and the latter a more inland route to Aomori (青森) in the extreme north of the main island.

[8]Saitama, 埼玉.

[9]Kokubu, 國分, the present city of Sendai (仙臺).

[10]Naniwakō, 浪華講, an association of inns first established in the early nineteenth century for the purpose of providing hostelries cleansed of lewd practices.

[11]Gifu, 岐阜.

[12]*Kokutai,* 國體.

[13]Tsuda here refers to his proposal in 1869 to the deliberative assembly known as the *Kōgisho* (公議所) that the government forbid traffic in human beings. The government three years later halted such human traffic, and slaves and prostitutes were declared legally free. The action was taken after the arrival of the Peruvian ship *Maria Luz* in Yokohama with 232 Chinese coolies aboard. The coolies were freed and returned to China.

On Change

Nishimura Shigeki

My fellow member Sakatani has previously explained the hinge of change.[1] I shall also discuss what I call change, but my thought is quite my own even though my title is the same as Sakatani's.

In the world generally, there are natural changes and changes in human affairs. The alternations of night and day and the shifting seasons are minor natural changes, while the progress from the world of fire, turbulence, and stone to the world of mud, water, and stone and then to the world of human beings involved great natural changes. The rise of a poor farmer to become a large landholder and the bankruptcy of a millionaire are small changes in human affairs. In terms of our country alone, the rise of the samurai clique with the decline of imperial power and the restoration of imperial power with the destruction of the samurai clique were great changes in human affairs.[2]

It is futile now to discuss the advances and regressions in natural change since they are the Creator's work, which cannot be influenced by human power. While it is essential to consider the changes in human affairs as they are often related to our human interests, we naturally can leave out of consideration the minor changes that affect an individual or a family. Great changes determine in large measure the happiness and well-being of the people of an entire country. More especially, we must give some thought to such changes as those in recent years since we too are deeply influenced by their benefits. Changes in human affairs invariably have their fundamental characters and their fundamental roots.[3] I shall not speak of fundamental roots since these relate to past events and are not important for the future. But it is imperative to discuss fundamental characters in detail because they are the essence of these changes and generally develop the pressure for change. Sometimes fundamental characters are unique; sometimes, multiple. The American war for independence arose from a unique fundamental character, the preservation of national independence. The great disturbance of the French Revolution arose from multiple fundamental characters, which are said to have included popular revulsion against royal oppression and the full expression of aspirations by all the people. The recent great changes in our country initially developed from the theme of "Revere the Emperor and Expel the Barbarian" (*Sonnō Jōi*),[4] but this later became mixed with what is known as "Civilization and Enlightenment" (*Bummei Kaika*).[5] I would call "Revere the Emperor and Expel the Barbarian" the first fundamental character and "Civilization and Enlightenment" the second fundamental character.

The first fundamental character embraces yearning for the past and disparaging the present, honoring the rulers and detesting the ruled, greatly respecting ourselves and arrogantly hating other countries. The second fundamental character involves adopting the new after casting off the old, helping the ruled by curtailing the rulers, and broadening the amenities of intercourse after dropping arrogant customs. These two fundamental characters, therefore, seem as mutually contradictory as black and white or ice and charcoal that cannot be mixed. Their simultaneous coalescence in one government and one people should be judged a truly extraordinary phenomenon.

The power of the first fundamental character was so extremely strong in the beginning that it rapidly achieved change, but the second fundamental character later gathered strength so that its power was often actually employed, albeit in the guise of the first fundamental character. There is no need to speak of this fact here since it is known to all from its clear manifestation in government.

The first fundamental character was beneficial in hastening the achievement of change. Nevertheless, if there had been only the first character, [our country] ultimately would have fallen into bigoted and narrow ways without being able to achieve equal standing among the nations. Once we reached the great change [of the Meiji Restoration], however, the merging of the two fundamental characters, whether by the spirit of our ancestors or the Will of the Creator, was really a great blessing.

Yet if one views [the Restoration] in terms of the status of the people, are their blessings more numerous in today's society than before the change? Judging from present conditions, it cannot be said that today's blessings greatly exceed yesterday's. What if there had been only the first fundamental character and not the second? Again, judging from today's conditions, I do not know that the blessings of the people have greatly increased, the addition of the second fundamental character notwithstanding. If you ask why I do not know, it is because the heads of the people today are permeated with a mixture of both fundamental characters.

What is the situation when the minds of the people are permeated by the first fundamental character? The people indeed pay taxes, but they know not how the government uses these taxes. The high regional officials are like territorial lords of old, and even the lower, unranked clerks trifle with the people oppressively. Legislation is entirely in the hands of officials who cause the people to obey the law whether they agree or not and who punish those who disobey. Such being the rule that emerged from the first fundamental character, feudal government of the past was also entirely of this nature.

What is the situation when the minds of the people are permeated by the second fundamental character? The people are forced to send their young men for military service, to pay the cost of roads, bridges, police, flood control, and embankments, and to provide funds for schools, the construction and maintenance of which have been established by law. It is practically impossible to observe and abide by the numerous changes in the rigorous and vexing laws relating to census registration, land surveys, and taxation. These trials are all the consequences of the second fundamental character that were extremely rare in old feudal society.

There are advantages and disadvantages for the people in the first fundamental character. What I have recorded above are disadvantages for the people, but there are also advantages. Thus the upper classes are themselves practitioners of frugality who lighten the tax burdens of the people. In troubled times of flood, draught, or epidemic, they make large grants in money and rice or help the distressed people by lending these essentials. When there are venerable elders or admirable persons, such as filial sons and loyal retainers, the rulers help the aged and encourage the virtuous by granting them rice stipends for life. But whereas one often heard of these advantages in feudal society, the people cannot receive such favors today. They have only destroyed such despotic measures as forced loans, compulsory assistance to neighboring villages, and property confiscations that were practiced during feudal days.

The first fundamental character regards the people as the treasure of the nation and is concerned to train and nurture them as well as to shield them from calamities and dangers. Yet it assumes the people to be completely ignorant and holds that they should not be allowed to participate in governmental affairs. Therefore, government is extremely benevolent toward the people when tyrants arise. Between the extremes of benevolence and despotism, there is the [type] of rule that, as previously explained, is sometimes advantageous and sometimes disadvantageous for the people.

Since the second fundamental character assumes the people to be the main body of the country and the government to be established by the people, the people themselves then formulate the laws, and they pay taxes the level of which they themselves have established. Public expenditures of the entire nation are wholly subscribed by the people and devoted to their needs, since the people can dismiss officials if they arbitrarily exert tyrannical power and change the government if it rules autocratically. It is then naturally unnecessary to draw a distinction between the people's expenses and official expenses. If these rights are withheld and if the people are subjected to the aforementioned arbitrary ways, they should become extremely vexed even though they may not call the practices autocratic. At present, the advantages devolving on the people from the second fundamental character are limited to such items as the adoption of family names, permission to ride on horseback, bringing outcasts into the ranks of the common people, and elimination of the requirement that the people sit on gravel in the courts of justice.

As I have said before, the minds of the people today are permeated by two fundamental characters. More especially, it is also not unreasonable that the people voice annoyance and distress since the disadvantages they derive from these characters are more numerous than the advantages. The first fundamental character, however, is gradually being extinguished, while the second fundamental character is daily more flourishing. And since even the government really intends to revive the people's strength and to plan benefits for the entire nation, the advantages no less than the disadvantages of the second fundamental character will ultimately pass to the people. Since the present is a time of change when the people are gaining their freedom as they abandon the old for the new, they should surely reach a fine season once they have endured and moved through this present troublesome period. I feel, therefore, that there was a change of governing power in the year of Teibō (1867)[6] and that there will be a shift to people's rights not long hereafter.

Should you ask when we will shift to people's rights, the change will come when the people grasp the legislative power that is for them most precious and most noble. To acquire this legislative power, however, they must be endowed with both education and spirit. Without these two, they cannot hold the power even if it is given to them by the government. If the people prematurely try to grasp the power forcefully, they will actually foment disturbances in the country, ultimately injuring their own well-being. Therefore, I earnestly beg you: train the people in letters, cultivate their spirit, avoid bowing to authority and force, and ignore hardships. Then when the people are able to grasp the legislative power, their other disadvantages will melt away like ice. The people's power being strong and flourishing, national power will also be strong and flourishing. When such comes to pass, we shall conform with the intent in the Imperial Oath (*Goseimon*)[7] regarding our country's position among the nations and reach the point where high and low both receive blessings. Should we not then rejoice?

Honoring the Emperor and Expelling the Barbarians

Sakatani Shiroshi

If I now take up such a theme as *Sonnō Jōi,*[8] "Honoring the Emperor and Expelling the Barbarians," I fear that people will scoff and wonder whether the toothless Sakatani has become mad since he is reviving an outdated issue that is as old as the *tengu*'s loin cloth hanging from Heaven.[9] My ideas on patriotism may indeed be mistaken, but I must set right in this speech how I feel in my heart on the matter. There was discussion of *Sonnō,* "Honoring the Emperor," in Katō's recent speech, and Fukuzawa also touched on this theme.[10] Their arguments were different even though they reached the same conclusions. Differing opinions should be welcomed in society because they enhance discernment. I also differ from them since I shall discuss both *Sonnō,* "Honoring the Emperor," and *Jōi,* "Expelling the Barbarians." Although this may not benefit others, I beg your indulgence since I am setting forth my views on these two themes for my own benefit.

I shall not be understood unless I return to fundamentals. There is an anecdote that contains my cherished views on the slogan "Honor the Emperor and Expel the Barbarians." In the fourth month of the first year of Ganji [1864],[11] Nakamura Kurō and Kusaka Gisuke (formerly Genzui) of Chōshū[12] called at my house in Bitchū when they were returning home together from Bizen.[13] When we touched on the phrase during an evening of delightful conversation, I observed:

> You may ridicule me or become angry, but I would say a word since it would be flattery and deception for me to hide what is in my heart. While the peace following your defeat in the fighting at Shimonoseki last year did no honor to your *han,*[14] I must say that it was extremely commendable since the reputation of the empire was established thereby. To explain this, under old laws, foreign ships were invariably repulsed when they brought castaways to Japan, and we always drove away the distressed vessels that sought help or asked for fuel and water. Was it not extremely savage that we regarded such impolite, unfeeling, and inhuman conduct as appropriate? Let us set aside the possibilities that our people would have been completely destroyed or that we would have been shouldered with an indemnity of many millions after enemies had been provoked to attack on all sides by an initial victory on our part at Shimonoseki. If we had fortunately won victory after victory, foreign states would have warned against approaching a country of tigers and wolves like Japan. Our empire would then be known through the world as

a land of savage wolves, and our unparalleled emperor, representing an unbroken line, would be regarded as the chief of savage wolves. Could a man with the least degree of spirit permit his sovereign to be thus demeaned rather than honored? How splendid it was for the empire that you were fortunately defeated and pacified before we suffered great shame.

When Kusaka asked if then the opening of the country by the bakufu[15] was good, I responded:

No, no, its professions are good, but its heart is bad, and its conduct is still worse. If you look at the bakufu, it undertakes to open the country saying that there is no alternative, even though at heart it hates foreign countries and would be guilty of savagery by expelling them. It is without courage or policy, still less settled convictions. It invariably acts like women and children confronted by robbers. Its every act and every word being subservient and fawning, it resorts only to flattery without expressing its true convictions. It explains that we must await the right time as it is too early to expel the barbarians [foreigners], and it is no less savage for having changed from tigers and wolves into rats and monkeys. I can only be really enraged that the [bakufu] has demeaned the sovereign, brought shame on the nation, and brewed great harm for future foreign relations.

To Kusaka's inquiry as to what we should do under the circumstances, I responded:

The word barbarians (*i*)[16] was applied to those who did not comport themselves according to the manners and ways of China. Barbarians, therefore, refers to savages (*yaban*).[17] How can we think of Westerners as barbarians when we were savages in the first place? When a flying bullet suddenly fell before two men who had set out in the night, one drew his sword in fury, and the other prostrated himself and begged for mercy. Their aversion for ghosts was the same even though their conduct was different. They were both no more than savages insofar as they were at a loss to distinguish between bullets and ghosts. The king is the leader of the country who protects the people by following the virtuous path. Should he stray in the least from this virtuous path, [the country] will surely decline if it is not destroyed. We should reflect on the clear lessons of history. Take the fellow who lacks the courage to defend the virtuous path in the country whose rice he eats and from which he receives remuneration. Like a drunkard who expands his ego, he is arrogant and arbitrary if he is not flattering and servile, and he will bring shame on the country and weaken the monarch. That is, he is savage and barbarian. If one tries to love the country and honor the king with barbaric ways, how is this different from honoring barbarians and demeaning one's sovereign? Even great treachery like that of a Yoshitoki or a Takauji[18] cannot destroy the principle that we should honor emperor and country. This is because the principle is inherent and thus immutable. Nevertheless, the monarchy will clearly fall into confusion and decline if it loses the virtuous path by turning toward injustice. Society is finally becoming enlightened, and there are many who understand the nature of things. By the end of the Chou Dynasty,[19] there were no longer efforts to mix administration with the mysterious teachings of religion or to stimulate loyalty [to the throne] with miraculous theories. The way to honor the emperor lies entirely in expelling our barbaric customs by acting in conformity with the virtuous and just path that extends through the whole world. To open the ports today is both just and in conformity with the times, and this is why opening the ports is honoring the emperor.

Without replying, Kusaka left after giving me a small volume on facts relating to imperial edicts. The book is still in my home, the bequest from a dead friend. Being pressed to defend his *han* against false charges, Kusaka was too diverted to comment on my opinions. I cannot again discuss [with my dead friend], but my views have not changed. At this time, therefore, we should consider foreign and domestic conditions when we treat such current matters as Korean relations. And when we decide, we should act in accordance with the just path that is common to all nations.

At the time of my conversation with Kusaka, I was unacquainted with Western studies and the trends of the times, as I was a dullard who had lived long in the country. I only contemplated these problems by relying on the one righteous and just path. Since recently joining your society, I have come to appreciate many things from listening to your discussions, and I have increasingly learned that I shall not be far from the mark if I consider matters in light of the righteous and just path.

When I earlier asked you to correct what I had written on a popularly elected assembly, you may have laughed at my essay, as there were many rough places that I was unable to revise quickly. My purport, however, was that the way to honor the emperor and to expel barbarism is surely as I have explained here. The expositions by Fukuzawa and Katō were indeed not the same, but they agreed in detesting subservience. Even though I have many fears, they all amount to a fear of flattery. Flattery is the source of subservience, and subservience is the source of flattery. When there is flattery and subservience, it is like the parent who gives poison to a child in compliance with his willful demands. Such conduct is really contemptible even though it arises from a true feeling of affection. To honor the emperor is but to expel barbarism. If we want to honor the emperor, we shall defend the virtuous path by invariably casting out barbaric customs of flattery and by standing up independently. A flatterer is one who tries to realize his personal ambitions by resorting to words and conduct that he knows in his heart to be wrong. His direct speech and exalted theories at times may surprise others, but the injury of his crafty conduct is even greater than subservience. These flatterers mislead the king down the wrong path by playing with him like a toy and pandering to his wishes, and they seek advantages for themselves by talking behind his back. There are those in society whom we call jesters and brothel touts. Such persons are invariably flatterers and sycophants who on occasion may startle their guests with their straight arguments. But they only degrade their patrons even though they may include one or two sincere words.

Just reflect how many in old China and Japan were not touts and jesters. Leading examples of such persons were Dōkyō,[20] Takauji, Wang Mang,[21] Ts'ao Ts'ao,[22] Chao Kao under Ch'in,[23] Ishida Mitsunari under Hō Taikō,[24] the Egyptian Cleopatra who captivated two great warriors, and John Law who threw France into confusion. Truly, there are innumerable people who take fancy to trifling honors that resemble hundreds of flowers. Those who flatter invariably enjoy flattery by others since it is also human nature to detest bitter words, to enjoy pleasantries, and to desire the realization of one's personal ambitions.

When touts and buffoons become patrons, they boast of their luxury and find pleasure in foolish conduct until they themselves unwittingly become fools. Flattery is really more to be feared than opium-smoking. This is why some of reputed brilliance in the past became fools as they rose in the world. Slander cannot induce changes in conduct and morality even though it harms reputations. But flattery blunts man's discernment, upsets his mind, and leads him down the evil path. Moreover, slander generally arises from flattery. Those who are free from flattery are extremely firm of character, and those produced by flattery are crafty tricksters whose injuries are incalculable.

From antiquity, persons who have subverted dynasties were all the creatures of flattery. Drawing close to those of like opinions, detesting those who differed, and striving to achieve only their own profit by means of divisive factionalism, these flatterers inevitably end in destruction, treason, or tyranny after suppressing national public opinion. The country is not a house of ill fame, and the monarch is the protector of the country, not its patron. To honor the ruler is to secure adoption of the virtuous path of protection even at the risk of opposing him. No country in the world is without a leader, even though monarchial traditions differ. The leader is an individual, and the subjects are many. What can even kings like the notorious Chou and Chieh[25] accomplish by themselves if the people all act in accordance with the righteous path of self-reliant independence without resorting to flattery? Still less will there emerge dull kings and tyrants to jeopardize the succession once a constitution is determined by public opinion.

If we review and compare history with statistical methods, however, [it will be seen] that people actually demean the ruler and bring ruin when they assume that they do him honor by following the savage path of flattery. Fellows who thus reduce rulers to misery are as numerous in history as swarms of maggots. Instances of their bravery, independence, and success have only been isolated achievements, the end results of which have really been to increase oppression and nurture flattery until there was no salvation. Under such circumstances, all things flow toward temporizing.

By what means can we then achieve enlightenment? And by what means can we establish the practices of honoring the emperor and expelling barbarism? There cannot indeed be established laws against flattery. We can only make flattery unprofitable. The various enlightened countries of Europe are noteworthy in this respect. They have made clear the principle of public conduct of national affairs and devised political structures that provide for harmonious rule by high and low [limited monarchy]. In their system, there is no room for flattery and subservience since those guilty of such conduct only suffer loss and shame without deriving any profit. Even the Chao Kaos and the Mitsunaris only cultivate their intellects on behalf of their country without practicing their deceptions. [Western countries] have been able to avoid disturbances by establishing good laws and constitutions through public discussion. Their finances are not doubted as they are public; appointments can bring no complaints as they are fair. In these strong and prosperous countries, the people exert themselves to the utmost to honor the emperor and expel barbarism, loving their countries ardently, performing their duties with high spirits, and departing from the bigoted customs of the past.

The Chinese, on the other hand, admire savage ways, willfully follow customs of flattery and oppression, and are content with methods that degrade the sovereign, even though they were the first to advocate honoring the emperor and expelling barbarism. I hear that the Americans are debating whether to expel the Chinese immigrants whose disturbance to customs they loathe. This truly is expelling barbarians, a twist in circumstances at which some may snicker or grieve. When I pondered on the causes of national misfortune, they all came down to temporizing by the officials and the people. Men are without backbone when they cajole and oppress each other with flattery and subservience, and they hasten aimlessly hither and yon when they are without backbone. It can be clearly and factually demonstrated in the case of China that nothing can be accomplished in the face of such confusion and irresolution. We detest these old customs in our country, and we are trying to adopt the fine points of Western civilization before we are overtaken by disaster. There have already been the Imperial Oath enjoining the determination of all matters by public discussion and the imperial edict calling upon the people to assist the throne in its efforts to establish a constitutional system.[26] Honoring the emperor and expelling barbarism formerly lay in opening the ports after rejecting flattery. Today it lies in determining the methods for public discussion by high and low after rejecting flattery. If asked where we should start from, I would begin with the nation's public finance.

These are my views on honoring the emperor and expelling barbarism. Some may complain that theories at times contradict facts. Looking at this contention more closely, however, there have actually been no facts either good or bad in the course of history that have not arisen from theories. I honor most divergent views and dissenting opinions that do not arise from flattery. This is why I previously contributed the article on honoring differences to the journal of the society.[27] I beg you to favor me with your criticisms.

[1]See Issue Thirty-Eight for Sakatani Shiroshi's speech on "Pivotal Times of Change."

[2]Nishimura here refers to the rise of the military houses (*buke*, 武家) to win power from the old court nobility (*kuge*, 公家) in the late twelfth century and the destruction of the prerequisites of the *buke* after the Meiji Restoration of 1868.

[3]Fundamental roots (*gen-in*, 原因) and fundamental character (*genshitsu*, 原質).

[4]*Sonnō Jōi*, 尊王攘夷, the slogan of the critics of the Tokugawa bakufu (徳川幕府) before 1868.

[5]*Bummei Kaika*, 文明開化, a slogan of the era of enlightenment during the decade after 1868.

[6]Teibō, 丁卯, the calendrical combination for 1867, the year in which the last shōgun (將軍) returned his powers to the emperor.

[7][*Gokajō no*] *Goseimon*, 五箇條ノ御誓文, the Five Article Imperial Oath of 6 April 1868.

[8]In this essay, Sakatani has tried to modify the meaning of the phrase *Sonnō Jōi* so that it could be applied in the era of the enlightenment. Whereas in the decade before 1868 it was a call to honor the emperor and expel the Western barbarians from Japan, Sakatani would have it mean to honor the emperor by expelling from Japan the barbaric elements that did not conform with the mores of an enlightened and civilized world.

[9]Sakatani here refers to a folk legend of the *tengu* (天狗) whose loincloth (*fundoshi*, 褌) was so long that it reached from Heaven to earth. If men compared Sakatani with the *tengu*'s loin cloth, therefore, they would think him a long-winded bore.

[10]Although Sakatani does not specify the occasion for the statements by Fukuzawa Yukichi and Katō Hiroyuki, it is entirely possible that he refers to a meeting of the Meirokusha, which was reported in the *Chōya Shimbun* (朝野新聞) the previous 7 May. While Katō held that the Japanese people were not yet ready to grasp liberty since they had been ground down by 2500 years of despotism, Fukuzawa claimed that the liberties of the people had been greatly expanded since the abolition of the domains (*han*, 藩) in 1871. In an article on dividing the national power in the *Minkan Zasshi*

(民間雜誌) the following month, Fukuzawa further argued that the Meiji Restoration was really a movement by the people in the guise of an imperial restoration that aimed to overthrow the despotism of the bakufu. See Keiō Gijuku Hensan, 慶應義塾編纂, *Fukuzawa Yukichi Zenshū*, 福澤諭吉全集 (22 vols.: Tokyo, 1958–1964), XIX, 525–536, and XXI, 296–299.

[11]Ganji, 元治, 1864.

[12]Kusaka Gisuke (Genzui), 日下義助 (元瑞), 1840–1864, and Nakamura Kurō, 中村九郎, 1828–1864, two extremist supporters of *Sonnō Jōi* ideology from Chōshū (長州). Kusaka killed himself in battle before the imperial palace in Kyōto, and Nakamura was executed by the conservative faction in Chōshū.

[13]Bitchū, 備中, and Bizen, 備前, two provinces on the northern shores of the Inland Sea.

[14]The destruction of the Chōshū forts on the Straits of Shimonoseki (下ノ關) by a combined flotilla of English, French, Dutch, and American vessels in retaliation against Chōshū's efforts to close the straits to Western ships by force. The bakufu thereafter undertook to pay the Western powers an indemnity of $3,000,000.

[15]The bakufu was then following a moderate policy toward the West while trying to mollify the *jōi* sentiment within the country.

[16]*I*, 夷.

[17]*Yaban*, 野蠻.

[18][Hōjō] Yoshitoki, 北條義時, and [Ashikaga] Takauji, 足利尊氏, both took up arms against imperial armies, the former in the Jōkyū (承久) Disturbance of 1219–1222 and the latter against Emperor Go-Daigo (後醍醐) in 1336.

[19]Chou (周) Dynasty, 1122–256 B.C.

[20]Dōkyō, 道鏡, the handsome priest who tried to induce the Empress Shōtoku (稱德) to abdicate in his favor in 769.

[21]Wang Mang, 王莽, 33 B.C.–23 A.D., the minister who overthrew the Former Han (漢) Dynasty and proclaimed himself emperor in 9 A.D.

[22]Ts'ao Ts'ao, 曹操, 155–220 A.D., traditionally regarded as the bold and wicked minister who brought the downfall of the Later Han Dynasty in 220 A.D.

[23]Chao Kao, 趙高, –207 B.C., the eunuch who conspired to win power for himself during the Ch'in Dynasty.

[24]Ishida Mitsunari, 石田三成, the follower of Toyotomi Hideyoshi (Hō Taikō), 豐臣秀吉(豐太閤), who led forces opposing the Tokugawa (德川) in the decisive battle of Sekigahara (關が原) on 21 October 1600.

[25]Kings Chieh (桀) and Chou (紂), respectively, the last evil kings of the semi-legendary Hsia (夏) and Shang (商) Dynasties of China.

[26]The Five Article Imperial Oath of 6 April 1868 and the rescript of 4 April 1875 that confirmed the intent to establish constitutional government.

[27]See Issue Nineteen for Sakatani's essay on honoring differences.